SUBJECT and STRATEGY

A Rhetoric Reader

EDITORS:

Paul Eschholz
Alfred Rosa
UNIVERSITY OF VERMONT

ST. MARTIN'S PRESS • New York

EDITOR: Jimmy Fleming
MANAGER, PUBLISHING SERVICES: Emily Berleth
PUBLISHING SERVICES ASSOCIATE: Meryl Perrin
PROJECT MANAGEMENT: Omega Publishing Services, Inc.
PRODUCTION SUPERVISOR: Melissa Kaprelian
TEXT DESIGN: Anna George
COVER DESIGN: Lucy Krikorian
COVER ART: Andy Goldsworthy, *Leaf Works*

Library of Congress Catalog Card Number: 97-67055

Manufactured in the United States of America.
0 9 8 7 6
f e d c b

For information write:
St. Martin's Press, Inc.
175 Fifth Avenue
New York, NY 10010

ISBN: 0-312-11528-8

Acknowledgments

Diane Ackerman, "Why Leaves Turn Color in the Fall," pages 256–260 from *A Natural History of the Senses* by Diane Ackerman. Copyright © 1990 by Diane Ackerman. Reprinted by permission of Random House, Inc.

Marcia Aldrich, "Hair," from *Northwest Review* (1992). Copyright © 1992 by Marcia Aldrich. Reprinted by permission of the author.

Nicholson Baker, "Clip Art," from *The New Yorker* magazine (November 7, 1994). Copyright © 1994 by Nicholson Baker. Reprinted by permission of the author.

Russell Baker, "The Plot against People," *The New York Times* (1968). Copyright © 1968 by The New York Times Company. Reprinted by permission.

William Bennett, "Should Drugs Be Legalized?" Reprinted with permission from the March 1990 *Reader's Digest*. Copyright © 1990 by The Reader's Digest Associa-tion, Inc.

Suzanne Britt, "Neat People versus Sloppy People," from *Show and Tell* by Suzanne Britt. Copyright © 1982 by Suzanne Britt. Reprinted by permission of the author.

Acknowledgments and copyrights are continued at the back of the book on pages 526–528, which constitute an extension of the copyright page.
It is a violation of the law to reproduce these selections by any means whatsoever without the written permission of the copyright holder.

CONTENTS

CONTENTS **xi**

THEMATIC
CONTENTS

A SENSE OF SELF

PEOPLE AND PERSONALITIES

CONTEMPORARY SOCIAL ISSUES

WOMEN AND MEN

MINORITIES AND THE POOR

HISTORICAL PERSPECTIVES

PREFACE

Subject and Strategy: A Rhetoric Reader, Seventh Edition, is an anthology of essays for college writing courses. Each of the first nine chapters focuses on a particular rhetorical strategy: narration, description, illustration, process analysis, comparison and contrast, division and classification, definition, cause and effect analysis, and argumentation. In the final chapter, "Combining Strategies," we present four essays that illustrate how writers often use several rhetorical strategies together.

Of the fifty-two readings by professional writers in this seventh edition, seventeen have been retained from the sixth edition and thirty-five are new. These selections represent a range of topics and purposes that students have found exciting.

Our general introduction stresses the role of reading (particularly, analytical reading and critical thinking) in the student writer's development. First, using a brief selection from Laurence Perrine's *Sound and Sense,* we provide an example of how to analyze a text and how to discover the craft involved in its composition and the strategies the writer employed. Further, we suggest procedures for using the readings concurrently and interactively throughout the writing process. To illustrate the writing process, we present a student essay and describe the process that student followed from initial notes to completed final draft.

New to the general introduction to this edition is a section on writing the documented essay. Here we offer students advice on notetak-

ing, and how to summarize, paraphrase, or directly quote sources, as
well as information on how to integrate these materials into their texts.
To assist students with the documentation of their researched papers,
we include advice with examples using the MLA and APA in-text citation systems. Finally, we conclude with a note on plagiarism.

We offer advice in our introductions to each of the rhetorical chapters that includes a definition of the rhetorical strategy under discussion,
an explanation of why writers use the strategy, a look at several examples, and a consideration of how to write an essay using that strategy. In
this edition we have moved the student essays, a regular feature of the
text, into the chapter introductions. This has allowed us to annotate
them and to discuss how the students wrote them, making these student essays even more instructive. The student writers chose their own
topics and each essay is, we believe, comparable in length and quality to
what most instructors expect from students in writing courses today.
These essays will help students establish realistic goals and standards for
their writing, as well as suggest ways of identifying and solving the sorts
of problems a particular assignment may present.

In the seventh edition we have modified the organization of the
argumentation chapter, believing that students should approach argumentation in several different ways. We start the chapter with four
essays on different issues in order to introduce students to some of the
fundamentals of argumentation. We then move to a pro and con
approach to argument with two pairs of essays on "The Legalization of
Drugs" and "Biotechnology: A Moral Dilemma." Finally, we conclude
with a mini-casebook of four arguments on "Violence in Movies and
Television," in which writers explore various aspects of the role violence
in the media plays in our culture. Taken together, these essays provide
an overview of the subject and specific ideas and examples for writing
a controlled research paper.

We have again included a thematic contents that groups all the
essays in the text according to sixteen broad subject categories. We
believe that this listing will provide further opportunities for classroom
discussion and student writing, based both on the content of individual
essays and on various rhetorical approaches to common themes.

In selecting the readings for this edition, we have continued to
prize readability, whether in such classic selections as Bruce Catton's
"Grant and Lee," Eudora Welty's "A Worn Path," E. B. White's
"Once More to the Lake," James Thurber's "Courtship through the
Ages," Virginia Woolf's "The Death of the Moth," and Mary Wollstonecraft's "The Playthings of Tyrants," or in such contemporary
writings as Gretel Ehrlich's "Spring," Cynthia Ozick's "On Excel-

lence," Nicholson Baker's "Clip Art," Joseph Mitchell's "McSorley's Wonderful Saloon," Barry Lopez's "The Arctic Forest," and Toni Morrison's "When Language Dies." We have also been conscious of the length of essays, generally preferring those in the three- to five-page range, although several longer ones demanded to be included. Above all, we have chosen essays that are well written.

Most of the essays in *Subject and Strategy* are followed by four kinds of study questions: "Questions on Subject," "Questions on Strategy," "Questions on Language," and "Writing Assignments." In addition, "Writing Suggestions" for each rhetorical method of development are provided at the end of each chapter.

Questions on Subject, designed to focus on the content of the essay as well as on the author's purpose, help students check their comprehension of the essays and also form a basis for classroom discussion.

Questions on Strategy focus on the various rhetorical strategies the authors have employed. Students are encouraged to put themselves in the author's place and consider how they might employ these strategies in their own writing. At least one of the questions in this group focuses on the writer's use of one rhetorical method to enhance or develop the dominant strategy.

Questions on Language emphasize the importance of each author's choice of appropriate words and phrases and remind students of the importance of the verbal context in which diction and vocabulary choices are made. Each set of language questions ends with an exercise in vocabulary building in which the reader is asked to use a desk dictionary to determine the meanings of words as they are used in the selection.

The Writing Assignments following individual essays are of two types: the first assignment generally focuses on the particular method of development under discussion; the second focuses more on the content of the essay, sometimes providing practice in the rhetorical strategy as well. Instructors wishing to have students work on different assignments, or on topics of their own choosing, may find these writing assignments helpful in generating good classroom discussions. Such discussions can often help students discover issues that they wish to pursue on their own.

The Writing Suggestions at the end of each chapter provide additional topics suitable to each particular strategy. Instructors may use these writing suggestions as complements to—or substitutes for—the more focused writing suggestions that accompany individual essays.

A Glossary of Rhetorical Terms at the end of the book provides concise definitions of terms. Wherever we have felt that information in the glossary might assist students in answering a study question, we have placed a cross-reference to the appropriate glossary entry next to the question.

The arrangement of chapters in *Subject and Strategy* suggests one possible sequence for using the book: an overview of analytical reading and the writing process in the general introduction followed by the movement from narration and description through exposition to argumentative writing, and ending with a look at writing in which authors have combined rhetorical strategies. Each chapter is self-contained, however, and instructors may follow any sequence, omitting or emphasizing particular chapters according to students' needs.

We are gratified by the acceptance of the six previous editions of *Subject and Strategy*. Composition teachers in hundreds of community colleges, liberal arts colleges, and universities have used the book. Several teachers responded to a detailed questionnaire that tremendously helped us revise this book. We thank A. M. Beckett, California State University at Northridge; Virginia Carruthers, University of Baltimore; M. B. Duffey, Mt. St. Mary's College; Thomas R. Klevan, The Pennsylvania State University, Altoona Campus; Mary McCombs, Eastern Oregon State; Adele S. Newson; Carol Orlock, Shoreline Community College; Kathryn Pixley, SUNY College at Oneonta; Patricia Rink, College of Du Page; Anne Slater, Frederick Community College; Lynne M. Sparks, Drury College; Ilha Udvardy, Jefferson Community College; and Kay Walder, Texas A&M University.

We have also benefited inestimably from the comments and suggestions of Linda A. Blatt, Central College; Art Hansen, University of Nebraska at Kearney; Stephen Hathaway, Wichita State University; Patricia Hutchins, Delta College; and Donnie Yeilding, Central Texas College. We would also like to thank Sam Potts, Edward Hutchinson, and Meg Spilleth of St. Martin's Press for their insightful editorial guidance; Emily Berleth and Rich Wright for their help in seeing the project through from manuscript to bound book; and Rick Eschholz and Melody Ziff for their assistance in developing the questions and instructor's manual.

We are especially grateful to those students whose essays appear in *Subject and Strategy* for their willingness to contribute their time and effort. Finally, we are grateful to all our writing students at the University of Vermont for their enthusiasm for writing and their invaluable responses to materials included in this book.

Paul Eschholz
Alfred Rosa

INTRODUCTION

Subject and Strategy is a reader for writers. The selections in this book will entertain you, inform you, even contribute to your self-awareness and understanding of the world around you. But, above all, they have been chosen to help you become a better writer—and especially to help you grasp and master nine versatile and widely used writing strategies. The first nine chapters are devoted to these strategies: narration, description, illustration, process analysis, comparison and contrast, division and classification, definition, cause and effect analysis, and argumentation. In each chapter an introduction first defines the strategy, explains its purpose, illustrates it with brief examples, tells how you can analyze the strategy as you read, presents an annotated student essay using the strategy, and finally offers suggestions for using the strategy in your own writing. This leads into a collection of essays that demonstrate how the strategy can be used with various subjects. In Chapter 10, "Combining Strategies," we demonstrate how professional writers employ thoughtful combinations of developmental strategies to advantage. The essays in all sections are drawn from various magazines and books, and each is accompanied by questions that direct your attention to aspects of its content and form or that offer writing assignments. At the end of each chapter are suggested topics for writing to help you continue your practice of the strategy.

Subject and Strategy, as its title suggests, places equal emphasis on the content and form of an essay—that is, on what an essay has to say and on the strategy used to say it. All readers pay attention to content, to the substance of what an author is saying. Far fewer, however, notice the strategies that authors use to organize their writing, to make it understandable and effective. Yet using these strategies is an essential element of the writer's craft, an element that must be mastered if one is to write well. Because these strategies are such an essential element of the writer's craft, you will need first to become more aware of them and then to master your use of them in order to write well.

There is nothing mysterious or difficult about the strategies themselves. You're probably familiar with some of them already. When you want to tell a story, for example, you naturally use the strategy called *narration*. When you want to make a choice, you naturally *compare and contrast* the things you must choose between. When you want to explain how to make a pizza, you fall automatically into the strategy called *process analysis*. These and the other strategies are ways we think about the world and our experiences in it. What makes them seem mysterious, especially in writing, is that most people use them more or less unconsciously, with little awareness that they're doing so. Sophisticated thinking and writing do not come from simply using these structures—everyone does that—but from using them consciously and purposefully.

A writing strategy, however, is not like a blueprint or a plaster mold that determines in advance exactly how the final product will be shaped. Rather, these forms of thought are flexible and versatile, with only a few simple rules or directions to define their shape, like the rules for basketball, chess, and other strategic games. Such directions leave plenty of room for all the imagination and variety you can put into your writing and for all the many things you may want to write about.

As the readings that make up this text will demonstrate, content and form are unified. Indeed, the two actually help determine one another. A writer who wants to tell what happened, for example, will naturally choose narration; at the same time, the requirements of the narrative form will influence the content of the written story. On the other hand, if the writer wants to tell *why* something happened, no amount of storytelling will do the job: it will be necessary to use the strategy of analyzing *cause and effect,* and this strategy will determine the ultimate content. As you write, you will often tentatively plan your strategy before you start, consciously deciding which one or which combination you think best fits what you have to say and what you want to accomplish. Sooner or later, you will have to look back at what you have written, making sure your choice of strategy was a good one and that it expresses your content accurately and effectively. The sort of reading this text encourages will help you become more skilled at making such decisions about your own writing.

READING AS A WRITER

You read for many reasons and in different ways. But reading is most rewarding when you do it actively, in a thoughtful spirit and with an alert and inquiring mind. One of the greatest benefits of active reading is that it can help you become a better writer. To read as a writer, you must know how to analyze what you read. You must be able to discover what is going on in an essay, to figure out the writer's reasons for shaping the essay in a particular way, to decide whether the result works well or poorly—and why. Such digging into an essay may seem odd, and for good reason: like writing itself, analytical reading is a skill that takes time to acquire. But the skill is necessary if you are to understand the craft of a piece of writing.

Another important reason to master the skills of analytical reading is that, for everything you write, you will be your own first reader and critic. How well you are able to analyze your own drafts will powerfully affect how well you revise them; and revising well is crucial to writing well. So reading others' writings analytically is useful and important practice.

Getting the Most Out of Your Reading

Practice in analytical reading requires, first, a commitment of time and effort. Second, you should try to take a positive interest in the act of reading, even if the subject matter is not immediately appealing. Remember, you are reading not for content alone, but also to understand a writer's methods.

Here are some further tips to follow:

READ AND REREAD.   Always read the selection at least twice, no matter how long it is. The first reading is a chance to get acquainted with the essay and to form your first impressions of it. The essay will offer you information, ideas, and arguments—some that you may not have expected; as you read you will find yourself continually modifying your sense of its purpose and its strategy.

Your second reading should be quite different from the first. You will know what the essay is about, where is it going, and how it gets there; now you can relate the parts more accurately to the whole. You can test your first impressions against the words on the page, developing and deepening your sense of how the essay is written, and how well. You can pay special attention to the author's purpose and means of achieving that purpose, looking for features of organization and style that you can learn from and adapt to your own work.

ASK YOURSELF QUESTIONS. As you probe the essay, focus your attention by asking yourself some basic questions about its content and its form. Here are some you may find useful:

1. What does the author want to say? What is his or her main point or thesis?
2. Why does the author want to say it? What is his or her purpose?
3. What strategy or strategies does the author use?
4. Why and how does the author's writing strategy suit both subject and purpose?
5. What, if anything, is noteworthy about the way the author uses the strategy?
6. How effective is the essay? Why?

Each selection in *Subject and Strategy* is followed by questions for analysis similar to the ones suggested here, but usually more specific. These questions will work best when you try to answer them as fully as you can, remembering and considering many details from the selection to support your answers.

ANNOTATE THE TEXT. As you read, keep a pencil in hand and use it. Mark the selection's main point when you find it stated directly. Look for the strategy or strategies the author uses to develop that point, and jot the information down. If you disagree with a fact or a conclusion, object in the margin: *"No!"* If you feel skeptical, indicate that response: *"Why?"* If you are impressed by an argument or a turn of phrase, compliment the author: *"Good!"* Write in whatever marginal notes come naturally to you. These quick, brief responses will help you later when you begin asking and answering for yourself more specific analytical questions.

When annotating a text, don't be timid. Mark up your book as much as you like. Jot down as many responses in your notebook as you think will be helpful. But don't let annotating become burdensome. It should be an aid, not a chore; and a word or phrase is usually as good as a sentence. You may, in fact, want to delay much of your annotating until a second reading, so that your first can be fast and free.

An Example: Reading Laurence Perrine's "Paradox"

The following brief selection is from Laurence Perrine's engaging text *Sound and Sense: An Introduction to Poetry*. First published in 1956, this textbook has introduced generations of high school and college students to the excitement and art of poetry.

As you read this through the first time, try not to stop—take it all in as if in one breath. The second time, however, pause to annotate the text as often as you like, keeping in mind the six basic questions we mentioned earlier:

1. What does Perrine want to say?
2. Why does Perrine want to say it?
3. What strategy or strategies does Perrine use?
4. Why and how does Perrine's strategy suit his subject and purpose?
5. What is noteworthy about Perrine's use of the strategy?
6. How effective is the essay? Why?

PARADOX

Aesop tells the tale of a traveler who sought refuge with a Satyr on a bitter winter night. On entering the Satyr's lodging, he blew on his fingers, and was asked by the Satyr what he did it for. "To warm them up," he explained. Later, on being served with a piping hot bowl of porridge, he blew also on it, and again was asked what he did it for. "To cool it off," he explained. The Satyr thereupon thrust him out of doors, for he would have nothing to do with a man who could blow hot and cold with the same breath.

A *paradox* is an apparent contradiction that is nevertheless somehow true. It may be either a situation or a statement. Aesop's tale of the traveler illustrates a paradoxical situation. As a figure of speech, paradox is a statement. When Alexander Pope wrote that a literary critic of his time would "damn with faint praise," he was using a verbal paradox, for how can a man damn by praising?

When we understand all the conditions and circumstances involved in a paradox, we find that what at first seemed impossible is actually entirely plausible and not strange at all. The paradox of the cold hands and hot porridge is not strange to a man who knows that a stream of air directed upon an object of different temperature will tend to bring that object closer to its own temperature. And Pope's paradox is not strange when we realize the *damn* is being used figuratively, and that Pope means only that a too reserved praise may damage an author with the public almost as much as adverse criticism. In a paradoxical statement the contradiction usually stems from one of the words being used figuratively or in more than one sense.

The value of paradox is its shock value. Its seeming impossibility startles the reader into attention and, thus, by the fact of its apparent absurdity, it underscores the truth of what is being said.

Once you have read and reread Perrine's essay, write your own answers to the six basic questions listed earlier. Then compare your answers with the set of answers that follows.

1. What does Perrine want to say?

Perrine wants to tell his readers what paradox is: "An apparent contradiction that is nevertheless somehow true." He also wants to show why paradox can be useful for writers. His main point seems to be that "The value of paradox is its shock value. Its seeming impossibility startles the reader into attention and, thus, by the fact of its apparent absurdity, it underscores the truth of what is being said."

2. Why does Perrine want to say it?

Perrine's purpose is to explain the meaning of the word *paradox* so that his readers can better understand the concept and how it works. He would also like his readers to appreciate how valuable and interesting examples of paradox can be to storytellers, poets, and writers in general. So Perrine's purpose is *to inform* and *to persuade*.

3. What strategy or strategies does Perrine use?

Overall, Perrine uses the strategy of *definition*. He gives what seems like a dictionary definition in the second paragraph ("A *paradox* is an apparent contradiction that is nevertheless somehow true"); but he elaborates on this formal definition in several ways, mainly through *illustration* or examples. The first paragraph is a *narration* that serves as an example of a paradoxical situation, while the quotation from Alexander Pope at the end of paragraph 2 provides an example of a paradoxical statement.

4. Why and how does Perrine's strategy suit his subject and purpose?

It is natural for Perrine to select definition as a strategy, because his purpose is to explain the meaning of a term unfamiliar to his readers. And for a complicated abstraction like *paradox,* the two specific examples he points out are crucial to illustrate his meaning.

5. What is noteworthy about Perrine's use of the strategy?

The concrete examples he includes serve to show rather than merely tell what paradox is and how it works. By beginning his essay with a clever story that provides a good example of his subject, Perrine is able to catch his readers' attention immediately and to prepare them for the formal definition of paradox in paragraph 2.

6. How effective is the essay? Why?

Perrine's essay is effective because it serves its purpose very well. He helps his readers understand what paradox is and appreciate what it does. His definition is to the point and easy to follow, while his examples from Aesop and Pope show how interesting the idea of paradox can be and clearly demonstrate why writers use paradox.

USING READING IN THE WRITING PROCESS

What does reading have to do with your own writing? Analytical reading is not simply an end in itself; it is also a means to help you become a better writer. At the simplest level, reading stimulates your thinking; it provides you with information and ideas to enliven your writing and often with subjects to write about. In a more subtle way, analytical reading can increase your awareness of how others' writing affects you, and thus can make you more sensitive to how your own writing will affect your readers. If you've ever been impressed by an author who uses convincing supporting evidence to document each one of his or her claims, you might be more likely to back up your own claims carefully. If you've been impressed by an apt turn of phrase or absorbed by a new idea, you might be less inclined to feed your readers clichés and platitudes. Gradually, you will discover yourself becoming more sensitive to how readers will be likely to respond.

More to the point, however, analytical reading of the kind you'll be encouraged to do in this text will help you master important strategies of thinking and writing that you can use very specifically throughout the writing process. During the early stages of your writing, you will need to focus on the large issues of choosing a subject, gathering information, planning a strategy suited to your purpose, and organizing your ideas. As you move from a first draft through further revisions, your concerns will begin to narrow. In conference with your instructor, you may discover a faulty beginning or ending, or realize that your tone is inappropriate, or see that the various parts of your essay are not quite connected, or notice awkward repetitions in your choice of words and phrases. Analytical reading can lead you to solutions for such problems at every stage of the writing process: prewriting, writing a draft, and revising.

THE WRITING PROCESS

Prewriting

Of course, reading can give you ideas and information. But reading also helps expand your knowledge of the writing strategies available to you and, consequently, can help direct all your prewriting activities. Let us explain how this works.

CHOOSING A TOPIC.   In a composition course, you may be given the freedom to choose your own subject matter. In selecting your topic, you should consider whether you know something about it and also whether it interests you.

Begin by determining a broad subject that you like to think about and might enjoy writing about—a subject like "music" or "relationships" or "college" or "sports." Something you read—one of the essays in this book, for example—may help bring particular subjects to mind. Or consider the possibilities of your career ambitions: business, journalism, law, sports, medicine, computer programming, whatever. Or list some subjects you like discussing with friends: food, perhaps, or motorcycles or soap operas or the next election. Focus on a likely subject; then let your mind explore its possibilities.

Suppose, for example, you're interested in journalism and have even done some writing for your school newspaper. Here's what you might come up with when you think about possible topics for your writing:

Broad Subject:	JOURNALISM	
Possible Topics:	print news	*ABC Nightly News*
	television news	*CBS Evening News*
	press freedom	*NBC Nightly News*
	press control	CNN
	Time	editorial writing
	Newsweek	advertising
	USA Today	censorship

Once you have such a list, you can choose from among the possible topics one that interests you most, that you have several ideas about.

GATHERING INFORMATION AND IDEAS. Even the most experienced writers need to generate information and ideas to use in their writing. Once you have begun to read analytically and thus to increase your command of the general writing strategies, you can use those strategies to get your mind working, to make associations, to find meaningful things to say about your topic. Remember that writing strategies are more than composing techniques; they are basic ways of thinking.

Suppose that you decide to write about the different ways your classsmates dress. First, you decide to identify the most common stylistic groups—to use the strategy of *division and classification:*

casual
preppie
the cowboy look
mixed
miscellaneous

Next, you might want to use the strategy of *illustration.* In order to do this you would choose one or more students to represent each style of dress, to provide a typical *example* of that style:

casual: me

preppie: Joanie Cabot

the cowboy look: Fred Williams

mixed: Jim Lee

miscellaneous: Emilia Sanchez—the young executive look; Bill Glass—the punk look; Judy Davidovich—the socialite/fashion model look

Then it would be natural to *describe* a typical outfit for each of your exemplary classmates. You would try to capture specific details of how each looks and, if necessary, to point out clearly why each is representative of a particular style:

JOANIE: loose, thick wool sweaters; tweedy skirts; loafers; muted greens and browns. Right out of the *Lands' End Catalog.*
BILL: black leather jacket and black denim jeans. Lots of metal.
JUDY: a different ensemble every day, down to the shoes and accessories; every one of them looks like it cost hundreds of dollars. Even wears perfume.

Other strategies you might choose include *narration*—thinking of brief stories or anecdotes that would add interest; *cause and effect*—analyzing how your classmates' dress affects the impression they make on others; even *comparison and contrast*—pointing out points of similarity and difference between the various styles.

Of course, you probably won't use all the material you gather this way; and you won't necessarily organize your writing using the same strategies that helped you find your ideas. At this stage, what you're concerned with is mining your memory for material. The writing strategies you learn through your reading can help immensely.

DETERMINING YOUR STRATEGY.   Once you decide what you want to write about and come up with some ideas for what you might like to say, your next task is to jot down the main ideas for your essay in an order that seems both natural and logical to you. In other words, make a scratch outline. This outline will often suggest to you one of the basic writing strategies you have learned from your reading. Or a strategy that was particularly helpful to you in generating ideas may well work for you now as an overall organizing principle.

If you're still confused about what strategy to use for your essay, however, try this: (1) sum up the point you want to make in a single phrase or sentence; (2) restate the point as a question, in effect the question your essay will answer; (3) look closely at both the summary and the question for key words or concepts that go with a particular strategy. Here are some examples:

SUMMARY: Michael Jordan is the best player in basketball.

QUESTION: How does Michael Jordan compare with other basketball players?

STRATEGY: Comparison and contrast. The writer must compare Jordan and other players and provide evidence to support the claim that Jordan is "the best."

SUMMARY: How to make chili.

QUESTION: How do you make chili?

STRATEGY: Process analysis. The word *how,* especially in the phrase *how to,* implies a procedure that can be explained in steps or stages.

SUMMARY: Systems malfunction and human error made the disaster happen at the Chernobyl nuclear power facility.

QUESTION: Why did the Chernobyl disaster happen?

STRATEGY: Cause and effect. The word *why* demands reasons in the answer, and the strongest kinds of reasons are causes.

SUMMARY: Petroleum and natural gas prices should be federally controlled.

QUESTION: What should be done about petroleum and natural gas prices?

STRATEGY: Argument or persuasion. The word *should* signals an argument, calling for evidence and reasoning in support of the conclusion.

These are just a few examples of how to decide on a writing strategy that is suitable for your topic and what you want to say about that topic. In every case, your reading can guide you in recognizing the best plan to follow.

ORGANIZING THE PAPER.   Before you start a draft, it's a good idea to organize your material according to the strategy you will use—to create a working plan. Different strategies, of course, will suggest different kinds of working plans. An *argumentative* essay, for example, might be mapped out in this way:

Point to be proved: _____

Supporting arguments:

1. _____

2. _____

3. _____

Opposing arguments: _____

Rebuttal: _____

Final argument: _____

A working plan for an essay in *comparison and contrast,* however, would naturally look quite different—perhaps like this:

OBJECT A	OBJECT B
Point 1: _____	Point 1: _____
Point 2: _____	Point 2: _____
Point 3: _____	Point 3: _____
Point 4: _____	Point 4: _____

A working plan for a *process analysis,* on the other hand, might look like this:

Step 1: _____

Step 2: _____

Step 3: _____

Step 4: _____

A working plan is similar to a scratch outline; but it is determined much more specifically by the requirements of the particular writing strategy you intend to use. You have a great deal of flexibility in determining the format of your working plan—the models provided here are only suggestions. Your reading will help you understand the kinds of modifications that are acceptable and useful for a given strategy.

Writing Your First Draft

First drafts are exploratory and sometimes unpredictable. While writing your first draft, you may find yourself getting away from your original plan; for example, what started as a definition may develop as you write into a process analysis or an effort at persuasion. If you notice something like this happening, don't force yourself to revert to your original plan. Allow your inspiration to take you where it will. Later, when you finish your draft, you can see whether the new strategy works better than the old or whether it would be best to go back to your former strategy.

It may also happen, however, that while writing your rough draft you run into a difficulty that prevents you from moving forward. For example, you want to tell the story of something that happened to you but aren't certain whether you should be using the pronoun *I* so often. If you turn to the essays in Chapter 1 to see how authors of narrations handle this problem, you will find that it's no problem at all: for an account of a personal experience, it's perfectly acceptable to say *I* as often as you need to. Or, while trying to describe someone you think is quite a character, you find you've been writing for pages, but your draft seems flat and doesn't begin to express how lively and funny your friend really is. If you look through the introduction to Chapter 2 you will come across the advice that descriptions need lots of factual, concrete detail, and the selections in this section give further proof of this. You suddenly realize that just such detail is what's missing from your draft. Reading, then, is helpful because it enables you to see how other writers successfully dealt with problems similar to yours.

Revising

Once you have completed your first draft, it is crucial that you set it aside and give yourself a rest. Then you can come back to it with some freshness and some objectivity. When you do, resist the temptation to plunge immediately into a second draft: mere changes are not necessarily improvements. Try to tackle your writing problems systematically. It's better to reread and analyze carefully what you have written, perhaps using the six basic questions (p. 4) you apply to other people's essays to criticize your own.

One way to begin the revision process is to make an outline of your first draft—not as you meant it to be, but as it actually came out. What does your outline tell you about the strategy you have used? Does it suit your purpose? Perhaps you meant to compare your two grandmothers, but you have not clearly shown their similarities and differences. Consequently, your draft is not one unified essay in comparison and contrast, but two descriptive essays under one roof. Or perhaps you set out to write about your grandmothers, but did not have a definite purpose in mind. Outlining your rough draft helps you see that, despite some differences in looks and habits, both grandmothers are essentially alike in all the ways that matter. This gives you both a point to make and a strategy for making it: comparison and contrast.

Even if you are satisfied with the overall strategy of your draft, an outline can still help you make improvements. Perhaps your directions for preparing a pizza leave out an important step in the process—adding oregano to the tomato sauce, for example. Or perhaps your classification essay on types of college students is confused because you create overlapping categories—computer majors, athletes, and foreign students (a computer major could, of course, be a foreign student, an athlete, or both). You may uncover a flaw in your organization and strategy, such as lack of coherence in an argument or of parallelism in a comparison and contrast. Now is the time to discover these problems and fix them. Return to the appropriate section in *Subject and Strategy*. Review the introductory discussion, especially the annotated student piece, and reread one or more of the essays.

Before beginning a second draft, you should consider constructing a formal outline of your paper, one that reflects all the changes you want to make. At the beginning of this outline include your title, a brief statement of your purpose, and your thesis statement. As a general rule, it's advisable to write in complete sentences unless your meaning is immediately clear from a phrase. In order to divide any of your main categories into subcategories, make sure that you have at least two subcategories. Otherwise, a division would make no sense. Finally, you should observe the conventions of formal outlining. Notice how each new level of specificity in the pattern below is given a new letter or number designation.

Title:
Purpose:
Thesis:
   I. _____
      A. _____
      B. _____
          1. _____
          2. _____
      C. _____
  II. _____
      A. _____
          1. _____
             a. _____
             b. _____
          2. _____
      B. _____
 III. _____

Finally, if you find yourself dissatisfied with specific elements of your draft, look at several essays to see how other writers have dealt with the particular situation you are confronting. For example, if you don't like the way your essay starts, find some beginnings you think are particularly effective; if your paragraphs don't seem to flow into one another, examine how various writers use transitions; if your essay seems too general, examine the way other writers include details and examples to substantiate their ideas. Analytical reading can provide you with any number of solutions to the problems you may have with your own writing.

WRITING AN EXPOSITORY ESSAY

A Student Essay in Progress

Keith Eldred, while a first-year student at the University of Vermont, was assigned to write an essay using the strategy of definition; he was able to choose whatever topic he wished. Eldred began by reading the introduction and all the essays in the definition section of this text. Then, because he had been recently introduced to the Hindu concept of the *mantra,* he decided he would like to explore this concept as it pertained to the secular world. Having made this decision, he began to generate some notes that would help to get him started writing. These notes provided him with several examples of what he intended to call "secular mantras"; a dictionary definition of the word *mantra;* and the idea that a good starting point for his rough draft might be the story of "The Little Engine That Could."

counting ten when angry

Dunkin' Donuts commercial—"Gotta make the donuts!"

"Little Engine That Could" (possible beginning)

Mantra—"a mystical formula of invocation or incantation" (Webster's)

"Let's Go Celtics" → action because crowd wants players to say it to self

swearing (not always a mantra)

John McEnroe—"Get serious!"

"Come on, come on" (at traffic light)

"Geronimo" "Ouch!"

Hindu mythology

After mulling over his list, Eldred began to organize his ideas with the following scratch outline:

1. begin with story of "Little Engine That Could"
2. talk about the magic of secular mantras
3. dictionary definition and Hindu connections
4. examples of individuals using mantras
5. crowd chants as mantras—Celtics
6. conclusion—talk about how you can't get through the day without using mantras

Based on this outline, as well as on what he had learned through his reading about definition as a writing strategy, Eldred came up with the following rough draft.

SECULAR MANTRAS: MAGIC WORDS

Remember "The Little Engine That Could"? That's the story about the tiny locomotive that pulled the train over the mountain when the big locomotives wouldn't. Remember how the Little Engine strained and chugged, "I think I can—I think I can—I think I can" until she reached the top of the mountain? That's a perfect example of a secular mantra in action.

A secular mantra (pronounced man-truh) is any word or group of words that helps a person use his energy. The key word there is "helps"—repeating a secular mantra doesn't create energy; it just makes it easier to channel a given amount. The Little Engine, for instance, obviously had the strength to pull the train up the mountain; apparently, she could have done it without saying a word. But we all know she wouldn't have been able to, any more than any one of us would be able to sky-dive the first time without yelling, "Geronimo" or not say "Ouch" if we touched a hot stove. Some words and phrases simply have a certain magic that makes a job easier or that makes us feel better when we repeat them. Those are secular mantras.

It is because of their magical quality that these expressions are called "secular mantras" in the first place. A mantra (Sanskrit for "sacred counsel") is literally "a mystical formula of invocation or incantation" used in Hinduism (Webster's). According to Hindu mythology, Manu, lawgiver and progenitor of mankind, created the first language by teaching men the thought-forms of objects and substances. "VAM," for example, is the thought-form of what we call "water." Mantras, groups of these ancient words, can summon any object or deity if they are miraculously revealed to a seer and properly repeated silently or vocally. Hindus use divine mantras to communicate with gods, acquire superhuman powers, and cure diseases, and for many other purposes. Hence, everyday words that a person concentrates on to help him accomplish tasks or cope with stress act as secular mantras.

All sorts of people use all sorts of secular mantras for all sorts of reasons. A father counts to 10 before saying anything when his son brings the car home dented. A tennis player faults and chides himself, "Get serious!" A frustrated mother pacing with her wailing baby mutters, "You'll have your own kids someday." A college student writhing before an exam instructs himself not to panic. A freshly spanked child glares at his mother's back and repeatedly promises himself never to speak to her again. Secular mantras are everywhere.

Usually, we use secular mantras to make ourselves walk faster or keep silent or do some other act. But we can also use them to influence the actions of other persons. Say, for instance, the Boston Celtics are behind in the final minutes of a game. 10,000 fans who want them to win scream, "Let's go, Celtics!" The Celtics are roused and win by 20 points. Chalk up the victory to the fans' secular mantra, which transferred their energy to the men on the court.

If you're not convinced of the power of secular mantras, try to complete a day without using any. Don't mutter anything to force yourself out of bed. Don't utter a sound when the water in the shower is cold. Don't grumble when the traffic lights are long. Don't speak to the TV when it's slow warming up. And don't be surprised if you have an unusually long, painful, frustrating day.

In class Eldred read his paper aloud, and other students had an opportunity to ask him questions about secular mantras. As a result of this class conference, Eldred had a good idea of what he needed to do in subsequent drafts, and he made the following notes to himself so that he wouldn't forget:

get more examples, especially from everyday experiences

class thought Celtics example didn't work—expand or cut

be more specific in my definition of secular mantra—maybe tell what secular mantras are *not*

make use of "The Little Engine That Could" example in the body of the paper

get new conclusion—present conclusion doesn't follow from paper

explain how mantras might work and why they are important

don't eliminate background information about mantras

In subsequent drafts, Eldred worked on each of the areas he had listed. While doing so, he found it helpful to reread particular portions of the essays on definition. Several of these led him to new insights about how to accomplish the changes he wanted to make. He found that, as he revised his paper, he needed to make yet other changes that he had not anticipated. For example, when he made his definition more specific, he found that he needed to do some reorganization (moving the background information on mantras to a position later in the paper) and to develop a new paragraph. By the deadline, Eldred had completed the following final draft. To help you see more clearly what he retained from his rough draft, we have underlined those portions. Marginal annotations point to the revisions he has made and comment on the overall structure of the paper.

SECULAR MANTRAS

Introductory Example (from first draft)

Remember "The Little Engine That Could"? That's the story about the tiny locomotive that hauled the train over the mountain when the big, rugged locomotives wouldn't. Remember how the Little Engine strained and heaved and chugged, "I think I can—I think I can—I think I can" until she reached the top of the mountain? That's a perfect example of a secular mantra in action.

Formal Definition (revised)

Controlling Sentence (new)

You probably have used a secular mantra— pronounce it "mantruh"—already today. It's any word or group of words that helps you use your energy when you consciously repeat it to yourself. You must understand two things about secular mantras to be able to recognize one.

Qualifier No. 1 (new)

First of all, a secular mantra is not simply any word or phrase you say to yourself. It must help you use your energy. Thus, "I wish I were home" is not a secular mantra if you just think the words. But the sentence is a secular mantra if, walking home on a cold day, you repeat it each time you take a step, willing your feet to move in a fast rhythm. By the same token, every swear word you mutter to bear down on a job is a secular mantra, while every one you unthinkingly repeat is simple profanity.

Qualifier No. 2 (slightly revised)

Secondly, secular mantras only help you use your energy. They don't create energy. The Little Engine, for instance, obviously had enough power to pull the train up the mountainside—she could have done it without a peep. But we all know that puffing "I think I can" somehow made her job easier, just like, say, chanting "left-right-left" makes it easier for us to march in step. Any such word or phrase that magically seems to help you perform an action when you purposefully utter it is a secular mantra.

In fact, it is to highlight this apparent magic that
I dubbed these expressions with so odd a title as
"secular mantras."

Historical
Definition of
Mantra *(slightly*
revised)

"Mantra" means "sacred counsel" in Sanskrit.
The term refers to a "mystical formula of invocation
or incantation" used in Hinduism (Webster's). According to Hindu mythology, the god Manu created
the first language by teaching humans the thought-
form of every object and substance. "VAM," for example, was what he told them to call the stuff we call
"water." But men altered or forgot most of Manu's
thought-forms. Followers of Hinduism believe mantras, groups of these ancient words revealed anew by
gods to seers, can summon specific objects or deities
if they are properly repeated, silently or vocally.
Hindus repeat mantras to gain superhuman powers,
cure diseases, and for many other purposes. Sideshow
fakirs chant "AUM" ("I agree" or "I accept") to become immune to pain when lying on beds of nails.

Definition of
Secular
(expanded)

Our "mantras" are "secular" because, unlike
Hindus, we do not attribute them to gods. Instead,
we borrow them from tradition or invent them to fit
a situation, as the Little Engine did. They work not
by divine power but because they help us, in a way,
to govern transmissions along our central nervous
systems.

Explanation
(new)

Secular mantras give our brains a sort of dual
signal-boosting and signal-damping capacity. The act
of repeating them pushes messages, or impulses, with
extra force along our nerves or interferes with incom-
ing messages we would rather ignore. We can then
perform actions more easily or cope with stress that
might keep us from functioning the way we want to.
We may even accomplish both tasks at once. A sky-

Example
(elaborated)

diver might yell "Geronimo," for example, both to
louden the signals telling his legs to jump and to
drown out the ones warning him he's dizzy or scared.

More Examples
(new)

Any one of us can use any words in this way to
help himself do any task. A father might count to ten

to keep from bellowing when Junior brings the car home dented. A tennis player who faults may chide himself "Get serious!" as he swings, to concentrate harder on directing the ball. A sleepy mother pacing with her wailing baby can make her chore less painful by muttering, "You'll have kids someday." Chanting "Grease Cartridge" always cools my temper because doing that once kept me from exploding at my father when we were working on a meddlesome Buick.

Personal Example (new)

You probably have favorite secular mantras already. Think about it. How about those phrases you mumble to force yourself from your warm bed on chilly mornings? And those words you chant to ease your impatience when the traffic lights are endless. And the reminders you mutter so you'll remember to buy bread at the store. You know what I'm talking about. And you must see how much less painful and frustrating your life is because of those magic words and phrases.

Revised Conclusion (more positive)

5

"Secular Mantras" is a fine essay of definition. Keith Eldred provides a clear explanation of the concept, offers numerous examples to illustrate it, and suggests how mantras work and how we use them. More importantly, the notes and the two drafts of Eldred's paper show how writing is accomplished. By reading analytically—both his own writing and the writing of others more experienced than he—Eldred has discovered the requirements of the strategy and how best to achieve them. Then an honest and thorough appraisal of his rough draft has led to thoughtful revisions, resulting in a stronger and more effective piece of writing.

WRITING A DOCUMENTED ESSAY

A documented paper is not unlike the other writing that you will be doing in your college writing course. You will find yourself drawing heavily on what you learned about writing essays in the earlier parts of our general introduction (pages 7–18). First you determine what you want to say, then you decide on a purpose, develop a thesis, consider your audience, collect your evidence, write a first draft, revise and edit, and prepare a final copy. What differentiates the documented paper from other kinds of papers is your use of outside sources and how you acknowledge them.

In writing a documented paper you will learn how to take useful notes, how to summarize, paraphrase, and quote your sources, how to integrate your notes into your paper, how to acknowledge your sources, and how to avoid plagiarism.

A good place to begin is to read assigned articles from *Subject and Strategy* together with articles on the same subject that you located in your college's library. After you have completed your reading, you will be in a good position to decide upon a topic and to develop a preliminary thesis—the main idea of what you want to say in your paper. At this point you'll be ready to begin carefully rereading those articles that directly relate to your topic.

NOTETAKING

As you read, take notes. You're looking for ideas, facts, opinions, statistics, examples, and evidence that you think will be useful in writing your paper. As you work through the articles, look for recurring themes and notice where the writers are in agreement and where they differ in their views. Try to remember that the effectiveness of your paper is largely determined by the quality—and not necessarily the quantity—of your notes. The purpose of a research paper is not to present a collection of quotes that show you've read all the material and can report what others have said about your topic. Your goal is to analyze, evaluate, and synthesize the information you collect—in other words, to enter into the discussion of the issues and thereby take ownership of your topic. You want to view the results of your research from your own perspective and arrive at an informed opinion of your topic.

Now for some practical advice on taking notes: First and foremost, be systematic in your notetaking. As a rule, write one note on a card, and use cards of uniform size, preferably 4 × 6-inch cards because they are large enough to accommodate even a long note on a single card and yet small enough to be easily handled and conveniently carried. More importantly, when you get to planning and writing your paper, you will be able to sequence your notes according to the plan you have envisioned for your paper. Furthermore, should you decide to alter your organizational plan, you can easily reorder your cards to reflect those revisions.

Second, try not to take too many notes. One good way to help you decide whether or not to take a note is to ask yourself "How exactly does this material help prove or disprove my thesis?" You might even try envisioning where you could use the information in your paper. If it does not seem relevant to your thesis, don't bother to take a note. Once you decide to take a note, you must decide whether to summarize, paraphrase, or quote directly. The approach that you take is largely determined by the content of the passage and the way you envision using it in your paper. All of the examples in the following discussion are taken from articles in *Subject and Strategy*.

Summary

When you *summarize* material from one of your sources, you capture in condensed form the essential idea of a passage, article, or entire chapter. Summaries are particularly useful when you are working with lengthy, detailed arguments or long passages of narrative or descriptive background information where the details are not germane to the overall thrust of your paper. You simply want to capture the essence of the passage while dispensing with the details because you are confident that your readers will readily understand the point being made or do not need to be convinced about the validity of the point. Because you are distilling information, a summary is always shorter than the original; often a chapter or more can be reduced to a paragraph, or several paragraphs to a sentence or two. Remember, in writing a summary you should use your own words.

Consider the following long descriptive paragraph in which Diane Ackerman classifies trees by the color their leaves turn in the fall.

> Not all leaves turn the same colors. Elms, weeping willows, and the ancient ginkgo all grow radiant yellow, along with hickories, aspens, bottlebrush buckeyes, cottonweeds, and tall, keening poplars. Basswood turns bronze, birches bright gold. Water-loving maples put on a symphonic display of scarlets. Sumacs turn red, too, as do flowering dogwoods, black gums, and sweet gums. Though some oaks yellow, most turn a pinkish brown. The farmlands also change color, as tepees of cornstalks and bales of shredded-wheat-textured hay stand drying in the fields. In some spots, one slope of a hill may be green and the other already in bright color, because the hillside facing south gets more sun and heat than the northern one.
> —DIANE ACKERMAN
> "Why Leaves Turn Color in the Fall," page 187

A student wishing to capture the gist of Ackerman's point without repeating her detailed account, wrote the following summary:

SUMMARY NOTE CARD

Leaf color

Ackerman notes that the leaves of different types of trees predictably turn certain colors in the fall.

Ackerman, 187

Paraphrase

When you *paraphrase* a source you restate the information in your own words instead of quoting directly. Unlike a summary, which gives a brief overview of the essential information in the original, a paraphrase seeks to maintain the same level of detail as the original to aid readers in understanding or believing the information presented. A paraphrase presents the original information in approximately the same number of words, but in your own wording. In other words, your paraphrase should closely parallel the presentation of ideas in the original, but not use the same words or sentence structure as the original. Even though you are using your own words with a paraphrase, it's important to remember that you are borrowing ideas and therefore must acknowledge the source of these ideas with a citation.

How would you paraphrase the following passage from Martin Luther King's book?

> Before it is too late, we must narrow the gaping chasm between our proclamations of peace and our lowly deeds which precipitate and perpetuate war. We are called upon to look up from the quagmire of military programs and defense commitments and read the warnings on history's signposts.
> —MARTIN LUTHER KING JR.
> "Where Do We Go from Here: Community or Chaos?" page 400

The following note card illustrates how a student paraphrased the passage from King:

PARAPHRASE NOTE CARD

Action needed

People need to close the gap between words of peace and provocative, hostile behavior before they have no alternatives. History tells us that military build-ups and a strong defense are not the solution, the road to peace.

King, 400

In most cases it is better to summarize or paraphrase materials—which by definition means using your own words—instead of quoting verbatim (word-for-word). To capture an idea in your own words ensures that you have thought about and understand what your source is saying.

Direct Quotation

When you directly *quote* a source, you copy the words of your source exactly, putting all quoted material in quotation marks. When you take a quoted note, carefully check for accuracy, including punctuation and capitalization. Be selective about what you choose to quote; reserve direct quotation for important ideas stated memorably, for especially clear explanations by authorities, and for proponents of a particular position to argue in their own words.

Consider, for example, Joyce Carol Oates powerful description of a premiere high-performance automobile:

> The Testarossa!—that domestic rocket of a sports car, sleek, low-slung, aggressively wide; startlingly beautiful even in the eyes of non–car aficionados; so spectacular a presence on the road that—as I

can personally testify—heads turn, faces break into childlike smiles in its wake.

—JOYCE CAROL OATES
"'State-of-the-Art Car': The Ferrari Testarossa," page 88

QUOTATION NOTE CARD

Presence of car

"The Testarossa!—that domestic rocket of a sports car, sleek, low-slung, aggressively wide; startlingly beautiful even in the eyes of non-car aficionados; so spectacular a presence on the road that—as I can personally testify—heads turn, faces break into childlike smiles in its wake."

Oates, 88

On occasion you'll find a useful passage with some memorable wording in it. Avoid the temptation to quote the whole passage; instead you can combine summary or paraphrase with direct quotation.

Consider the following paragraph from Barbara Hattemer's essay on violence in the media.

Television and violence have been almost synonymous since television became a part of nearly every home. As far back as 1977, 9 of every 10 TV programs contained violence. Today, while there is more variety, there are more sources of violence than ever before. In addition to violent action-adventure movies and television dramas, violence pervades music videos, rap songs, documentaries, commercials, and news broadcasts. The networks provide up to 10 violent acts per hour; cable, up to 18 violent acts per hour; and children's cartoons, 32 violent acts per hour. Movies like *Teenage Mutant Ninja Turtles* raise the count to 133 violent acts per hour. The body count is rising, too: *Total Recall*, 74 dead; *Robocop 2*, 81 dead; *Rambo III*, 106 dead; and *Die Hard 2*, 264 dead.

—BARBARA HATTEMER
"Cause and Violent Effect: Media and Our Youth," page 463

Note how the student in taking this note was careful to put quotation marks around all words that have been borrowed directly.

QUOTATION AND SUMMARY CARD

Violent acts

The link between television and violence has al-
ways existed, but today it's more varied. "The
networks provide up to 10 violent acts per hour;
cable, up to 18 violent acts per hour; and children's
cartoons, 32 violent acts per hour. Movies like Teen-
age Mutant Ninja Turtles raise the count to 133
violent acts per hour. The body count is rising, too:
Total Recall, 74 dead; Robocop 2, 81 dead; Rambo
III, 106 dead; and Die Hard 2, 264 dead."

Hattemer, 463

INTEGRATING QUOTES INTO YOUR TEXT

Whenever you want to use borrowed material, be it a summary, paraphrase, or quotation, it's best to introduce the material with a signal phrase—a phrase that alerts the reader that borrowed information is going to come. A signal phrase usually consists of the author's name and a verb. Well-chosen signal phrases help you to integrate quotations, paraphrases, and summaries into the flow of your paper. Besides, signal phrases let your reader know who is speaking and, in the case of summaries and paraphrases, exactly where your ideas end and someone else's begin. Never confuse your reader with a quotation that appears suddenly without introduction in your paper.

UNANNOUNCED QUOTATION

Many Americans believe that our war on drugs is a losing battle and that we would be far better off to make drugs legal. "The legalizers want peace at any price, even though it means the inevitable proliferation of a practice that degrades, impoverishes and kills" (Bennett 415).

INTEGRATED QUOTATION

Many Americans believe that our war on drugs is a losing battle and that we would be far better off to make drugs legal. According to former drug czar William Bennett, "the legalizers want peace at any price, even though it means the inevitable proliferation of a practice that degrades, impoverishes and kills" (415).

How well you integrate a quote, paraphrase, or summary into your paper depends partly on varying your signal phrases and, in particular, choosing a verb for the signal phrase that accurately conveys the tone and intent of the writer. If a writer is arguing, use the verb *argues* (or *asserts, claims,* or *contends*); if the writer contests a particular position or fact, use the verb *contests* (or *denies, disputes, refutes,* or *rejects*). In using verbs that are specific to the situation in your paper, you bring your readers into the intellectual debate as well as avoid the monotony of repeating such all-purpose verbs as *says* or *writes*.

You should always try to use a signal phrase that fits the situation in your essay. The following are just a few examples of how you can vary signal phrases to add interest to your paper:

Malcolm X confesses that ". . . ."
As linguist Deborah Tannen has observed, ". . . ."
According to television watchdog Marie Winn, ". . . ."
Bruce Catton, noted Civil War historian, emphasizes ". . . ."
Gloria Naylor rejects the widely held belief that ". . . ."
Cynthia Ozick enriches our understanding of ". . . ."

Other verbs that you should keep in mind when constructing signal phrases include the following:

acknowledges	declares	points out
adds	endorses	reasons
admits	grants	reports
believes	implies	responds
compares	insists	suggests
confirms		

DOCUMENTING YOUR SOURCES

Whenever you summarize, paraphrase, or quote a person's thoughts and ideas, and when you use facts or statistics that are not commonly known or believed, you must properly acknowledge the source of your information. These acknowledgments are called *citations.* Your citations must consistently follow either Modern Language Association (MLA) or American Psychological Association (APA) style. The MLA documentation system is used in English and the humanities, while the APA system is used throughout the social sciences. (Your instructor will tell you which system to use.)

There are two components of documentation in a research paper:
the *in-text citation*, placed in the body of your paper, and the *list of
works cited*, which provides complete publication data on your sources
and is placed at the end of your paper.

In-Text Citations

Most in-text citations consist of only the author's last name and a
page reference. Usually the author's name is given in an introductory or
signal phrase at the beginning of the borrowed material and the page
reference is given in parentheses at the end. If the author's name is not
given at the beginning, put it in the parentheses along with the page
reference. The parenthetical reference signals the end of the borrowed
material and directs your reader to the list of works cited should he or
she want to pursue a source. Consider the following examples of in-text
citations from a student paper.

IN-TEXT CITATION (MLA STYLE)

Citation with author's name in the signal phrase

> One widespread stereotype holds that the poor
> are out of work and on welfare. But Edwards reminds
> us of the plight of the laboring poor, the "4 million
> people in the United States today who still live
> miserable and know not why" (135). The effects
> of such poverty can often be debilitating because,
> as one person who has experienced poverty ad-
> mits, "poverty is an acid that drips on pride until all

Citation with author's name in parentheses

> pride is worn away" (Parker 305). The government
> needs to address the issue of poverty before it is
> too late.

IN-TEXT CITATION (APA STYLE)

Citation with author's name and date in the signal phrase

> One widespread stereotype holds that the poor
> are out of work and on welfare. But Edwards (1978)
> reminds us of the plight of the laboring poor, the "4
> million people in the United States today who still
> live miserable and know not why" (p. 135). The ef-
> fects of such poverty can often be debilitating be-
> cause, as one person who has experienced poverty
> admits, "poverty is an acid that drips on pride until

Citation with author's name and date in parentheses   all pride is worn away" (Parker, 1971, p. 305). Our government needs to address the issue of poverty before it is too late.

In both the above examples page references are to the articles as they appear here in *Subject and Strategy*. If you were using these sources from the books in which they appeared, your page references would be to the originals.

List of Works Cited

LIST OF WORKS CITED ENTRY (MLA STYLE)

Edwards, Flora Mancuso. "Elvira's Story." Subject and Strat-
  egy. 7th ed. Eds. Paul Eschholz and Alfred Rosa. New
  York: St. Martin's, 1996. 135–138.
Parker, Jo Goodwin. "What Is Poverty?" Subject and Strategy.
  7th ed. Eds. Paul Eschholz and Alfred Rosa. New York: St.
  Martin's, 1996. 302–307.

REFERENCES ENTRY (APA STYLE)

Edwards, F. M. Elvira's story. (1978). In P. Eschholz & A. Rosa
  (Eds.), Subject and Strategy (7th ed.) (pp. 135–138). New
  York: St. Martin's.
Parker, J. G. What is poverty? (1971). In P. Eschholz & A. Rosa
  (Eds.), Subject and Strategy (7th ed.) (pp. 302–307). New
  York: St. Martin's.

You should use one of the above formats when citing articles included in *Subject and Strategy*. For articles and books located in your college's library, consult either the *MLA Handbook for Writers of Research Papers* (4th ed., 1995) or the *Publication Manual of the American Psychological Association* (4th ed., 1994). In addition, there is a model *List of Works Cited* at the end of the student paper on page 35.

A NOTE ON PLAGIARISM

The importance of honesty and accuracy in doing library research can't be stressed enough. Any material borrowed word-for-word must be placed within quotation marks and be properly cited; any idea, explanation, or argument you have paraphrased or summarized must be documented, and it must be clear where the paraphrased material begins and ends. In short, to use someone else's ideas whether in their original form or in an altered form without proper acknowledgment is to be guilty of *plagiarism*. And plagiarism is plagiarism even if it is accidental.

A little attention and effort at the notetaking stage can go a long way toward eliminating the possibility of inadvertent plagiarism. Check all direct quotations against the wording of the original, and double check your paraphrases to be sure that you have not used the writer's wording or sentence structure. It is easy to forget to put quotation marks around material taken verbatim or to use the same sentence structure and most of the same words—substituting a synonym here and there—and record it as a paraphrase. In working closely with the ideas and words of others, intellectual honesty demands that we distinguish between what we borrow—and therefore acknowledge in a citation—and what is our own.

While writing your paper, be careful whenever you incorporate one of your notes into your paper; make sure that you put quotation marks around material taken verbatim, and double check your text against your note card—or better yet, the original if you have it on hand—to make sure that your quotation is accurate. When paraphrasing or summarizing, make sure you haven't inadvertently borrowed key words or sentence structures from the original.

Finally, as you proofread your final draft, check all your citations one last time. If at any time while you are taking notes or writing your paper you have a question about plagiarism, consult your instructor for clarification and guidance before proceeding.

A DOCUMENTED STUDENT ESSAY

Melanie Milks's essay grew out of her reading in *Subject and Strategy*. Her assignment was to write her own essay in response to one that she had read. She knew from past experience that in order to write a good essay, she would have to write on a topic she cared about. She also knew that she should allow herself a reasonable amount of time to gather her ideas and to focus her topic. After reading Marie Winn's "Television and Family Life" in Chapter 8, Milks knew that she'd found her topic—television and how it affects family. She started to see this paper as an opportunity to become more informed about the issue, to explore her own childhood experiences, and to articulate her own position on it.

Milks began by brainstorming about her topic. She made lists of all the ideas, facts, questions, arguments, opposing arguments, and refutations that came to mind as a result of her own reflections about television viewing. She then went to the library to find additional information and was successful in locating several helpful sources. Once she was confident that she had enough information to begin writing, she made a rough outline of an organizational pattern she believed would work for her. Keeping this pattern in mind, Milks wrote a first draft of her essay, then went back and examined it carefully, assessing how it could be improved.

Milks was writing this particular essay in the second half of the semester after she had read and written a number of essays and had learned the importance of such matters as good paragraphing, unity, and sound organization. In revising her first draft, Milks realized that a chronological organizational pattern would best suit her purpose and rearranged her discussion of family experiences accordingly. She also found places where phrases and even whole sentences could be added to make her meaning clearer. She repositioned some sentences, added some key transitions, and rewrote her concluding paragraphs to make them forceful as well as more persuasive.

As you read Milks's final draft notice how she develops each of her paragraphs, uses specific information and examples to support her thesis and purpose, and how she has used the MLA in-text citation system to acknowledge her sources. Finally, notice how Milks uses her opening paragraph to establish a context for her essay and her concluding paragraph to bring her essay full circle back to her parents' decision to not have television in their home.

THE ABSENCE OF TELEVISION IN MY FAMILY
Melanie Milks

> I believe television is going to be the test of the modern
> world, and that in this new opportunity to see beyond the
> range of our vision we shall discover either a new and
> unbearable disturbance of the general peace or a saving
> radiance in the sky. We shall stand or fall by television—
> of that I am quite sure.
>
> —E. B. White, from "One Man's Meat,"
> Harper's (October 1938)

About two months ago at a dinner for the runners in the Montreal Marathon, my father and I had a discussion with a woman concerning the effects of television on family life. At one point in our conversation, my father mentioned to her that I grew up in a television-free environment. This woman, Elizabeth, looked at my father and asked, "How did you do it?" Elizabeth said she would prefer not having a television in her home but she relies on television for her own stimulation as well as an outlet for her children. Admitting that television disrupted her family harmony, Elizabeth confessed it would be nearly impossible to eliminate television from her daily routine. Nevertheless she applauded the decision my parents made in 1973 to exclude television from our home. In The New Read-Aloud Handbook, Jim Trelease reports that, "Both children and adults average nearly four hours a day [in front of the television] passively letting someone else do all the thinking, speaking, imagining, and exploring" (118). My parents feared that a television would dominate our lives and provide an unnecessary disruption of family.

As a child, I never developed a real appetite for television; I had too many things to keep me occupied. If I weren't looking through a stack of books, I could be found cutting purses out of colorful sheets of construction paper, singing to my favorite records, or coloring with my crayons. There was never enough time, or need, to fit television programs like Mr. Rogers, Sesame Street, or The Electric Company into my day. My mother shuddered at the thought of relying on these programs to teach me how to count from one to ten and recite my ABC's. She and my father gladly undertook this project themselves. We used flashcards and pieces of paper labeling every inch of our house to begin my reading instruction.

Story time became a nightly ritual for both my parents and me. Cuddling up next to them was the best part of my day. I could have spent hours listening to them read while I gazed at the illustrations in front of me. The beautiful drawings pulled me into the story, mesmerizing me. My favorite read-aloud books were The Beatrix Potter series, The Little Princess and The Secret Garden by Francis Hodge Burnette, and Anne of Green Gables by Lucy M. Montgomery. Each story contained lovely illustrations that made my imagination soar.

Reading became a pleasure for me, and consequently I never considered it a chore in school. In second and third grade the public library became my second home. With encouragement from my parents I got my first library card. While many of my friends sat in front of the television after school, I roamed every aisle in the children's section. I read everything from the Anastasia Krupnink series to Superfudge. In third grade I begged my teacher Mrs. Coombs to be allowed to read from the fourth grade book section. After two or three sample novels, I was permitted to choose my first novel from the infamous shelves. I proudly chose a book entitled Roll of Thunder Hear My Cry, one of the best young adult books I have ever read. While my friends were busy reenacting their favorite episodes of Chips, or The Dukes of Hazard, I lingered on every word in my book.

As I got older, I'd often postpone bedtime reading to play checkers or backgammon with my dad. We spent hours huddled over game boards, waiting in silence as the other person developed a strategy for their next move. The silence was always broken by a story or a question. We exchanged details from our day that we failed to mention at the dinner table, and often my dad would tell hilarious stories from his childhood. Laughter continually rang throughout our house. Marie Winn, a nationally recognized television critic and author of The Plug-In-Drug, asserts that there are "decreased opportunities for simple conversation between parents and children in a television-centered home" (346). I believe this. My dad and I might not have done so many things together if we had a television in our house.

Without a television to turn on, I had to use my imagination to its fullest. When we lived in Illinois, I had access to the local library, great playground structures to explore at my elementary school, and friends' houses close by. When we moved to rural Vermont, all my freedoms slipped away from me. I found it difficult acclimating myself to my new surroundings. My parents showed me that Vermont had as much to offer as our urban community in Illinois. Our weekends were packed with camping trips in the Green Mountains and biking along the shores of Lake Champlain. In the winter we cross-country skied in the pastures behind our house. I don't remember having many dull moments growing up.

Nevertheless, at the age of nine I had my own battle with television. Without the accessibility to the local library in our little Vermont town, I would race to my friend Julie's house after school. Instead of enjoying a beautiful fall day outside discovering a new corner of the woods, we sat glued in front of her television watching the last twenty five minutes of Guiding Light, a soap opera I became hooked on. Looking back now, I realize how true Urie Bronfenbrenner's statement about television is. He said, "the television casts its magic spell, freezing speech and action, turning the living into silent statues as long as the enchantments lasts. . . . turning on the television set can turn off the process that transforms children into people" (Winn 341). Never before did I actually realize the addicting qualities of television. I know watching television requires no intelligence because the mind is engaged in the activity on the screen.

Eventually my parents would not let me go to Julie's after school. They witnessed a deterioration in my attention span because of too many afternoons spent in front of what Marie Winn calls the "plug-in-drug." In the evenings I would be somewhat dazed from hours of watching television. My parents constantly reminded me why they chose not to purchase one. But I did not want to listen to their explanations. Sometimes I felt like an outsider at school because I had not seen a particular episode of Silver Spoons or Who's the Boss. However, my parents would not give in to my pestering. They did not want me to grow up like they did, spending beautiful afternoons in front of the television.

At my grandparents' house the television was always on. My father's parents ran a store and my mother's parents both worked. Much of the time my parents spent with their family was done silently, watching evening sitcoms. Jim Trelease states that "conversation during [a television] program is seldom if ever encouraged by the child or the parents" (122). Parenting becomes easy without much interaction between parent and child. Family activities have diminished since the development of television. My parents were afraid of falling into this trap.

At college, my roommate and I have a television in our apartment, and even though it is hardly on, we have favorite shows we occasionally sit down to watch, or catch during dinner. 60 Minutes on Sunday, Melrose Place on Monday, 90210 and Party of Five on Wednesday, Seinfeld and ER on Thursday, and of course CNN. I rarely have time to watch all of these shows in a given week, but there are many people who do. I have found that after a full day of work the lure of the television presents a distraction, and sometimes it is very difficult to turn it off and do my work. Growing up I never had the desire to spend hours in front of the television following a certain show or avoiding something that I had to do. Now, I realize the challenge my parents had keeping the television out of our home, and they were very courageous to raise two children in a television-free environment. I wish I still lived there.

Works Cited

Russell, Christine. "Study: Teens Sitting through Life." Burlington Free Press 8 Nov. 1994: A1.

Trelease, Jim. The New Read-Aloud Handbook. New York: Penguin, 1989.

White, E. B. "One Man's Meat." Harper's Magazine Oct. 1938: 553–56.

Winn, Marie. "Television and Family Life." Subject and Strategy. 7th ed. Eds. Paul Eschholz and Alfred Rosa. New York: St. Martin's, 1995. 341–351.

1
NARRATION

WHAT IS NARRATION?

We all love a good story. We're interested to discover "what happened." The tremendous popularity of current fiction and biography speaks to our avid interest in stories. And, knowing of our interest in stories, many writers and speakers use stories to advantage. A science writer, for example, wishing to make the point that many important scientific discoveries have been made by accident, could tell the story of how Sir Alexander Fleming happened to discover penicillin one day when he saw that a bit of mold that had fallen from a culture plate in his laboratory had destroyed bacteria around it. Or a minister, in writing a sermon about charity, could illustrate and emphasize the point that charity should not always be measured in monetary terms by telling the story of the old woman who spent hours every week visiting hospital patients. Or a politician or after-dinner speaker, taking a cue from comedians, could engage the audience by starting off with a humorous story, either true or fictitious.

Whenever you recount an event, or tell a story or anecdote to illustrate an idea, you are using *narration*. In its broadest sense, narration includes all writing that provides an account of an event or a series of events. Although you are already very familiar with narratives, you probably, like the rest of us, associate narration with novels and short fiction. But narration is effective and useful in nonfiction writing as well. A good narrative essay provides a meaningful account of some significant event—anything from the history of America's involvement in Vietnam to a personal experience that gave you new insight about yourself or others.

A good narrative essay has four essential features. The first is *context:* the writer makes clear when the action happened, where it happened, and to whom. The second is *point of view:* the writer establishes and maintains a consistent relationship to the action, either as a participant or as a reporter simply looking on. The third is *selection of detail:* the writer carefully chooses what to include, focusing on those actions and details that are most important to the story while merely mentioning or actually eliminating others. The fourth is *organization:* the writer organizes the events of the narrative into an appropriate sequence, often a strict chronology with a clear beginning, middle, and end. As you read the selections in this chapter, watch for these features and for how each author uses them to tell his or her story.

WHY DO WRITERS USE NARRATION?

People have been telling stories since the dawn of time and for purposes that have apparently changed very little over the millennia. Perhaps the most basic of these purposes is to entertain. Children love to tell stories and to have stories told to them, and even adults never seem to outgrow their taste for a well-told narrative. People read novels and biographies and watch dramatized stories on television, at the movies, and in the theater, all for the same reason: to be entertained. Certainly, Langston Hughes's "Salvation," a narrative you will find in the following pages, is richly entertaining. But as you will see, this essay does more than entertain, for narration has other purposes as well.

Another of those purposes is to report—to give the facts, to tell what happened. Journalists and historians, in reporting events of the near and more distant past, provide us with information that we can use in our own ways, perhaps to form an opinion about a current issue or to understand why the world is as it is. A biographer gives us another person's life as a document of an individual past but also, perhaps, as a portrait of more general human potential. Scientists recount their experiments so that we may judge for ourselves whether their conclusions are to be believed. We often expect such narratives to be objective, to "stick to the facts," or at least to make clear the difference between facts and opinions.

Perhaps the most important purpose of narration is to instruct. A story may represent a straightforward moral, or it may make a more subtle point about ourselves and the world we live in. In "Letting in Light," Patricia Raybon reassesses the value of women's work as she prepares to pass this work on to her daughter. Langston Hughes, on the other hand, in "Salvation," finds an equally important significance in the story he tells of his early childhood experiences in church.

Finally, it is well worth noting that narration is often used in conjunction with all of the other rhetorical modes. So, in an essay that is primarily explaining a process, how to take a job interview, for example, a writer might find it useful to tell a brief story or anecdote about how the process worked especially well or even failed to work, in a particular instance. Similarly, a writer attempting to define the term *irony*, for example, may find it very useful to tell several stories in which irony figures prominently or is the point of the narrative. Narration, then, can be put to several purposes at once.

LOOKING AT NARRATION

First, make sure that you can follow the events of the narrative, that you understand what's happening. Then, define the writer's purpose and how the various features of the narrative work together to support this purpose.

Consider, for example, the following paragraph from Willie Morris's "On a Commuter Train":

> One afternoon in late August, as the summer's sun streamed into the [railroad] car and made little jumping shadows on the windows, I sat gazing out at the tenement-dwellers, who were themselves looking out of their windows from the gray crumbling buildings along the tracks of upper Manhattan. As we crossed into the Bronx, the train unexpectedly slowed down for a few miles. Suddenly from out of my window I saw a large crowd near the tracks, held back by two policemen. Then, on the other side from my window, I saw a sight I would never be able to forget: a little boy almost severed in halves, lying at an incredible angle near the track. The ground was covered with blood, and the boy's eyes were opened wide, strained and disbelieving in his sudden oblivion. A policeman stood next to him, his arms folded, staring straight ahead at the windows of our train. In the orange glow of late afternoon the policemen, the crowd, the corpse of the boy were for a brief moment immobile, motionless, a small tableau to violence and death in the city. Behind me, in the next row of

seats, there was a game of bridge. I heard one of the four men say as he looked out at the sight, "God, that's horrible." Another said, in a whisper, "Terrible, terrible." There was a momentary silence, punctuated only by the clicking of the wheels on the track. Then, after the pause, I heard the first man say: "Two hearts."

Clearly, few readers would have difficulty understanding what happens here. This is partly because the narrative is so brief and partly because the events are so memorable. More important, though, is the fact that Morris has used the four essential features of narration and has used them effectively. First, he establishes a clear context for his narrative from the very beginning. He tells when the action happened: "One afternoon in late August." He tells where: on the railroad where it crosses from Manhattan into the Bronx. And he tells who it happened to: the passengers on the train, including himself. Next, Morris establishes a first-person point of view (he uses the first-person pronoun *I*) because he is reporting his own experience, and his point of view allows readers to take in the events of the narrative directly, as if through his eyes and ears. He also chooses his details carefully and well. He provides just enough information about the train, the passengers, and the accident so that readers know what they need to know without being overwhelmed or bored. He does not bother with needless data such as the name of the railroad or the precise time; yet he gives significant attention to the boy's corpse and to the other passengers' reactions, placing the emphasis squarely on these aspects of his story. Every detail is there for a purpose. Finally, Morris organizes his story chronologically, so that the events follow each other as they actually occurred. Notice his use of well-placed words and phrases such as *suddenly, then, momentary silence,* and *after the pause* to make transitions between events and clearly indicate how long each event lasted.

Morris's purpose in telling this story is to make a point. He doesn't state his point directly, but it comes out in the closing sentences where he reports the bridge players' reactions to the grisly sight of the dead boy's corpse: first, "God, that's horrible," and "Terrible, terrible"; then, "Two hearts." Morris does not tell his readers what to think of this, and different readers will probably respond in different ways. Some will conclude that the bridge players were unmoved by the boy's death, that they were so callous that they could return to their bridge game after only a "momentary silence." Others may feel that despite everything, even a tragedy such as the death of the boy, life goes on—that it *must* go on—and that the bridge players were not insensitive, merely coping in a typical way with one of life's shocks. You might draw a quite different conclusion of your own. Morris's essay is not a puzzle with a single "right" answer, but an opportunity to broaden your experience and discover your own values and beliefs.

Morris might have told his story from the third-person point of view, as if he were not a participant in the action but merely a reporter of it. Doing so would have cost him some of the immediacy and authority he achieves—it's hard to dispute the facts as he states them, since he was there—but the relative impersonality, the "distance," of third-person point of view has its advantages too. Consider, for example, the following paragraph by William Allen White, from an obituary for his daughter. Again it's a young person who has died and, of course, White was writing from firsthand experience just as Morris was. But he chooses instead to write in the third person:

> The last hour of her life was typical of its happiness. She came home from a day's work at school, topped off by a hard grind with the copy on the High School Annual, and felt that a ride would refresh her. She climbed into her khakis, chattering to her mother about the work she was doing, and hurried to get her horse and be out on the dirt roads for the country air and the radiant green fields of the spring. As she rode through the town on an easy gallop she kept waving at passersby. She knew everyone in town. For a decade the little figure with the long pig-tail and the red hair ribbon has been familiar on the streets of Emporia, and she got in the way of speaking to those who nodded at her. She passed the Kerrs, walking the horse, in front of the Normal Library, and waved at them; passed another friend a few hundred feet further on, and waved at her. The horse was walking and, as she turned into North Merchant street she took off her cowboy hat, and the horse swung into a lope. She passed the Tripletts and waved her cowboy hat at them, still moving gaily north on Merchant street. A Gazette carrier passed—a High School boy friend—and she waved at him, but with her bridle hand: the horse veered quickly, plunged into the parking lot where the low-hanging limb faced her, and, while she still looked back waving, the blow came. But she did not fall from the horse, she slipped off, dazed a bit, staggered and fell in a faint. She never quite recovered consciousness.

White's third-person point of view keeps the focus squarely on his young daughter and her activities. He himself never appears, never comments, never states his feelings. This objectivity—the psychological distance he sets between himself and his subject—might at first seem strange, even inappropriate, in so personal a narrative. But by presenting the girl in this way, White hopes to make the reader mourn her death as he did. His love for his daughter comes through without his having to assert it, and by keeping his distance he prevents any possibility that sorrow for his daughter will be diluted by sympathy for himself.

Note also that, unlike Morris, White states the point of his story explicitly, indeed in the first sentence: his daughter was a happy little girl. It's this sentence that determines what events he will report, how he will arrange them, and how much detail he will supply about each.

READING NARRATION IN AN ANNOTATED STUDENT ESSAY

Andrew Kauser, a student at the University of Vermont, was born in Montreal, Canada, where he grew up and still makes his home. As a youngster, he often went on weekend-long flying trips with his father, who is a pilot, and these experiences instilled in him a passion for flying and a desire to get his own pilot's license one day. In the following essay, Kauser writes how he felt as he took that most important step in becoming a licensed pilot, the first solo flight.

CHALLENGING MY FEARS
Andrew Kauser

Context

Cedars Airport, just off the western tip of Montreal, is about a half-hour drive from my house. Today's drive is boring as usual except for the chill which runs up the back of my legs because of the cold breeze entering through the rusted floorboards. I peer through the dew-covered windshield to see the leaves changing color. Winter is on its way. 1

Chronological order

Finally, I arrive at the airport; while my instructor waits, I do my aircraft check. I curse as I touch the steely cold parts of the aircraft. Even though the discomfort is great, I do my check slowly. Hurrying could make me miss a potential problem. It is better to find a problem on the ground instead of in the air. The check takes about fifteen minutes, and by this time my fingertips are white. Everything appears to be in order so now it is time to start up. 2

My instructor and I climb into the cockpit of the airplane and strap ourselves in. The plane has been out all night, and it is just as cold inside as it is outside. My back shivers as I sit in the seat, and the 3 controls are painfully cold to the touch. The plane starts without a hint of trouble, and in one continuous motion I taxi onto the runway. At full throttle we begin to increase our speed down the runway. In a matter of seconds we leave the ground. The winds are calm and the visibility is endless. It's a beautiful day to fly.

Purpose of the flight

The object of today's lesson is to practice taking   4 off and landing. The first "touch and go" is so smooth that I surprise both myself and my instructor. Unfortunately, my next two attempts are more like "smash and goes." I land once more; this time it is not as jarring as my last two, and my instructor gives me the O.K. to do a circuit alone. We taxi to the hangar and he gets out.

Confined in the small cockpit with my seatbelt   5 strapped around me as tightly as it will go, I look out the window and watch my human security blanket walking back toward the hangars. The calm feeling with which I began the day quickly disappears. I feel like a soldier being sent to the front lines. I begin to feel smothered by the enclosed cockpit. My stomach tightens around the breakfast I ate and squeezes out my last breath. I gulp for air, and my breathing becomes irregular. My mind still functions, though, and I begin to taxi toward the runway.

Key word transition

Showing rather than telling

It is a long taxi, and I have ample time to think   6 about what I am about to do. I remember the time when my father had to land on a football field when his engine quit. My eyes scan the instruments quickly in hope of finding something comforting in all the dials. My hands are still feeling quite cool. I reach out and pull the lever for cabin heat. A rush of warm air saturated with the smell of the engine fills the cockpit. This allows me some comfort and my mind begins to wander. The radio crackles and breaks my train of thought. A student pilot in the air with his instructor announces that he is on final approach for landing. While still taxiing, I look through the Plexiglas windscreen to watch him land. The plane hits hard and bounces right back into the air from which it came. It comes down again and, as though on springs, leaps back into the air. Once again it comes down and this time stays.

At the parking area off the runway, I close the throttle and bring the plane to a stop. I check the instruments and request clearance for take-off from the tower. While I wait I try to calm down. 7

*Key idea
transition*

Now hold your breath and count to ten. Look, the chances of dying in a car accident are twenty times greater, I think to myself. Somehow that wasn't very comforting. The radio crackles, and I exhale quickly. Permission is granted. 8

I taxi onto the runway and come to a stop. I mentally list my options, but they are very few. One is to get up the courage to challenge my fears; the other, to turn the plane around and shamefully go back to the hangar. Well, the choices are limited, but the ultimate decision seems fairly obvious. I reach out and push the throttle into the full open position. The engine roars to life. The decision to go has been made. The plane screams down the runway, and at fifty-five knots I pull back on the controls. In one clean movement, the plane and I leave the ground. 9

*Connection is
made to title*

The noise of the engine is the only thing I can hear as the air pressure begins to clog my ears. My mind still racing, I check my instruments. The winds are still calm, and the plane cuts through the air without a hint of trouble. Warm gas-laden air streams through the vents as the sun streaks into the cockpit through the passenger window, and I begin to feel quite hot. At seven hundred feet above the ground, I turn left, check for any traffic, and continue climbing. At twelve hundred feet, I turn left onto the downwind portion of the circuit which is parallel to the runway. 10

*"This" used as a
pronoun
transition*

This is a longer stretch, and I take a moment to gaze down at the ground below. The view is simply amazing. The trees are all rich bright colors, and I can 11 see for miles. Then it hits me. I'm flying alone. It's great, almost tranquil, no instructor yelling things into my ear, just the machine and myself. A calm feeling begins to come over me, and I start to enjoy the flight. I check my instruments again and start to descend as I turn left.

More commentary that reveals the author "challenging his fears"

Author addresses himself directly

Turning onto the final approach, I announce my intentions on the radio. The nice feeling of calm leaves me just as quickly as it came. What is there to worry about, Andrew? All you have to do is land the airplane, preferably on the runway. My heart starts to pound quickly, almost to the beat of the motor. Where is my instructor? Why am I alone? 12

Lower the nose, Andrew, don't lose speed. Give it some more power, maintain your glidepath, that's it. Bank a little to the left, that's it, now you're doing it, just a little further. My ears begin to pop as the pressure on them decreases and the motor gets quieter as I start to decrease power. The plane passes over the threshold of the runway, and I begin to raise the nose. The wheels utter a squeal as they touch down, but the impact quickly sends the plane back into the air. The wheels hit again and this time they stay down. A few seconds later my nose wheel touches down, and I roll to a stop. 13

Comments that relate to the author's purpose

Reference to key words in title

Back at the hangar, I climb out of the plane and shudder as the cool air hits me again. A smile comes across my face, and it persists. I told myself that I would just be cool about it and not try to show any emotion but it isn't going to work. I can't stop smiling as my instructor congratulates me. I smile because I know that I was successful in challenging and overcoming my fear. 14

In commenting on how important it was for him to set a context for the essay, Andrew Kauser said the following: "Context is very important in anything that you write, but especially in a narrative. The experience I recount in my essay took place in a specific time and place. It wouldn't have been the same narrative if it had taken place in some other city or country. Basically, the narrative is specific to that situation, and it wouldn't be credible to me in another situation."

In reflecting on the purpose of his essay, Kauser said, "The experience I had with flying was fresh in my mind, and at the time it seemed to be the most interesting thing that had happened to me recently. The purpose of the narrative was to share my experience of flying with the class. When I used to fly with my dad, I was afraid of flying because I didn't know how to operate the plane. In a way, it was a challenge to myself to find out how to fly. I guess I just wanted to tell the readers that you don't get anywhere by just sitting around being afraid."

WRITING A NARRATIVE ESSAY

Once you have decided upon the story you want to tell and have determined your purpose, you should keep in mind the basic features of narration and use them when planning, writing, and revising your narrative essay. How you use those features will depend on the story you have to tell and your purpose for telling it.

Purpose

Right from the beginning, ask yourself *why* you are telling your story. Your purpose in writing will influence which events and details you include and which you leave out. Suppose, for example, you choose to write about how you learned to ride a bicycle. If you mean mainly to entertain, you will probably include a number of unusual and amusing incidents, unique to your experience. If your purpose is mainly to report or inform, it will make more sense to concentrate on the kinds of details that are common to most people's experience. (However, if your purpose is to tell your readers step-by-step how to ride a bicycle, you should use process analysis and not narration.)

The most successful narrative essays, however, often do more than entertain or inform. Readers will more than likely expect your story to have a point; certainly, you will not be happy if your story is dismissed as essentially "pointless." As you prepare to write, then, look for some significance in the story you want to tell—some broader, more instructive points it may make about the ways of the world. Learning to ride a bicycle may not suggest such points, and it may therefore not be a very good subject for an essay. However, the subject does have possibilities. Here's one: learning to master a difficult, even dangerous, but definitely useful skill like riding a bike is an important experience to have early in life. Here's another: learning to ride a bicycle requires you to acquire and use some basic physics such as the laws of gravity and the behavior of a gyroscope. Maybe you can think of others. If, however, your story seems pointless even to you, perhaps you can find another, more interesting story to tell.

Context

Early in your essay, often in the first paragraph or two, you should establish the context, or setting, of your story—the world within which its action took place:

When it happened—morning, afternoon, 11:37 on the dot.

Where it happened—in the street, at Wendy's, in Pocatello, Idaho.

To whom it happened—to me, to my father, to the secretary, to Teri Hopper.

Without a clear context, your readers can easily get confused or even completely lost.

Point of View

You should consider what point of view to take in your narrative. Did you take part in the action? If so, it will seem most natural for you to use the first-person point of view. On the other hand, if you weren't there at all and must rely on other sources for your information, you will probably choose the third-person point of view without even thinking about it. However, if you were a witness to part or all of what happened but not a participant, then you will need to choose between the more immediate and subjective quality of the first person and the more distanced, objective effect of the third person. Whichever you choose, you should maintain that same point of view throughout your narrative, as Willie Morris and William Allen White did in theirs.

Selection of Events and Details

The proper use of details in an essay can help your reader understand and appreciate your message. Andrew Kauser learned this lesson from his classmates: "I had a problem trying to make the audience grasp what I was talking about. The first time I read my essay to the class, their reaction was that I didn't use enough detail and so they really didn't feel as though they were there with me. I consequently included many more details when I read the essay, and they were able to understand the experience better."

When writing your essay, you should include enough detail about the action and its context so that your readers can understand what is going on. In addition, you will want to select and emphasize events and details that serve your purpose. Nonetheless, you should not get so carried away with details that your readers become confused or bored by an excess of information. In good storytelling, deciding what to include is as important as deciding what to leave out.

Organization

Storytellers tend to follow an old rule: "Begin at the beginning and go on till you come to the end; then stop." Chronological organization is natural in narration, because it is a reconstruction of the original order of events; it is also easiest for the writer to manage and the reader to understand.

Interestingly, Andrew Kauser chose a chronological ordering for his narrative because, as he said, "I didn't think much about patterns other than chronological. For the most part, I felt I had no choice but to write it that way. I did have difficulty in beginning the narrative because I wasn't sure whether I wanted to write it in the past or the present tense. I made many attempts at different beginnings, from describing waking up on the morning of my flight to describing how I spent my summer flying. Once I found a beginning that I liked, it was relatively easy to write the rest of the essay because I just wrote about the events in the order that they happened. The beginning solved my tense problem as well."

Some narratives, however, are organized using a technique common in movies and the theater called *flashback:* the writer may begin midway through the story with an important or exciting event, then use flashbacks to fill in what happened earlier. Whatever the organization, words and phrases like *for a month, afterward,* and *three days earlier* are examples of devices that will help you and your reader keep the sequence of events straight.

It may help you in organizing to jot down a scratch outline before tackling the first draft of your narrative. Here's an outline of the Willie Morris selection—not by him, of course, but still a useful model:

NARRATION ABOUT AN ACCIDENT ON THE TRAIN LINE.

Point: the way the bridge players responded to the boy's death.

Context: commuter train, leaving Manhattan, afternoon, late August.

1. I'm riding along, looking at the tenements.
2. The train slows, I see a crowd out my window.
3. I look out the opposite window, see boy killed by train. Lots of detail.
4. Bridge players' first comments—quote them.
5. Bridge players resume their game as if accident hadn't happened.

Such an outline can remind you of your point, your organization, and the emphasis you want when you write your first draft.

More Helpful Suggestions

VERB TENSE.　Most narratives are in the past tense, and this is logical: they recount events that have already happened, even if very recently. But writers sometimes like to use the present tense to create an effect of intense immediacy, as if the events were happening as you read about them. The essay by Andrew Kauser, "Challenging My Fears," is an example of the use of present-tense narrative.

NARRATIVE TIME.　The number of words or pages you devote to an event does not usually correspond to the number of minutes or hours the event took to happen. You may require several pages to recount an important or complex quarter of an hour, but then pass over years in a sentence or two. Length has to do not with chronological time but with the amount of detail you include, and that's a function of the amount of emphasis you want to give.

TRANSITIONAL WORDS.　Words like *next, then,* or *and* are useful, as they help you to carry your readers smoothly through the sequence of events that makes up your narrative. But inexperienced writers sometimes repeat these words needlessly, and this makes their writing style wordy and tiresome. Use these conventional transitions when you really need them, but when you don't—when your readers can follow your story without them—leave them out.

DIALOGUE.　Having people in a narrative speak in a very effective way of "showing rather than telling," of making a story come alive and be immediate. Sometimes dialogue can be very cleverly made a part of a narrative. When it was observed that Andrew Kauser appeared not to have used any dialogue in his "Challenging My Fears" essay, he disagreed, "In paragraphs 12 and 13 of the narration I do use dialogue— dialogue without quotation marks, however. It is a kind of interior monologue in which I hear my instructor talking to me. I tried other ways of writing the paragraph, but it really didn't come off as well. This passage was very easy for me to write because it was exactly what I was thinking when I was up there."

Coming to an Awareness of Language
MALCOLM X

Malcolm X, leader of the Black Muslims, was shot and killed at the age of thirty-nine on February 21, 1965, as he addressed an afternoon rally in Harlem. In his short lifetime, Malcolm X rose from a life on the streets to become one of the most controversial and articulate spokesmen for African Americans in the 1960s. With Alex Haley, later the author of Roots, *Malcolm X wrote* The Autobiography of Malcolm X.*

In the following chapter from his book, Malcolm X explains how his frustration at being unable to express his ideas led to his determination to master the skills of reading and writing while he was serving time in a federal prison.

I've never been one for inaction. Everything I've ever felt strongly 1 about, I've done something about. I guess that's why, unable to do anything else, I soon began writing to people I had known in the hustling world, such as Sammy the Pimp, John Hughes, the gambling house owner, the thief Jumpsteady, and several dope peddlers. I wrote them all about Allah and Islam and Mr. Elijah Muhammad. I had no idea where most of them lived. I addressed their letters in care of the Harlem or Roxbury bars and clubs where I'd known them.

I never got a single reply. The average hustler and criminal was too 2 uneducated to write a letter. I have known many slick, sharp-looking hustlers, who would have you think they had an interest in Wall Street; privately, they would get someone else to read a letter if they received one. Besides, neither would I have replied to anyone writing me something as wild as "the white man is the devil."

What certainly went on the Harlem and Roxbury wires was that 3 Detroit Red was going crazy in stir, or else he was trying some hype to shake up the warden's office.

During the years that I stayed in the Norfolk Prison Colony, never 4 did any official directly say anything to me about those letters, although, of course, they all passed through the prison censorship. I'm sure, however, they monitored what I wrote to add to the files which every state and federal prison keeps on the conversion of Negro inmates by the teachings of Mr. Elijah Muhammad.

But at that time, I felt that the real reason was that the white man 5
knew that he was the devil.

Later on, I even wrote to the Mayor of Boston, to the Governor of 6
Massachusetts, and to Harry S. Truman. They never answered; they
probably never even saw my letters. I handscratched to them how the
white man's society was responsible for the black man's condition in
this wilderness of North America.

It was because of my letters that I happened to stumble upon 7
starting to acquire some kind of a homemade education.

I became increasingly frustrated at not being able to express what 8
I wanted to convey in letters that I wrote, especially those to Mr. Elijah
Muhammad. In the street, I had been the most articulate hustler out
there—I had commanded attention when I said something. But now,
trying to write simple English, I not only wasn't articulate, I wasn't
even functional. How would I sound writing in slang, the way I would
say it, something such as, "Look, daddy, let me pull your coat about a
cat. Elijah Muhammad—"

Many who today hear me somewhere in person, or on television, or 9
those who read something I've said, will think I went to school far beyond the eighth grade. This impression is due entirely to my prison
studies.

It had really begun back in the Charlestown Prison, when Bimbi 10
first made me feel envy of his stock of knowledge. Bimbi had always
taken charge of any conversation he was in, and I had tried to emulate
him. But every book I picked up had few sentences which didn't contain anywhere from one to nearly all of the words that might as well
have been in Chinese. When I just skipped those words, of course, I
really ended up with little idea of what the book said. So I had come to
the Norfolk Prison Colony still going through only book-reading
motions. Pretty soon, I would have quit even these motions, unless I
had received the motivation that I did.

I saw that the best thing I could do was get hold of a dictionary—to 11
study, to learn some words. I was lucky enough to reason also that I
should try to improve my penmanship. It was sad. I couldn't even write
in a straight line. It was both ideas together that moved me to request
a dictionary along with some tablets and pencils from the Norfolk
Prison Colony school.

I spent two days just riffling uncertainly through the dictionary's 12
pages. I'd never realized so many words existed! I didn't know *which*
words I needed to learn. Finally, just to start some kind of action, I
began copying.

In my slow, painstaking, ragged handwriting, I copied into my tablet everything printed on that first page, down to the punctuation marks. 13

I believe it took me a day. Then, aloud, I read back, to myself, everything I'd written on the tablet. Over and over, aloud, to myself, I read my own handwriting. 14

I woke up the next morning, thinking about those words— immensely proud to realize that not only had I written so much at one time, but I'd written words that I never knew were in the world. Moreover, with a little effort, I also could remember what many of these words meant. I reviewed the words whose meanings I didn't remember. Funny thing, from the dictionary first page right now, that "aardvark" springs to my mind. The dictionary had a picture of it, a long-tailed, long-eared, burrowing African mammal, which lives off termites caught by sticking out its tongue as an anteater does for ants. 15

I was so fascinated that I went on—I copied the dictionary's next page. And the same experience came when I studied that. With every succeeding page, I also learned of people and places and events from history. Actually the dictionary is like a miniature encyclopedia. Finally the dictionary's A section had filled a whole tablet—and I went on into the B's. That was the way I started copying what eventually became the entire dictionary. It went a lot faster after so much practice helped me to pick up handwriting speed. Between what I wrote in my tablet, and writing letters, during the rest of my time in prison I would guess I wrote a million words. 16

I suppose it was inevitable that as my word-base broadened, I could for the first time pick up a book and read and now begin to understand what the book was saying. Anyone who has read a great deal can imagine the new world that opened. Let me tell you something: from then until I left that prison, in every free moment I had, if I was not reading in the library, I was reading on my bunk. You couldn't have gotten me out of books with a wedge. Between Mr. Muhammad's teachings, my correspondence, my visitors . . . and my reading of books, months passed without my even thinking about being imprisoned. In fact, up to then, I never had been so truly free in my life. 17

QUESTIONS ON SUBJECT

1. Exactly what inspired Malcolm X to "acquire some kind of homemade education"?

2. What are the "Harlem and Roxbury wires" Malcolm X refers to in paragraph 3? Who is Detroit Red?

3. In paragraph 8, Malcolm X refers to the difference between being "articulate" and being "functional" in his speaking and writing. What is the distinction he makes? In your opinion is it a valid one? Why or why not?

4. Malcolm X offers two possible reasons for the warden's keeping track of Negroes' conversion to Muhammadanism. One he states directly; one he implies. What are those two assertions, and what is their effect on the reader?

5. What did Malcolm X hope to learn by copying the dictionary? What unexpected discovery did he make?

QUESTIONS ON STRATEGY

1. Malcolm X narrates his experiences as a prisoner in the first person. Why is the first person particularly appropriate?

2. In his opening paragraph, Malcolm X refers to himself as a man of action and conviction. What details does he include to support this assertion?

3. In the opening paragraph, the author presents a list of the names of people he wrote to. How does this list help to establish the context of the story? In what ways is it appropriate?

4. What point is Malcolm X trying to make with his narration? Is it stated directly, or is it implied?

5. Malcolm X makes several references to Muhammad throughout his essay. What effect do these repetitions have on the reader? In what way do they add to the narration?

6. Is Malcolm X more interested in causes or effects in this essay, or is he interested in both equally? Explain. (Glossary: *Cause and Effect*)

QUESTIONS ON LANGUAGE

1. Although Malcolm X taught himself to be articulate, we can still "hear" the voice of the inner city. Cite examples of his diction that help him to maintain a streetwise sound.

2. Malcolm X took great care to copy the dictionary cover to cover. The painstaking nature of this work is apparent in his writing. Cite examples of his choice of phrasing that enable you to feel the almost plodding care he brings to any task.

3. Refer to your desk dictionary to determine the meanings of the following words as they are used in this selection: *hustler* (paragraph 2), *slick* (2), *hype* (3), *frustrated* (8), *articulate* (8), *functional* (8), *emulate* (10), *inevitable* (17).

WRITING SUGGESTIONS

1. Using Malcolm X's essay as a model, write a narrative about some goal you have set and achieved in which you were motivated by a strong inner conflict. What was the nature of your conflict? What feeling did it arouse in you, and how did it help you to accomplish your goal?

2. Malcolm X expresses his anger at the white man, but he never asks the reader to feel sorry for him. Write a narrative in which you describe your own anger at some injustice to you or someone you know. How can you convey your sense of anger without resorting to a "whining" plea for sympathy?

Letting in Light

PATRICIA RAYBON

Patricia Raybon, a journalist and professor of journalism at the University of Colorado, was born in 1949. Raybon worked as a reporter and feature writer for the Rocky Mountain News *and later edited the weekend magazine for the* Denver Post. *Her articles have appeared in* Newsweek, USA Today, *and* The New York Times Magazine.

In the following piece, which was first published in The New York Times, *Raybon reassesses the value of women's work. Action and perception melt into the metaphor of washing windows, as Raybon examines her own feelings toward women's work and passing this work on to her daughter as this work had been passed to her by her grandmother and mother.*

The windows were a gift or maybe a bribe—or maybe a bonus—for 1 falling in love with such a dotty old house. The place was a wreck. A showoff, too. So it tried real hard to be more. But it lacked so much—good heat, stable floors, solid walls, enough space. A low interest rate.

But it had windows. More glass and bays and bows than people on 2 a budget had a right to expect. And in unlikely places—like the window inside a bedroom closet, its only view a strawberry patch planted by the children next door.

None of it made sense. So we bought the place. We saved up and 3 put some money down, then toasted the original builder—no doubt some brave and gentle carpenter, blessed with a flair for the grand gesture. A romantic with a T-square.

We were young then and struggling. Also, we are black. We looked 4 with irony and awe at the task now before us. But we did not faint.

The time had come to wash windows. 5

Yes, I do windows. Like an amateur and a dabbler, perhaps, but the 6 old-fashioned way—one pane at a time. It is the best way to pay back something so plain for its clear and silent gifts—the light of day, the glow of moon, hard rain, soft snow, dawn's early light.

The Romans called them *specularia*. They glazed their windows 7 with translucent marble and shells. And thus the ancients let some light into their world.

In my own family, my maternal grandmother washed windows—   8
and floors and laundry and dishes and a lot of other things that needed
cleaning—while doing day work for a rich, stylish redhead in her Southern hometown.

To feed her five children and keep them clothed and happy, to help   9
them walk proudly and go to church and sing hymns and have some
change in their pockets—and to warm and furnish the house her dead
husband had built and added onto with his own hands—my grandmother went to work.

She and her third daughter, my mother, put on maids' uniforms   10
and cooked and sewed and served a family that employed my grandmother until she was nearly 80. She called them Mister and Missus—
yes, ma'am and yes, sir—although she was by many years their elder.
They called her Laura. Her surname never crossed their lips.

But her daughter, my mother, took her earnings from the cooking   11
and serving and window washing and clothes ironing and went to
college, forging a life with a young husband—my father—that granted
me, their daughter, a lifetime of relative comfort.

I owe these women everything.   12

They taught me hope and kindness and how to say thank you.   13

They taught me how to brew tea and pour it. They taught me how   14
to iron creases and whiten linen and cut hair ribbon on the bias so it
doesn't unravel. They taught me to carve fowl, make butter molds and
cook a good cream sauce. They taught me "women's work"—secrets
of home, they said, that now are looked on mostly with disdain: how to
sweep, dust, polish, and wax. How to mow, prune, scrub, scour, and
purify.

They taught me how to wash windows.   15

Not many women do anymore, of course. There's no time. Life has   16
us all on the run. It's easier to call a "window man," quicker to pay and,
in the bargain, forget about the secret that my mother and her mother
learned many years before they finally taught it to me.

Washing windows clears the cobwebs from the corners. It's plain   17
people's therapy, good for troubles and muddles and other consternations. It's real work, I venture—honest work—and it's a sound thing to
pass on. Mother to daughter. Daughter to child. Woman to woman.

This is heresy, of course. Teaching a girl to wash windows is now an   18
act of bravery—or else defiance. If she's black, it's an act of denial, a
gesture that dares history and heritage to make something of it.

But when my youngest was 5 or 6, I tempted fate and ancestry and   19
I handed her a wooden bucket. Together we would wash the outdoor
panes. The moment sits in my mind.

She works a low row. I work the top. Silently we toil, soaping and 20
polishing, each at her own pace—the only sounds the squeak of glass,
some noisy birds, our own breathing.

Then, quietly at first, this little girl begins to hum. It's a nonsense 21
melody, created for the moment. Soft at first, soon it gets louder. And
louder. Then a recognizable tune emerges. Then she is really singing.
With every swish of the towel, she croons louder and higher in her
little-girl voice with her little-girl song. "This little light of mine—I'm
gonna let it shine! Oh, this little light of mine—I'm gonna let it shine!"
So, of course, I join in. And the two of us serenade the glass and the
sparrows and mostly each other. And too soon our work is done.

"That was fun," she says. She is innocent, of course, and does this 22
work by choice, not by necessity. But she's not too young to look at
truth and understand it. And her heart, if not her arm, is resolute and
strong.

Those years have passed. And other houses and newer windows— 23
and other "women's jobs"—have moved through my life. I have
chopped and pureed and polished and glazed. Bleached and folded and
stirred. I have sung lullabies.

I have also marched and fought and prayed and taught and tes- 24
tified. Women's work covers many bases.

But the tradition of one simple chore remains. I do it without apology. 25

Last week, I dipped the sponge into the pail and began the gentle 26
bath—easing off the trace of wintry snows, of dust storms and dead,
brown leaves, of too much sticky tape used to steady paper pumpkins
and Christmas lights and crepe-paper bows from holidays now past.
While I worked, the little girl—now 12—found her way to the bucket,
proving that her will and her voice are still up to the task, but mostly,
I believe, to have some fun.

We are out of step, the two of us. She may not even know it. But we 27
can carry a tune. The work is never done. The song is two-part harmony.

QUESTIONS ON SUBJECT

1. What distinction does the author make between amateur and professional?
   Why is she proud to be an amateur?

2. Why do you think Raybon chose to use "window man" instead of window
   person in paragraph 16? What is she saying about women's work?

3. How is teaching a black girl to wash windows an act of denial?

4. What truth does Raybon's daughter see and understand? Is it important
   that her daughter was working by choice and not out of necessity? Explain.

QUESTIONS ON STRATEGY

1. How do the first five paragraphs serve as an introduction to this essay? What parallels do you see between the author's first house and the narrative that follows?

2. Raybon writes about washing windows with her daughter, when her daughter was 5 or 6, in the present tense. Try changing the verb tense from past to present in another one of her paragraphs. What's different? Why do you think she chose to use the present tense while writing about washing windows with her daughter?

3. The author uses several one sentence paragraphs. Re-read these paragraphs by themselves. How do they read differently on their own? What effect do they have within the essay?

4. In a relatively short narrative essay, Raybon moves back and forth through time and focuses on several characters. What holds everything together?

5. In paragraphs 8–11, Raybon uses cause and effect analysis to discuss how window washing changed her family. What exactly are the effects of washing windows on this family? (Glossary: *Cause and Effect Analysis*)

6. At several points in her essay, Raybon seems on the verge of telling us how to wash windows. Why do you suppose she doesn't give us a step-by-step description of how she and her daughter wash windows? (Glossary: *Process Analysis*)

QUESTIONS ON LANGUAGE

1. Raybon writes that she and her husband looked at the task of fixing and paying for their first house with "irony and awe". What irony do you see in these first few paragraphs?

2. Look up *specularia* in your dictionary. If you can't find it, look for some derivatives. What does this add to your understanding of the essay?

3. Using your desk dictionary, look up the following words as they appear in the essay: *dotty* (paragraph 1), *translucent* (7), *consternations* (17), *heresy* (18).

WRITING ASSIGNMENTS

1. Write a narrative essay dealing with work that receives little or no recognition. What is enjoyable about this work? What is the popular conception of this work? What would you like people to value in this work?

2. Write a narrative essay examining what women's work means to you. What work do the women around you perform? Compare it with the work you see men doing. What people and literature have influenced your views on this subject? Have your views changed recently? If so, how and why?

Salvation

LANGSTON HUGHES

Born in Joplin, Missouri, Langston Hughes (1902–1967) wrote poetry, fiction, and drama and regularly contributed a column to the New York Post. *An important figure in the Harlem Renaissance, he is best known for* Weary Blues, The Negro Mother, Shakespeare in Harlem, *and* Ask Your Mama, *collections of poetry that reflect his racial pride, his familiarity with the traditions of African Americans, and his knowledge of jazz rhythms.*

In this selection taken from his autobiography, The Big Sea, *Hughes narrates his experiences at a church revival meeting he attended when he was twelve years old.*

I was saved from sin when I was going on thirteen. But not really 1 saved. It happened like this. There was a big revival at my Auntie Reed's church. Every night for weeks there had been much preaching, singing, praying, and shouting, and some very hardened sinners had been brought to Christ, and the membership of the church had grown by leaps and bounds. Then just before the revival ended, they held a special meeting for children, "to bring the young lambs to the fold." My aunt spoke of it for days ahead. That night I was escorted to the front row and placed on the mourners' bench with all the other young sinners, who had not yet been brought to Jesus.

My aunt told me that when you were saved you saw a light, and 2 something happened to you inside! And Jesus came into your life! And God was with you from then on! She said you could see and hear and feel Jesus in your soul. I believed her. I have heard a great many old people say the same thing and it seemed to me they ought to know. So I sat there calmly in the hot, crowded church, waiting for Jesus to come to me.

The preacher preached a wonderful rhythmical sermon, all moans 3 and shouts and lonely cries and dire pictures of hell, and then he sang a song about the ninety and nine safe in the fold, but one little lamb was left out in the cold. Then he said: "Won't you come? Won't you come to Jesus? Young lambs, won't you come?" And he held out his arms to all us young sinners there on the mourners' bench. And the little girls cried. And some of them jumped up and went to Jesus right away. But most of us just sat there.

A great many old people came and knelt around us and prayed, old 4 women with jet-black faces and braided hair, old men with work-gnarled hands. And the church sang a song about the lower lights are burning, some poor sinners to be saved. And the whole building rocked with prayer and song.

Still I kept waiting to *see* Jesus.   5

Finally all the young people had gone to the altar and were saved,   6 but one boy and me. He was a rounder's son named Westley. Westley and I were surrounded by sisters and deacons praying. It was very hot in the church, and getting late now. Finally Westley said to me in a whisper: "God damn! I'm tired o' sitting here. Let's get up and be saved." So he got up and was saved.

Then I was left all alone on the mourners' bench. My aunt came   7 and knelt at my knees and cried, while prayers and songs swirled all around me in the little church. The whole congregation prayed for me alone, in a mighty wail of moans and voices. And I kept waiting serenely for Jesus, waiting, waiting—but he didn't come. I wanted to see him, but nothing happened to me. Nothing! I wanted something to happen to me, but nothing happened.

I heard the songs and the minister saying: "Why don't you come?   8 My dear child, why don't you come to Jesus? Jesus is waiting for you. He wants you. Why don't you come? Sister Reed, what is this child's name?"

"Langston," my aunt sobbed.   9

"Langston, why don't you come? Why don't you come and be   10 saved? Oh, Lamb of God! Why don't you come?"

Now it was really getting late. I began to be ashamed of myself,   11 holding everything up so long. I began to wonder what God thought about Westley, who certainly hadn't seen Jesus either, but who was now sitting proudly on the platform, swinging his knickerbockered legs and grinning down at me, surrounded by deacons and old women on their knees praying. God had not struck Westley dead for taking his name in vain or for lying in the temple. So I decided that maybe to save further trouble, I'd better lie, too, and say that Jesus had come, and get up and be saved.

So I got up.   12

Suddenly the whole room broke into a sea of shouting, as they saw   13 me rise. Waves of rejoicing swept the place. Women leaped in the air. My aunt threw her arms around me. The minister took me by the hand and led me to the platform.

When things quieted down, in a hushed silence, punctuated by a   14 few ecstatic "Amens," all the new young lambs were blessed in the name of God. Then joyous singing filled the room.

That night, for the last time in my life but one—for I was a big boy   15 twelve years old—I cried. I cried, in bed alone, and couldn't stop. I buried my head under the quilts, but my aunt heard me. She woke up and told my uncle I was crying because the Holy Ghost had come into my life, and because I had seen Jesus. But I was really crying because I couldn't bear to tell her that I had lied, that I had deceived everybody in the church, that I hadn't seen Jesus, and that now I didn't believe there was a Jesus any more, since he didn't come to help me.

QUESTIONS ON SUBJECT

1. Why does the young Langston expect to be saved at the revival meeting? Once the children are in church, what appeals are made to them to encourage them to seek salvation?

2. Trace the various pressures working on Hughes that lead to his decision to "get up and be saved" (paragraph 11). What important realization finally convinces him to lie about being saved?

3. Even though Hughes's account of the events at the revival is at points humorous, the experience was nonetheless painful for him. Why does he cry on the night of his "salvation"? Why does his aunt think he is crying? What significance is there in the disparity between their views?

QUESTIONS ON STRATEGY

1. What paradox or apparent contradiction does Hughes present in the first two sentences of the narrative? Why do you suppose he uses this device? (Glossary: *Paradox*)

2. What is the function of the third sentence, "It happened like this"?

3. Hughes consciously varies the structure and length of his sentences to create different effects. What effect does he create through the short sentences in paragraphs 2 and 3 and the long sentence that concludes the final paragraph? How do the short, one-sentence paragraphs aid the author in telling his story?

4. Although Hughes tells most of his story himself, he allows Auntie Reed, the minister, and Westley to speak for themselves. What does Hughes gain by having his characters speak for themselves?

5. Explain how Hughes uses comparison and contrast to differentiate himself from Westley. (Glossary: *Comparison and Contrast*)

QUESTIONS ON LANGUAGE

1. How does Hughes's choice of words help to establish a realistic atmosphere for a religious revival meeting? Does he use any traditional religious figures of speech? (Glossary: *Figures of Speech*)

2. Why does Hughes italicize the word *see* in paragraph 5? What do you think he means by *see*? What do you think his aunt means by *see* (2)? Explain.

3. Refer to your desk dictionary to determine the meanings of the following words as they are used in this selection: *dire* (paragraph 3), *gnarled* (4), *vain* (11), *punctuated* (14), *ecstatic* (14).

WRITING ASSIGNMENTS

1. Like the young Langston Hughes, we sometimes find ourselves in situations in which, for the sake of conformity, we do things or act in ways we do not believe in. Consider one such experience you have had. What is it about human nature that makes us occasionally act in ways that contradict our inner feelings? Write an essay in which you explore that experience.

2. Any narrative requires that the writer gather information concerning a particular incident from his or her own experience or from other reliable sources. Interview a member of your class so as to obtain enough information to write a brief narrative about an interesting event in that person's life. Write your narrative in the third-person point of view.

A Worn Path

EUDORA WELTY

Eudora Welty was born in 1909 in Jackson, Mississippi, and has lived there for most of her life. Her father was president of an insurance company, and she was able to go away to the University of Wisconsin and then take a postgraduate course in advertising at Columbia University's business school. Advertising jobs being scarce during the Depression, Welty returned home and began to write. The American South has brought forth more than its share of fine writers, and Welty holds an honored place among them. Her published works include many short stories, now available as her Collected Stories *(1980), five novels, and a collection of her essays,* The Eye of the Story *(1975). Welty's* One Writer's Beginnings *(1987) recounts the events in childhood that influenced her development as a writer.*

In "A Worn Path" we meet old Phoenix Jackson, one of Welty's memorable characters, on her way to town on a vital errand.

It was December—a bright frozen day in the early morning. Far out in the country there was an old Negro woman with her head tied in a red rag, coming along a path through the pinewoods. Her name was Phoenix Jackson. She was very old and small and she walked slowly in the dark pine shadows, moving a little from side to side in her steps, with the balanced heaviness and lightness of a pendulum in a grandfather clock. She carried a thin, small cane made from an umbrella, and with this she kept tapping the frozen earth in front of her. This made a grave and persistent noise in the still air, that seemed meditative like the chirping of a solitary little bird.

She wore a dark striped dress reaching down to her shoe tops, and an equally long apron of bleached sugar sacks, with a full pocket: all neat and tidy, but every time she took a step she might have fallen over her shoelaces, which dragged from her unlaced shoes. She looked straight ahead. Her eyes were blue with age. Her skin had a pattern all its own of numberless branching wrinkles and as though a whole little tree stood in the middle of her forehead, but a golden color ran underneath, and the two knobs of her cheeks were illumined by a yellow burning under the dark. Under the red rag her hair came down on her neck in the frailest of ringlets, still black, and with an odor like copper.

Now and then there was a quivering in the thicket. Old Phoenix 3 said, "Out of my way, all you foxes, owls, beetles, jack rabbits, coons and wild animals! . . . Keep out from under these feet, little bob-whites. . . . Keep the big wild hogs out of my path. Don't let none of those come running my direction. I got a long way." Under her small black-freckled hand her cane, limber as a buggy whip, would switch at the brush as if to rouse up any hiding things.

On she went. The woods were deep and still. The sun made the 4 pine needles almost too bright to look at, up where the wind rocked. The cones dropped as light as feathers. Down in the hollow was the mourning dove—it was not too late for him.

The path ran up a hill. "Seem like there is chains about my feet, 5 time I get this far," she said, in the voice of argument old people keep to use with themselves. "Something always take a hold of me on this hill—pleads I should stay."

After she got to the top she turned and gave a full, severe look 6 behind her where she had come. "Up through pines," she said at length. "Now down through oaks."

Her eyes opened their widest, and she started down gently. But 7 before she got to the bottom of the hill a bush caught her dress.

Her fingers were busy and intent, but her skirts were full and long, 8 so that before she could pull them free in one place they were caught in another. It was not possible to allow the dress to tear. "I in the thorny bush," she said. "Thorns, you doing your appointed work. Never want to let folks pass, no sir. Old eyes thought you was a pretty little *green* bush."

Finally, trembling all over, she stood free, and after a moment dared 9 to stoop for her cane.

"Sun so high!" she cried, leaning back and looking, while the thick 10 tears went over her eyes. "The time getting all gone here."

At the foot of this hill was a place where a log was laid across the 11 creek.

"Now comes the trial," said Phoenix. 12

Putting her right foot out, she mounted the log and shut her eyes. 13 Lifting her skirt, leveling her cane fiercely before her, like a festival figure in some parade, she began to march across. Then she opened her eyes and she was safe on the other side.

"I wasn't as old as I thought," she said. 14

But she sat down to rest. She spread her skirts on the bank around 15 her and folded her hands over her knees. Up above her was a tree in a pearly cloud of mistletoe. She did not dare to close her eyes, and when a little boy brought her a plate with a slice of marble-cake on it she spoke to him. "That would be acceptable," she said. But when she went to take it there was just her own hand in the air.

So she left that tree, and had to go through a barbed-wire fence. 16 There she had to creep and crawl, spreading her knees and stretching her fingers like a baby trying to climb the steps. But she talked loudly to herself: she could not let her dress be torn now, so late in the day, and she could not pay for having her arm or her leg sawed off if she got caught fast where she was.

At last she was safe through the fence and risen up out in the 17 clearing. Big dead trees, like black men with one arm, were standing in the purple stalks of the withered cotton field. There sat a buzzard.

"Who you watching?"   18

In the furrow she made her way along.   19

"Glad this not the season for bulls," she said, looking sideways, 20 "and the good Lord made his snakes to curl up and sleep in the winter. A pleasure I don't see no two-headed snake coming around that tree, where it come once. It took a while to get by him, back in the summer."

She passed through the old cotton and went into a field of dead 21 corn. It whispered and shook and was taller than her head. "Through the maze now," she said, for there was no path.

Then there was something tall, black, and skinny there, moving 22 before her.

At first she took it for a man. It could have been a man dancing in 23 the field. But she stood still and listened, and it did not make a sound. It was as silent as a ghost.

"Ghost," she said sharply, "who be you the ghost of? For I have 24 heard of nary death close by."

But there was no answer—only the ragged dancing in the wind.   25

She shut her eyes, reached out her hand, and touched a sleeve. She 26 found a coat and inside that an emptiness, cold as ice.

"You scarecrow," she said. Her face lighted. "I ought to be shut up 27 for good," she said with laughter. "My senses is gone. I too old. I the oldest people I ever know. Dance, old scarecrow," she said, "while I dancing with you."

She kicked her foot over the furrow, and with mouth drawn down, 28 shook her head once or twice in a little strutting way. Some husks blew down and whirled in streamers about her skirts.

Then she went on, parting her way from side to side with the cane, 29 through the whispering field. At last she came to the end, to a wagon track where the silver grass blew between the red ruts. The quail were walking around like pullets, seeming all dainty and unseen.

"Walk pretty," she said. "This the easy place. This the easy going." 30

She followed the track, swaying through the quiet bare fields, 31 through the little strings of trees silver in their dead leaves, past cabins silver from weather, with the doors and windows boarded shut, all like old women under a spell siting there. "I walking in their sleep," she said, nodding her head vigorously.

In a ravine she went where a spring was silently flowing through a 32 hollow log. Old Phoenix bent and drank. "Sweetgum makes the water sweet," she said, and drank more. "Nobody know who made this well, for it was here when I was born."

The track crossed a swampy part where the moss hung as white as 33 lace from every limb. "Sleep on, alligators, and blow your bubbles." Then the track went into the road.

Deep, deep the road went down between the high green-colored 34 banks. Overhead the live-oaks met, and it was as dark as a cave.

A black dog with a lolling tongue came up out of the weeds by the 35 ditch. She was meditating, and not ready, and when he came at her she only hit him a little with her cane. Over she went in the ditch, like a little puff of milkweed.

Down there, her senses drifted away. A dream visited her, and she 36 reached her hand up, but nothing reached down and gave her a pull. So she lay there and presently went to talking. "Old woman," she said to herself, "that black dog come up out of the weeds to stall you off, and now there he sitting on his fine tail, smiling at you."

A white man finally came along and found her—a hunter, a young 37 man, with his dog on a chain.

"Well, Granny!" he laughed. "What are you doing there?" 38

"Lying on my back like a June-bug waiting to be turned over, 39 mister," she said, reaching up her hand.

He lifted her up, gave her a swing in the air, and set her down. 40 "Anything broken, Granny?"

"No sir, them old dead weeds is springy enough," said Phoenix, 41 when she had got her breath. "I thank you for your trouble."

"Where do you live, Granny?" he asked, while the two dogs were 42 growling at each other.

"Away back yonder, sir, behind the ridge. You can't even see it 43 from here."

"On your way home?" 44

"No sir, I going to town." 45

"Why, that's too far! That's as far as I walked when I come out 46
myself, and I get something for my trouble." He patted the stuffed bag
he carried, and there hung down a little closed claw. It was one of the
bob-whites, with its beak hooked bitterly to show it was dead. "Now
you go on home, Granny!"

"I bound to go to town, mister," said Phoenix. "The time come 47
around."

He gave another laugh, filling the whole landscape. "I know you 48
old colored people! Wouldn't miss going to town to see Santa Claus!"

But something held old Phoenix very still. The deep lines in her 49
face went into a fierce and different radiation. Without warning, she
had seen with her own eyes a flashing nickel fall out of the man's pocket
onto the ground.

"How old are you, Granny?" he was saying.   50

"There is no telling, mister," she said, "no telling."   51

Then she gave a little cry and clapped her hands and said, "Git on 52
away from here, dog! Look! Look at that dog!" She laughed as if in
admiration. "He ain't scared of nobody. He a big black dog." She whispered, "Sic him!"

"Watch me get rid of that cur," said the man. "Sic him, Pete! Sic 53
him!"

Phoenix heard the dogs fighting, and heard the man running and 54
throwing sticks. She even heard a gunshot. But she was slowly bending
forward by that time, further and further forward, the lids stretched
down over her eyes, as if she were doing this in her sleep. Her chin was
lowered almost to her knees. The yellow palm of her hand came out
from the fold of her apron. Her fingers slid down and along the ground
under the piece of money with the grace and care they would have in
lifting an egg from under a setting hen. Then she slowly straightened up,
she stood erect, and the nickel was in her apron pocket. A bird flew by.
Her lips moved. "God watching me the whole time. I come to stealing."

The man came back, and his own dog panted about them. "Well, 55
I scared him off that time," he said, and then he laughed and lifted his
gun and pointed it at Phoenix.

She stood straight and faced him.   56

"Doesn't the gun scare you?" he said, still pointing it.   57

"No, sir, I seen plenty go off closer by, in my day, and for less than 58
what I done," she said, holding utterly still.

He smiled, and shouldered the gun. "Well, Granny," he said, "you 59
must be a hundred years old, and scared of nothing. I'd give you a dime
if I had any money with me. But you take my advice and stay home, and
nothing will happen to you."

"I bound to go on my way, mister," said Phoenix. She inclined her 60
head in the red rag. Then they went in different directions, but she
could hear the gun shooting again and again over the hill.

She walked on. The shadows hung from the oak trees to the road 61
like curtains. Then she smelled wood-smoke, and smelled the river, and
she saw a steeple and the cabins on their steep steps. Dozens of little
black children whirled around her. There ahead was Natchez shining.
Bells were ringing. She walked on.

In the paved city it was Christmas time. There were red and green 62
electric lights strung and crisscrossed everywhere, and all turned on in
the daytime. Old Phoenix would have been lost if she had not distrusted
her eyesight and depended on her feet to know where to take her.

She paused quietly on the sidewalk where people were passing by. 63
A lady came along in the crowd, carrying an armful of red-, green-, and
silver-wrapped presents; she gave off perfume like the red roses in hot
summer, and Phoenix stopped her.

"Please, missy, will you lace up my shoe?" She held up her foot. 64

"What do you want, Grandma?" 65

"See my shoe," said Phoenix. "Do all right for out in the country, 66
but wouldn't look right to go in a big building."

"Stand still then, Grandma," said the lady. She put her packages 67
down on the sidewalk beside her and laced and tied both shoes tightly.

"Can't lace 'em with a cane," said Phoenix. "Thank you, missy. I 68
doesn't mind asking a nice lady to tie up my shoe, when I gets out on
the street."

Moving slowly and from side to side, she went into the big build- 69
ing, and into a tower of steps, where she walked up and around and
around until her feet knew to stop.

She entered a door, and there she saw nailed up on the wall the 70
document that had been stamped with the gold seal and framed in the
gold frame, which matched the dream that was hung up in her head.

"Here I be," she said. There was a fixed and ceremonial stiffness 71
over her body.

"A charity case, I suppose," said an attendant who sat at the desk 72
before her.

But Phoenix only looked above her head. There was sweat on her 73
face, the wrinkles in her skin shone like a bright net.

"Speak up, Grandma," the woman said. "What's your name? We 74
must have your history, you know. Have you been here before? What
seems to be the trouble with you?"

Old Phoenix only gave a twitch to her face as if a fly were bothering 75
her.

"Are you deaf?" cried the attendant.   76

But then the nurse came in.   77

"Oh, that's just old Aunt Phoenix," she said. "She doesn't come   78
for herself—she has a little grandson. She makes these trips just as regular as clockwork. She lives away back off the Old Natchez Trace." She
bent down. "Well, Aunt Phoenix, why don't you just take a seat? We
won't keep you standing after your long trip." She pointed.

The old woman sat down, bolt upright in the chair.   79

"Now, how is the boy?" asked the nurse.   80

Old Phoenix did not speak.   81

"I said, how is the boy?"   82

But Phoenix only waited and stared straight ahead, her face very   83
solemn and withdrawn into rigidity.

"Is his throat any better?" asked the nurse. "Aunt Phoenix, don't   84
you hear me? Is your grandson's throat any better since the last time
you came for the medicine?"

With her hands on her knees, the old woman waited, silent, erect   85
and motionless, just as if she were in armor.

"You mustn't take up our time this way, Aunt Phoenix," the nurse   86
said. "Tell us quickly about your grandson, and get it over. He isn't
dead, is he?"

At last there came a flicker and then a flame of comprehension   87
across her face, and she spoke.

"My grandson. It was my memory had left me. There I sat and   88
forgot why I made my long trip."

"Forgot?" The nurse frowned. "After you came so far?"   89

Then Phoenix was like an old woman begging a dignified forgive-   90
ness for waking up frightened in the night. "I never did go to school,
I was too old at the Surrender," she said in a soft voice. "I'm an old
woman without an education. It was my memory fail me. My little
grandson, he is just the same, and I forgot it in the coming."

"Throat never heals, does it?" said the nurse, speaking in a loud,   91
sure voice to old Phoenix. By now she had a card with something
written on it, a little list. "Yes. Swallowed lye. When was it?—January—
two-three years ago—"

Phoenix spoke unasked now. "No, missy, he not dead, he just the   92
same. Every little while his throat begin to close up again, and he not
able to swallow. He not get his breath. He not able to help himself. So
the time come around, and I go on another trip for the soothing
medicine."

"All right. The doctor said as long as you came to get it, you could   93
have it," said the nurse. "But it's an obstinate case."

"My little grandson, he sit up there in the house all wrapped up, 94 waiting by himself," Phoenix went on. "We is the only two left in the world. He suffer and it don't seem to put him back at all. He got a sweet look. He going to last. He wear a little patch quilt and peep out holding his mouth open like a little bird. I remembers so plain now. I not going to forget him again, no, the whole enduring time. I could tell him from all the others in creation."

"All right." The nurse was trying to hush her now. She brought 95 her a bottle of medicine. "Charity," she said, making a check mark in a book.

Old Phoenix held the bottle close to her eyes, and then carefully 96 put it into her pocket.

"I thank you," she said. 97

"It's Christmas time, Grandma," said the attendant. "Could I give 98 you a few pennies out of my purse?"

"Five pennies is a nickel," said Phoenix stiffly. 99

"Here's a nickel," said the attendant. 100

Phoenix rose carefully and held out her hand. She received the 101 nickel and then fished the other nickel out of her pocket and laid it beside the new one. She stared at her palm closely, with her head on one side.

Then she gave a tap with her cane on the floor. 102

"This is what come to me to do," she said. "I going to the store 103 and buy my child a little windmill they sells, made out of paper. He going to find it hard to believe there such a thing in the world. I'll march myself back where he waiting, holding it straight up in this hand."

She lifted her free hand, gave a little nod, turned around, and 104 walked out of the doctor's office. Then her slow step began on the stairs, going down.

QUESTIONS ON SUBJECT

1. Why is Old Phoenix going to Natchez? Who does she tell, and why?

2. What obstacles does Phoenix meet on the way? How, emotionally, does she cope with those obstacles? What does this reveal about her character?

3. How does Phoenix get the money she plans to spend at the end of the story? What will she be bringing home to her grandson? What is the significance of this gift?

4. In paragraph 90 Phoenix says, "I never did go to school, I was too old at the Surrender." What does this mean?

5. What does the title of the story mean to you? Does the name Phoenix or the title have any metaphorical meaning? Explain.

6. After reading this story, many people have asked: "Is Phoenix Jackson's grandson really dead?" Did this question occur to you? Is an answer to this question important to an understanding of Welty's story? Explain.

QUESTIONS ON STRATEGY

1. Why do we only learn about the grandson through Phoenix and the nurse? What effect does this have on the reader?

2. Compare Phoenix's speech with that of the hunter and the nurse. When Phoenix talks to another character does she seem to understand what's going on? Does a difference in age account for the difference in speech? Explain.

3. How would the story be different if Phoenix had good eyesight? What role does sight play in this story?

4. Comment on the landscape in this story. How does it change? Which characters blend in with it and which characters stick out? Why does Welty end her story in the city of Natchez?

5. Identify several passages in which Welty uses vivid description to give her readers verbal pictures of her characters, the setting, and the action. What, for you, does this description add to her narrative? (Glossary: *Description*)

QUESTIONS ON LANGUAGE

1. How does the diction of the characters vary according to their background? Use examples.

2. Using your desk dictionary look up the following words as they appear in the story: *nary* (paragraph 24), *furrow* (28), *pullets* (29), *cur* (53), *lye* (91).

WRITING ASSIGNMENTS

1. Write a character sketch of an old person you know well. Use narration to organize your sketch by showing your subject engaged in some typical activity.

2. Family obligations can be tiresome chores, or willing acts of love, or even both. What family obligations do you have—or do others have toward you? How do you feel about these obligations? Write an essay in which you explain your thoughts on these obligations, drawing on "A Worn Path" and Patricia Raybon's "Letting in Light."

3. Though brought up in a time and place where racial discrimination and hatred were widespread, Eudora Welty writes of Phoenix Jackson with understanding and love. Is this typical of Welty? Read some of her other works—perhaps the story "Powerhouse" or the essay "A Pageant of Birds"—and then write an essay in which you assess the image of African Americans in her work.

WRITING SUGGESTIONS
FOR NARRATION

1. Each of us can tell of an experience that has been unusually significant. Think about your past, identify one experience that has been especially important for you, and write an essay in which you recount it. In preparing to write your narrative, you may find it helpful to ask such questions as: Why is the experience important for me? What details are necessary for me to recreate the experience in an interesting and engaging way? How can my narrative of the experience be most effectively organized? What point of view will work best?

2. Using Malcolm X's essay as a model, narrate an experience that gave you a new awareness of yourself. Use enough telling detail in your narrative to allow your reader to visualize that experience and understand its significance for you. You may find the following suggestions helpful in choosing an experience to narrate in the first person.

   a. my greatest success
   b. my biggest failure
   c. my most embarrassing moment
   d. my happiest moment
   e. my first truly frightening experience
   f. an experience that turned my hero or idol into an ordinary person
   g. an experience that turned an ordinary person I know into a hero

3. Sometimes the little, insignificant, seemingly trivial experiences in our daily lives can provide the material for entertaining personal narratives—narratives that reveal something about ourselves and the world we live in. Select one of the following experiences, or one of your own choosing, and write an essay in which you narrate that experience and its significance for you.

   a. having your name misspelled and/or mispronounced
   b. being confused with another person in your family
   c. rushing to keep an appointment, only to find that you are a day early or a day late
   d. dialing the wrong telephone number more than once
   e. moving to avoid someone who is moving to avoid you and bumping into that person
   f. sleeping through the alarm clock
   g. not being able to find a parking space
   h. getting "ripped off" by a vending machine

4. As a way of gaining experience with third-person narration, write an essay in which you report what happened at one of the following:

   a. the visit of a state or national figure to your campus
   b. a dormitory meeting

    c. a current event of local, state, or national significance

    d. an important sports event

    e. the current research of one of your professors

    f. a campus demonstration or gathering

5. Tell the story of a trip you once took that is still memorable for you because of what you learned. First get the events of the trip and the sequence in which they occurred clearly in mind. In light of what you learned, which events need to be emphasized? Experiment with various organizational patterns so as not to render the account of the trip in strictly chronological sequence.

6. Most experiences that we have for the first time leave an indelible impression on us. For example, we can all remember the first day we drove a car, our first college class, our first date or love, the first time we voted, the day we discovered the meaning of teamwork, or the day we first felt like an adult. Select one of these experiences, or one of your own choosing, and present it in a narrative essay.

7. Write a narrative of a humorous incident that happened to you or that you witnessed that carries some insight into our common humanity. The humor may derive from the juxtaposition of a funny action with a serious setting, a miscommunication that turned out well, or contrasting perceptions of a situation or event.

8. You are a member of a campus organization that is seeking volunteers for a community project. You have been asked to write a piece for the school newspaper to solicit help. Support your call for help by narrating one or more stories about the rewards of lending a hand to others within the community.

2
DESCRIPTION

WHAT IS DESCRIPTION?

Description is conveying, through words alone, the perceptions of our senses. We see, hear, smell, taste, and feel; and through description we try to re-create those sensations in order to share them with others. Some sensations are so basic that they almost precede thought: the color and dazzle of aerial fireworks, the crunch of snow underfoot, the savory aroma of fried onion rings, the tartness of lemonade, the soothing coolness of suntan lotion on burning skin, the pleasant tiredness of leg muscles after a brisk run. Other perceptions appeal more directly to the mind, like the intricate architecture of a spider web or the elaborate complexity of a piece of music. All are the province of description.

It is often said that to describe is to paint a verbal picture—of a thing, a place, a person. The comparison is helpful because it suggests some truths. Both description and painting seek to transform fleeting perceptions into lasting images through the use of a foreign medium, words in the case of description, oils or watercolors in the case of painting. Although the original perception may have taken place in a flash, both description and painting are created bit by bit, word by word, or brushstroke by brushstroke. But the comparison goes only so far. We grasp a painting at a single glance (though appreciation may take longer); but we take in a description only piece by piece, or word by word, just as the writer created it. And, of course, a picture is purely visual, while description may draw on all of our sense perceptions.

There are essentially two types of description—objective and subjective. *Objective description* is as factual as possible, emphasizing the actual qualities of the subject being described, while subordinating the writer's personal responses. For example, a holdup victim would try to give authorities a precise, objective description of the criminal, uncolored by emotional responses, so that positive identification could be made—and so that an innocent person would not be arrested by mistake. *Subjective* or *impressionistic description,* on the other hand, conveys the writer's personal view or impression of the object, often in language rich in modifiers and figures of speech. A food critic describing a memorable meal would inevitably write about it impressionistically, using colorful or highly subjective language; there are, in fact, relatively few words in English to describe objectively the subtleties of smell and taste. Notice that with objective description it is usually the person, place, or thing being described that stands out, whereas with subjective description it is the response of the person doing the describing that is the most prominent feature of the description. Most subjects, however, lend themselves to both objective and subjective description, depending on your purpose. You could write, for example, that you had "exactly four weeks" to finish a history term paper (objective), or that you had "all the time in the world" or "an outrageously short amount of time" (subjective). Each type of description can be accurate and useful in its own way.

WHY DO WRITERS USE DESCRIPTION?

Description, especially when it is impressionistic and original, can give pleasure, and so one of a writer's purposes in using description may be to entertain. When Jim Tassé in "Trailcheck" describes the scenery he observes and the sensations he experiences while taking the first run of the day on the ski slope where he works, he paints a vivid word-picture that allows us to share in his ecstasy.

Description can also be used to inform—to provide readers with specific data. You may need to describe the results of a chemical reaction for a lab report; the style of a Renaissance painting for an art history term paper; the physical capabilities and limitations of a stroke patient for a case study; or the acting of Jodie Foster in a movie you want your friends to see. Such descriptions will sometimes be scientifically objective, sometimes intensely impressionistic, depending on the subject itself and the information you want to communicate about it.

Another important use of description is to create a mood or atmosphere, or even to convey your own views—to develop a *dominant impression*. In "My Father, the Prince," Phyllis Theroux creates a loving, full-length portrait of a man she wants us to know and like; she builds this impression with such carefully chosen details as that he "wore penny loafers on business trips" and "a Mouseketeer hat to pick up my brother on his first movie date." In "McSorley's Wonderful Saloon," Joseph Mitchell captures the dominant impression of unchanging drowsiness of one of America's most famous saloons. Each of the descriptions in this chapter, whether entertaining, informative, or both, is distinguished by the strong dominant impression the writer wishes to create.

Although descriptive writing can stand alone, and often does, it is also used with other types of writing. In a narrative, for example, descriptions provide the context for the story—the background and setting—and make the characters come alive for us. Description may also help to define a word like *giraffe* or *windmill*, or to clarify the steps of a process such as diagnosing an illness or making butter. Wherever it is used, and for whatever purpose, good description creates vivid and specific pictures that clarify, create a mood, build a dominant impression, and inform and entertain.

LOOKING AT DESCRIPTION

First, allow the words of the description to build up a mental image for you. Try to see in your mind's eye what the writer actually saw; try to hear or smell or taste or feel what the writer's words suggest. Put together the jigsaw puzzle of words and details into a complete picture. Then, define the dominant impression the writer creates.

Consider, for example, this paragraph by writer Roger Angell, in which he describes a baseball:

> It weighs just over five ounces and measures between 2.86 and 2.94 inches in diameter. It is made of a composition-cork nucleus encased in two thin layers of rubber, one black and one red, surrounded by 121 yards of tightly wrapped blue-gray wool yarn, 45 yards of white wool yarn, 53 more yards of blue-gray wool yarn, 150 yards of fine cotton yarn, a coat of rubber cement, and a cowhide (formerly horsehide) exterior, which is held together with 216 slightly raised red cotton stitches. Printed certifications, endorsements, and outdoor advertising spherically attest to its authenticity. Like most institutions, it is considered inferior in its present form to its ancient

archetypes, and in this case the complaint is probably justified; on occasion in recent years it has actually been known to come apart under the demands of its brief but rigorous active career. Baseballs are assembled and hand-stitched in Taiwan (before this year the work was done in Haiti, and before 1973 in Chicopee, Massachusetts), and contemporary pitchers claim that there is a tangible variation in the size and feel of the balls that now come into play in a single game; a true peewee is treasured by hurlers, and its departure from the premises, by fair means or foul, is secretly mourned. But never mind: any baseball is beautiful. No other small package comes as close to the ideal in design and utility. It is a perfect object for a man's hand. Pick it up and it instantly suggests its purpose; it is meant to be thrown a considerable distance—thrown hard and with precision. Its feel and heft are the beginning of the sport's critical dimensions; if it were a fraction of an inch larger or smaller, a few centigrams heavier or lighter, the game of baseball would be utterly different. Hold a baseball in your hand. As it happens, this one is not brand-new. Here, just to one side of the curved surgical welt of stitches, there is a pale-green grass smudge, darkening on one edge almost to black—the mark of an old infield play, a tough grounder now lost in memory. Feel the ball, turn it over in your hand; hold it across the seam or the other way, with the seam just to the side of your middle finger. Speculation stirs. You want to get outdoors and throw this spare and sensual object to somebody or, at the very least, watch somebody else throw it.

The first thing you probably noticed here is the amount of detail Angell provides about something as seemingly simple as a baseball. But perhaps you noticed, as well, that he leaves out some facts that most readers would find unnecessary—the pattern of the stitches, for example, and the color of the cowhide cover. In forming your mental picture of a baseball, you probably supplied that information from your own experience.

Is Angell's description objective or impressionistic? Actually, it is both. The author begins objectively and tells us not only about a baseball's obvious features—its weight, diameter, covering, stitching, and endorsements—but also about its innards. About halfway through, however, he changes his approach. Starting with the sentence "But never mind: any baseball is beautiful," Angell puts the greatest emphasis on his own attitudes and opinions. This part of his description is impressionistic and highly personal; who else, for example, would say of a baseball that "no other small package comes as close to the ideal in design and utility"?

Does the description create a unified, dominant impression? At first you might think not, because of the sudden switch from objective to impressionistic detail. Yet by the end of the description it's clear that Angell sees a baseball as something of rare perfection, deserving a kind of reverence. And the factual information with which he begins contributes to this impression: anything so complex, made with such extraordinary care and precision, may indeed be called "beautiful."

Angell's description can stand by itself, as it does here. In fact, however, he wrote it to appear at the beginning of a 400-page book about baseball called *Five Seasons*. He chose this description as his starting point because, as he says immediately afterward, "Thinking of the ball and its attributes seems to refresh our appreciation of this game." Certainly, the sort of freshness and enthusiasm Angell reveals in his description can lead readers to an appreciation of any subject, familiar or not.

READING DESCRIPTION IN AN ANNOTATED STUDENT ESSAY

Jim Tassé wrote the following essay while a student at the University of Vermont where he majored in English and religion. Tassé hopes eventually to teach, perhaps at the college level, but his most immediate interests include biking and singing with a rock band. As his essay "Trailcheck" reveals, Tassé is also an enthusiastic skier; his experience working on the ski patrol during the winter breaks provides him with the subject for a striking description.

TRAILCHECK
James C. Tassé

Context set—
early morning in
January and
preparations for
trailcheck.

    At a quarter to eight in the morning, the sharp   1
cold of the mid-winter night still hangs in the air of
Smuggler's Notch. At the base of Madonna Mountain,
we stamp our feet and turn up our collars while waiting for Dan to get the chair lift running. Trailcheck
always begins with this cold, sleepy wait—but it can

Description of
trailcheck begins
with explanation
of what one is.

continue in many different ways. The ski patrol has
to make this first run every morning to assess the
trail conditions before the mountain opens—and you
never know what to expect on top of the Mad Dog,
Madonna Mountain. Sometimes we take our first

run down the sweet, light powder that fell the night
before; sometimes we have to ski the rock-hard boiler-
plate ice that formed when yesterday's mush froze.
But there's always the cold—the dank, bleary cold of
8 A.M. in January.

*Use of present
tense gives imme-
diacy to the
description.*

I adjust my first-aid belt and heft my backpack up   2
a little higher, cinch it tight. I shiver, and pull my hat
down a bit lower. I am sleepy, cold, impatient. Dan's
finally got the lift running, and the first two patrollers, Ken and Chuck, get on. Three more chairs get
filled, and then there's me. Looks like I'm riding up
alone. The chair lift jars me a little more awake as it
hits the back of my boots. I sit down and am scooped
into the air.

*Description of the
total experience is
enhanced by ap-
pealing to the
reader's senses—
especially touch,
hearing, and
sight.*

It's a cold ride up, and I snuggle my chin deep   3
into my parka. The bumps of the chair going over the
lift tower rollers help keep me awake. Trees piled
high and heavy with snow move silently past. Every
so often, in sudden randomness, a branch lets go a
slide and the air fills with snowdust as the avalanche
crashes from branch to branch, finally landing with a
soft thud on the ground. Snow dances in the air with
kaleidoscopic colors, shining in the early daylight. I
imagine what it would have been like on the moun-

*Well-selected de-
tails contribute to
the description of
the wintry moun-
tain and the
magic of the day.*

tain on a similar day three hundred years ago. A day
like this would have been just as beautiful, or maybe
even more—the silent mountain, all trees and cold
and sunshine, with no men and no lifts. I think of
days when the fog rolls out of the Notch, and the
wind blows cold and damp, and the trees are close
and dark in the mist, and I try to imagine how terrify-
ingly wild the mountain would have been centuries
ago, before the white man came and installed the
chair lift that takes me to the top so easily. I think
how difficult it would have been to climb through the
thick untamed forest that bristles out of the mountain's flanks, and I am glad that I don't have to walk
up Madonna this sleepy-eyed morning.

I watch the woods pass, looking for the trails of   4
small animals scrolled around the trees. Skiing
should be nice with all the new snow. Arriving at the
top, I throw up the safety bar, tip my skis up, make
contact, stand, ski clear of the lift. The view from the
mountaintop is incredible. I can see over to the slopes
of Stowe, where another patrol is running trailcheck
just as we are. Across the state, Mt. Washington hangs
above the horizon like a mirage. Back towards
Burlington, I can see the frozen lake sprawling like
a white desert.

I toss my backpack full of lunch and books to   5
Marty, who's going into the patrol shack to get the
stove fired up. I stretch my legs a little as we share
some small talk, waiting for the mountain captain to
say we can go on down. Tighten my boots. Finally
Ken's radio crackles out the word, and I pull down
my goggles and pole forward.

Opening sentence and two fragments following signal the end of the ride up the mountain and the beginning of the trailcheck.

Wake up! The first run of the day. Trailcheck.   6
Today the run is heaven—eight inches of light dry
powder. My turns are relaxed giant slaloms that leave
neat S's in the snow behind me. No need to worry
about ice or rocks—the snow covers everything with
an airy cushion that we float on, fly on, our skis
barely on the ground. We split up at the first intersection, and I bear to the left, down into the Glades. My
skis gently hiss as they break the powder, splitting the
snow like a boat on calm water. I blast through deep
drifts of snow, sending gouts and geysers of snow up
around me. The air sparkles with snow, breaking the
light into tiny flecks of color.

Strong action verbs bring the description alive.

What a day! Some mornings I ride up in fifteen-   7
below-zero cold, only to ski down icy hardpack on
which no new snow has fallen for days. There are
rocks and other hazards to be noted and later marked
with bamboo poles so skiers don't hit them. Fallen
branches must be cleared from the trail. On days like
that, when the snow is lousy and I have to worry

*Contrast en-
hances description
of the trailcheck.*

about rocks gouging the bottoms of my skis, trailcheck is work—cold, necessary work done too early in the morning. But when the run is like it is today, that suffering is worthwhile.

Dominant impression of ecstatic playfullness emerges.

I yelp with pleasure as I launch myself off a knoll 8 and gently land in the soft whiteness, blasting down a chute of untracked powder that empties out into a flatter run. I can hear the other patrollers whooping and yelling with me in the distance. Turns are effortless; a tiny shift of weight and the skis respond like wings. I come over the next pitch, moving fast, and my skis hit an unseen patch of ice, my tails slide, too late to get the edge in, POOF! I tumble into the snow in an explosion of snowdust. For a second I lie panting. Then I wallow in ecstasy, scooping handfuls of powder over myself, the sweet light snow tingling in the air. After a moment I hop up and continue down, sluicing more S-turns on the whipped-cream powder.

Reaching the patrol room, I click off my skis and 9 stamp the snow from myself. No longer do I feel the night's cold breath in the air—just the sting of the melting snow on my face. Ken looks at me as I drip

Concluding comment sums up the writer's experience in one word

and glisten over my trail report, and asks: "Good run, Jim?"

I grin at him and say, "Beau-ti-ful!"   10

In discussing what he finds most difficult about writing Tassé was revealing, "Clarity, I guess. Like I said, I'm hardly ever satisfied with anything I've written, and I always think I could make it better by doing another draft. And the more drafts you do, the more challenging it gets, because the work you do seems to be finer and finer. You're looking for rough spots to polish, and as a piece gets better and you find more and more good about it, the rough spots become hidden even more. So each draft becomes more of a challenge, but I'm always eager to get at it."

As an illustration of what he means, Tassé pointed to paragraph 3 of "Trailcheck." He revised his first draft in order to eliminate shifts in person from *one* to *you* to *I* to *we* and to heighten the effect of the dominant impression of beauty by showing rather than telling: "Instead of saying that the mountain is beautiful, I tried to show how beautiful it was." Here are the two drafts of paragraph 3 reprinted side-by-side so you can see the changes:

<table>
<tr><td>FIRST DRAFT</td><td>FINAL DRAFT</td></tr>
</table>

FIRST DRAFT	FINAL DRAFT
The ride up gives one a chance to do some serious thinking. You're barely awake, and your first question is usually, "What the hell am I doing here?" But when you see the sun racing between tree branches piled high with snow, and bathing Mt. Mansfield in early morning coral light—you let that question slide. There is great beauty to mountain in the winter, and the patrol is always the first to see it. Inevitable I wonder what the mountain would've been like had it remained as it was a hundred years ago: silent, cold, all trees and animals—a lonely, dangerous place for a man to be.	It's a cold ride up, and I snuggle my chin deep into my parka. The bumps of the chair going over the lift tower rollers help keep me awake. Trees piled high and heavy with snow move silently past. Every so often, in sudden randomness, a branch lets go a slide and the air fills with snowdust as the avalanche crashes from branch to branch, finally landing with a soft thud on the ground. Snow dances in the air with kaleidoscopic colors, shining in the early daylight. I imagine what it would have been like on the mountain on a similar day three hundred years ago. A day like this would have been just as beautiful, or maybe even more—the silent mountain, all trees and cold and sunshine, with no men and no lifts. I think of days when the fog rolls out of the Notch, and the wind blows cold and damp, and the trees are close and dark in the mist, and I try to imagine how terrifyingly wild the mountain would have been centuries

ago, before the white man
came and installed the chair
lift that takes me to the top so
easily. I think how difficult it
would have been to climb
through the thick untamed
forest that bristles out of the
mountain's flanks, and I am
glad that I don't have to walk
up Madonna this sleepy-eyed
morning.

Finally, Tassé offered important information regarding the purpose
of his description. He mentioned that paragraph 7 had been added at
the final draft stage of his work on the essay. "My instructor suggested
it; he said he wasn't sure what a trailcheck is for, and by telling about
the hazards we sometimes have to deal with I could make that day's run
seem even more perfect. I didn't have to add this but it seemed worth
trying, and I liked the result. I like to get feedback from a reader. It
helps me to have things like this pointed out."

WRITING A DESCRIPTIVE ESSAY

You should begin by fixing the subject of your description firmly in
your mind. If it's an inanimate object, get it and keep it handy as you
work on your essay; if it's a place, go there and spend some time taking
in the sights, sounds, and smells; if it's a person, dig out old photographs and letters, or try to make a visit. Observe, observe, observe, and
make notes of your sense impressions. If you must work from memory—
if, for example, you are describing your great-grandmother—try to
"observe" with your mind's eye, to conjure up the half-forgotten face,
the quirky way of talking, the special walk. If you must rely on others'
writing (for example, to describe Pompeii before the eruption of Vesu-
vius), try to put together your own picture from the pieces you find in
your sources. Without vivid perceptions of your own to work from, you
can hardly create a detailed, accurate description.

The way you develop your perceptions will depend, first, on your
purpose for writing the description and the audience you are writing
for.

Purpose

Why you are writing will influence the kinds of descriptive details you use and the way you use them. Let's say, for example, that you want to describe the emergency room of your local hospital. If your purpose is mainly to entertain, then you might want to create an atmosphere of looming, intricate technology as in a mad scientist's laboratory, or of controlled chaos as in the operating room on *M*A*S*H*. If you mean mainly to inform your readers, however, you will use a more objective approach, relying on factual descriptions of individual staff members and pieces of emergency equipment, as well as explaining the functions of each.

Audience

Whom do you expect to read your essay? What do they know, and what do they want to learn from you? If you are describing the hospital emergency room for an audience of medical professionals, you will only need to mention a nuclear magnetic resonance scanner for them to know what it looks like and what it does. A less specialized audience, however, will appreciate a more detailed discussion. In addition, the general audience will be more receptive to impressionistic description and to details such as the staff's uniforms and the strong antiseptic smell; the professional readers will consider such things obvious or irrelevant.

Gathering Details

Once you have considered your purpose and your audience, writing a description requires that you gather a great many details about your subject, more, in fact, than you are likely to use. Like a reporter at the scene of an accident, you will write notes about what you see and hear directly; but you may also need to list details that you remember or that you have learned from other sources.

When collecting descriptive details, it's easy to forget to use *all* your senses. Sight is so important to us that we tend to pay attention only to what we can see, and inexperienced writers often rely almost completely on visual detail. While making observations of an emergency room, you would by all means take notes about the medical equipment, the blank white walls, the unnaturally brilliant lighting, and the brisk, efficient movements of the medical staff. But don't stop there. Keep your ears open for the hiss of trolley tires on linoleum and the odd, mechanical noises that interrupt the emergency room hush;

sniff the hospital smell; touch the starched sheets on the stretchers and the cold stainless steel that seems to be everywhere. Your observations, and the notes you make about them, will give you the details you need when you write your description.

Creating a Dominant Impression

From the catalog of details that you have collected, select those that will be most helpful in developing a dominant impression. Suppose that you wish to create a dominant impression of the hospital emergency room as a place of great tension. You will then naturally choose details to reinforce that sense of tension: the worried looks on the faces of a man and woman sitting in the corner, the quick movements of the medical staff as they tend a patient on a wheeled stretcher, the urgent whisperings of two interns out in the hallway, the incessant paging of Dr. Thomas. A dominant impression of the emergency room's sterility, however, will call for different details: the smell of disinfectant, the spotless white uniforms of the staff members, the stainless steel tables and chairs, the gleaming instruments a nurse hands to the physician. Building an effective and convincing dominant impression depends on the selection of such details.

Of course, it is equally important to omit any details that conflict with the dominant impression. Perhaps there was an orderly lounging in a corner, chewing gum and reading a magazine, who did not feel the tension of the emergency room; perhaps a room's sterility was marred by several used Styrofoam coffee cups left on a corner table. Deciding what details to include and exclude is up to you.

Organization

A photographer can capture a large, complicated scene with the press of a button. The writer has to put descriptive details down on paper one at a time. It's not enough to decide which details to include and which to leave out; you also need to arrange your chosen details in a particular order, one that serves your purpose and is easy for the reader to follow.

Visual details, for example, may be presented as if your eyes are moving from left to right, from bottom to top, from far to near, or the reverse of any of these. A description of an emergency room could begin at the entrance, move through the waiting area, pass the registration desk, and proceed into the treatment cubicles. A description of a restaurant kitchen might conjure up the smells and sounds that escape through the swinging doors even before moving on to the first glimpse inside.

Other patterns of organization include moving from the general to the specific, from smallest to largest, from least important to most important, or from the usual to the unusual. Roger Angell's description of a baseball moves from the objective to the impressionistic and subjective. In any case, keep in mind that the very last details you present will probably stay in the reader's mind the longest, and that the very first details will also have special force; those in the middle of your description, though they will have their effect, may not have the same impact as those before and after them.

Before you begin your first draft, you may find it useful to sketch out a scratch outline of your description. Here's a sample of such an outline for the Angell excerpt:

Description of a baseball.

Dominant impression: a baseball is a perfectly beautiful thing.

Objective details: weight, size, manufacture.

Impressions: perfectly suited for its purpose—if it were different, the game would be different—describe a used baseball, how it looks, how to hold it.

Such an outline can remind you of the dominant impression you want to create and suggest which specific details may be most useful to you.

Being Specific

Inexperienced writers often believe that adjectives and adverbs are the basis for effective descriptions. They're right in a sense, but not wholly so: while strong adjectives and adverbs are crucial, description also depends on well-chosen nouns and verbs. *Vehicle* is not nearly so descriptive as something more specific—*jeep, snowmobile,* or *Honda Civic.* Why write *see* when what you mean is *glance, stare, spy, gaze, peek, examine,* or *witness?* The more specific and strong you make your nouns and verbs, the more lively and interesting your descriptions will be.

"State-of-the-Art Car": The Ferrari Testarossa

JOYCE CAROL OATES

Novelist, essayist, and short story writer, Joyce Carol Oates was born in 1938 in Lockport, New York. After receiving her B.A. from Syracuse University and her M.A. in English from the University of Wisconsin, she taught English and creative writing at the University of Detroit and the University of Windsor (Ontario, Canada). She later became an English professor and writer-in-residence at Princeton University. Today, Oates lives near Princeton University. Her first collection of short stories By the North Gate *(1963), published when she was only twenty-five, received rave reviews in which she was compared to William Faulkner. Among her many works of fiction and nonfiction are:* Expensive People *(1968),* Unholy Loves *(1979),* Angel of Light *(1981),* Solstice *(1985), and* On Boxing *(1987). Her books on literary criticism include* The Edge of Impossibility *(1971),* The Poetry of D. H. Lawrence *(1973), and* New Heaven, New Earth *(1974).*

In the following essay, Oates describes with abandon the aesthetic, philosophical, and physical pleasures of the Testarossa, a premiere high-performance automobile made by Ferrari.

Speak of the Ferrari Testarossa to men who know cars and observe 1 their immediate visceral response: the virtual dilation of their eyes in sudden focused *interest*. The Testarossa!—that domestic rocket of a sports car, sleek, low-slung, aggressively wide; startlingly beautiful even in the eyes of non–car aficionados; so spectacular a presence on the road that—as I can personally testify—heads turn, faces break into childlike smiles in its wake. As one observer has noted, the Testarossa drives "civilians" crazy.

Like a very few special cars, the Ferrari Testarossa is in fact a meta- 2 car, a poetic metaphor or trope: an *object* raised to the level of a near-spiritual *value*. Of course it has a use—as a Steinway concert grand or a Thoroughbred racing horse has a use—but its significance hovers above and around mere use. What can one say about a street car (as opposed to a racing car) capable of traveling 177 effortless miles per hour?—accelerating, as it does, again without effort, from 0 mph to 60 mph in 5 seconds, 107 mph in 13.3 seconds? A car that sells for approximately $104,000—if you can get one? (The current waiting period is twelve months and will probably get longer). There are said to be no more than 450 Testarossas in private ownership in the United States; only about three hundred models are made by Ferrari yearly. So popular has the model become, due in part to its much-publicized presence in the television series *Miami Vice* (in which, indeed, fast cars provide a sort of subtextual commentary on the men who drive them), that a line of child-sized motorized "Testarossas" is now being marketed—which extravagant toys range in price from $3,500 to $13,000. (Toys bought by parents who don't want to feel guilty, as one Ferrari dealer remarked.)

For all its high-tech styling, its racing-car image, the Ferrari Testa- 3 rossa is a remarkably easy car to drive: its accelerative powers are first unnerving, then dangerously seductive. You think you are traveling at about 60 miles per hour when in fact you are moving toward 100 miles per hour (with your radar detector—"standard issue for this model"— in operation). In the luxury-leather seats, low, of course, and accommodatingly wide, you have the vertiginous impression of being somehow below the surface of the very pavement, skimming, flying, *rocketing* past vehicles moving at ordinary speeds; as if in a dream, or an "action" film. (Indeed, viewed through the discreetly tinted windshield of a Testarossa, the world, so swiftly passing, looks subtly altered: less assertive in its dimensions, rather more like "background.") Such speeds are heady, intoxicating, clearly addictive: if you are moving at 120 mph so smoothly, why not 130 mph? why not 160 mph? why not the limit—if, indeed, there is a limit? "Gusty/Emotions on wet roads on autumn nights" acquire a new significance in a car of such unabashed romance. What godly maniacal power: you have only to depress the accelerator of the Ferrari Testarossa and you're at the horizon. Or beyond.

The mystique of high-performance cars has always intrigued me 4 with its very opacity. Is it lodged sheerly in speed?—mechanical ingenuity?—the "art" of a finely tuned beautifully styled vehicle (as the mere physical fact of a Steinway piano constitutes "art")?—the adrenal thrill of courting death? Has it primarily to do with display (that of male game fowl, for instance)? Or with masculine prowess of a fairly obvious sort? (Power being, as the cultural critic Henry Kissinger once observed, the ultimate aphrodisiac.)

Or is it bound up with the phenomenon of what the American 5 economist Thorstein Veblen so wittily analyzed as "conspicuous consumption" in his classic *Theory of the Leisure Class* (1899)—Veblen's theory being that the consumption of material goods is determined not by the inherent value of goods but by the social standing derived from their consumption. (Veblen noted how in our capitalistic-democratic society there is an endless "dynamics" of style as the wealthiest class ceaselessly strives to distinguish itself from the rest of society and its habits of consumption trickle down to lower levels.)

Men who work with high-performance cars, however, are likely to 6 value them as ends in themselves: they have no time for theory, being so caught up, so mesmerized, in practice. To say that certain cars at certain times determine the "state-of-the-art" is to say that such machinery, on its most refined levels, constitutes a serious and speculative and ever-changing (improving?) art. The Ferrari Testarossa is not a *car* in the generic sense in which, say, a Honda Accord—which my husband and I own—is a *car.* (For one thing, the Accord has about 90 horsepower; the Testarossa 380.) Each Ferrari is more or less unique, possessed of its own mysterious personality; its peculiar ghost-in-the-machine. "It's a good car," I am told, with typical understatement, by a Testarossa owner named Bill Kontes, "—a *good* car." He pauses, and adds, "But not an antique. This is a car you can actually drive."

(Though it's so precious—the lipstick-red model in particular such 7 an attention-getter—that you dare not park it in any marginally public place. Meta-cars arouse emotions at all points of the spectrum.)

Bill Kontes, in partnership with John Melniczuk, owns and oper- 8 ates Checkered Flag Cars in Vineland, New Jersey—a dealership of such choice content (high-performance exotic cars, "vintage" classics, others) as to make it a veritable Phillips Collection amid its larger rivals in the prestige car market. It was by way of their hospitality that I was invited to test-drive the Ferrari Testarossa for *Quality,* though my only qualifications would seem to have been that I knew how to drive a car. (Not known to Mr. Kontes and Mr. Melniczuk was the ambiguous fact that I did once own, in racier days, a sports car of a fairly modest species—a Fiat Spider also in audacious lipstick-red. I recall that it was always stalling. That it gave up, so to speak, along a melancholy stretch of interstate highway in the approximate vicinity of Gary, Indiana, emitting actual flames from its exhaust. That the garage owner to whose garage it was ignominiously towed stared at it and said contemptuously, "A pile of junk!" That we sold it soon afterward and never bought another "sports" car again.)

It was along a semideserted stretch of South Jersey road that Mr. 9 Kontes turned the Ferrari Testarossa over to me, gallantly, and surely bravely: and conscious of the enormity of the undertaking—a sense, very nearly, that the honor of "woman writerhood" might be here at stake, a colossal blunder or actual catastrophe reflecting not only upon the luckless perpetrator but upon an entire generation and gender—I courageously drove the car, and, encouraged by Mr. Kontes, and by the mysterious powers of the radar detector to detect the presence of uniformed and sanctioned enforcers of the law (which law, I fully understand, *is* for our own good and in the best and necessary interests of the commonwealth), I did in fact accelerate through all five gears to a speed rather beyond one I'd anticipated: though not to 120 mph, which was Mr. Kontes's fairly casual speed a few minutes previously. (This particular Testarossa, new to Vineland, had been driven at 160 mph by Mr. Melniczuk the other day, along a predawn stretch of highway presumably sanctioned by the radar detector. To drive behind the Testarossa, as I also did, and watch it—suddenly—ease away toward the horizon is an eerie sight: if you don't look closely you're likely to be startled into asking, Where did it go?)

But the surprise of the Testarossa, *pace Miami Vice* and the hyped-up 10 media image, is that it is an easy, even comfortable car to drive: userfriendly, as the newly coined cliché would have it. It reminded me not at all of the tricky little Spider I'd quite come to hate by the time of our parting but, oddly, of the unnerving but fiercely exhilarating experience of being behind the controls—so to speak—of a two-seater open-cockpit plane. (My father flew sporty airplanes years ago, and my childhood is punctured with images of flight: the wind-ravaged open-cockpit belonged to a former navy bomber recycled for suburban airfield use.) As the Testarossa was accelerated I felt that visceral sense of an irresistibly gathering and somehow condensing power—"speed" being in fact a mere distillation or side effect of power—and, within it, contained by it, an oddly humble sense of human smallness, frailty. One of the perhaps unexamined impulses behind high-speed racing must be not the mere "courting" of death but, on a more primary level, its actual preexperience; its taste.

But what have such thoughts to do with driving a splendid red 11 Ferrari Testarossa in the environs of Vineland, New Jersey, one nearperfect autumn day, an afternoon shading romantically into dusk? Quite beyond, or apart from, the phenomenal machinery in which Bill Kontes and I were privileged to ride I was acutely conscious of the spectacle we and it presented to others' eyes. Never have I seen so many heads turn!—so much staring!—*smiling!* While the black Testarossa may very well resemble, as one commentator has noted, Darth Vader's personal warship, the lipstick-red model evokes smiles of pleasure, envy, awe—most pointedly in young men, of course, but also in older, even elderly women. Like royalty, the Testarossa seems to bestow a gratuitous benison upon its spectators. Merely to watch it pass is to feel singled out, if, perhaps, rather suddenly drab and anonymous. My thoughts drifted onto the pomp of kings and queens and maharajahs, the legendary excesses of the Gilded Age of Morgan, Carnegie, Rockefeller, Mellon, Armour, McCormick, et al.—Edith Rockefeller McCormick, just to give one small example, served her dinner guests on china consisting of over a thousand pieces containing 11,000 ounces of gold— the Hope Diamond, and Liz Taylor's diamonds, and the vision of Mark Twain, in impeccably dazzling white, strolling on Fifth Avenue while inwardly chafing at his increasing lack of privacy. If one is on public display one is of course obliged not to be conscious of it; driving a $104,000 car means being equal to the car in dignity and style. Otherwise the public aspect of the performance is contaminated: we are left with merely conspicuous consumption, an embarrassment in such times of economic trepidation and worldwide hunger.

Still, it's the one incontrovertible truth about the Ferrari Testarossa: no matter who is behind the wheel people stare, and they stare in admiration. Which might not otherwise be the case. 12

QUESTIONS ON SUBJECT

1. Early in her essay Oates says the Testarossa has a "near-spiritual value." Where in her essay does she support this claim?

2. Oates asks several questions in paragraph 4. How does she answer them? How would you answer them?

3. In your own words, what is the "conspicuous consumption" Oates refers to in paragraph 5? According to Oates, how does the driver of the Testarossa escape this label?

4. In what way do high-performance cars become "ends in themselves"? (6)

5. In what way was "woman writerhood" at stake for Oates?

6. What was the "surprise of the Testarossa"?

QUESTIONS ON STRATEGY

1. What is Oates's purpose in writing this essay? Where is it stated? (Glossary: *Purpose*)

2. In what way do the first three paragraphs of Oates's description serve as an introduction to the rest of her essay? (Glossary: *Beginnings*)

3. Throughout her essay, Oates uses parenthetical expressions. What sort of comments does she typically make in parentheses? Why do you think she does so?

4. Make a list of the qualities Oates assigns to drivers and spectators of the Testarossa. How does she distinguish between the two? What is the effect of this contrast she draws for her readers?

5. In what way do Oates's references to members of royalty, Mark Twain, and other rich and famous people function in the context of her description?

6. What does Oates give as the causes for the Testarossa's great appeal to both spectators and drivers? (Glossary: *Cause and Effect*)

QUESTIONS ON LANGUAGE

1. Oates manages to create an impression of speed and power in her description. What kinds of words does she use to create this impression? Does she rely more heavily on verbs or on adjectives? Cite examples of her diction to support your answer.

2. Refer to your desk dictionary to determine the meanings of the following words as they are used in this selection: *visceral* (paragraph 1), *vertiginous* (3), *opacity* (4), *inherent* (5), *mesmerized* (6), *audacious* (8), *ignominiously* (8), *perpetrator* (9), *eerie* (9), *environs* (11), *evokes* (11), *gratuitous* (11), *trepidation* (11), *incontrovertible* (12).

WRITING SUGGESTIONS

1. Write a short descriptive essay about your own or your family's car in which you evoke all the emotions you experience when you drive it. (Your challenge may be even greater if your car is ordinary rather than spectacular.) What kinds of verbs or adjectives will you use to describe something that is not wonderful or exciting?

2. Write an essay in which you describe the greatest thrill of your life. Then, just to make the assignment more challenging, make your description objective rather than subjective. Which version of the experience do you prefer? Why?

McSorley's Wonderful Saloon

JOSEPH MITCHELL

Joseph Mitchell, born in 1908, grew up in North Carolina and graduated from the University of North Carolina in 1929. He worked for several New York City newspapers before joining the staff of The New Yorker *in 1938. Mitchell established a reputation for himself as both a journalist and a fiction writer through his eccentric, and often peripheral, New York City characters.*

The following is an excerpt from a true story, first published in 1943 and most recently in Up in the Old Hotel and Other Stories *(1992), depicting the life of John McSorley, original proprietor of New York City's oldest bar. Through selection of detail, Mitchell gives us an unadorned glimpse into a life preserved in memory and brick.*

McSorley's occupies the ground floor of a red-brick tenement at 15 1 Seventh Street, just off Cooper Square, where the Bowery ends. It was opened in 1854 and is the oldest saloon in New York City. In eighty-eight years it has had four owners—an Irish immigrant, his son, a retired policeman, and his daughter—and all of them have been opposed to change. It is equipped with electricity, but the bar is stubbornly illuminated with a pair of gas lamps, which flicker fitfully and throw shadows on the low, cobwebby ceiling each time someone opens the street door. There is no cash register. Coins are dropped in soup bowls—one for nickels, one for dimes, one for quarters, and one for halves—and bills are kept in a rosewood cashbox. It is a drowsy place; the bartenders never make a needless move, the customers nurse their mugs of ale, and the three clocks on the walls have not been in agreement for many years. The clientele is motley. It includes mechanics from the many garages in the neighborhood, salesmen from the restaurant-supply houses on Cooper Square, truck-drivers from Wanamaker's, internes from Bellevue, students from Cooper Union, and clerks from the row of second-hand bookshops just north of Astor Place. The backbone of the clientele, however, is a rapidly thinning group of crusty old men, predominantly Irish, who have been drinking there since they were youths and now have a proprietary feeling about the place. Some of them have tiny pensions, and are alone in the world; they sleep in Bowery hotels and spend practically all their waking hours in McSorley's. A few of these veterans clearly remember John McSorley, the founder, who died in 1910 at the age of eighty-seven. They refer to him as Old John, and they like to sit in rickety armchairs around the big belly stove which heats the place, gnaw on the stems of their pipes, and talk about him.

Old John was quirky. He was normally affable but was subject to spells of unaccountable surliness during which he would refuse to answer when spoken to. He went bald in early manhood and began wearing scraggly, patriarchal sideburns before he was forty. Many photographs of him are in existence, and it is obvious that he had a lot of unassumed dignity. He patterned his saloon after a public house he had known in his hometown in Ireland—Omagh, in County Tyrone—and originally called it the Old House at Home; around 1908 the signboard blew down, and when he ordered a new one he changed the name to McSorley's Old Ale House. That is still the official name; customers never have called it anything but McSorley's. Old John believed it impossible for men to drink with tranquillity in the presence of women; there is a fine back room in the saloon, but for many years a sign was nailed on the street door, saying, "NOTICE. NO BACK ROOM IN HERE FOR LADIES." In McSorley's entire history, in fact, the only woman customer ever willingly admitted was an addled old peddler called Mother Fresh-Roasted, who claimed her husband died from the bite of a lizard in Cuba during the Spanish-American War and who went from saloon to saloon on the lower East Side for a couple of generations hawking peanuts, which she carried in her apron. On warm days, Old John would sell her an ale, and her esteem for him was such that she embroidered him a little American flag and gave it to him one Fourth of July; he had it framed and placed it on the wall above his brass-bound ale pump, and it is still there. When other women came in, Old John would hurry forward, make a bow, and say, "Madam, I'm sorry, but we don't serve ladies." If a woman insisted, Old John would take her by the elbow, head her toward the door, and say, "Madam, please don't provoke me. Make haste and get yourself off the premises, or I'll be obliged to forget you're a lady." This technique, pretty much word for word, is still in use.

In his time, Old John catered to the Irish and German workingmen—carpenters, tanners, bricklayers, slaughter-house butchers, teamsters, and brewers—who populated the Seventh Street neighborhood, selling ale in pewter mugs at five cents a mug and putting out a free lunch inflexibly consisting of soda crackers, raw onions, and cheese; present-day customers are wont to complain that some of the cheese Old John laid out on opening night in 1854 is still there. Adjacent to the free lunch he kept a quart crock of tobacco and a rack of clay and corncob pipes—the purchase of an ale entitled a man to a smoke on the house; the rack still holds a few of the communal pipes. Old John was thrifty and was able to buy the tenement—it is five stories high and holds eight families—about ten years after he opened the saloon in it. He distrusted banks and always kept his money in a cast-iron safe; it still stands in the back room, but its doors are loose on their hinges and there is nothing in it but an accumulation of expired saloon licenses and several McSorley heirlooms, including Old John's straight razor. He lived with his family in a flat directly over the saloon and got up every morning at five and took a long walk before breakfast, no matter what the weather. He unlocked the saloon at seven, swept it out himself, and spread sawdust on the floor. Until he became too feeble to manage a racing sulky, he always kept a horse and a nanny goat in a stable around the corner on St. Mark's Place. He kept both animals in the same stall, believing, like many horse-lovers, that horses should have company at night. During the lull in the afternoon a stablehand would lead the horse around to a hitching block in front of the saloon, and Old John, wearing his bar apron, would stand on the curb and groom the animal. A customer who wanted service would tap on the window and Old John would drop his currycomb, step inside, draw an ale, and return at once to the horse. On Sundays he entered sulky races on uptown highways.

From the time he was twenty until he was fifty-five, Old John drank 4
steadily, but throughout the last thirty-two years of his life he did not take a drop, saying, "I've had my share." Except for a few experimental months in 1905 or 1906, no spirits ever have been sold in McSorley's; Old John maintained that the man never lived who needed a stronger drink than a mug of ale warmed on the hob of a stove. He was a big eater. Customarily, just before locking up for the night, he would grill himself a three-pound T-bone, placing it on a coal shovel and holding it over a bed of oak coals in the back-room fireplace. He liked to fit a whole onion into the hollowed-out heel of a loaf of French bread and eat it as if it were an apple. He had an extraordinary appetite for onions, the stronger the better, and said that "Good ale, raw onions, and no ladies" was the motto of his saloon. About once a month during the winter he presided over an on-the-house beefsteak party in the back room, and late in life he was president of an organization of gluttons called the Honorable John McSorley Pickle, Beefsteak, Baseball Nine, and Chowder Club, which held hot-rock clambakes in a picnic grove on North Brother Island in the East River. On the walls are a number of photographs taken at outings of the club, and in most of them the members are squatting around kegs of ale; except for the president,

they all have drunken, slack-mouthed grins and their eyes look dazed. Old John had a bull-frog bass and enjoyed harmonizing with a choir of drunks. His favorite songs were "Muldoon, the Solid Man," "Swim Out, You're Over Your Head," "Maggie Murphy's Home," and "Since the Soup House Moved Away." These songs were by Harrigan and Hart, who were then called "the Gilbert and Sullivan of the U.S.A." He had great respect for them and was pleased exceedingly when, in 1882, they made his saloon the scene of one of their slum comedies; it was called "McSorley's Inflation."

Although by no means a handshaker, Old John knew many prominent men. One of his closest friends was Peter Cooper, president of the North American Telegraph Company and founder of Cooper Union, which is a half-block west of the saloon. Mr. Cooper, in his declining years, spent so many afternoons in the back room philosophizing with the workingmen that he was given a chair of his own; it was equipped with an inflated rubber cushion. (The chair is still there; each April 4th for a number of years after Mr. Cooper's death, on April 4, 1883, it was draped with black cloth.) Also, like other steadfast customers, Mr. Cooper had a pewter mug on which his name had been engraved with an icepick. He gave the saloon a life-sized portrait of himself, which hangs over the mantel in the back room. It is an appropriate decoration, because, since the beginning of prohibition, McSorley's has been the official saloon of Cooper Union students. Sometimes a sentimental student will stand beneath the portrait and drink a toast to Mr. Cooper.

QUESTIONS ON SUBJECT

1. What do Old John's past-times tell us about his character?

2. Why wouldn't Old John allow women in his pub? Why did he allow Mother Fresh-Roasted in his pub?

3. Who were Old John's patrons? What did they have in common with him? What historical changes do you see reflected in the difference between Old John's patrons and McSorley's customers at the time Mitchell wrote this selection?

4. What qualities did Old John reveal through the care of his racing sulky? Are these qualities different than those he showed while in the pub? Explain.

QUESTIONS ON STRATEGY

1. What is the dominant impression of Old John and his pub given in this essay? What details does the author emphasize to create this impression? (Glossary: *Dominant Impression*)

2. The author never ventures to guess what Old John might have thought. Why do you think Mitchell chose to detach himself from his subject in this way?

3. In paragraph 3, Mitchell writes about Old John's customers, his finances and investments, and his racing sulky. What do you suppose Mitchell was trying to achieve in writing long, discursive paragraphs? What would have been lost had he used shorter paragraphs?

4. We see Old John through the eyes of those who knew him and through the author's description of his saloon. Why do you think Mitchell found a group of crusty old men his best source?

5. Mitchell only mentions McSorley's family once, in the middle of paragraph 3. What would have happened to the dominant impression of McSorley and his pub had the author given us more information about Old John's family?

6. Identify some narrative techniques that Mitchell uses in recounting the history of Old John and his wonderful saloon. (Glossary: *Narration*)

QUESTIONS ON LANGUAGE

1. Mitchell writes of McSorley's, "It is a drowsy place; the bartenders never make a needless move." Explain how Mitchell's language and sentence structure reinforce the feeling of drowsiness.

2. Refer to your desk dictionary to determine the meanings of the following words as they are used in this selection: *motley* (paragraph 1), *proprietary* (1), *addled* (2), *wont* (3), *steadfast* (5).

WRITING SUGGESTIONS

1. Write an essay describing a person you know. Brainstorm for ideas: what are this person's eccentricities, where do you usually see this person, what objects remind you of him or her, how does he or she dress, what kind of impression does this person make on people? Finally, consider the tone you want to use in describing the person you've chosen and the situation you wish to place that person in.

2. Write an essay describing an historic place or simply a place you enjoy visiting. Consider what details you want to mention and what kind of an impression those details will make on your audience.

My Father, the Prince

PHYLLIS THEROUX

Phyllis Theroux was born in San Francisco in 1939. A graduate of Manhattanville College, she has worked as a secretary, a school teacher, and a legal researcher. As a writer she has been a frequent contributor to the "Hers" column in the New York Times *as well as to* Reader's Digest, *the* Washington Post, *and* McCall's. *In 1980, Theroux published her first book,* California and Other States of Grace: A Memoir. *She followed this collection with two others,* Peripheral Visions *and* Night Lights: Bedtime Stories for Parents in the Dark.

"My Father, the Prince" is taken from her second book, Peripheral Visions, *a collection of autobiographical essays. In describing her father and his special gift to her, Theroux also probes the crucial relationship that exists between all fathers and daughters.*

Fathers. They say that a woman seeks—in love, marriage, or any 1 male-female relationship of real heft—to approximate the father she had, the father she didn't have but wanted, or the father minus the attributes that caused her mother to leave him for good and sufficient reason. In the winnowing-out process that precedes deep commitment to a new man, the daughter subconsciously throws up the wheat of her father's virtues along with the chaff of his faults, and her decision to commit is strongly influenced by that first experience of male companionship.

I think they're right. 2

We all know that men consider their mothers when they choose a 3 woman for themselves, but fathers have traditionally been considered mere linkage in the rosary of wombs that produce progeny from one decade to the next. Accessories to the fact, off-campus providers, fathers are six o'clock visitors to the nursery tended by all-powerful mothers.

One can scarcely overestimate the influence that mothers have 4 upon their sons. But fathers have yet to be properly weighed in as determinative factors in the lives of their daughters. To my way of thinking, this is a terrible oversight.

In a grayer, more small-minded period of my life, I used to in- 5 wardly gripe at the inaccuracy of the Cinderella story. Cinderella does not go from ashes to amethysts. In real life the brooms and the dustpans materialize after the wedding, whereupon she spends forever after staring out the window wondering where her father—the real prince in her life—has gone.

Of course, women are now rewriting that old script, and this is an 6 age in which we are forming piano-moving companies, hiking up telephone poles, and swimming along with Jacques Cousteau. But I live with a little woman, aged seven, who recently gave me to understand that liberation is an acquired taste and no substitute for gut feeling.

"What's this?" I asked as she handed me a crayon drawing of a little 7 girl next to what looked like a giant lollipop.

"Me," she answered. (There was a crown drawn on the little girl's 8 head.)

"And what are you doing?" I pursued, searching the drawing for 9 some evidence of a plot line.

"Nothing," she said matter-of-factly. "Just standing by the bus 10 stop waiting for the prince."

I put the drawing aside, looked at my matter-of-fact daughter, and 11 thought with chagrin, "Aren't we all!" Spoiled or despoiled by the first prince in our life, we understand, either way, what it means to be born to the purple. No, Cinderella did not accidentally fall for royalty. Her dear departed father had given her an early taste for it. My father did the same.

He was a tall, crooked-toothed, curly-haired man, who smelled of 12 Lucky Strikes and St. Johns Bay Rum shaving lotion. He was the only father who wore penny loafers on business trips, a Mouseketeer hat to pick up my brother on his first movie date, and had the delicious gall to invite the richest girl in my class (she had her own pool but an exclusive number of invitations) to come on over to the house ("When you're free, of course") and watch our lawn sprinklers.

"Sometimes we get them going in opposite directions to each 13 other," he said dryly, "and it's terribly amusing."

The richest girl in the class laughed nervously, I choked back my bor- 14 rowed triumph, and savored the fact that once again my father had effectively punched out the opposition on my behalf. He had a gift for it.

Yet, unlike other men blessed with a quick wit and a rare natural 15 electricity of being, my father was oddly incapable of parlaying his gifts to his own long-range advantage.

As I grew older and more able to observe him objectively in group 16 situations, I noticed that in a room full of peers he would usually back up against the mantel and go into a sort of social receivership that did not jibe with my understanding of him. It made me impatient. He was far and away the largest talent in the room, and it seemed a terrible waste to give over the floor to anyone else. Yet he consistently passed up opportunities to reveal himself in public, and it was many years before I realized that my wonderful father was *shy*.

I was thunderstruck. Is Douglas Fairbanks, Jr., shy? Does Cary Grant [17] falter? Should my father have anything in the world to hesitate over?

It was one thing to be a pudgy, preadolescent girl trying to make [18] it in a class full of gazelles, but quite another thing to be that little girl's handsome father, who at various crucial junctures had told her that all she had to do in order to succeed was to take this step, or that action, and—for heaven's sake—was the world such a difficult nut to crack after all? Of course not!

If there was any one thing that my father did for me when I was [19] growing up it was to give me the promise that ahead of me was dry land—a bright, marshless territory, without chuckholes or traps, where one day I would walk easily and as befitting my talents. The fact that I didn't know what my talents were did not put my father off in the slightest. He knew potential when he saw it.

Thus it was, when he came upon me one afternoon sobbing out my [20] unsuccesses into a wet pillow, that he sat down on the bed and, like a strong, omniscient archangel, assured me that my grief was only a temporary setback.

Oh, very temporary! Why he couldn't think of any other little girl [21] who was so talented, so predestined to succeed in every department as I was. "And don't forget," he added with a smile, "that we can trace our ancestry right back to Pepin the Stupid!"[1]

That last piece of news turned out to be true, but whether he be- [22] lieved the rest of his words or not I don't know. He was, after all, gazing down upon a disheveled ten-year-old who was too embarrassed to shift her gum from one cheek to the other.

But I listened to him carefully, and by the time he had finished [23] talking I really did understand that someday I would live among rational beings, and walk with kind, unvindictive people who, by virtue of their maturity and mine, would take no pleasure in cruelty and would welcome my presence among them as an asset. It was only a question of time before I came ripping out of my cocoon, a free-flying butterfly that would skim triumphantly over the meadow of my choice. I cannot say that my father was completely wrong.

Time has passed. Choices have been made. I am no longer a pre- [24] teen in a net formal who secretly hoped that all the other girls at the

---

[1] A medieval French ruler.

Father-Daughter Dance were eating their hearts out. My father's crooked front tooth was replaced several years ago by a nice, straight, shiny one. He has passed through the hospital several times. There are grandchildren. I sometimes think that it is not the same between us, or perhaps it never was what I thought.

One's memory is selective, and I admit that it's to my advantage to recall only those moments when my father rose to the occasion and parted another Red Sea of Impossibility[2] and elbowed me across. Yet these moments really did happen and I am not the same because of them. 25

There are some people, my father is one of them, who carry the flint that lights other people's torches. They get them all excited about the possibilities of an idea, the "can-do" potential of one's own being. 26

That was my father's gift to me, and whatever psychic wounds remain to be thrashed out between us are still lying on the floor of my unconscious, waiting for deep therapy to uncover. The fact is that I am closer to my mother. But they say that a daughter carries around the infection of her father for life. 27

They are right. 28

QUESTIONS ON SUBJECT

1. What does Theroux mean by her title, "My Father, the Prince"? In what way was her father a prince?

2. How does the Cinderella story fit into Theroux's description? What point is she making with the anecdote about her daughter's drawing?

3. What was Theroux's father's special "gift" to her? What does this gift have to do with his ability to "punch out the opposition" (paragraph 14), as well as his shyness?

4. Has Theroux's view of her father changed over the years? If so, how?

QUESTIONS ON STRATEGY

1. Theroux's description of her father doesn't actually begin until paragraph 12. What function or functions do paragraphs 1–11 serve? (Glossary: *Beginnings*)

2. Two paragraphs in the essay—the second and the last—are linked in several interesting ways. What function do they serve in the overall context?

---

[2]Refers to the miraculous parting of the actual Red Sea by Moses during the Israelites' escape from Egypt (Exodus 21–29).

3. Theroux tells us very little about her father's physical appearance. How, then, does she actually describe him? Do you feel that you know what he is like?

4. Theroux's essay is drawn from her own experience and observations, yet she writes: "They say that . . ." (1); "We all know that . . ." (3); "One can scarcely overestimate . . ." (4); and, again, "But they say that . . ." (27). Why do you suppose Theroux chooses not to limit herself to the first-person *I*, particularly at the beginning and the end?

5. Is there an element of argument in Theroux's essay? What is that argument? Do you agree with it? Why or why not? (Glossary: *Argumentation*)

QUESTIONS ON LANGUAGE

1. Theroux makes effective use of figurative language in this essay. For example, she says "the daughter subconsciously throws up the wheat of her father's virtues along with the chaff of his faults" (1), and she refers to herself as a "pudgy, preadolescent girl trying to make it in a class full of gazelles" (18). Locate several other figures of speech and comment on their contributions to this essay. (Glossary: *Figures of Speech*)

2. Refer to your desk dictionary to determine the meanings of the following words as they are used in this selection: *heft* (paragraph 1), *amethysts* (5), *chagrin* (11), *despoiled* (11), *gall* (12), *parlaying* (15), *receivership* (16), *omniscient* (20), *psychic* (27).

WRITING ASSIGNMENTS

1. In an essay, describe your mother, your father, or another adult who has been an important influence in your life. Use your description not only to create a portrait of the person, but also to clarify your relationship and its effect on you. In selecting details for your description, keep in mind that personality traits can be just as important, if not more so, than physical characteristics.

2. Using library sources, write a descriptive essay about a person you have never met, perhaps a present-day celebrity or a historical figure. Whether your description is objective or impressionistic, try to create a dominant impression of your subject.

Once More to the Lake

E. B. WHITE

Master essayist, storyteller, and poet, Elwyn Brooks (1899–1985) White was born in Mount Vernon, New York, lived some years in New York City, and for many years made his home on a salt-water farm in Maine. After studying at Cornell University, he joined the staff of The New Yorker *in 1926, where he wrote essays, editorials, anonymous fillers, and even cartoon captions that helped to establish the magazine's and his own reputation for witty and graceful prose. For some years he also wrote a monthly column for* Harper's *with his observations and reflections on topics both humorous and serious, personal and political. A selection of his essays is available in* The Essays of E. B. White. *He is the author of the classic children's stories* Stuart Little *and* Charlotte's Web *and has revised William Strunk's celebrated work,* The Elements of Style.

"Once More to the Lake," first published in Harper's *in 1941, is an account of a trip White took with his son to the site of his own childhood vacations. White uses vivid description to establish the context for his narrative and to recall childhood trips to the lake with his family.*

One summer, along about 1904, my father rented a camp on a lake 1 in Maine and took us all there for the month of August. We all got ringworm from some kittens and had to rub Pond's Extract on our arms and legs night and morning, and my father rolled over in a canoe with all his clothes on; but outside of that the vacation was a success and from then on none of us ever thought there was any place in the world like that lake in Maine. We returned summer after summer—always on August 1st for one month. I have since become a salt-water man, but sometimes in summer there are days when the restlessness of the tides and the fearful cold of the sea water and the incessant wind which blows across the afternoon and into the evening make me wish for the placidity of a lake in the woods. A few weeks ago this feeling got so strong I bought myself a couple of bass hooks and a spinner and returned to the lake where we used to go, for a week's fishing and to revisit old haunts.

I took along my son, who had never had any fresh water up his nose 2 and who had seen lily pads only from train windows. On the journey over to the lake I began to wonder what it would be like. I wondered how time would have marred this unique, this holy spot—the coves and streams, the hills that the sun set behind, the camps and the paths behind the camps. I was sure that the tarred road would have found it out and I wondered in what other ways it would be desolated. It is strange how much you can remember about places like that once you allow your mind to return into the grooves which lead back. You remember one thing, and that suddenly reminds you of another thing. I guess I remembered clearest of all the early mornings, when the lake was cool and motionless, remembered how the bedroom smelled of the lumber it was made of and of the wet woods whose scent entered through the screen. The partitions in the camp were thin and did not extend clear to the top of the rooms, and as I was always the first up I would dress softly so as not to wake the others, and sneak out into the sweet outdoors and start out in the canoe, keeping close along the shore in the long shadows of the pines. I remembered being very careful never to rub my paddle against the gunwale for fear of disturbing the stillness of the cathedral.

The lake had never been what you would call a wild lake. There 3 were cottages sprinkled around the shores, and it was in farming country although the shores of the lake were quite heavily wooded. Some of the cottages were owned by nearby farmers, and you would live at the shore and eat your meals at the farmhouse. That's what our family did. But although it wasn't wild, it was a fairly large and un-disturbed lake and there were places in it which, to a child at least, seemed infinitely remote and primeval.

I was right about the tar: it led to within half a mile of the shore. 4 But when I got back there, with my boy, and we settled into a camp near a farmhouse and into the kind of summertime I had known, I could tell that it was going to be pretty much the same as it had been before—I knew it, lying in bed the first morning, smelling the bed-room, and hearing the boy sneak quietly out and go off along the shore in a boat. I began to sustain the illusion that he was I, and therefore, by simple transposition, that I was my father. This sensation persisted, kept cropping up all the time we were there. It was not an entirely new feeling, but in this setting it grew much stronger. I seemed to be living a dual existence. I would be in the middle of some simple act, I would be picking up a bait box or laying down a table fork, or I would be saying something, and suddenly it would be not I but my father who was saying the words or making the gesture. It gave me a creepy sensation.

We went fishing the first morning. I felt the same damp moss 5 covering the worms in the bait can, and saw the dragonfly alight on the tip of my rod as it hovered a few inches from the surface of the water. It was the arrival of this fly that convinced me beyond any doubt that everything was as it always had been, that the years were a mirage and there had been no years. The small waves were the same, chucking the rowboat under the chin as we fished at anchor, and the boat was the same boat, the same color green and the ribs broken in the same places, and under the floor-boards the same freshwater leavings and débris— the dead helgramite, the wisps of moss, the rusty discarded fishhook, the dried blood from yesterday's catch. We stared silently at the tips of our rods, at the dragonflies that came and went. I lowered the tip of mine into the water, tentatively, pensively dislodging the fly, which darted two feet away, poised, darted two feet back, and came to rest again a little farther up the rod. There had been no years between the ducking of this dragonfly and the other one—the one that was part of memory. I looked at the boy, who was silently watching his fly, and it was my hands that held his rod, my eyes watching. I felt dizzy and didn't know which rod I was at the end of.

We caught two bass, hauling them in briskly as though they were 6 mackerel, pulling them over the side of the boat in a businesslike manner without any landing net, and stunning them with a blow on the back of the head. When we got back for a swim before lunch, the lake was exactly where we had left it, the same number of inches from the dock, and there was only the merest suggestion of a breeze. This seemed an utterly enchanted sea, this lake you could leave to its own devices for a few hours and come back to, and find that it had not stirred, this constant and trustworthy body of water. In the shallows, the dark, water-soaked sticks and twigs, smooth and old, were undulating in clusters on the bottom against the clean ribbed sand, and the track of the mussel was plain. A school of minnows swam by, each minnow with its small individual shadow, doubling the attendance, so clear and sharp in the sunlight. Some of the other campers were in swimming, along the shore, one of them with a cake of soap, and the water felt thin and clear and unsubstantial. Over the years there had been this person with the cake of soap, this cultist, and here he was. There had been no years.

Up to the farmhouse to dinner through the teeming, dusty field, 7 the road under our sneakers was only a two-track road. The middle track was missing, the one with the marks of the hooves and the splotches of dried, flaky manure. There had always been three tracks to choose from in choosing which track to walk in; now the choice was narrowed down to two. For a moment I missed terribly the middle alternative. But the way led past the tennis court, and something about the way it lay there in the sun reassured me; the tape had loosened along the backline, the alleys were green with plantains and other weeds, and the net (installed in June and removed in September) sagged in the dry noon, and the whole place steamed with midday heat and hunger and emptiness. There was a choice of pie for dessert, and one was blueberry and one was apple, and the waitresses were the same country girls, there having been no passage of time, only the illusion of it as in a dropped curtain—the waitresses were still fifteen; their hair had been washed, that was the only difference—they had been to the movies and seen the pretty girls with the clean hair.

Summertime, oh summertime, pattern of life indelible, the fade-proof lake, the woods unshatterable, the pasture with the sweet-fern and the juniper forever and ever, summer without end; this was the background, and the life along the shore was the design, the cottages with their innocent and tranquil design, their tiny docks with the flagpole and the American flag floating against the white clouds in the blue sky, the little paths over the roots of the trees leading from camp to camp and the paths leading back to the outhouses and the can of lime for sprinkling, and at the souvenir counters at the store the miniature birch-bark canoes and the post cards that showed things looking a little better than they looked. This was the American family at play, escaping the city heat, wondering whether the newcomers in the camp at the head of the cove were "common" or "nice," wondering whether it was true that the people who drove up for Sunday dinner at the farmhouse were turned away because there wasn't enough chicken. 8

It seemed to me, as I kept remembering all this, that those times and those summers had been infinitely precious and worth saving. There had been jollity and peace and goodness. The arriving (at the beginning of August) had been so big a business in itself, at the railway station the farm wagon drawn up, the first smell of the pine-laden air, the first glimpse of the smiling farmer, and the great importance of the trunks and your father's enormous authority in such matters, and the feel of the wagon under you for the long ten-mile haul, and at the top of the last long hill catching the first view of the lake after eleven months of not seeing this cherished body of water. The shouts and cries of the other campers when they saw you, and the trunks to be unpacked, to give up their rich burden. (Arriving was less exciting nowadays, when you sneaked up in your car and parked it under a tree near 9 the camp and took out the bags and in five minutes it was all over, no fuss, no loud wonderful fuss about trunks.)

Peace and goodness and jollity. The only thing that was wrong 10 now, really, was the sound of the place, an unfamiliar nervous sound of the outboard motors. This was the note that jarred, the one thing that would sometimes break the illusion and set the years moving. In those other summertimes all motors were inboard; and when they were at a little distance, the noise they made was a sedative, an ingredient of summer sleep. They were one-cylinder and two-cylinder engines, and some were make-and-break and some were jump-spark, but they all made a sleepy sound across the lake. The one-lungers throbbed and fluttered, and the twin-cylinder ones purred and purred, and that was a quiet sound too. But now the campers all had outboards. In the daytime, in the hot mornings, these motors made a petulant, irritable sound; at night, in the still evening when the afterglow lit the water, they whined about one's ears like mosquitoes. My boy loved our rented outboard, and his great desire was to achieve singlehanded mastery over it, and authority, and he soon learned the trick of choking it a little (but not too much), and the adjustment of the needle valve. Watching him I would remember the things you could do with the old one-cylinder engine with the heavy flywheel, how you could have it eating out of your hand if you got really close to it spiritually. Motor boats in those days didn't have clutches, and you would make a landing by shutting off the motor at the proper time and coasting in with a dead rudder. But there was a way of reversing them, if you learned the trick, by cutting the switch and putting it on again exactly on the final dying revolution of the flywheel, so that it would kick back against compression and begin reversing. Approaching a dock in a strong following breeze, it was difficult to slow up sufficiently by the ordinary coasting method, and if a boy felt he had complete mastery over his motor, he was tempted to keep it running beyond its time and then reverse it a few feet from the dock. It took a cool nerve, because if you threw the switch a twentieth of a second too soon you could catch the flywheel when it still had speed enough to go up past center, and the boat would leap ahead, charging bull-fashion at the dock.

We had a good week at the camp. The bass were biting well and the 11 sun shone endlessly, day after day. We would be tired at night and lie down in the accumulated heat of the little bedrooms after the long hot day and the breeze would stir almost imperceptibly outside and the smell of the swamp drift in through the rusty screens. Sleep would come easily and in the morning the red squirrel would be on the roof, tapping out his gay routine. I kept remembering everything, lying in bed in the mornings—the small steamboat that had a long rounded stern like the lip of a Ubangi, and how quietly she ran on the moonlight sails, when the older boys played their mandolins and the girls sang and we ate doughnuts dipped in sugar, and how sweet the music was on the water in the shining night, and what it had felt like to think about girls then. After breakfast we would go up to the store and the things were in the same place—the minnows in a bottle, the plugs and spinners disarranged and pawed over by the youngsters from the boys' camp, the fig newtons and the Beeman's gum. Outside, the road was tarred and cars stood in front of the store. Inside, all was just as it had always been, except there was more Coca-Cola and not so much Moxie and root beer and birch beer and sarsaparilla. We would walk out with a bottle of pop apiece and sometimes the pop would backfire up our noses and hurt. We explored the streams, quietly, where the turtles slid off the sunny logs and dug their way into the soft bottom; and we lay on the town wharf and fed worms to the tame bass. Everywhere we went I had trouble making out which was I, the one walking at my side, the one walking in my pants.

One afternoon while we were there at that lake a thunderstorm 12 came up. It was like the revival of an old melodrama that I had seen long ago with childish awe. The second-act climax of the drama of the electrical disturbance over a lake in America had not changed in any important respect. This was the big scene, still the big scene. The whole thing was so familiar, the first feeling of oppression and heat and a general air around camp of not wanting to go very far away. In mid-afternoon (it was all the same) a curious darkening of the sky, and a lull in everything that had made life tick; and then the way the boats suddenly swung the other way at their moorings with the coming of a breeze out of the new quarter, and the premonitory rumble. Then the kettle drum, then the snare, then the bass drum and cymbals, then crackling light against the dark, and the gods grinning and licking their chops in the hills. Afterward the calm, the rain steadily rustling in the calm lake, the return of light and hope and spirits, and the campers running out in joy and relief to go swimming in the rain, their bright cries perpetuating the deathless joke about how they were getting simply drenched, and the children screaming with delight at the new sensation of bathing in the rain, and the joke about getting drenched linking the generations in a strong indestructible chain. And the comedian who waded in carrying an umbrella.

When the others went swimming my son said he was going in too. 13 He pulled his dripping trunks from the line where they had hung all through the shower, and wrung them out. Languidly, and with no thought of going in, I watched him, his hard little body, skinny and bare, saw him wince slightly as he pulled up around his vitals the small, soggy, icy garment. As he buckled the swollen belt suddenly my groin felt the chill of death.

QUESTIONS ON SUBJECT

1. What compelled White to return to the lake?

2. White returns to the lake wondering whether it will be as he remembers it from childhood vacations. What remains the same? What significance does White attach to the changes in the road, the waitresses, and the outboard-motor boats?

3. In paragraph 4 White tells us, "I began to sustain the illusion that my son was I, and therefore, by simple transposition, that I was my father." What first prompts this "illusion"? Where else does White refer to it? How does it affect your understanding of what the week at the lake means to White?

4. The closing sentence takes many readers by surprise. Why did White feel the "chill of death"? Has he prepared for this surprise earlier in the essay? If so, where?

QUESTIONS ON STRATEGY

1. The first three paragraphs serve as an introduction to White's essay. Taken together, how do they prepare for what follows? (Glossary: *Beginnings*) What does each paragraph contribute?

2. In paragraph 12 White describes a late afternoon thunderstorm at the lake. How does White organize his description of the storm? (Glossary: *Organization*) What does the metaphor of the old melodrama contribute to that description? (Glossary: *Figure of Speech*)

3. What dominant impression does White create of the lake when he visits it with his son? What is the dominant impression of the lake during his earlier visits?

4. Why is it inevitable that this essay be written in the first person? Copy out several paragraphs, changing the point of view to third person. What is the effect? (Glossary: *Narration*)

5. White's essay is about a trip to a lake in Maine that he took with his son. Discuss the ways in which he uses comparison and contrast to develop his story. (Glossary: *Comparison and Contrast*)

QUESTIONS ON LANGUAGE

1. Comment on the connotations of each of the following phrases:
   a. "the stillness of the cathedral" (2)

b. "infinitely remote and primeval" (3)

c. "utterly enchanted sea" (6)

d. "the woods unshatterable" (8)

e. "nervous sound of outboard motors" (10)

What is the cumulative effect of such connotative language on you as a reader? (Glossary: *Connotation/Denotation*)

2. What is the tone of this essay, and how is it reflected in the diction that White uses? (Glossary: *Tone*) What does White's tone reveal about his attitude toward his experience? Give examples to support your answer.

3. Refer to your desk dictionary to determine the meanings of the following words as they are used in this selection: *placidity* (1), *haunts* (1), *partitions* (2), *primeval* (3), *transposition* (4), *tentatively* (5), *pensively* (6), *petulant* (10), *premonitory* (12).

WRITING SUGGESTIONS

1. Have you ever returned to a place you once knew well but have not seen for some time—a house or city where you once lived, a school you once attended, a favorite vacation spot? Write an essay in which you describe your return visit. What memories did the visit bring back? Did you, like White, find that little had changed and feel that time had stood still, or were there many changes? If possible, you should choose a spot you can actually revisit, to reflect on what has happened to the place—and to you—since you were last there.

2. What, for you, is the ideal vacation? Where would you go and what would you do? What do you hope and expect that a good vacation will do for you? Write an essay about your ideal vacation, concentrating on what this ideal reveals about you.

Spring

GRETEL EHRLICH

Gretel Ehrlich was born in Santa Barbara, California, in 1946. She attended Bennington College in Vermont, the UCLA Film School, and the New School for Social Research in New York. While working as a documentary filmmaker in Wyoming she became enraptured by the area and has lived there ever since. Ehrlich is an essayist, poet, and a journalist, and has published The Solace of Open Spaces *in 1985,* Islands, the Universe, Home *in 1987, both collections of essays, and* Heart Mountain, *a novel, published in 1988.*

In "Spring," which first appeared in the journal Antaeus *in 1986, Ehrlich describes what spring is like in Wyoming and how it affects her mind, her heart, and her soul.*

We have a nine-acre lake on our ranch and a warm spring that feeds 1 it all winter. By mid-March the lake ice begins to melt where the spring feeds in, and every year the same pair of mallards come ahead of the others and wait. Though there is very little open water, they seem content. They glide back and forth through a thin estuary, brushing watercress with their elegant, folded wings, then tip end-up to eat and, after, clamber onto the lip of ice that retreats, hardens forward, and retreats again.

Mornings, a transparent pane of ice lies over the meltwater. I peer 2 through and see some kind of waterbug—perhaps a leech—paddling like a sea turtle between green ladders of lakeweed. Cattails and sweet grass from the previous summer are bone dry, marked with black mold spots, and bend like elbows into the ice. They are swords that cut away the hard tenancy of winter. At the wide end, a mat of dead water plants has rolled back into a thick, impregnable breakwater. Near it, bubbles trapped under the ice are lenses focused straight up to catch the coming season.

It's spring again, and I wasn't finished with winter. That's what I 3 said at the end of summer too. I stood on the ten-foot-high haystack and yelled, "No!" as the first snow fell. We had been up since four in the morning, picking the last bales of hay from the oat field by hand, slipping under the weight of them in the mud, and by the time we finished the stack, six inches of snow had fallen.

It's spring, but I was still cataloguing the different kinds of snow: 4
snow that falls dry but is rained on; snow that melts down into hard
crusts; wind-driven snow that looks blue; powder snow on hard pack
on powder—a Linzer torte of snow. I look up. The troposphere is
the five-mile-wide sleeve of air out of which all our weather shakes.
A bank of clouds drives in from the south. Where in it, I wonder, does
a snowflake take on its thumbprint uniqueness? Inside the cloud,
where schools of flakes like schools of fish are flung this way and that?
What gives the snowflake its needle, plate, column, branching shapes—
the battering wind or the dust particles around which water vapor
clings?

Near town the river ice breaks up and lies stacked in industrial-sized 5
hunks on the banks—big as railway cars—and is flecked black by wheel-
ing hurricanes of plowed topsoil. That's how I feel when winter breaks
up inside me: heavy, upended, inert against the flow of a new season. I
had thought about ice during the cold months too. How it is movement betrayed, water seized in the moment of falling. In November, ice
thickened over the lake like a cataract and from the air looked like a
Cyclops: one bad eye. Under its milky spans over irrigation ditches, the
sound of water running south was muffled. One solitary spire of ice
hung noiselessly against dark rock at the falls, as if mocking or mirror-
ing the broomtail comet on the horizon. Then, in February, I tried for
words not about ice but words hacked from it—the ice at the end of the
mind, so to speak—and failed.

Those were winter things, and now it is spring, though one name 6
can't describe what, in Wyoming, is a three-part affair: false spring, the
vernal equinox, and the spring in June, when flowers come and the
grass grows.

Spring means restlessness. The physicist I've been talking to all 7
winter says if I look more widely, deeply, and microscopically all at once,
I might see how springlike the whole cosmos is. What I see as order and
stillness, the robust, time-bound determinacy of my life, is really a
mirage suspended above chaos. "There's a lot of random jiggling going
on everywhere," he tells me. Winter's tight sky hovers. Under it, hayfields are green, then white, then green growing under white. The
confinement I've felt since November resembles the confinement of
subatomic particles, I'm told. A natural velocity finally shows itself.
Particles move and become waves.

Sap rises in trees and in me, and the hard knot of perseverance I 8
cultivated to meet winter dissipates; I walk away from the obsidian of
bitter nights. Now snow comes wet and heavy, but the air it traverses
feels light. I sleep less and dream not of human entanglements but of

animals I've never seen: a caterpillar fat as a man's thumb, made of linked silver tubes, has two heads—one human, one a butterfly's.

Last spring at this time I was coming out of a bout with pneu- 9 monia. I went to bed on January 1 and didn't get up until the end of February. Winter was a cocoon in which my gagging, basso cough shook the dark figures at the end of my bed. Had I read too much Hemingway? Or was I dying? I'd lie on my stomach and look out. Nothing close-up interested me. All engagements of mind—the circumlocutions of love interests and internal gossip—appeared false. Only my body was true. And my body was trying to close down, go out the window without me.

I saw things out there. Our ranch faces south down a long treeless 10 valley whose vanishing point is two gray hills folded one in front of the other like two hands, beyond which is space, cerulean air, pleated clouds, and red mesas standing up like breaching whales in a valley three thousand feet below. Afternoons, our young horses played, rearing up on back legs and pawing oh so carefully at each other, reaching around, ears flat back, nipping manes and withers. One of those times their falsetto squeals looped across the pasture and hung, but when I tried to intone their sounds of delight, I found my lungs had no air.

It was thirty-five below zero that night. Our plumbing froze and 11 because I was very weak my husband had to bundle me up and help me to the outhouse. Nothing close at hand seemed to register with me: neither the cold nor the semicoziness of an uninsulated house. But the stars were lurid. For a while I thought I saw dead horses, eating one another's manes and tails, spinning above my head in the ice fall.

Scientists talk animatedly about how insignificant we humans are 12 when placed against the time scale of geology and the cosmos. I had heard it a hundred times but never felt it truly. Back in bed, I felt the black room was a screen through which parts of my body traveled, leaving the rest behind. I thought I was a sun flying over a barge whose iron holds soaked me up until I became rust, floating on a bright river. A ferocious loneliness took hold of me. That night a luscious, creamy fog rolled in like a roll of fat hugging me, but it was snow.

Recuperation is like spring: dormancy and vitality collide. In any 13 year I'm like a bear, a partial hibernator. During January thaws I stick my nose out and peruse the frozen desolation as if reading a book whose language I don't know. In March I'm ramshackle, weak in the knees, giddy, dazzled by broken-backed clouds, the passing of Halley's comet, the on-and-off strobe of sun. Like a sheepherder, I x out each calendar day as if time were a forest through which I could clear-cut a way to the future. The physicist straightens me out on this point too. The notion of "time passing," like a train through a landscape, is an illusion, he says. I hold the Big Ben clock taken from a dead sheep-herder's wagon. The clock measures intervals of time, not the speed of time, and the calendar is a scaffolding we hang as if time were rushing water we could harness. Time-bound, I hinge myself to a linear bias—cause and effect all laid out in a neat row.

Julius Caesar had a sense of humor about time. The Roman calen- 14 dar with its kalends, nones, and ides—counting days—changed according to who was in power. Caesar serendipitously added days, changed the names of certain months, and when he was through, the calendar was so skewed, January fell in autumn.

Einsteinian time is too big for even Julius Caesar to have touched. 15 It stretches and shrinks and dilates. Indecipherable from space, time is not one thing but an infinity of space-times, overlapping and interfering. There is no future that is not now, no past that is not now. Time includes every moment.

It's the Ides of March today. 16

I've walked to a hill a mile from the house. It's not really a hill but 17 a mountain slope that heaves up, turns sideways, and comes straight down to a foot-wide creek. Everything I can see from here used to be a flatland covered with shallow water. "Used to be" means several hundred million years ago, and the land itself was not really "here" at all but part of a continent floating near Bermuda. On top is a fin of rock, a marine deposition from Jurassic times created by small waves moving in and out from the shore.

I've come here for peace and quiet and to see what's going on in 18 this secluded valley away from ranch work and sorting corrals, but what I get is a slap on the ass by a prehistoric wave, gains and losses in altitude and aridity, outcrops of mud composed of rotting volcanic ash which fell continuously for ten thousand years, a hundred million years ago. The soils are a geologic flag—red, white, green, and gray. On one side of the hill, mountain mahogany gives off a scent like orange blossoms; on the other, colonies of sagebrush root wide in ground the color of Spanish roof tiles. And it still looks like the ocean to me. "How much truth can a man stand, sitting by the ocean, all that perpetual motion . . . ," Mose Allison, the jazz singer, sings.

The wind picks up and blusters. Its fat underbelly scrapes uneven 19 ground, twisting toward me like taffy, slips up over the mountain and showers out across the Great Plains. The sea smell it carried all the way from Seattle has long since been absorbed by pink gruss—the rotting granite that spills down the slopes of the Rockies. Somewhere over the Midwest the wind slows, tangling in the hair of hardwood forests, and finally drops into the corridors of cities, past Manhattan's World Trade Center, ripping free again as it skims the Atlantic's green swell.

Spring jitterbugs inside me. Spring *is* wind, symphonic and billow- 20 ing. A dark cloud pops like a blood blister, spraying red hail down. The sky widens, breaking itself. Wind concusses. It is a cloth that sails so birds have something to fly on.

A message reports to my brain, but I can't believe my eyes. The 21 sheet of wind had a hole in it: an eagle just fell out of the sky as if down the chute of a troubled airplane. Landed, falling. Is there a leg broken? The sides of this narrow valley, a seashore 170,000 years ago, now lift like a medic's litter to catch up this bird.

Hopping, she flaps seven feet of wing and sways near a dead fawn 22 whose carcass had recently been feasted upon. When I approached, all I could see of the animal was a rib cage rubbed red with fine tissue and the decapitated head lying peacefully against sagebrush, eyes closed.

Friends who have investigated eagles' nests have literally feared for 23 their lives. An eagle's talons are a powerful jaw. Their grip is so strong the talons can slice through flesh to bone in one motion.

I had come close to seeing what was wrong, to seeing what I could 24 do. An eagle with a bum leg will starve to death, but when I approached again she lifted her wings threateningly and, craning her neck, first to one side, then to the other, she stared hard, giving me "the eagle eye." Best to leave her alone. My husband dragged a road-killed deer up the mountain slope so she could eat, and I brought a bucket of water.

A golden eagle is not golden but black with yellow spots on the 25 neck and wings. Looking at her, I had wondered how feathers—the rachis, vane, and quill—came to be.

Birds are glorified flying lizards. Positioned together, feathers are 26 like hundreds of smaller wings, evolved from reptilian scales. Ancestral birds had thirteen pairs of cone-shaped teeth that grew in separate sockets like a snake's, rounded ribs, and bony tails. Archaeopteryx was half bird, half dinosaur, and glided instead of flying; ichthyornis was a fish-bird, a relative of the pelican; diatryma was a seven-foot-tall giant with a huge beak and with wings so absurdly small they must have been useless, though later the wing bone sprouted from them. *Aquila chrysaëtos,* the modern golden eagle, has seven thousand contour feathers, no teeth, and weighs about one pound. I think about the eagle on the hill. How big she was, how each time she spread her wings it was like a thought stretching between two seasons.

Back at the house, I relax with a beer. At 5:03 the vernal equinox 27
occurs. I go outside and stand in the middle of a hayfield with my eyes
closed. The universe is restless, but I want to feel celestial equipoise:
twelve hours of daylight, twelve of dark, and the earth ramrod straight
on its axis. Straightening my posture to resist the magnetic tilt back into
dormancy, spiritual and emotional reticence, I imagine the equatorial
sash, now nose-to-nose with the sun, sizzling like a piece of bacon, and
the earth slowly tilting.

In the morning I walk to the valley. The eagle isn't there. The hind- 28
quarters of the road-killed deer have been eaten. Coyote tracks circle
the carcass. Did they have eagle for dinner too?

Afternoon. I return. Far up on the opposite hill I see her, flapping 29
and hopping to the top. When I stop, she stops and turns her head.
Even at two hundred yards, I can feel the heat of her stare.

Later, looking through my binoculars, I try to see the world with 30
eagle eyes. After glassing the crescent moon, I dream it has grown full
and doubled. One moon is pink and spins fast; the other is an eagle's
head, turning slowly in the opposite direction. Then both moons
descend, and it is day.

At first light I clamber up the hill. Now the dead deer my husband 31
brought is only a hoop of ribs, two forelegs, and hair. The eagle is not
here or along the creek or on either hill. I climb the slope and sit. After
a long wait she careens out from the narrow slit of the red-walled canyon whose creek drains into this valley. Surely it's the same bird. Flying
by, she cocks her head and looks at me. I smile. What is a smile to her?
Now she is not flying but lifting above the planet, far from me.

Late March. The emerald of the hayfields brightens. A flock of 32
gray-capped rosy finches who overwintered here swarms a leafless apple
tree, then falls from the smooth boughs like cut grass. The tree was
planted by the Texan who homesteaded this ranch. As I walk past, one
of the boughs, shaped like an undulating dragon, splits off from the
trunk and drops.

Space is an arena where the rowdy particles that are the building 33
blocks of life perform their antics. All spring, things fall; the general law
of increasing disorder is on the rise. What is it to be a cause without an
effect, an effect without a cause, to abandon time-bound thinking, the
use of tenses, the temporally related emotions of impatience, expectation, hope, and fear? But I can't. At the edge of the lake I watch ducks.
Like them, my thinking rises and falls on the same water.

Another day. Feeling small-minded, I take a plane ride over Wyom- 34
ing. As we take off, the plane resists accepting air under its wings. Is this

how an eagle feels? Ernst Mach's principle tells me that an object's resistance against being accelerated is not the intrinsic property of matter but a measure of its interaction with the universe; that matter has inertia only because it exists in relation to other matter.

Airborne, we fly southeast from Heart Mountain across the Big 35 Horn River, over the long red wall where Butch Cassidy trailed stolen horses, across the high plains to Laramie. Coming home, we hit clouds. Turbulence, like many forms of trouble, cannot always be seen. We bounce so hard my arms sail helplessly above my head. In evolution, wing bones became arms and hands; perhaps I'm de-evolving.

From ten thousand feet I can see that spring is only half here: the 36 southern part of the state, being higher in altitude, is white; the northern half is green. Time is one of spring's greening forms, a clock whose hands are blades of grass moving vertically, up through the fringe of numbers, spreading across the middle of the face, sinking again as the sun moves from one horizon to the other. Time doesn't go anywhere; the shadow of the plane, my shadow, moves across it.

To sit on a plane is to sit on the edge of sleep, where the mind's 37 forge brightens into incongruities. Down there I see disparate wholenesses strung together and the string dissolving. Mountains run like rivers; I fly through waves and waves of chiaroscuro light. The land looks bare but is articulate. The body of the plane is my body, pressing into spring, pressing matter into relation with matter. Is it even necessary to say the obvious? That spring brings on surges of desire? From this disinterested height I say out loud what Saint Augustine wrote: "My love is my weight. Because of it I move."

Directly below us now is the fine old Wyoming ranch where Joel, 38 Mart, Dave, Hughy, and I have moved thousands of head of cattle. Joel's father, Smokey, was one of two brothers who put the outfit together. They worked hard, lived frugally, and even after his brother died, Smokey did not marry until his late fifties. As testimony to a long bachelorhood, there is no kitchen in the main house. The cookhouse stands separate from all the other buildings. In back is a bedroom and bath, which has housed a list of itinerant cooks ten pages long.

Over the years I've helped during roundup and branding. We'd rise 39 at four. Smokey, then in his eighties, cooked flapjacks and boiled coffee on the wood cookstove. There was a long table. Joel and Smokey always sat at one end.

QUESTIONS ON SUBJECT

1. What, in particular, does Ehrlich like about spring?

2. What exactly does Ehrlich mean when she writes in paragraph 35, "perhaps I'm de-evolving"?

3. Is spring "out there" only? Why do you think Ehrlich continually tells us what's she feeling and thinking while describing?

4. Explain what the vernal equinox is. Has Ehrlich done an adequate job of explaining it? Why, or why not?

QUESTIONS ON STRATEGY

1. How is Ehrlich's essay organized? (Glossary: *Organization*)

2. How are the eagle Ehrlich describes, the plane ride she takes, and spring related in this essay and for what purpose?

3. How does Ehrlich relate time and space? What or who does she use to help her explain these concepts?

4. Ehrlich tends to move between minute observation and expansive abstractions in her description of spring. What benefits does she achieve from her ability to focus in and out in this manner? What stylistic effect is created through this strategy?

5. Ehrlich uses a number of figures of speech to make spring come alive for us. Give ten examples of where she uses figures of speech. (Glossary: *Figures of Speech*)

6. Having read Ehrlich's description of spring, her attempts to come to terms with it, how would you briefly define that time of year in Wyoming? (Glossary: *Description*)

QUESTIONS ON LANGUAGE

1. In paragraph 17, Ehrlich says, "It's the Ides of March today." What does she mean? How has she prepared us to understand the term?

2. Look closely at the verbs Ehrlich uses in her sentences. What characterizes those verbs?

3. Refer to your desk dictionary to determine the meanings of the following words as they are used in this selection: *robust* (paragraph 7), *obsidian* (8), *basso* (9), *circumlocutions* (9), *cerulean* (10), *mesas* (10), *withers* (10), *lurid* (11), *ramshackle* (13), *strobe* (13), *corrals* (18), *gruss* (19), *equipoise* (27), *careens* (31), *chiaroscuro* (37).

WRITING SUGGESTIONS

1. Gretel Ehrlich is very clever in describing her subject both objectively, at times scientifically, and impressionistically, almost poetically. Using her essay as a model, try rendering a place you know well with some of the

same alternations of objective and subjective description. Try, as well, to infuse your description with some statements that reveal your own philosophic outlook about the place you describe.

2. Write a descriptive essay in which you describe what you value most in life, whether it be family, solitude, your work, a special friend, or a combination of things. Along with telling details about that thing or person, be sure to include your reasons for valuing it, him, or her above everything (or everyone) else.

WRITING SUGGESTIONS FOR DESCRIPTION

1. Most description is predominantly visual; that is, it appeals to our sense of sight. Good description, however, often goes beyond the visual; it appeals as well to one or more of the other senses—hearing, smelling, tasting, and touching. One way to heighten your awareness of these other senses is purposefully to deemphasize the visual impressions you receive. For example, while standing on a busy street corner, sitting in a classroom, or shopping in a supermarket, carefully note what you hear, smell, taste, or feel. (It may actually help to close your eyes to eliminate visual distraction as you carry out this experiment.) Use these sense impressions to write a brief description of the street corner, the classroom, or the supermarket.

2. Select one of the following topics, and write an objective description of it. Remember that your task in writing objective description is to inform the reader about the object, not to convey to the reader the mood or feeling that the object evokes in you.

   a. a pine tree
   b. a personal computer
   c. a bake shop
   d. a dictionary
   e. a fast-food restaurant

   f. a football field
   g. the layout of your campus
   h. a stereo system
   i. a houseplant
   j. your room

3. Writers of description often rely on factual information to give substance and interest to their writing. Using facts, statistics, or other information found in standard reference works in your college library (encyclopedias, dictionaries, almanacs, atlases, biographical dictionaries, or yearbooks), write an essay of several paragraphs describing one of the people, places, or things from the following list. Be sure that you focus your description, that you have a purpose for your description, and that you present your facts in an interesting manner.

   a. the Statue of Liberty
   b. the telephone
   c. Sandra Day O'Connor
   d. Niagara Falls
   e. the Great Wall of China
   f. Michael Jordan
   g. Bonnie Raitt

   h. the Tower of London
   i. the sun
   j. Disney World
   k. Princess Diana
   l. Julia Roberts
   m. Hillary Clinton

4. Select one of the following places and write a multiparagraph description that captures your subjective sense impressions of that particular place.

a. a busy downtown intersection
b. a bakery
c. an auction
d. a factory
e. a service station
f. a zoo

g. a cafeteria
h. a farmers' market
i. a concert hall
j. a locker room
k. a bank
l. a library

3
ILLUSTRATION

WHAT IS ILLUSTRATION?

Illustration is the use of examples—facts, anecdotes, samples, and many other kinds of specific information—to make a generalization more vivid, understandable, or persuasive. Here are a few typical generalizations:

The films coming out of Hollywood place too much emphasis on violence.

Modern art is characterized by the fragmentation of form, composition, color, and image.

Americans are a pain-conscious people who would rather get rid of pain than seek and cure its root causes.

Each of these statements is very broad and vague, even open to challenge. Yet each point could be strengthened and made meaningful through illustration. The first assertion could be given depth and impact with detailed examples taken from actual movies. The second, though puzzling to readers who have not seen much modern art, could be clarified with descriptions of specific paintings and sculptures. And the third claim could be supported with examples of situations and even specific cases in which Americans have gone to the drugstore instead of to the doctor.

Writing that consists wholly of generalizations strung together page after page can be extremely difficult to read. Good writers recognize this fact and try to provide just the right kind and number of examples to make their ideas clear or understandable, interesting, and convincing. In fact, illustration is so useful and versatile a writing strategy that it may be found in all kinds of writing; there is hardly an essay in this book that does not use examples in one way or another.

An example may be anything from a statistic to a story; it may be stated in a few words or go on for several pages. What is required of an example is that it be closely *relevant* to the idea or generalization it is meant to illustrate. While a statistic showing how much of a particular drug Americans purchased in a given year might be interesting, a statistic showing that over the past ten years painkiller sales have increased more rapidly than the population would be relevant to the idea that Americans are a pain-conscious people, and so could be used as an example to support the author's assertion.

To be most effective, an example should be *representative*. The story it tells or the fact it presents should be typical of many others that readers are sure to think of. Figures showing how many people use aspirin, and what for, would be representative, since aspirin is the most widely used painkiller in America. Statistics about a newly discovered and highly specialized barbiturate might well show a tremendous increase in its use, but the example would be unrepresentative and, therefore, less persuasive.

WHY DO WRITERS USE ILLUSTRATION?

Illustrating a point with examples seems to be a basic strategy of human communication—and serves several purposes for writers. First, examples are used to make writing more vivid or entertaining. An essay about television bloopers will be dull and pointless without some examples of on-screen blunders—"tips of the slongue," as one writer calls them. A more serious essay on the danger of drunken driving will gain in impact if it is illustrated with descriptions of the victims' shattered lives and the grief and outrage of their family and friends.

Writers also use illustration to explain or clarify their ideas. In an essay on political leadership, the assertion "Successful leaders are often a product of their times" will certainly require further explanation. Such explanation could very effectively be provided through examples: Franklin Roosevelt in 1932, Winston Churchill in 1940, and Charles de Gaulle in 1958 all rose to power because their people were looking for

ILLUSTRATION   125

leadership in a national crisis, as did Lenin, Hitler, and Mussolini. In her essay "How to Give Orders Like a Man" later in this chapter, Deborah Tannen presents a number of examples to help her illustrate the topic she presents in the title to her essay.

Examples like Tannen's also demonstrate another important function of illustration: to support a generalization and make it more convincing. James Thurber, in "Courtship through the Ages," uses examples from the animal kingdom to illustrate the "sorrowful lengths to which all males must go to arouse the interest of a lady." And in "Elvira's Story," Flora Mancuso Edwards provides an extended, detailed example to support her point that the poor "live miserable and know not why."

LOOKING AT ILLUSTRATION

First, try to discover what general point the author is making; then, determine how the author has presented examples to develop that point. Sometimes you will find the point stated early on to introduce the examples. At other times you may have to look further for the generalization. Consider this brief discussion by George Orwell:

> The other night a barmaid informed me that if you pour beer into a damp glass it goes flat much more quickly. She added that to dip your mustache into your beer also turns it flat. I immediately accepted this without further inquiry; in fact, as soon as I got home I clipped my mustache, which I had forgotten to do for some days.
>
> Only later did it strike me that this was probably one of those superstitions which are able to keep alive because they have the air of being scientific truths. In my notebook I have a long list of fallacies which were taught to me in my childhood, in each case not as an old wives' tale but as a scientific fact. I can't give the whole list, but here are a few hardy favorites: that a swan can break your leg with a blow of its wing; that if you cut yourself between the thumb and forefinger you get lockjaw; that powdered glass is poisonous; that if you wash your hands in the water eggs have been boiled in (why anyone should do this is a mystery) you will get warts; that bulls become infuriated at the sight of red; that sulphur in a dog's drinking water acts as a tonic.
>
> And so on and so forth. Almost everyone carries some or other of these beliefs into adult life. I have met someone of over thirty who still retained the second of the beliefs I have listed above. As for the third, it is still so widespread that in India, for instance, people are constantly trying to poison one another with powdered glass, with disappointing results.

Not until the third paragraph does Orwell make his generalization: "Almost everyone carries some or other of these beliefs into adult life." Already in paragraphs 1 and 2, Orwell has illustrated such beliefs by referring to numerous examples: first, those told him by the barmaid and, then, a further list of "hardy favorites." These help explain and clarify what Orwell means when he talks about superstitions "that have the air of being scientific truths." Following his generalization Orwell offers two more specific cases: an adult who believes that a cut on the hand causes lockjaw, and people in India who believe that powdered glass is poisonous. Here, again, is a group of examples (obvious even without the telltale phrase *for instance* in the last sentence); but these are offered to support the generalization and persuade readers that it is true, rather than to explain what the generalization means. So Orwell has used two sets of examples for two different purposes in the space of three short paragraphs.

You may even conclude that Orwell has yet another purpose in mind with this collection of examples—to entertain. Certainly the superstitions he lists are particularly silly, even funny: at the end he sketches in the would-be Indian poisoners with dry humor, and in the first paragraph he even makes fun of himself for accepting a barmaid as an expert on the science of beer foam and mustaches. Orwell's point is no deep insight into the human condition but an amused observation about how silly people can be. It's through his examples that he creates his humorous tone.

Are Orwell's examples good ones? Certainly. They serve his purposes, and each is relevant to the generalization it develops. Most readers would also agree that the examples are representative. The superstitions he mentions are typical of pseudoscientific "laws" familiar to all (that lightning never strikes twice in the same place, that handling toads causes warts); and his two final examples bring to mind other adults, even sensible ones, who believe such nonsense.

Are there enough examples? Orwell provides plenty to explain what he means by "superstitions which . . . have the air of being scientific truths." For his concluding generalization, however, he supplies only two examples. Are these enough to support his claim that "almost everyone" believes superstitions such as these? Here, readers will make their own judgments, and opinions may differ. Those who disagree with Orwell may well feel that two examples are not sufficient to prove his point.

Sometimes, however, just one example will do, if it is representative and if the writer develops it well. Here is such an example by basketball all-star Bill Russell from his autobiographical *Second Wind:*

ILLUSTRATION 127

Every champion athlete has a moment when everything goes so perfectly for him he slips into a gear that he didn't know was there. It's easy to spot that perfect moment in a sport like track. I remember watching the 1968 Olympics in Mexico City, where the world record in the long jump was just under 27 feet. Then Bob Beamon flew down the chute and leaped out over the pit in a majestic jump that I have seen replayed many times. There was an awed silence when the announcer said that Beamon's jump measured 29 feet 2¼ inches. Generally world records are broken by fractions of inches, but Beamon had exceeded the existing record by more than two feet. On learning what he had done, Beamon slumped down on the ground and cried. To all those who saw it, this was an unforgettable moment in sport. Most viewers' image of Beamon ends with the picture of him weeping on the ground, but in fact he got up and took some more jumps that day. I like to think that he did so because he had jumped for so long at his best that *even then* he didn't know what might come out of him. At the end of that day he wanted to be absolutely sure that he'd had his perfect day.

Few readers have been world-class athletes and known that "extra gear" Russell describes, so he illustrates what he means with a single, extended example—in this case an anecdote that gives substance to the idea he wants us to understand.

READING ILLUSTRATION IN AN ANNOTATED STUDENT ESSAY

Originally from New York City, Eleanor DeLisa wrote this essay while a student at the University of Vermont. She later transferred to California State University, Long Beach, where she majored in education in preparation for a career as a Language Arts teacher at the middle school level. In this essay, DeLisa presents many examples to explain why fad diets are so popular and yet do not fulfill their promise.

DIETS—DO THEY WORK?
Eleanor DeLisa

Attention-grabbing lead sentence

Three examples from surveys establish Americans obsession with weight.

Americans are obsessed with thinness. A recent article in *Time* reported on a *Better Homes and Gardens* study that showed "nearly 90 percent of Americans think that they weigh too much." According to a Gallup poll, approximately "31 percent of American

women ages 19 to 39 diet at least once a month, and
16 percent of them consider themselves to be per-

*MLA in-text
citation of sources*

petual dieters" (Toulexis 54). It seems as if almost all
Americans consider themselves in need of some type
of diet. One of the most alluring characteristics of diets is that they promise quick weight loss. But in the
long term nearly everyone who goes on some type of
a diet risks failure. Another survey on the results of
dieting showed that "two-thirds of people who lose
weight gain it all back, and then some, within a few
years. After seven years, only 2 percent can still

Thesis statement

flaunt svelter selves" (Toulexis 55). The key to real
weight loss is not dieting. The best results come from
a long-term weight-control plan.

*Discussion of
quick weight-loss
schemes*

        Most quick weight-loss schemes fall into two cat-   2
egories, fasting and crash dieting. Both of these methods will in fact allow people to lose pounds, but will
they allow them to keep the weight off? Also, such
programs can be dangerous if continued for a long
period of time. Although there is a technical differ-

*Example of
fasting*

ence between fasting and starving, metabolically the
human body can't tell the difference. If a person fasts,
the body has to rely on producing energy from its
own resources. In order to conserve fuel, the body
then lowers its metabolism. A few days of fasting may
produce lost pounds on the scale, but it's not the fat
loss most dieters aim for. It's mainly water loss,
which is almost immediately regained once the fast is
broken. Moreover, the longer the fast continues, the
greater the serious risk to the body's protein reserves.
There is also a greater risk of gaining even more
weight after coming off a fast because the body will
still function at a lower metabolic rate, allowing a
more rapid weight gain on fewer calories. Many
people believe that a one-or-two-day fast helps reduce
the appetite. While this is true, repeated fasting can
permanently alter the body's base metabolic rate.

        The other major quick weight-loss scheme, crash   3
dieting, is no better than its counterpart. Most crash

ILLUSTRATION   129

Multiple examples of crash diets

diets promise quick weight loss by limiting the amount of food eaten. They also tend to emphasize certain food groups, while excluding others. The Beverly Hills Diet, for example, requires only fresh fruits during the first two or three weeks of the regimen. Because diets do restrict food, it is very important to maintain good nutrition. Crash diets do not. If a person eats too many foods from one food group and doesn't eat any from another, the body will not be able to function correctly. The infamous Last Chance Diet, with its emphasis on liquid protein, led to numerous heart attacks and over sixty deaths among users. The Scarsdale Diet, an enormously popular diet from a decade ago, is another prime example. Neither medically sound nor nutritionally safe, this diet results in a rapid and dangerous drop in weight caused by fluid and protein loss. The diet permits only limited amounts of bread and cereal, allows no dairy products, and results in carbohydrate and calcium deficiencies. Protein, niacin, and vitamins A and C intake far exceeds the recommended daily amount. Meat is also emphasized to the exclusion of other foods, making the diet high in cholesterol. In spite of the fact that this and other diets like it can destroy a person's health, people actually follow these diets to shed their excess pounds.

It is obvious from even this cursory examination   4
of the negative effects of fad dieting that the "get-thin-quick" schemes offer little more than empty promises.

Transitional paragraph turns focus to weight control plans.

Dieters ought to consider a weight-control plan instead. Weight control is commonsense eating—foods high in nutrition and low in fat and sugar—in conjunction with an exercise program. The weight-control method can't offer fast results, but it can be successful where diets fail. Here's why.

Losing weight is a slow process. Given an ad-   5

Example of how weight-control plan works: eating

equate period of time, along with a sensible eating and exercise plan, the body will naturally start to slim down. Eating a well-balanced diet with foods from the four food groups gives the body all the essentials it needs. The high amounts of fiber in these foods make the stomach feel full and satisfied. When the body receives the nutrients it needs, it functions better as well. Studies show that depression, migraine headaches, and lethargy are triggered by certain nutritional deficiencies. Once these deficiencies are eliminated, the ailments tend to disappear.

Example of how weight-control plan works: exercise

Most fad diets don't advocate exercise, but "working out" is an essential ingredient in the weight-control program. Exercise tones up the body and gives people more energy and life. Moderate exercise such as walking can rev-up the metabolism and help the body burn calories more efficiently. Regular exercise has the additional benefit of increasing over time the body's base metabolic rate, so that more food may be eaten with no weight gain.   6

Conclusion summarizes key points of essay

Fad dieting as practiced in the 1980s just doesn't work. Fasting and crash dieting in particular often do more harm than good in terms of nutrition and general well-being. A weight-control program, however, offers success where diets fail. When overweight people forsake the lure of quick weight loss and understand all the negative aspects of dieting, they will look to weight control for the solution to their health problem.   7

Works Cited

MLA-style list of works cited

Farley, Dixie. "Eating Disorders: When Thinness Becomes an Obsession." *FDA Consumer* May 1986.
"Is Fasting Safe for Quick Weight Loss?" *Glamour* Mar. 1987.
Toulexis, Anastasia. "Dieting: The Losing Game." *Time* 20 Jan. 1986.

DeLisa came up with her topic in a kind of roundabout way. She recalls, "I originally wanted to do a paper on starvation—I was interested in the famine in Africa. While researching this topic in the library, I discovered an abundance of material on anorexia nervosa and, on a

ILLUSTRATION   **131**

broader scale, dieting. The topic itself is a good one because diets and weight control interest a great many people nowadays because of the recent drive to promote better health awareness and because people are more conscious of their appearance." The more DeLisa read and the more she talked with her friends, the more she liked the idea of diets. "It was a subject I felt more comfortable with. Besides, a lot of my friends were talking about quick and easy ways to lose those extra pounds, and I always had my suspicions." And it was her suspicions that led DeLisa to ask the question that became the focus for her essay. "It just seemed to me that if these diets really worked, why were my friends constantly looking for new ones? I also wondered if these diets posed any special risks, especially when I saw the crazy regimens that other students followed." The result—an essay entitled "Diets—Do They Work?"

WRITING AN ESSAY USING ILLUSTRATION

Begin by thinking of ideas and generalizations about your topic that you can make clearer and more persuasive by illustrating them in your writing with facts, anecdotes, or other specifics. Most important, of course, is your main point, the central generalization that you will develop in your essay. But also be alert for other statements or references that may gain from illustration—as Orwell did in writing about superstition. Those that are already clear and uncontroversial, that your readers will understand and immediately agree with, can stand on their own as you pass along quickly to your next point; belaboring the obvious wastes your time and energy, as well as your readers'. Often, however, you will find that examples add clarity, color, and weight to what you want to say.

Gathering Examples

Before beginning to write, bring together as many examples as you can think of that are related to your subject, more even than you can possibly use. Then you will be able to choose the strongest and most representative for your essay, not merely the first that come to mind. This abundance of materials will also make it less likely that you will have to stop in mid-draft and hunt for further examples, losing the thread of your ideas. In addition, the more examples you gather, the more you are likely to learn about your subject.

What kinds of examples you look for and where you look for them will depend, of course, on your subject and the point you want to make about it. If you plan to write about all the quirky, fascinating individuals who make up your family, you can gather your examples without leaving your room: descriptions of their habits and clothing, stories about their strange adventures, facts about their backgrounds, quotations from their talk. If, however, you are writing an essay on book censorship in American public schools, you will need to go to the library and read many sources there to supply yourself with examples. Your essay might well include accounts drawn from newspapers; statistics published by librarians' or teachers' professional organizations; court transcripts and judicial opinions on censorship; and interviews with school board members, parents, book publishers, even the authors whose work has been pulled off library shelves or kept out of the classroom. The range of sources and the variety of examples are limited only by your own imagination and the time you can spend on research. DeLisa remembers her work in the library well. "It's really not that difficult if you stay organized. I started with the *Reader's Guide to Periodical Literature*. I also thought it was wise to use a variety of magazines, ranging from women's magazines, such as *Glamour*, to popular newsmagazines such as *Time* and *U.S. News and World Report*. I did a lot of reading before I selected the examples that seemed best suited to illustrate what I wanted to say in my essay."

Testing Examples

First, make sure that your examples are, in fact, relevant. Do they concern the points you want to make, or the ideas you want to clarify? If not, then they aren't really examples at all. Suppose the main point of your planned essay is that book censorship has spread throughout American public education. A newspaper story about the banning of *Catcher in the Rye* and *The Merchant of Venice* from the local high school's English curriculum would clearly be relevant, since it concerns book censorship at a public school. But the fact that James Joyce's novel *Ulysses* was first banned as obscene and then vindicated in a famous trial, although an important case of censorship, has nothing to do with books in public schools. Consequently, it is not relevant to your essay.

Next, determine which of your examples are most representative. If, while working on the censorship paper, you have found a dozen quiet administrative hearings and orderly court cases reported, but only one sensational incident where books were actually burned in a school parking lot, the latter, however dramatic, is clearly not a representative example. You might want to mention the book-burning in your essay, but you could not present it as typical of how censorship is handled.

ILLUSTRATION 133

What if your examples do not support your point? Perhaps you have missed some important information and need to look further. But perhaps the problem is with the point itself. For example, you intend your censorship paper to illustrate the following generalization: "Book censorship has spread throughout American public education." However, you have not found very many examples in which specific books were actually censored or banned outright. Although many attempts at censorship have been made, most were ultimately prevented or overturned in the courts. You might then have to revise your original generalization: "Although there have been many well-publicized attempts to censor books in public schools, actual censorship is comparatively rare."

DeLisa found it particularly helpful to share the drafts of her essay with other students in her writing class. "In total, I probably wrote five or six different versions of this essay. I shared them with members of the class, and their comments were extremely insightful. I remember one student's questions in particular, because she really got me to focus on the problems with fad diets. The students also helped me to see where I needed examples to explain what I was talking about. The very first draft that I wrote is completely different from the one I submitted in class."

Organization

It is important to arrange your examples in an order that serves your purpose, is easy for readers to follow, and will have maximum effect. Some possible patterns of organization include chronological order and spatial order, as well as moving from the simplest example to the most difficult, from the least to the most controversial, or from the least to the most important. If your examples are fairly brief, similar to each other, and equally important, you may hit upon an order that "feels right" to you, as George Orwell did in his paragraphs about superstitions.

Before starting the first draft, it may help you to work out your pattern of organization in a scratch outline, using only enough words so that you will be able to tell which example each entry refers to. Here's a scratch outline of the Orwell selection:

Examples of common superstitions.

> Generalization: some superstitions are carried into adult life because they seem like scientific truths.

> what turns beer flat—I believed a barmaid

swan's wing

lockjaw—some adults still believe it

powdered glass—Indians still believe this one

bulls see red

sulphur & water a tonic for dogs

You could add another line, right after "generalization," to remind yourself of your pattern of organization, perhaps "order: increasing importance." Such an outline can help you keep track of which examples you mean to use and your order of presentation.

Elvira's Story

FLORA MANCUSO EDWARDS

Flora Mancuso Edwards has been the president of Middlesex County College in Edison, New Jersey, since 1986. Prior to coming to Middlesex County College, Edwards was president of Hostos Community College of the City University of New York. She earned her B.A., M.A., and Ph.D. in Romance languages and linguistics from New York University. She also taught at Columbia University, New York City Community College, and LaGuardia Community College, where she was an academic dean.

In "Elvira's Story," first published in 1978, Edwards uses a single extended example to explain the particular plight of the laboring poor.

Over 150 years ago the English historian Thomas Carlyle had this to say about Victorian society:

> It is not to die, or even to die of hunger, that makes a man wretched; many men have died; all men must die. . . . But it is to live miserable we know not why; to work sore and yet gain nothing; to be heartworn, weary, yet isolated, unrelated, girt in with a cold, universal Laissez-faire.[1]

There are over 4 million people in the United States today who still live miserable and know not why, who still "work sore and yet gain nothing." They are our laboring poor.

Elvira Ramirez is just one example of those who must sell their labor so cheaply that the necessities of life are just barely met. Elvira is a soft-spoken, cheerful, well-mannered woman who works in a luxurious East Side beauty salon doing shampoos and manicures. Her average day is filled by serving New York's well-to-do matrons who spend spring in New York, winter in Miami, and summer on Cape Cod. Elvira listens sympathetically to their problems in getting "reliable help" or to their last-minute preparations for a child's wedding in Switzerland.

---

[1]Quoted in Robert Hunter, *Poverty,* ed. Peter d'A. Jones (New York: Macmillan, 1904; Harper & Row, 1965), p. 1 [Author's note]. *Laissez-faire:* loosely translated, this French expression means "let-things-be."

For her services and good company she receives $0.25 to $0.50 [4] from each one and occasionally $1.00 from a more generous customer. These tips bring up her total salary of $90.00 to approximately $110.00 a week. On this salary, Elvira supports herself, her son, a teen-age daughter, and her mother in a one-bedroom apartment in the Nathan Strauss Housing Projects in the Chelsea section on Manhattan's West Side.

Her apartment is on the third floor of a building whose elevators [5] are as offensive as they are nonfunctioning. Elvira, her mother, her daughter, and her son all used to sleep in one room, but now the boy is older and has inherited the sofa in the living room, which doubles as his bedroom. The apartment has no closets, and there is little room even for the metal Woolworth's wardrobes. The kitchen is so small that there is no place for a table, so when the family must eat together, the sofa is moved and a table set up in the living room.

Elvira receives no health insurance from her job, nor does she [6] receive a vacation or overtime pay. Her mother is only sixty and neither blind nor technically disabled, so she receives no social security or public assistance. Elvira's income—marginal as it may be—is too high for Medicaid, so Elvira works fourteen to sixteen hours a day, six days a week, and prays that no one will get sick. But, because the windows of the third-floor apartment keep getting broken, New York's winter always seems to take its toll in doctor bills, which each year are increasingly hard to pay.

When Elvira was hospitalized several years ago, the Department of [7] Social Services came to her rescue. But it did not take long for Elvira to realize that the benefits came at a high price.

> No, the welfare is all waiting with the children crying, waiting outside the office for hours in the freezing cold, sick hungry waiting all day in the clinic, waiting to be looked down on, insulted, and humiliated. No, I'm not earning much more—but it's better than waiting.
> God willing, I don't get sick again.[2]

Elvira has no savings and therefore cannot move to larger quarters. [8] As it is, rent is her biggest expenditure. Her hopes?

> Maybe I go back to the Island[3] when Michele finish school. You know, I guess I didn't do so bad after all. Michele finish fourth in her class. Now she goes to Harpur College. She got a scholarship, you know. I thought when she finish high school she would get a job and

---

[2]Personal interviews conducted between May and December 1973 [Author's note].
[3]Puerto Rico, her birthplace.

help out, but maybe it's better like this. Now she'll be somebody. . . . You know, like a teacher or a nurse or something. That's the most important thing—the kids. Sure I work hard—but the kids—they're going to be something.

Am I poor? No, not really. Really poor people take the welfare. Most of the time we manage to get by.[4]

Elvira receives no benefits, no medical coverage, no public assis- 9 tance. She earns $6,000 a year before taxes. She works harder and longer than most people and earns considerably less. She eats little meat and indulges herself in no luxuries. She does not own a car, goes on no vacations, eats in few restaurants, and buys a minimum of clothing.

Elvira's job is similar to almost one-third of all the jobs in New 10 York, and Elvira is one of 600,000 New Yorkers who live below the poverty line and struggle on day by day, eking out a marginal existence in New York, one of the richest cities in the world.

On a national level, over 4.5 million people (not counting rural 11 sharecroppers) are employed full time and are still poor. In almost half of these families, two people work full time in order to reap the bitter rewards of poverty and want.

QUESTIONS ON SUBJECT

1. Who is Elvira Ramirez? How does she earn her living? What distinguishes her position from that of middle-class laborers?
2. What is Elvira Ramirez's attitude toward welfare?
3. What is the relevance of Edwards's quotation from Carlyle (paragraph 1)? What does it add to her essay?
4. What hope, if any, does Edwards offer that the "laboring poor" can be helped?

QUESTIONS ON STRATEGY

1. What is Edwards's purpose in this essay? How does the extended example of Elvira Ramirez serve that purpose? (Glossary: *Purpose*)
2. Edwards points up several ironies in Elvira's situation and attitude. What are they, and where do you find them? Is her use of irony effective? (Glossary: *Irony*)
3. Is the treatment of Elvira's situation objective or subjective? Why do you think so? (Glossary: *Objective/Subjective*)

---

[4]See note 2.

4. How does Edwards use definition to make her readers understand the meaning of the phrase "laboring poor"? Where in the essay does she come closest to defining the term? (Glossary: *Definition*)

QUESTIONS ON LANGUAGE

1. What details of Elvira's speech, as quoted in paragraphs 7 and 8, reveal her not to be a native speaker of English? Why do you think Edwards did not silently correct Elvira's mistakes?

2. What details in the quotation from Carlyle indicate that this is not contemporary American prose? Pay attention not only to the diction but to how the sentences are composed.

3. Refer to your dictionary to determine the meanings of the following words as they are used in this selection: *Laissez-faire* (paragraph 1), *marginal* (6), *eking* (10), *sharecroppers* (11).

WRITING ASSIGNMENTS

1. When asked if she is poor, Elvira Ramirez says "no, not really. Really poor people take the welfare. Most of the time we manage to get by." Yet Flora Mancuso Edwards has chosen Elvira as a prime example of the "laboring poor." Obviously, they have different views of the same situation, different definitions of the word *poor*. Consider how psychological factors such as pride, self-respect, and control over one's life, as well as employment, income, and the cost of living, affect different people's views of what poverty is and who the poor are. Write an essay illustrating some common definitions of poverty.

2. Gather examples from your personal experience or your reading and write an essay illustrating one of the following generalizations:
   a. Being involved in politics is/isn't a very rewarding experience.
   b. Most products do/don't live up to the claims of their advertisements.
   c. You are what you say.
   d. Nature works in mysterious ways.
   e. Television teaches us as many bad things as good.

A Crime of Compassion

BARBARA HUTTMANN

Barbara Huttmann, a nurse, a teacher, and a writer, was born in Oakland, California, in 1935. Her intense interest in the patients' rights issue is expressed in her two books, The Patient's Advocate *and* Code Blue: A Nurse's True-Life Story. *Currently, she is associate director of nursing services at Children's Hospital of San Francisco.*

In the following essay, which first appeared in Newsweek *in 1983, Huttmann narrates the final months in the life of Mac, one of her favorite patients. Her story serves as an extended example to support her emotional plea for new legislation that would give terminally ill patients the right to die with dignity.*

"Murderer," a man shouted. "God help patients who get *you* for 1 a nurse."

"What gives you the right to play God?" another one asked. 2

It was the Phil Donahue Show where the guest is a fatted calf 3 and the audience a 200-strong flock of vultures hungering to pick at the bones. I had told them about Mac, one of my favorite cancer patients. "We resuscitated him 52 times in just one month. I refused to resuscitate him again. I simply sat there and held his hand while he died."

There wasn't time to explain that Mac was a young, witty, macho 4 cop who walked into the hospital with 32 pounds of attack equipment, looking as if he could single-handedly protect the whole city, if not the entire state. "Can't get rid of this cough," he said. Otherwise, he felt great.

Before the day was over, tests confirmed that he had lung cancer. 5 And before the year was over, I loved him, his wife, Maura, and their three kids as if they were my own. All the nurses loved him. And we all battled his disease for six months without ever giving death a thought. Six months isn't such a long time in the whole scheme of things, but it was long enough to see him lose his youth, his wit, his macho, his hair, his bowel and bladder control, his sense of taste and smell, and his ability to do the slightest thing for himself. It was also long enough to watch Maura's transformation from a young woman into a haggard, beaten old lady.

When Mac had wasted away to a 60-pound skeleton kept alive by 6 liquid food we poured down a tube, i.v. solutions we dripped into his veins, and oxygen we piped to a mask on his face, he begged us: "Mercy . . . for God's sake, please just let me go."

The first time he stopped breathing, the nurse pushed the button 7 that calls a "code blue" throughout the hospital and sends a team rushing to resuscitate the patient. Each time he stopped breathing, sometimes two or three times in one day, the code team came again. The doctors and technicians worked their miracles and walked away. The nurses stayed to wipe the saliva that drooled from his mouth, irrigate the big craters of bedsores that covered his hips, suction the lung fluids that threatened to drown him, clean the feces that burned his skin like lye, pour the liquid food down the tube attached to his stomach, put pillows between his knees to ease the bone-on-bone pain, turn him every hour to keep the bedsores from getting worse, and change his gown and linen every two hours to keep him from being soaked in perspiration.

At night I went home and tried to scrub away the smell of decaying 8 flesh that seemed woven into the fabric of my uniform. It was in my hair, the upholstery of my car—there was no washing it away. And every night I prayed that Mac would die, that his agonized eyes would never again plead with me to let him die.

Every morning I asked his doctor for a "no-code" order. Without 9 that order, we had to resuscitate every patient who stopped breathing. His doctor was one of several who believe we must extend life as long as we have the means and knowledge to do it. To not do it is to be liable for negligence, at least in the eyes of many people, including some nurses. I thought about what it would be like to stand before a judge, accused of murder, if Mac stopped breathing and I didn't call a code.

And after the fifty-second code, when Mac was still lucid enough to 10 beg for death again, and Maura was crumbled in my arms again, and when no amount of pain medication stilled his moaning and agony, I wondered about a spiritual judge. Was all this misery and suffering supposed to be building character or infusing us all with the sense of humility that comes from impotence?

Had we, the whole medical community, become so arrogant that 11 we believed in the illusion of salvation through science? Had we become so self-righteous that we thought meddling in God's work was our duty, our moral imperative and our legal obligation? Did we really believe that we had the right to force "life" on a suffering man who had begged for the right to die?

Such questions haunted me more than ever early one morning 12 when Maura went home to change her clothes and I was bathing Mac.

He had been still for so long, I thought he at last had the blessed relief of coma. Then he opened his eyes and moaned, "Pain . . . no more . . . Barbara . . . do something . . . God, let me go."

The desperation in his eyes and voice riddled me with guilt. "I'll 13 stop," I told him as I injected the pain medication.

I sat on the bed and held Mac's hands in mine. He pressed his bony 14 fingers against my hand and muttered, "Thanks." Then there was one soft sigh and I felt his hands go cold in mine. "Mac?" I whispered, as I waited for his chest to rise and fall again.

A clutch of panic banded my chest, drew my finger to the code 15 button, urged me to do something, anything . . . but sit there alone with death. I kept one finger on the button, without pressing it, as a waxen pallor slowly transformed his face from person to empty shell. Nothing I've ever done in my 47 years has taken so much effort as it took *not* to press that code button.

Eventually, when I was as sure as I could be that the code team 16 would fail to bring him back, I entered the legal twilight zone and pushed the button. The team tried. And while they were trying, Maura walked into the room and shrieked, "No . . . don't let them do this to him . . . for God's sake . . . please, no more."

Cradling her in my arms was like cradling myself, Mac, and all those 17 patients and nurses who had been in this place before, who do the best they can in a death-denying society.

So a TV audience accused me of murder. Perhaps I am guilty. If a 18 doctor had written a no-code order, which is the only *legal* alternative, would he have felt any less guilty? Until there is legislation making it a criminal act to code a patient who has requested the right to die, we will all of us risk the same fate as Mac. For whatever reason, we developed the means to prolong life, and now we are forced to use it. We do not have the right to die.

QUESTIONS ON SUBJECT

1. Why did people in the audience at the Phil Donahue Show call Huttmann a "murderer" (paragraph 1)? Is there any sense in which their accusation is justified?

2. Why, according to Huttmann, do some doctors refuse to give a "no-code" order?

3. What made Huttmann's decision not to press the code button so difficult? Why didn't she stop resuscitation efforts earlier? Why did she finally decide not to press the button?

4. What does Huttmann mean when she calls America "a death-denying society" (17)? Do you agree with her characterization? Why, or why not?

5. Huttmann concludes her essay with the statement, "We do not have the right to die" (18). What does this mean? Is she overstating the situation, or telling the simple truth?

QUESTIONS ON STRATEGY

1. A good narrative frequently has an attention-grabbing opening and a thought-provoking closing. Explain how this is true of Huttmann's essay. (Glossary: *Beginnings/Endings*)

2. What part do the questions in paragraphs 10 and 11 play in the overall narration? Why are they important to Huttmann's strategy? (Glossary: *Rhetorical Question*)

3. Explain Huttmann's use of dialogue in this essay. What purpose does the use of dialogue help her to achieve? (Glossary: *Dialogue*)

4. Huttmann's narrative covers a period of six months. In paragraphs 4 through 6, she tells us about the first five months of Mac's illness; in paragraphs 7 through 10, the sixth month; and in paragraphs 11 through 17, the final morning. In what ways do Huttmann's selection of detail and use of time reflect her reason for telling her story? Explain. (Glossary: *Narration*)

5. Huttmann believes that new legislation is needed to cover the "coding" of patients who have requested the right to die. How does she attempt to persuade readers to her position? Do you find her argument convincing? Why, or why not? (Glossary: *Argumentation*)

QUESTIONS ON LANGUAGE

1. Huttmann calls each successful resuscitation of Mac a "miracle" (7). What attitude does she express with this word? (Glossary: *Attitude*)

2. The right-to-die issue is indeed an emotional one. Discuss how Huttmann uses connotation to involve readers emotionally in Mac's case and in the issue in general. (Glossary: *Connotation/Denotation*)

3. Refer to your desk dictionary to determine the meanings of the following words as they are used in this selection: *resuscitate* (paragraph 3), *irrigate* (7), *lucid* (10), *imperative* (11), *waxen* (15), *pallor* (15).

WRITING ASSIGNMENTS

1. Huttmann says, "Nothing I've ever done in my 47 years has taken so much effort as it took *not* to press that code button" (15). Using Huttmann's

essay as a model, relate an episode in which you have had to make an important and difficult decision. Be careful to show your readers why the incident was significant for you, why it was hard to arrive at your decision, and what generalization your story illustrates.

2. Select a controversial issue—such as the death penalty, school prayer, military service, or welfare—in which the law and morality seem to you to be in conflict. Write an essay in which you explain the nature of that conflict and attempt to resolve the issue convincingly. Be sure to include enough information to justify your opinions.

Courtship through the Ages

JAMES THURBER

James Thurber (1894–1961), writer and cartoonist, has been one of America's favorite and most prolific humorists for more than fifty years. Most of his early essays, short stories, and line drawings appeared in the New Yorker *after he joined its editorial staff in 1925. Some of his books include* Is Sex Necessary? *(1929, with E. B. White),* The Thurber Carnival *(1945), and* Alarms and Diversions *(1957).*

In the following essay, first published in My World—And Welcome to It, *Thurber makes a masterful use of absurd and ironic examples to poke fun at the mating rituals of humans and animals alike.*

Surely nothing in the astonishing scheme of life can have non- 1
plussed Nature so much as the fact that none of the females of any of the species she created really cared very much for the male, as such. For the past ten million years Nature has been busily inventing ways to make the male attractive to the female, but the whole business of courtship, from the marine annelids up to man, still lumbers heavily along, like a complicated musical comedy. I have been reading the sad and absorbing story in Volume 6 (Code to Dama) of the *Encyclopaedia Britannica.* In this volume you can learn all about cricket, cotton, costume designing, crocodiles, crown jewels, and Coleridge, but none of these subjects is so interesting as the Courtship of Animals, which recounts the sorrowful lengths to which all males must go to arouse the interest of a lady.

We all know, I think, that Nature gave man whiskers and a mus- 2
tache with the quaint idea in mind that these would prove attractive to the female. We all know that, far from attracting her, whiskers and mustaches only made her nervous and gloomy, so that man had to go in for somersaults, tilting with lances, and performing feats of parlor magic to win her attention; he also had to bring her candy, flowers, and the furs of animals. It is common knowledge that in spite of all these "love displays" the male is constantly being turned down, insulted, or thrown out of the house. It is rather comforting, then, to discover that the peacock, for all his gorgeous plumage, does not have a particularly easy time in courtship; none of the males in the world do. The first

peahen, it turned out, was only faintly stirred by her suitor's beautiful train. She would often go quietly to sleep while he was whisking it around. The *Britannica* tells us that the peacock actually had to learn a certain little trick to wake her up and revive her interest: he had to learn to vibrate his quills so as to make a rustling sound. In ancient times man himself, observing the ways of the peacock, probably tried vibrating his whiskers to make a rustling sound; if so, it didn't get him anywhere. He had to go in for something else; so, among other things, he went in for gifts. It is not unlikely that he got this idea from certain flies and birds who were making no headway at all with rustling sounds.

One of the flies of the family Empidae, who had tried everything, 3 finally hit on something pretty special. He contrived to make a glistening transparent balloon which was even larger than himself. Into this he would put sweetmeats and tidbits and he would carry the whole elaborate envelope through the air to the lady of his choice. This amused her for a time, but she finally got bored with it. She demanded silly little colorful presents, something that you couldn't eat but that would look nice around the house. So the male Empis had to go around gathering flower petals and pieces of bright paper to put into his balloon. On a courtship flight a male Empis cuts quite a figure now, but he can hardly be said to be happy. He never knows how soon the female will demand heavier presents, such as Roman coins and gold collar buttons. It seems probable that one day the courtship of the Empidae will fall down, as man's occasionally does, of its own weight.

The bowerbird is another creature that spends so much time court- 4 ing the female that he never gets any work done. If all the male bowerbirds became nervous wrecks within the next ten or fifteen years, it would not surprise me. The female bowerbird insists that a playground be built for her with a specially constructed bower at the entrance. This bower is much more elaborate than an ordinary nest and is harder to build; it costs a lot more, too. The female will not come to the playground until the male has filled it up with a great many gifts: silvery leaves, red leaves, rose petals, shells, beads, berries, bones, dice, buttons, cigar bands, Christmas seals, and the Lord knows what else. When the female finally condescends to visit the playground, she is in a coy and silly mood and has to be chased in and out of the bower and up and down the playground before she will quit giggling and stand still long enough even to shake hands. The male bird is, of course, pretty well done in before the chase starts, because he has worn himself out hunting for eyeglass lenses and begonia blossoms. I imagine that many a bowerbird, after chasing a female for two or three hours, says the hell with it and goes home to bed. Next day, of course, he telephones someone else and the same trying ritual is gone through with again. A male bowerbird is as exhausted as a night-club habitué before he is out of his twenties.

The male fiddler crab has a somewhat easier time, but it can hardly 5 be said that he is sitting pretty. He has one enormously large and powerful claw, usually brilliantly colored, and you might suppose that all he had to do was reach out and grab some passing cutie. The very earliest fiddler crabs may have tried this, but, if so, they got slapped for their pains. A female fiddler crab will not tolerate any caveman stuff; she never has and she doesn't intend to start now. To attract a female, a fiddler crab has to stand on tiptoe and brandish his claw in the air. If any female in the neighborhood is interested—and you'd be surprised how many are not—she comes over and engages him in light badinage, for which he is not in the mood. As many as a hundred females may pass the time of day with him and go on about their business. By nightfall of an average courting day, a fiddler crab who has been standing on tiptoe for eight or ten hours waving a heavy claw in the air is in pretty sad shape. As in the case of the male of all species, however, he gets out of bed next morning, dashes some water on his face, and tries again.

The next time you encounter a male web-spinning spider, stop and 6 reflect that he is too busy worrying about his love life to have any desire to bite you. Male web-spinning spiders have a tougher life than any other males in the animal kingdom. This is because the female web-spinning spiders have very poor eyesight. If a male lands on a female's web, she kills him before he has time to lay down his cane and gloves, mistaking him for a fly or a bumblebee who has tumbled into her trap. Before the species figured out what to do about this, millions of males were murdered by ladies they called on. It is the nature of spiders to perform a little dance in front of the female, but before a male spinner could get near enough for the female to see who he was and what he was up to, she would lash out at him with a flat-iron or a pair of garden shears. One night, nobody knows when, a very bright male spinner lay awake worrying about calling on a lady who had been killing suitors right and left. It came to him that this business of dancing as a love display wasn't getting anybody anywhere except the grave. He decided to go in for web-twitching, or strand-vibrating. The next day he tried it on one of the nearsighted girls. Instead of dropping in on her suddenly, he stayed outside the web and began monkeying with one of its strands. He twitched it up and down and in and out with such a lilting rhythm that the female was charmed. The serenade worked beautifully; the female let him live. The *Britannica*'s spider-watchers, however, report that this system is not always successful. Once in a while, even now, a female will fire three bullets into a suitor or run him through with a kitchen knife. She keeps threatening him from the moment he strikes the first low notes on the outside strings, but usually by the time he has got up to the high notes played around the center of the web, he is going to town and she spares his life.

Even the butterfly, as handsome a fellow as he is, can't always win a mate merely by fluttering around and showing off. Many butterflies have to have scent scales on their wings. Hepialus carries a powder puff in a perfumed pouch. He throws perfume at the ladies when they pass. The male tree cricket, Oecanthus, goes Hepialus one better by carrying a tiny bottle of wine with him and giving drinks to such doxies as he has designs on. One of the male snails throws darts to entertain the girls. So it goes, through the long list of animals, from the bristle worm and his rudimentary dance steps to man and his gift of diamonds and sapphires. The goldeneye drake raises a jet of water with his feet as he flies over a lake; Hepialus has his powder puff, Oecanthus his wine bottle, man his etchings. It is a bright and melancholy story, the age-old desire of the male for the female, the age-old desire of the female to be amused and entertained. Of all the creatures on earth, the only males who could be figured as putting any irony into their courtship are the grebes and certain other diving birds. Every now and then a courting grebe slips quietly down to the bottom of a lake and then, with a mighty "Whoosh!" pops out suddenly a few feet from his girl friend, splashing water all over her. She seems to be persuaded that this is a purely loving display, but I like to think that the grebe always has a faint hope of drowning her or scaring her to death.

I will close this investigation into the mournful burdens of the male with *Britannica*'s story about a certain Argus pheasant. It appears that the Argus displays himself in front of a female who stands perfectly still without moving a feather. . . . The male Argus the *Britannica* tells about was confined in a cage with a female of another species, a female who kept moving around, emptying ashtrays and fussing with lampshades all the time the male was showing off his talents. Finally, in disgust, he stalked away and began displaying in front of his water trough. He reminds me of a certain male (*Homo sapiens*) of my acquaintance who one night after dinner asked his wife to put down her detective magazine so that he could read a poem of which he was very fond. She sat quietly enough until he was well into the middle of the thing, intoning with great ardor and intensity. Then suddenly there came a sharp, disconcerting *slap!* It turned out that all during the male's display, the female had been intent on a circling mosquito and had finally trapped it between the palms of her hands. The male in this case did not stalk away and display in front of a water trough; he went over to Tim's and had a flock of drinks and recited the poem to the fellas. I am sure they all told bitter stories of their own about how their displays had been interrupted by females. I am also sure that they all ended up singing "Honey, Honey, Bless Your Heart."

QUESTIONS ON SUBJECT

1. What are some of the "love displays" common to both men and animals?

2. How are females' reactions to male overtures similar among species? Can you think of other traits they have in common?

3. Which species has a "tougher life than any other males in the animal kingdom"? Why is this so? Of the species Thurber names, which seems to have the easiest time courting females? Explain your answer.

QUESTIONS ON STRATEGY

1. What is the thesis of Thurber's essay? Where is it stated? Thurber is, of course, known for his witty writing. Do you think he intends his thesis to be serious? How do you know? (Glossary: *Thesis*)

2. Thurber uses several lengthy examples of animal behavior to show the many ways nature has come up with to make males attractive to females. What figure of speech does Thurber use throughout his essay to remind us that these rules apply to humans as well? Is this device effective? Explain your answer using examples from the text. (Glossary: *Figures of Speech*)

3. Review the eessay, and identify the topic sentences in each paragraph. What do they have in common? How do they work to achieve unity in this essay? (Glossary: *Unity*)

4. Reread the concluding sentence in each of Thurber's paragraphs. What do the sentences have in common? How do they work to illustrate his point?

5. Thurber mixes fact and fiction to achieve humor in his essay. For example, in paragraph 7, Thurber describes how many butterflies have scent scales on their wings but the male tree cricket goes him one better by carrying "a tiny bottle of wine with him." Find other examples of his mixing fact and fiction to achieve humor in the essay. What does this technique add to the essay?

6. What, if anything, is Thurber arguing for, or to what view is he trying to persuade us? What type of argument does he use? (Glossary: *Argumentation*)

QUESTIONS ON LANGUAGE

1. Thurber takes delight at making fun of men's foolishness as they show off for their ladies, but he also commiserates with them. Cite examples from

the text of the words Thurber uses that show he also feels sorry for his hapless comrades.

2. Refer to your desk dictionary to determine the meaning of the following words as they are used in this selection: *nonplussed* (paragraph 1), *lumbers* (1), *quaint* (2), *coy* (4), *badinage* (5), *doxies* (7).

WRITING ASSIGNMENTS

1. Write an essay offering the point of view opposite from that of Thurber's essay. That is, explain the ways females traditionally have been frustrated in their efforts to attract males.

2. Thurber is telling us that the animal kingdom supplies many helpful insights into our own behavior. What other areas of human behavior can you illustrate using examples from the world of insects, mammals, or reptiles? The possibilities cover the same range as human behavior: work habits, parenting habits, couples' behavior, and shopping habits are just a few.

How to Give Orders Like a Man

DEBORAH TANNEN

Deborah Tannen, professor of linguistics at Georgetown University, was born on June 7, 1945, in Brooklyn, New York. Tannen received her BA in English from the State University of New York at Binghamton in 1966 and taught English in Greece until 1968. She then earned an MA in English literature from Wayne State University in 1970. While pursuing her Ph.D. in linguistics at the University of California, Berkeley, she received several prizes for her poetry and short fiction. Her work has appeared in New York, Vogue, *and* The New York Times Magazine, *and she has authored three best-selling linguistics books including her latest release,* Talking from Nine to Five: How Women's and Men's Conversational Styles Affect Who Gets Heard, Who Gets Credit, and What Gets Done at Work.

In this essay, first published in The New York Times Magazine *in August 1994, Tannen looks at the variety of ways that orders are given and received. Interestingly, she concludes that, "Directness is not necessarily logical or effective. Indirectness is not necessarily manipulative or insecure."*

A university president was expecting a visit from a member of the 1 board of trustees. When her secretary buzzed to tell her that the board member had arrived, she left her office and entered the reception area to greet him. Before ushering him into her office, she handed her secretary a sheet of paper and said: "I've just finished drafting this letter. Do you think you could type it right away? I'd like to get it out before lunch. And would you please do me a favor and hold all calls while I'm meeting with Mr. Smith?"

When they sat down behind the closed door of her office, Mr. Smith 2 began by telling her that he thought she had spoken inappropriately to her secretary. "Don't forget," he said. *"You're* the president!"

Putting aside the question of the appropriateness of his admonish- 3 ing the president on her way of speaking, it is revealing—and representative of many Americans' assumptions—that the indirect way in which the university president told her secretary what to do struck him as self-deprecating. He took it as evidence that she didn't think she had the right to make demands of her secretary. He probably thought he was giving her a needed pep talk, bolstering her self-confidence.

I challenge the assumption that talking in an indirect way neces- 4
sarily reveals powerlessness, lack of self-confidence or anything else
about the character of the speaker. Indirectness is a fundamental element in human communication. It is also one of the elements that
varies most from one culture to another, and one that can cause confusion and misunderstanding when speakers have different habits with
regard to using it. I also want to dispel the assumption that American
women tend to be more indirect than American men. Women and men
are both indirect, but in addition to differences associated with their
backgrounds—regional, ethnic and class—they tend to be indirect in
different situations and in different ways.

At work, we need to get others to do things, and we all have 5
different ways of accomplishing this. Any individual's ways will vary
depending on who is being addressed—a boss, a peer or a subordinate.
At one extreme are bald commands. At the other are requests so indirect that they don't sound like requests at all, but are just a statement
of need or a description of a situation. People with direct styles of
asking others to do things perceive indirect requests—if they perceive
them as requests at all—as manipulative. But this is often just a way of
blaming others for our discomfort with their styles.

The indirect style is no more manipulative than making a telephone 6
call, asking "Is Rachel there?" and expecting whoever answers the
phone to put Rachel on. Only a child is likely to answer "Yes" and continue holding the phone—not out of orneriness but because of inexpe-
rience with the conventional meaning of the question. (A mischievous
adult might do it to tease.) Those who feel that indirect orders are
illogical or manipulative do not recognize the conventional nature of
indirect requests.

Issuing orders indirectly can be the prerogative of those in power. 7
Imagine, for example, a master who says "It's cold in here" and expects
a servant to make a move to close a window, while a servant who says
the same thing is not likely to see his employer rise to correct the situation and make him more comfortable. Indeed, a Frenchman raised in
Brittany tells me that his family never gave bald commands to their
servants but always communicated orders in indirect and highly polite
ways. This pattern renders less surprising the finding of David Bellinger
and Jean Berko Gleason that fathers' speech to their young children
had a higher incidence than mothers' of both direct imperatives like
"Turn the bolt with the wrench" *and* indirect orders like "The wheel
is going to fall off."

The use of indirectness can hardly be understood without the cross- 8
cultural perspective. Many Americans find it self-evident that directness

is logical and aligned with power while indirectness is akin to dishonesty and reflects subservience. But for speakers raised in most of the world's cultures, varieties of indirectness are the norm in communication. This is the pattern found by a Japanese sociolinguist, Kunihiko Harada, in his analysis of a conversation he recorded between a Japanese boss and a subordinate.

The markers of superior status were clear. One speaker was a Jap- 9 anese man in his late 40's who managed the local branch of a Japanese private school in the United States. His conversational partner was a Japanese-American woman in her early 20's who worked at the school. By virtue of his job, his age and his native fluency in the language being taught, the man was in the superior position. Yet when he addressed the woman, he frequently used polite language and almost always used indirectness. For example, he had tried and failed to find a photography store that would make a black-and-white print from a color negative for a brochure they were producing. He let her know that he wanted her to take over the task by stating the situation and allowed her to volunteer to do it: (This is a translation of the Japanese conversation.)

> On this matter, that, that, on the leaflet? This photo, I'm think-
> ing of changing it to black-and-white and making it clearer. . . . I
> went to a photo shop and asked them. They said they didn't do black-
> and-white. I asked if they knew any place that did. They said they
> didn't know. They weren't very helpful, but anyway, a place must be
> found, the negative brought to it, the picture developed.

Harada observes, "Given the fact that there are some duties to be 10 performed and that there are two parties present, the subordinate is supposed to assume that those are his or her obligation." It was precisely because of his higher status that the boss was free to choose whether to speak formally or informally, to assert his power or to play it down and build rapport—an option not available to the subordinate, who would have seemed cheeky if she had chosen a style that enhanced friendliness and closeness.

The same pattern was found by a Chinese sociolinguist, Yuling Pan, 11 in a meeting of officials involved in a neighborhood youth program. All spoke in ways that reflected their place in the hierarchy. A subordinate addressing a superior always spoke in a deferential way, but a superior addressing a subordinate could either be authoritarian, demonstrating his power, or friendly, establishing rapport. The ones in power had the option of choosing which style to use. In this spirit, I have been told by people who prefer their bosses to give orders indirectly that those who issue bald commands must be pretty insecure; otherwise why would they have to bolster their egos by throwing their weight around?

I am not inclined to accept that those who give orders directly are 12
really insecure and powerless, any more than I want to accept that judgment of those who give indirect orders. The conclusion to be drawn is
that ways of talking should not be taken as obvious evidence of inner
psychological states like insecurity or lack of confidence. Considering
the many influences on conversational style, individuals have a wide
range of ways of getting things done and expressing their emotional
states. Personality characteristics like insecurity cannot be linked to
ways of speaking in an automatic, self-evident way.

Those who expect orders to be given indirectly are offended when 13
they come unadorned. One woman said that when her boss gives her
instructions, she feels she should click her heels, salute, and say "Yes,
boss!" His directions strike her as so imperious as to border on the
militaristic. Yet I received a letter from a man telling me that indirect
orders were a fundamental part of his military training. He wrote:

> Many years ago, when I was in the Navy, I was training to be a
> radio technician. One class I was in was taught by a chief radioman, a
> regular Navy man who had been to sea, and who was then in his third
> hitch. The students, about 20 of us, were fresh out of boot camp, with
> no sea duty and little knowledge of real Navy life. One day in class the
> chief said it was hot in the room. The students didn't react, except
> perhaps to nod in agreement. The chief repeated himself: "It's hot in
> this room." Again there was no reaction from the students.
>
> Then the chief explained. He wasn't looking for agreement or
> discussion from us. When he said that the room was hot, he expected
> us to do something about it—like opening the window. He tried it
> one more time, and this time all of us left our workbenches and
> headed for the windows. We had learned. And we had many oppor-
> tunities to apply what we had learned.

This letter especially intrigued me because "It's cold in here" is the 14
standard sentence used by linguists to illustrate an indirect way of getting someone to do something—as I used it earlier. In this example, it
is the very obviousness and rigidity of the military hierarchy that makes
the statement of a problem sufficient to trigger corrective action on the
part of subordinates.

A man who had worked at the Pentagon reinforced the view that 15
the burden of interpretation is on subordinates in the military—and he
noticed the difference when he moved to a position in the private
sector. He was frustrated when he'd say to his new secretary, for example, "Do we have a list of invitees?" and be told, "I don't know; we
probably do" rather than "I'll get it for you." Indeed, he explained, at
the Pentagon, such a question would likely be heard as a reproach that
the list was not already on his desk.

The suggestion that indirectness is associated with the military   16
must come as a surprise to many. But everyone is indirect, meaning
more than is put into words and deriving meaning from words that are
never actually said. It's a matter of where, when and how we each tend
to be indirect and look for hidden meanings. But indirectness has a
built-in liability. There is a risk that the other will either miss or choose
to ignore your meaning.

On January 13, 1982, a freezing cold, snowy day in Washington,   17
Air Florida Flight 90 took off from National Airport, but could not get
the lift it needed to keep climbing. It crashed into a bridge linking Washington to the state of Virginia and plunged into the Potomac. Of the 79
people on board, all but 5 perished, many floundering and drowning in
the icy water while horror-stricken bystanders watched helplessly from
the river's edge and millions more watched, aghast, on their television
screens. Experts later concluded that the plane had waited too long
after deicing to take off. Fresh buildup of ice on the wings and engine
brought the plane down. How could the pilot and co-pilot have made
such a blunder? Didn't at least one of them realize it was dangerous to
take off under these conditions?

Charlotte Linde, a linguist at the Institute for Research on Learning   18
in Palo Alto, Calif., has studied the "black box" recordings of cockpit
conversations that preceded crashes as well as tape recordings of conversations that took place among crews during flight simulations in which
problems were presented. Among the black box conversations she
studied was the one between the pilot and co-pilot just before the Air
Florida crash. The pilot, it turned out, had little experience flying in icy
weather. The co-pilot had a bit more, and it became heartbreakingly clear
on analysis that he had tried to warn the pilot, but he did so indirectly.

The co-pilot repeatedly called attention to the bad weather and to   19
ice building up on other planes:

> Co-pilot: Look how the ice is just hanging on his, ah, back, back
> there, see that?
> . . .
> Co-pilot: See all those icicles on the back there and everything?
> Captain: Yeah.

He expressed concern early on about the long waiting time be-   20
tween de-icing:

> Co-pilot: Boy, this is a, this is a losing battle here on trying to
> de-ice those things, it [gives] you a false feeling of security, that's all
> that does.

Shortly after they were given clearance to take off, he again ex- 21
pressed concern:

> Co-pilot: Let's check these tops again since we been setting here
> awhile.
> Captain: I think we get to go here in a minute.

When they were about to take off, the co-pilot called attention to 22
the engine instrument readings, which were not normal:

> Co-pilot: That don't seem right, does it? [three-second pause]
> Ah, that's not right. . . .
> Captain: Yes, it is, there's 80.
> Co-pilot: Naw, I don't think that's right. [seven-second pause]
> Ah, maybe it is.
> Captain: Hundred and twenty.
> Co-pilot: I don't know.

The takeoff proceeded, and 37 seconds later the pilot and co-pilot 23
exchanged their last words.

The co-pilot had repeatedly called the pilot's attention to danger- 24
ous conditions but did not directly suggest they abort the takeoff. In
Linde's judgment, he was expressing his concern indirectly, and the
captain didn't pick up on it—with tragic results.

That the co-pilot was trying to warn the captain indirectly is sup- 25
ported by evidence from another airline accident—a relatively minor
one—investigated by Linde that also involved the unsuccessful use of
indirectness.

On July 9, 1978, Allegheny Airlines Flight 453 was landing at 26
Monroe County Airport in Rochester, when it overran the runway by
728 feet. Everyone survived. This meant that the captain and co-pilot
could be interviewed. It turned out that the plane had been flying too
fast for a safe landing. The captain should have realized this and flown
around a second time, decreasing his speed before trying to land. The
captain said he simply had not been aware that he was going too fast.
But the co-pilot told interviewers that he "tried to warn the captain in
subtle ways, like mentioning the possibility of a tail wind and the slow-
ness of flap extension." His exact words were recorded in the black box.
The crosshatches indicate words deleted by the National Transportation Safety Board and were probably expletives:

> Co-pilot: Yeah, it looks like you got a tail wind here.
> Captain: Yeah.
> [?]: Yeah [it] moves awfully # slow.
> Co-pilot: Yeah the # flaps are slower than a #.

Captain: We'll make it, gonna have to add power.
Co-pilot: I know.

The co-pilot thought the captain would understand that if there 27
was a tail wind, it would result in the plane going too fast, and if the
flaps were slow, they would be inadequate to break the speed sufficiently for a safe landing. He thought the captain would then correct
for the error by not trying to land. But the captain said he didn't interpret the co-pilot's remarks to mean they were going too fast.

Linde believes it is not a coincidence that the people being indirect 28
in these conversations were the co-pilots. In her analyses of flight-crew
conversations she found it was typical for the speech of subordinates to
be more mitigated—polite, tentative or indirect. She also found that
topics broached in a mitigated way were more likely to fail, and that
captains were more likely to ignore hints from their crew members than
the other way around. These findings are evidence that not only can
indirectness and other forms of mitigation be misunderstood, but they
are also easier to ignore.

In the Air Florida case, it is doubtful that the captain did not realize 29
what the co-pilot was suggesting when he said, "Let's check these tops
again since we been setting here awhile" (though it seems safe to assume
he did not realize the gravity of the co-pilot's concern). But the indirectness of the co-pilot's phrasing certainly made it easier for the pilot
to ignore it. In this sense, the captain's response, "I think we get to go
here in a minute," was an indirect way of saying, "I'd rather not." In
view of these patterns, the flight crews of some airlines are now given
training to express their concerns, even to superiors, in more direct ways.

The conclusion that people should learn to express themselves 30
more directly has a ring of truth to it—especially for Americans. But
direct communication is not necessarily always preferable. If more direct expression is better communication, then the most direct-speaking
crews should be the best ones. Linde was surprised to find in her research that crews that used the most mitigated speech were often
judged the best crews. As part of the study of talk among cockpit crews
in flight simulations, the trainers observed and rated the performances
of the simulation crews. The crews they rated top in performance had
a higher rate of mitigation than crews they judged to be poor.

This finding seems at odds with the role played by indirectness in 31
the examples of crashes that we just saw. Linde concluded that since
every utterance functions on two levels—the referential (what it says)
and the relational (what it implies about the speaker's relationships),
crews that attend to the relational level will be better crews. A similar
explanation was suggested by Kunihiko Harada. He believes that the

secret of successful communication lies not in teaching subordinates to be more direct, but in teaching higher-ups to be more sensitive to indirect meaning. In other words, the crashes resulted not only because the co-pilots tried to alert the captains to danger indirectly but also because the captains were not attuned to the co-pilots' hints. What made for successful performance among the best crews might have been the ability—or willingness—of listeners to pick up on hints, just as members of families or longstanding couples come to understand each other's meaning without anyone being particularly explicit.

It is not surprising that a Japanese sociolinguist came up with this 32 explanation; what he described is the Japanese system, by which good communication is believed to take place when meaning is gleaned without being stated directly—or at all.

While Americans believe that "the squeaky wheel gets the grease" 33 (so it's best to speak up), the Japanese say, "The nail that sticks out gets hammered back in" (so it's best to remain silent if you don't want to be hit on the head). Many Japanese scholars writing in English have tried to explain to bewildered Americans the ethics of a culture in which silence is often given greater value than speech, and ideas are believed to be best communicated without being explicitly stated. Key concepts in Japanese give a flavor of the attitudes toward language that they reveal—and set in relief the strategies that Americans encounter at work when talking to other Americans.

Takie Sugiyama Lebra, a Japanese-born anthropologist, explains 34 that one of the most basic values in Japanese culture is *omoiyari*, which she translates as "empathy." Because of *omoiyari*, it should not be necessary to state one's meaning explicitly; people should be able to sense each other's meaning intuitively. Lebra explains that it is typical for a Japanese speaker to let sentences trail off rather than complete them because expressing ideas before knowing how they will be received seems intrusive. "Only an insensitive, uncouth person needs a direct, verbal, complete message," Lebra says.

Sasshi, the anticipation of another's message through insightful 35 guesswork, is considered an indication of maturity.

Considering the value placed on direct communication by Ameri- 36 cans in general, and especially by American business people, it is easy to imagine that many American readers may scoff at such conversational habits. But the success of Japanese businesses makes it impossible to continue to maintain that there is anything inherently inefficient about such conversational conventions. With indirectness, as with all aspects of conversational style, our own habitual style seems to make sense—

seems polite, right and good. The light cast by the habits and assumptions of another culture can help us see our way to the flexibility and respect for other styles that is the only best way of speaking.

QUESTIONS ON SUBJECT

1. How does Tannen define indirect speech? What does she see as the built-in liability of indirect speech? Do you see any comparable liability inherent to direct speech?

2. Tannen doesn't contest a finding that fathers had a higher incidence of direct imperatives and indirect orders than mothers. How does she interpret the meaning of these results?

3. How does Tannen see bosses who give bald commands rather than indirect requests? Does she think that they are insecure? Why or why not?

4. Why doesn't Tannen tell her audience how to deal with an insecure boss?

5. Why is it typical for the Japanese to let their sentences trail off?

QUESTIONS ON STRATEGY

1. What is Tannen's thesis and where does she present it? (Glossary: *Thesis*)

2. Tannen only uses examples where men give orders. In what ways do these examples support her thesis?

3. For what audience has Tannen written this essay? (Glossary: *Audience*) Does this help to explain why she focuses primarily on indirect communication? Why or why not?

4. Tannen gives two harrowing examples of misunderstanding as a result of indirect speech and then reveals that top performing flight teams used indirect speech more often than those teams that performed poorly. How do these seemingly contradictory examples support the author's thesis?

5. Tannen uses several examples from other cultures. What do these examples help to show us about Americans?

6. Explain how Tannen uses comparison and contrast to document the assertion that "indirectness is a fundamental element in human communication. It is also one of the elements that varies most from one culture to another, and one that can cause confusion and misunderstanding when speakers have different habits with regard to using it." (Glossary: *Comparison and Contrast*)

QUESTIONS ON LANGUAGE

1. What irony does Tannen point out in the popular understanding of the word *militaristic*?

2. Refer to your desk dictionary to determine the meanings of the following words as they are used in this selection: *admonishing* (paragraph 3), *self-deprecating* (3), *subservience* (8), *cheeky* (10), *deferential* (11), *imperious* (13), *mitigated* (28), *broached* (28), *gleaned* (32), *relief* (33).

WRITING SUGGESTIONS

1. Write an essay comparing the command styles of people you know or fictional characters. You might consider your parents, teachers, professors, coaches, television characters like Captain Picard and Captain Kirk, or characters in a novel.

2. Tannen concludes that, "The light cast by the habits and assumptions of another culture can help us see our way to the flexibility and respect for other styles that is the only best way of speaking." Write an essay in which you use examples from your own experience, observation, or readings to agree or disagree with her conclusion.

WRITING SUGGESTIONS
FOR ILLUSTRATION

1. Write an essay on one of the following statements, using examples to illustrate your ideas. You should be able to draw your examples primarily from personal experience and firsthand observation. As you plan your essay, consider whether you will want to use a series of short examples or one or more extended examples.

   a. Fads never go out of style.
   b. Television has produced a number of "classic" programs.
   c. Every college campus has its own slang terms.
   d. Making excuses sometimes seems like a national pastime.
   e. A liberal arts education can have many practical applications.
   f. College students are not often given credit for the community volunteer work that they do.
   g. Clothes make the person.
   h. All good teachers have certain traits in common.
   i. Graffiti can tell us a good deal about our life and times.
   j. There are a number of simple strategies one can use to relax.

2. Write an essay on one of the following statements using examples to illustrate your ideas. Draw your examples from as many sources as necessary: your reading, the media, interviews, conversations, lectures, and whatever else may be helpful. As you plan your essay, consider whether you will want to use a series of short examples or one or more extended examples.

   a. Much has been (*or* should still be) done to eliminate barriers for the physically handicapped.
   b. Nature's oddities are numerous.
   c. Throughout history dire predictions have been made about the end of the world.
   d. The past predictions of science fiction are today's realities.
   e. Boxing should be outlawed.
   f. The world has seen no absence of wars since World War II.
   g. The Japanese have developed many innovative management strategies.
   h. A great work of art may come out of an artist's most difficult period.
   i. The misjudgments and mistakes of our presidents can be useful lessons in leadership.
   j. Genius is 10 percent talent and 90 percent hard work.
   k. Drugs have taken an economic toll on American business.
   l. Democracy is enjoying a renewed interest in countries outside of the United States.

4
PROCESS ANALYSIS

WHAT IS PROCESS ANALYSIS?

A process is a series of actions or stages that follow one another in a specific, unchanging order and lead to a particular end. People have invented many processes, like assembling pickup trucks or making bread; others occur naturally, like the decay of uranium or the development of a fetus in its mother's womb. All are processes because, if each step occurs correctly and in the right order, the results will be predictable: a completed pickup will roll off the assembly line, and a fully formed baby will be born. Process analysis involves separating such an event or operation or cycle of development into distinct steps, describing each step precisely, and arranging it in its proper order.

Whenever you explain how plants create oxygen, tell how to make ice cream, or merely give directions to your house, you are using process analysis. Each year thousands of books and magazine articles tell us how to make home repairs, how to lose weight and get physically fit, how to improve our memories, how to play better tennis, how to manage our money; they try to satisfy our curiosity about how television shows are made, how plants grow, how jet planes work, and how monkeys, bees, or whales mate. People simply want to know how things work and how to do things for themselves, so it's not surprising that process analysis is one of the most widespread and popular forms of writing today.

Process analysis resembles narration, because both strategies present a series of events occurring over time. But a narration is the story of how things happened in a particular way during one particular period of time; process analysis relates how things always happen (or always should happen) in essentially the same way time after time.

WHY DO WRITERS USE PROCESS ANALYSIS?

There are essentially two reasons for writing a process analysis. One is to provide a reader with the necessary directions to achieve a desired result; this kind of writing is called, naturally enough, *directional process analysis*. The directions may be as short and simple as the instructions on a frozen-food package ("Heat over a low flame for 45 minutes, stir, and serve") or as long and complex as the operator's manual for a mainframe computer. But all directions have the same purpose: to guide the reader through a series of steps, resulting in a particular goal. William Peterson's "I Bet You Can" and Paul Roberts's "How to Say Nothing in 500 Words," later in this chapter, are examples of directional process analysis.

Informational process analysis, however, deals not with processes that readers want to perform for themselves, but with processes that readers are curious about or would like to understand: how presidents are elected, how soil is eroded, how an elevator works, how the brain functions. Virginia Woolf's "The Death of the Moth" and Alexander Petrunkevitch's "The Spider and the Wasp," later in this chapter, analyze natural processes that fascinate readers because they are so unlike anything they will experience on their own.

LOOKING AT PROCESS ANALYSIS

First, decide whether the process analysis is directional or informational—whether it describes something you can do or something you can only observe. Then, as you read, try to "see" the process with your mind's eye. If it is directional, imagine yourself following the directions; if it is informative, try to visualize the process as the author describes it.

Consider, for example, Bernard Gladstone's piece about building a fire in a fireplace, taken from *The New York Times Complete Manual of Home Repair:*

Though "experts" differ as to the best technique to follow when building a fire, one generally accepted method consists of first laying a generous amount of crumpled newspaper on the hearth between the andirons. Kindling wood is then spread generously over this layer of newspaper and one of the thickest logs is placed across the back of the andirons. This should be as close to the back of the fireplace as possible, but not quite touching it. A second log is then placed an inch or so in front of this, and a few additional sticks of kindling are laid across these two. A third log is then placed on top to form a sort of pyramid with air space between all logs so that flames can lick freely up between them.

A mistake frequently made is in building the fire too far forward so that the rear wall of the fireplace does not get properly heated. A heated back wall helps increase the draft and tends to suck smoke and flames rearward with less chance of sparks or smoke spurting out into the room.

Another common mistake often made by the inexperienced fire-tender is to try to build a fire with only one or two logs, instead of using at least three. A single log is difficult to ignite properly, and even two logs do not provide an efficient bed with adequate fuel-burning capacity.

Use of too many logs, on the other hand, is also a common fault and can prove hazardous. Building too big a fire can create more smoke and draft than the chimney can safely handle, increasing the possibility of sparks or smoke being thrown out into the room. For best results, the homeowner should start with three medium-size logs as described above, then add additional logs as needed if the fire is to be kept burning.

In the very first sentence, Gladstone indicates what process he is going to describe: a generally accepted method for building a fire. Even a reader who never wants to build a fire—who doesn't have a fireplace—can quickly see that this is a "how-to" discussion, a directional process analysis. Gladstone takes his readers through six steps which, if followed to the letter, will result in a wood-and-paper structure that will light at the touch of a match and stay lit. Each step is described in a sentence or less, but Gladstone provides enough specific detail so that his directions will be clear, easy to understand, and easy to follow. The process analysis portion of the selection is over in a paragraph.

Even so, Gladstone goes on, describing three mistakes that people often make when building a fire. Note that anyone who follows Gladstone's six steps exactly could not possibly make any of these mistakes; but the writer recognizes that many of us are careless about following directions. Having told us what to do, he reinforces his instructions by telling us what *not* to do, as well.

Here's another process analysis, in which Alan Devoe explains what happens to an animal when it goes into hibernation. The selection is from *Lives Around Us:*

> The woodchuck's hibernation usually starts about the middle of September. For weeks he has been foraging with increased appetite among the clover blossoms and has grown heavy and slow-moving. Now, with the coming of mid-September, apples and corn and yarrow tops have become less plentiful, and the nights are cool. The woodchuck moves with slower gait, and emerges less and less frequently for feeding trips. Layers of fat have accumulated around his chest and shoulders, and there is thick fat in the axils of his legs. He has extended his summer burrow to a length of nearly thirty feet, and has fashioned a deep nest-chamber at the end of it, far below the level of the frost. He has carried in, usually, a little hay. He is ready for the Long Sleep.
>
> When the temperature of the September days falls below 50 degrees or so, the woodchuck becomes too drowsy to come forth from his burrow in the chilly dusk to forage. He remains in the deep nest-chamber, lethargic, hardly moving. Gradually, with the passing of hours or days, his coarse-furred body curls into a semicircle, like a foetus, nose-tip touching tail. The small legs are tucked in, the hand-like clawed forefeet folded. The woodchuck has become a compact ball. Presently the temperature of his body begins to fall.
>
> In normal life the woodchuck's temperature, though fluctuant, averages about 97 degrees. Now, as he lies tight-curled in a ball with the winter sleep stealing over him, this body heat drops ten degrees, twenty degrees, thirty. Finally, by the time the snow is on the ground and the woodchuck's winter dormancy has become complete, his temperature is only 38 or 40. With the falling of the body heat there is a slowing of his heartbeat and his respiration. In normal life he breathes thirty or forty times each minute; when he is excited, as many as a hundred times. Now he breathes slower and slower—ten times a minute, five times a minute, once a minute, and at last only ten or twelve times in an hour. His heartbeat is a twentieth of normal. He has entered fully into the oblivion of hibernation.

The process Devoe describes is natural to woodchucks but not to humans, so obviously he cannot be giving instructions. Rather, he has created an informational process analysis to help us understand what happens during the remarkable process of hibernation. As Devoe's analysis reveals, hibernation is not a series of well-defined steps but a long, slow change from the activity of late summer to the immobility of a deep winter's sleep. The woodchuck does not suddenly stop feeding, nor do his temperature, pulse, and rate of respiration plummet at once. Using transitional expressions and time markers, Devoe shows us that this process lasts for weeks, even months. He connects the progress of hibernation with changes in the weather because the woodchuck's body responds to the dropping temperature as autumn sets in rather than to the passage of specific periods of time.

READING PROCESS ANALYSIS IN
AN ANNOTATED STUDENT ESSAY

Bill Peterson grew up in New Hartford, New York. After completing a business major at the University of Vermont, he entered the music business and now works as a booking agent. He had extensive experience organizing campus concerts for the UVM Student Association. Peterson is also an avid juggler, and he enjoys teaching others the craft. In "I Bet You Can," he shares with us, step by step, the basics of how to juggle. Try it.

I BET YOU CAN
William Peterson

Introduction invites reader to learn how to juggle

Have you ever seen Michael Davis on television? 1 He's a standup comic and a juggler. His antics got me interested in learning how to juggle. Several years ago after watching his act on "Saturday Night Live" I went out to my garage and started to experiment with some tennis balls. At first I felt helpless after tossing and chasing the balls for what seemed like countless hours. However, I actually did start to learn how to juggle. To my surprise I discovered that juggling is much easier than it had at first appeared. If you'd like to learn how to juggle, I recommend that you find some

Transition

tennis balls or lacrosse balls and continue reading.

First step in process: the simple toss

Step one is the simple toss. Stand erect and hold 2 one ball in your right hand. Carefully toss the ball up to approximately an inch above your head and to about half an arm's length in front of you. The ball should arch from your right hand across to your left.

This step should now be repeated, starting with your left hand and tossing to your right. Be sure that the ball reaches the same height and distance from you and is not simply passed from your left hand to your right. Keep tossing the ball back and forth until you have become thoroughly disgusted with this step. If you have practiced this toss enough we can now call this step "the perfect toss." If it is not quite perfect, then you have not become disgusted enough with the step. We'll assume that you've perfected it. Now you're ready to take a little breather and move on.

Recommendation to practice first step until perfected

Labeling of step one as "the perfect toss"

Transition

Second step in process: the toss and return

Step two is the toss and return. Get back on your feet and this time hold a ball in each hand. Take a deep breath and make a perfect toss with the ball in your right hand. As that ball reaches its peak make another perfect toss with the ball in your left hand. The second ball should end up passing under the first one and reaching approximately the same height. When the second ball peaks you should be grabbing— or already have grabbed, depending on timing—the first ball. The second ball should then gently drop into your awaiting right hand. If it was not that easy, then don't worry about the "gently" bit. Most people do not achieve perfection at first. Step two is the key factor in becoming a good juggler and should be practiced at least five times as much as step one.

Emphasis on need to practice step two

Don't deceive yourself after a few successful completions. This maneuver really must be perfected before step three can be approached. As a way to improve dexterity, you should try several tosses and returns starting with your left hand. Let's call step two "the exchange." You're now ready for another well-deserved breather before you proceed.

Helpful suggestion

Labeling of step two as "the exchange"

Third step in process: addition of third ball

Ready or not, here it goes. Step three is merely a continuum of "the exchange" with the addition of a third ball. Don't worry if you are confused—I will explain. Get back up again and now hold two balls in your right hand and one in your left. Make a perfect toss with one of the balls in your right hand and then an exchange with the one in your left hand. The ball coming from your left hand should now be exchanged with the, as of now, unused ball in your right hand. This process should be continued until you find yourself reaching under nearby chairs for bouncing tennis balls. It is true that many persons' backs and legs become sore when learning how to juggle because they've been picking up balls that they've inadvertently tossed around the room. Try practicing over a bed; you won't have to reach down so far. Don't get too upset if things aren't going well, you're probably keeping the same pace as everyone else at this stage. You're certainly doing better than I was because you've had me as a teacher.

Transitional paragraph

Don't worry, this teacher is not going to leave you stranded with hours of repetition of the basic steps. I am sure that you have already run into some basic problems. I will now try to relate some of my beginners' troubles and some of the best solutions you can try for them. 6

Discussion of problem one and solutions

Problem one, you are getting nowhere after the simple toss. This requires a basic improvement of hand to eye coordination. Solution one is to just go back and practice the simple toss again and again. Unfortunately, this becomes quite boring. Solution two is not as tedious and involves quite a bit of skill. Try juggling two balls in one hand. Some people show me this when I ask them if they can juggle— they're not fooling anyone. Real juggling is what you're here to learn. First try circular juggling in one hand. This involves tosses similar to "the perfect toss." They differ in that the balls go half as far towards the opposite hand, are tossed and grabbed by the same hand, and end up making their own circles (as opposed to going up and down in upside down V-s like exchanges). Then try juggling the balls in the same line style—I think this is harder. You have to keep two balls traveling in their own vertical paths (the balls should go as high as they do in a "perfect 7 toss") with only one hand. I think this is harder than the circular style because my hands normally tend to make little circles when I juggle.

Discussion of problem two and solution

Problem two, you can make exchanges but you just can't accomplish step three. The best solution to this is to just continue practicing step two, but now add a twist. As soon as the first ball is caught by the left hand in our step two, throw it back up in another perfect toss for another exchange. Continue this and increase speed up to the point where two balls just don't seem like enough. You should now be ready to add the third ball and accomplish what you couldn't before—real Michael Davis kind of juggling. 8

Discussion of problem three and solutions

Problem three, you have become the "runaway juggler." This means you can successfully achieve numerous exchanges but you're always chasing after balls tossed too far in front of you. The first solution is to stand in front of a wall. This causes you to end up catching a couple of balls bouncing off the wall or else you'll end up consciously keeping your tosses in closer to your body. The second solution is to put your back up against a wall. This will tend to make you toss in closer to yourself because you will be restricted to keeping your back up against the wall. This solution can work but more often than not you'll find yourself watching balls fly across the room in front of you! I've told you about the back on the wall method because some people find it effective. As you can tell, I don't. 9

Step 1	Step 2	Step 3

Conclusion with visual presenta-tion of three-step process

Juggling is a simple three-step process. Following my routine is the easiest way to get from being a spas-tic ball chaser to an accomplished juggler. Patience and coordination are really not required. The only requirements are a few tennis balls, the ability to fol-low some basic instructions, and the time to have some fun.

10

It's always important to be both enthusiastic and knowledgeable about one's subject when writing. When asked why he wrote an essay on juggling, Peterson replied, "Well, I've been juggling for almost ten years, and in that time I've taught many people how to juggle. It's very easy to teach another person, especially one-on-one. All I need is a set of tennis balls. It's just something that comes easily to most people once they are shown how to do it. And my friends tell me that I'm pretty successful at showing others just how to do it. As a result, I thought I'd try to explain the process on paper." Peterson went on to explain how he'd had a chance to rehearse this topic in a speech class he'd taken earlier. "In all honesty, I'd done a speech on juggling before writing this essay. In class, I discovered that the neat three-step process fit perfectly into the process analysis strategy. It's a natural. I started by making a thorough outline of the process. That made writing the rough draft relatively easy."

WRITING A PROCESS ANALYSIS ESSAY

In a process analysis, always aim for precision and clarity. Few things are more frustrating to readers of directions than an unclear or misplaced step that prevents them from achieving the result you have promised. The same sort of error in an informational process analysis will cause misunderstanding and confusion. Whatever your purpose, process analysis requires a systematic, logical approach.

Dividing the Process into Steps

As much as possible, make each step a simple and well-defined action, preferably a single action. To guide yourself in doing so, write up a scratch outline listing the steps. Here, for example, is an outline of Bernard Gladstone's directions for building a fire.

Process analysis of building a fire in a fireplace

Directional

1. put down crumpled newspaper
2. lay kindling
3. place back log near rear wall but not touching
4. place front log an inch forward
5. bridge logs with kindling
6. place third log on top of kindling bridge

Next, check your outline to make sure that the steps are in the right order and that none has been omitted. Then analyze your outline more carefully. Are any steps so complex that they need to be described in some detail—or perhaps divided into more steps? Will you need to explain the purpose of a certain step because the reason for it is not obvious? Especially in an informational process analysis, it may happen that two steps take place at the same time; perhaps they are performed by different people or different parts of the body. Does your outline make this clear? (One solution is to assign both steps the same number but label one of them "A" and the other "B.") When you feel certain that the steps of the process are complete and correct, ask yourself two more questions. Will the reader need any other information to understand the process—definitions of unusual terms, for example, or descriptions of special equipment? Should you anticipate common mistakes or misunderstandings and discuss them, as Gladstone does? If so, be sure to add an appropriate note or two to your scratch outline as a reminder.

Testing Your Process Analysis

After finishing a first draft of your essay, have someone else read it. If you are writing a directional process analysis, ask your reader to follow the instructions and then to tell you whether he or she was able to understand each step and perform it satisfactorily. Was the desired result achieved? Did the fire burn well, the computer program run, the lasagna taste good? If not, examine your process analysis step by step, looking for errors and omissions that would explain the unsatisfactory result (no kindling wood, perhaps, or a loop in the program, or too much garlic).

In fact, William Peterson gave his essay on juggling to some friends to have them test his directions. "I gave it to people who had never tried juggling to see if there were any 'bugs' or unclear sections in my instructions. This helped me a lot as a writer because they told me where certain things were not clear or outright confusing. This enabled me to go back and revise, knowing exactly what the problem was." Peterson's readers had difficulty understanding his directions for the simple toss in his rough draft. Peterson agreed with their criticism; "I just couldn't get detailed enough in my rough draft. I had real trouble with paragraph 2, the explanation of the simple toss. See what I mean:

> Step one is the simple toss. Stand erect and hold one object (we'll call it a ball from now on) in your most adroit hand (we'll say the right). Toss the ball into the air to approximately an inch above your head and to about half an arm's length in front of you. The ball should take an arched path traveling from your right hand to your left. This step should now be repeated using your left hand first and returning it to your right hand. Repeat this until completely proficient. We'll now call this action the "perfect toss." Take a breather and then move on.

"After several drafts, I finally felt satisfied with my directions." To see what changes Peterson made, compare the paragraph above with paragraph 2 in his final copy on pages 165–166.

For an informational process analysis, it may be a bit trickier to make sure that your reader really understands. Test your reader's comprehension by asking a few questions. If there seems to be any confusion, try rereading what you have written with an objective eye. Sometimes an especially intricate or otherwise difficult step can be made clear by rewriting it in everyday language; sometimes a recognizable comparison or analogy will help, especially if you are analyzing a scientific or otherwise unfamiliar process. (For example, American readers might better understand the British game of rugby if it was compared with American football; nonspecialists might grasp the circulation of the blood more easily through an analogy between the cardiovascular system and domestic plumbing. See Chapter 5 for discussions of *comparison and contrast* and *analogy*.) Again, try to pin down the specific cause of any misunderstanding, the step or steps that are confusing your reader. Keep on revising until he or she can demonstrate a clear understanding of what you've tried to say.

Using Transitional Words

Transitional words and phrases such as *then, next, after doing this,* and *during the summer months* can both emphasize and clarify the sequence of steps in your process analysis. The same is true of sequence markers like *first, second, third,* and so on. The Devoe piece uses such words effectively to make it clear which stages in the process of hibernation are simultaneous and which are not; Gladstone includes an occasional *first* or *then* to alert us to shifts from one step to the next. But both writers are careful not to overuse these words, and so should you be. Transitions are a resource of language, but they should not be used routinely.

How to Say Nothing in 500 Words

PAUL ROBERTS

Paul Roberts (1917–1967) was a linguist, a teacher, and a writer. His books on writing, including English Syntax *(1954) and* Patterns of English *(1956), have helped generations of high school and college students to become better writers.*

"How to Say Nothing in 500 Words" is taken from his best-known book, Understanding English *(1958). Although written over thirty years ago, the essay is still relevant for student writers today. Good writing, Roberts tells us, is not simply a matter of filling up a page; rather, the words have to hold the reader's interest and they must say something. In this essay, the author uses lively prose and a step-by-step process to guide the student from the blank page to the finished essay. His bag of writing tricks is good advice to anyone who wants to write well.*

NOTHING ABOUT SOMETHING

It's Friday afternoon, and you have almost survived another week 1 of classes. You are just looking forward dreamily to the week end when the English instructor says: "For Monday you will turn in a five-hundred word composition on college football."

Well, that puts a good big hole in the weekend. You don't have any 2 strong views on college football one way or the other. You get rather excited during the season and go to all the home games and find it rather more fun than not. On the other hand, the class has been reading Robert Hutchins in the anthology and perhaps Shaw's "Eighty-Yard Run," and from the class discussion you have got the idea that the instructor thinks college football is for the birds. You are no fool, you. You can figure out what side to take.

After dinner you get out the portable typewriter that you got for 3 high school graduation. You might as well get it over with and enjoy Saturday and Sunday. Five hundred words is about two double-spaced pages with normal margins. You put in a sheet of paper, think up a title, and you're off:

WHY COLLEGE FOOTBALL SHOULD BE ABOLISHED

College football should be abolished because it's bad for the school and also bad for the players. The players are so busy practicing that they don't have any time for their studies.

173

This, you feel, is a mighty good start. The only trouble is that it's 4
only thirty-two words. You still have four hundred and sixty-eight to
go, and you've pretty well exhausted the subject. It comes to you that
you do your best thinking in the morning, so you put away the typewriter and go to the movies. But the next morning you have to do your
washing and some math problems, and in the afternoon you go to the
game. The English instructor turns up too, and you wonder if you've
taken the right side after all. Saturday night you have a date, and Sunday
morning you have to go to church. (You shouldn't let English assignments interfere with your religion.) What with one thing and another,
it's ten o'clock Sunday night before you get out the typewriter again.
You make a pot of coffee and start to fill out your views on college
football. Put a little meat on the bones.

WHY COLLEGE FOOTBALL SHOULD BE ABOLISHED

In my opinion, it seems to me that college football should be
abolished. The reason why I think this to be true is because I feel that
football is bad for the colleges in nearly every respect. As Robert
Hutchins says in his article in our anthology in which he discusses
college football, it would be better if the colleges had race horses and
had races with one another, because then the horses would not have
to attend classes. I firmly agree with Mr. Hutchins on this point, and
I am sure that many other students would agree too.

One reason why it seems to me that college football is bad is that
it has become too commercial. In the olden times when people played
football just for the fun of it, maybe college football was all right, but
they do not play football just for the fun of it now as they used to in
the old days. Nowadays college football is what you might call a big
business. Maybe this is not true at all schools, and I don't think it is
especially true here at State, but certainly this is the case at most colleges and universities in America nowadays, as Mr. Hutchins points
out in his very interesting article. Actually the coaches and alumni go
around to the high schools and offer the high school stars large salaries to come to their colleges and play football for them. There was
one case where a high school star was offered a convertible if he would
play football for a certain college.

Another reason for abolishing college football is that it is bad for
the players. They do not have time to get a college education, because
they are so busy playing football. A football player has to practice
every afternoon from three to six, and then he is so tired that he can't
concentrate on his studies. He just feels like dropping off to sleep after
dinner, and then the next day he goes to his classes without having
studied and maybe he fails the test.

(Good ripe stuff so far, but you're still a hundred and fifty-one words
from home. One more push.)

Also I think college football is bad for the colleges and the universities because not very many students get to participate in it. Out of a college of ten thousand students only seventy-five or a hundred play football, if that many. Football is what you might call a spectator sport. That means that most people go to watch it but do not play it themselves.

(Four hundred and fifteen. Well, you still have the conclusion, and when you retype it, you can make the margins a little wider.)

These are the reasons why I agree with Mr. Hutchins that college football should be abolished in American colleges and universities.

On Monday you turn it in, moderately hopeful, and on Friday it 5 comes back marked "weak in content" and sporting a big "D."

This essay is exaggerated a little, not much. The English instructor 6 will recognize it as reasonably typical of what an assignment on college football will bring in. He knows that nearly half of the class will contrive in five hundred words to say that college football is too commercial and bad for the players. Most of the other half will inform him that college football builds character and prepares one for life and brings prestige to the school. As he reads paper after paper all saying the same thing in almost the same words, all bloodless, five hundred words dripping out of nothing, he wonders how he allowed himself to get trapped into teaching English when he might have had a happy and interesting life as an electrician or a confidence man.

Well, you may ask, what can you do about it? The subject is one on 7 which you have few convictions and little information. Can you be expected to make a dull subject interesting? As a matter of fact, this is precisely what you are expected to do. This is the writer's essential task. All subjects, except sex, are dull until somebody makes them interesting. The writer's job is to find the argument, the approach, the angle, the wording that will take the reader with him. This is seldom easy, and it is particularly hard in subjects that have been much discussed: College Football, Fraternities, Popular Music, Is Chivalry Dead?, and the like. You will feel that there is nothing you can do with such subjects except repeat the old bromides. But there are some things you can do which will make your papers, if not throbbingly alive, at least less insufferably tedious than they might otherwise be.

AVOID THE OBVIOUS CONTENT

Say the assignment is college football. Say that you've decided to be 8 against it. Begin by putting down the arguments that come to your mind: it is too commercial, it takes the students' minds off their studies, it is hard on the players, it makes the university a kind of circus instead of an intellectual center, for most schools it is financially ruinous. Can you think of any more arguments just off hand? All right. Now when you write your paper, *make sure that you don't use any of the material on this list.* If these are the points that leap to your mind, they will leap to everyone else's too, and whether you get a "C" or a "D" may depend on whether the instructor reads your paper early when he is fresh and tolerant or late, when the sentence "In my opinion, college football has become too commercial," inexorably repeated, has brought him to the brink of lunacy.

Be against college football for some reason or reasons of your own. 9 If they are keen and perceptive ones, that's splendid. But even if they are trivial or foolish or indefensible, you are still ahead so long as they are not everybody else's reasons too. Be against it because the colleges don't spend enough money on it to make it worthwhile, because it is bad for the characters of the spectators, because the players are forced to attend classes, because the football stars hog all the beautiful women, because it competes with baseball and is therefore un-American and possibly Communist inspired. There are lots of more or less unused reasons for being against college football.

Sometimes it is a good idea to sum up and dispose of the trite and 10 conventional points before going on to your own. This has the advantage of indicating to the reader that you are going to be neither trite nor conventional. Something like this:

> We are often told that college football should be abolished because it has become too commercial or because it is bad for the players. These arguments are no doubt very cogent, but they don't really go to the heart of the matter.

Then you go to the heart of the matter.

TAKE THE LESS USUAL SIDE

One rather simple way of getting interest into your paper is to take 11 the side of the argument that most of the citizens will want to avoid. If the assignment is an essay on dogs, you can, if you choose, explain that dogs are faithful and lovable companions, intelligent, useful as guardians of the house and protectors of children, indispensable in police work—in short, when all is said and done, man's best friends. Or you can suggest that those big brown eyes conceal, more often than not, a vacuity of mind and an inconstancy of purpose; that the dogs you have known most intimately have been mangy, ill-tempered brutes, incapable of instruction; and that only your nobility of mind and fear of arrest prevent you from kicking the flea-ridden animals when you pass them on the street.

Naturally, personal convictions will sometimes dictate your approach. If the assigned subject is "Is Methodism Rewarding to the Individual?" and you are a pious Methodist, you have really no choice. But few assigned subjects, if any, will fall in this category. Most of them will lie in broad areas of discussion with much to be said on both sides. They are intellectual exercises and it is legitimate to argue now one way and now another, as debaters do in similar circumstances. Always take the side that looks to you hardest, least defensible. It will almost always turn out to be easier to write interestingly on that side. 12

This general advice applies where you have a choice of subjects. If you are to choose among "The Value of Fraternities" and "My Favorite High School Teacher" and "What I Think about Beetles," by all means plump for the beetles. By the time the instructor gets to your paper, he will be up to his ears in tedious tales about the French teacher at Bloombury High and assertions about how fraternities build character and prepare one for life. Your views on beetles, whatever they are, are bound to be a refreshing change. 13

Don't worry too much about figuring out what the instructor thinks about the subject so that you can cuddle up with him. Chances are his views are no stronger than yours. If he does have convictions and you oppose them, his problem is to keep from grading you higher than you deserve in order to show he is not biased. This doesn't mean that you should always cantankerously dissent from what the instructor says; that gets tiresome too. And if the subject assigned is "My Pet Peeve," do not begin, "My pet peeve is the English instructor who assigns papers on 'my pet peeve.'" This was still funny during the War of 1812, but it has sort of lost its edge since then. It is in general good manners to avoid personalities. 14

SLIP OUT OF ABSTRACTION

If you will study the essay on college football . . . you will perceive that one reason for its appalling dullness is that it never gets down to particulars. It is just a series of not very glittering generalities: "football is bad for the colleges," "it has become too commercial," "football is a big business," "it is bad for the players," and so on. Such round 15 phrases thudding against the reader's brain are unlikely to convince him, though they may well render him unconscious.

If you want the reader to believe that college football is bad for the players, you have to do more than say so. You have to display the evil. Take your roommate, Alfred Simkins, the second-string center. Picture poor old Alfy coming home from football practice every evening, bruised and aching, agonizingly tired, scarcely able to shovel the mashed potatoes into his mouth. Let us see him staggering up to the room, getting out his econ textbook, peering desperately at it with his good eye, falling asleep and failing the test in the morning. Let us share his unbearable tension as Saturday draws near. Will he fail, be demoted, lose his monthly allowance, be forced to return to the coal mines? And if he succeeds, what will be his reward? Perhaps a slight ripple of applause when the third-string center replaces him, a moment of elation in the locker room if the team wins, of despair if it loses. What will he look back on when he graduates from college? Toil and torn ligaments. And what will be his future? He is not good enough for pro football, and he is too obscure and weak in econ to succeed in stocks and bonds. College football is tearing the heart from Alfy Simkins and, when it finishes with him, will callously toss aside the shattered hulk. 16

This is no doubt a weak enough argument for the abolition of college football, but it is a sight better than saying, in three or four variations, that college football (in your opinion) is bad for the players. 17

Look at the work of any professional writer and notice how constantly he is moving from the generality, the abstract statement, to the concrete example, the facts and figures, the illustration. If he is writing on juvenile delinquency, he does not just tell you that juveniles are (it seems to him) delinquent and that (in his opinion) something should be done about it. He shows you juveniles being delinquent, tearing up movie theatres in Buffalo, stabbing high school principals in Dallas, smoking marijuana in Palo Alto. And more than likely he is moving toward some specific remedy, not just a general wringing of the hands. 18

It is no doubt possible to be *too* concrete, too illustrative or anecdotal, but few inexperienced writers err this way. For most the soundest advice is to be seeking always for the picture, to be always turning general remarks into seeable examples. Don't say, "Sororities teach girls the social graces." Say, "Sorority life teaches a girl how to carry on a conversation while pouring tea, without sloshing the tea into the saucer." Don't say, "I like certain kinds of popular music very much." Say, "Whenever I hear Gerber Spinklittle play 'Mississippi Man' on the trombone, my socks creep up my ankles." 19

GET RID OF OBVIOUS PADDING

The student toiling away at his weekly English theme is too often 20
tormented by a figure: five hundred words. How, he asks himself, is he
to achieve this staggering total? Obviously by never using one word
when he can somehow work in ten.

He is therefore seldom content with a plain statement like "Fast 21
driving is dangerous." This has only four words in it. He takes thought,
and the sentence becomes:

> In my opinion, fast driving is dangerous.

Better, but he can do better still:

> In my opinion, fast driving would seem to be rather dangerous.

If he is really adept, it may come out:

> In my humble opinion, though I do not claim to be an expert on
> this complicated subject, fast driving, in most circumstances, would
> seem to be rather dangerous in many respects, or at least so it would
> seem to me.

Thus four words have been turned into forty, and not an iota of content
has been added.

Now this is a way to go about reaching five hundred words, and if 22
you are content with a "D" grade, it is as good a way as any. But if you
aim higher, you must work differently. Instead of stuffing your sentences with straw, you must try steadily to get rid of the padding, to
make your sentences lean and tough. If you are really working at it,
your first draft will greatly exceed the required total, and then you will
work it down, thus:

> It is thought in some quarters that fraternities do not contribute
> as much as might be expected to campus life.

> Some people think that fraternities contribute little to campus
> life.

> The average doctor who practices in small towns or in the
> country must toil night and day to heal the sick.

> Most country doctors work long hours.

> When I was a little girl, I suffered from shyness and embarrass-
> ment in the presence of others.

> I was a shy little girl.

It is absolutely necessary for the person employed as a marine fireman to give the matter of steam pressure his undivided attention at all times.

The fireman has to keep his eye on the steam gauge.

You may ask how you can arrive at five hundred words at this rate. 23 Simply. You dig up more real content. Instead of taking a couple of obvious points off the surface of the topic and then circling warily around them for six paragraphs, you work in and explore, figure out the details. You illustrate. You say that fast driving is dangerous, and then you prove it. How long does it take to stop a car at forty and at eighty? How far can you see at night? What happens when a tire blows? What happens in a head-on collision at fifty miles an hour? Pretty soon your paper will be full of broken glass and blood and headless torsos, and reaching five hundred words will not really be a problem.

CALL A FOOL A FOOL

Some of the padding in freshman themes is to be blamed not on 24 anxiety about the word minimum but on excessive timidity. The student writes, "In my opinion, the principal of my high school acted in ways that I believe every unbiased person would have to call foolish." This isn't exactly what he means. What he means is, "My high school principal was a fool." If he was a fool, call him a fool. Hedging the thing about with "in-my-opinion's" and "it-seems-to-me's" and "as-I-see-it's" and "at-least-from-my-point-of-view's" gains you nothing. Delete these phrases whenever they creep into your paper.

The student's tendency to hedge stems from a modesty that in 25 other circumstances would be commendable. He is, he realizes, young and inexperienced, and he half suspects that he is dopey and fuzzy-minded beyond the average. Probably only too true. But it doesn't help to announce your incompetence six times in every paragraph. Decide what you want to say and say it as vigorously as possible, without apology and in plain words.

Linguistic diffidence can take various forms. One is what we call 26 *euphemism*. This is the tendency to call a spade "a certain garden implement" or women's underwear "unmentionables." It is stronger in some eras than others and in some people than others but it always operates more or less in subjects that are touchy or taboo: death, sex, madness, and so on. Thus we shrink from saying "He died last night" but say instead "passed away," "left us," "joined his Maker," "went to his reward." Or we try to take off the tension with a lighter cliché: "kicked the bucket," "cashed in his chips," "handed in his dinner pail." We have found all sorts of ways to avoid saying *mad:* "mentally ill," "touched," "not quite right upstairs," "feeble-minded," "innocent," "simple," "off his trolley," "not in his right mind." Even such a now plain word as *insane* began as a euphemism with the meaning "not healthy."

Modern science, particularly psychology, contributes many poly- 27 syllables in which we can wrap our thoughts and blunt their force. To many writers there is no such thing as a bad schoolboy. Schoolboys are maladjusted or unoriented or misunderstood or in need of guidance or lacking in continued success toward satisfactory integration of the personality as a social unit, but they are never bad. Psychology no doubt makes us better men or women, more sympathetic and tolerant, but it doesn't make writing any easier. Had Shakespeare been confronted with psychology, "To be or not to be" might have come out, "To continue as a social unit or not to do so. That is the personality problem. Whether 'tis a better sign of integration at the conscious level to display a psychic tolerance toward the maladjustments and repressions induced by one's lack of orientation in one's environment or—" But Hamlet would never have finished the soliloquy.

Writing in the modern world, you cannot altogether avoid modern 28 jargon. Nor, in an effort to get away from euphemism, should you salt your paper with four-letter words. But you can do much if you will mount guard against those roundabout phrases, those echoing polysyllables that tend to slip into your writing to rob it of its crispness and force.

BEWARE OF THE PAT EXPRESSION

Other things being equal, avoid phrases like "other things being 29 equal." Those sentences that come to you whole, or in two or three doughy lumps, are sure to be bad sentences. They are no creation of yours but pieces of common thought floating in the community soup.

Pat expressions are hard, often impossible, to avoid, because they 30 come too easily to be noticed and seem too necessary to be dispensed with. No writer avoids them altogether, but good writers avoid them more often than poor writers.

By "pat expressions" we mean such tags as "to all practical intents 31 and purposes," "the pure and simple truth," "from where I sit," "the time of his life," "to the ends of the earth," "in the twinkling of an eye," "as sure as you're born," "over my dead body," "under cover of darkness," "took the easy way out," "when all is said and done," "told him time and time again," "parted the best of friends," "stand up and be counted," "gave him the best years of her life," "worked her fingers to the bone." Like other clichés, these expressions were once forceful. Now we should use them only when we can't possibly think of anything else.

Some pat expressions stand like a wall between the writer and 32 thought. Such a one is "the American way of life." Many student writers feel that when they have said that something accords with the American way of life or does not they have exhausted the subject. Actually, they have stopped at the highest level of abstraction. The American way of life is the complicated set of bonds between a hundred and eighty million ways. All of us know this when we think about it, but the tag phrase too often keeps us from thinking about it.

So with many another phrase dear to the politician: "this great land 33 of ours," "the man in the street," "our national heritage." These may prove our patriotism or give a clue to our political beliefs, but otherwise they add nothing to the paper except words.

COLORFUL WORDS

The writer builds with words, and no builder uses a raw material 34 more slippery and elusive and treacherous. A writer's work is a constant struggle to get the right word in the right place, to find that particular word that will convey his meaning exactly, that will persuade the reader or soothe him or startle or amuse him. He never succeeds altogether— sometimes he feels that he scarcely succeeds at all—but such successes as he has are what make the thing worth doing.

There is no book of rules for this game. One progresses through 35 everlasting experiment on the basis of ever-widening experience. There are few useful generalizations that one can make about words as words, but there are perhaps a few.

Some words are what we call "colorful." By this we mean that they 36 are calculated to produce a picture or induce an emotion. They are dressy instead of plain, specific instead of general, loud instead of soft. Thus, in place of "Her heart beat," we may write "Her heart *pounded, throbbed, fluttered, danced.*" Instead of "He sat in his chair," we may say, "He *lounged, sprawled, coiled.*" Instead of "It was hot," we may say, "It was *blistering, sultry, muggy, suffocating, steamy, wilting.*"

However, it should not be supposed that the fancy word is always 37 better. Often it is as well to write "Her heart beat" or "It was hot" if that is all it did or all it was. Ages differ in how they like their prose. The nineteenth century liked it rich and smoky. The twentieth has usually preferred it lean and cool. The twentieth-century writer, like all writers, is forever seeking the exact word, but he is wary of sounding feverish. He tends to pitch it low, to understate it, to throw it away. He knows that if he gets too colorful, the audience is likely to giggle.

See how this strikes you: "As the rich, golden glow of the sunset 38 died away along the eternal western hills, Angela's limpid blue eyes looked softly and trustingly into Montague's flashing brown ones, and her heart pounded like a drum in time with the joyous song surging in her soul." Some people like that sort of thing, but most modern readers would say, "Good grief," and turn on the television.

COLORED WORDS

Some words we would call not so much colorful as colored—that 39 is, loaded with associations, good or bad. All words—except perhaps structure words—have associations of some sort. We have said that the meaning of a word is the sum of the contexts in which it occurs. When we hear a word, we hear with it an echo of all the situations in which we have heard it before.

In some words, these echoes are obvious and discussable. The word 40 *mother*, for example, has, for most people, agreeable associations. When you hear *mother* you probably think of home, safety, love, food, and various other pleasant things. If one writes, "She was like a mother to me," he gets an effect which he would not get in "She was like an aunt to me." The advertiser makes use of the associations of *mother* by working it in when he talks about his product. The politician works it in when he talks about himself.

So also with such words as *home, liberty, fireside, contentment,* 41 *patriot, tenderness, sacrifice, childlike, manly, bluff, limpid*. All of these words are loaded with favorable associations that would be rather hard to indicate in a straightforward definition. There is more than a literal difference between "They sat around the fireside" and "They sat around the stove." They might have been equally warm and happy around the stove, but *fireside* suggests leisure, grace, quiet tradition, congenial company, and *stove* does not.

Conversely, some words have bad associations. *Mother* suggests 42 pleasant things, but *mother-in-law* does not. Many mothers-in-law are heroically lovable and some mothers drink gin all day and beat their children insensible, but these facts of life are beside the point. The thing is that *mother* sounds good and *mother-in-law* does not.

Or consider the word *intellectual*. This would seem to be a com- 43
plimentary term, but in point of fact it is not, for it has picked up associations of impracticality and ineffectuality and general dopiness. So also with such words as *liberal, reactionary, Communist, Socialist, capitalist, radical, schoolteacher, truck driver, undertaker, operator, salesman, huckster, speculator.* These convey meanings on the literal level, but beyond that—sometimes, in some places—they convey contempt on the part of the speaker.

The question of whether to use loaded words or not depends on 44
what is being written. The scientist, the scholar, try to avoid them; for the poet, the advertising writer, the public speaker, they are standard equipment. But every writer should take care that they do not substitute for thought. If you write, "Anyone who thinks that is nothing but a Socialist (or Communist or capitalist)" you have said nothing except that you don't like people who think that, and such remarks are effective only with the most naïve readers. It is always a bad mistake to think your readers more naïve than they really are.

COLORLESS WORDS

But probably most student writers come to grief not with words 45
that are colorful or those that are colored but with those that have no color at all. A pet example is *nice*, a word we would find it hard to dispense with in casual conversation but which is no longer capable of adding much to a description. Colorless words are those of such general meaning that in a particular sentence they mean nothing. Slang adjectives, like *cool* ("That's real cool") tend to explode all over the language. They are applied to everything, lose their original force, and quickly die.

Beware also of nouns of very general meaning, like *circumstances,* 46
cases, instances, aspects, factors, relationships, attitudes, eventualities, etc. In most circumstances you will find that those cases of writing which contain too many instances of words like these will in this and other aspects have factors leading to unsatisfactory relationships with the reader resulting in unfavorable attitudes on his part and perhaps other eventualities, like a grade of "D." Notice also what "etc." means. It means "I'd like to make this list longer, but I can't think of any more examples."

QUESTIONS ON SUBJECT

1. According to Roberts, what is the job of the writer? Why, in particular, is it difficult for college students to do this job well? Discuss how your college experience leads you to agree or disagree with Roberts.

2. The author offers several "tricks" of good writing in his essay. What are they? Do you find some of them more useful than others? Explain.

3. If, according to Roberts, a good writer never uses unnecessary words, what then are the legitimate ways a student can reach the goal of a 500-word essay?

4. How has modern psychology made it more difficult to write well?

QUESTIONS ON STRATEGY

1. Make a scratch outline of Roberts's essay. What are the similarities between his organization of material and the process analyses he outlines for students? Explain. (Glossary: *Organization*)

2. Roberts's writing style is clearly well-suited to his student audience. How would you describe his writing style? What are some of the ways he uses humor, diction, and illustration to make the process analyses easy to follow? (Glossary: *Diction; Illustration*)

3. What kind of information does the title of Roberts's essay lead you to expect? Does the author deliver what he promises in the title? Why do you think he chose this title?

4. What is Roberts' tone in this essay? (Glossary: *Tone*) Is it an appropriate one for his purpose? Explain.

5. Explain how Roberts' use of examples helps him to further the points he wishes to make. (Glossary: *Illustration*)

QUESTIONS ON LANGUAGE

1. Roberts wrote this essay nearly forty years ago. Is there anything in his diction that gives this away, or does his writing sound contemporary? Choose examples from the text to support your answer. (Glossary: *Diction*)

2. Refer to your desk dictionary to determine the meanings of the following words as they are used in this selection: *contrive* (paragraph 6), *bromides* (7), *tedious* (7), *inexorably* (8), *trite* (10), *cogent* (10), *vacuity* (11), *cantankerously* (14), *iota* (21), *diffidence* (26), *soliloquy* (27).

WRITING ASSIGNMENTS

1. Pick up a copy of your college newspaper and find an article that uses the dull, limp writing Roberts talks about. Using an editor's eye (almost every-

one can edit other people's writing), rewrite the article eliminating unnecessary words, substituting colorful verbs and adjectives for dull ones, and perhaps even shifting the focus of the article to make it more interesting. Then consider how you can edit your own writing in this way.

2. In paragraph 16, Roberts explains how a brief but good essay on college football might be written. He obeys the first rule of good writing—show don't tell. Thus, instead of a dry lump of words, his essay uses humor, exaggeration, and particulars to breathe life into the football player. Review Roberts's tricks for good writing, choose one of the dull topics he suggests or one of your own, and, following the steps he lays out in his essay, write a 500-word process analysis.

Why Leaves Turn Color in the Fall

DIANE ACKERMAN

Born in Waukegan, Illinois, in 1948, Diane Ackerman received degrees from Pennsylvania State University and Cornell University. She has written several books of poetry, a prose memoir, and a play, and has directed the Writers' Program at Washington University in St. Louis. Ackerman's most recent book is A Natural History of the Senses *(1990), from which the following selection has been taken. She is currently a staff writer at the* New Yorker *and lives in upstate New York.*

Every October, nature surprises us all with a spectacular color show that leaves us wondering "Where do the colors come from?" We know when to expect the beautiful leaves, but we don't know how the color change happens. In this selection, Ackerman lets us in on one of nature's secrets. Notice the way in which she shares her enthusiasm for the natural world as she explains the process by which autumn leaves assume their brilliant color.

The stealth of autumn catches one unaware. Was that a goldfinch 1 perching in the early September woods, or just the first turning leaf? A red-winged blackbird or a sugar maple closing up shop for the winter? Keen-eyed as leopards, we stand still and squint hard, looking for signs of movement. Early-morning frost sits heavily on the grass, and turns barbed wire into a string of stars. On a distant hill, a small square of yellow appears to be a lighted stage. At last the truth dawns on us: Fall is staggering in, right on schedule, with its baggage of chilly nights, macabre holidays, and spectacular, heart-stoppingly beautiful leaves. Soon the leaves will start cringing on the trees, and roll up in clenched fists before they actually fall off. Dry seedpods will rattle like tiny gourds. But first there will be weeks of gushing color so bright, so pastel, so confettilike, that people will travel up and down the East Coast just to stare at it—a whole season of leaves.

Where do the colors come from? Sunlight rules most living things 2 with its golden edicts. When the days begin to shorten, soon after the summer solstice on June 21, a tree reconsiders its leaves. All summer it feeds them so they can process sunlight, but in the dog days of summer the tree begins pulling nutrients back into its trunk and roots, pares down, and gradually chokes off its leaves. A corky layer of cells forms at

187

the leaves' slender petioles, then scars over. Undernourished, the leaves stop producing the pigment chlorophyll, and photosynthesis ceases. Animals can migrate, hibernate, or store food to prepare for winter. But where can a tree go? It survives by dropping its leaves, and by the end of autumn only a few fragile threads of fluid-carrying xylem hold leaves to their stems.

A turning leaf stays partly green at first, then reveals splotches of 3 yellow and red as the chlorophyll gradually breaks down. Dark green seems to stay longest in the veins, outlining and defining them. During the summer, chlorophyll dissolves in the heat and light, but it is also being steadily replaced. In the fall, on the other hand, no new pigment is produced, and so we notice the other colors that were always there, right in the leaf, although chlorophyll's shocking green hid them from view. With their camouflage gone, we see these colors for the first time all year, and marvel, but they were always there, hidden like a vivid secret beneath the hot glowing greens of summer.

The most spectacular range of fall foliage occurs in the northeast- 4 ern United States and in eastern China, where the leaves are robustly colored, thanks in part to a rich climate. European maples don't achieve the same flaming reds as their American relatives, which thrive on cold nights and sunny days. In Europe, the warm, humid weather turns the leaves brown or mildly yellow. Anthocyanin, the pigment that gives apples their red and turns leaves red or red-violet, is produced by sugars that remain in the leaf after the supply of nutrients dwindles. Unlike the carotenoids, which color carrots, squash, and corn, and turn leaves orange and yellow, anthocyanin varies from year to year, depending on the temperature and amount of sunlight. The fiercest colors occur in years when the fall sunlight is strongest and the nights are cool and dry (a state of grace scientists find vexing to forecast). This is also why leaves appear dizzyingly bright and clear on a sunny fall day: The anthocyanin flashes like a marquee.

Not all leaves turn the same colors. Elms, weeping willows, and the 5 ancient ginkgo all grow radiant yellow, along with hickories, aspens, bottlebrush buckeyes, cottonweeds, and tall, keening poplars. Basswood turns bronze, birches bright gold. Water-loving maples put on a symphonic display of scarlets. Sumacs turn red, too, as do flowering dogwoods, black gums, and sweet gums. Though some oaks yellow, most turn a pinkish brown. The farmlands also change color, as tepees of cornstalks and bales of shredded-wheat-textured hay stand drying in the fields. In some spots, one slope of a hill may be green and the other already in bright color, because the hillside facing south gets more sun and heat than the northern one.

An odd feature of the colors is that they don't seem to have any   6
special purpose. We are predisposed to respond to their beauty, of
course. They shimmer with the colors of sunset, spring flowers, the
tawny buff of a colt's pretty rump, the shuddering pink of a blush.
Animals and flowers color for a reason—adaptation to their environment—but there is no adaptive reason for leaves to color so beautifully
in the fall any more than there is for the sky or ocean to be blue. It's just
one of the haphazard marvels the planet bestows every year. We find the
sizzling colors thrilling, and in a sense they dupe us. Colored like living
things, they signal death and disintegration. In time, they will become
fragile and, like the body, return to dust. They are as we hope our own
fate will be when we die: Not to vanish, just to sublime from one beautiful state into another. Though leaves lose their green life, they bloom
with urgent colors, as the woods grow mummified day by day, and
Nature becomes more carnal, mute, and radiant.

We call the season "fall," from the Old English *feallan*, to fall,   7
which leads back through time to the Indo-European *phol*, which also
means to fall. So the word and the idea are both extremely ancient, and
haven't really changed since the first of our kind needed a name for
fall's leafy abundance. As we say the word, we're reminded of that other
Fall, in the garden of Eden, when fig leaves never withered and scales
fell from our eyes. Fall is the time when leaves fall from the trees, just
as spring is when flowers spring up, summer is when we simmer, and
winter is when we whine from the cold.

Children love to play in piles of leaves, hurling them into the air like   8
confetti, leaping into soft unruly mattresses of them. For children, leaf
fall is just one of the odder figments of Nature, like hailstones or
snowflakes. Walk down a lane overhung with trees in the never-never
land of autumn, and you will forget about time and death, lost in the
sheer delicious spill of color. Adam and Eve concealed their nakedness
with leaves, remember? Leaves have always hidden our awkward secrets.

But how do the colored leaves fall? As a leaf ages, the growth hor-   9
mone, auxin, fades, and cells at the base of the petiole divide. Two or
three rows of small cells, lying at right angles to the axis of the petiole,
react with water, then come apart, leaving the petioles hanging on by
only a few threads of xylem. A light breeze, and the leaves are airborne.
They glide and swoop, rocking in invisible cradles. They are all wing
and may flutter from yard to yard on small whirlwinds or updrafts,
swiveling as they go. Firmly tethered to earth, we love to see things rise
up and fly—soap bubbles, balloons, birds, fall leaves. They remind us
that the end of a season is capricious, as is the end of life. We especially
like the way leaves rock, careen, and swoop as they fall. Everyone knows

the motion. Pilots sometimes do a maneuver called a "falling leaf," in which the plane loses altitude quickly and on purpose, by slipping first to the right, then to the left. The machine weighs a ton or more, but in one pilot's mind it is a weightless thing, a falling leaf. She has seen the motion before, in the Vermont woods where she played as a child. Below her the trees radiate gold, copper, and red. Leaves are falling, although she can't see them fall, as she falls, swooping down for a closer view.

At last the leaves leave. But first they turn color and thrill us for 10 weeks on end. Then they crunch and crackle underfoot. They *shush,* as children drag their small feet through leaves heaped along the curb. Dark, slimy mats of leaves cling to one's heels after a rain. A damp, stuccolike mortar of semidecayed leaves protects the tender shoots with a roof until spring, and makes a rich humus. An occasional bulge or ripple in the leafy mounds signals a shrew or a field mouse tunneling out of sight. Sometimes one finds in fossil stones the imprint of a leaf, long since disintegrated, whose outlines remind us how detailed, vibrant, and alive are the things of this earth that perish.

QUESTIONS ON SUBJECT

1. According to Ackerman, exactly what causes leaves to change color? What particular conditions cause the brightest colors in autumn leaves?

2. Why, according to Ackerman, do we call the season "fall"? Why do you suppose she bothers to gives us this language lesson in paragraph 7?

3. What does Ackerman mean when she says, "Leaves have always hidden our awkward secrets"? Explain.

4. What, according to Ackerman, is the function of leaves underfoot? Explain.

5. Reread Ackerman's concluding sentence. What does she mean? Why do you suppose she has chosen to end her essay in this way? In what ways, if any, is it a particularly appropriate ending for her essay? (Glossary: *Beginnings and Endings*)

QUESTIONS ON STRATEGY

1. Briefly summarize the steps of the process by which leaves change color in autumn.

2. How has Ackerman organized her essay? (Glossary: *Organization*) Explain why this organization seems most appropriate for her subject.

3. What is Ackerman's attitude toward her subject? (Glossary: *Attitude*) Cite examples of her diction to support your answer. (Glossary: *Diction*)

4. Ackerman is fond of asking questions. Locate four or five that she uses, and explain the different functions they serve within the context of this essay.

5. Not only does Ackerman describe the process by which leaves change color, she includes other information as well. For example, she uses cause and effect analysis to explain what causes leaves to be particularly bright some years, to explain why trees turn color at different rates, and to explain why leaves finally lose their grip and fall from the trees. (Glossary: *Cause and Effect Analysis*) Did you find this information useful? What, if anything, did it add to your appreciation of her process analysis?

QUESTIONS ON LANGUAGE

1. Explain how Ackerman personifies autumn in paragraph 1. (Glossary: *Figurative Language*) What do you think this personification adds to her essay? Explain.

2. Identify several similes and metaphors that Ackerman uses, and explain how each functions in the context of the essay. (Glossary: *Figurative Language*)

3. How would you describe Ackerman's diction in this essay? Does she ever get too scientific for the general reader? If so, where do you think her language gets too technical?

4. Refer to your desk dictionary to determine the meanings of the following words as they are used in this selection: *stealth* (paragraph 1), *clenched* (1), *gushing* (1), *camouflage* (3), *tawny* (6), *figments* (8), *stuccolike* (10), *vibrant* (10).

WRITING ASSIGNMENTS

1. Our world is filled with hundreds of natural processes—for example, the cycle of the moon, the "rising" and "setting" of the sun, the germination of a seed, the movement of the tides, the formation of a tornado, and the flowering of a tree. Write an informational process analysis explaining one such natural process.

2. Use a directional process analysis for a "simple" task that could prove disastrous if not explained precisely. For example, changing a tire, driving a standard shift car, packing for a weekend camp in the woods, or loading film into a camera.

Unchopping a Tree

W. S. MERWIN

W(illiam) S(tanley) Merwin, poet, short story writer, essayist, autobiographer, dramatist, translator, and editor, was born in 1927 in New York City. He grew up in Union City, New Jersey, and Scranton, Pennsylvania, and graduated from Princeton University in 1947. His poetry has received many awards including the Pulitzer Prize for The Carrier of Ladders (1970). In the New York Review of Books, Stephen Spender wrote of Merwin's poetical insight, "These poems communicate a sense of someone watching and waiting, surrounding himself with silence, so that he can see minute particles, listen to infinitesimal sounds, with a passivity of attention, a refusal to disturb with his own observing consciousness the object observed. It is as though things write their own poems through Merwin. At their best they are poems of total attention and as such they protest against our world of total distraction." Ecology and human separation from nature are two issues that have remained central to Merwin's work.

In this essay, Merwin questions the impact of development and progress. His ironic use of process analysis lets him convey a very serious ecological message.

Start with the leaves, the small twigs, and the nests that have been 1 shaken, ripped, or broken off by the fall; these must be gathered and attached once again to their respective places. It is not arduous work, unless major limbs have been smashed or mutilated. If the fall was carefully and correctly planned, the chances of anything of the kind happening will have been reduced. Again, much depends upon the size, age, shape, and species of the tree. Still, you will be lucky if you can get through this stage without having to use machinery. Even in the best of circumstances it is a labor that will make you wish often that you had won the favor of the universe of ants, the empire of mice, or at least a local tribe of squirrels, and could enlist their labors and their talents. But no, they leave you to it. They have learned, with time. This is men's work. It goes without saying that if the tree was hollow in whole or in part, and contained old nests of bird or mammal or insect, or hoards of nuts or such structures as wasps or bees build for their survival, the contents will have to be repaired where necessary, and reassembled, insofar as possible, in their original order, including the shells of nuts already opened. With spiders' webs you must simply do the best you can. We do not have the spider's weaving equipment, nor any substitute for the leaf's living bond with its point of attachment and nourishment. It is even harder to simulate the latter when the leaves have once become dry—as they are bound to do, for this is not the labor of a moment. Also it hardly needs saying that this is the time for repairing any neighboring trees or bushes or other growth that may have been damaged by the fall. The same rules apply. Where neighboring trees were of the same species it is difficult not to waste time conveying a detached leaf back to the wrong tree. Practice, practice. Put your hope in that.

Now the tackle must be put into place, or the scaffolding, depend- 2 ing on the surroundings and the dimensions of the tree. It is ticklish work. Almost always it involves, in itself, further damage to the area, which will have to be corrected later. But as you've heard, it can't be helped. And care now is likely to save you considerable trouble later. Be careful to grind nothing into the ground.

At last the time comes for the erecting of the trunk. By now it will 3 scarcely be necessary to remind you of the delicacy of this huge skeleton. Every motion of the tackle, every slight upward heave of the trunk, the branches, their elaborately reassembled panoply of leaves (now dead) will draw from you an involuntary gasp. You will watch for a leaf or a twig to be snapped off yet again. You will listen for the nuts to shift in the hollow limb and you will hear whether they are indeed falling into place or are spilling in disorder—in which case, or in the event of anything else of the kind—operations will have to cease, of course, while you correct the matter. The raising itself is no small enterprise, from the moment when the chains tighten around the old bandages until the bole hangs vertical above the stump, splinter above splinter. Now the final straightening of the splinters themselves can take place (the preliminary work is best done while the wood is still green and soft, but at times when the splinters are not badly twisted most of the straightening is left until now, when the torn ends are face to face with each other). When the splinters are perfectly complementary the appropriate fixative is applied. Again we have no duplicate of the original substance. Ours is extremely strong, but it is rigid. It is limited to surface, and there is no play in it. However the core is not the part of the trunk that conducted life from the roots up into the branches and back again. It was relatively inert. The fixative for this part is not the same as the one for the outer layers and the bark, and if either of these is involved in the splintered section they must receive applications of the

appropriate adhesives. Apart from being incorrect and probably ineffective, the core fixative would leave a scar on the bark.

When all is ready the splintered trunk is lowered onto the splinters 4
of the stump. This, one might say, is only the skeleton of the resurrection. Now the chips must be gathered, and the sawdust, and returned
to their former positions. The fixative for the wood layers will be applied to chips and sawdust consisting only of wood. Chips and sawdust
consisting of several substances will receive applications of the correct
adhesives. It is as well, where possible, to shelter the materials from the
elements while working. Weathering makes it harder to identify the
smaller fragments. Bark sawdust in particular the earth lays claim to
very quickly. You must find your own ways of coping with this problem.
There is a certain beauty, you will notice at moments, in the pattern of
the chips as they are fitted back into place. You will wonder to what
extent it should be described as natural, to what extent man-made. It
will lead you on to speculations about the parentage of beauty itself, to
which you will return.

The adhesive for the chips is translucent, and not so rigid as that for 5
the splinters. That for the bark and its subcutaneous layers is transparent and runs into the fibers on either side, partially dissolving them into
each other. It does not set the sap flowing again but it does pay a kind
of tribute to the preoccupations of the ancient thoroughfares. You
could not roll an egg over the joints but some of the mine-shafts would
still be passable, no doubt, for the first exploring insect who raises its
head in the tight echoless passages. The day comes when it is all restored, even to the moss (now dead) over the wound. You will sleep
badly, thinking of the removal of the scaffolding that must begin the
next morning. How you will hope for sun and a still day!

The removal of the scaffolding or tackle is not so dangerous, per- 6
haps, to the surroundings, as its installation, but it presents problems.
It should be taken from the spot piece by piece as it is detached and
stored at a distance. You have come to accept it there, around the tree.
The sky begins to look naked as the chains and struts one by one vacate
their positions. Finally the moment arrives when the last sustaining
piece is removed and the tree stands again on its own. It is as though
its weight for a moment stood on your heart. You listen for a thud of
settlement, a warning creak deep in the intricate joinery. You cannot
believe it will hold. How like something dreamed it is standing there all
by iteself. How long will it stand there now? The first breeze that
touches its dead leaves all seems to flow into your mouth. You are afraid
the motion of the clouds will be enough to push it over. What more can
you do? What more can you do?

But there is nothing more you can do.   7

Others are waiting.   8

Everything is going to have to be put back.   9

QUESTIONS ON SUBJECT

1. What practical goal(s) do you think Merwin wants to achieve through his impractical directions?

2. Why can't the unchopper enlist the aid of nature? What makes this "men's work"?

3. In paragraph 2 Merwin writes, "But as you've heard, it can't be helped." Who has told us that "it can't be helped"?

4. In the process of unchopping the tree, what information does Merwin give the reader about a tree and its environment?

5. Merwin concludes the first paragraph by asking the reader to, "Practice, practice. Put your hope in that." What do you think he means here?

QUESTIONS ON STRATEGY

1. Why do you suppose Merwin chose process analysis as the organizational strategy for this essay? What other strategies might he have used? (Glossary: *Purpose*) Explain.

2. Is Merwin's essay a directional process analysis or an informational one? How do you know?

3. What is Merwin's tone in this essay? (Glossary: *Tone*) Point to specific words or sentences that led you to this conclusion.

4. As Merwin gives the steps for his process analysis he repeatedly tells us that certain things go without saying, even as he explains them to us. What effect do you think Merwin is trying to have on his readers? How do you react to this?

5. Identify any language Merwin uses that suggests "unchopping a tree" is akin to a major construction project. How well does this analogy hold up throughout the essay? What does it add to your understanding of the essay? (Glossary: *Analogy*)

QUESTIONS ON LANGUAGE

1. Comment on the following verbs Merwin uses: *shaken, ripped, broken, smashed, mutilated*. What do they have in common? In what context does Merwin use them? Do you think these verbs are appropriate, given the context and Merwin's purpose?

2. What effect did Merwin's use of the second-person pronoun "you" have on you? Explain. (Glossary: *Audience*)

3. Refer to your desk dictionary to determine the meanings of the following words as they are used in this selection: *respective* (paragraph 1), *arduous* (1), *panoply* (3), *bole* (3), *fixative* (3), *subcutaneous* (5), *preoccupations* (5).

WRITING SUGGESTIONS

1. Using Merwin's essay as a model, write an un-directional process analysis. Consider how describing undoing something will make your reader reconsider the act of doing. Also, keep in mind that undoing something doesn't have to be impossible and that you don't have to select a destructive act.

2. Write a directional process analysis for an activity or action that you do on a regular basis—shining shoes, jogging, making a "to do" list, making coffee, cutting your fingernails/toenails, and so forth. Think carefully about all the steps that you go through each time that you do it? Do you have any tips or short-cuts that would be of particular interest to readers? If most people already know how to do this activity, why would they want to read your directions?

The Death of the Moth

VIRGINIA WOOLF

Virginia Woolf was born in London in 1882, the daughter of the distinguished scholar Leslie Stephen. She was educated at home with the resources of her father's superb library, and after his death she moved with her sister and brothers to London's Blooms-bury district. There they became friends with a circle of writers and artists that included the novelist E. M. Forster and the economist John Maynard Keyes. Woolf started her writing career as a literary critic for the Times Literary Supplement *and in 1917 founded with her husband Leonard the Hogarth Press, which published many of the writers associated with the Blooms-bury group, including Woolf herself. She is best known for her novels, including* Jacob's Room *(1922),* Mrs. Dalloway *(1925),* To the Lighthouse *(1927), and* The Waves *(1931). Her essays have been published in the four-volume* Collected Essays *(1966– 1967). In her later life Woolf was subject to periods of depression and anxiety, and in 1941 she took her own life.*

In the following essay, first published in 1942, she tells how witnessing the final stages of the death of a moth brought home to her the power of life and the enormity of death.

Moths that fly by day are not properly to be called moths; they do 1 not excite that pleasant sense of dark autumn nights and ivy-blossom which the commonest yellow-underwing asleep in the shadow of the curtain never fails to rouse in us. They are hybrid creatures, neither gay like butterflies nor sombre like their own species. Nevertheless the present specimen, with his narrow hay-colored wings, fringed with a tassel of the same color, seemed to be content with life. It was a pleasant morning, mid-September, mild, benignant, yet with a keener breath than that of the summer months. The plough was already scoring the field opposite the window, and where the share had been, the earth was pressed flat and gleamed with moisture. Such vigor came rolling in from the fields and the down beyond that it was difficult to keep the eyes strictly turned upon the book. The rooks too were keeping one of their annual festivities; soaring around the tree tops until it looked as if a vast net with thousands of black knots in it had been cast up into the air; which, after a few moments sank slowly down upon the trees until every twig seemed to have a knot at the end of it. Then, suddenly, the net would be thrown into the air again in a wider circle this time, with the utmost clamor and vociferation, as though to be thrown into the air and settle slowly down upon the tree tops were a tremendously exciting experience.

The same energy which inspired the rooks, the ploughmen, the 2 horses, and even, it seemed, the lean bare-backed downs, sent the moth fluttering from side to side of his square of the window-pane. One could not help watching him. One was, indeed, conscious of a queer feeling of pity for him. The possibilities of pleasure seemed that morning so enormous and various that to have only a moth's part in life, and a day moth's at that, appeared a hard fate, and his zest in enjoying his meagre opportunities to the full, pathetic. He flew vigorously to one corner of his compartment, and, after waiting there a second, flew across to the other. What remained for him but to fly to a third corner and then to a fourth? That was all he could do, in spite of the size of the downs, the width of the sky, the far-off smoke of houses, and the romantic voice, now and then, of a steamer out at sea. What he could do he did. Watching him, it seemed as if a fibre, very thin but pure, of the enormous energy of the world had been thrust into his frail and diminutive body. As often as he crossed the pane, I could fancy that a thread of vital light became visible. He was little or nothing but life.

Yet, because he was so small, and so simple a form of the energy 3 that was rolling in at the open window and driving its way through so many narrow and intricate corridors in my own brain and in those of other human beings, there was something marvelous as well as pathetic about him. It was as if someone had taken a tiny bead of pure life and decking it as lightly as possible with down and feathers, had set it dancing and zigzagging to show us the true nature of life. Thus displayed one could not get over the strangeness of it. One is apt to forget all about life, seeing it humped and bossed and garnished and cumbered so that it has to move with the greatest circumspection and dignity. Again, the thought of all that life might have been had he been born in any other shape caused one to view his simple activities with a kind of pity.

After a time, tired by his dancing apparently, he settled on the 4 window ledge in the sun, and, the queer spectacle being at an end, I forgot about him. Then, looking up, my eye was caught by him. He was trying to resume his dancing, but seemed either so stiff or so awkward that he could only flutter to the bottom of the window-pane; and when he tried to fly across it he failed. Being intent on other matters I watched these futile attempts for a time without thinking, unconsciously waiting for him to resume his flight, as one waits for a machine, that has stopped momentarily, to start again without considering the reason of its failure. After perhaps a seventh attempt he slipped from the wooden ledge and fell, fluttering his wings, onto his back on the window sill. The helplessness of his attitude roused me. It flashed upon me he was in difficulties; he could no longer raise himself; his legs struggled vainly. But, as I stretched out a pencil, meaning to help him to right himself, it came over me that the failure and awkwardness were the approach of death. I laid the pencil down again.

The legs agitated themselves once more. I looked as if for the 5 enemy against which he struggled. I looked out of doors. What had happened there? Presumably it was midday, and work in the fields had stopped. Stillness and quiet had replaced the previous animation. The birds had taken themselves off to feed in the brooks. The horses stood still. Yet the power was there all the same, massed outside indifferent, impersonal, not attending to anything in particular. Somehow it was opposed to the little hay-colored moth. It was useless to try to do anything. One could only watch the extraordinary efforts made by those tiny legs against an oncoming doom which could, had it chosen, have submerged an entire city, not merely a city, but masses of human beings; nothing, I knew, had any chance against death. Nevertheless after a pause of exhaustion the legs fluttered again. It was superb this last protest, and so frantic that he succeeded at last in righting himself. One's sympathies, of course, were all on the side of life. Also, when there was nobody to care or to know, this gigantic effort on the part of an insignificant little moth, against a power of such magnitude, to retain what no one else valued or desired to keep, moved one strangely. Again, somehow, one saw life, a pure bead. I lifted the pencil again, useless though I knew it to be. But even as I did so, the unmistakable tokens of death showed themselves. The body relaxed, and instantly grew stiff. The struggle was over. The insignificant little creature now knew death. As I looked at the dead moth, this minute wayside triumph of so great a force over so mean an antagonist filled me with wonder. Just as life had been strange for a few minutes before, so death was now as strange. The moth having righted himself now lay most decently and uncomplainingly composed. O yes, he seemed to say, death is stronger than I am.

QUESTIONS ON SUBJECT

1. Why do you think Woolf chose a common moth for the subject of her essay? Why do you suppose she focuses on the unattractive features of the moth in the first half of her essay?

2. What does the moth represent in this essay? What does the scene outdoors represent? How are they parallel?

3. Why does Woolf feel pity for the moth? Although the creature is obviously symbolic, how does Woolf convey its concrete reality? What visual details does she provide?

4. What does Woolf mean when she writes, "One is apt to forget all about life, seeing it humped and bossed and garnished and cumbered so that it has to move with the greatest circumspection and dignity"?

5. Why does Woolf say in conclusion, "Just as life had been strange for a few minutes before, so death was now as strange"? What, in her description, was "strange" about both life and death?

6. Woolf describes the scene outside her window with urgency in the first two paragraphs, then doesn't mention it at all except to describe the indifference of this world to the moth's struggle. What has brought about this change in her attitude toward the outside scene?

7. Woolf's essay is about much more than the death of a moth. What insights into life does she gain through the contemplation of the moth?

QUESTIONS ON STRATEGY

1. How would you describe Woolf's tone in the first paragraph? (Glossary: *Tone*) What unrealistic expectations does she hold?

2. What happens outdoors during the moth's death throes? What is the tone of Woolf's descriptions of the moth and the outdoors? (Glossary: *Tone*) How does this tone contribute to the essay's meaning and effect?

3. Reread the first sentence of this essay and the last two. How do the last two contrast with the first? What strengths would you attribute to each sentence?

4. What stages does Woolf delineate in her description of the moth's struggle with death?

5. Describe the difference in the author's vision between the following two passages: "What remained for him but to fly to a third corner and then to a fourth? That was all he could do, in spite of the size of the downs, the width of the sky, the far-off smoke of houses, and the romantic voice, now and then, of a steamer out at sea." "It was as if someone had taken a tiny bead of pure life and decking it as lightly as possible with down and feathers, had set it dancing and zigzagging to show us the true nature of life."

6. What advantages do you see in the author's long paragraphs? What would have been lost had she broken them up?

7. Woolf relies heavily on description to set the scene in her opening two paragraphs. What dominant impression does she create for the reader?

(Glossary: *Dominant Impression*) What specific details help her create this impression?

QUESTIONS ON LANGUAGE

1. In paragraph 3, Woolf writes, "One is apt to forget all about life, seeing it humped and bossed and garnished and cumbered so that it has to move with the greatest circumspection and dignity." How has Woolf's language moved with circumspection and dignity to this point?

2. What figures of speech does Woolf use to describe the scene outdoors and the moth's actions? How do these add to your understanding and enjoyment of the essay?

3. Refer to your desk dictionary to determine the meanings of the following words as they are used in this selection: *rouse* (paragraph 1), *hybrid* (1), *benignant* (1), *vociferation* (1), *diminutive* (2), *garnished* (3), *cumbered* (3), *vainly* (4), *magnitude* (5), *minute* (5), *composed* (5).

WRITING SUGGESTIONS

1. As the seventeenth-century English writer Sir Thomas Browne once wrote, "The long habit of living indisposeth us for dying"—yet we must all die, of course. Do thoughts of death come to you from time to time? Under what circumstances? How do they affect your attitude toward life, if they do? Write an essay in which you present your thoughts on death.

2. Like Virginia Woolf, many writers have found in small, apparently insignificant things the occasion for reflection on large topics. Choose an apparently trivial object or event, then meditate on it, allowing it to suggest deeper thoughts and associations. Write an essay in which you present not only the larger ideas at which you arrived but the little one with which you began.

3. Recall a job you find boring or tedious, and describe the steps you take to add variety and interest to an otherwise impossible task. For example, you might write about cleaning your room, mowing the lawn, paying your bills, or grocery shopping.

The Spider and the Wasp

ALEXANDER PETRUNKEVITCH

Alexander Petrunkevitch (1875–1964), a Russian-born zoologist, was a leading authority on spiders. He published his first important work, The Index Catalogue of Spiders of North, Central, and South America, *in 1911. In addition to his scientific research, Petrunkevitch was widely recognized for his accomplished translations of English and Russian poetry.*

In this essay, first published in 1952 in Scientific American, *Petrunkevitch describes the way in which the "intelligence" of digger wasps is pitted against the "instincts" of tarantula spiders.*

In the feeding and safeguarding of their progeny insects and spiders 1
exhibit some interesting analogies to reasoning and some crass examples of blind instinct. The case I propose to describe here is that of the
tarantula spiders and their arch-enemy, the digger wasps of the genus
Pepsis. It is a classic example of what looks like intelligence pitted
against instinct—a strange situation in which the victim, though fully
able to defend itself, submits unwittingly to its destruction.

Most tarantulas live in the tropics, but several species occur in the 2
temperate zone and a few are common in the southern U.S. Some
varieties are large and have powerful fangs with which they can inflict a
deep wound. These formidable looking spiders do not, however, attack
man; you can hold one in your hand, if you are gentle, without being
bitten. Their bite is dangerous only to insects and small mammals such
as mice; for man it is no worse than a hornet's sting.

Tarantulas customarily live in deep cylindrical burrows, from which 3
they emerge at dusk and into which they retire at dawn. Mature males
wander about after dark in search of females and occasionally stray into
houses. After mating, the male dies in a few weeks, but a female lives
much longer and can mate several years in succession. In a Paris museum is a tropical specimen which is said to have been living in captivity
for 25 years.

A fertilized female tarantula lays from 200 to 400 eggs at a time; 4
thus it is possible for a single tarantula to produce several thousand
young. She takes no care of them beyond weaving a cocoon of silk to
enclose the eggs. After they hatch, the young walk away, find conve-

nient places in which to dig their burrows and spend the rest of their lives in solitude. The eyesight of tarantulas is poor, being limited to a sensing of change in the intensity of light and to the perception of moving objects. They apparently have little or no sense of hearing, for a hungry tarantula will pay no attention to a loudly chirping cricket placed in its cage unless the insect happens to touch one of its legs.

But all spiders, and especially hairy ones, have an extremely delicate 5 sense of touch. Laboratory experiments prove that tarantulas can distinguish three types of touch: pressure against the body wall, stroking of the body hair, and riffling of certain very fine hairs on the legs called trichobothria. Pressure against the body, by the finger or the end of a pencil, causes the tarantula to move off slowly for a short distance. The touch excites no defensive response unless the approach is from above where the spider can see the motion, in which case it rises on its hind legs, lifts its front legs, opens its fangs and holds this threatening posture as long as the object continues to move.

The entire body of a tarantula, especially its legs, is thickly clothed 6 with hair. Some of it is short and woolly, some long and stiff. Touching this body hair produces one of two distinct reactions. When the spider is hungry, it responds with an immediate and swift attack. At the touch of a cricket's antennae the tarantula seizes the insect so swiftly that a motion picture taken at the rate of 64 frames per second shows only the result and not the process of capture. But when the spider is not hungry, the stimulation of its hairs merely causes it to shake the touched limb. An insect can walk under its hairy belly unharmed.

The trichobothria, very fine hairs growing from disclike mem- 7 branes on the legs, are sensitive only to air movement. A light breeze makes them vibrate slowly, without disturbing the common hair. When one blows gently on the trichobothria, the tarantula reacts with a quick jerk of its four front legs. If the front and hind legs are stimulated at the same time, the spider makes a sudden jump. This reaction is quite independent of the state of its appetite.

These three tactile responses—to pressure on the body wall, to 8 moving of the common hair, and to flexing of the trichobothria—are so different from one another that there is no possibility of confusing them. They serve the tarantula adequately for most of its needs and enable it to avoid most annoyances and dangers. But they fail the spider completely when it meets its deadly enemy, the digger wasp Pepsis.

These solitary wasps are beautiful and formidable creatures. Most 9 species are either a deep shiny blue all over, or deep blue with rusty wings. The largest have a wing span of about four inches. They live on nectar. When excited, they give off a pungent odor—a warning that they are ready to attack. The sting is much worse than that of a bee or common wasp, and the pain and swelling last longer. In the adult stage the wasp lives only a few months. The female produces but a few eggs, one at a time at intervals of two or three days. For each egg the mother must provide one adult tarantula, alive but paralyzed. The mother wasp attaches the egg to the paralyzed spider's abdomen. Upon hatching from the egg, the larva is many hundreds of times smaller than its living but helpless victim. It eats no other food and drinks no water. By the time it has finished its single Gargantuan meal and become ready for wasphood, nothing remains of the tarantula but its indigestible chitinous skeleton.

The mother wasp goes tarantula-hunting when the egg in her 10 ovary is almost ready to be laid. Flying low over the ground late on a sunny afternoon, the wasp looks for its victim or for the mouth of a tarantula burrow, a round hole edged by a bit of silk. The sex of the spider makes no difference, but the mother is highly discriminating as to species. Each species of Pepsis requires a certain species of tarantula, and the wasp will not attack the wrong species. In a cage with a tarantula which is not its normal prey, the wasp avoids the spider and is usually killed by it in the night.

Yet when a wasp finds the correct species, it is the other way about. 11 To identify the species the wasp apparently must explore the spider with her antennae. The tarantula shows an amazing tolerance to this exploration. The wasp crawls under it and walks over it without evoking any hostile response. The molestation is so great and so persistent that the tarantula often rises on all eight legs, as if it were on stilts. It may stand this way for several minutes. Meanwhile the wasp, having satisfied itself that the victim is of the right species, moves off a few inches to dig the spider's grave. Working vigorously with legs and jaws, it excavates a hole 8 to 10 inches deep with a diameter slightly larger than the spider's girth. Now and again the wasp pops out of the hole to make sure that the spider is still there.

When the grave is finished, the wasp returns to the tarantula to 12 complete her ghastly enterprise. First she feels it all over once more with her antennae. Then her behavior becomes more aggressive. She bends her abdomen, protruding her sting, and searches for the soft membrane at the point where the spider's legs join its body—the only spot where she can penetrate the horny skeleton. From time to time, as the exasperated spider slowly shifts ground, the wasp turns on her back and slides along with the aid of her wings, trying to get under the tarantula for a shot at the vital spot. During all this maneuvering, which can last for several minutes, the tarantula makes no move to save itself. Finally the wasp corners it against some obstruction and grasps one of its legs in her powerful jaws. Now at last the harassed spider tries a desperate but vain defense. The two contestants roll over and over on the ground. It is a terrifying sight and the outcome is always the same. The wasp finally manages to thrust her sting into the soft spot and holds it there for a few seconds while she pumps in the poison. Almost immediately the tarantula falls paralyzed on its back. Its legs stop twitching; its heart stops beating. Yet it is not dead, as is shown by the fact that if taken from the wasp it can be restored to some sensitivity by being kept in a moist chamber for several months.

After paralyzing the tarantula, the wasp cleans herself by dragging 13 her body along the ground and rubbing her feet, sucks the drop of blood oozing from the wound in the spider's abdomen, then grabs a leg of the flabby, helpless animal in her jaws and drags it down to the bottom of the grave. She stays there for many minutes, sometimes for several hours, and what she does all that time in the dark we do not know. Eventually she lays her egg and attaches it to the side of the spider's abdomen with a sticky secretion. Then she emerges, fills the grave with soil carried bit by bit in her jaws, and finally tramples the ground all around to hide any trace of the grave from prowlers. Then she flies away, leaving her descendant safely started in life.

In all this the behavior of the wasp evidently is qualitatively differ- 14 ent from that of the spider. The wasp acts like an intelligent animal. This is not to say that instinct plays no part or that she reasons as man does. But her actions are to the point; they are not automatic and can be modified to fit the situation. We do not know for certain how she identifies the tarantula—probably it is by some olfactory or chemo-tactile sense—but she does it purposefully and does not blindly tackle a wrong species.

On the other hand, the tarantula's behavior shows only confusion. 15 Evidently the wasp's pawing gives it no pleasure, for it tries to move away. That the wasp is not simulating sexual stimulation is certain be-cause male and female tarantulas react in the same way to its advances. That the spider is not anesthetized by some odorless secretion is easily shown by blowing lightly at the tarantula and making it jump suddenly. What, then, makes the tarantula behave as stupidly as it does?

No clear, simple answer is available. Possibly the stimulation by the 16 wasp's antennae is masked by a heavier pressure on the spider's body, so that it reacts as when prodded by a pencil. But the explanation may be much more complex. Initiative in attack is not in the nature of taran-tulas; most species fight only when cornered so that escape is impos-sible. Their inherited patterns of behavior apparently prompt them to avoid problems rather than attack them. For example, spiders always weave their webs in three dimensions, and when a spider finds that there is insufficient space to attach certain threads in the third dimension, it leaves the place and seeks another, instead of finishing the web in a single plane. This urge to escape seems to arise under all circumstances, in all phases of life, and to take the place of reasoning. For a spider to change the pattern of its web is as impossible as for an inexperienced man to build a bridge across a chasm obstructing his way.

In a way the instinctive urge to escape is not only easier but often   17
more efficient than reasoning. The tarantula does exactly what is most efficient in all cases except in an encounter with a ruthless and determined attacker dependent for the existence of her own species on killing as many tarantulas as she can lay eggs. Perhaps in this case the spider follows its usual pattern of trying to escape, instead of seizing and killing the wasp, because it is not aware of its danger. In any case, the survival of the tarantula species as a whole is protected by the fact that the spider is much more fertile than the wasp.

QUESTIONS ON SUBJECT

1. What is Petrunkevitch's purpose in this essay? Where is his purpose revealed? (Glossary: *Purpose*)

2. Petrunkevitch contrasts the behavior of the tarantula with that of the wasp. What significant differences does he note? How are these differences related to his overall purpose in the essay?

3. Briefly describe the process that the mother wasp follows in hunting a tarantula.

QUESTIONS ON STRATEGY

1. Petrunkevitch describes the way the wasp hunts the tarantula in order to use it as food for its young. How is the author's description of this process related to his overall purpose in the essay?

2. How has Petrunkevitch organized his essay? You may find it helpful to outline the essay in answering this question. (Glossary: *Organization*)

3. In paragraphs 10–13, Petrunkevitch describes what happens when the wasp encounters the tarantula. How has the author organized this process analysis? What transitional or linking devices has he used to give coherence to his description of the process? (Glossary: *Transitions*)

4. Why do you think Petrunkevitch goes into such detail in his description of the tarantula and the wasp? (Glossary: *Description*)

QUESTIONS ON LANGUAGE

1. Identify some examples in the text of informal or colloquial expressions (for example, "pitted against" [1]) and impressionistic words and phrases (for example, "ghastly enterprise," [12]), which, while not appropriate in a technical report, engage the nonscientific reader. What specifically do they add to Petrunkevitch's essay?

2. Refer to your desk dictionary to determine the meanings of the following words as they are used in this selection: *progeny* (paragraph 1), *crass* (1), *unwittingly* (1), *fangs* (2), *riffling* (5), *tactile* (8), *qualitatively* (14).

WRITING ASSIGNMENTS

1. Using Petrunkevitch's essay as a model, write an essay in which you describe and explain a recurring natural process—for example, seed germination, bird migration, pollination, hibernation, an eclipse, or digestion.

2. In his essay, Petrunkevitch closely examines the interdependent relationship between the tarantula and the digger wasp. What other interdependent relationships do you know about in your own experience of the natural world? Write an essay in which you explore one of these relationships. What do such relationships seem to tell us about life itself?

WRITING SUGGESTIONS
FOR PROCESS ANALYSIS

1. Write a directional process analysis on one of the following topics:
   a. how to make chocolate-chip cookies
   b. how to adjust brakes on a bicycle
   c. how to change a tire
   d. how to give a permanent
   e. how to use the memory function on a calculator
   f. how to add, drop, or change a course
   g. how to play a specific card game
   h. how to wash a sweater
   i. how to develop film
   j. how to make a pizza
   k. how to make a long-distance call from a phone booth and charge it to your home phone
   l. how to do batik dyeing
   m. how to select a major course of study
   n. how to winterize a car
   o. how to rent an apartment
   p. how to develop confidence
   q. how to operate a small business
   r. how to run for a student government office
   s. how to do a magic trick

2. Write an informational process analysis on one of the following topics:
   a. how your heart functions
   b. how a United States president is elected
   c. how ice cream is made
   d. how a hurricane forms
   e. how hailstones are formed
   f. how a volcano erupts
   g. how the circulatory system works
   h. how a camera works
   i. how photosynthesis takes place
   j. how an atomic bomb works
   k. how fertilizer is made
   l. how a refrigerator works
   m. how water evaporates
   n. how flowers bloom
   o. how a recession occurs
   p. how an automobile is made

q. how a bill becomes law in your state
r. how a caterpillar becomes a butterfly
s. how the judicial appeals process works
t. how a video camera works

5
COMPARISON AND CONTRAST

WHAT ARE COMPARISON AND CONTRAST?

A *comparison* presents two or more objects, considers them together, and shows in what ways they are alike; a *contrast* shows how the objects differ. These two perspectives, apparently in opposition to each other, actually work so often in conjunction that they are commonly considered a single strategy, called *comparison and contrast* or simply *comparison* for short.

Comparison and contrast are so much a part of daily life that people are often not aware of using them. Whenever you make a choice—what to wear, where to eat, what college to attend, what career to pursue—you implicitly use comparison and contrast to arrive at your decision. Consider an easy choice, like picking what shirt or blouse to wear for the day. You probably have a fair number to choose from, neatly stowed in a drawer. All are comparable in certain ways—they all fit you, they are all clean and ready to wear, and they all reflect your taste in clothes. But they also contrast with each other. Some have short sleeves, others have long; some are lightweight, others are warm; some are plain white or pale blue, others are in bright colors and patterns; one is a DisneyWorld T-shirt, another a sweatshirt stenciled "Property of Tampa Bay Rowdies." Eventually, you select from among them the shirt that suits your purpose, that fits where you are going, who you will see, and the weather you will be passing through on the way. You make your choice by comparing and contrasting the items in your wardrobe, even though you may not consciously realize exactly what you are doing.

The strategy of comparison and contrast works best when the objects under discussion belong to the same class or general category of things: four makes of car, for example, or two candidates for the Senate. (See Chapter 6, "Division and Classification," for a fuller discussion of classes.) Such objects are said to be comparable, or to have a strong *basis for comparison.*

Once a basis for comparison has been established, an effective comparison and contrast does not dwell on obvious similarities and differences; rather, it tells readers something significant that they do not already know. As a rule, therefore, writers tend to emphasize either the contrast between obviously similar objects or the comparison between objects usually thought to be quite different. For example, although an essay about Minneapolis and St. Paul might begin by showing why they are called the Twin Cities, it would likely give more attention to the contrasts that reveal how much the two communities differ. On the other hand, a consumer magazine might mention the contrasting claims made for a dozen different brands of frozen dinners, but the purpose of the article would be to demonstrate that, under all the packaging, the products are very much the same.

ANALOGY: A SPECIAL FORM OF COMPARISON AND CONTRAST

When a subject is unobservable, complex, or abstract—when it is so generally unfamiliar that readers may have trouble understanding it—*analogy* can be most effective. Analogy is really a special form of comparison. By pointing out the certain similarities between a difficult subject and a more familiar or concrete subject, writers can help their readers achieve a firmer grasp of the difficult subject. Unlike a true comparison, though, which analyzes items that belong to the same class—breeds of dogs or types of engines—analogy pairs things from different classes, things that have nothing in common except through the imagination of the writer. In addition, whereas comparison seeks to illuminate specific features of both subjects, the primary purpose of analogy is to clarify the one subject that is complex or unfamiliar. For example, an exploration of the similarities (and differences) between short stories and novels—two forms of fiction—would constitute a logical comparison: short stories and novels belong to the same class, and your purpose would be to learn something about both. If, however, your purpose was to explain the craft of fiction writing, you might note its similarities to the craft of carpentry. Then, you would be drawing an analogy, because the two subjects clearly belong to different classes. Carpentry is the more concrete subject and the one more people will have direct experience with. If you use your imagination, you will easily see many ways the tangible work of the carpenter can be used to help readers understand the more abstract work of the novelist. Depending on its purpose, an analogy can be made in one or two paragraphs to clarify a particular aspect of the larger topic being discussed; or it can provide the organizational strategy for an entire essay.

Observe in the following example from *The Mysterious Sky* how Lester Del Rey explains the functions of the earth's atmosphere (a subject that people have difficulty with because they can't "see" it) by referring to an ordinary window.

> The atmosphere of Earth acts like any window in serving two very important functions. It lets light in and it permits us to look out. It also serves as a shield to keep out dangerous or uncomfortable things. A normal glazed window lets us keep our houses warm by keeping out cold air, and it prevents rain, dirt, and unwelcome insects and animals from coming in. As we have already seen, Earth's atmospheric window also helps to keep our planet at a comfortable temperature by holding back radiated heat and protecting us from dangerous levels of ultraviolet light.
>
> Lately, we have discovered that space is full of a great many very dangerous things against which our atmosphere guards us. It is not a perfect shield, and sometimes one of these dangerous objects does get through. There is even some evidence that a few of these messengers from space contain life, though this has by no means been proved yet.

You'll notice that Del Rey's analogy establishes no *direct* relationship between the earth's atmosphere and a window. The analogy is effective precisely because it enables the reader to "visualize" something that is unobservable by comparing it to something quite different from it, but familiar and concrete.

WHY DO WRITERS USE COMPARISON AND CONTRAST?

Comparison and contrast can serve a number of writing purposes. One of these is to inform, to point out similarities or differences that are interesting in themselves. Bruce Catton's essay "Grant and Lee: A Study in Contrasts," which appears later in this chapter, is primarily informative. A writer may also seek to emphasize the particular qualities of two types of people by comparing and contrasting them, as Suzanne Britt does in "Neat People versus Sloppy People." Another use of comparison and contrast is to explain the unfamiliar in terms of the familiar; yet another is to evaluate, to show that an object is not only different from but better than others of its kind, whether kitchen appliances or tennis players. Finally, comparison and contrast can be used in various ways to make a persuasive point. Student writer Barbara Bowman does this in her essay "Guns and Cameras," setting up a comparison between hunting and photography to show that there is an alternative to killing animals for sport.

LOOKING AT COMPARISON AND CONTRAST

First, determine what objects are being compared and the basis of comparison; then consider why and how the comparisons are made. Sometimes the subjects of the comparison will be clear from the beginning, as in Catton's "Grant and Lee: A Study in Contrasts." At other times you may be well into your reading before you even realize that the author is using comparison and contrast. In the following selection from *Why They Behave Like Russians* by John Fischer, the author declares his subject and strategy in the first sentence:

> The Ukrainians are the Texans of Russia. They believe they can fight, drink, ride, sing, and make love better than anybody else in the world, and if pressed will admit it. Their country, too, was a borderland—that's what "Ukraine" means—and like Texas it was originally settled by outlaws, horse thieves, land-hungry farmers, and people who hadn't made a go of it somewhere else. Some of these hard cases banded together, long ago, to raise hell and livestock. They called themselves Cossacks, and they would have felt right at home in any Western movie. Even today the Ukrainians cherish a wistful tradition of horsemanship, although most of them would feel as uncomfortable in a saddle as any Dallas banker. They still like to wear knee-high boots and big, furry hats, made of gray or black Persian lamb, which are the local equivalent of the Stetson.
>
> Even the country looks a good deal like Texas—flat, dry prairie, shading off in the south to semidesert. Through the middle runs a strip of dark, rich soil, the Chernozom Belt, which is almost identical with the black waxy soil of central Texas. It grows the best wheat in the Soviet Union. The Ukraine is also famous for its cattle, sheep, and cotton, and—again like Texas—it has been in the throes of an industrial boom for the last twenty years. On all other people the Ukrainians look

with a sort of kindly pity. They might have thought up for their own use
the old Western rule of etiquette: "Never ask a man where he comes
from. If he's a Texan, he'll tell you; if he's not, don't embarrass him.''

It is immediately clear that these paragraphs compare the Soviet
region of the Ukraine with the state of Texas and the people of the
Ukraine with Texans. Close attention to the writer's methods reveals
further information.

What is Fischer's basis of comparison? Both objects are members of
the same class or general category, *geographic regions and their people.*

What is the purpose of this comparison? Fischer helps us understand an unfamiliar region, the Ukraine, by comparing it with a more
familiar one, Texas.

What comparisons does he make? There are almost too many
points of comparison to count—six in the second sentence alone—but
they can be summed up in this way: paragraph 1 compares the self-
image of Ukrainians with that of Texans, the early history of each group,
and their current life-style; paragraph 2 compares the geography of the
two regions and ends with a comparison of Ukrainian and Texan attitudes toward the rest of the world. Often the comparisons are explicit,
as when Fischer says, "Even the country looks a good deal like Texas—
flat, dry prairie, shading off in the south to semidesert.'' Sometimes,
however, the comparison may be implicit, taking for granted what readers already know. In the second sentence, Fischer suggests that Ukrainians "believe they can fight, drink, ride, sing, and make love better than
anybody else . . .''; he assumes that his readers know Texan mythology
well enough to spot his implied comparison.

How does Fischer organize his comparison? He uses a pattern
called *point-by-point comparison*. He starts by comparing both objects
in terms of a particular point, then moves on to a second point and
compares both objects, then moves on to a third point, and so on.

The other way to organize a comparison is called *block comparison*.
In this pattern the information about one object is gathered into a
block, which is set against a block of comparable information about the
second object. Here is an example of block comparison, from "There
Are 00 Trees in Russia'' by Otto Friedrich:

> There is an essential difference between a news story, as under-
> stood by a newspaperman or a wire-service writer, and a newsmaga-
> zine story. The chief purpose of the conventional news story is to tell
> what happened. It starts with the most important information and
> continues into increasingly inconsequential details, not only because
> the reader may not read beyond the first paragraph, but because an

editor working on galley proofs a few minutes before press time likes to be able to cut freely from the end of the story.

A newsmagazine is very different. It is written to be read consecutively from beginning to end, and each of its stories is designed, following the critical theories of Edgar Allan Poe, to create one emotional effect. The news, what happened that week, may be told in the beginning, the middle, or the end; for the purpose is not to throw information at the reader but to seduce him into reading the whole story, and into accepting the dramatic (and often political) point being made.

A quick reading of Friedrich's paragraphs shows that his objects of comparison are a newspaper story and a newsmagazine story; both of these certainly belong to the same class. But what is Friedrich's purpose? First of all, he offers information about particular journalistic practices his readers may not be aware of. He also uses his comparison for emphasis, to strengthen a reader's sense of each kind of news story by contrasting it with the other. He may even have a further purpose in mind: to persuade his reader that newsmagazine stories tend to be more biased than the standard newspaper story.

Each pattern of comparison, point-by-point and block, has its own advantages and disadvantages. Point-by-point comparison allows the reader to grasp fairly easily the specific points of comparison the author is making; it may be harder, though, to pull together the details and form a distinct impression of what each object is like. The block comparison, on the other hand, guarantees that each object will receive a more unified discussion; however, the points of comparison between the different objects may be less clear. (These two patterns of organization are discussed more fully on pages 221–223.)

READING COMPARISON AND CONTRAST IN AN ANNOTATED STUDENT ESSAY

A studio art major from Pittsburgh, Pennsylvania, Barbara Bowman has a special interest in photography. She was particularly pleased, therefore, to receive an internship as a photographer's assistant at Vermont Shelburne Museum. In her writing courses, Bowman has discovered many similarities between the writing process and the process that an artist follows. Her essay "Guns and Cameras," however, explores similarities of another kind: those between hunting with a gun and hunting with a camera.

GUNS AND CAMERAS
Barbara Bowman

Discussion of the objects of comparison.

With a growing number of animals heading toward extinction, and with the idea of protecting such animals on game reserves increasing in popularity, photographic safaris are replacing hunting safaris. This may seem odd because of the obvious differences between guns and cameras. Shooting is aggressive, photography is passive; shooting eliminates, photography preserves. However, some hunters are willing to trade their guns for cameras because of similarities in the way the equipment is used, as well as in the relationship among equipment, user, and "prey."

Block 1 (The Hunter) begins.

The hunter has a deep interest in the apparatus he uses to kill his prey. He carries various types of guns, different kinds of ammunition, and special sights and telescopes to increase his chances of success. He knows the mechanics of his guns and understands how and why they work. This fascination with the hardware of his sport is practical—it helps him achieve his goal—but it frequently becomes an end, almost a hobby in itself.

Point A: equipment

Point B: stalking

Not until the very end of the long process of stalking an animal does a game hunter use his gun. First he enters into the animal's world. He studies his prey, its habitat, its daily habits, its watering holes and feeding areas, its migration patterns, its enemies and allies, its diet and food chain. Eventually the hunter himself becomes animal-like, instinctively sensing the habits and moves of his prey. Of course, this instinct gives the hunter a better chance of killing the animal; he knows where and when he will get the best shot. But it gives him more than that. Hunting is not just pulling the trigger and killing the prey. Much of it is a multifaceted and ritualistic identification with nature.

Point C: the
result

After the kill, the hunter can do a number of things with his trophy. He can sell the meat or eat it himself. He can hang the animal's head on the wall, or lay its hide on the floor or even sell these objects. But any of these uses is a luxury, and its cost is high. An animal has been destroyed; a life has been eliminated.   4

Block 2 (The Pho-
tographer) begins

Point A:
equipment

Like the hunter, the photographer has a great interest in the tools he uses. He carries various types of cameras, lenses, and film to help him get the picture he wants. He understands the way cameras work, the uses of telephoto and micro lenses, and often the technical procedures of printing and developing. Of course, the time and interest a photographer invests in these mechanical aspects of his art allow him to capture and produce the image he wants. But as with the hunter, these mechanics can and often do become fascinating in themselves.   5

Point B: stalking

The wildlife photographer also needs to stalk his "prey" with knowledge and skill in order to get an accurate "shot." Like the hunter, he has to understand the animal's patterns, characteristics, and habitat, must become animal-like, in order to succeed; and like the hunter's, his pursuit is much more prolonged and complicated than the shot itself. The stalking processes are almost identical and give many of the same satisfactions.   6

Point C: the
result

The successful photographer also has something tangible to show for his efforts. A still picture of an animal can be displayed in a home, a gallery, a shop; it can be printed in a publication, as a postcard, or as a poster. In fact, a single photograph can be used in all these ways at once, can in fact be reproduced countless times. And despite all these ways of using his "trophies," the photographer continues to preserve his prey.   7

Conclusion: The
two activities are
similar and give
the same satisfac-
tion, so why kill.

Photography is obviously the less violent and to me the more acceptable method for obtaining a trophy of a wild animal. We no longer need to hunt in order   8

to feed or clothe ourselves, and hunting for "sport"
seems to be barbaric. Luckily, the excitement of pursuing an animal, learning its habits and patterns, out-
smarting it on its own level, and finally "getting" it
can all be done with a camera. So why use guns?

In discussing how she came to write about cameras and guns, Bowman said, "Photography is a big part of my life right now. I'm a studio
art major, and this summer I'll be an intern with the local weekly newspaper, their only staff photographer. So you can see why my bias is
toward cameras instead of guns." As for how she came up with the idea
of comparing guns and cameras, she said, "I was reading a photography
book and it mentioned a safari in Africa that used cameras instead of
guns. I thought that was very interesting, so I thought I'd use it for a
writing subject. I don't know that much about guns, but there's a guy
in my English class who's a big hunter—he wrote a paper for the class
about hunting—so I asked him about it. I could tell from what he said
that he got the same gratification from it that a nature photographer
would. Other people I know who hunt do it mostly for the meat and
for the adventure of stalking the prey. So that's how I got what I needed
to know about hunting. Photography I knew lots about already, of
course."

As to why she chose to use a block method of organization over a
point-by-point method, Bowman explained, "Well, the first draft was a
point-by-point comparison, and it was very bumpy, shifting back and
forth between the hunter and the photographer, and I thought it was
probably confusing. As I kept developing the paper, it just made more
sense to switch to block comparison. Unfortunately, this meant that I
had to throw out some paragraphs in the first draft that I liked. That's
hard for me—to throw out some writing that seems different and new—
but it wasn't fitting right, so I had to make the cuts."

Asked if she made any other large-scale changes as she revised,
Bowman responded, "Nothing in particular, but each time I revised I
threw things out that I didn't need, and now the essay is only half as
long as it used to be. For example, here's a sentence from the next-
to-last draft: "Guns kill, cameras don't; guns use ammunition, cameras
use film; shooting eliminates, photography preserves." Everybody
knows this, and the first and last parts say the same thing. I liked the last
part, the way the words go together, so I kept that, but I cut out the
rest. I did a lot of that."

Finally, in reflecting on the purpose of her writing, Bowman turned
to her dislike of killing, "I don't like the idea of killing things for sport.

I can see the hunter's argument that you've got to keep the animals' numbers under control, but I still would rather they weren't shot to death. That was the point of the comparison right from the first draft."

WRITING AN ESSAY OF COMPARISON AND CONTRAST

As you choose your objects of comparison and contrast, keep in mind the requirements of this writing strategy. These requirements, along with your purpose for using the strategy, will guide you as you plan, write, and revise your essay.

Objects

Remember that the objects of your comparison should be in the same class or general category—that you should be able to define a clear basis for comparison. (There are any number of possible classes, such as particular types of persons, places, and things, as well as occupations, activities, philosophies, points in history, even concepts and internal qualities.) Remember also that, if the similarities and differences between the objects are all simply obvious, the reader of the essay is certain to be bored.

Purpose

Suppose you choose to compare and contrast solar energy with wind energy. It is clear that both are members of the same class, *energy,* so there is a basis for comparing them; there also seem to be enough interesting differences to make a comparison and contrast possible. But before going any further, you must ask yourself *why* you want to compare and contrast these particular objects. Do you want to inform, to emphasize, to explain, to evaluate, to persuade? Do you have more than one purpose? Whatever your purpose, it will influence the content and organization of your comparison.

Comparing and contrasting solar and wind energy, you will certainly provide information; but more than likely you will also want to evaluate—to determine whether one or the other or both is a practical means of producing significant amounts of energy. You may also want to persuade your readers that one technology is superior to the other.

Points of Comparison

What qualities and features of your chosen objects do you want to base your comparison on? At this stage, if you don't yet know very much about the objects of your comparison, you may only be able to guess. Perhaps wind energy means no more to you than an image of giant windmills lined up on a California ridge, and solar energy brings to mind only the odd-looking glassy roof on a Colorado ski lodge. Even so, list possible points of comparison that will be relevant to your objects and your purpose. For example:

cost
convenience
efficiency
environmental impact

Of course, as you learn more about your objects and think about what you are learning, you may want to change some of these points or add new ones. But meanwhile a tentative list will help you by suggesting the kind of information you need to gather for your comparison and contrast.

Gathering Information

For some comparisons you will find the information you need in your own head; for others you will have to search for that information in books, magazines, and newspapers. Let your tentative points of comparison be your guide, but remain alert for other points you may not have thought of. For example, you may find that maintenance requirements are an important factor in considering energy systems and so want to add that point to your list:

cost
convenience
efficiency
maintenance
environmental impact

Organization

Remember that there are two patterns for structuring a comparison and contrast: block and point-by-point. Once you have gathered the necessary information, you should decide which pattern will serve your purpose best. It may help you to jot down a scratch outline before beginning your draft.

Block organization works best when the two objects of comparison are relatively simple, when the points of comparison are rather general and few in number, and when the amount of information you have to present is not great. As a scratch outline indicates, block organization makes for a unified discussion of each object, which can help your readers absorb the information you have to give them:

Solar energy
    Cost
    Efficiency
    Convenience
    Maintenance
    Environmental impact
Wind energy
    Cost
    Efficiency
    Convenience
    Maintenance
    Environmental impact

If your essay will be more than two or three pages long, however, block organization may be a poor choice. By the time your readers come to your discussion of the cost of wind energy, they may well have forgotten what you had to say about solar energy costs several pages earlier and have to flip back and forth to grasp the comparison. If such difficulties are possible, you would do better to use point-by-point organization, in which comparisons are made immediately as each point is raised:

Cost
    Solar energy
    Wind energy
Efficiency
    Solar energy
    Wind energy
Convenience
    Solar energy
    Wind energy

Maintenance
  Solar energy
  Wind energy
Environmental impact
  Solar energy
  Wind energy

Drawing a Conclusion

Only after you have gathered your information and made your comparisons are you really ready to decide what your conclusion should be. Perhaps, for example, your comparison shows that solar and wind energy are both feasible, with solar energy having a slight edge on most points. Then, if your purpose has been evaluation, you might conclude, "Both solar energy and wind energy are practical alternatives to conventional energy sources." If you wish to convince your readers that one of the technologies is superior to the other, your comparison will support a more persuasive conclusion: "While both solar and wind energy are practical technologies, solar energy now seems the better investment."

Two Ways of Seeing a River

MARK TWAIN

Mark Twain (1835–1910), the pen name of Samuel L. Clemens, was born in Mississippi and raised in Hannibal, Missouri. He created Huckleberry Finn *(1884),* Tom Sawyer *(1876),* The Prince and the Pauper *(1882), and* A Connecticut Yankee in King Arthur's Court *(1889), among other classics. One of America's most popular writers, Twain is generally regarded as the most important practitioner of the realistic school of writing, a style that emphasizes observable details.*

The following passage is taken from Life on the Mississippi *(1883), Twain's study of that great river and his account of his early experiences learning to be a river steamboat pilot. As you read the passage, notice how Twain makes use of figurative language in offering two quite different ways of seeing the Mississippi River.*

Now when I had mastered the language of this water and had come to know every trifling feature that bordered the great river as familiarly as I knew the letters of the alphabet, I had made a valuable acquisition. But I had lost something, too. I had lost something which could never be restored to me while I lived. All the grace, the beauty, the poetry, had gone out of the majestic river! I still kept in mind a certain wonderful sunset which I witnessed when steamboating was new to me. A broad expanse of the river was turned to blood; in the middle distance the red hue brightened into gold, through which a solitary log came floating, black and conspicuous; in one place a long, slanting mark lay sparkling upon the water; in another the surface was broken by boiling, tumbling rings that were as many-tinted as an opal; where the ruddy flush was faintest was a smooth spot that was covered with graceful circles and radiating lines, ever so delicately traced; the shore on our left was densely wooded, and the somber shadow that fell from this forest was broken in one place by a long, ruffled trail that shone like silver; and high above the forest wall a clean-stemmed dead tree waved a single leafy bough that glowed like a flame in the unobstructed splendor that was flowing from the sun. There were graceful curves, reflected images, woody heights, soft distances, and over the whole scene, far and near, the dissolving lights drifted steadily, enriching it every passing moment with new marvels of coloring.

I stood like one bewitched. I drank it in, in a speechless rapture. 2 The world was new to me and I had never seen anything like this at home. But as I have said, a day came when I began to cease from noting the glories and the charms which the moon and the sun and the twilight wrought upon the river's face; another day came when I ceased altogether to note them. Then, if that sunset scene had been repeated, I should have looked upon it without rapture and should have commented upon it inwardly after this fashion: "This sun means that we are going to have wind tomorrow; that floating log means that the river is rising, small thanks to it; that slanting mark on the water refers to a bluff reef which is going to kill somebody's steamboat one of these nights, if it keeps on stretching out like that; those tumbling 'boils' show a dissolving bar and a changing channel there; the lines and circles in the slick water over yonder are a warning that that troublesome place is shoaling up dangerously; that silver streak in the shadow of the forest is the 'break' from a new snag and he has located himself in the very best place he could have found to fish for steamboats; that tall dead tree, with a single living branch, is not going to last long, and then how is a body ever going to get through this blind place at night without the friendly old landmark?"

No, the romance and beauty were all gone from the river. All the 3 value any feature of it had for me now was the amount of usefulness it could furnish toward compassing the safe piloting of a steamboat. Since those days, I have pitied doctors from my heart. What does the lovely flush in a beauty's cheek mean to a doctor but a "break" that ripples above some deadly disease? Are not all her visible charms sown thick with what are to him the signs and symbols of hidden decay? Does he ever see her beauty at all, or doesn't he simply view her professionally and comment upon her unwholesome condition all to himself? And doesn't he sometimes wonder whether he has gained most or lost most by learning his trade?

QUESTIONS ON SUBJECT

1. What two attitudes toward the Mississippi River does Twain discuss? What was his first attitude toward the river? His second? What brought about the change? (Glossary: *Attitude*)

2. What points of contrast does Twain refer to in his two ways of seeing the river?

3. What point does Twain make in this selection regarding the difference between appearance and reality, between romance and practicality? What role does knowledge play in Twain's inability to see the river as he once did?

4. Now that he has learned the trade of steamboating, does Twain feel he has "gained most or lost most"?

QUESTIONS ON STRATEGY

1. What method of organization does Twain use in this selection? What alternative methods might he have used? What would have been gained or lost? (Glossary: *Organization*)

2. Explain the analogy that Twain uses in paragraph 3. What is his purpose in using the analogy? (Glossary: *Analogy*)

3. Reread Twain's conclusion. How effective do you find it? (Glossary: *Beginnings/Endings*)

4. What is Twain's tone in this essay? (Glossary: *Tone*)

5. Does Twain rely on subjective, objective, or a combination of both forms of description? Explain. (Glossary: *Description*)

QUESTIONS ON LANGUAGE

1. Twain uses a number of similes and metaphors in this passage. Identify three of each, and explain what is being compared in each case. (Glossary: *Figures of Speech*)

2. What effect do the italicized words have in each of the following quotations from this selection? How do these words contribute to Twain's description?
   a. "ever so *delicately* traced" (paragraph 1)
   b. "shadow that *fell* from this forest" (1)
   c. "*wrought* upon the river's face" (2)
   d. "show a *dissolving* bar" (2)
   e. "to get through this *blind* place at night" (2)
   f. "lovely *flush* in a beauty's cheek" (3)

3. Refer to your desk dictionary to determine the meanings of the following words as they are used in this selection: *acquisition* (paragraph 1), *hue* (1), *opal* (1), *rapture* (2), *romance* (3).

WRITING ASSIGNMENTS

1. Write an essay modeled on Twain's in which you offer your two different views of a particular scene, event, or issue. Describe how you once regarded your subject, and then describe how you now view the subject. For exam-

ple, you might wish to present the way you once viewed your hometown or high school, and the way you now view it. Be sure that you consider both your purpose in writing and the manner in which you conclude your essay.

2. Write an essay in which you use comparison and/or contrast to help you describe one of the following places or another place of your choice:

a. a place of worship
b. a fast-food restaurant
c. your dormitory
d. your college library
e. your favorite place on campus
f. your college student center
g. your hometown

Neat People versus Sloppy People

SUZANNE BRITT

*Born in Winston-Salem, North Carolina, Suzanne Britt now
makes her home in Raleigh. She graduated from Salem College
and Washington University, where she received her M.A. in
English. A freelance writer, Britt has a regular column in* North
Carolina Gardens & Homes. *Her work appears from time to
time in the* New York Times, Newsweek, *and the* Boston Globe.
Her essays have been collected in two books, People Are Dull and
Crunchy like Carrots *and* Show and Tell. *Currently she teaches
English at Meredith College in North Carolina and continues to
write.*

In the following essay taken from Show and Tell, *Britt takes
a humorous look at the differences between neat and sloppy people
by giving us some serious insights about several important personality traits.*

I've finally figured out the difference between neat people and 1
sloppy people. The distinction is, as always, moral. Neat people are
lazier and meaner than sloppy people.

Sloppy people, you see, are not really sloppy. Their sloppiness is 2
merely the unfortunate consequence of their extreme moral rectitude.
Sloppy people carry in their mind's eye a heavenly vision, a precise plan,
that is so stupendous, so perfect, it can't be achieved in this world or
the next.

Sloppy people live in Never-Never Land. Someday is their métier. 3
Someday they are planning to alphabetize all their books and set up
home catalogs. Someday they will go through their wardrobes and
mark certain items for tentative mending and certain items for passing on to relatives of similar shape and size. Someday sloppy people
will make family scrapbooks into which they will put newspaper clippings, postcards, locks of hair, and the dried corsage from their senior
prom. Someday they will file everything on the surface of their desks,
including the cash receipts from coffee purchases at the snack shop.
Someday they will sit down and read all the back issues of *The New
Yorker.*

For all these noble reasons and more, sloppy people never get neat. 4
They aim too high and wide. They save everything, planning some-

day to file, order, and straighten out the world. But while these ambitious plans take clearer and clearer shape in their heads, the books spill from the shelves onto the floor, the clothes pile up in the hamper and closet, the family mementos accumulate in every drawer, the surface of the desk is buried under mounds of paper and the unread magazines threaten to reach the ceiling.

Sloppy people can't bear to part with anything. They give loving attention to every detail. When sloppy people say they're going to tackle the surface of the desk, they really mean it. Not a paper will go unturned; not a rubber band will go unboxed. Four hours or two weeks into the excavation, the desk looks exactly the same, primarily because the sloppy person is meticulously creating new piles of papers with new headings and scrupulously stopping to read all the old book catalogs before he throws them away. A neat person would just bulldoze the desk. 5

Neat people are bums and clods at heart. They have cavalier attitudes toward possessions, including family heirlooms. Everything is just another dust-catcher to them. If anything collects dust, it's got to go and that's that. Neat people will toy with the idea of throwing the children out of the house just to cut down on the clutter. 6

Neat people don't care about process. They like results. What they want to do is get the whole thing over with so they can sit down and watch the rasslin' on TV. Neat people operate on two unvarying principles: never handle any item twice, and throw everything away. 7

The only thing messy in a neat person's house is the trash can. The minute something comes to a neat person's hand, he will look at it, try to decide if it has immediate use and, finding none, throw it in the trash. 8

Neat people are especially vicious with mail. They never go through their mail unless they are standing directly over a trash can. If the trash can is beside the mailbox, even better. All ads, catalogs, pleas for charitable contributions, church bulletins and money-saving coupons go straight into the trash can without being opened. All letters from home, postcards from Europe, bills and paychecks are opened, immediately responded to, then dropped in the trash can. Neat people keep their receipts only for tax purposes. That's it. No sentimental salvaging of birthday cards or the last letter a dying relative ever wrote. Into the trash it goes. 9

Neat people place neatness above everything, even economics. They are incredibly wasteful. Neat people throw away several toys every time they walk through the den. I knew a neat person once who threw away a perfectly good dish drainer because it had mold on it. The 10 drainer was too much trouble to wash. And neat people sell their furniture when they move. They will sell a La-Z-Boy recliner while you are reclining in it.

Neat people are no good to borrow from. Neat people buy everything in expensive little single portions. They get their flour and sugar in two-pound bags. They wouldn't consider clipping a coupon, saving a leftover, reusing plastic nondairy whipped cream containers or rinsing off tin foil and draping it over the unmoldy dish drainer. You can never borrow a neat person's newspaper to see what's playing at the movies. Neat people have the paper all wadded up and in the trash by 7:05 A.M.

Neat people cut a clean swath through the organic as well as the inorganic world. People, animals, and things are all one to them. They are so insensitive. After they've finished with the pantry, the medicine cabinet, and the attic, they will throw out the red geranium (too many leaves), sell the dog (too many fleas), and send the children off to boarding school (too many scuffmarks on the hardwood floors).

QUESTIONS ON SUBJECT

1. Why do you suppose Britt characterizes the distinction between sloppy and neat people as a "moral" one? What is she really poking fun at with this reference?

2. In your own words, what is the "heavenly vision," the "precise plan," Britt refers to in paragraph 2? How does Britt use this idea to explain why sloppy people can never be neat?

3. Choose one sentence in Britt's essay that best sums up her idea of a neat person.

4. Exaggeration, as Britt uses it, is only effective if it departs from some shared idea of the truth. What commonly understood ideas about sloppy and neat people does Britt rely on? Do you agree with her? Why or why not?

QUESTIONS ON STRATEGY

1. Note Britt's use of transitions as she moves from trait to trait. How well does she use transitions to achieve unity in her essay? Explain. (Glossary: *Transitions*)

2. Britt uses a block system of contrast. Why do you suppose she has chosen this strategy? What would have been gained or lost had she used a point-by-point system of contrast?

3. One of the ways Britt achieves a sense of the ridiculous in her essay is to switch the attributes of sloppy and neat people. Cite examples of this tech-

nique and discuss the ways in which it adds to her essay. What does it reveal to the reader about her purpose in writing this essay? (Glossary: *Purpose*)

4. Britt uses a block system of contrast to point out the differences between sloppy and neat people. Make a side-by-side list of the traits of sloppy and neat people; now see if you can determine any ways in which they may be similar. Why do you suppose Britt does not include some of the ways in which they are the same?

5. How effective do you find Britt's use of example in this essay? Cite five to ten examples that Britt uses to illustrate the points she makes. (Glossary: *Illustration*)

QUESTIONS ON LANGUAGE

1. Cite examples of Britt's diction that indicate her change of tone when she is talking about either sloppy or neat people. (Glossary: *Tone*)

2. Refer to your desk dictionary to determine the meanings of the following words as they are used in this selection: *rectitude* (paragraph 2), *stupendous* (2), *tentative* (3), *excavation* (5), *meticulously* (5), *scrupulously* (5), *heirlooms* (6), *vicious* (9), *salvaging* (9), *swath* (12).

WRITING SUGGESTIONS

1. Write an essay in which you describe yourself as either sloppy or neat. In what ways does your behavior compare or contrast with the traits Britt offers?

2. Compare and contrast two personality traits that are typically seen as opposites such as stingy and generous, serious and silly, emotional and rational, responsible and flighty, or choose two of your own. Remember that to be convincing you will have to base your analysis on a germ of truth even if you are speaking tongue-in-cheek.

Letters Are Acts of Faith;
Telephone Calls Are a Reflex

VIVIAN GORNICK

Vivian Gornick, a journalist and feminist, was born in New York City in 1935 and grew up there. She has taught English at the State University of New York at Stony Brook and Hunter College of the City University of New York. Gornick worked as a staff writer for The Village Voice *from 1969 to 1977. She has authored several books including* In Search of Ali Mahmoud: An American Woman in Egypt *(1973) and* Women in Science: Portraits from a World in Transition *(1983).*

In this selection, first published in The New York Times Book Review *on July 31, 1994, Gornick finds that although letters and phone calls serve the same need for communication, the two processes share little else in common.*

In 1920, when my mother was 18 years old, she worked in the 1 accounts department of a large wholesale bakery in lower Manhattan. The chief bookkeeper was, like herself, a European immigrant who read books and listened to music. Mr. Levinson (an unhappily married man who lived in the Bronx) saw in my mother (a soulful young woman who lived on the Lower East Side) a kindred spirit. When they parted at the end of the working day his need for her conversation had often not run its course, and he fell into the habit of writing to her late at night.

These letters were remarkably varied in mood and content. They 2 might begin reflectively at the point where the discussion had ended that day, or announce suddenly that he'd been to the theater and was drenched in longing for he knew not what, or that a child was sick, the apartment in chaos and his life a hell. The language might be poetic in tone or cynical or despairing: variations of response he allowed himself only in writing, never face to face at the bakery.

Whatever the subject, whatever the mood, when Mr. Levinson sat 3 down at midnight to write to My Dear Friend he wrote at length and at leisure. If he'd been to the theater he described the play, the acting, the crowd on 14th Street; if a child was sick he confided the atmosphere in the room, the look of the patient, how the doctor had conducted himself; if he was continuing an earlier conversation he included nuance and digression freely and fully. Inevitably, he would speak of how many were his thoughts and how hungry his spirit; he'd observe the weather at the present moment, the way the street looked from the window beyond the table where he sat writing; and often he ended by telling my mother he was now going down to the corner to mail this letter so that she would read it at 8 in the morning before they met an hour later at work. This last—that she'd read it in the morning—he predicted with an assurance he was entitled to: there were then five mail deliveries a day in New York.

This morning my phone rang at 9 o'clock. It was my friend Laura, an academic, calling from Iowa City where she works and lives. I said hello, and she launched into a familiar tale of discontent: her need for a more enlivening conversation with her husband than the one she has. The subject is territory we have traversed many times over many years, yet it remains absorbing to both of us. Useful, in fact. My friendship with Laura is an intimacy of more than two decades, characterized by a running commentary on the dailiness of our lives and conducted almost entirely on the telephone. When we talk we each cradle the receiver, stare unseeing into the emptiness of the rooms we occupy, and concentrate on the exchange.

Inevitably, these conversations are laced with our mutual intensities—literature, politics, analysis—yet they do not wander, and within minutes it is clear that once again we are pursuing our continuing interest—the nature of true well-being—as though the call were a seminar session in a course we are both permanently enrolled in. Now, this morning, in the well-worn arguments for and against Laura remaining in her marriage, the give and take was rapid, informed, sympathetic. It supplied instant catharsis. Entertained and refreshed by the wisdom of our insights, the range of our references, the sophistication of our gossip (comparable situations provide necessary texture), we were soon persuaded that we were going forward. At the end of an hour, Laura felt renewed and I felt clarified. We replaced our receivers fortified against the anxiety of the coming day.

Seventy years ago, when Mr. Levinson wanted to relieve his overflowing heart he wrote a letter to my mother. This morning, when the same need drove my friend Laura she picked up the telephone and called me. The result, in a sense, was also the same—connection had been made, a vital exchange extended, the courage for life restored—but surely the difference signifies. Mr. Levinson's letter was discursive, and narrative in nature. He had a subject (that is, a reason for writing), but he didn't hesitate to ramble, digress, describe everything in sight, give in restlessly to the easy pull of mood change (in the letters he sighs, he yearns, he accuses). As he writes he is placing himself in the world: alone, and with the rapture of the poet. Laura's call was focused and analytic in nature. She did not really digress, nor could she indulge herself in mood change at my expense—I was right there on the line—but as she spoke she too was placing herself: on the landscape inside her head, and with the absorption of an analysand.

Mr. Levinson's letter resembles the social novel of a hundred years   7 ago and Laura's phone call a piece of 20th-century minimalism. Each performs a task of the human intelligence: they are comparable but not equivalent. Yet one has all but replaced the other. Why? And what does it mean?

QUESTIONS ON SUBJECT

1. What do you think Gornick means by an act of faith? How is this different from a reflex?

2. What do Mr. Levinson's letters and the author's phone calls have in common?

3. Why do you suppose the author describes an hour phone call as an example of "20th-century minimalism"? Do you agree with her assessment? Why or why not?

4. Mr. Levinson would describe his environment in detail while writing; Gornick, however, remains oblivious to her surroundings while on the phone. What explanation does she offer for this difference?

5. Parenthetically, Gornick writes, "comparable situations provide necessary texture." Why do you think she says this about her phone conversation and not about letter writing?

QUESTIONS ON STRATEGY

1. Make an outline of the information the author gives in her essay. What is there about the way she arranges her information that facilitates a comparison and contrast? (Glossary: *Organization*)

2. How is the tone of paragraph 5 different from the preceding paragraphs? What does this change in tone have to do with the subject of Gornick's essay? (Glossary: *Tone*)

3. Gornick uses Mr. Levinson, a turn-of-the-century gentleman, as her example of a letter writer. How would using a modern-day letter writer change her essay?

4. Gornick begins her essay by telling about Mr. Levinson and her mother. How would this selection be different if she began by describing one of her phone calls? (Glossary: *Beginnings and Endings*)

5. Throughout her essay Gornick develops the examples of Mr. Levinson and Laura. Explain how these two specific examples enhance her comparison of letters and telephone calls. (Glossary: *Illustration*)

QUESTIONS ON LANGUAGE

1. Without using excerpts from letters or dialogue, the author gives the reader a flavor of the examples she compares. What about the author's language enables her to do this? Give examples to support your answer.

2. Refer to your desk dictionary to determine the meanings of the following words as they are used in this selection: *catharsis* (paragraph 5), *discursive* (6), *analysand* (6).

WRITING SUGGESTIONS

1. Write an essay comparing one of your phone calls to Gornick's call. What difference do age and education make? What other factors are important in this comparison? What feelings do you share with the author? Do you agree with her generalizations about phone calls?

2. Write your own essay comparing phone calls and letters. Do you favor one to the exclusion of the other? Why or why not? Do your peers share your habits?

Grant and Lee: A Study in Contrasts

BRUCE CATTON

Bruce Catton (1899–1978) was born in Petoskey, Michigan, and attended Oberlin College. Early in his career, Catton worked as a reporter for various newspapers, among them the Cleveland Plain Dealer. *Having an interest in history, Catton became a leading authority on the Civil War and published a number of books on this subject. These include* Mr. Lincoln's Army, Glory Road, A Stillness at Appomattox, This Hallowed Ground, The Coming Fury, Never Call Retreat, *and* Gettysburg: The Final Fury. *Catton was awarded both the Pulitzer Prize and the National Book Award in 1954.*

The following selection was included in The American Story, *a collection of historical essays edited by Earl Schenk Miers. In it Catton considers "two great Americans, Grant and Lee—very different, yet under everything very much alike."*

When Ulysses S. Grant and Robert E. Lee met in the parlor of a modest house at Appomattox Court House, Virginia, on April 9, 1865, to work out the terms for the surrender of Lee's Army of Northern Virginia, a great chapter in American life came to a close, and a great new chapter began. 1

These men were bringing the Civil War to its virtual finish. To be sure, other armies had yet to surrender, and for a few days the fugitive Confederate government would struggle desperately and vainly, trying to find some way to go on living now that its chief support was gone. But in effect it was all over when Grant and Lee signed the papers. And the little room where they wrote out the terms was the scene of one of the poignant, dramatic contrasts in American history. 2

They were two strong men, these oddly different generals, and they represented the strengths of two conflicting currents that, through them, had come into final collision. 3

Back of Robert E. Lee was the notion that the old aristocratic concept might somehow survive and be dominant in American life. 4

Lee was tidewater Virginia, and in his background were family, culture, and tradition . . . the age of chivalry transplanted to a New World which was making its own legends and its own myths. He embodied a way of life that had come down through the age of knight- 5

236

hood and the English country squire. America was a land that was beginning all over again, dedicated to nothing much more complicated than the rather hazy belief that all men had equal rights and should have an equal chance in the world. In such a land Lee stood for the feeling that it was somehow of advantage to human society to have a pronounced inequality in the social structure. There should be a leisure class, backed by ownership of land; in turn, society itself should be keyed to the land as the chief source of wealth and influence. It would bring forth (according to this ideal) a class of men with a strong sense of obligation to the community; men who lived not to gain advantage for themselves, but to meet the solemn obligations which had been laid on them by the very fact that they were privileged. From them the country would get its leadership; to them it could look for the higher values—of thought, of conduct, of personal deportment—to give it strength and value.

Lee embodied the noblest elements of this aristocratic ideal. 6 Through him, the landed nobility justified itself. For four years, the Southern states had fought a desperate war to uphold the ideals for which Lee stood. In the end, it almost seemed as if the Confederacy fought for Lee; as if he himself was the Confederacy . . . the best thing that the way of life for which the Confederacy stood could ever have to offer. He had passed into legend before Appomattox. Thousands of tired, underfed, poorly clothed Confederate soldiers, long since past the simple enthusiasm of the early days of the struggle, somehow considered Lee the symbol of everything for which they had been willing to die. But they could not quite put this feeling into words. If the Lost Cause, sanctified by so much heroism and so many deaths, had a living justification, its justification was General Lee.

Grant, the son of a tanner on the Western frontier, was everything 7 Lee was not. He had come up the hard way and embodied nothing in particular except the eternal toughness and sinewy fiber of the men who grew up beyond the mountains. He was one of a body of men who owed reverence and obeisance to no one, who were self-reliant to a fault, who cared hardly anything for the past but who had a sharp eye for the future.

These frontier men were the precise opposite of the tidewater 8 aristocrats. Back of them, in the great surge that had taken people over the Alleghenies and into the opening Western country, there was a deep, implicit dissatisfaction with a past that had settled into grooves. They stood for democracy, not from any reasoned conclusion about the proper ordering of human society, but simply because they had grown up in the middle of democracy and knew how it worked. Their society might have privileges, but they would be privileges each man had won for himself. Forms and patterns meant nothing. No man was born to anything, except perhaps to a chance to show how far he could rise. Life was competition.

Yet along with this feeling had come a deep sense of belonging to 9 a national community. The Westerner who developed a farm, opened a shop, or set up in business as a trader, could hope to prosper only as his own community prospered—and his community ran from the Atlantic to the Pacific and from Canada down to Mexico. If the land was settled, with towns and highways and accessible markets, he could better himself. He saw his fate in terms of the nation's own destiny. As its horizons expanded, so did his. He had, in other words, an acute dollars-and-cents stake in the continued growth and development of his country.

And that, perhaps, is where the contrast between Grant and Lee 10 becomes most striking. The Virginia aristocrat, inevitably, saw himself in relation to his own region. He lived in a static society which could endure almost anything except change. Instinctively, his first loyalty would go to the locality in which that society existed. He would fight to the limit of endurance to defend it, because in defending it he was defending everything that gave his own life its deepest meaning.

The Westerner, on the other hand, would fight with an equal 11 tenacity for the broader concept of society. He fought so because everything he lived by was tied to growth, expansion, and a constantly widening horizon. What he lived by would survive or fall with the nation itself. He could not possibly stand by unmoved in the face of an attempt to destroy the Union. He would combat it with everything he had, because he could only see it as an effort to cut the ground out from under his feet.

So Grant and Lee were in complete contrast, representing two 12 diametrically opposed elements in American life. Grant was the modern man emerging; beyond him, ready to come on the stage, was the great age of steel and machinery, of crowded cities and a restless burgeoning vitality. Lee might have ridden down from the old age of chivalry, lance in hand, silken banner fluttering over his head. Each man was the perfect champion of his cause, drawing both his strengths and his weaknesses from the people he led.

Yet it was not all contrast, after all. Different as they were—in 13 background, in personality, in underlying aspiration—these two great soldiers had much in common. Under everything else, they were marvelous fighters. Furthermore, their fighting qualities were really very much alike.

Each man had, to begin with, the great virtue of utter tenacity 14
and fidelity. Grant fought his way down the Mississippi Valley in spite
of acute personal discouragement and profound military handicaps.
Lee hung on in the trenches at Petersburg after hope itself had died.
In each man there was an indomitable quality . . . the born fighter's
refusal to give up as long as he can still remain on his feet and lift his two
fists.

Daring and resourcefulness they had, too; the ability to think faster 15
and move faster than the enemy. These were the qualities which gave
Lee the dazzling campaigns of Second Manassas and Chancellorsville
and won Vicksburg for Grant.

Lastly, and perhaps greatest of all, there was the ability, at the end, 16
to turn quickly from war to peace once the fighting was over. Out of the
way these two men behaved at Appomattox came the possibility of a
peace of reconciliation. It was a possibility not wholly realized, in the
years to come, but which did, in the end, help the two sections to
become one nation again . . . after a war whose bitterness might have
seemed to make such a reunion wholly impossible. No part of either
man's life became him more than the part he played in their brief
meeting in the McLean house at Appomattox. Their behavior there put
all succeeding generations of Americans in their debt. Two great Americans, Grant and Lee—very different, yet under everything very much
alike. Their encounter at Appomattox was one of the great moments of
American history.

QUESTIONS ON SUBJECT

1. In paragraphs 10 through 12, Catton discusses what he considers to be the
   most striking contrast between Grant and Lee. What is that difference?
2. List the similarities that Catton sees between Grant and Lee. Which similarity does Catton feel is most important? Why?
3. What attitudes and ideas does Catton describe to support his view that
   tidewater Virginia was a throwback to the "age of chivalry" (paragraph 5)?
4. Catton says that Grant was "the modern man emerging" (12). How does
   he support that statement? Do you agree?

QUESTIONS ON STRATEGY

1. What would have been lost had Catton compared Grant and Lee before
   contrasting them? Would anything have been gained?
2. How does Catton organize the body of his essay (3–16)? You may find it
   helpful in answering this question to summarize the point of comparison

in each paragraph and label it as being concerned with Lee, Grant, or both. (Glossary: *Organization*)

3. Catton has carefully made clear transitions between paragraphs. For each paragraph, identify the transitional devices he uses. How do they help your reading? (Glossary: *Transitions*)

4. How does Catton use cause and effect to explain Grant and Lee's respective natures? Cite several examples to illustrate your answer. (Glossary: *Cause and Effect*)

QUESTIONS ON LANGUAGE

1. Identify at least two metaphors that Catton uses, and explain what each contributes to his comparison. (Glossary: *Figures of Speech*)

2. Refer to your desk dictionary to determine the meanings of the following words as they are used in this selection: *poignant* (paragraph 2), *chivalry* (5), *sanctified* (6), *sinewy* (7), *obeisance* (7), *tidewater* (8), *tenacity* (11), *aspiration* (13).

WRITING ASSIGNMENTS

1. Select one of the following topics for an essay of comparison and contrast. In selecting your topic, you should consider (a) what your purpose will be, (b) whether you will emphasize similarities or differences, (c) what specific points you will discuss, and (d) what organizational pattern will best suit your purpose. As you plan your essay, consider whether the objects of your comparison can be discussed as representatives of particular types, the way Catton does with Grant and Lee.
   a. two actors or actresses
   b. two friends or roommates
   c. two books by the same author
   d. two paintings
   e. two popular campus hangouts
   f. two musical groups

2. Compare and contrast two famous people whose careers have at some point crossed in a dramatic or decisive way: John F. Kennedy and Richard Nixon, for example, or Ernest Hemingway and F. Scott Fitzgerald, or Sir Thomas More and Henry VIII, or Franklin Roosevelt and Winston Churchill.

The Attic of the Brain

LEWIS THOMAS

Physician, administrator, teacher, and writer, Lewis Thomas was born in 1913 in New York and attended Princeton and the Harvard Medical School. A former president of the Memorial Sloan-Kettering Cancer Center, Lewis began his writing career in 1971 with a series of essays for the New England Journal of Medicine. *The best of them were collected in his book* The Lives of a Cell: Notes of a Biology Watcher, *winner of a National Book Award in 1974. Four other collections have followed:* The Medusa and the Snail: More Notes of a Biology Watcher, Late Night Thoughts on Listening to Mahler's Ninth Symphony, Etcetera, Etcetera: Notes of a Word-Watcher, *and* The Fragile Species: Notes of an Earth Watcher. *Thomas died in 1993.*

In the following essay, taken from Late Night Thoughts, *Lewis cautions against the irreverent and ill-advised intrusion into the unconscious by using the analogy of the attic to explain complexities and mysteries of the human brain.*

My parents' house had an attic, the darkest and strangest part of 1 the building, reachable only by placing a stepladder beneath the trapdoor and filled with unidentifiable articles too important to be thrown out with the trash but no longer suitable to have at hand. This mysterious space was the memory of the place. After many years all the things deposited in it became, one by one, lost to consciousness. But they were still there, we knew, safely and comfortably stored in the tissues of the house.

These days most of us live in smaller, more modern houses or in 2 apartments, and attics have vanished. Even the deep closets in which we used to pile things up for temporary forgetting are rarely designed into new homes.

Everything now is out in the open, openly acknowledged and dis- 3 played, and whenever we grow tired of a memory, an old chair, a trunkful of old letters, they are carted off to the dump for burning.

This has seemed a healthier way to live, except maybe for the 4 smoke—everything out to be looked at, nothing strange hidden under the roof, nothing forgotten because of no place left in impenetrable darkness to forget. Openness is the new life-style, no undisclosed belongings, no private secrets. Candor is the rule in architecture. The house is a machine for living, and what kind of a machine would hide away its worn-out, obsolescent parts?

But it is in our nature as human beings to clutter, and we hanker for places set aside, reserved for storage. We tend to accumulate and outgrow possessions at the same time, and it is an endlessly discomforting mental task to keep sorting out the ones to get rid of. We might, we think, remember them later and find a use for them, and if they are gone for good, off to the dump, this is a source of nervousness. I think it may be one of the reasons we drum our fingers so much these days.

We might take a lesson here from what has been learned about our brains in this century. We thought we discovered, first off, the attic, although its existence has been mentioned from time to time by all the people we used to call great writers. What we really found was the trapdoor and a stepladder, and off we clambered, shining flashlights into the corners, vacuuming the dust out of bureau drawers, puzzling over the names of objects, tossing them down to the floor below, and finally paying around fifty dollars an hour to have them carted off for burning.

After several generations of this new way of doing things we took up openness and candor with the febrile intensity of a new religion, everything laid out in full view, and as in the design of our new houses it seemed a healthier way to live, except maybe again for smoke.

And now, I think, we have a new kind of worry. There is no place for functionless, untidy, inexplicable notions, no dark comfortable parts of the mind to hide away the things we'd like to keep but at the same time forget. The attic is still there, but with the trapdoor always open and the stepladder in place we are always in and out of it, flashing lights around, naming everything, unmystified.

I have an earnest proposal for psychiatry, a novel set of therapeutic rules, although I know it means waiting in line.

Bring back the old attic. Give new instructions to the patients who are made nervous by our times, including me, to make a conscious effort to hide a reasonable proportion of thought. It would have to be a gradual process, considering how far we have come in the other direction talking, talking all the way. Perhaps only one or two thoughts should be repressed each day, at the outset. The easiest, gentlest way might be to start with dreams, first by forbidding the patient to mention any dream, much less to recount its details, then encouraging the outright forgetting that there was a dream at all, remembering nothing beyond the vague sense that during sleep there had been the familiar sound of something shifting and sliding, up under the roof.

We might, in this way, regain the kind of spontaneity and zest for 11
ideas, things popping into the mind, uncontrollable and ungovernable
thoughts, the feel that this notion is somehow connected unaccount-
ably with that one. We could come again into possession of real memory, the kind of memory that can come from jumbled forgotten
furniture, old photographs, fragments of music.

It has been one of the great errors of our time to think that by 12
thinking about thinking, and then talking about it, we could possibly
straighten out and tidy up our minds. There is no delusion more damaging than to get the idea in your head that you understand the
functioning of your own brain. Once you acquire such a notion, you
run the danger of moving in to take charge, guiding your thoughts,
shepherding your mind from place to place, *controlling* it, making lists
of regulations. The human mind is not meant to be governed, certainly
not by any book of rules yet written; it is supposed to run itself, and we
are obliged to follow it along, trying to keep up with it as best we can.
It is all very well to be aware of your awareness, even proud of it, but
never try to operate it. You are not up to the job.

I leave it to the analysts to work out the techniques for doing what 13
now needs doing. They are presumably the professionals most familiar
with the route, and all they have to do is turn back and go the other
way, session by session, step by step. It takes a certain amount of hard
swallowing and a lot of revised jargon, and I have great sympathy for
their plight, but it is time to reverse course.

If after all, as seems to be true, we are endowed with unconscious 14
minds in our brains, these should be regarded as normal structures,
installed wherever they are for a purpose. I am not sure what they are
built to contain, but as a biologist, impressed by the usefulness of
everything alive, I would take it for granted that they are useful, probably indispensable organs of thought. It cannot be a bad thing to own
one, but I would no more think of meddling with it than trying to
exorcise my liver, an equally mysterious apparatus. Until we know a lot
more, it would be wise, as we have learned from other fields in medicine, to let them be, above all not to interfere. Maybe, even—and this
is the notion I wish to suggest to my psychiatric friends—to stock them
up, put more things into them, make *use* of them. Forget whatever you
feel like forgetting. From time to time, practice *not* being open, discover new things *not* to talk about, learn reserve, hold the tongue. But
above all, develop the human talent for forgetting words, phrases,
whole unwelcome sentences, all experiences involving wincing. If we
should ever lose the loss of memory, we might lose as well that most
attractive of signals ever flashed from the human face, the blush. If we

should give away the capacity for embarrassment, the touch of fingertips might be the next to go, and then the suddenness of laughter, the
unaccountable sure sense of something gone wrong, and, finally, the
marvelous conviction that being human is the best thing to be.

Attempting to operate one's own mind, powered by such a magi-   15
cal instrument as the human brain, strikes me as rather like using the
world's biggest computer to add columns of figures, or towing a Rolls-
Royce with a nylon rope.

I have tried to think of a name for the new professional activity, but   16
each time I think of a good one I forget it before I can get it written
down. Psychorepression is the only one I've hung on to, but I can't
guess at the fee schedule.

QUESTIONS ON SUBJECT

1. To what does Thomas liken psychoanalysis?

2. What is Thomas's proposal for psychiatry? What does he want us to get
   back? Why?

3. How does Thomas define "real memory" (paragraph 11)? How is it associated with the "blush" he refers to in paragraph 14?

4. What does Thomas say is the danger in imagining we can control our
   brains? Do you agree? Why or why not?

5. What exactly does Thomas mean when he says operating one's own mind
   is like "towing a Rolls-Royce with a nylon rope"?

QUESTIONS ON STRATEGY

1. Explain the analogy Thomas uses to discuss the unconscious. Is it effective?

2. How has Thomas organized his essay? (Glossary: *Organization*) What one
   sentence provides the unifying idea for his essay? (Glossary: *Thesis*)

3. Point out a few of the specific examples Thomas uses to compare the
   human brain to an attic. Explain in what way these examples contribute to
   your understanding of the subject.

4. What is Thomas arguing for in this essay? (Glossary: *Argument*) How do
   you know that his purpose is to argue and not, say, to inform? Explain.

5. Although the use of analogy can be a powerful strategy in an argument, it
   alone cannot "prove" a position. What kinds of evidence does Thomas use
   to support his argument? (Glossary: *Argument* and *Evidence*) Which kind
   did you find most persuasive? Why?

6. In paragraph 16, Thomas coins the term "psychorepression." How has he
   prepared the reader to understand this new term? Has he defined it?
   (Glossary: *Definition*) Explain.

QUESTIONS ON LANGUAGE

1. In addition to the analogy of the attic, Thomas uses other figures of speech in his essay. Identify them and explain in what way each of them contributes to the overall effectiveness of his essay. (Glossary: *Figures of Speech*)

2. Does Thomas intend for his essay to be taken seriously? How do you know? Cite examples of his diction to support your answer.

3. Refer to your desk dictionary to determine the meanings of the following words as they are used in this selection: *candor* (paragraph 4), *obsolescent* (4), *hanker* (5), *clambered* (6) *febrile* (7), *repressed* (10), *vague* (10), *spontaneity* (11), *delusion* (12), *jargon* (13), *meddling* (14), *exorcise* (14), *apparatus* (14), *wincing* (14), *blush* (14).

WRITING SUGGESTIONS

1. Write an essay in which you develop an analogy to explain some abstract notion of interest to you such as mathematics, faith, friendship, commitment, jealousy, infatuation, or music.

2. For one week, use your journal to keep track of the times you find yourself or others you know with "everything looked at, nothing . . . hidden under the roof." Also record the times you gave into the need for "private secrets." What, if anything, did the events in each group have in common? What feelings do you associate with those moments? Do you find yourself hankering "for places set aside"? At the end of the week, write about your findings in an essay. In what way did your research support Thomas's essay?

WRITING SUGGESTIONS
FOR COMPARISON AND CONTRAST

1. Write an essay in which you compare and/or contrast two objects, persons, or events to show at least one of the following:

   a. their important differences
   b. their significant similarities
   c. their relative value
   d. their distinctive qualities

2. Select a topic from the list that follows. Write an essay using comparison and/or contrast as your primary means of development. Be sure that your essay has a definite purpose and a clear direction.

   a. two methods of dieting
   b. two television situation comedies
   c. two types of summer employment
   d. two people who display different attitudes toward responsibility
   e. two restaurants
   f. two courses in the same subject area
   g. two friends who exemplify different life-styles
   h. two network television or local news programs
   i. two professional quarterbacks
   j. two ways of studying for an exam
   k. two rooms in which you have classes
   l. two of your favorite magazines
   m. two attitudes toward death
   n. two ways to heat a home

3. Use one of the following "before and after" situations as the basis for an essay of comparison and/or contrast:

   a. before and after an examination
   b. before and after seeing a movie
   c. before and after reading an important book
   d. before and after dieting
   e. before and after a long trip

4. The following poems attempt to capture the essence of a moment of poetic truth in baseball and basketball, respectively. After reading the two poems, write an essay in which you compare and contrast the subjects and/or the way the poets have treated them.

THE BASE STEALER

Poised between going on and back, pulled
Both ways taut like a tightrope-walker,

246

Fingertips pointing the opposites,
Now bouncing tiptoe like a dropped ball
Or a kid skipping rope, come on, come on,
Running a scattering of steps sidewise,
How he teeters, skitters, tingles, teases,
Taunts them, hovers like an ecstatic bird,
He's only flirting, crowd him, crowd him,
Delicate, delicate, delicate, delicate—now!

                                        —ROBERT FRANCIS

FOUL SHOT

With two 60's stuck on the scoreboard
And two seconds hanging on the clock,
The solemn boy in the center of eyes,
Squeezed by silence,
Seeks out the line with his feet,
Soothes his hands along his uniform,
Gently drums the ball against the floor,
Then measures the waiting net,

Raises the ball on his right hand,
Balances it with his left,
Calms it with fingertips,
Breathes,
Crouches,
Waits,
And then through a stretching of stillness,
Nudges it upward.

The ball
Slides up and out,
Lands,
Leans,
Wobbles,
Wavers,
Hesitates,
Exasperates,
Plays it coy
Until every face begs with unsounding screams—
And then

        And then
                And then,
Right before ROAR-UP,
Dives down and through.

                                        —EDWIN A. HOEY

6
DIVISION AND CLASSIFICATION

WHAT ARE DIVISION AND CLASSIFICATION?

Like comparison and contrast, division and classification are separate yet closely related mental operations. Division involves breaking down a single large unit into smaller subunits, or separating a group of items into discrete categories. For example, a state government can be divided into its various branches and even further into departments or agencies; the whole pool of registered voters in the United States can be divided among political affiliations—Democrat, Republican, Independent, and so forth. Classification, on the other hand, entails sorting individual items and placing them into established categories: a boxer is classified with other boxers according to weight, a movie is placed in a particular rating category, a library book is shelved according to an elaborate system of subject codes, and a voter is categorized with others in his or her political party. Division, then, takes apart, whereas classification groups together. But even though the two processes can operate separately, the activity of dividing and classifying is more often circular.

Another example may help clarify how division and classification work hand in hand. Suppose a sociologist wants to determine whether the socioeconomic status of the people in a particular neighborhood has any influence on their voting behavior. Having decided on her purpose, the sociologist chooses as her subject the fifteen families living on Maple Street. Her goal then becomes to group these families in a way that will be relevant to her purpose. She immediately knows that she wants to divide the neighborhood in two ways—(1) according to socioeconomic status (low-income earners, middle-income earners, and high-income earners) and (2) according to voting behavior (voters and nonvoters). However, her process of division won't be complete until she can classify individual families into her various groupings.

In confidential interviews with each family, the sociologist learns first its income and then whether or not any member of the household has voted in a state or federal election during the last four years. Based on this information, she begins to classify each family according to her established categories and at the same time to divide the neighborhood into the subclasses crucial to her study. Her work leads her to construct a diagram of her divisions/classifications (see page 251). This diagram allows the sociologist to visualize her division and classification system and its essential components: *subject, basis* or *principle of division; subclasses* or *categories;* and *conclusion.* It is clear that her ultimate conclusion depends on her ability to work back and forth between the potential divisions or subclasses and the actual families to be classified.

WHY DO WRITERS USE DIVISION AND CLASSIFICATION?

As the work of the Maple Street sociologist shows, division and classification are used primarily to demonstrate a particular point about the subject under discussion. In a paper about the emphasis a television network places on reaching various audiences, you could begin by dividing prime-time programing into suitable subclasses: shows primarily for adults, shows for families, shows for children, and so forth. You could then classify each of that network's individual programs into one of these categories. Ultimately, you would want to analyze how the programs are divided among the various categories; in this way you could make a point about which audiences the network works hardest to reach.

Classification and division can also help to explain a broadly complicated subject by reducing it to its more manageable parts. In an essay later in this chapter, for example, William Lutz focuses his discussion on identifying and classifying different types of deceptive language.

Another purpose of division and classification can be to help writers and readers make choices. A voter may classify politicians on the basis of their attitudes toward nuclear energy or abortion; *Consumer Reports* classifies refrigerators on the basis of capacity, energy efficiency, repair

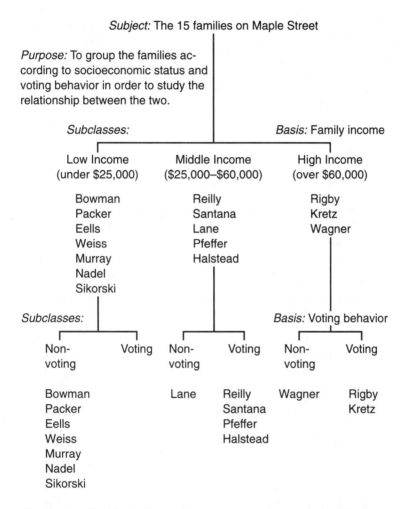

Subject: The 15 families on Maple Street

Purpose: To group the families according to socioeconomic status and voting behavior in order to study the relationship between the two.

Subclasses: *Basis:* Family income

Low Income (under $25,000)	Middle Income ($25,000–$60,000)	High Income (over $60,000)
Bowman	Reilly	Rigby
Packer	Santana	Kretz
Eells	Lane	Wagner
Weiss	Pfeffer	
Murray	Halstead	
Nadel		
Sikorski		

Subclasses: *Basis:* Voting behavior

Non-voting	Voting	Non-voting	Voting	Non-voting	Voting
Bowman		Lane	Reilly	Wagner	Rigby
Packer			Santana		Kretz
Eells			Pfeffer		
Weiss			Halstead		
Murray					
Nadel					
Sikorski					

Conclusion: On Maple Street there seems to be a relationship between socioeconomic status and voting behavior: the low-income families are nonvoters.

record, freezer size, and warranty; high school seniors classify colleges and universities on the basis of the programs available at each. In such cases, division and classification have an absolutely practical end—making a decision about whom to vote for, which refrigerator to buy, and where to apply for admission to college.

Finally, division and classification can serve as a basic organizational strategy, one that is particularly helpful in informal essays. As you'll see later in this chapter, Russell Baker's system of classification in "The Plot against People" is hardly scientific; but his three categories of inanimate objects (those that break down, those that get lost, and those that don't work) create a clear and logical structure for his tongue-in-cheek musings.

LOOKING AT DIVISION AND CLASSIFICATION

First, be sure that you understand the writer's classification system; pay particular attention to the principle of division, the specific categories or subclasses, and how individual items can be grouped. Then, see how the writer's system of dividing and classifying helps to clarify the subject for you.

Consider, for example, the following passage from E. B. White's "Here Is New York," in which he discusses New Yorkers and their city:

> There are roughly three New Yorks. There is, first, the New York of the man or woman who was born here, who takes the city for granted and accepts its size and its turbulence as natural and inevitable. Second, there is the New York of the commuter—the city that is devoured by locusts each day and spat out each night. Third, there is the New York of the person who was born somewhere else and came to New York in quest of something. Of these three trembling cities the greatest is the last—the city of final destination, the city that is a goal. It is this third city that accounts for New York's highstrung disposition, its poetical deportment, its dedication to the arts, and its incomparable achievements. Commuters give the city its tidal restlessness; natives give it solidarity and continuity; but the settlers give it passion. And whether it is a farmer arriving from Italy to set up a small grocery store in a slum, or a young girl arriving from a small town in Mississippi to escape the indignity of being observed by her neighbors, or a boy arriving from the Corn Belt with a manuscript in his suitcase and a pain in his heart, it makes no difference: each embraces New York with the intense excitement of first love, each absorbs New York with the fresh eyes of an adventurer, each generates heat and light to dwarf the Consolidated Edison Company.

In his opening sentences, White suggests a principle for dividing the population of New York, establishing his three categories on the basis of a person's relation to the city. There is the New York of the native, the New York of the worker who commutes to the city, and the New York of the immigrant. (White's only specific examples belong to his third grouping; it is easy to see, however, where any individual would be classified.) The purpose and result of White's divisions are clear and effective: they help him make a point about the characteristics of New York City, its restlessness, its solidarity, and its passion.

Division and classification can also make it considerably easier for you to follow a writer's ideas. In the following paragraphs from *Rhetorical Models for Effective Writing,* a text for college composition courses, note how J. Karl Nicholas and James R. Nicholl use this strategy to organize their discussion of prose writing:

> Prose writing may be divided into three types based on the effect the writing is supposed to have on its audience. The first, *narrative-descriptive writing,* strives to make readers see and feel as it presents a scene or series of actions witnessed or imagined by the writer. Travelogs, news accounts, short stories, and novels are examples of narrative-descriptive writing.
>
> The second kind of writing is called *exposition.* In expository writing the writer presumes that readers do not know some piece of information and therefore seeks to explain it. Textbooks, essays and reports, instruction manuals, and legal documents furnish examples of expository writing. It is the most common type of writing in both school and work situations.
>
> The third type of writing is *argumentation,* in which the writer presumes that readers already hold an opinion concerning the subject matter. It is not the purpose of argumentation to add new information (although this is sometimes necessary), but to discuss known information in a way that will persuade readers to change their minds about it, adopting the writer's opinion on the matter. Advertisements, scholarly and scientific treatises, debates, congressional speeches, and editorials offer examples of this kind of writing.
>
> It is important that you understand these divisions . . . because they will help you answer the most important question that will confront you as a writer: What is my purpose in writing? If you want to make your audience see, you will write in a narrative-descriptive mode and use narrative-descriptive techniques. If you want to inform, to educate, to add to the reader's fund of information, then you will write expositorily, using expository techniques. And if you want to change the minds of your readers, you will write persuasively, using the techniques of argumentation.

Nicholas and Nicholl divide prose writing into three basic types: narrative–descriptive writing, exposition, and argumentation. In the first sentence, they announce that their basis of division is "the effect the writing is supposed to have on its audience." The authors then briefly describe each type of subclass of writing and classify individual examples accordingly. The value of their system of division and classification is clear in the final paragraph: understanding the three types of prose writing will help a writer determine the purpose suitable to a particular task and the techniques suitable to a particular purpose. Readers of this passage are given practical information to help them make a decision; the organizational strategy helps make that information absolutely clear.

READING DIVISION AND CLASSIFICATION IN AN ANNOTATED STUDENT ESSAY

Gerald Cleary graduated with a B. S. in mathematics from the University of Vermont in 1986, and later attended law school at Cornell University. He grew up in Burlington, Vermont, but spent his last two years of high school in West Germany as a military dependent. During that time, Cleary sold stereo equipment at a large Post Exchange. In this essay, Cleary has fun dividing and classifying the different types of customers he dealt with during his time on the job.

HOW LOUD? HOW GOOD?
HOW MUCH? HOW PRETTY!
Gerald Cleary

Introduction

As stereo equipment gets better and prices go   1
down, stereo systems are becoming household necessities rather than luxuries. People are buying stereos by the thousands. During my year as a stereo salesman, I witnessed this boom firsthand. I dealt with hundreds of customers, and it didn't take long for me to learn that people buy stereos for different reasons.

Division of stereo buyers into four categories.
Labels make for ease of reference.

Eventually, though, I was able to divide all the stereo buyers into four basic categories: the looks buyer, the wattage buyer, the price buyer, and the quality buyer.

The looks buyer cannot be bothered with the   2
question of how her stereo will sound. Her only concern is how the stereo *looks*, making her the buyer

Organization: Least appealing buyer to salesperson is discussed.

least respected by the stereo salesperson. The looks buyer has an irresistible attraction to flashing lights, knobs, switches, and frivolous features. Even the loudspeakers are chosen on the basis of appearance—

the looks buyer always removes the grill to make sure
a couple of knobs are present. Enjoyment for her is
watching the output meters flash on her amplifier, or
playing with her cassette deck's remote control. No
matter what component she is shopping for, the looks
buyer always decides on the flashiest, exclaiming,
"Wait 'til my friends see this!"

*Typical statement
used as example.*

*Organization:
Second, more ap-
pealing, buyer is
discussed.*

Slightly more respected is the wattage buyer, who   3
is most easily identified by his trademark question:
"How many watts does it put out?" He will not settle
for less than 100 watts from his amp, and his speakers must be able to handle all this power. He is interested only in the volume level his stereo can produce,
for the wattage buyer always turns it up loud—so
loud that most would find it painful. The wattage
buyer genuinely enjoys his music—either soul or
heavy metal—at this volume. He is actually proud of
his stereo's ability to put out deafening noise. As a
result, the wattage buyer becomes as well-known to
his neighbors as he is to the salesperson. His competitive nature makes him especially obvious as he pays

*Typical statement
used as example.*

for his new system, telling his friend, "Man, this is
gonna blow Jones's stereo away!"

*Organization:
Third, yet more
appealing, buyer
is discussed.*

In this money-conscious world, the price buyer   4
has the understanding, if not the respect, of the salesperson. Often, she is ashamed of her budget limitations and will try to disguise herself as one of the
other types of buyers, asking, "What's the loudest receiver I can buy for $200?" Or, "What's the best turn-
table for under $150?" It is always obvious that price
is the price buyer's greatest worry—she doesn't really
want the "loudest" or the "best." The price buyer can
be spotted looking over the sale items, or staring
open-mouthed at the price tag of an expensive unit.
After asking the salesperson where the best deal in
the store can be found, she cringes at the standard

Dialogue

reply: "You usually get what you pay for." But the
price buyer still picks the cheapest model, telling her
friends, "You won't believe the deal I got on this!"

Organization: Fourth, and most appealing, buyer is discussed.

Only one category remains: the quality buyer. He 5 is the buyer most respected by the salesperson, although he is often not even in the store to buy—he may simply want to listen to the new compact-disc player tested in his latest issue of *High Fidelity*. The quality buyer never buys on impulse; he has already read about and listened to any piece of equipment he finally buys. But along with high quality comes high price. The quality buyer can often be seen fingering the price tag of that noise reduction unit he just has to own but can't yet afford. He never considers a cheaper model, preferring to wait until he can afford the high standard of quality he demands. The quality buyer shuns salespeople, believing that he knows more than them anyway. Asking him "May I help you?" is the greatest insult of all.

Conclusion: How classifying buyers helped the author do his job.

Recognizing the kind of buyer I was dealing with 6 helped me steer her to the right corner of the store. I took looks buyers to the visually dazzling working displays, and wattage buyers into the soundproof speaker rooms. I directed price buyers to the sale items, and left quality buyers alone. By the end of the year, I was able to identify the type of buyer almost instantly. My expertise paid off, making me the most successful salesperson in the store.

In reflecting on the writing of his essay, particularly his need to revise several times before producing a satisfactory draft, Gerry Cleary shed some light on the difficulty of introducing an essay of division and classification: "One of the things I spent the most time working on and did the most revisions of was the introduction to the paper. I think it's probably always a problem with division and classification, a problem of how to get the reader into your actual divisions and get going on them. How do you prepare readers for the divisions that they're about to read about? In my first draft I went out of my way trying to explain how I came up with the classifications and why I was going to do it. I went on about how I had the job for a year and had helped hundreds of customers. I began to notice that each customer seemed to belong to one of four general categories. I felt that in that rough draft of my introduction I was really going out of my way to explain where the categories came from and why I was going to write about them. I had a couple [of] people read my rough draft during class and it really didn't work for any of them. By the time I came up with the final introduction, I realized that I wanted to keep the introduction short. I didn't need to go out of my way to explain as I did in that first draft, so I kept the introductory paragraph very brief. Simply, I told readers that I was a stereo salesman and I was able to divide the buyers up into four categories. I thought that's all the readers needed to get them hooked on my essay."

Another very difficult part of an essay of division and classification is to make its purpose clear to the reader. Gerry Cleary struggled with this aspect of his essay, determining finally that "the purpose of the paper is to entertain. I think that what I tried to do is talk about buyers in general. I think these buyers aren't just stereo buyers—they're buyers of almost every high-priced product. Buyers are buyers. You have the same thing for cars, for furniture, for virtually anything. What I wanted to do was to let readers see a little part of themselves and their buying behavior. Depending on what they're looking for, they've probably been "looks buyers" at some times and "quality buyers" at others. It was my hope that people would learn something about themselves or laugh at themselves or be entertained when reading the essay. I think mainly the point of the paper is to entertain and to show us something about ourselves."

"Deciding what order to put the four categories of stereo buyers into was one of the hardest things I had to deal with," Cleary noted. "At first I was going to do it in order of least common to most common, but that wasn't really working out. At that point I knew I wanted to have something in my essay about the respect that the stereo salesperson has for each buyer. So I decided to have the respect element run through each of the four groups and put them in order of the respect—from least to most—that they received from the salesperson."

WRITING AN ESSAY OF DIVISION AND CLASSIFICATION

Begin by making certain that your subject, in fact, represents a single, coherent entity. In order to do so, you will have to set definite limits for yourself and then stick to them. For example, the sociologist whose purpose was to survey relationships between family income and voting patterns limited her study to residents of Maple Street. Including a family from Oak Street would upset the established system and, consequently, suggest the need to set new limits. Similarly, if you take as your subject for classification the student body at your school, you obviously cannot include students who are visiting from somewhere else, unless you first redefine your subject.

As you redefine your essay of classification, pay particular attention to your purpose, the divisions of your subject, your organization, and your conclusion. Your further process of planning and writing will depend on your purpose and on how that purpose leads you to divide your subject.

Purpose

The principle you use to divide your subject into classes or categories depends on your larger purpose for writing. It is crucial, then, that you determine a clear purpose for your division and classification before you begin to examine your subject in detail. For example, a study of the student body at your school might have any number of purposes: to discover how much time your classmates spend in the library during a week, to explain how financial aid is distributed among majors, to discuss the types of movies that are most popular on campus, to describe styles of dorm-room decor. The categories into which you divide the student body will vary according to your chosen purpose.

Dividing Your Subject

In many cases, once you have decided on a subject and determined a purpose, your principle of division will be obvious. The sociologist studying voting patterns on Maple Street could immediately divide her topic into three standard socioeconomic classes and into voters or nonvoters. Her important task was then to classify families according to these divisions. In a study of how much time students spend in the library, you might just as readily divide your subject into categories: for example, those who spend less than one hour a week, those who spend between one and four hours, and those who spend more than four hours. You would then use these categories as your basis for classifying various individuals.

Just make certain, first, that your principle of division is appropriate to your purpose. In determining financial aid distribution you might consider family income, academic major, or athletic participation; but obviously you would not consider dancing ability or brand of toothpaste. Second, make sure that the categories you come up with are consistent and mutually exclusive. For example, trying to work with the classes *men, women,* and *athletes* would only be confusing, because *athletes* could include *men* or *women.* Rather, the student body could be divided into *male athletes, female athletes, male nonathletes,* and *female nonathletes.* Third, make sure your categories are complete and that they will account for all the members of your subject class. In dividing the student body according to place of birth, it would be inaccurate to consider only home states; such a division could never account for foreign students or citizens born outside of the country. A diagram (such as the one of families on Maple Street) can often help you determine whether or not your classes are consistent, mutually exclusive, and complete.

For some subjects and purposes, however, appropriate divisions will not be immediately apparent. In fact, your most challenging task can often be the creation of interesting and accurate classes based on careful observation. Dividing dorm rooms according to style of decor, for example, will require some canvassing before a system of classification becomes clear. Once you have developed a system, though, you can easily classify individual rooms: *homey, spartan, childish, contemporary, cluttered,* and so on. The effect of many informal essays depends on the writer's ability to establish clever yet useful divisions and classifications that might not otherwise be noticed by the reader.

Organization

Essays of division and classification, when sensibly planned, can generally be organized with little trouble; the essay's chief divisions will reflect the classes into which the subject itself has been divided. A scratch outline can help you see those divisions and plan your order of presentation. For example, here is an outline of the preceding passage from Nicholas and Nicholl's *Rhetorical Models for Effective Writing:*

Three types of writing

1. Narrative–descriptive to make readers see and feel examples

2. Expository to explain examples

3. Argumentative to persuade examples

Such an outline clearly reveals the essay's overall structure.

Stating Your Conclusion

Your purpose for writing will determine the kinds of conclusions you reach. For example, a study of the student body might show that

67 percent of all male athletes receive financial aid, compared with 46 percent of all female athletes, 45 percent of all male nonathletes, and 44 percent of all female nonathletes. These facts could provide a conclusion in themselves, or they might be the basis for a more controversial assertion about your school's athletic program. A study of dorm-room decor might conclude with the observation that juniors and seniors tend to have more elaborate rooms than first-year students. Your conclusions will depend on the way you work back and forth between the various classes you establish and the individual objects available for you to classify.

The Plot against People

RUSSELL BAKER

Born in Virginia in 1925, Russell Baker graduated from Johns Hopkins University in 1947 and began his career as a newspaper reporter with the Baltimore Sun. *He joined the* New York Times *in 1954; after eight years with its Washington bureau covering national politics, he began writing his syndicated "Observer" column, which is now published four times a week. In 1979, he was awarded the Pulitzer Prize, journalism's highest award, for his column. Baker's books include* An American in Washington, No Cause for Panic, Poor Russell's Almanac, So This Is Depravity, *and the autobiographical* Growing Up, *which won a Pulitzer in 1983, and* The Good Times.*

In the following essay, which first appeared in the New York Times *in 1968, Baker humorously classifies inanimate objects according to the method they use "to resist man and ultimately to defeat him."*

Inanimate objects are classified scientifically into three major categories—those that break down, those that get lost, and those that don't work. 1

The goal of all inanimate objects is to resist man and ultimately to defeat him, and the three major classifications are based on the method each object uses to achieve its purpose. As a general rule, any object capable of breaking down at the moment when it is most needed will do so. The automobile is typical of the category. 2

With the cunning peculiar to its breed, the automobile never breaks down while entering a filling station which has a large staff of idle mechanics. It waits until it reaches a downtown intersection in the middle of the rush hour, or until it is fully loaded with family and luggage on the Ohio Turnpike. Thus it creates maximum inconvenience, frustration, and irritability, thereby reducing its owner's lifespan. 3

Washing machines, garbage disposals, lawn mowers, furnaces, TV sets, tape recorders, slide projectors—all are in league with the automobile to take their turn at breaking down whenever life threatens to flow smoothly for their enemies. 4

Many inanimate objects, of course, find it extremely difficult to break down. Pliers, for example, and gloves and keys are almost totally 5 incapable of breaking down. Therefore, they have had to evolve a different technique for resisting man.

They get lost. Science has still not solved the mystery of how they 6 do it, and no man has ever caught one of them in the act. The most plausible theory is that they have developed a secret method of loco-motion which they are able to conceal from human eyes.

It is not uncommon for a pair of pliers to climb all the way from the 7 cellar to the attic in its single-minded determination to raise its owner's blood pressure. Keys have been known to burrow three feet under mat-tresses. Women's purses, despite their great weight, frequently travel through six or seven rooms to find hiding space under a couch.

Scientists have been struck by the fact that things that break down 8 virtually never get lost, while things that get lost hardly ever break down. A furnace, for example, will invariably break down at the depth of the first winter cold wave, but it will never get lost. A woman's purse hardly ever breaks down; it almost invariably chooses to get lost.

Some persons believe this constitutes evidence that inanimate ob- 9 jects are not entirely hostile to man. After all, they point out, a furnace could infuriate a man even more thoroughly by getting lost than by breaking down, just as a glove could upset him far more by breaking down than by getting lost.

Not everyone agrees, however, that this indicates a conciliatory 10 attitude. Many say it merely proves that furnaces, gloves and pliers are incredibly stupid.

The third class of objects—those that don't work—is the most 11 curious of all. These include such objects as barometers, car clocks, cig-arette lighters, flashlights and toy-train locomotives. It is inaccurate, of course, to say that they *never* work. They work once, usually for the first few hours after being brought home, and then quit. Thereafter, they never work again.

In fact, it is widely assumed that they are built for the purpose of 12 not working. Some people have reached advanced ages without ever seeing some of these objects—barometers, for example—in working order.

Science is utterly baffled by the entire category. There are many 13 theories about it. The most interesting holds that the things that don't work have attained the highest state possible for an inanimate object, the state to which things that break down and things that get lost can still only aspire.

They have truly defeated man by conditioning him never to expect 14 anything of them. When his cigarette lighter won't light or his flashlight fails to illuminate, it does not raise his blood pressure. Objects that don't work have given man the only peace he receives from inanimate society.

QUESTIONS ON SUBJECT

1. Into what three broad categories does Baker classify inanimate objects? How do you suppose he arrived at these particular categories? In what other ways might inanimate objects be classified?

2. What is the relationship between objects that break down and objects that get lost?

3. According to Baker, what is the highest possible state an inanimate object can reach? What does he mean when he says, "Objects that don't work have given man the only peace he receives from inanimate society" (paragraph 14)?

4. Explain the meaning of Baker's title. Why does he use the word *plot*?

QUESTIONS ON STRATEGY

1. How does Baker make it clear at the beginning of the essay that his approach to the subject is humorous? How does he succeed in being more than simply silly? Point to several passages to illustrate your answer.

2. How does Baker organize his essay? Why do you think he waits until the conclusion to discuss objects "that don't work"? (Glossary: *Organization*)

3. How does paragraph 5 act as a transition? (Glossary: *Transitions*)

4. Baker personifies inanimate objects in his essay. What is the effect of his doing so? Identify several specific examples of personification. (Glossary: *Figures of Speech*)

5. What is the relationship between paragraphs 6 and 7? Where else does Baker use examples, as he does in paragraph 7? For what purposes does he use them? (Glossary: *Illustration*)

QUESTIONS ON LANGUAGE

1. How would you describe Baker's tone? Point to specific words and phrases to explain your answer. (Glossary: *Tone*)

2. How would you describe Baker's attitude toward inanimate objects? How does his diction help reveal his attitude? (Glossary: *Diction*)

3. Refer to your desk dictionary to determine the meanings of the following words as they are used in this selection: *cunning* (paragraph 3), *league* (4), *plausible* (6), *conciliatory* (10), *baffled* (13).

WRITING ASSIGNMENTS

1. Using Baker's essay as a model, create a system of classification for one of the following topics. Then write an essay like Baker's, classifying objects within that system.
   a. cars
   b. friends
   c. recreational activities
   d. sports
   e. drivers
   f. students
   g. music
   h. pet peeves

2. Most of us have had frustrating experiences with mechanical objects that seem to have perverse minds of their own. Write a narrative recounting one such experience—with a vending machine, a television set, an automobile, a computer, a pay telephone, a typewriter, or any other such object. Be sure to establish a clear context for your essay.

Types of Doublespeak

WILLIAM LUTZ

William Lutz, professor of English at Rutgers University and chair of the National Council of Teachers of English's Committee on Public Doublespeak, has long been a watchdog of public officials who use language to "mislead, distort, deceive, inflate, circumvent, and obfuscate." Each year the committee presents the Orwell Awards, recognizing the most outrageous uses of public doublespeak in the world of government and business. In the following essay, Lutz begins with a definition of doublespeak and then moves on to classify its major types.

There are no potholes in the streets of Tucson, Arizona, just "pavement deficiencies." The Reagan Administration didn't propose any new taxes, just "revenue enhancement" through new "user's fees." Those aren't bums on the street, just "non-goal oriented members of society." There are no more poor people, just "fiscal underachievers." There was no robbery of an automatic teller machine, just an "unauthorized withdrawal." The patient didn't die because of medical malpractice, it was just a "diagnostic misadventure of a high magnitude." The U.S. Army doesn't kill the enemy anymore, it just "services the target." And the doublespeak goes on.

Doublespeak is language that pretends to communicate but really doesn't. It is language that makes the bad seem good, the negative appear positive, the unpleasant appear attractive or at least tolerable. Doublespeak is language that avoids or shifts responsibility, language that is at variance with its real or purported meaning. It is language that conceals or prevents thought; rather than extending thought, doublespeak limits it.

Doublespeak is not a matter of subjects and verbs agreeing; it is a matter of words and facts agreeing. Basic to doublespeak is incongruity, the incongruity between what is said or left unsaid, and what really is. It is the incongruity between the word and the referent, between seem and be, between the essential function of language—communication—and what doublespeak does—mislead, distort, deceive, inflate, circumvent, obfuscate.

How can you spot doublespeak? Most of the time you will recognize doublespeak when you see or hear it. But, if you have any doubts, you can identify doublespeak just by answering these questions: Who is saying what to whom, under what conditions and circumstances, with what intent, and with what results? Answering these questions will usually help you identify as doublespeak language that appears to be legitimate or that at first glance doesn't even appear to be doublespeak.

There are at least four kinds of doublespeak. The first is the euphemism, an inoffensive or positive word or phrase used to avoid a harsh, unpleasant, or distasteful reality. But a euphemism can also be a tactful word or phrase which avoids directly mentioning a painful reality, or it can be an expression used out of concern for the feelings of someone else, or to avoid directly discussing a topic subject to a social or cultural taboo.

When you use a euphemism because of your sensitivity for someone's feelings or out of concern for a recognized social or cultural taboo, it is not doublespeak. For example, you express your condolences that someone has "passed away" because you do not want to say to a grieving person, "I'm sorry your father is dead." When you use the euphemism "passed away," no one is misled. Moreover, the euphemism functions here not just to protect the feelings of another person, but to communicate also your concern for that person's feelings during a period of mourning. When you excuse yourself to go to the "rest room," or you mention that someone is "sleeping with" or "involved with" someone else, you do not mislead anyone about your meaning, but you do respect the social taboos about discussing bodily functions and sex in direct terms. You also indicate your sensitivity to the feelings of your audience, which is usually considered a mark of courtesy and good manners.

However, when a euphemism is used to mislead or deceive, it becomes doublespeak. For example, in 1984 the U.S. State Department announced that it would no longer use the word "killing" in its annual report on the status of human rights in countries around the world. Instead, it would use the phrase "unlawful or arbitrary deprivation of life," which the department claimed was more accurate. Its real purpose for using this phrase was simply to avoid discussing the embarrassing situation of goverment-sanctioned killings in countries that are supported by the United States and have been certified by the United States as respecting the human rights of their citizens. This use of a euphemism constitutes doublespeak, since it is designed to mislead, to cover up the unpleasant. Its real intent is at variance with its apparent intent. It is language designed to alter our perception of reality.

The Pentagon, too, avoids discussing unpleasant realities when it refers to bombs and artillery shells that fall on civilian targets as "incontinent ordnance." And in 1977 the Pentagon tried to slip funding for the neutron bomb unnoticed into an appropriations bill by calling it a "radiation enhancement device."

A second kind of doublespeak is jargon, the specialized language of 9 a trade, profession, or similar group, such as that used by doctors, lawyers, engineers, educators, or car mechanics. Jargon can serve an important and useful function. Within a group, jargon functions as a kind of verbal shorthand that allows members of the group to communicate with each other clearly, efficiently, and quickly. Indeed, it is a mark of membership in the group to be able to use and understand the group's jargon.

But jargon, like the euphemism, can also be doublespeak. It can 10 be—and often is—pretentious, obscure, and esoteric terminology used to give an air of profundity, authority, and prestige to speakers and their subject matter. Jargon as doublespeak often makes the simple appear complex, the ordinary profound, the obvious insightful. In this sense it is used not to express but impress. With such doublespeak, the act of smelling something becomes "organoleptic analysis," glass becomes "fused silicate," a crack in a metal support beam becomes a "discontinuity," conservative economic policies become "distributionally conservative notions."

Lawyers, for example, speak of an "involuntary conversion" of prop- 11 erty when discussing the loss or destruction of property through theft, accident, or condemnation. If your house burns down or if your car is stolen, you have suffered an involuntary conversion of your property. When used by lawyers in a legal situation, such jargon is a legitimate use of language, since lawyers can be expected to understand the term.

However, when a member of a specialized group uses its jargon 12 to communicate with a person outside the group, and uses it knowing that the nonmember does not understand such language, then there is doublespeak. For example, on May 9, 1978, a National Airlines 727 airplane crashed while attempting to land at the Pensacola, Florida airport. Three of the fifty-two passengers aboard the airplane were killed. As a result of the crash, National made an after-tax insurance benefit of $1.7 million, or an extra 18¢ a share dividend for its stockholders. Now National Airlines had two problems: It did not want to talk about one of its airplanes crashing, and it had to account for the $1.7 million when it issued its annual report to its stockholders. National solved the problem by inserting a footnote in its annual report which explained that the $1.7 million income was due to "the involuntary conversion of a 727." National thus acknowledged the crash of its airplane and the subsequent profit it made from the crash, without once mentioning the accident or the deaths. However, because airline officials knew that most stockholders in the company, and indeed most of the general public, were not familiar with legal jargon, the use of such jargon constituted doublespeak.

A third kind of doublespeak is gobbledygook or bureaucratese. 13 Basically, such doublespeak is simply a matter of piling on words, of overwhelming the audience with words, the bigger the words and the longer the sentences the better. Alan Greenspan, then chair of President Nixon's Council of Economic Advisors, was quoted in *The Philadelphia Inquirer* in 1974 as having testified before a Senate committee that "It is a tricky problem to find the particular calibration in timing that would be appropriate to stem the acceleration in risk premiums created by falling incomes without prematurely aborting the decline in the inflation-generated risk premiums."

Nor has Mr. Greenspan's language changed since then. Speaking to 14 the meeting of the Economic Club of New York in 1988, Mr. Greenspan, now Federal Reserve chair, said "I guess I should warn you, if I turn out to be particularly clear, you've probably misunderstood what I've said." Mr. Greenspan's doublespeak doesn't seem to have held back his career.

Sometimes gobbledygook may sound impressive, but when the 15 quote is later examined in print it doesn't even make sense. During the 1988 presidential campaign, vice-presidential candidate Senator Dan Quayle explained the need for a strategic-defense initiative by saying, "Why wouldn't an enhanced deterrent, a more stable peace, a better prospect to denying the ones who enter conflict in the first place to have a reduction of offensive systems and an introduction to defensive capability? I believe this is the route the country will eventually go."

The investigation into the Challenger disaster in 1986 revealed the 16 doublespeak of gobbledygook and bureaucratese used by too many involved in the shuttle program. When Jesse Moore, NASA's associate administrator, was asked if the performance of the shuttle program had improved with each launch or if it had remained the same, he answered, "I think our performance in terms of the liftoff performance and in terms of the orbital performance, we knew more about the envelope we were operating under, and we have been pretty accurately staying in that. And so I would say the performance has not by design drastically improved. I think we have been able to characterize the performance more as a function of our launch experience as opposed to it improving as a function of time." While this language may appear to be jargon, a close look will reveal that it is really just gobbledygook laced with jargon. But you really have to wonder if Mr. Moore had any idea what he was saying.

The fourth kind of doublespeak is inflated language that is designed 17
to make the ordinary seem extraordinary; to make everyday things
seem impressive; to give an air of importance to people, situations, or
things that would not normally be considered important; to make the
simple seem complex. Often this kind of doublespeak isn't hard to spot,
and it is usually pretty funny. While car mechanics may be called "auto-
motive internists," elevator operators members of the "vertical transportation corps," used cars "pre-owned" or "experienced cars," and
black-and-white television sets described as having "non-multicolor
capability," you really aren't misled all that much by such language.

However, you may have trouble figuring out that, when Chrysler 18
"initiates a career alternative enhancement program," it is really laying off five thousand workers; or that "negative patient care outcome"
means the patient died; or that "rapid oxidation" means a fire in a
nuclear power plant.

The doublespeak of inflated language can have serious conse- 19
quences. In Pentagon doublespeak, "pre-emptive counterattack" means
that American forces attacked first; "engaged the enemy on all sides"
means American troops were ambushed; "backloading of augmenta-
tion personnel" means a retreat by American troops. In the doublespeak of the military, the 1983 invasion of Grenada was conducted not
by the U.S. Army, Navy, Air Force, and Marines, but by the "Caribbean
Peace Keeping Forces." But then, according to the Pentagon, it wasn't
an invasion, it was a "predawn vertical insertion."

QUESTIONS ON SUBJECT

1. What, according to Lutz, is doublespeak? What are its characteristics?

2. What precisely does Lutz mean when he writes in paragraph 3 that doublespeak "is the incongruity between the word and the referent, between
   seem and be . . ."?

3. How does Lutz say one should detect doublespeak? Have you detected
   examples of doublespeak in the language you encounter?

4. Are euphemism, jargon, bureaucratese, and inflated language another way
   of describing doublespeak? Are all uses of euphemism, jargon, bureaucratese, and inflated language to be avoided? Why or why not?

QUESTIONS ON STRATEGY

1. How well does Lutz's first paragraph function as a beginning for his essay?
   (Glossary: *Beginnings and Endings*)

2. Lutz discusses four types of doublespeak. How does his classification help to clarify his discussion of the language of distortion? Explain.
3. Lutz uses the word *gobbledygook*. Does he define it? How would you define it?
4. Where in his essay does Lutz define doublespeak (Glossary: *Definition*)? Try defining doublespeak in your own words.
5. Lutz is careful to illustrate each of his points with examples. Why is it important for him to use plenty of examples in an essay like this? What do his examples reveal about Lutz's expertise on this subject? (Glossary: *Illustration*)

QUESTIONS ON LANGUAGE

1. Choose a profession (e.g., medicine, the law, education) and prepare a list of jargon terms used in that profession. Evaluate the usefulness of the terms you have gathered. Are they all necessary or could simpler language be used?
2. Refer to your desk dictionary to determine the meanings of the following words as they are used in this selection: *incongruity* (paragraph 3), *circumvent* (3), *obfuscate* (3), *condolences* (6), *"incontinent ordnance"* (8), *esoteric* (10).

WRITING SUGGESTIONS

1. Test the principle of Lutz's division and classification by finding a dozen or two new examples of doublespeak in your own reading, listening to the radio, and television viewing. Write an essay in which you discuss how your examples fit or fail to fit Lutz's classification.
2. Write an essay in which you argue that the consequences of doublespeak can run the range from benign or harmless to seriously malevolent, even deadly, and that as responsible citizens we need to become more sensitive to doublespeak and call the public's attention to it whenever we encounter it.

The Truth about Lying

Judith Viorst

Judith Viorst, poet, journalist, author of children's books, and novelist, was born in 1931. She has chronicled her life in such books as It's Hard to Be Hip Over Thirty and Other Tragedies of Married Life (1968), How Did I Get to Be Forty and Other Atrocities (1976), *and* When Did I Stop Being Twenty and Other Injustices: Selected Prose from Single to Mid-Life (1987). *In 1981 she went back to school, taking courses at the Washington Psychoanalytic Institute. This study, along with her personal experience of psychoanalysis, helped to inspire* Necessary Losses (1986), *a popular and critical success. Combining theory, poetry, interviews, and anecdotes, Viorst approaches personal growth as a shedding of illusions. Her most recent work, a novel,* Murdering Mr. Monti: A Merry Little Tale of Sex and Violence, *was published in 1994.*

In this essay, first published in the March 1981 issue of Redbook *where Viorst works as a contributing editor, the author approaches lying with delicacy and candor as she carefully classifies the different types of lies we all encounter.*

I've been wanting to write on a subject that intrigues and chal- 1
lenges me: the subject of lying. I've found it very difficult to do. Everyone I've talked to has a quite intense and personal but often rather intolerant point of view about what we can—and can never *never*—tell lies about. I've finally reached the conclusion that I can't present any ultimate conclusions, for too many people would promptly disagree. Instead, I'd like to present a series of moral puzzles, all concerned with lying. I'll tell you what I think about them. Do you agree?

SOCIAL LIES

Most of the people I've talked with say that they find social lying 2
acceptable and necessary. They think it's the civilized way for folks to behave. Without these little white lies, they say, our relationships would be short and brutish and nasty. It's arrogant, they say, to insist on being so incorruptible and so brave that you cause other people unnecessary

embarrassment or pain by compulsively assailing them with your honesty. I basically agree. What about you?

Will you say to people, when it simply isn't true, "I like your new   3
hairdo," "You're looking much better," "It's so nice to see you," "I had a wonderful time"?

Will you praise hideous presents and homely kids?   4

Will you decline invitations with "We're busy that night—so sorry   5
we can't come," when the truth is you'd rather stay home than dine with the So-and-sos?

And even though, as I do, you may prefer the polite evasion of   6
"You really cooked up a storm" instead of "The soup"—which tastes like warmed-over coffee—"is wonderful," will you, if you must, proclaim it wonderful?

There's one man I know who absolutely refuses to tell social lies. "I 7
can't play that game," he says; "I'm simply not made that way." And his answer to the argument that saying nice things to someone doesn't cost anything is, "Yes, it does—it destroys your credibility." Now, he won't, unsolicited, offer his views on the painting you just bought, but you don't ask his frank opinion unless you want *frank*, and his silence at those moments when the rest of us liars are muttering, "Isn't it lovely?" is, for the most part, eloquent enough. My friend does not indulge in what he calls "flattery, false praise and mellifluous comments." When others tell fibs he will not go along. He says that social lying is lying, that little white lies are still lies. And he feels that telling lies is morally wrong. What about you?

PEACE-KEEPING LIES

Many people tell peace-keeping lies; lies designed to avoid irrita-   8
tion or argument; lies designed to shelter the liar from possible blame or pain; lies (or so it is rationalized) designed to keep trouble at bay without hurting anyone.

I tell these lies at times, and yet I always feel they're wrong. I   9
understand why we tell them, but still they feel wrong. And whenever I lie so that someone won't disapprove of me or think less of me or holler at me, I feel I'm a bit of a coward, I feel I'm dodging responsibility, I feel . . . guilty. What about you?

Do you, when you're late for a date because you overslept, say that   10
you're late because you got caught in a traffic jam?

Do you, when you forget to call a friend, say that you called several 11
times but the line was busy?

Do you, when you didn't remember that it was your father's birth- 12
day, say that his present must be delayed in the mail?

And when you're planning a weekend in New York City and you're 13
not in the mood to visit your mother, who lives there, do you
conceal—with a lie, if you must—the fact that you'll be in New York?
Or do you have the courage—or is it the cruelty?—to say, "I'll be in
New York, but sorry—I don't plan on seeing you"?

(Dave and his wife Elaine have two quite different points of view on 14
this very subject. He calls her a coward. She says she's being wise. He
says she must assert her right to visit New York sometimes and not see
her mother. To which she always patiently replies: "Why should we
have useless fights? My mother's too old to change. We get along much
better when I lie to her.")

Finally, do you keep the peace by telling your husband lies on the 15
subject of money? Do you reduce what you really paid for your shoes?
And in general do you find yourself ready, willing and able to lie to him
when you make absurd mistakes or lose or break things?

"I used to have a romantic idea that part of intimacy was confessing 16
every dumb thing that you did to your husband. But after a couple of
years of that," says Laura, "have I changed my mind!"

And having changed her mind, she finds herself telling peace- 17
keeping lies. And yes, I tell them too. What about you?

PROTECTIVE LIES

Protective lies are lies folks tell—often quite serious lies—because 18
they're convinced that the truth would be too damaging. They lie because they feel there are certain human values that supersede the wrong
of having lied. They lie, not for personal gain, but because they believe
it's for the good of the person they're lying to. They lie to those they
love, to those who trust them most of all, on the grounds that breaking
this trust is justified.

They may lie to their children on money or marital matters. 19

They may lie to the dying about the state of their health. 20

They may lie about adultery, and not—or so they insist—to save 21
their own hide, but to save the heart and the pride of the men they are
married to.

They may lie to their closest friend because the truth about her tal- 22
ents or son or psyche would be—or so they insist—utterly devastating.

I sometimes tell such lies, but I'm aware that it's quite presump- 23
tuous to claim I know what's best for others to know. That's called

playing God. That's called manipulation and control. And we never can be sure, once we start to juggle lies, just where they'll land, exactly where they'll roll.

And furthermore, we may find ourselves lying in order to back up 24 the lies that are backing up the lie we initially told.

And furthermore—let's be honest—if conditions were reversed, we 25 certainly wouldn't want anyone lying to us.

Yet, having said all that, I still believe that there are times when 26 protective lies must nonetheless be told. What about you?

If your Dad had a very bad heart and you had to tell him some bad 27 family news, which would you choose: to tell him the truth or lie?

If your former husband failed to send his monthly child-support 28 check and in other ways behaved like a total rat, would you allow your children—who believed he was simply wonderful—to continue to believe that he was wonderful?

If your dearly beloved brother selected a wife whom you deeply 29 disliked, would you reveal your feelings or would you fake it?

And if you were asked, after making love, "And how was that for 30 you?" would you reply, if it wasn't too good, "Not too good"?

Now, some would call a sex lie unimportant, little more than social 31 lying, a simple act of courtesy that makes all human intercourse run smoothly. And some would say all sex lies are bad news and unacceptably protective. Because, says Ruth, "a man with an ego that fragile doesn't need your lies—he needs a psychiatrist." Still others feel that sex lies are indeed protective lies, more serious than simple social lying, and yet at times they tell them on the grounds that when it comes to matters sexual, everybody's ego is somewhat fragile.

"If most of the time things go well in sex," says Sue, "I think 32 you're allowed to dissemble when they don't. I can't believe it's good to say, 'Last night was four stars, darling, but tonight's performance rates only a half.'"

I'm inclined to agree with Sue. What about you?   33

TRUST-KEEPING LIES

Another group of lies are trust-keeping lies, lies that involve trian- 34 gulation, with *A* (that's you) telling lies to *B* on behalf of *C* (whose trust you'd promised to keep). Most people concede that once you've agreed not to betray a friend's confidence, you can't betray it, even if you must lie. But I've talked with people who don't want you telling them anything that they might be called on to lie about.

"I don't tell lies for myself," says Fran, "and I don't want to have 35 to tell them for other people." Which means, she agrees, that if her best friend is having an affair, she absolutely doesn't want to know about it.

"Are you saying," her best friend asks, "that if I went off with a 36 lover and I asked you to tell my husband I'd been with you, that you wouldn't lie for me, that you'd betray me?"

Fran is very pained but very adamant. "I wouldn't want to betray 37 you, so . . . don't ask me."

Fran's best friend is shocked. What about you? 38

Do you believe you can have close friends if you're not prepared to 39 receive their deepest secrets?

Do you believe you must always lie for your friends? 40

Do you believe, if your friend tells a secret that turns out to be quite 41 immoral or illegal, that once you've promised to keep it, you must keep it?

And what if your friend were your boss—if you were perhaps one 42 of the President's men—would you betray or lie for him over, say, Watergate?

As you can see, these issues get terribly sticky. 43

It's my belief that once we've promised to keep a trust, we must tell 44 lies to keep it. I also believe that we can't tell Watergate lies. And if these two statements strike you as quite contradictory, you're right—they're quite contradictory. But for now they're the best I can do. What about you?

Some say that truth will out and thus you might as well tell the truth. 45 Some say you can't regain the trust that lies lose. Some say that even though the truth may never be revealed, our lies pervert and damage our relationships. Some say . . . well, here's what some of them have to say.

"I'm a coward," says Grace, "about telling close people important, 46 difficult truths. I find that I'm unable to carry it off. And so if something is bothering me, it keeps building up inside till I end up just not seeing them any more."

"I lie to my husband on sexual things, but I'm furious," says Joyce, 47 "that he's too insensitive to know I'm lying."

"I suffer most from the misconception that children can't take 48 the truth," says Emily. "But I'm starting to see that what's harder and more damaging for them is being told lies, is *not* being told the truth."

"I'm afraid," says Joan, "that we often wind up feeling a bit of contempt 49 for the people we lie to."

And then there are those who have no talent for lying. 50

"Over the years, I tried to lie," a friend of mine explained, "but I 51 always got found out and I always got punished. I guess I gave myself

away because I feel guilty about any kind of lying. It looks as if I'm
stuck with telling the truth."

For those of us, however, who are good at telling lies, for those of   52
us who lie and don't get caught, the question of whether or not to lie
can be a hard and serious moral problem. I liked the remark of a friend
of mine who said, "I'm willing to lie. But just as a last resort—the
truth's always better."

"Because," he explained, "though others may completely accept   53
the lie I'm telling, I don't."

I tend to feel that way too.   54

What about you?   55

QUESTIONS ON SUBJECT

1. Why is Viorst wary of giving advice on this subject?

2. Into what main categories does Viorst divide lying? Do you agree with her
   division?

3. Viorst admits to contradicting herself in her section on trust-keeping lies.
   Where else do you see contradictions, either the author's or our own?

4. In telling a protective lie, what assumption would you make?

5. What's the difference between a peace-keeping lie and a protective lie?

QUESTIONS ON STRATEGY

1. Viorst recognizes that many people have steadfast views on lying. What
   accommodations does she make for this audience? How does she challenge
   this audience? (Glossary: *Audience*)

2. There are at least two parties involved in a lie, a liar and a listener. How
   much significance does the author give to each of these?

3. Viorst presents the reader with a series of moral puzzles. Do these puzzles
   succeed in encouraging further thought on the subject of lying? Why or
   why not?

4. Viorst chooses an unconventional way to wrap up her essay. What do you
   think she's doing in this last section, beginning in paragraph 45? Does
   this ending intensify any of the points she has made? Explain. (Glossary:
   Beginnings and Endings)

QUESTIONS ON LANGUAGE

1. How would you characterize Viorst's diction in this essay? Consider her
   subject and the way she approaches this essay. Cite specific examples of her
   word choice to support your conclusions.

2. Refer to your desk dictionary to determine the meaning of the following words as they are used in this selection: *mellifluous* (paragraph 7), *supersede* (18).

WRITING SUGGESTIONS

1. Write a response to Viorst's essay. Is she too wishy-washy about lying? Do you feel there are situations in which a person absolutely should not lie? What are they?

2. Viorst wrote this essay for *Redbook,* a woman's magazine. Do you think her categories work well for men, too? Do you think men are more likely to tell lies from a certain category? Explain. If you were writing this essay for a male audience, would you change the examples? If so, how would you change them? If not, why not?

Hair

MARCIA ALDRICH

Marcia Aldrich currently teaches at Michigan State University where she specializes in twentieth-century poetry. Selected for inclusion in Best American Essays 1993, *"Hair" first appeared in the* Northwest Review. *In addition, "Hair" is part of a larger manuscript of prose pieces, inspired by letters of the alphabet, called* The X-Woman. *At present Aldrich is writing "Lethal Brevity: Louise Bogan, Modernism, and the Feminine Lyric."*

In the following essay, Aldrich not only classifies the various hair styles of the women in her family, she presents hair style and the individual's attitude toward it as representative of a wide variety of character traits, one's position in the family, and as a record of one's movement across the years.

I've been around and seen the Taj Mahal and the Grand Canyon and Marilyn Monroe's footprints outside Grauman's Chinese Theater, but I've never seen my mother wash her own hair. After my mother married, she never washed her own hair again. As a girl and an unmarried woman—yes—but, in my lifetime, she never washed her hair with her own two hands. Upon matrimony, she began weekly treks to the beauty salon where Julie washed and styled her hair. Her appointment on Fridays at two o'clock was never canceled or rescheduled; it was the bedrock of her week, around which she pivoted and planned. These two hours were indispensable to my mother's routine, to her sense of herself and what, as a woman, she should concern herself with—not to mention their being her primary source of information about all sorts of things she wouldn't otherwise come to know. With Julie my mother discussed momentous decisions concerning hair color and the advancement of age and what could be done about it, hair length and its effect upon maturity, when to perm and when not to perm, the need to proceed with caution when a woman desperately wanted a major change in her life like dumping her husband or sending back her newborn baby and the only change she could effect was a change in her hair. That was what Julie called a "dangerous time" in a woman's life. When my mother spoke to Julie, she spoke in conspiratorial, almost confessional, tones I had never heard before. Her voice was usually tense, on guard, the laughter forced, but with Julie it dropped much lower, the timbre darker than the upper-register shrills sounded at home. And most remarkably, she listened to everything Julie said.

As a child I was puzzled by the way my mother's sense of self-worth and mood seemed dependent upon how she thought her hair looked, how the search for the perfect hair style never ended. Just as Mother seemed to like her latest color and cut, she began to agitate for a new look. The cut seemed to have become a melancholy testimony, in my mother's eyes, to time's inexorable passage. Her hair never stood in and of itself; it was always moored to a complex set of needs and desires her hair couldn't in itself satisfy. She wanted her hair to illuminate the relationship between herself and the idea of motion while appearing still, for example. My mother wanted her hair to be fashioned into an event with a complicated narrative past. However, the more my mother attempted to impose a hair style pulled from an idealized image of herself, the more the hair style seemed to be at odds with my mother. The more the hair style became substantial, the more the woman underneath was obscured. She'd riffle through women's magazines and stare for long dreamy hours at a particular woman's coiffure. Then she'd ask my father in an artificially casual voice: "How do you think I'd look with really short hair?" or "Would blonde become me?" My father never committed himself to an opinion. He had learned from long experience that no response he made could turn out well; anything he said would be used against him, if not in the immediate circumstances, down the line, for my mother never forgot anything anyone ever said about her hair. My father's refusal to engage the "hair question" irritated her.

So too, I was puzzled to see that unmarried women washed their own hair, and married women, in my mother's circle at least, by some unwritten dictum never touched their own hair. I began studying before and after photographs of my mother's friends. These photographs were all the same. In the pre-married mode, their hair was soft and unformed. After the wedding, the women's hair styles bore the stamp of property, looked constructed from grooming talents not their own, hair styles I'd call produced, requiring constant upkeep and technique to sustain the considerable loft and rigidity—in short, the antithesis of anything I might naively call natural. This was hair no one touched, crushed, or ran fingers through. One poked and prodded various hair masses back into formation. This hair presented obstacles to embrace, the scent of the hair spray alone warded off man, child, and pests. I never saw my father stroke my mother's head. Children whimpered when my mother came home fresh from the salon with a potent do. Just when a woman's life was supposed to be opening out into daily affection, *the* sanctioned affection of husband and children, the women

of my mother's circle encased themselves in a helmet of hair not unlike
Medusa's.

In so-called middle age, my mother's hair never moved, never blew, 4
never fell in her face: her hair became a museum piece. When she went
to bed, she wore a blue net, and when she took short showers, short
because, after all, she wasn't washing her hair and she was seldom dirty,
she wore a blue plastic cap for the sake of preservation. From one
appointment to the next, the only change her hair could be said to
undergo was to become crestfallen. Taking extended vacations presented problems sufficiently troublesome to rule out countries where
she feared no beauty parlors existed. In the beginning, my parents took
over-nighters, then week jaunts, and thereby avoided the whole hair
dilemma. Extending their vacations to two weeks was eventually managed by my mother applying more hair spray and sleeping sitting up.
But after the two-week mark had been reached, she was forced to either
return home or venture into an unfamiliar salon and subject herself to
scrutiny, the kind of scrutiny that leaves no woman unscathed. Then
she faced Julie's disapproval, for no matter how expensive and expert
the salon, my mother's hair was to be lamented. Speaking just for myself, I had difficulty distinguishing Julie's cunning from the stranger's.
In these years my mother's hair looked curled, teased, and sprayed into
a waved tossed monument with holes poked through for glasses. She
believed the damage done to her hair was tangible proof she had been
somewhere, like stickers on her suitcases.

My older sisters have worked out their hair positions differently. 5
My oldest sister's solution has been to fix upon one hair style and never
change it. She wants to be thought of in a singular fashion. She may
vary the length from long to longer, but that is the extent of her al-
teration. Once, after having her first baby, the "dangerous time" for
women, she recklessly cut her hair to just below the ear. She immediately regretted the decision and began growing it back as she walked
home from the salon, vowing not to repeat the mistake. Her signature
is dark, straight hair pulled heavily off her face in a large silver clip,
found at any Woolworth's. When one clip breaks, she buys another just
like it. My mother hates the timelessness of my sister's hair. She equates
it with a refusal to face growing old. My mother says, "It's immature to
wear your hair the same way all your life." My sister replies,

"It's immature to never stop thinking about your hair. If this hair 6
style was good enough when I was twenty, it's good enough when I'm
forty, if not better."

"But what about change?" my mother asks. 7

"Change is overrated," my sister says, flipping her long hair over 8 her shoulder definitively. "I feel my hair."

My other sister was born with thin, lifeless, nondescript hair: a cross 9 she has had to bear. Even in the baby pictures, the limp strands plastered on her forehead in question marks wear her down. Shame and self-effacement are especially plain in the pictures where she posed with our eldest sister, whose dark hair dominates the frame. She's spent her life attempting to disguise the real state of her hair. Some years she'd focus on style, pulling it back in ponytails so that from the front no one could see there wasn't much hair in the back. She tried artless, even messy styles—as if she had just tied it up any old way before taking a bath or bunched it to look deliberately snarled. There were the weird years punctuated by styles that looked as if she had taken sugar water and lemon juice and squeezed them onto her wet hair and then let them crystallize. The worst style was when she took her hair and piled it on the top of her head in a cone shape and then crimped the ponytail into a zigzag. Personally, I thought she had gone too far. No single approach solved the hair problem, and so now, in maturity, she combines the various phases of attack in hope something will work. She frosts both the gray strands and the pale brown, and then perms for added body and thickness. She's forced to keep her hair short because chemicals do tend to destroy. My mother admires my sister's determination to transform herself, and never more than in my sister's latest assault upon middle age. No one has known for many years nor does anyone remember what the untreated color or texture of either my mother's or my sister's hair might be.

As the youngest by twelve years, there was little to distract Mother's 10 considerable attention from the problem of my hair. I had cowlicks, a remarkable number of them, which like little arrows shot across my scalp. They refused to be trained, to lie down quietly in the same direction as the rest of my hair. One at the front insisted on sticking straight up while two on either side of my ears jutted out seeking sun. The lack of uniformity, the fact that my hair had a mind of its own, infuriated my mother and she saw to it that Julie cut my hair as short as possible in order to curtail its wanton expression. Sitting in the swivel chair before the mirror while Julie snipped, I felt invisible, as if I was unattached to my hair.

Just when I started to menstruate, my mother decided the battle 11 plan needed a change, and presto, the page boy replaced the pixie. Having not outgrown the thicket of cowlicks, Mother bought a spectrum of brightly colored stretch bands to hold my hair back off my face. Then she attached thin pink plastic curlers with snap-on lids to the ends of my hair to make them flip up or under, depending on her mood. The stretch bands pressed my hair flat until the very bottom, at which point the ends formed a tunnel with ridges from the roller caps—a point of emphasis, she called it. Coupled with the aquamarine eyeglasses, newly acquired, I looked like an overgrown insect that had none of its kind to bond with.

However, I was not alone. Unless you were the last in a long line 12 of sisters, chances were good that your hair would not go unnoticed by your mother. Each of my best friends was subjected to her mother's hair dictatorship, although with entirely different results. Perry Jensen's mother insisted that all five of her daughters peroxide their hair blonde and pull it back into hair ponytails. All the girls' hair turned green in the summer from chlorine. Melissa Matson underwent a look-alike "home perm" with her mother, an experience she never did recover from. She developed a phobic reaction to anything synthetic, which made life very expensive. Not only did mother and daughter have identical tight curls and wear mother-daughter outfits, later they had look-alike nose jobs.

In my generation, many women who survived hair bondage to 13 their mothers now experiment with hair styles as one would test a new design: to see how it works, what it will withstand, and how it can be improved. Testing requires boldness, for often the style fails dramatically, as when I had my hair cut about a half inch long at the top, and it stood straight up like a tacky shag carpet. I had to live with the results, bear daily witness to the kinks in its design for nine months until strategies of damage control could be deployed. But sometimes women I know create a look that startles in its originality and suggests a future not yet realized.

The women in my family divide into two general groups: those 14 who fasten upon one style, become identified with a look, and are impervious to change, weathering the years steadfastly, and those who, for a variety of reasons, are in the business of transforming themselves. In my sister's case, the quest for perfect hair originates in a need to mask her own appearance; in my mother's case, she wants to achieve a beauty of person unavailable in her own life story. Some women seek transformation, not out of dissatisfaction with themselves, but because hair change is a means of moving along in their lives. These women create portraits of themselves that won't last forever, a new hair style will write over the last.

Since my mother dictated my hair, I never took a stand on the hair 15 issue. In maturity, I'm incapable of assuming a coherent or consistent philosophy. I have wayward hair: it's always becoming something else. The moment it arrives at a recognizable style, it begins to undo itself, it grows, the sun colors it, it waves. When one hair pin goes in, another seems to come out. Sometimes I think I should follow my oldest sister— she claims to never give more than a passing thought to her hair and can't see what all the angst is about. She asks, "Don't women have better things to think about than their hair?"

I bite back: "But don't you think hair should reflect who you are?" 16

"To be honest, I've never thought about it. I don't think so. Cut 17 your hair the same way, and lose yourself in something else. You're distracted from the real action."

I want to do what my sister says, but when I walk out into shop- 18 lined streets, I automatically study women's hair and always with the same question: How did they arrive at their hair? Lately, I've been feeling more and more like my mother. I hadn't known how to resolve the dilemma until I found Rhonda. I don't know if I found Rhonda or made her up. She is not a normally trained hairdresser: she has a different set of eyes, unaffected. One day while out driving around to no place in particular, at the bottom of a hill, I found: "Rhonda's Hair Salon—Don't Look Back" written on a life-size cardboard image of Rhonda. Her shop was on the top of this steep orchard-planted hill, on a plateau with a great view that opened out and went on forever. I parked my car at the bottom and walked up. Zigzagging all the way up the hill, leaning against or sticking out from behind the apple trees, were more life-size cardboard likenesses of Rhonda. Except for the explosive sunbursts in her hair, no two signs were the same. At the bottom, she wore long red hair falling below her knees and covering her entire body like a shawl. As I climbed the hill, Rhonda's hair gradually became shorter and shorter, and each length was cut differently, until when I reached the top, her head was shaved and glistening in the sun. I found Rhonda herself out under one of the apple trees wearing running shoes. Her hair was long and red and looked as if it had never been cut. She told me she had no aspirations to be a hairdresser, "she just fell into it." "I see hair," she continued, "as an extension of the head and therefore I try to do hair with a lot of thought." Inside there were no mirrors, no swivel chairs, no machines of torture with their accompanying stink. She said, "Nothing is permanent, nothing is forever. Don't feel hampered or hemmed in by the shape of your face or the shape of your past. Hair is vital, sustains mistakes, can be born again. You don't have to marry it. Now tip back and put your head into my hands."

QUESTIONS ON SUBJECT

1. What categories of hair does the author explore in her essay? Does the author fit in an established category or does she create her own? Explain your answer.

2. Aldrich's mother and the younger of her two sisters both constantly change their hairstyles. According to the author, what makes each distinct?

3. What hair ritual did the women friends of Aldrich's mother practice on their daughters? Has the author freed herself from this legacy? Explain.

4. Aldrich writes, "I don't know if I found Rhonda or made her up." Why might the author have made Rhonda up? What purpose does Rhonda serve in this essay?

QUESTIONS ON STRATEGY

1. Reread Aldrich's last paragraph. What conclusions does the author come to? How does she characterize Rhonda? How does Rhonda feel about hair? How do the author's categories logically lead up to the last paragraph?

2. How would you describe the author's tone as she describes her mother and two sisters? Would you say that the author is ever cynical? Explain. (Glossary: *Tone*)

3. The author spends much of this essay examining the whimsical and austere hair philosophies of her mother and two sisters. How does her writing help to make these two categories more extreme?

4. What effect does the author achieve by using her viewpoint as a child? Where does the author decide not to do this?

5. The author's voice emerges at the end of this essay through the bold character of Rhonda. What does she say through Rhonda, and how is this a reaction to her experiences with hair?

6. Aldrich uses description to enhance her essay of classification. (Glossary: *Description*) What dominant impression does she create of her mother's hair? Her two sisters' hair?

QUESTIONS ON LANGUAGE

1. Locate an example of hyperbole and one of understatement in this essay. Explain how you react to each and what tone each helps to create.

2. Refer to your desk dictionary to determine the meaning of the following words as they appear in this selection: *shrills* (paragraph 1), *inexorable* (2), *moored* (2), *riffle* (2) *dictum* (3), *antithesis* (3), *crestfallen* (4), *unscathed* (4), *self-effacement* (9), *curtail* (10), *wanton* (10), *steadfastly* (14).

WRITING SUGGESTIONS

1. Write your own division and classification essay on hair or another beauty-related subject. How do race and sex effect the hair question? Were your family members or peers more influential in determining how you look at hair? What's your hair history?

2. How did your parents and siblings influence the way you dressed as you grew up? What impressions have they left on your sense of style? Write a division and classification essay examining style?

Writing Suggestions
for Division and Classification

1. To write a meaningful paper of classification, you must analyze a body of unorganized material, arranging it for a particular purpose. For example, in order to identify for a buyer the most economical cars currently on the market, you might initially determine which cars can be purchased for under $10,000, which cost between $10,000 and $15,000, and which cost more than $15,000. Then, using a second basis of selection—fuel economy—you could determine which cars have the best gas mileage within each price range. A different purpose would result in a different classification. For example, you might initially want to determine which cars on the market comfortably accommodate a family of six. Next, using a second principle of selection—price—you could determine which vehicles might be purchased for under $10,000. Such a classification would identify for a buyer all six-passenger cars available for under $10,000.

   Select one of the following subjects, and write a paper of classification. Be sure that your purpose is clearly explained and that your bases of selection are chosen and ordered in accordance with your purpose.

   a. attitudes toward physical fitness
   b. contemporary American music
   c. reading materials
   d. reasons for going to college
   e. attitudes toward the religious or spiritual side of life
   f. choosing a hobby
   g. television comedies
   h. college professors
   i. local restaurants
   j. choosing a career
   k. college courses
   l. recreational activities
   m. ways of financing a college education
   n. parties or other social events

2. We sometimes resist classifying other people because it can seem like "pigeonholing" or stereotyping individuals unfairly. In an essay, compare and contrast two or more ways of classifying people—at least one that you would call legitimate and one that you would call misleading. What conclusions can you draw about the difference between useful classifications and damaging stereotypes?

7
DEFINITION

WHAT IS DEFINITION?

A definition explains the meaning of a word or phrase, as everyone who has ever used a dictionary knows. Words need to be defined because their sounds and spelling hardly ever indicate exactly what they are intended to mean. A word like *draft* can refer to a current of air, conscription, a ship's depth in the water, a bank check, or the first attempt at a piece of writing. It's amazing that this jumble of apparently unrelated meanings can all belong to one simple set of letters and sounds; but, then, words are abstract symbols and represent a large and complex world of things and ideas. We can only communicate with each other properly when we agree on a definition for the words we use. To assure such agreement, writers have a variety of techniques at their disposal.

A *formal definition* explains the meaning of a word by assigning it to a class and then differentiating it from other members of that class.

TERM		CLASS	DIFFERENTIATION
Music	is	sound	made by voices or instruments and characterized by melody, harmony, or rhythm.

Note how crucial the differentiation is here: there are many sounds—from the roar of a passing jet airplane to the fizz of soda in a glass—that must be excluded for the definition to be precise and useful. Dictionary entries often follow the class–differentiation pattern of the formal definition.

A *synonymous definition* explains a word by pairing it with another word of similar but perhaps more limited meaning.

> Music is melody.

Synonymous definition can never be as precise as formal definition, because few words share exactly the same meaning. But, particularly when the word being defined is reasonably familiar and somewhat broad, a well-chosen synonym can provide readers with a surer sense of its meaning in context. Occasionally, a synonymous definition may even be metaphorical.

A *negative definition* explains a word by saying what it does not mean.

> Music is not silence, and it is not noise.

Such a definition must obviously be incomplete: there are sounds which are neither silence nor noise and yet are not music—quiet conversation, for example. But specifying what something is *not* may often help to clarify other statements about what it *is*.

An *etymological definition* also seldom stands alone, but by tracing a word's origins it helps readers understand its meaning.

> Music is descended from the Greek word *mousikē*, meaning literally "the art of the Muse."

The Muses, according to Greek mythology, were deities and the sources of inspiration in the arts. Thus, the etymology suggests why we think of music as an art and as the product of inspiration. Etymological definitions can often reveal surprising sources that suggest new ways of looking at ideas or objects.

A *stipulative definition* is a definition invented by a writer to convey a special or unexpected sense of an existing and often familiar word.

> Music is a language, but a language of the intangible, a kind of soul-language.   —EDWARD MACDOWELL
> Music is the arithmetic of sounds.   —CLAUDE DEBUSSY

Although these two examples seem to disagree with each other, and perhaps also with your idea of what music is, note that neither is arbitrary. (That is, neither assigns to the word *music* a completely foreign meaning, as Humpty-Dumpty did in *Through the Looking-Glass* when he defined *glory* as "a nice knock-down argument.") The stipulative definitions by MacDowell and Debussy help explain each composer's conception of the subject and can lead, of course, to further elaboration. Stipulative definitions almost always provide the basis for a more complex discussion.

Sometimes a word, or the idea it stands for, requires more than a sentence of explanation. Such a longer definition—called, naturally enough, *extended definition*—may go on for a paragraph, a page, an essay, or even an entire book. It may employ any of the techniques mentioned already in this chapter, as well as the various strategies discussed throughout the text. An extended definition of music might provide *examples*, ranging from African drumming to a Bach fugue to a Bruce Springsteen song, in order to develop a fuller and more vivid sense of what music is. A writer might *describe* music in detail by showing its characteristic features, or explain the *process* of composing music, or *compare and contrast* music with language (according to MacDowell's stipulative definition) or arithmetic (according to Debussy's). Any of these strategies, and others too, will help to make the meaning of a writer's words and ideas clear.

WHY DO WRITERS USE DEFINITION?

Since most readers have dictionaries, it might seem that writers would hardly ever have to define their terms. In fact, they seldom do, even when using an unusual word like *tergiversation*, which few readers will have in their active vocabularies; if readers don't know it, the reasoning goes, let them look it up. But there are times when a definition is really necessary. One is when a writer uses a word so specialized, or so new, that it simply won't be in the dictionaries; another is when a writer must use a number of unfamiliar technical terms within only a few sentences. Also, when a word has several different meanings or may mean different things to different people, authors will often state exactly the sense in which they are using the word. In each of these cases, definition serves the purpose of achieving clarity.

But writers also use definition, particularly extended definition, to explain the essential nature of the things and ideas they write about. Such writing goes beyond answering the question, "What does _____ mean?" to tackle the much broader and deeper question, "What is _____?" And while this may be the primary object of such a definition, an author may also go further and use extended definition to make a persuasive point. That's what Ellen Goodman does in "The Company Man" and Jo Goodwin Parker does in "What Is Poverty?" later in this chapter.

LOOKING AT DEFINITION

First, determine what word or idea the definition is about—what subject it seeks to explain. Sometimes the title will tell you, as with "What Is Poverty?" and "Best Friends"; at other times you may have to read further into the essay. Then, consider the writer's purpose, and pay attention to the strategies and techniques the writer uses to develop the definition.

The subject of the following extended definition by Robert Keith Miller is clear, if not from the title ("Discrimination Is a Virtue"), then from the second sentence.

> We have a word in English which means "the ability to tell differences." That word is *discrimination*. But within the last twenty years, this word has been so frequently misused that an entire generation has grown up believing that "discrimination" means "racism." People are always proclaiming that "discrimination" is something that should be done away with. Should that ever happen, it would prove to be our undoing.
>
> Discrimination means discernment; it means the ability to perceive the truth, to use good judgment and to profit accordingly. "The Oxford English Dictionary" traces this understanding of the word back to 1648 and demonstrates that for the next 300 years, "discrimination" was a virtue, not a vice. Thus, when a character in a nineteenth-century novel makes a happy marriage, Dickens has another character remark, "It does credit to your discrimination that you should have found such a very excellent young woman."
>
> Of course, "the ability to tell differences" assumes that differences exist, and this is unsettling for a culture obsessed with the notion of equality. The contemporary belief that discrimination is a vice stems from the compound "discriminate against." What we need to remember, however, is that some things deserve to be judged harshly: we should not leave our kingdoms to the selfish and the wicked.
>
> Discrimination is wrong only when someone or something is discriminated against because of prejudice. But to use the word in this sense, as so many people do, is to destroy its true meaning. If you discriminate against something because of general preconceptions rather than particular insights, then you are not discriminating—bias has clouded the clarity of vision which discrimination demands.

The subject of Miller's extended definition is, of course, the word *discrimination*. His purpose, however, is less immediately obvious. At first it appears that he wants only to explain what the word *discrimination* means. But by the third sentence he is distinguishing what it does *not* mean, and at the end it's clear he's trying to persuade readers to use the word correctly, and thus discriminate more sharply and more justly themselves.

Miller begins with a very brief formal definition of discrimination: "the ability [class] to tell differences" [differentiation]. He then offers a negative definition (discrimination is not racism) and a synonymous definition (discrimination is discernment). Next he cites the entry in a great historical dictionary of English to support his claim and quotes an example to illustrate his definition. He concludes by contrasting the word *discrimination* with the compound "discriminate against." Each of these techniques helps make the case that the most precise meaning of discrimination is in direct opposition to its common usage today.

For an analysis of another extended definition, consult the discussion of Laurence Perrine's "Paradox," pp. 5–6.

READING DEFINITION IN AN ANNOTATED STUDENT ESSAY

A native of New York City, Howard Solomon now lives in Lincoln, Vermont. He studied in France as part of the AFS program in high school and he majored in French at the University of Vermont. Solomon's other interests include foreign affairs, languages, photography, and cycling; in his wildest dreams, he imagines becoming an international lawyer. For the following essay, Solomon began by interviewing students in his dormitory, collecting information and opinions that he eventually brought together with his own experiences to develop a definition of "best friends."

BEST FRIENDS

Howard Solomon Jr.

Introduction: brief definition of best friend.

Best friends, even when they are not a part of our 1 day-to-day lives, are essential to our well-being. They supply the companionship, help, security, and love that we all need. It is not easy to put into words exactly what a best friend is, because the matter is so personal. From time to time, however, we may think about our best friends—who they are, what characteristics they share, and why they are so important to

us—in order to gain a better understanding of ourselves and our relationships.

I recently asked several people for their opinions   2
on the subject, beginning with the qualities they valued in their own best friends. They all agreed on
three traits: reciprocity, honesty, and love. Reciprocity
means that one can always rely on a best friend in
times of need. A favor doesn't necessarily have to be
returned; but best friends will return it anyway, because they want to. Best friends are willing to help
each other for the sake of helping and not just for personal gain. One woman said that life seemed more
secure because she knew her best friend was there if
she ever needed help.

Honesty in a best friendship is the sharing of feel-   3
ings openly and without reserve. The people I interviewed said they could rely on their best friends as
confidants: they could share problems with their best
friends and ask for advice. They also felt that, even if
best friends were critical of each other, they would
never be hurtful or spiteful.

Love is probably the most important quality of a   4
best friend relationship, according to the people I interviewed. They very much prized the affection and
enjoyment they felt in the company of their best
friends. One man described it as a "gut reaction," and
all said it was a different feeling from being with
other friends. Private jokes, looks, and gestures create
personal communication between best friends that is
at a very high level—many times one person knows
what the other is thinking without anything being
said. The specifics differ, but most everyone I talked
to agreed that a special feeling exists, which is best
described as love.

I next asked who could be a best friend and who   5
could not. My sources all felt it was impossible for
parents, other relatives, and people of the opposite
sex (especially husbands or wives) to be best friends.

One woman said such people were "too inhibitive."
Personally, I disagree—I have two best friends who
are women. However, I may be an exception, and
most best friends may fit the above requirements.
There could be a good reason for this, too: most of the
people I interviewed felt that their best friends were
not demanding, while relatives and partners of the
opposite sex can be very demanding.

Answers to question 3: How many best friends can a person have?   To the question of how many best friends one can 6
have, some in my sample responded that it is possible
to have several best friends, although very few people
can do so; others said it was possible to have only a
very few best friends; and still others felt they could
have just one—that single friend who is most out-
standing. It was interesting to see how ideas varied on
this question. Although best friends may be no less
special for one person than another, people do define
the concept differently.

Answers to question 4: How long does it take to become best friends?   Regarding how long it takes to become best 7
friends and how long the relationship lasts, all were
in agreement. "It is a long hard process which takes a
lot of time," one woman explained. "It isn't something that can happen overnight," suggested another.
One man said, "You usually know the person very
well before you consider him your best friend. In fact
you know everything about him, his bad points as
well as his good points, so there is little likelihood
that you can come into conflict with him." In addition, everyone thought that once a person has become
a best friend, he or she remains so for the rest of one's
life.

Differences in responses from men and women.   During the course of the interviews I discovered 8
one important and unexpected difference between
men and women regarding the qualities of their best
friends. The men all said that a best friend usually
possessed one quality that stood out above all
others—an easygoing manner or humor or sympathy,
for example. One of them told me that he looked not

for loyalty but for honesty, for someone who was truthful, because it was so rare to find this quality in anyone. The women I surveyed, however, all responded that they looked for a well-rounded person who had many good qualities. One said that a person who had just one good quality and not several would be "too boring to associate with." Does this difference hold true beyond my sample? If so, it means that men and women have quite different definitions of their best friends.

Personal example: what the writer learned about best friends at the time of his father's death.

I have always wondered why my own best friends were so important to me; but it wasn't until recently that something happened to make me really understand my relationship with my best friends. My father died, and this was a crisis for me. Most of my friends gave me their condolences. But my best friends did more than that: they actually supported me. They called long distance to see how I was and what I needed, to try and help me work out my problems or simply to talk. Two of my best friends even took time from their spring break and, along with two other best friends, attended my father's memorial service; none of my other friends came. Since then, these are the only people who have continued to worry about me and talk to me about my father. I know that, whenever I need someone, they will be there and willing to help me. I know also that, whenever they need help, I will be ready to do the same for them. 9

Conclusion: personal definition of best friends.

Yet, I don't value my best friends so much just for what they do for me. I simply enjoy their company more than anyone else's. We talk, joke, play sports, and do all kinds of things when we are together. I never feel ill at ease, even after we've been apart for a while. However, the most important thing for me about best friends is the knowledge that I am never alone, that there are others in the world who care about my well-being as much as I do about theirs. Surely this is a comforting feeling for everyone. 10

Thesis

WRITING AN ESSAY OF EXTENDED DEFINITION

Whatever your subject, make sure you have a clear sense of your purpose. Why are you writing a definition? If it's only to explain what a word or phrase means, you'll probably run out of things to say in a few sentences—or find that a good dictionary has already said them for you. An effective extended definition should attempt to explain the essential nature of a thing or an idea, whether photosynthesis or spring fever or Republicanism or prison or common sense.

Student Howard Solomon Jr. hit on the idea of defining what a best friend is. He recalls that "a friend of mine had become a best friend, and I was trying to figure out what had happened, what was different. So I decided to explore what was on my mind." At the beginning, you have at least a general idea of what your subject means to you, as well as a sense of the audience you are writing your definition for and the impact you want your definition to achieve. The following advice will guide you as you plan and draft your essay.

Considering the Nature of Your Subject

Certain subjects, like Republicanism and discrimination, lend themselves to different interpretations depending on the writer's point of view. While readers may agree in general about what such subjects mean, there will be much disagreement over particulars—and, therefore, room for you to propose and defend your own definitions. A subject like photosynthesis, though, is a specific natural process, so all definitions of it must agree very closely on particulars—even though your general approach to the definition may be quite original. In preparing to define a specific subject like photosynthesis, your preparations will include some reading and note-taking to make sure that you've got your facts right. If your subject is more general or subjective, there may be fewer facts to look for; but it is wise to take your readers' probable views into account, and possibly the views of other writers on the subject—not necessarily to change your own definition, but to present it more effectively to your audience.

Solomon remembers the difficulties he had getting started with his essay on best friends. "The first draft I wrote was nothing. I tried to get a start with the dictionary definition, but it didn't help—it just put into two words what really needs hundreds of words to explain, and the words it used had to be defined, too. My teacher suggested I might get going better if I talked about my topic with other people. I decided to make it semiformal, so I made up a list of a few specific questions—five questions—and went to about a dozen people I knew and asked them. Questions like, "What qualities do your best friends have?" and "What are some of the things they've done for you?" And I took notes on the answers. I was surprised when so many of them agreed. It isn't a scientific sampling, but the results helped get me started."

Considering Your Audience

What do your readers know? If you're an economics major in an undergraduate writing course, you can safely assume that you know your subject better than your readers do and so will have to explain even very basic terms and ideas. If, however, you're writing a paper for your course in econometrics, your most important reader—the one who grades your paper—won't even slow down at your references to *monetary aggregates* and *Philips Curves,* provided, of course, that you obviously know what you mean.

Choosing a Technique or Techniques of Definition

The choices you make depend on your subject and your readers. Photosynthesis, for example, is a natural process, so a good choice of strategy in defining it would be a process analysis; readers who know little about biology may better understand photosynthesis if you draw an analogy with the eating and breathing of human beings. Common sense is an abstract concept, so its meaning could certainly be illustrated with concrete examples; in addition, its special nature would emerge more sharply through comparison and contrast with other ways of thinking. To define a salt marsh, you might choose a typical marsh and describe it. To define economic inflation or a particular disease, you might discuss causes and effects. Only two requirements limit your choice of definition strategy: the strategy must be appropriate to your subject, and it must help you explain your subject's essential nature. Solomon builds his essay of definition around the many examples he garnered from his interviews with other students and his own personal experiences.

Many inexperienced writers believe that any extended definition, no matter what the subject, should begin with a formal "dictionary" definition, or at least introduce one before the essay has proceeded very far. This is not necessarily so; you will find that most of the following essays include no such formal definition. Assume that your readers have dictionaries and know how to use them. If, however, you think your readers do require a short, formal definition at some point, don't simply quote from a dictionary. Unless you have some very good reason for doing otherwise, put the definition into your own words, words that suit your approach and the probable readers of your essay. (Certainly, nonscientists would be baffled by an essay that began, "The dictionary defines photosynthesis as 'the process by which chlorophyll-containing cells in green plants convert incident light to chemical energy and synthesize organic compounds from inorganic compounds, especially carbohydrates from carbon dioxide and water, with the simultaneous release of oxygen.'") There's another advantage to using your own words: you won't have to write "The dictionary defines . . ." or "According to Webster's . . ."; stock phrases like these almost immediately put the reader's mind to sleep.

Developing Your Strategy

The various strategies for developing essays of extended definition are discussed fully in the introductions to the other nine chapters in *Subject and Strategy*. If you need to, look up the strategy you have chosen—illustration or comparison and contrast, for example—and review the suggestions there on gathering and organizing information and ideas for your essay. Solomon can trace at least several distinct stages that his paper went through before he settled upon the plan of organizing his examples around the items on his interview questionnaire.

"Doing this paper showed me that writing isn't all that easy. Boy, I went through so many copies—adding some things, taking out some things, reorganizing. At one point half the paper was a definition of *friends,* so I could contrast them with *best friends.* That wasn't necessary. Then, I've said that the personal stuff came in late. In fact, my father died after I'd begun writing the paper, so that paragraph came in almost last of all. On the next-to-last draft everything was there, but it was put together in a sort of random way—not completely random, one idea would lead to the next and then the next, but there was a lot of circling around. My teacher pointed this out and suggested I outline what I'd written and work on the outline. So I tried it and I saw what the problem was and what I had to do. It was just a matter of getting my examples into the right order, and finally everything clicked into place."

The Company Man

ELLEN GOODMAN

Ellen Goodman was born in Boston in 1941. After graduating cum laude from Radcliffe College in 1963, she worked as a reporter and researcher for Newsweek. *In 1967, she began working at the* Boston Globe *and, since 1974, has been a full-time columnist. Her regular column, "At Large," is syndicated by the* Washington Post *Writer's Group and appears in nearly four hundred newspapers across the country. In addition, her writing has appeared in* McCall's, Harper's Bazaar, *and* Family Circle, *and her commentaries have been broadcast on radio and television. In 1979, Goodman published* Close to Home, *a collection of her columns; several other collections have appeared since then, including* At Large, Keeping in Touch, *and* Making Sense.

In "The Company Man," taken from Close to Home, *Goodman defines the "workaholic" by offering a poignant case-in-point example.*

He worked himself to death, finally and precisely, at 3:00 A.M. Sunday morning.

The obituary didn't say that, of course. It said that he died of a coronary thrombosis—I think that was it—but everyone among his friends and acquaintances knew it instantly. He was a perfect Type A, a workaholic, a classic, they said to each other and shook their heads—and thought for five or ten minutes about the way they lived.

This man who worked himself to death finally and precisely at 3:00 A.M. Sunday morning—on his day off—was fifty-one years old and a vice-president. He was, however, one of six vice-presidents, and one of three who might conceivably—if the president died or retired soon enough—have moved to the top spot. Phil knew that.

He worked six days a week, five of them until eight or nine at night, during a time when his own company had begun the four-day week for everyone but the executives. He worked like the Important People. He had no outside "extracurricular interests," unless, of course, you think about a monthly golf game that way. To Phil, it was work. He always ate egg salad sandwiches at his desk. He was, of course, overweight, by 20 or 25 pounds. He thought it was okay, though, because he didn't smoke.

On Saturdays, Phil wore a sports jacket to the office instead of a 5
suit, because it was the weekend.

He had a lot of people working for him, maybe sixty, and most of 6
them liked him most of the time. Three of them will be seriously considered for his job. The obituary didn't mention that.

But it did list his "survivors" quite accurately. He is survived by his 7
wife, Helen, forty-eight years old, a good woman of no particular marketable skills, who worked in an office before marrying and mothering.
She had, according to her daughter, given up trying to compete with
his work years ago, when the children were small. A company friend
said, "I know how much you will miss him." And she answered, "I
already have."

"Missing him all these years," she must have given up part of her- 8
self which had cared too much for the man. She would be "well taken
care of."

His "dearly beloved" eldest of the "dearly beloved" children is a 9
hard-working executive in a manufacturing firm down South. In the
day and a half before the funeral, he went around the neighborhood
researching his father, asking the neighbors what he was like. They were
embarrassed.

His second child is a girl, who is twenty-four and newly married. 10
She lives near her mother and they are close, but whenever she was
alone with her father, in a car driving somewhere, they had nothing to
say to each other.

The youngest is twenty, a boy, a high-school graduate who has 11
spent the last couple of years, like a lot of his friends, doing enough odd
jobs to stay in grass and food. He was the one who tried to grab at his
father, and tried to mean enough to him to keep the man at home. He
was his father's favorite. Over the last two years, Phil stayed up nights
worrying about the boy.

The boy once said, "My father and I only board here."   12

At the funeral, the sixty-year-old company president told the forty- 13
eight-year-old widow that the fifty-one-year-old deceased had meant
much to the company and would be missed and would be hard to
replace. The widow didn't look him in the eye. She was afraid he would
read her bitterness and, after all, she would need him to straighten out
the finances—the stock options and all that.

Phil was overweight and nervous and worked too hard. If he wasn't 14
at the office, he was worried about it. Phil was a Type A, a heart-attack
natural. You could have picked him out in a minute from a lineup.

So when he finally worked himself to death, at precisely 3:00 A.M. 15
Sunday morning, no one was really surprised.

By 5:00 P.M. the afternoon of the funeral, the company president 16
had begun, discreetly of course, with care and taste, to make inquiries
about his replacement. One of three men. He asked around: "Who's
been working the hardest?"

QUESTIONS ON SUBJECT

1. In paragraph 4, Goodman says that Phil worked like "Important People."
   What does she mean?

2. Why did Phil's son go around the neighborhood researching his father?
   What is ironic about this? What significance do you see in the fact that
   Phil's son is an executive in a manufacturing plant down South? (Glossary:
   Irony)

3. In your own words, explain the meaning of paragraph 11.

4. Do you think Phil's problems were all his own? Does Goodman suggest
   that the "system" may, in part, also be responsible for Phil's untimely end?
   Explain.

QUESTIONS ON STRATEGY

1. What is Goodman's purpose in this essay? Goodman's tone is unemo-
   tional. Why is that tone especially fitting for her purpose? (Glossary: *Purpose; Tone*)

2. In your own words, give a brief definition of *workaholic* based on the
   information that Goodman provides in this essay. What information, if any,
   has the author failed to provide?

3. What significance do you see in the statement "I think that was it" (paragraph 2)?

4. In paragraphs 1, 3, and 15, Goodman tells us the precise time of Phil's
   death. Why do you suppose this is an important fact for Goodman? Why
   do you think she repeats the information?

5. Comment on the effectiveness of Goodman's last sentence. (Glossary:
   Beginnings/Endings)

6. What dominant impression of the company man does Goodman create in
   this essay? (Glossary: *Dominant Impression*) What details does she use to
   describe him?

QUESTIONS ON LANGUAGE

1. Why does the author place the phrase "dearly beloved" in quotation marks
   in paragraph 9?

2. Refer to your desk dictionary to determine the meanings of the following words as they are used in this selection: *coronary thrombosis* (paragraph 2), *workaholic* (2), *conceivably* (3), *obituary* (6), *marketable* (7), *deceased* (13), *discreetly* (16).

WRITING ASSIGNMENTS

1. The procrastinator—the type of person who continually puts off responsibilities and jobs—is very different from the workaholic. Write an essay, modeled on Goodman's if you like, that attempts to use an extended example to define this interesting personality type.

2. One issue that Goodman does not raise is how a person becomes a workaholic. Write an essay in which you speculate about some reasons for such an addiction. How might workaholism be avoided? Or should it be?

What Is Poverty?

Jo Goodwin Parker

All we know about Jo Goodwin Parker is that when George Henderson, a professor at the University of Oklahoma, was preparing his 1971 book, America's Other Children: Public Schools Outside Suburbia, *the following essay was mailed to him from West Virginia under Parker's name. Henderson included Parker's essay in his book, and according to him, her piece was an unpublished speech, given in Deland, Florida, on December 27, 1965. Perhaps she is, as her essay says, one of the rural poor who eke out a hardscrabble living just beyond view of America's middle-class majority; or perhaps she is a spokesperson for them, writing not from her own experience but from long and sympathetic observation. In either case, her definition of poverty is so detailed and forceful as to convey, even to those who have never known it, the nature of poverty.*

You ask me what is poverty? Listen to me. Here I am, dirty, smelly, 1 and with no "proper" underwear on and with the stench of my rotting teeth near you. I will tell you. Listen to me. Listen without pity. I cannot use your pity. Listen with understanding. Put yourself in my dirty, worn out, ill-fitting shoes, and hear me.

Poverty is getting up every morning from a dirt- and illness-stained 2 mattress. The sheets have long since been used for diapers. Poverty is living in a smell that never leaves. This is a smell of urine, sour milk, and spoiling food sometimes joined with the strong smell of long-cooked onions. Onions are cheap. If you have smelled this smell, you did not know how it came. It is the smell of the outdoor privy. It is the smell of young children who cannot walk the long dark way in the night. It is the smell of the mattresses where years of "accidents" have happened. It is the smell of the milk which has gone sour because the refrigerator long has not worked, and it costs money to get it fixed. It is the smell of rotting garbage. I could bury it, but where is the shovel? Shovels cost money.

Poverty is being tired. I have always been tired. They told me at the 3 hospital when the last baby came that I had chronic anemia caused from poor diet, a bad case of worms, and that I needed a corrective operation. I listened politely—the poor are always polite. The poor always listen. They don't say that there is no money for iron pills, or better food, or worm medicine. The idea of an operation is frightening and costs so much that, if I had dared, I would have laughed. Who takes care of my children? Recovery from an operation takes a long time. I have three children. When I left them with "Granny" the last time I had a job, I came home to find the baby covered with fly specks, and a diaper that had not been changed since I left. When the dried diaper came off, bits of my baby's flesh came with it. My other child was playing with a sharp bit of broken glass, and my oldest was playing alone at the edge of a lake. I made twenty-two dollars a week, and a good nursery school costs twenty dollars a week for three children. I quit my job.

Poverty is dirt. You say in your clean clothes coming from your 　4 clean house, "Anybody can be clean." Let me explain about housekeeping with no money. For breakfast I give my children grits with no oleo or cornbread without eggs and oleo. This does not use up many dishes. What dishes there are, I wash in cold water and with no soap. Even the cheapest soap has to be saved for the baby's diapers. Look at my hands, so cracked and red. Once I saved for two months to buy a jar of Vaseline for my hands and the baby's diaper rash. When I had saved enough, I went to buy it and the price had gone up two cents. The baby and I suffered on. I have to decide every day if I can bear to put my cracked, sore hands into the cold water and strong soap. But you ask, why not hot water? Fuel costs money. If you have a wood fire it costs money. If you burn electricity, it costs money. Hot water is a luxury. I do not have luxuries. I know you will be surprised when I tell you how young I am. I look so much older. My back has been bent over the wash tubs for so long, I cannot remember when I ever did anything else. Every night I wash every stitch my school age child has on and just hope her clothes will be dry by morning.

Poverty is staying up all night on cold nights to watch the fire, 　5 knowing one spark on the newspaper covering the walls means your sleeping children die in flames. In summer poverty is watching gnats and flies devour your baby's tears when he cries. The screens are torn and you pay so little rent you know they will never be fixed. Poverty means insects in your food, in your nose, in your eyes, and crawling over you when you sleep. Poverty is hoping it never rains because diapers won't dry when it rains and soon you are using newspapers. Poverty is seeing your children forever with runny noses. Paper handkerchiefs cost money and all your rags you need for other things. Even more costly are antihistamines. Poverty is cooking without food and cleaning without soap.

Poverty is asking for help. Have you ever had to ask for help, know- 6 ing your children will suffer unless you get it? Think about asking for a loan from a relative, if this is the only way you can imagine asking for help. I will tell you how it feels. You find out where the office is that you are supposed to visit. You circle that block four or five times. Thinking of your children, you go in. Everyone is very busy. Finally, someone comes out and you tell her that you need help. That never is the person you need to see. You go see another person, and after spilling the whole shame of your poverty all over the desk between you, you find that this isn't the right office after all—you must repeat the whole process, and it never is any easier at the next place.

You have asked for help, and after all it has a cost. You are again 7 told to wait. You are told why, but you don't really hear because of the red cloud of shame and the rising black cloud of despair.

Poverty is remembering. It is remembering quitting school in 8 junior high because "nice" children had been so cruel about my clothes and my smell. The attendance officer came. My mother told him I was pregnant. I wasn't but she thought that I could get a job and help out. I had jobs off and on, but never long enough to learn anything. Mostly I remember being married. I was so young then. I am still young. For a time, we had all the things you have. There was a little house in another town, with hot water and everything. Then my husband lost his job. There was unemployment insurance for a while and what few jobs I could get. Soon, all our nice things were repossessed and we moved back here. I was pregnant then. This house didn't look so bad when we first moved in. Every week it gets worse. Nothing is ever fixed. We now had no money. There were a few odd jobs for my husband, but everything went for food then, as it does now. I don't know how we lived through three years and three babies, but we did. I'll tell you something, after the last baby I destroyed my marriage. It had been a good one, but could you keep on bringing children in this dirt? Did you ever think how much it costs for any kind of birth control? I knew my husband was leaving the day he left, but there were no good-byes between us. I hope he has been able to climb out of this mess some-where. He never could hope with us to drag him down.

That's when I asked for help. When I got it, you know how much 9 it was? It was, and is, seventy-eight dollars a month for the four of us; that is all I ever can get. Now you know why there is no soap, no needles and thread, no hot water, no aspirin, no worm medicine, no hand cream, no shampoo. None of these things forever and ever and ever. So that you can see clearly, I pay twenty dollars a month rent, and most of the rest goes for food. For grits and cornmeal, and rice and milk and beans. I try my best to use only the minimum electricity. If I use more, there is that much less for food.

Poverty is looking into a black future. Your children won't play 10 with my boys. They will turn to other boys who steal to get what they want. I can already see them behind the bars of their prison instead of behind the bars of my poverty. Or they will turn to the freedom of alcohol or drugs, and find themselves enslaved. And my daughter? At best, there is for her a life like mine.

But you say to me, there are schools. Yes, there are schools. My 11 children have no extra books, no magazines, no extra pencils, or crayons, or paper and the most important of all, they do not have health. They have worms, they have infections, they have pinkeye all summer. They do not sleep well on the floor, or with me in my one bed. They do not suffer from hunger, my seventy-eight dollars keeps us alive, but they do suffer from malnutrition. Oh yes, I do remember what I was taught about health in school. It doesn't do much good. In some places there is a surplus commodities program. Not here. The county said it cost too much. There is a school lunch program. But I have two children who will already be damaged by the time they get to school.

But, you say to me, there are health clinics. Yes, there are health 12 clinics and they are in the towns. I live out here eight miles from town. I can walk that far (even if it is sixteen miles both ways), but can my little children? My neighbor will take me when he goes; but he expects to get paid, *one way or another.* I bet you know my neighbor. He is that large man who spends his time at the gas station, the barbershop, and the corner store complaining about the government spending money on the immoral mothers of illegitimate children.

Poverty is an acid that drips on pride until all pride is worn away. 13 Poverty is a chisel that chips on honor until honor is worn away. Some of you say that you would do *something* in my situation, and maybe you would, for the first week or the first month, but for year after year after year?

Even the poor can dream. A dream of a time when there is money. 14 Money for the right kinds of food, for worm medicine, for iron pills, for toothbrushes, for hand cream, for a hammer and nails and a bit of screening, for a shovel, for a bit of paint, for some sheeting, for needles and thread. Money to pay *in money* for a trip to town. And, oh, money for hot water and money for soap. A dream of when asking for help does not eat away the last bit of pride. When the office you visit is as nice as the offices of other governmental agencies, when there are enough workers to help you quickly, when workers do not quit in defeat and despair. When you have to tell your story to only one person, and that person can send you for other help and you don't have to prove your poverty over and over and over again.

I have come out of my despair to tell you this. Remember I did not 15 come from another place or another time. Others like me are all around you. Look at us with an angry heart, anger that will help you help me. Anger that will let you tell of me. The poor are always silent. Can you be silent too?

QUESTIONS ON SUBJECT

1. Why did Parker not have the operation that was recommended for her? Why did she quit her job?

2. In Parker's view, what makes asking for help such a difficult and painful experience? What compels her to do so anyway?

3. Why did Parker's husband leave her? How does she justify her attitude toward his leaving? (Glossary: *Attitude*)

4. In paragraph 12, Parker says the following about a neighbor giving her a ride to the nearest health clinic: "My neighbor will take me when he goes; but he expects to get paid, *one way or another.* I bet you know my neighbor." What is she implying in these sentences and in the rest of the paragraph?

5. What are the chances that the dreams described in paragraph 14 will come true? What do you think Parker would say?

QUESTIONS ON STRATEGY

1. What is Parker's purpose in defining poverty as she does? (Glossary: *Purpose*) Why has she cast her essay in the form of an extended definition?

2. What techniques of definition does Parker use? What is missing that you would expect to find in a more general and impersonal definition of poverty? Why does Parker leave such information out?

3. How would you characterize Parker's tone and her style? How do you respond to her presentation? Point to specific examples as support for your view. (Glossary: *Style; Tone*)

4. Parker repeats words and phrases throughout this essay. Choose some typical examples and explain how they work. What do they accomplish? (Glossary: *Coherence*)

5. In describing what poverty looks like, Parker creates a vivid verbal picture for her readers. What for you are the most striking details that she uses? How do you account for the emotional impact of some of her details and images? (Glossary: *Description*)

QUESTIONS ON LANGUAGE

1. Although her essay is written for the most part in simple, straightforward language, Parker does make use of an occasional striking figure of speech. Identify three such figures of speech—you might begin with those in paragraph 13—and explain their effect on the reader. (Glossary: *Figures of Speech*)

2. In paragraph 10, Parker makes a paradoxical statement. Identify the statement and explain why it is paradoxical. (Glossary: *Paradox*)

3. Refer to your desk dictionary to determine the meanings of the following words as they are used in this selection: *chronic* (paragraph 3), *anemia* (3), *grits* (4), *oleo* (4), *antihistamines* (5).

WRITING ASSIGNMENTS

1. Using Parker's essay as a model, write an extended definition of a general topic from the firsthand perspective of an expert. Choose as your subject a particular environment (suburbia, the inner city, a frat house) or way of living (children of divorce, the physically handicapped, the working student).

2. Write an essay of your own defining poverty. You may wish to gather statistical data on the problem as it exists today in the United States and abroad, or draw exclusively on personal observations and experiences.

What's in a Name?

GLORIA NAYLOR

American novelist and essayist Gloria Naylor was born in 1950 in New York City. She worked first as a missionary for the Jehovah's Witnesses from 1967 to 1975, then as a telephone operator until 1981. That year she graduated from Brooklyn College of the City of New York and began graduate work in African American studies at Yale University. In addition to winning numerous academic and literary awards, Naylor has been a Guggenheim Fellow and a National Endowment for the Arts Fellow. Her visiting professorships have taken her to Africa, England, and India and to universities across the United States. She has published four novels on the "black experience": The Women of Brewster Place *(1982),* Linden Hills *(1985),* Mama Day *(1988), and* Bailey's Cafe *(1993).* The Women of Brewster Place *won the American Book Award for first fiction and was adapted for television in 1989.*

The following essay first appeared in the New York Times *in 1986. In it Naylor examines the ways in which words can take on meaning depending on who uses them and to what purpose.*

Language is the subject. It is the written form with which I've 1 managed to keep the wolf away from the door and, in diaries, to keep my sanity. In spite of this, I consider the written word inferior to the spoken, and much of the frustration experienced by novelists is the awareness that whatever we manage to capture in even the most transcendent passages falls far short of the richness of life. Dialogue achieves its power in the dynamics of a fleeting moment of sight, sound, smell, and touch.

I'm not going to enter the debate here about whether it is language 2 that shapes reality or vice versa. That battle is doomed to be waged whenever we seek intermittent reprieve from the chicken and egg dispute. I will simply take the position that the spoken word, like the written word, amounts to a nonsensical arrangement of sounds or letters without a consensus that assigns "meaning." And building from the meanings of what we hear, we order reality. Words themselves are innocuous; it is the consensus that gives them true power.

I remember the first time I heard the word *nigger.* In my third-grade 3
class, our math tests were being passed down the rows, and as I handed
the papers to a little boy in back of me, I remarked that once again he had
received a much lower mark than I did. He snatched his test from me and
spit out that word. Had he called me a nymphomaniac or a necrophiliac,
I couldn't have been more puzzled. I didn't know what a nigger was, but
I knew that whatever it meant, it was something he shouldn't have called
me. This was verified when I raised my hand, and in a loud voice repeated
what he had said and watched the teacher scold him for using a "bad"
word. I was later to go home and ask the inevitable question that every
black parent must face—"Mommy, what does *nigger* mean?"

And what exactly did it mean? Thinking back, I realize that this 4
could not have been the first time the word was used in my presence.
I was part of a large extended family that had migrated from the rural
South after World War II and formed a close-knit network that gravi-
tated around my maternal grandparents. Their ground-floor apartment
in one of the buildings they owned in Harlem was a weekend mecca for
my immediate family, along with countless aunts, uncles, and cousins
who brought along assorted friends. It was a bustling and open house
with assorted neighbors and tenants popping in and out to exchange
bits of gossip, pick up an old quarrel, or referee the ongoing checkers
game in which my grandmother cheated shamelessly. They were all
there to let down their hair and put up their feet after a week of labor
in the factories, laundries, and shipyards of New York.

Amid the clamor, which could reach deafening proportions—two 5
or three conversations going on simultaneously, punctuated by the
sound of a baby's crying somewhere in the back rooms or out on the
street—there was still a rigid set of rules about what was said and how.
Older children were sent out of the living room when it was time to get
into the juicy details about "you-know-who" up on the third floor who
had gone and gotten herself "p-r-e-g-n-a-n-t!" But my parents, knowing that I could spell well beyond my years, always demanded that I
follow the others out to play. Beyond sexual misconduct and death,
everything else was considered harmless for our young ears. And so
among the anecdotes of the triumphs and disappointments in the various workings of their lives, the word *nigger* was used in my presence,
but it was set within contexts and inflections that caused it to register
in my mind as something else.

In the singular, the word was always applied to a man who had 6
distinguished himself in some situation that brought their approval for
his strength, intelligence, or drive:

"Did Johnny *really* do that?"   7

"I'm telling you, that nigger pulled in $6,000 of overtime last year.   8
Said he got enough for a down payment on a house."

When used with a possessive adjective by a woman—"my nigger"—   9
it became a term of endearment for her husband or boyfriend. But it
could be more than just a term applied to a man. In their mouths it
became the pure essence of manhood—a disembodied force that chan-
neled their past history of struggle and present survival against the odds
into a victorious statement of being: "Yeah, that old foreman found out
quick enough—you don't mess with a nigger."

In the plural, it became a description of some group within the   10
community that had overstepped the bounds of decency as my family
defined it. Parents who neglected their children, a drunken couple who
fought in public, people who simply refused to look for work, those
with excessively dirty mouths or unkempt households were all "trifling
niggers." This particular circle could forgive hard times, unemployment, the occasional bout of depression—they had gone through all of
that themselves—but the unforgivable sin was a lack of self-respect.

A woman could never be a "nigger" in the singular, with its con-   11
notation of confirming worth. The noun *girl* was its closest equivalent
in that sense, but only when used in direct address and regardless of the
gender doing the addressing. *Girl* was a token of respect for a woman.
The one-syllable word was drawn out to sound like three in recognition
of the extra ounce of wit, nerve, or daring that the woman had shown
in the situation under discussion.

"G-i-r-l, stop. You mean you said that to his face?"   12

But if the word was used in a third-person reference or shortened   13
so that it almost snapped out of the mouth, it always involved some
element of communal disapproval. And age became an important factor
in these exchanges. It was only between individuals of the same generation, or from any older person to a younger (but never the other way
around), that *girl* would be considered a compliment.

I don't agree with the argument that use of the word *nigger* at this   14
social stratum of the black community was an internalization of racism.
The dynamics were the exact opposite: the people in my grandmother's
living room took a word that whites used to signify worthlessness or
degradation and rendered it impotent. Gathering there together, they
transformed *nigger* to signify the varied and complex human beings
they knew themselves to be. If the word was to disappear totally from
the mouths of even the most liberal of white society, no one in that

room was naive enough to believe it would disappear from white minds. Meeting the word head-on, they proved it had absolutely nothing to do with the way they were determined to live their lives.

So there must have been dozens of times that *nigger* was spoken in 15 front of me before I reached the third grade. But I didn't "hear" it until it was said by a small pair of lips that had already learned it could be a way to humiliate me. That was the word I went home and asked my mother about. And since she knew that I had to grow up in America, she took me in her lap and explained.

QUESTIONS ON SUBJECT

1. How does Naylor explain her preference for the spoken word over the written word? What does she mean by "context"?

2. How, according to Naylor, do words get their meanings?

3. Naylor says she must have heard the word *nigger* many times while she was growing up; yet she "heard" it for the first time when she was in the third grade. How does she explain this seeming contradiction?

4. In the context of her family, what does the word *nigger* mean to Naylor? Why do you suppose she offers so little in the way of definition of her classmate's use of the word? What is the effect on you as a reader? Explain.

5. In what context is *girl* "a token of respect for a woman"? How do you think women in general would—or should—react to being called "girls"? Explain.

QUESTIONS ON STRATEGY

1. What is Naylor's thesis, and where is it stated? (Glossary: *Thesis*)

2. What are the two meanings of the word *nigger* as Naylor uses it in her essay? Where in the essay is the clearest definition of each use of the word presented?

3. What is Naylor's purpose in writing this essay? (Glossary: *Purpose*) Where in her essay is Naylor's purpose most evident?

4. What is the meaning of Naylor's last sentence? How well does it work as an ending for her essay? Explain. (Glossary: *Endings*)

5. Naylor gives a detailed narration of her family and its lifestyle in paragraphs 4 and 5. What kinds of details does she include in her brief story? How does this narration contribute to your understanding of the word *nigger* as used by her family? (Glossary: *Narration*)

QUESTIONS ON LANGUAGE

1. Would you characterize Naylor's tone as angry, objective, cynical, or something else? (Glossary: *Tone*) Cite examples of her diction to support your answer. (Glossary: *Diction*)

2. Consult an unabridged dictionary for the history of the word *nigger*. When was the word first used? How has its meaning changed over time?

3. Refer to your desk dictionary to determine the meanings of the following words as they are used in this selection: *transcendent* (1), *consensus* (2), *innocuous* (2), *nymphomaniac* (3), *necrophiliac* (3), *mecca* (4), *clamor* (5), *anecdotes* (5), *inflections* (5), *unkempt* (10), *trifling* (10), *internalization* (14), *impotent* (14).

WRITING ASSIGNMENTS

1. Write an essay in which you define a word that has more than one meaning, depending on one's point of view. For example, consider *wife, macho, liberal, success, chick, radical, homosexual,* and *marriage.*

2. Naylor disagrees with the notion that use of the word *nigger* in the African American community can be taken as an "internalization of racism." Reexamine her essay and discuss in what ways her definition of the word *nigger* affirms or denies her position. Draw on your own experiences, observations, and reading to add support to your answer.

3. Look up the words *black* and *white* in your dictionary. What are the connotations of most phrases and metaphors that include the word *black*? the word *white*? Why do you suppose the word *black* has more negative connotations? Do you think it has any racist overtones? Discuss your opinion and your reasons for having it in an essay.

On Excellence

CYNTHIA OZICK

Cynthia Ozick, novelist, short-fiction writer, essayist, critic, and translator, was born in 1928 in New York City. She graduated from New York University in 1949 and received her Masters from Ohio State University in 1950. She has worked as an advertising copywriter in Boston for Filene's and as an English professor at New York University. Ozick has contributed four times to the annual collection Best American Short Stories *and received three O. Henry first prize awards. Her work is critically praised for its diversity, combining Judaic law and history, science fiction and fantasy, with comedy, as well as for the precision of her word selection and prose.*

In this essay, first published in Ms. *magazine in January 1985, Ozick tries to define* excellence, *a surprisingly uncomfortable task for a precise writer.*

In my Depression childhood, whenever I had a new dress, my 1 cousin Sarah would get suspicious. The nicer the dress was, and especially the more expensive it looked, the more suspicious she would get. Finally she would lift the hem and check the seams. This was to see if the dress had been bought or if my mother had sewed it. Sarah could always tell. My mother's sewing had elegant outsides, but there was something catch-as-catch-can about the insides. Sarah's sewing, by contrast, was as impeccably finished inside as out; not one stray thread dangled.

My uncle Jake built meticulous grandfather clocks out of rose- 2 wood; he was a perfectionist, and sent to England for the clockworks. My mother built serviceable radiator covers and a serviceable cabinet, with hinged doors, for the pantry. She built a pair of bookcases for the living room. Once, after I was grown and in a house of my own, she fixed the sewer pipe. She painted ceilings, and also landscapes; she re-upholstered chairs. One summer she planted a whole yard of tall corn. She thought herself capable of doing anything, and did everything she imagined. But nothing was perfect. There was always some clear flaw, never visible head-on. You had to look underneath where the seams were. The corn thrived, though not in rows. The stalks elbowed one another like gossips in a dense little village.

"Miss Brrrrooooobaker," my mother used to mock, rolling her 3
Russian *r*s, whenever I crossed a *t* she had left uncrossed, or corrected
a word she had misspelled, or became impatient with a *v* that had
tangled itself up with a *w* in her speech. ("V*vv*entriloquist," I would
say. "V*vv*entriloquist," she would obediently repeat. And the next time
it would come out "wiolinist.") Miss Brubaker was my high school
English teacher, and my mother invoked her name as an emblem of
raging finical obsession. "Miss Brrrrooooobaker," my mother's voice
hoots at me down the years, as I go on casting and recasting sentences
in a tiny handwriting on monomaniacally uniform paper. The loops of
my mother's handwriting—it was the Palmer Method—were as big as
hoops, spilling generous splashy ebullience. She could pull off, at five
minutes' notice, a satisfying dinner for 10 concocted out of nothing
more than originality and panache. But the napkin would be folded a
little off-center, and the spoon might be on the wrong side of the knife.
She was an optimist who ignored trifles; for her, God was not in the
details but in the intent. And all these culinary and agricultural efflorescences were extracurricular, accomplished in the crevices and niches of
a 14-hour business day. When she scribbled out her family memoirs, in
heaps of dog-eared notebooks, or on the backs of old bills, or on the
margins of last year's calendar, I would resist typing them; in the speed
of the chase she often omitted words like "the," "and," "will." The
same flashing and bountiful hand fashioned and fired ceramic pots, and
painted brilliant autumn views and vases of imaginary flowers and ferns,
and decorated ordinary Woolworth platters and lavish enameled gardens. But bits of the painted petals would chip away.

Lavish: my mother was as lavish as nature. She woke early and sat- 4
urated the hours with work and inventiveness, and read late into the
night. She was all profusion, abundance, fabrication. Angry at her children, she would run after us whirling the cord of the electric iron, like
a lasso or a whip; but she never caught us. When, in the seventh grade,
I was afraid of failing the Music Appreciation final exam because I could
not tell the difference between "To a Wild Rose" and "Barcarolle," she
got the idea of sending me to school with a gauze sling rigged up on my
writing arm, and an explanatory note that was purest fiction. But the
sling kept slipping off. My mother gave advice like mad—she boiled
over with so much passion for the predicaments of strangers that they
turned into permanent cronies. She told intimate stories about people
I had never heard of.

Despite the gargantuan Palmer loops (or possibly because of 5
them), I have always known that my mother's was a life of—intricately
abashing word!—excellence: insofar as excellence means ripe generos-

ity. She burgeoned, she proliferated; she was endlessly leafy and flowering. She wore red hats, and called herself a Gypsy. In her girlhood she
marched with the suffragettes and for Margaret Sanger and called herself a Red. She made me laugh, she was so varied: like a tree on which
lemons, pomegranates, and prickly pears absurdly all hang together.
She had the comedy of prodigality.

My own way is a thousand times more confined. I am a pinched per- 6
fectionist, the ultimate fruition of Miss Brubaker; I attend to crabbed
minutiae and am self-trammeled through taking pains. I am a kind of
human snail, locked in and condemned by my own nature. The ancients
believed that the moist track left by the snail as it crept was the snail's
own essence, depleting its body little by little; the farther the snail
toiled, the smaller it became, until it finally rubbed itself out. This is
how perfectionists are. Say to us Excellence, and we will show you how
we use up our substance and wear ourselves away, while making scarcely
any progress at all. The fact that I am an exacting perfectionist in a narrow strait only, and nowhere else, is hardly to the point, since nothing
matters to me so much as a comely and muscular sentence. It is my
narrow strait, this snail's road: the track of the sentence I am writing
now; and when I have eked out the wet substance, ink or blood, that
is its mark, I will begin the next sentence. Only in reading out sentences
am I perfectionist; but then there is nothing else I know how to do, or
take much interest in. I miter every pair of abutting sentences as scrupulously as Uncle Jake fitted one strip of rosewood against another. My
mother's worldly and bountiful hand has escaped me. The sentence I
am writing is my cabin and my shell, compact, self-sufficient. It is the
burnished horizon—a merciless planet where flawlessness is the single
standard, where even the inmost seams, however hidden from a laser
eye, must meet perfection. Here "excellence" is not strewn casually
from a tipped cornucopia, here disorder does not account for charm,
here trifles rule like tyrants.

I measure my life in sentences, and my sentences are superior to my 7
mother's, pressed out, line by line, like the lustrous ooze on the underside of the snail, the snail's secret open seam, its wound, leaking attar.
My mother was too mettlesome to feel the force of a comma. She
scorned minutiae. She measured her life according to what poured
from the horn of plenty, which was her ample, cascading, elastic, susceptible, inexact heart. My narrower heart rides between the tiny horns
of the snail, dwindling as it goes.

And out of this thinnest thread, this ink-wet line of words, must 8
rise a visionary fog, a mist, a smoke, forging cities, histories, sorrows,
quagmires, entanglements, lives of sinners, even the life of my furnace-

hearted mother: so much wilderness, waywardness, plentitude on the head of the precise and impeccable snail, between the horns.

QUESTIONS ON SUBJECT

1. How does the author define *excellence?* Does Ozick use the same definition of *excellence* for her mother and herself? Explain.
2. What is a suffragette? Who was Margaret Sanger? What is a Red? What do these references tell us about Ozick's mother?
3. What reason does Ozick give for her discomfort with defining *excellence?*
4. Ozick begins her essay by telling about the imperfect seams of the dresses her mother made for her. What do these seams mean to Ozick as she begins writing about herself? Does she find anything positive in them? Explain.

QUESTIONS ON STRATEGY

1. Why do you think Ozick begins her essay by writing about her mother's imperfections? (Glossary: *Beginnings and Endings*) How does this lead into a definition of excellence?
2. Make a case for paragraph 6 in this essay. Does the author's self-raillery belong in this essay? What purpose does it serve? What does it add to the reader's understanding of excellence?
3. How do you see the author's definition of excellence developing in this essay? Do you see any stages to the way Ozick organizes her essay? Explain. (Glossary: *Organization*)
4. What significant tone changes do you sense in this essay? Where do you see them, and what significance do you attach to them? (Glossary: *Tone*)
5. Explain how Ozick uses comparison and contrast to develop her definition of *excellence.* (Glossary: *Comparison and Contrast*)

QUESTIONS ON LANGUAGE

1. Ozick characterizes herself as an exacting perfectionist and her mother as exemplifying generosity. Locate an exact sentence and a generous sentence. After finding them, explain how your definition of exact and generous directed your search for sentences.
2. What extended metaphor does Ozick employ in her essay? Do you think it resonates for both the author and her mother? Explain.
3. Refer to your desk dictionary to determine the meanings of the following words as they are used in this selection: *finical* (paragraph 3), *monomaniacally* (3), *ebullience* (3), *panache* (3), *efflorescences* (3), *profusion* (4),

cronies (4), *abashing* (5), *burgeoned* (5), *proliferated* (5), *prodigality* (5), *fruition* (6), *minutiae* (6), *burnished* (6), *cornucopia* (6), *quagmires* (8).

WRITING SUGGESTIONS

1. Write your own essay defining *excellence*. How do you define excellence and in what activities do you pursue excellence? What people in your life exemplify excellence? Can your definition encompass all of the different kinds of excellence you've encountered?

2. *Excellence* is an abstract term, open to interpretation, yet any definition of it must still be supported with credible evidence. Write an essay in which you define one of the following abstract terms. Include in your definition of the word a definition of what it is "not."

choice	honesty
peace	discrimination
patriotism	morality
civil disobedience	responsibility
censorship	rights

Clip Art

NICHOLSON BAKER

Nicholson Baker was born on January 7, 1957, in New York City. He attended the Eastman School of Music and later graduated from Haverford College in 1980. After working variously as an oil analyst, word processor, and technical writer, he embarked on a full-time writing career in 1987. Although best known for his quirky, innovative fiction including the novels The Mezzanine *(1988) and* Room Temperature *(1990), Baker contributes stories and essays to such magazines as* Atlantic *and* The New Yorker. U and I, *a work of nonfiction, appeared in 1991.*

In the following essay, first published in The New Yorker *on November 7, 1994, Nicholson Baker provides a witty definition of the "homeliest and most durable of our fashion accessories," the fingernail clipper.*

Professional men can't sport much in the way of jewelry. The gemless wedding band, the watch, the belt buckle, the key chain, the car, possibly the quietly costly blue-enamelled pen in a shirt pocket are among the few sanctioned outlets for the male self-embellishing urge. Occasionally permissible are the shirt stud, the cufflink, and the nautical brass blazer button. Bas-relief suspender clasps, various forms of tie and collar tackle, and chunky nonmarital fingerware are allowable on men who make a living by commission. The demotion of smoke has eliminated the ornate cigarette lighter. Neck and wrist chains are inadvisable. Metalwork for the male nostril, tongue, ear, or foreskin is an option only in outlying areas.

But fingernail and toenail clippers—the unworn but elegant accessories to all men's fashion, since no man has ever looked presentable with long nails (long being anything over three-sixteenths of an inch)—continue to glitter legitimately in an otherwise unpolished age. Like fancy pens and pocket watches, these palmable curios have a function—that of severing corneous shrapnel from key areas of the human body with a bracing abruptness, a can-do metallic snap, that leaves their user with the illusion that he is progressively, clip by hardened-steel clip, gaining control of his shambling life. They offer some of the satisfactions of working out on exercise machines without the sweat and gym shorts; some of the pleasures of knuckle manipulation without the risk of arthritic deformity; some of the rewards of cracking a nut without having to eat it. You may crouch over the wastebasket while you operate, but there is happily no assurance that anything clipped will end up there; for just as certain insects will hop or fly off so fast that they seem not to displace themselves physically but simply to disappear on the spot, so the clipper chip vanishes at the very instant the jaws meet and chime, propelled toward a windowsill or on some untraceable tangent, never to trouble anyone again unless a bare foot happens to rediscover it.

The market for clippers is apparently unsaturable. This year, mil- 3 lions of men will buy one, as they have for decades, despite the fact that these maintenance tools almost never wear out and are entirely unnecessary. You can cut your nails just fine with a decent pair of scissors, assuming a rudimentary ambidextrousness; in fact, from one point of view a scissor cut is less labor-intensive than clipping, since, despite the helpful curvature of the clipper jaws, it often takes three angled snips to approximate the arc of a given fingernail. (The cut facets thus formed are surprisingly sharp the first time you scratch an itch, but they wear away in a day.) Clippers sell steadily because, like clippings, they disappear (in the backs of drawers, in glove compartments) and must be replaced, and because they are beautiful and cheap. A big clear drum of ninety-nine-cent Trim-brand clippers sitting near the drugstore's cash register like a bucket of freshly netted minnows is an almost irresistible sight. They are the ideal weight and smoothness; they exploit the resiliency of their material both to maintain their assembly without rattling and to hold their business edges apart. They appear to have aerodynamic virtues. And, once bought, they can alter their profile in a single puzzle-solving flip-and-pivot of the lever arm, without excessive play or roughness or torn rotator cuffs, from minnow shape to grasshopper shape and back again. True children of the dexter brain, they were our first toy Transformers: metallic dual-phase origamis that seem triumphantly Japanese and yet happen to be, in their perfected form, a product of the small town of Derby, in southern Connecticut, near the Sikorsky helicopter plant.

In the forties, the W. E. Bassett Company made washers for the 4 rubber heel pieces on men's shoes (these stopped nails from piercing through to the foot area) and artillery components for the United States Army. After the war, William E. Bassett, founder, retooled his equipment in Derby, and devoted himself to the production of a superior jaw-style nail clipper, the Trim clipper. The jawed design had been around since the nineteenth century, but Bassett was its Bernini. He added, for example, two thoughtful nibs near the base of the tiny (and, in the experience of some, unused) nail file which together keep the lever arm aligned in its closed position; and he replaced the unsatisfactory pinned rivet with the lovely *notched* rivet. (The Chinese still use pinned rivets in their mediocre baby-nail clipper, manufactured for Evenflo.) The stylish, and patented, thumb-swerve in the Trim's lever was Bassett's idea, too.

According to William's brother Henry (who died, as the chairman 5 of the board, in May of 1994, at the age of eighty-four), the best fingernail clipper Bassett ever made was the Croydon model of the late forties. It was stamped with a clipper-ship emblem and was promoted in *Esquire* for the jewelry-store trade. But William Bassett's sons William C. Bassett, now the president and treasurer, and Dave Bassett, now the company's manufacturing engineering manager, continue the work of innovation and cost-manicuring. Despite some exciting recent work by the Koreans, who manufacture all Revlon's more expensive but not quite so well-finished clippers, along with the Gem line, the Trim clipper by Bassett continues its reign as the best on the planet. (Clippers are chrome-plated after being assembled. The finished Revlon clippers frequently betray their undercoating in those areas where one part obscured another in the electrolyte solution; Trim clippers, on the other hand, because they are designed to minimize this shadowing, almost never do.)

All Bassett's grooming aids—from emery boards to tweezers—earn 6 high marks among power users, in fact; this past August, for example, Jerry Lewis's secretary called the company directly to order a dozen five-inch triple-cut Trim nail files (with accompanying blue vinyl protective sheaths), because Mr. Lewis couldn't obtain them locally. "The tweezer is a very fussy item," Dave Bassett said recently. Each Bassett tweezer tip (its inner edge ground "to help grab that hair") is inspected manually, under a magnifier. The company makes nail clippers plated in gold as well as in chrome; its Heirloom line offers gift sets like the Saddlebag, which includes scissors, a bottle opener, and folding nail files, along with an anchor pair of clippers. This Christmas, Bassett will be selling the Holiday Family Manicure Kit, with a fingernail clipper and a toenail clipper, two wooden cuticle pokers, some emery boards, and a pair of tweezers, displayed against a background of falling snow and rising reindeer. (What better way to spend Christmas morning with one's loved ones?) For Dr. Scholl's, Bassett has created an extraordinary matte-black and gold-plated piece of toenail-cleaving insanity that would not be out of place dangling from the rearview mirror of a new forty-valve 3.5-litre Ferrari F355.

It won't do to labor the parallels between caring for a fingernail and 7 manufacturing a fingernail clipper. Making a clipper is considerably more complex. Still, it is striking how reminiscent of human clippings are the spurned little pieces of scrap metal exiting from the side of the deafening Minster stamping press. Once cut (from rolls of Midwestern steel, at an impact force of roughly fifteen tons), the clipper "blanks" must be cleaned of oil, spot-welded, racked, hardened for two hours in a massive furnace, then oil-quenched, cleaned again, tempered in a second furnace to limber them up a little, and finally revolved in huge barrels with sixty thousand of their fellows for several days in a slurry of metal slugs, abrasives, and lime, to smooth away unhandy burrs. Vibrating bowls jiggle the components into sequential position, preparing them for a definitive riveting, which is accompanied by a Fred Astaire-like volley of air-cylinder tappings and flourishes. Each clipper gets a sharpened cutting edge; a digital imaging system checks the finished edges for parallelism. Eyelets, shot in at the caudal end, affix the nail files; then the entire splayed clipper, racked on hooks, proceeds through the plating sequence—ten minutes in a warm nickel bath, a minute or two of chrome. A nimble piece of pneumatics straightens the akimbo file and closes the lever. At last the basic Bassett fingernail clipper is ready for action. You can determine the year your clipper was made by referring to the inside of the lever arm.

    Nail care has been weighing on my thoughts recently, I confess, be- 8 cause the great Stephen King, in an introduction to his recent short-story collection, "Nightmares & Dreamscapes," describes one of my books as a "meaningless little fingernail paring." Are we to infer from "paring" that the Bard of Bangor doesn't possess or know how to operate a Trim (or a Gem, or a Revlon, or even a La Cross) clipper of his own? Does he envision himself as the heir of Joyce's artist-hero, in "A Portrait of the Artist as a Young Man," who was "refined out of existence, indifferent, paring his fingernails"? Does he still whittle? (Bassett's sales are "really taking off" in Ireland right now, according to Barbara Shannon, the company's marketing manager; it seems that the Irish are through with Joyce's manual methods and insist on taking, with Trim's help, the shortcut to artistry.) Or is Mr. King rather implying that someone like me disdainfully pares and fiddles while he, market-wise progressivist, hacks on with the latest technology?

    If so, I can assure Mr. King that I, too, clip—not as often as I 9 should, perhaps, but with genuine enthusiasm. When I want a really authentic experience, I sometimes use a toenail clipper on my fingernails, shuddering with the thrill of fulcrumed power; and then, for my toes, I step on up to Revlon's veterinary-gauge Nipper, a parrot-beaked personal-pruning weapon that, but for its chrome plate, looks as if it should be stored in the garage. A dense, semi-opaque shard cut by this nineteen-dollar piece of spring-loaded Brazilian craftsmanship recently rose from what was left of my ravished toenail and travelled across the room, landing in a box of tax records, where it remains.

We can say with some certainty (and sadness) that Nabokov did *not* 10 use nail clippers. That is, John Shade, "Pale Fire"'s poet, did not:

> *The little scissors I am holding* are
> A dazzling synthesis of sun and star.
> I stand before the window and I pare
> My fingernails. . . .

(Italics mine.) The cutting of a fingernail is important in Nabokov: 11 it may constitute for him the act of self-liberation from annotative servitude, since he is demonstrably aware of the traditional scholarly use of the nail's edge as a marginal place-inscriber. In Pushkin's "Eugene Onegin," Tatiana learns about Onegin's mind by studying his library, and she notices (in Nabokov's translation) that

> Many pages preserved
> the trenchant mark of fingernails.

Nabokov's commentary to these lines mentions Sheridan's "The 12 Rivals" (dismissing it in passing, with his usual harshness, as a "singularly inept comedy"), in which someone "cherishes her nails for the convenience of making marginal notes." Nabokov adds, puzzlingly, "The art is a lost one today." Hardly so: even with a closely clipped and manly thumbnail, the reader can and very often does, today, in America, score a visible double line to mark an interesting passage, if it appears in a book that he is prevented for one reason or another from defacing. In those midnight moments of the misplaced pencil, too, a nail impression is a less destructive and more spatially precise aid to memory than a turned-down corner. Moreover, the pressure of the reader's nail, deformed by its momentary trenchancy, against the tender hyponychial tissues it protects creates a transient thumbwide pleasure that is, or can be, more than literary.

But the most troubling feature of Stephen King's assessment of my 13 alleged "nail paring" of a novel is his apparent belief that a bookish toe- or fingernail scrap can be justifiably brushed off as meaningless. Last September, Allen Ginsberg sold a bag of his beard hair to Stanford. Surely Mr. King ought to be saving for the ages whatever gnarled relics he clips or pares? And the Master Spellbinder, of all people, should be able to detect the secret terrors, the moans of the severed but unquiet soul, that reside in these disjecta. Think of the fearful Norse ship of the apocalypse, Naglfar, made of dead men's nails, which will break loose from its moorings during the Monstrous Winter, when the Wolf has swallowed the Sun—"a warning," in Brian Branston's retelling, "that if a man dies with his nails unshorn he is adding greatly to the materials for Naglfar (a thing both gods and men would be slow to do)." Gertrude Jobes's mythological dictionary cites a related Finno-Ugric tradition in which the Evil One collects any Sunday nail parings and "with them builds the boat for transporting the dead." Lithuanian folklore contends (per Stith Thompson) that "from the parings of man's nails devils make little caps for themselves." I didn't have a chance to ask any of the employees at the factory in Derby, Connecticut, many of whom are first- or second-generation Polish, whether they had heard similar tales.

Lest someone unknowingly aid the devils in their hattery (would a 14 fingernail hat resemble a miniature wicker knickknack basket, one wonders, or would the snippets be sewn or glued on, like sequins?), the Bassett Company, in 1990, launched the Easy Hold clipper. The Easy Hold line features an unusual pair of ambidextrous cuticle scissors, with forefinger-rests that aid fine work (U.S. Design Patent No. 331,867); a foam emery-board holder; and an enhanced tweezer that makes the removal of other people's splinters even more of a wicked joy than it always has been. But the new nail clippers go further: in addition to a considerate plastic thumb element, they include a housing for the jaw which catches nearly every snippet the moment it is clipped.

Eric Rommerdale, the head of laboratory technology at the Uni- 15 versity of Mississippi School of Dentistry, in Jackson, is the unexpected principal figure behind the development of all the Easy Hold grooming products. Mr. Rommerdale, fifty-two, a white-mustached ex-Navy man, is no stranger to inventive self-care, having in his off-hours developed Sunbeam's triple-brush, hands-free toothbrushing system (now sold by DKI Inc.) and the mouth-stick-activated urine-bag release valve, both for the disabled. His big fingernail moment came in November, 1987, in a Stop-n-Go, while he was watching a man in his seventies with "hands the size of baseball mitts" trying to clip his nails. Three times the clipper fell to the floor. Out of polymer resin (often used in dental work) Rommerdale built a pair of add-on clipper grips and tried to interest Revlon in them. Revlon said no, unequivocally. But in 1988 William Bassett the younger listened to a pitch by Rommerdale in the lobby of the Bridgeport Hilton, liked what he heard, and asked the inventor to rethink the graspability of the entire manicure line. The University of Mississippi Medical Center then evaluated and refined the prototypes (under a grant from the Bassett Company), videotaping and surveying a group of talkative elderly beta-testers.

Although Rommerdale's original rounded design gained, in its final, 16 blister-packed form, a few unwelcome projections and some squared-off edges that cry out for smoothing ("We could have done a better job on that," William Bassett admits), it is nonetheless heartening to find that the stylistic history of the clipper—one of the great bureau-top products of the century—is far from over. This coming January, all plastic Easy Hold fittings, presently colored a battleship gray, will turn teal green, after extensive mall-site interviewing. Eric Rommerdale, using his patent royalties, recently expanded his back-yard workshop, and he is currently developing safer tools for meat cutters and a jar opener for the disabled. It seems there is still time for all of us to clip our nails closely and carefully before the coming of the Monstrous Winter, when Naglfar will set sail.

QUESTIONS ON SUBJECT

1. According to Baker, what are some of the defining characteristics of fingernail clippers? What satisfactions do these clippers offer?

2. What innovations did William E. Bassett bring to the clipper after World War II? What new features were introduced in 1990 with the Easy Hold clipper?

3. Why, according to Baker, is Bassett's Trim clipper superior to others on the market?

4. In paragraphs 8–13, Baker introduces such writers as King, Joyce, Nabokov, Pushkin, Sheridan, and Ginsberg. In what ways, if any, are these literary figures important to a discussion of fingernail clippers? Explain.

5. What is the meaning of Baker's last line? Does his final paragraph effectively conclude this essay? Why, or why not?

QUESTIONS ON STRATEGY

1. How does Baker's opening paragraph prepare us for a discussion of fingernail clippers? (Glossary: *Beginnings*)

2. What techniques does Baker use to define fingernail clippers? Does he ever present a formal definition of fingernail clippers? If so, where?

3. How would you describe Baker's tone in this essay? (Glossary: *Tone*) Is this tone appropriate for his subject and his *New Yorker* audience? Explain.

4. Baker uses parentheses a great deal in this essay. Examine the types of information that he includes parenthetically. What conclusions can you draw about his use of parentheses?

5. What rhetorical strategy does Baker use in paragraph 7 to explain the manufacturing process of fingernail clippers?

QUESTIONS ON LANGUAGE

1. How would you characterize Baker's diction in this essay? (Glossary: *Diction*) Why do you suppose he uses such language to discuss the everyday fingernail clipper? Explain with reference to specific words that Baker uses.

2. Identify four or more figures of speech that Baker uses, and explain how each works in the context of this essay.

3. Refer to your desk dictionary to determine the meanings of the following words as they are used in this selection: *sanctioned* (1), *curios* (2), *shambling* (2), *unsaturable* (3), *resiliency* (3), *caudal* (7), *splayed* (7), *akimbo* (7), *annotative* (11), *trenchancy* (12).

WRITING ASSIGNMENTS

1. Using Baker's essay as a model, write an essay of definition about some commonplace item such as a paper clip, chewing gum, a TV remote control, a key ring, or a belt.

2. Every generation develops its own slang, which generally enlivens the speech and writing of those who use it. Ironically, however, no generation can arrive at a consensus definition of even its most popular slang terms— for example, *bummer, dork,* and *air-head.* Select a slang term that you use frequently, and write an essay in which you define the term. Read your definition aloud in class. Do the other members of your class agree with your definition?

WRITING SUGGESTIONS FOR DEFINITION

1. Some of the most pressing social issues in American life today are further complicated by imprecise definition of critical terms. Various medical cases, for example, have brought worldwide attention to the legal and medical definitions of the word *death*. Debates continue about the meanings of other controversial words such as:

   a. morality
   b. minority (ethnic)
   c. alcoholism
   d. cheating
   e. pornography
   f. kidnapping
   g. drugs
   h. censorship
   i. remedial
   j. insanity
   k. monopoly (business)
   l. literacy
   m. success
   n. happiness
   o. life
   p. equality

   Select one of these words, and write an essay in which you discuss not only the definition of the term but also the problems associated with defining it.

2. Write an essay in which you define one of the words listed below by telling not only what it *is* but also what it *is not*. (For example, it has been said that "poetry is that which cannot be expressed in any other way.") Remember, however, that defining by negation does not relieve you of the responsibility of defining the term in other ways as well.

   a. intelligence
   b. leadership
   c. fear
   d. patriotism
   e. wealth
   f. failure
   g. family
   h. style
   i. loyalty
   j. selflessness
   k. creativity
   l. humor

8

CAUSE AND EFFECT ANALYSIS

WHAT IS CAUSE AND EFFECT ANALYSIS?

From the time children begin to talk, they exhibit a natural curiosity about the world by asking questions. Such questioning is among the most common of human activities: "Why are babies born?" "Why do people cheat?" "Why can't we find a cure for cancer?" "Why are there homeless and hungry people in America?" "What if grades were abolished in college?" "What if the stock market crashed again?" "What would happen if drunk drivers were given mandatory jail sentences?" "What would happen if the U.S. space program were expanded?" Answering questions like these means engaging in the process of *cause and effect analysis*. Whenever a question asks *why*, answering it will require discovering a *cause* or series of causes for a particular *effect*; whenever a question asks *what if*, its answer will point out the effect or effects that can result from a particular cause. Cause and effect analysis, then, is a way of discovering important relationships between events or circumstances.

You will have frequent opportunity to use cause and effect analysis in the writing you do in college. For example, a history instructor might ask you to explain the causes of the Seven-Day War between Egypt and Israel. In a paper for an American literature course, you might try to determine why *The Adventures of Huckleberry Finn* has sparked so much controversy in a number of schools and communities. On an environmental studies exam, you might have to speculate about the effects acid rain will have on the ecology of northeastern Canada and the United States. Demonstrating an understanding of cause and effect is crucial to the process of learning.

While the ultimate purpose of cause and effect analysis may seem simple—*to know* or *to understand*—determining causes and effects is often a thought-provoking and complex strategy. One reason for this complexity is that some causes are less obvious than others. *Immediate causes* are readily apparent, because they are closest in time to the effect; the immediate cause of a flood, for example, may be the collapse of a dam. However, *remote causes* may be just as important, even though they are not so apparent and perhaps even hidden. The remote (and, in fact, primary) cause of the flood might have been an engineering error or the use of substandard building materials or the failure of personnel to relieve the pressure on the dam caused by unseasonably heavy rains. In many cases it is necessary to look beyond the most immediate causes to discover the true sources of an event.

Furthermore, it may be necessary to trace a *causal chain:* an initial cause may bring about a particular effect, which in turn becomes the immediate cause of a further effect, and so on down to the effect that interests you. Before a computer salesperson approaches an important client about a big sale, she prepares extensively for the meeting (initial cause). Her preparation leads her to impress the client (effect A), which guarantees her the big sale (effect B), which results in her promotion to district sales manager (effect C). The sale she made is the most immediate and the most obvious cause of her promotion; but it is possible to trace the chain back to its more essential cause, her hard work preparing for the meeting.

A second reason for the complexity of this strategy is the difficulty of distinguishing between possible and actual causes, as well as between possible and actual effects. An upset stomach may be caused by spoiled food; but it may also be caused by overeating, by flu, by nervousness, by pregnancy, or by a combination of factors. Similarly, an increase in the cost of electricity may have multiple effects: higher profits for utility companies, fewer sales of electrical appliances, higher prices for other products that depend on electricity in their manufacture, even the development of alternative sources of energy. Making reasonable choices among the various possibilities requires thought and care.

WHY DO WRITERS USE CAUSE AND EFFECT ANALYSIS?

Writers may use cause and effect analysis for three essential purposes: to inform, to speculate, and to argue. Most commonly, they will want to inform, to help their readers understand some identifiable fact. A state wildlife biologist, for example, might wish to tell the public about the effects severe winter weather has had on the state's deer herd; or in a newsletter a member of Congress might explain to his or her constituency the reasons changes are being made in the Social Security system. In an essay later in this chapter ("Television and Family Life"), Marie Winn uses cause and effect analysis to inform, by exploring the effects television has on American parents and their children.

Cause and effect analysis may also allow writers to speculate, to consider what might be or what might have been. To satisfy the Board of Trustees, for example, a university treasurer could discuss the impact a raise in tuition will have on the school's budget; a columnist for *People* magazine might speculate about the reasons for a new singer's increasing popularity. Similarly, pollsters are estimating the effects the female vote will have on future elections, and historians are evaluating how the Kennedy presidency will continue to influence American government in the closing decade of this century.

Finally, cause and effect analysis provides an excellent basis from which to argue a given position or point of view. Parents, for example, might argue that the ill effects of curtailing extracurricular activities in their children's high school far outweigh the potential savings. An editorial writer could argue that bringing a professional ball club into the area would have many positive effects on the local economy and on the community as a whole. And educators who think that video games are a cause of delinquency and poor school performance have argued in newspapers and professional journals against the widespread acceptance of such games. Alice Walker's essay "My Daughter Smokes" is an excellent example of how cause and effect analysis can provide the basis for an effective argument.

LOOKING AT CAUSE AND EFFECT ANALYSIS

First, determine whether the author is more interested in the causes or the effects of the action, event, or object under discussion. Then consider how reasonable, effective, and helpful the author's analysis actually seems to be.

One common use of the strategy is for the writer to identify the particular causal agent or circumstance and then discuss the consequences or effects it has had (or may have). In the following passage from his book *The Telephone*, it is clear from the first sentence that John Brooks is primarily concerned with the effects that the telephone has had (or may have had) on modern life.

What has the telephone done to us, or for us, in the hundred years of its existence? A few effects suggest themselves at once. It has saved lives by getting rapid word of illness, injury, or famine from remote places. By joining with the elevator to make possible the multistory residence or office building, it has made possible—for better or worse—the modern city. By bringing about a quantum leap in the speed and ease with which information moves from place to place, it has greatly accelerated the rate of scientific and technological change and growth in industry. Beyond doubt it has crippled if not killed the ancient art of letter writing. It has made living alone possible for persons with normal social impulses; by so doing, it has played a role in one of the greatest social changes of this century, the breakup of the multigenerational household. It has made the waging of war chillingly more efficient than formerly. Perhaps (though not provably) it has prevented wars that might have arisen out of international misunderstanding caused by written communication. Or perhaps—again not provably—by magnifying and extending irrational personal conflicts based on voice contact, it has caused wars. Certainly it has extended the scope of human conflicts, since it impartially disseminates the useful knowledge of scientists and the babble of bores, the affection of the affectionate and the malice of the malicious.

The bulk of Brooks's paragraph is devoted to a catalog that answers the very question he poses in his opening sentence: "What has the telephone done to us, or for us, in the hundred years of its existence?" Notice that even though many of the effects Brooks discusses are verifiable or probable, he is willing to admit that he is speculating about those effects that he cannot prove.

Another common use of the strategy is for the writer to describe an important event or problem (effect) and then to examine the possible reasons (causes) for it. For example, different experts might trace the causes of poverty to any or all of the following: poor education, a non-progressive tax system, declining commitment to social services, inflation, discrimination, or the very welfare system that is designed to help the poor.

A third use of the strategy is for the writer to explore a complex causal chain. In this selection from his book *The Politics of Energy*, Barry Commoner examines the series of malfunctions that led to the near disaster at Three Mile Island nuclear facility in Harrisburg, Pennsylvania.

On March 28, 1979, at 3:53 A.M., a pump at the Harrisburg plant failed. Because the pump failed, the reactor's heat was not drawn off in the heat exchanger and the very hot water in the primary loop overheated. The pressure in the loop increased, opening a release valve that was supposed to counteract such an event. But the valve stuck open and the primary loop system lost so much water (which ended up as a highly radioactive pool, six feet deep, on the floor of the reactor building) that it was unable to carry off all the heat generated within the reactor core. Under these circumstances, the intense heat held within the reactor could, in theory, melt its fuel rods, and the resulting "meltdown" could then carry a hugely radioactive mass through the floor of the reactor. The reactor's emergency cooling system, which is designed to prevent this disaster, was then automatically activated; but when it was, apparently, turned off too soon, some of the fuel rods overheated. This produced a bubble of hydrogen gas at the top of the reactor. (The hydrogen is dissolved in the water in order to react with oxygen that is produced when the intense reactor radiation splits water molecules into their atomic constituents. When heated, the dissolved hydrogen bubbles out of the solution.) This bubble blocked the flow of cooling water so that despite the action of the emergency cooling system the reactor core was again in danger of melting down. Another danger was that the gas might contain enough oxygen to cause an explosion that could rupture the huge containers that surround the reactor and release a deadly cloud of radioactive material into the surrounding countryside. Working desperately, technicians were able to gradually reduce the size of the gas bubble using a special apparatus brought in from the atomic laboratory at Oak Ridge, Tennessee, and the danger of a catastrophic release of radioactive materials subsided. But the sealed-off plant was now so radioactive that no one could enter it for many months—or, according to some observers, for years—without being exposed to a lethal dose of radiation.

Tracing a causal chain, as Commoner does here, is similar to narration: the writer must organize the events sequentially to show clearly how each one leads to the next.

READING CAUSE AND EFFECT ANALYSIS IN AN ANNOTATED STUDENT ESSAY

Born in Brooklyn, New York, Kevin Cunningham spent most of his life in Flemington, New Jersey. While enrolled in the mechanical engineering program at the University of Vermont, Cunningham shared an apartment near the Burlington waterfront with several other students. There he became interested in the effects that private real estate development—or gentrification—would have on his neighborhood. Such development is not peculiar to Burlington, Vermont; it is happening in the older sections of cities across the country. After gathering information for his essay by talking with the various people who live in the neighborhood, Cunningham found it useful to discuss both the causes and the effects of gentrification.

GENTRIFICATION
Kevin Cunningham

"I went back to Ohio, and my city was gone . . ."
—Chrissie Hynde, of the Pretenders

My city is in Vermont, not Ohio, but soon my   1
neighborhood will probably be gone, too. Or maybe
it's I that will be gone. My street, Lakeview Terrace,
lies unobtrusively in the old northwest part of Burlington and is notable, as its name suggests, for
spectacular views of Lake Champlain framed by the
Adirondacks. It's not that the neighborhood is going
to seed—no, quite the contrary. Recently it has been
Thesis   Discovered, and now it is on the verge of being Gen-
trified. For some of us who live here, that's bad.
Description of   Cities are often assigned human characteristics,   2
life-cycle of city   one of which is a life-cycle: they have a birth, a
neighborhoods.   youth, a middle age, and an old age. A neighborhood
is built and settled by young, vibrant people, proud of
their sturdy new homes. Together, residents and
houses mature, as families grow larger and extensions
get built on. Eventually, though, the neighborhood
begins to show its age. Buildings sag a little, houses
aren't repainted as quickly, and maintenance slips.
The neighborhood may grow poorer, as the young and
upwardly mobile find new jobs and move away, while
the older and less successful inhabitants remain.
Decay, renewal,   One of three fates awaits the aging neighborhood.   3
or redevelopment   Decay may continue until the neighborhood becomes
await aging   a slum. It may face urban renewal, with old buildings
neighborhoods   being razed and ugly, new apartment houses taking
Writer interested   their place. Or it may undergo redevelopment, in
in what happens   which government encourages the upgrading of exist-
when a neigh-   ing housing stock by offering low-interest loans or
borhood is
redeveloped.

outright grants; thus, the original character of the neighborhood may be retained or restored, allowing the city to keep part of its identity.

Example of Hoboken, New Jersey.

An example of redevelopment at its best is Hoboken, New Jersey. In the early 1970s Hoboken was a dying city, with rundown housing and many abandoned buildings. However, low-interest loans enabled some younger residents to begin to refurbish their homes, and soon the area began to show signs of renewed vigor. Even outsiders moved in and rebuilt some of the abandoned houses. Today, whole blocks have been restored, and neighborhood life is active again. The city does well too, because property values are higher and so are property taxes. And there, at least for my neighborhood, is the rub.

Effects of redevelopment on Hoboken.

Transition: writer moves from example of Hoboken to his Lakeview Terrace neighborhood.

Lakeview Terrace is a demographic potpourri of students and families, young professionals and elderly retirees, home-owners and renters. It's a quiet street where kids can play safely and the neighbors know each other. Most of the houses are fairly old and look it, but already some redevelopment has begun. Recently, several old houses were bought by a real estate company, rebuilt, and sold as condominiums; the new residents drive BMWs and keep to themselves. The house where I live is owned by a Young Urban Professional couple—he's an architect—and they have renovated the place to what it must have looked like when it was new. They did a nice job, too. These two kinds of development are the main forms of gentrification, and so far they have done no real harm.

Describes "gentrification" to date.

But the city is about to start a major property tax reappraisal. Because of the renovations, the houses on Lakeview Terrace are currently worth more than they used to be; soon there will be a big jump in property taxes. And then a lot of people will be hurt—even dispossessed from their own neighborhood.

Redevelopment causes property values to increase which in will cause property taxes to go up

Clem is a retired General Electric employee who has lived on Lakeview for over thirty years and who

*Effects of gentri-
fication on local
property owners.* owns his home. About three years ago some condos
were built on the lot next door, which didn't please
Clem—he says they just don't fit in. But with higher
property taxes, it may be Clem who no longer fits in.
At the very least, since he's on a fixed income, he
will have to make sacrifices in order to stay. Ryan
works as a mailman and also owns his Lakeview
Terrace home, which is across the street from the
houses that were converted into condos: same
cause, same effect.

*Effects of
gentrification on
renters.* Then there are those of us who rent. As our land- 8
lords have to pay higher property taxes, they will
naturally raise rents at least as much (and maybe
more, if they've spent money on renovations of their
own). Some of us won't be able to afford the increase
and will have to leave. "Some of us" almost certainly
includes me, as well as others who have lived on
Lakeview Terrace much longer than I have. In fact,
the exodus has already begun, with the people who
were displaced by the condo conversions.

Conclusion Of course, many people would consider what's 9
happening on Lakeview Terrace a genuine improvement in every way, resulting not only in better-
looking houses but also in a better class of people. I
dispute that. The new people may be more affluent
than those they displace, but certainly not "better,"
not by any standard that counts with me. Gentrifica-

*Restatement of
thesis* tion may do wonders for a neighborhood's aesthetics,
but it certainly can be hard on its soul.

WRITING A CAUSE AND EFFECT ANALYSIS

Begin by selecting a manageable topic for your essay. In making
your decision, you will need to consider both the amount of information available to you and the time you have to complete your research
and your writing. For a short essay due in two weeks, for example, you
might concentrate on what is causing increasing numbers of students in
your community to seek part-time jobs; you probably should not,

however, try to examine the reasons for the decline of American labor unions. The second topic will clearly require a significant amount of research and a more elaborate presentation; it is really more suitable for a term paper.

What is then necessary for a successful cause and effect analysis is a clear sense of purpose, as well as a careful and objective examination of the topic.

Establishing Your Focus

Decide whether your essay will propose causes, talk about effects, or analyze both causes and effects. Any research you do, any questions you ask, will depend on how you wish to concentrate your attention. For example, as a reporter for the school paper, you are writing a story about a fire that destroyed a high-rise apartment building in the neighborhood, killing four people. In doing so, you might focus on the cause of the fire (Was there more than one cause? Was carelessness to blame? Was the fire of suspicious origin?); you might focus on the effects of the fire (How much damage was done to the building? How many people were left homeless? What was the impact on the families of the four victims?); or you might cover both the reasons for this tragic event and its ultimate effects, setting up a sort of causal chain. Such a focus is crucial as you gather information. Early on Kevin Cunningham decided that he wanted to explore what would happen (the effects) if gentrification continued on his street.

Determining Your Purpose

Once you begin to draft your essay and as you continue to refine it, make sure your purpose or intention is clear. Do you wish your cause and effect analysis to be primarily informative, speculative, or argumentative? An informative essay allows readers to say, "I learned something from this; I didn't know that the fire was caused by faulty wiring." A speculative essay suggests to readers new possibilities: "That never occurred to me before; the high-rise could indeed be replaced by a professional building." An argumentative essay convinces readers that some sort of action should be taken: "I have to agree; fire inspections should occur more regularly in our neighborhood." Whatever your purpose, be sure to provide the information necessary to carry it through.

In his essay on "Gentrification," Cunningham uses cause and effect analysis to question the value of redevelopment and what it does to the heart and soul of a neighborhood.

Avoiding Oversimplification and Errors of Logic

Sound and thoughtful reasoning, while present in all good writing, is central to any analysis of cause and effect. Writers of convincing cause and effect analysis must examine their material objectively and develop their essays carefully, taking into account any potential objections that readers might raise. Therefore, do not jump to conclusions or let your own prejudices interfere with the logic of your interpretation or the completeness of your presentation. In gathering information for his essay, Kevin Cunningham discovered that he had to watch himself, that he had to distinguish between cause and effect and mere coincidence. "You have to know your subject, and you have to be honest. For example, my downstairs neighbors moved out last month because the rent was raised. Somebody who didn't know the situation might say, 'See? Gentrification.' But that wasn't the reason—it's that heating costs went up. This is New England, and we had a cold winter; gentrification had nothing to do with it. It's something that is just beginning to happen, and it's going to have a big effect, but we haven't actually felt many of the effects here yet."

Be sure that you do not oversimplify the cause and effect relationship you are writing about. A good working assumption is that most important matters cannot be traced to a single provable cause; similarly, a cause or set of causes rarely produces a single isolated effect. In order to be believable, your analysis of your topic must demonstrate a thorough understanding of the surrounding circumstances; there is often nothing less convincing than the single-minded determination to show one particular connection. Of course, to achieve coherence, you will want to emphasize the important causes or the most significant effects. But be careful not to lose your reader's trust by insisting on a simple "X leads to Y" relationship.

The other common problem of cause and effect analysis is the error known as the "after this, therefore because of this" fallacy (in Latin, *post hoc ergo propter hoc*). In attempting to discover an explanation for a particular event or circumstance, a writer may point to something that merely preceded it in time, assuming causal connection where none has in fact been proven. If you have dinner out one evening and the next day come down with stomach cramps, you may blame your illness on the restaurant where you ate the night before; but you do so without justification if your only proof is the fact that you ate there beforehand. More evidence would be required to establish a causal relationship. The *post hoc ergo propter hoc* fallacy is often harmlessly foolish ("I failed the exam because I lost my lucky key chain"). It can, however, lead writers into serious errors of judgment and blind them to more reasonable explanations of cause and effect. And, like oversimplification, such mistakes in logic can undercut a reader's confidence. Make sure that the causal relationships you see are, in fact, based on demonstrable evidence and not merely on a temporal connection.

Striking a Balanced Tone

Be careful neither to overstate nor to understate your position. Avoid superfluous exaggerations like *"there can be no question"* and *"the evidence speaks for itself."* Such diction is generally annoying and brings into question your confidence in the power of your interpretation. Instead, allow your analysis of the facts to convince readers of the cause and effect relationship you wish to suggest; do not be afraid to admit the possibility of other viewpoints. At the same time no analytical writer convinces by understating or qualifying information with words and phrases such as *perhaps, maybe, I think, sometimes, most often, nearly always,* or *in my opinion.* While it may be your intention to appear reasonable, overusing such words can make you sound unclear or indecisive, and your analysis, therefore, will be less convincing. Present your case forcefully, but do so honestly and sensibly.

The Arctic Forest

BARRY HOLSTUN LOPEZ

Barry Holstun Lopez, naturalist, writer, editor, and journalist, was born in 1945 in Port Chester, New York. After studying folklore in graduate school at the University of Oregon, Lopez decided in 1970 to become a full-time writer. He achieved a critical breakthrough in 1978 with Of Wolves and Men, *a comprehensive study of the wolf. Lopez examined scientific information, aboriginal lore, and the wolf in literature, and came to the conclusion that western portrayals of the wolf contrast the wolf's actual behavior, while revealing the fears of a voraciously expanding culture. His work has appeared in several anthologies including* Best American Essays 1987, *and in such magazines as* Harper's, Outside, *and* National Geographic.

In this selection, taken from Arctic Dreams: Imagination and Desire in a Northern Landscape *(1986), Lopez examines the reasons why Arctic trees are so tenacious.*

The northern limit of the continental forests in North America 1 seems anomalous if you try to make sense of the tree line. The boundary sweeps southwest from Labrador to pass beneath James Bay, then turns northwest, crossing Canada's Precambrian Shield and paralleling the Mackenzie River Valley nearly to the Arctic Ocean before zigzagging west through the valleys of the Brooks Range and the Kobuk River to Norton Sound. The explanation for the irregularity of the line lies with the seasonal climate—it marks the average southward extension of arctic air masses in summer.

The far northern trees, like the animals, constitute a very few 2 species—willows growing in valleys where they are protected from the wind and a dwarf form of birch. Along the tree line itself, the only successful strategists are species in the pine and birch families. Their numbers thin out over a span of several miles, with trees persisting farther north in isolated patches where there is a fortuitous conjunction of perennially calm air, moisture, and soil nutrients. Islands of trees in the tundra ocean.

The growth of trees in the Arctic is constrained by several factors. 3 Lack of light for photosynthesis of course is one; but warmth is another.

A tree, like an animal, needs heat to carry on its life processes. Solar radiation provides this warmth, but in the Arctic there is a strong correlation between this warmth and closeness to the ground. In summer there may be a difference of as much as 15°F in the first foot or so of air, because of the cooling effect of the wind above and the ability of dark soils to intensify solar radiation. To balance their heat budgets for growth and survival, trees must hug the ground—so they are short. Willows, a resourceful family to begin with, sometimes grow tall, but it is only where some feature of the land stills the drying and cooling wind.

Lack of water is another factor constraining the development of 4 trees. No more moisture falls on the arctic tundra in a year than falls on the Mojave Desert; and it is available to arctic plants in the single form in which they can use it—liquid water—only during the summer.

Permafrost, the permanently frozen soil that underlies the tundra, 5 presents arctic trees with still other difficulties. Though they can penetrate this rocklike substance with their roots, deep roots, which let trees stand tall in a windy landscape, and which can draw water from deep aquifers, serve no purpose in the Arctic. It's too cold to stand tall, and liquid water is to be found only in the first few inches of soil, for only this upper layer of the ground melts in the summer. (Ironically, since the permafrost beneath remains impervious, in those few weeks when water *is* available to them, arctic trees must sometimes cope with boglike conditions.)

Trees in the Arctic have an aura of implacable endurance about 6 them. A cross-section of the bole of a Richardson willow no thicker than your finger may reveal 200 annual growth rings beneath the magnifying glass. Much of the tundra, of course, appears to be treeless when, in many places, it is actually covered with trees—a thick matting of short, ancient willows and birches. You realize suddenly that you are wandering around on *top* of a forest.

QUESTIONS ON SUBJECT

1. According to Lopez, what causes the zigzag shape of the northern limit of the continental forests in North America?
2. If we found a tall tree in the Arctic, what assumption could we make?
3. How and when does permafrost help to create a boglike condition for Arctic trees?
4. What obstacles to growth do Arctic trees face?

QUESTIONS ON STRATEGY

1. This is a tight, readable work. What information does Lopez leave out? How would you define information pertinent to Lopez's essay?

2. Lopez writes that, "Trees in the Arctic have an aura of implacable endurance about them." How does he build up this aura for readers unfamiliar with the Arctic?

3. How has Lopez organized his essay? (Glossary: *Organization*)

4. What factors make this essay interesting and readable for a general audience? (Glossary: *Audience*)

5. Lopez has the ability to raise large environmental issues through focusing on a particular aspect of nature. What issues do you think Lopez raises in this essay, and how does he manage to bring them up?

6. Discuss the use that Lopez makes of illustration to explain each of the factors that affect the growth of trees in the Arctic. (Glossary: *Illustration*)

QUESTIONS ON LANGUAGE

1. Identify two examples of personification in this essay. How do they affect your reading of this selection?

2. Refer to your desk dictionary to determine the meaning of the following words as they are used in this selection: *anomalous* (paragraph 1), *fortuitous* (2), *perennially* (2), *aquifers* (5), *impervious* (5), *implacable* (6).

WRITING SUGGESTIONS

1. Pick a geographic region that interests you, and do a little research into the plants and animals that inhabit this region. Narrow your scope to one plant or animal within the region. Now, using Lopez's essay as your model, write a cause and effect essay explaining the relationship between your plant or animal and the region.

2. Write an essay about a favorite place. What are the most prominent features of this place? How do you get there? What importance does this place hold for you? What activities do you enjoy at this place?

Television and Family Life

MARIE WINN

Marie Winn was born in 1937 in Czechoslovakia and as a child came with her family to settle in New York City. She graduated from Radcliffe College, did graduate work at Columbia University, and then embarked on a career as a writer for and about children. Her articles have appeared in the New York Times Magazine *and the* Village Voice, *and she has written and edited books for children, including* What Shall We Do and Allee Galloo, *a collection of songs and singing games.*

The following selection is taken from her 1977 best-seller, The Plug-In Drug: Television, Children, and the Family, *in which Winn examines the effects of television on American parents and their children.*

Home and family life have changed in important ways since the advent of television. The peer group has become television-oriented, and much of the time children spend together is occupied by television viewing. Culture generally has been transformed by television. Therefore it is improper to assign to television the subsidiary role its many apologists (too often members of the television industry) insist it plays. Television is not merely one of a number of important influences upon today's child. Through the changes it has made in family life, television emerges as *the* important influence in children's lives today.

THE QUALITY OF FAMILY LIFE

Television's contribution to family life has been an equivocal one. For while it has, indeed, kept the members of the family from dispersing, it has not served to bring them *together*. By its domination of the time families spend together, it destroys the special quality that distinguishes one family from another, a quality that depends to a great extent on what a family *does*, what special rituals, games, recurrent jokes, familiar songs, and shared activities it accumulates.

"Like the sorcerer of old," writes Urie Bronfenbrenner, "the television set casts its magic spell, freezing speech and action, turning the living into silent statues so long as the enchantment lasts. The primary

danger of the television screen lies not so much in the behavior it produces—although there is danger there—as in the behavior it prevents:
the talks, the games, the family festivities and arguments through which
much of the child's learning takes place and through which his character is formed. Turning on the television set can turn off the process
that transforms children into people."[1]

Yet parents have accepted a television-dominated family life so   4
completely that they cannot see how the medium is involved in whatever problems they might be having. A first-grade teacher reports:

"I have one child in the group who's an only child. I wanted to find   5
out more about her family life because this little girl was quite isolated
from the group, didn't make friends, so I talked to her mother. Well,
they don't have time to do anything in the evening, the mother said.
The parents come home after picking up the child at the baby-sitter's.
Then the mother fixes dinner while the child watches TV. Then they
have dinner and the child goes to bed. I said to this mother, 'Well,
couldn't she help you fix dinner? That would be a nice time for the two
of you to talk,' and the mother said, 'Oh, but I'd hate to have her miss
"Zoom." It's such a good program!' "

Even when families make efforts to control television, too often its   6
very presence counterbalances the positive features of family life. A
writer and mother of two boys aged 3 and 7 described her family's television schedule in the *New York Times:*

> We were in the midst of a full-scale War. Every day was a new bat-
> tle and every program was a major skirmish. We agreed it was a bad
> scene all around and were ready to enter diplomatic negotiations. . . .
> In principle we have agreed on 2½ hours of TV a day, "Sesame Street,"
> "Electric Company" (with dinner gobbled up in between) and two
> half-hour shows between 7 and 8:30 which enables the grown-ups to
> eat in peace and prevents the two boys from destroying one another.
> Their pre-bedtime choice is dreadful, because, as Josh recently ad-
> mitted, "There's nothing much on I really like." So . . . it's "What's
> My Line" or "To Tell the Truth." . . . Clearly there is a need for first-
> rate children's shows at this time. . . .[2]

Consider the "family life" described here: Presumably the father   7
comes home from work during the "Sesame Street"–"Electric Com-

---

[1] Urie Bronfenbrenner, "Who Cares for America's Children?" Address presented at
the Conference of the National Association for the Education of Young Children, 1970.

[2] Eleanor Dienstag, "What Will the Kids Talk About? Proust?" *New York Times,*
December 24, 1972.

pany" stint. The children are either watching television, gobbling their dinner, or both. While the parents eat their dinner in peaceful privacy, the children watch another hour of television. Then there is only a half-hour left before bedtime, just enough time for baths, getting pajamas on, brushing teeth, and so on. The children's evening is regimented with an almost military precision. They watch their favorite programs, and when there is "nothing much on I really like," they watch whatever else is on—because *watching* is the important thing. Their mother does not see anything amiss with watching programs just for the sake of watching; she only wishes there were some first-rate children's shows on at those times.

8 Without conjuring up memories of the Victorian era with family games and long, leisurely meals, and large families, the question arises: isn't there a better family life available than this dismal, mechanized arrangement of children watching television for however long is allowed them, evening after evening?

9 Of course, families today still do *special* things together at times: go camping in the summer, go to the zoo on a nice Sunday, take various trips and expeditions. But their *ordinary* daily life together is diminished—that sitting around at the dinner table, that spontaneous taking up of an activity, those little games invented by children on the spur of the moment when there is nothing else to do, the scribbling, the chatting, and even the quarreling, all the things that form the fabric of a family, that define a childhood. Instead, the children have their regular schedule of television programs and bedtime, and the parents have their peaceful dinner together.

10 The author of the article in the *Times* notes that "keeping a family sane means mediating between the needs of both children and adults."[3] But surely the needs of adults are being better met than the needs of the children, who are effectively shunted away and rendered untroublesome, while their parents enjoy a life as undemanding as that of any childless couple. In reality, it is those very demands that young children make upon a family that lead to growth, and it is the way parents accede to those demands that builds the relationships upon which the future of the family depends. If the family does not accumulate its backlog of shared experiences, shared *everyday* experiences that occur and recur and change and develop, then it is not likely to survive as anything other than a caretaking institution.

---

[3]Ibid.

Family Rituals

Ritual is defined by sociologists as "that part of family life that the 11 family likes about itself, is proud of and wants formally to continue."[4] Another text notes that "the development of a ritual by a family is an index of the common interest of its members in the family as a group."[5]

What has happened to family rituals, those regular, dependable, 12 recurrent happenings that gave members of a family a feeling of *belonging* to a home rather than living in it merely for the sake of convenience, those experiences that act as the adhesive of family unity far more than any material advantages?

Mealtime rituals, going-to-bed rituals, illness rituals, holiday ritu- 13 als, how many of these have survived the inroads of the television set?

A young woman who grew up near Chicago reminisces about her 14 childhood and gives an idea of the effects of television upon family rituals:

"As a child I had millions of relatives around—my parents both 15 come from relatively large families. My father had nine brothers and sisters. And so every holiday there was this great swoop-down of aunts, uncles, and millions of cousins. I just remember how wonderful it used to be. These thousands of cousins would come and everyone would play and ultimately, after dinner, all the women would be in the front of the house, drinking coffee and talking, all the men would be in the back of the house, drinking and smoking, and all the kids would be all over the place, playing hide and seek. Christmas time was particularly nice because everyone always brought all their toys and games. Our house had a couple of rooms with go-through closets, so there were always kids running in a great circle route. I remember it was just wonderful.

"And then all of a sudden one year I remember becoming suddenly 16 aware of how different everything had become. The kids were no longer playing Monopoly or Clue or the other games we used to play together. It was because we had a television set which had been turned on for a football game. All of that socializing that had gone on previously had ended. Now everyone was sitting in front of the television set, on a holiday, at a family party! I remember being stunned by how awful that was. Somehow the television had become more attractive."

---

[4]James H. Bossard and Eleanor S. Boll, *Ritual in Family Living* (Philadelphia: University of Pennsylvania Press, 1950).

[5]Bossard and Boll, *The Sociology of Child Development* (New York: Harper & Row, 1960).

As families have come to spend more and more of their time to- 17
gether engaged in the single activity of television watching, those rituals
and pastimes that once gave family life its special quality have become
more and more uncommon. Not since prehistoric times when cave
families hunted, gathered, ate, and slept, with little time remaining to
accumulate a culture of any significance, have families been reduced to
such a sameness.

Real People

It is not only the activities that a family might engage in together 18
that are diminished by the powerful presence of television in the home.
The relationships of the family members to each other are also affected,
in both obvious and subtle ways. The hours that the young child spends
in a one-way relationship with television people, an involvement that
allows for no communication or interaction, surely affect his relationships with real-life people.

Studies show the importance of eye-to-eye contact, for instance, in 19
real-life relationships, and indicate that the nature of a person's eye-
contact patterns, whether he looks another squarely in the eye or looks
to the side or shifts his gaze from side to side, may play a significant role
in his success or failure in human relationships.[6] But no eye contact is
possible in the child-television relationship, although in certain children's programs people purport to speak directly to the child and the
camera fosters this illusion by focusing directly upon the person being
filmed. (Mr. Rogers is an example, telling the child "I like you, you're
special," etc.) How might such a distortion of real-life relationships
affect a child's development of trust, of openness, of an ability to relate
well to other *real* people?

Bruno Bettelheim writes: 20

> Children who have been taught, or conditioned, to listen pas-
> sively most of the day to the warm verbal communications coming
> from the TV screen, to the deep emotional appeal of the so-called TV
> personality, are often unable to respond to real persons because they
> arouse so much less feeling than the skilled actor. Worse, they lose the
> ability to learn from reality because life experiences are much more
> complicated than the ones they see on the screen. . . .[7]

---

[6]Ralph V. Extine, "Visual Interaction: The Glances of Power and Preference," in
Nonverbal Communication—Reading with Commentaries, ed. Shirley Weitz (New York:
Oxford University Press, 1974).

[7]Bruno Bettelheim, *The Informed Heart* (New York: The Free Press, 1960).

A teacher makes a similar observation about her personal viewing 21
experiences:

"I have trouble mobilizing myself and dealing with real people 22
after watching a few hours of television. It's just hard to make that transition from watching television to a real relationship. I suppose it's because there was no effort necessary while I was watching, and dealing
with real people always requires a bit of effort. Imagine, then, how
much harder it might be to do the same thing for a small child, particularly one who watches a lot of television every day."

But more obviously damaging to family relationships is the elimi- 23
nation of opportunities to talk, and perhaps more important, to argue,
to air grievances, between parents and children and brothers and sisters.
Families frequently use television to avoid confronting their problems,
problems that will not go away if they are ignored but will only fester
and become less easily resolvable as time goes on.

A mother reports: 24

"I find myself, with three children, wanting to turn on the TV set 25
when they're fighting. I really have to struggle not to do it because I
feel that's telling them this is the solution to the quarrel—but it's so
tempting that I often do it."

A family therapist discusses the use of television as an avoidance 26
mechanism:

"In a family I know the father comes home from work and turns on 27
the television set. The children come and watch with him and the wife
serves them their meal in front of the set. He then goes and takes a
shower, or works on the car or something. She then goes and has her
own dinner in front of the television set. It's a symptom of a deeper-
rooted problem, sure. But it would help them all to get rid of the set.
It would be far easier to work on what the symptom really means without the television. The television simply encourages a double avoidance of each other. They'd find out more quickly what was going on if
they weren't able to hide behind the TV. Things wouldn't necessarily
be better, of course, but they wouldn't be anesthetized."

The decreased opportunities for simple conversation between par- 28
ents and children in the television-centered home may help explain an
observation made by an emergency room nurse at a Boston hospital.
She reports that parents just seem to sit there these days when they
come in with a sick or seriously injured child, although talking to the
child would distract and comfort him. "They don't seem to know *how*
to talk to their own children at any length," the nurse observes. Similarly, a television critic writes in the *New York Times:* "I had just a day
ago taken my son to the emergency ward of a hospital for stitches above

his left eye, and the occasion seemed no more real to me than Maalot or 54th Street, south-central Los Angeles. There was distance and numbness and an inability to turn off the total institution. I didn't behave at all; I just watched. . . ."[8]

A number of research studies substantiate the assumption that [29] television interferes with family activities and the formation of family relationships. One survey shows that 78 percent of the respondents indicate no conversation taking place during viewing except at specified times such as commercials. The study notes: "The television atmosphere in most households is one of quiet absorption on the part of family members who are present. The nature of the family social life during a program could be described as 'parallel' rather than interactive, and the set does seem to dominate family life when it is on."[9] Thirty-six percent of the respondents in another study indicated that television viewing was the only family activity participated in during the week.[10]

In a summary of research findings on television's effect on family [30] interactions James Gabardino states: "The early findings suggest that television had a disruptive effect upon interaction and thus presumably human development. . . . It is not unreasonable to ask: 'Is the fact that the average American family during the 1950's came to include two parents, two children and a television set somehow related to the psychosocial characteristics of the young adults of the 1970's?' "[11]

Undermining the Family

In its effect on family relationships, in its facilitation of parental [31] withdrawal from an active role in the socialization of their children, and in its replacement of family rituals and special events, television has played an important role in the disintegration of the American family. But of course it has not been the only contributing factor, perhaps not even the most important one. The steadily rising divorce rate, the increase in the number of working mothers, the decline of the extended

---

[8]Cyclops, "Watching the World through TV-Colored Glasses," *New York Times,* June 2, 1974.

[9]E. Maccoby, "Television: Its Impact on School Children," *Public Opinion Quarterly,* Vol. 15, 1951.

[10]R. Hamilton and R. Lawless, "Television within the Social Matrix," *Public Opinion Quarterly,* Vol. 20, 1956.

[11]James Gabardino, "A Note on the Effects of Television Viewing," in Urie Bronfenbrenner and Maureen A. Mahoney, *Influences on Human Development,* 2nd ed. (Hinsdale, Illinois: The Dryden Press, 1975).

family, the breakdown of neighborhoods and communities, the growing isolation of the nuclear family—all have seriously affected the family.

As Urie Bronfenbrenner suggests, the sources of family breakdown [32] do not come from the family itself, but from the circumstances in which the family finds itself and the way of life imposed upon it by those circumstances. "When those circumstances and the way of life they generate undermine relationships of trust and emotional security between family members, when they make it difficult for parents to care for, educate and enjoy their children, when there is no support or recognition from the outside world for one's role as a parent and when time spent with one's family means frustration of career, personal fulfillment and peace of mind, then the development of the child is adversely affected," he writes.[12]

But while the roots of alienation go deep into the fabric of American [33] social history, television's presence in the home fertilizes them, encourages their wild and unchecked growth. Perhaps it is true that America's commitment to the television experience masks a spiritual vacuum, an empty and barren way of life, a desert of materialism. But it is television's dominant role in the family that anesthetizes the family into accepting its unhappy state and prevents it from struggling to better its condition, to improve its relationships, and to regain some of the richness it once possessed.

Others have noted the role of mass media in perpetuating an un- [34] satisfactory *status quo*. Leisure-time activity, writes Irving Howe, "must provide relief from work monotony without making the return to work too unbearable; it must provide amusement without insight and pleasure without disturbance—as distinct from art which gives pleasure through disturbance. Mass culture is thus oriented towards a central aspect of industrial society: the depersonalization of the individual."[13] Similarly, Jacques Ellul rejects the idea that television is a legitimate means of educating the citizen: "Education . . . takes place only incidentally. The clouding of his consciousness is paramount. . . ."[14]

And so the American family muddles on, dimly aware that some- [35] thing is amiss but distracted from an understanding of its plight by an endless stream of television images. As family ties grow weaker and vaguer, as children's lives become more separate from their parents', as parents' educational role in their children's lives is taken over by tele-

---

[12]Urie Bronfenbrenner, "The Origins of Alienation," *Scientific American*, August, 1974.

[13]Irving Howe, "Notes on Mass Culture," *Politics*, Spring, 1948.

[14]Jacques Ellul, *The Technological Society* (New York: Alfred A. Knopf, 1964).

vision and schools, family life becomes increasingly more unsatisfying for both parents and children. All that seems to be left is Love, an abstraction that family members *know* is necessary but find great difficulty giving each other because the traditional opportunities for expressing love within the family have been reduced or destroyed.

For contemporary parents, love toward each other has increasingly 36 come to mean successful sexual relations, as witnessed by the proliferation of sex manuals and sex therapists. The opportunities for manifesting other forms of love through mutual support, understanding, nurturing, even, to use an unpopular word, *serving* each other, are less and less available as mothers and fathers seek their independent destinies outside the family.

As for love of children, this love is increasingly expressed through 37 supplying material comforts, amusements, and educational opportunities. Parents show their love for their children by sending them to good schools and camps, by providing them with good food and good doctors, by buying them toys, books, games, and a television set of their very own. Parents will even go further and express their love by attending PTA meetings to improve their children's schools, or by joining groups that are acting to improve the quality of their children's television programs.

But this is love at a remove, and it is rarely understood by children. 38 The more direct forms of parental love require time and patience, steady, dependable, ungrudgingly given time actually spent *with* a child, reading to him, comforting him, playing, joking, and working with him. But even if a parent were eager and willing to demonstrate that sort of direct love to his children today, the opportunities are diminished. What with school and Little League and piano lessons and, of course, the inevitable television programs, a day seems to offer just enough time for a good-night kiss.

QUESTIONS ON SUBJECT

1. What is the central point Winn develops throughout her essay? Locate several different places where she states that point (or thesis) directly, in more or less detail. (Glossary: *Thesis*)

2. What does Winn mean when she says, "Television's contribution to family life has been an equivocal one" (paragraph 2)? What does she point to as television's specific negative effects?

3. According to Winn, family rituals have been undermined by television. What rituals does she mention? Can you think of any other family rituals that have been affected?

4. What does Winn mean when she states that television fosters only a "one-way relationship" (18)? How are people on television different from "real people"? Why isn't Mr. Rogers a real person?

5. How, according to Winn, is television used by families as a way to avoid confronting problems? What examples does she give?

6. Winn knows that television is not the sole cause of "the disintegration of the American family" (31). What other factors does she suggest have exerted an influence? How is television related to these other factors?

QUESTIONS ON STRATEGY

1. Winn believes that "parents have accepted a television-dominated family life so completely that they cannot see how the medium is involved in whatever problems they might be having" (4). How does she support this generalization? Are you convinced?

2. Before talking about the effects of television on family rituals, Winn offers several sociological definitions of *ritual* (11). Why do you suppose she thought it necessary to define the term? (Glossary: *Definition*)

3. Briefly describe the causal chain that Winn presents in paragraph 35. Why do you suppose she reserves her discussion of love until paragraphs 35 through 38?

4. How has Winn organized her essay? Do you find the headings helpful in understanding her organization? Why, or why not? (Glossary: *Organization*)

5. Analyze the effectiveness of the examples Winn quotes from various sources. Which quotations do you find most interesting and convincing? What other kinds of evidence does she use to document the effects television has on the American family? (Glossary: *Examples*)

QUESTIONS ON LANGUAGE

1. Winn italicizes a number of words in her essay, such as in paragraphs 1 and 2. Explain her reason for using italics in several specific instances. Do you find the emphasis particularly effective?

2. Comment on the connotative value of each of the following italicized words. (Glossary: *Connotation/Denotation*)
   a. "will only *fester* and become less easily resolvable" (23)
   b. "television has played an important role in the *disintegration* of the American family" (31)
   c. "while the *roots* of alienation go deep into the *fabric* of American social history, television's presence in the home *fertilizes* them" (33)
   d. "the American family *muddles* on" (35)
   e. "independent *destinies* outside the family" (36)

3. How does Winn's diction make a difference in the tone of her essay? You might contrast Winn's tone with Gloria Steinem's in "Why Young Women Are More Conservative." (Glossary: *Diction; Tone*)

4. Refer to your desk dictionary to determine the meanings of the following words as they are used in this selection: *apologists* (paragraph 1), *equivocal* (2), *conjuring* (8), *spontaneous* (9), *shunted* (10), *accede* (10), *purport* (19), *status quo* (34), *paramount* (34), *proliferation* (36), *ungrudgingly* (38).

WRITING ASSIGNMENTS

1. How do you feel about mathematics, English, science, art, or another general area of study? Write an essay discussing the causes and the effects of your attitude toward one of these subjects. What events or relationships in your past have led you to feel the way you do? How does this attitude determine the kinds of choices you make and other aspects of your behavior?

2. Write an essay in which you discuss the effects of television on you or on American society. You may wish to focus on the specific influences of one of the following aspects of television:
   a. advertising
   b. sports broadcasts
   c. cultural programming
   d. talk shows
   e. cartoons

My Daughter Smokes

ALICE WALKER

Alice Walker, novelist, poet, short story writer, and essayist, was born in 1944 in Eatonton, Georgia. She graduated from Sarah Lawrence College in 1965. She has registered voters, worked for Head Start and the New York City welfare department, and lectured at several universities including Wellesley College and the University of California, Berkeley. She became nationally recognized with the publication of The Color Purple, *which won the Pulitzer Prize and the American Book Award. Most of Walker's main characters are black women, and the issues of sexism and racism remain at the forefront of her work. Recently she has written* Warrior Marks: Female Genital Mutilation and the Sexual Blinding of Women *(1993), and* Everyday Use *(1994), a novel about southern quilters.*

In this essay, taken from the collection Living By the Word *(1988), Walker approaches the national health problem of smoking by revealing the impact it has had on her family.*

My daughter smokes. While she is doing her homework, her feet 1 on the bench in front of her and her calculator clicking out answers to her algebra problems, I am looking at the half-empty package of Camels tossed carelessly close at hand. Camels. I pick them up, take them into the kitchen, where the light is better, and study them— they're filtered, for which I am grateful. My heart feels terrible. I want to weep. In fact, I do weep a little, standing there by the stove holding one of the instruments, so white, so precisely rolled, that could cause my daughter's death. When she smoked Marlboros and Players I hardened myself against feeling so bad; nobody I knew ever smoked these brands.

She doesn't know this, but it was Camels that my father, her grand- 2 father, smoked. But before he smoked "ready-mades"—when he was very young and very poor, with eyes like lanterns—he smoked Prince Albert tobacco in cigarettes he rolled himself. I remember the bright-red tobacco tin, with a picture of Queen Victoria's consort, Prince Albert, dressed in a black frock coat and carrying a cane.

The tobacco was dark brown, pungent, slightly bitter. I tasted it 3 more than once as a child, and the discarded tins could be used for a number of things: to keep buttons and shoelaces in, to store seeds, and best of all, to hold worms for the rare times my father took us fishing.

By the late forties and early fifties no one rolled his own anymore 4 (and few women smoked) in my hometown, Eatonton, Georgia. The tobacco industry, coupled with Hollywood movies in which both hero and heroine smoked like chimneys, won over completely people like my father, who were hopelessly addicted to cigarettes. He never looked as dapper as Prince Albert, though; he continued to look like a poor, over-weight, overworked colored man with too large a family; black, with a very white cigarette stuck in his mouth.

I do not remember when he started to cough. Perhaps it was un- 5 noticeable at first. A little hacking in the morning as he lit his first cig-arette upon getting out of bed. By the time I was my daughter's age, his breath was a wheeze, embarrassing to hear; he could not climb stairs without resting every third or fourth step. It was not unusual for him to cough for an hour.

It is hard to believe there was a time when people did not under- 6 stand that cigarette smoking is an addiction. I wondered aloud once to my sister—who is perennially trying to quit—whether our father real-ized this. I wondered how she, a smoker since high school, viewed her own habit.

It was our father who gave her her first cigarette, one day when she 7 had taken water to him in the fields.

"I always wondered why he did that," she said, puzzled, and with 8 some bitterness.

"What did he say?" I asked. 9

"That he didn't want me to go to anyone else for them," she said, 10 "which never really crossed my mind."

So he was aware it was addictive, I thought, though as annoyed as 11 she that he assumed she would be interested.

I began smoking in eleventh grade, also the year I drank numerous 12 bottles of terrible sweet, very cheap wine. My friends and I, all boys for this venture, bought our supplies from a man who ran a segregated bar and liquor store on the outskirts of town. Over the entrance there was a large sign that said COLORED. We were not permitted to drink there, only to buy. I smoked Kools, because my sister did. By then I thought her toxic darkened lips and gums glamorous. However, my body simply would not tolerate smoke. After six months I had a chronic sore throat. I gave up smoking, gladly. Because it was a ritual with my buddies— Murl, Leon, and "Dog" Farley—I continued to drink wine.

My father died from "the poor man's friend," pneumonia, one 13 hard winter when his bronchitis and emphysema had left him low. I doubt he had much lung left at all, after coughing for so many years. He had so little breath that, during his last years, he was always leaning on something. I remember once, at a family reunion, when my daughter was two, that my father picked her up for a minute—long enough for me to photograph them—but the effort was obvious. Near the very end of his life, and largely because he had no more lungs, he quit smoking. He gained a couple of pounds, but by then he was so emaciated no one noticed.

When I travel to Third World countries I see many people like 14 my father and daughter. There are large billboards directed at them both: the tough, "take-charge," or dapper older man, the glamorous, "worldly" young woman, both puffing away. In these poor countries, as in American ghettos and on reservations, money that should be spent for food goes instead to the tobacco companies; over time, people starve themselves of both food and air, effectively weakening and addicting their children, eventually eradicating themselves. I read in the newspaper and in my gardening magazine that cigarette butts are so toxic that if a baby swallows one, it is likely to die, and that the boiled water from a bunch of them makes an effective insecticide.

My daughter would like to quit, she says. We both know the sta- 15 tistics are against her; most people who try to quit smoking do not succeed.*

There is a deep hurt that I feel as a mother. Some days it is a feeling 16 of futility. I remember how carefully I ate when I was pregnant, how patiently I taught my daughter how to cross a street safely. For what, I sometimes wonder; so that she can wheeze through most of her life feeling half her strength, and then die of self-poisoning, as her grandfather did?

But, finally, one must feel empathy for the tobacco plant itself. For 17 thousands of years, it has been venerated by Native Americans as a sacred medicine. They have used it extensively—its juice, its leaves, its roots, its (holy) smoke—to heal wounds and cure diseases, and in ceremonies of prayer and peace. And though the plant as most of us know it has been poisoned by chemicals and denatured by intensive monocropping and is therefore hardly the plant it was, still, to some modern Indians it remains a plant of positive power. I learned this when my Native American friends, Bill Wahpepah and his family, visited with me for a few days and the first thing he did was sow a few tobacco seeds in my garden.

---

*Three months after reading this essay my daughter stopped smoking.

Perhaps we can liberate tobacco from those who have captured and 18
abused it, enslaving the plant on large plantations, keeping it from freedom and its kin, and forcing it to enslave the world. Its true nature suppressed, no wonder it has become deadly. Maybe by sowing a few seeds
of tobacco in our gardens and treating the plant with the reverence it
deserves, we can redeem tobacco's soul and restore its self-respect.

Besides, how grim, if one is a smoker, to realize one is smoking a 19
slave.

There is a slogan from a battered women's shelter that I especially 20
like: "Peace on earth begins at home." I believe everything does. I
think of a slogan for people trying to stop smoking: "Every home a
smoke-free zone." Smoking is a form of self-battering that also batters
those who must sit by, occasionally cajole or complain, and helplessly
watch. I realize now that as a child I sat by, through the years, and literally watched my father kill himself: surely one such victory in my family,
for the rich white men who own the tobacco companies, is enough.

QUESTIONS ON SUBJECT

1. Why is her daughter's brand of cigarette's important to Walker?
2. What importance do you attach to Walker's father giving one of his daughters her first cigarette?
3. What is the relationship Walker establishes between those who grow tobacco and those who smoke it?
4. Walker writes of the segregated bar where she and her friends bought
   cheap wine, "We were not permitted to drink there, only to buy." What
   relationship do you see between this quote and the family history of
   smoking that Walker relates?
5. What do you think the author means when she suggests that we must feel
   empathy for the tobacco plant?

QUESTIONS ON STRATEGY

1. How does Walker's description of her father's tobacco tins affect you?
   How do you see such detail fitting into a cause and effect essay?
2. Make an outline of Walker's essay. Does your outline help you to see the
   cause and effect relationship Walker advances? Explain. What importance
   do you see in where she introduces family members and observations from
   outside her family?
3. Walker strives to make the reader recognize the issue of smoking on a personal level. Is she successful? Defend your answer by pointing to specific
   passages in the text.

4. How and to what advantage does the author use comparison and contrast in this essay? (Glossary: *Comparison and Contrast*)

QUESTIONS ON LANGUAGE

1. In the last paragraph, Walker states that, "Smoking is a form of self-battering that also batters those who sit by." How appropriate do you find this image of battering? Does Walker's diction throughout the essay prepare us for this conclusion? Explain.

2. Refer to your desk dictionary to determine the meanings of the following words as they are used in this selection: *consort* (paragraph 2), *pungent* (3), *perennially* (6), *emphysema* (13), *emaciated* (13), *empathy* (17), *cajole* (20).

WRITING SUGGESTIONS

1. Write a personal reaction to Walker's essay. Where do you agree and disagree with her? How are your viewpoint and experiences similar to or different from hers?

2. Walker observed billboards targeted at groups of people in the Third World. Write an essay examining advertising targeted at people like yourself. What messages do you detect in this advertising? Make sure to provide your audience with a sufficient foundation of description upon which to base your interpretation.

Eleven Blue Men

BERTON ROUECHÉ

Berton Roueché (pronounced Roo-shay), medical journalist and novelist, was born on April 16, 1911, in Kansas City, Missouri. After graduating from the University of Missouri, he worked as a reporter for the Kansas City Star *from 1934–1941. He also worked for the* St. Louis Globe-Democrat *and the* St. Louis Post-Dispatch *before joining the staff of* The New Yorker *in 1944, where he founded the "Annals of Medicine" department. Roueché has written four novels and received numerous awards including the Mystery Writers of America award (1954), the American Medical Writers Association annual award (1963 and 1978), and the American Medical Association Annual Journalism Award (1970).*

In this essay, published in a collection of stories that first appeared in The New Yorker—Eleven Blue Men, and Other Narratives of Medical Detection *(1953), Roueché reports a case involving a rare kind of poisoning. Through an interview, he retraces the steps of the two medical investigators in charge of the case as they solve the mystery of the eleven blue men.*

At about eight o'clock on Monday morning, September 25, 1944, 1
a ragged, aimless old man of eighty-two collapsed on the sidewalk on
Dey Street, near the Hudson Terminal. Innumerable people must have
noticed him, but he lay there alone for several minutes, dazed, doubled
up with abdominal cramps, and in an agony of retching. Then a policeman came along. Until the policeman bent over the old man, he may
have supposed that he had just a sick drunk on his hands; wanderers
dropped by drink are common in that part of town in the early morning. It was not an opinion that he could have held for long. The old
man's nose, lips, ears, and fingers were sky-blue. The policeman went to
a telephone and put in an ambulance call to Beekman-Downtown Hospital, half a dozen blocks away. The old man was carried into the emergency room there at eight-thirty. By that time, he was unconscious and
the blueness had spread over a large part of his body. The examining
physician attributed the old man's morbid color to cyanosis, a condition that usually results from an insufficient supply of oxygen in the
blood, and also noted that he was diarrheic and in a severe state of

shock. The course of treatment prescribed by the doctor was conventional. It included an instant gastric lavage, heart stimulants, bed rest, and oxygen therapy. Presently, the old man recovered an encouraging, if painful, consciousness and demanded, irascibly and in the name of God, to know what had happened to him. It was a question that, at the moment, nobody could answer with much confidence.

For the immediate record, the doctor made a freehand diagnosis of 2 carbon-monoxide poisoning—from what source, whether an automobile or a gas pipe, it was, of course, pointless even to guess. Then, because an isolated instance of gas poisoning is something of a rarity in a section of the city as crammed with human beings as downtown Manhattan, he and his colleagues in the emergency room braced themselves for at least a couple more victims. Their foresight was promptly and generously rewarded. A second man was rolled in at ten-twenty-five. Forty minutes later, an ambulance drove up with three more men. At eleven-twenty, two others were brought in. An additional two arrived during the next fifteen minutes. Around noon, still another was admitted. All of these nine men were also elderly and dilapidated, all had been in misery for at least an hour, and all were rigid, cyanotic, and in a state of shock. The entire body of one, a bony, seventy-three-year-old consumptive named John Mitchell, was blue. Five of the nine, including Mitchell, had been stricken in the Globe Hotel, a sunless, upstairs flophouse at 190 Park Row, and two in a similar place, called the Star Hotel at 3 James Street. Another had been found slumped in the doorway of a condemned building on Park Row, not far from City Hall Park, by a policeman. The ninth had keeled over in front of the Eclipse Cafeteria, at 6 Chatham Square. At a quarter to seven that evening, one more aged blue man was brought in. He had been lying, too sick to ask for help, on his cot in a cubicle in the Lion Hotel, another flophouse, at 26 Bowery, since ten o'clock that morning. A clerk had finally looked in and seen him.

By the time this last blue man arrived at the hospital, an investiga- 3 tion of the case by the Department of Health, to which all outbreaks of an epidemiological nature must be reported, had been under way for five hours. Its findings thus far had not been illuminating. The investigation was conducted by two men. One was the Health Department's chief epidemiologist, Dr. Morris Greenberg, a small, fragile, reflective man of fifty-seven, who is now acting director of the Bureau of Preventable Diseases; the other was Dr. Ottavio Pellitteri, a field epidemiologist, who, since 1946, has been administrative medical inspector for the Bureau. He is thirty-six years old, pale, and stocky, and has a bristling black mustache. One day, when I was in Dr. Greenberg's office, he and Dr. Pellitteri told me about the case. Their recollection of it is, understandably, vivid. The derelicts were the victims of a type of poisoning so rare that only ten previous outbreaks of it had been recorded in medical literature. Of these, two were in the United States and two in Germany; the others had been reported in France, England, Switzerland, Algeria, Australia, and India. Up to September 25, 1944, the largest number of people stricken in a single outbreak was four. That was in Algeria, in 1926.

The Beekman-Downtown Hospital telephoned a report of the 4 occurrence to the Health Department just before noon. As is customary, copies of the report were sent to all the Department's administrative officers. "Mine was on my desk when I got back from lunch," Dr. Greenberg said to me. "It didn't sound like much. Nine persons believed to be suffering from carbon-monoxide poisoning had been admitted during the morning, and all of them said they had eaten breakfast at the Eclipse Cafeteria, at 6 Chatham Square. Still, it was a job for us. I checked with the clerk who handles assignments and found that Pellitteri had gone out on it. That was all I wanted to know. If it amounted to anything, I knew he'd phone me before making a written report. That's an arrangement we have here. Well, a couple of hours later I got a call from him. My interest perked right up."

"I was at the hospital," Dr. Pellitteri told me, "and I'd talked to 5 the staff and most of the men. There were ten of them by then, of course. They were sick as dogs, but only one was in really bad shape."

"That was John Mitchell," Dr. Greenberg put in. "He died the 6 next night. I understand his condition was hopeless from the start. The others, including the old boy who came in last, pulled through all right. Excuse me, Ottavio, but I just thought I'd get that out of the way. Go on."

Dr. Pellitteri nodded. "I wasn't at all convinced that it was gas 7 poisoning," he continued. "The staff was beginning to doubt it, too. The symptoms weren't quite right. There didn't seem to be any of the headache and general dopiness that you get with gas. What really made me suspicious was this: Only two or three of the men had eaten breakfast in the cafeteria at the same time. They had straggled in all the way from seven o'clock to ten. That meant that the place would have had to be full of gas for at least three hours, which is preposterous. It also indicated that we ought to have had a lot more sick people than we did. Those Chatham Square eating places have a big turnover. Well, to make sure, I checked with Bellevue, Gouverneur, St. Vincent's and the other downtown hospitals. None of them had seen a trace of cyanosis. Then I talked to the sick men some more. I learned two interesting things.

One was that they had all got sick right after eating. Within thirty minutes. The other was that all but one had eaten oatmeal, rolls, and coffee. He ate just oatmeal. When ten men eat the same thing in the same place on the same day and then all come down with the same illness . . . I told Greenberg that my hunch was food poisoning."

"I was willing to rule out gas," Dr. Greenberg said. A folder containing data on the case lay on the desk before him. He lifted the cover thoughtfully, then let it drop. "And I agreed that the oatmeal sounded pretty suspicious. That was as far as I was willing to go. Common, ordinary, everyday food poisoning—I gathered that was what Pellitteri had in mind—wasn't a very satisfying answer. For one thing, cyanosis is hardly symptomatic of that. On the other hand, diarrhea and severe vomiting are, almost invariably. But they weren't in the clinical picture, I found, except in two or three of the cases. Moreover, the incubation periods—the time lapse between eating and illness—were extremely short. As you probably know, most food poisoning is caused by eating something that has been contaminated by bacteria. The usual offenders are the staphylococci—they're mostly responsible for boils and skin infections and so on—and the salmonella. The latter are related to the typhoid organism. In a staphylococcus case, the first symptoms rarely develop in under two hours. Often, it's closer to five. The incubation period in the other ranges from twelve to thirty-six hours. But here we were with something that hit in thirty minutes or less. Why, one of the men had got only as far as the sidewalk in front of the cafeteria before he was knocked out. Another fact that Pellitteri had dug up struck me as very significant. All of the men told him that the illness had come on with extraordinary suddenness. One minute they were feeling fine, and the next minute they were practically helpless. That was another point against the ordinary food-poisoning theory. Its onset is never that fast. Well, that suddenness began to look like a lead. It led me to suspect that some drug might be to blame. A quick and sudden reaction is characteristic of a great many drugs. So is the combination of cyanosis and shock."

"None of the men were on dope," Dr. Pellitteri said. "I told Greenberg I was sure of that. Their pleasure was booze."

"That was O.K.," Dr. Greenberg said. "They could have got a toxic dose of some drug by accident. In the oatmeal, most likely. I couldn't help thinking that the oatmeal was relevant to our problem. At any rate, the drug idea was very persuasive."

"So was Greenberg," Dr. Pellitteri remarked with a smile. "Actually, it was the only explanation in sight that seemed to account for everything we knew about the clinical and environmental picture."

"All we had to do now was prove it," Dr. Greenberg went on   12
mildly. "I asked Pellitteri to get a blood sample from each of the men
before leaving the hospital for a look at the cafeteria. We agreed he
would send the specimens to the city toxicologist, Dr. Alexander O.
Gettler, for an overnight analysis. I wanted to know if the blood contained methemoglobin. Methemoglobin is a compound that's formed
only when any one of several drugs enters the blood. Gettler's report
would tell us if we were at least on the right track. That is, it would give
us a yes-or-no answer on drugs. If the answer was yes, then we could go
on from there to identify the particular drug. How we could go about
that would depend on what Pellitteri was able to turn up at the cafeteria. In the meantime, there was nothing for me to do but wait for
their reports. I'd theorized myself hoarse."

Dr. Pellitteri, having attended to his bloodletting with reasonable   13
dispatch, reached the Eclipse Cafeteria at around five o'clock. "It was
about what I'd expected," he told me. "Strictly a horse market, and
dirtier than most. The sort of place where you can get a full meal for
fifteen cents. There was a grind house on one side, a cigar store on the
other, and the 'L' overhead. Incidentally, the Eclipse went out of business a year or so after I was there, but that had nothing to do with us.
It was just a coincidence. Well, the place looked deserted and the door
was locked. I knocked, and a man came out of the back and let me in.
He was one of our people, a health inspector for the Bureau of Food
and Drugs, named Weinberg. His bureau had stepped into the case as
a matter of routine, because of the reference to a restaurant in the
notification report. I was glad to see him and to have his help. For one
thing, he had put a temporary embargo on everything in the cafeteria.
That's why it was closed up. His main job, though, was to check the
place for violations of the sanitation code. He was finding plenty."

"Let me read you a few of Weinberg's findings," Dr. Greenberg   14
said, extracting a paper from the folder on his desk. "None of them had
any direct bearing on our problem, but I think they'll give you a good
idea of what the Eclipse was like—what too many restaurants are like.
This copy of his report lists fifteen specific violations. Here they are:
'Premises heavily infested with roaches. Fly infestation throughout
premises. Floor defective in rear part of dining room. Kitchen walls and
ceiling encrusted with grease and soot. Kitchen floor encrusted with
dirt. Refuse under kitchen fixtures. Sterilizing facilities inadequate. Sink
defective. Floor and walls at serving tables and coffee urns encrusted
with dirt. Kitchen utensils encrusted with dirt and grease. Storage-cellar
walls, ceiling, and floor encrusted with dirt. Floor and shelves in cellar
covered with refuse and useless material. Cellar ceiling defective. Sewer

pipe leaking. Open sewer line in cellar.' Well . . .'" He gave me a squeamish smile and stuck the paper back in the folder.

"I can see it now," Dr. Pellitteri said. "And smell it. Especially the 15 kitchen, where I spent most of my time. Weinberg had the proprietor and the cook out there, and I talked to them while he prowled around. They were very coöperative. Naturally. They were scared to death. They knew nothing about gas in the place and there was no sign of any, so I went to work on the food. None of what had been prepared for breakfast that morning was left. That, of course, would have been too much to hope for. But I was able to get together some of the kind of stuff that had gone into the men's breakfast, so that we could make a chemical determination at the Department. What I took was ground coffee, sugar, a mixture of evaporated milk and water that passed for cream, some bakery rolls, a five-pound carton of dry oatmeal, and some salt. The salt had been used in preparing the oatmeal. That morning, like every morning, the cook told me, he had prepared six gallons of oatmeal, enough to serve around a hundred and twenty-five people. To make it, he used five pounds of dry cereal, four gallons of water— regular city water—and a handful of salt. That was his term—a handful. There was an open gallon can of salt standing on the stove. He said the handful he'd put in that morning's oatmeal had come from that. He refilled the can on the stove every morning from a big supply can. He pointed out the big can—it was up on a shelf—and as I was getting it down to take with me, I saw another can, just like it, nearby. I took that one down, too. It was also full of salt, or, rather, something that looked like salt. The proprietor said it wasn't salt. He said it was saltpetre— sodium nitrate—that he used in corning beef and in making pastrami. Well, there isn't any harm in saltpetre; it doesn't even act as an anti-aphrodisiac, as a lot of people seem to think. But I wrapped it up with the other loot and took it along, just for fun. The fact, is, I guess, everything in that damn place looked like poison."

After Dr. Pellitteri had deposited his loot with a Health Depart- 16 ment chemist, Andrew J. Pensa, who promised to have a report ready by the following afternoon, he dined hurriedly at a restaurant in which he had confidence and returned to Chatham Square. There he spent the evening making the rounds of the lodging houses in the neighborhood. He had heard at Mr. Pensa's office that an eleventh blue man had been admitted to the hospital, and before going home he wanted to make sure that no other victims had been overlooked. By midnight, having covered all the likely places and having rechecked the downtown hospitals, he was satisfied. He repaired to his office and composed a formal progress report for Dr. Greenberg. Then he went home and to bed.

The next morning, Tuesday, Dr. Pellitteri dropped by the Eclipse, 17 which was still closed but whose proprietor and staff he had told to return for questioning. Dr. Pellitteri had another talk with the proprietor and the cook. He also had a few inconclusive words with the rest of the cafeteria's employees—two dishwashers, a busboy, and a counterman. As he was leaving, the cook, who had apparently passed an uneasy night with his conscience, remarked that it was possible that he had absent-mindedly refilled the salt can on the stove from the one that contained saltpetre. "That was interesting," Dr. Pellitteri told me, "even though such a possibility had already occurred to me, and even though I didn't know whether it was important or not. I assured him that he had nothing to worry about. We had been certain all along that nobody had deliberately poisoned the old men." From the Eclipse, Dr. Pellitteri went on to Dr. Greenberg's office, where Dr. Gettler's report was waiting.

"Gettler's test for methemoglobin was positive," Dr. Greenberg 18 said. "It had to be a drug now. Well, so far so good. Then we heard from Pensa."

"Greenberg almost fell out of his chair when he read Pensa's re- 19 port," Dr. Pellitteri observed cheerfully.

"That's an exaggeration," Dr. Greenberg said. "I'm not easily 20 dumbfounded. We're inured to the incredible around here. Why, a few years ago we had a case involving some numbskull who stuck a fistful of potassium-thiocyanate crystals, a very nasty poison, in the coils of an office water cooler, just for a practical joke. However, I can't deny that Pensa rather taxed our credulity. What he had found was that the small salt can and the one that was supposed to be full of sodium nitrate both contained sodium nitrite. The other food samples, incidentally, were O.K."

"That also taxed my credulity," Dr. Pellitteri said. 21

Dr. Greenberg smiled. "There's a great deal of difference between 22 nitrate and nitrite," he continued. "Their only similarity, which is an unfortunate one, is that they both look and taste more or less like ordinary table salt. Sodium nitrite isn't the most powerful poison in the world, but a little of it will do a lot of harm. If you remember, I said before that this case was almost without precedent—only ten outbreaks like it on record. Ten is practically none. In fact, sodium-nitrite poisoning is so unusual that some of the standard texts on toxicology don't even mention it. So Pensa's report was pretty startling. But we accepted it, of course, without question or hesitation. Facts are facts. And we were glad to. It seemed to explain everything very nicely. What I've been saying about sodium-nitrite poisoning doesn't mean that sodium nitrite itself is rare. Actually, it's fairly common. It's used in the manufacture of dyes and as a medical drug. We use it in treating certain heart conditions and for high blood pressure. But it also has another important use, one that made its presence at the Eclipse sound plausible. In recent years, and particularly during the war, sodium nitrite has been used as a substitute for sodium nitrate in preserving meat. The government permits it but stipulates that the finished meat must not contain more than one part of sodium nitrite per five thousand parts of meat. Cooking will safely destroy enough of that small quantity of the drug." Dr. Greenberg shrugged. "Well, Pellitteri had had the cook pick up a handful of salt—the same amount, as nearly as possible, as went into the oatmeal—and then had taken this to his office and found that it weighed approximately a hundred grams. So we didn't have to think twice to realize that the proportion of nitrite in that batch of cereal was considerably higher than one to five thousand. Roughly, it must have been around one to about eighty before cooking destroyed part of the nitrite. It certainly looked as though Gettler, Pensa, and the cafeteria cook between them had given us our answer. I called up Gettler and told him what Pensa had discovered and asked him to run a specific test for nitrites on his blood samples. He had, as a matter of course, held some blood back for later examination. His confirmation came through in a couple of hours. I went home that night feeling pretty good."

Dr. Greenberg's serenity was a fugitive one. He awoke on Wednes-   23
day morning troubled in mind. A question had occurred to him that he was unable to ignore. "Something like a hundred and twenty-five people ate oatmeal at the Eclipse that morning," he said to me, "but only eleven of them got sick. Why? The undeniable fact that those eleven old men were made sick by the ingestion of a toxic dose of sodium nitrite wasn't enough to rest on. I wanted to know exactly how much sodium nitrite each portion of that cooked oatmeal had contained. With Pensa's help again, I found out. We prepared a batch just like the one the cook had made on Monday. Then Pensa measured out six ounces, the size of the average portion served at the Eclipse, and analyzed it. It contained two and a half grains of sodium nitrite. That explained why the hundred and fourteen other people did not become ill. The toxic dose of sodium nitrite is three grains. But it didn't explain how each of our eleven old men had received an additional half grain. It seemed extremely unlikely that the extra touch of nitrite had been in the oatmeal when it was served. It had to come in later. Then I began to get a glimmer. Some people sprinkle a little salt, instead of sugar, on hot cereal. Suppose, I thought, that the busboy, or whoever had the job of keeping the table salt shakers filled, had made the same mistake that the cook had.

It seemed plausible. Pellitteri was out of the office—I've forgotten where—so I got Food and Drugs to step over to the Eclipse, which was still under embargo, and bring back the shakers for Pensa to work on. There were seventeen of them, all good-sized, one for each table. Sixteen contained either pure sodium chloride or just a few inconsequential traces of sodium nitrite mixed in with the real salt, but the other was point thirty-seven per cent nitrite. That one was enough. A spoonful of that salt contained a bit more than half a grain."

"I went over to the hospital Thursday morning," Dr. Pellitteri said. 24 "Greenberg wanted me to check the table-salt angle with the men. They could tie the case up neatly for us. I drew a blank. They'd been discharged the night before, and God only knew where they were."

"Naturally," Dr. Greenberg said, "it would have been nice to know 25 for a fact that the old boys all sat at a certain table and that all of them put about a spoonful of salt from that particular shaker on their oatmeal, but it wasn't essential. I was morally certain that they had. There just wasn't any other explanation. There was one other question, however. Why did they use so *much* salt? For my own peace of mind, I wanted to know. All of a sudden, I remembered Pellitteri had said they were all heavy drinkers. Well, several recent clinical studies have demonstrated that there is usually a subnormal concentration of sodium chloride in the blood of alcoholics. Either they don't eat enough to get sufficient salt or they lose it more rapidly than other people do, or both. Whatever the reasons are, the conclusion was all I needed. Any animal, you know, whether a mouse or a man, tends to try to obtain a necessary substance that his body lacks. The final question had been answered."

QUESTIONS ON SUBJECT

1. What did the eleven blue men have in common? Explain the importance of this information.
2. What circumstances made gas poisoning and food poisoning seem unlikely and why?
3. Why would sodium nitrite have been in the Eclipse at all?
4. Why does it appear that the Eclipse cook had spent an uneasy night with his conscience?

QUESTIONS ON STRATEGY

1. How do the first three paragraphs serve as an introduction to this medical case? What relevant information does the author present? (Glossary: *Beginnings*)

2. Briefly outline the causal chain of events that Roueché unravels in this story of medical detection.

3. Comment on the author's use of background information in paragraph 14 and in other parts of this essay. In your opinion, does Roueché give too much, too little, or about the right amount of background? Defend your answer using examples from this essay.

4. What do you see in the way Roueché transcribes his interview with Pelliteri and Greenberg that builds suspense and creates context?

5. What elements of narration does Roueché use in writing his cause and effect analysis of this perplexing medical mystery? (Glossary: *Narration*)

QUESTIONS ON LANGUAGE

1. Does the reader need to have any medical knowledge to follow this case? Defend your answer using examples of Roueché's diction from this essay.

2. Refer to your desk dictionary to determine the meanings of the following words as they are used in this selection: *irascibly* (paragraph 1), *consumptive* (2), *flophouse* (2), *epidemiological* (3), *moreover* (8), *repaired* (16), *inured* (20), *taxed* (20), *credulity* (20).

WRITING SUGGESTIONS

1. Using Roueché's work as your model, write an essay explaining an apparent mystery. For example, explain why your toaster hasn't been working, why a certain course is offered at your university, or why two people refuse to talk to each other. Roueché interviewed Pelliteri and Greenberg because they solved the case. Who solved your case, and are they the best source in explaining the mystery? Consider mysteries that you have solved and those solved by others before deciding how you want to approach your essay.

2. Create a causal chain of your own for some action or activity that culminated in community action in your town or your school. For example, a volunteer program in your school, the building of a new firehouse, a neighborhood watch committee, or a summer recreation program. Be sure that the different parts of your chain are authentically related and not *non sequiturs*. (Glossary: *Logical Fallacies*)

WRITING SUGGESTIONS
FOR CAUSE AND EFFECT ANALYSIS

1. Write an essay in which you analyze the most significant reasons why you went to college. You may wish to discuss such matters as your family background, your high-school experience, people and events that influenced your decision, and your goals in college as well as in later life.

2. It is interesting to think of ourselves in terms of the influences that have caused us to be who we are. Write an essay in which you discuss two or three of what you consider the most important influences on your life. Following are some areas you may wish to consider in planning and writing your paper:

   a. a parent   f. a friend
   b. a book or movie   g. a youth organization
   c. a member of the clergy   h. a coach
   d. a teacher   i. your neighborhood
   e. a hero   j. your ethnic background

3. Decisions often involve cause and effect relationships; that is, a person usually weighs the possible results of an action before deciding to act. Write an essay in which you consider the possible effects that would result from one decision or another in one of the following controversies:

   a. taxing cars on the basis of fuel consumption
   b. reinstituting the military draft
   c. legalizing marijuana
   d. mandatory licensing of handguns
   e. raising the legal drinking age to twenty-one
   f. ending subsidies to tobacco growers
   g. abolishing grades for college courses
   h. raising the minimum wage
   i. mandatory community service (one year) for all eighteen-year-olds
   j. banning the use of pesticides on produce
   k. requiring an ethics course in college

9

ARGUMENTATION

WHAT IS ARGUMENT?

The word *argument* probably brings to mind a verbal disagreement of the sort that everyone has at least witnessed, if not participated in directly. Such disputes are occasionally satisfying; you can take pleasure in knowing you have converted someone to your point of view. More often, though, arguments like these are inconclusive and result only in the frustration of realizing that you have failed to make your position understood, or in sputtering anger over your opponent's unreasonable stubbornness. Such dissatisfaction is inevitable, because verbal arguments generally arise spontaneously and so cannot be thoughtfully planned or researched; it is difficult to come up with appropriate evidence on the spur of the moment or to find the language that will make a point hard to deny. Indeed, it is often not until later, in retrospect, that the convincing piece of evidence, the forcefully phrased assertion, finally comes to mind.

Written arguments have much in common with spoken ones: they attempt to convince a reader to agree with a particular point of view, to make a particular decision, to pursue a particular course of action; they involve the presentation of well-chosen evidence and the artful control of language. However, writers of argument have no one around to dispute their words directly, so they must imagine their probable audience in order to predict the sorts of objections that may be raised. This requires that written arguments be much more carefully planned—the writer must settle in advance on a specific, sufficiently detailed thesis or proposition, rather than grope toward one as in a verbal argument. There is a greater need for organization, for choosing the most effective types of evidence from all that is available, for determining the strategies of rhetoric, language, and style that will best suit the argument's subject, its purpose, its thesis, as well as its effect on the intended audience. In the end, however, such work can be far more satisfying than the slapdash of a spontaneous oral argument.

Most people who specialize in the study of arguments identify two essential categories: persuasion and logic.

Persuasive argument relies primarily on appeals to emotion, to the subconscious, even to bias and prejudice. These appeals involve diction, slanting, figurative language, analogy, rhythmic patterns of speech, and the establishment of a tone that will encourage a positive response. Examples of persuasive argument are found in the exaggerated claims of advertisers and the speechmaking of political and social activists.

Logical argument, on the other hand, appeals primarily to the mind, to the audience's intellectual faculties, understanding, and knowledge. Such appeals depend on the reasoned movement from assertion to evidence to conclusion, and on an almost mathematical system of proof and counterproof. Logical argument, unlike persuasion, does not normally impel its audience to action. Logical argument is commonly found in scientific or philosophical articles, in legal decisions, and in technical proposals.

Most arguments, however, are neither purely persuasive nor logical in nature. A well-written newspaper editorial, for example, will rest on a logical arrangement of assertions and evidence, but it will employ striking diction and other persuasive patterns of language to reinforce it effectiveness. Thus, the kinds of appeals a writer emphasizes depend on the nature of the topic, the thesis or proposition of the argument, the various kinds of support (e.g., evidence, opinions, examples, facts, statistics) offered, and a thoughtful consideration of the audience. Knowing the differences between persuasive and logical arguments is, then, essential in learning both to read and write arguments.

There are some additional types of argument that are helpful in expanding your understanding.

Informational or Exploratory Argument

Often it is useful to provide a comprehensive layout of the various facets of an issue. This is done to inform an audience, especially one that may not understand why the issue is controversial in the first place, and to help that audience take a position. The writer of this type of argument does not take a position but aims, instead, to render the positions taken by the various sides in accurate and clear language. Your instructors may occasionally call for this kind of argumentative writing as a way of teaching you to explore the complexity of a particular issue.

Focused Argument

This kind of argument has only one objective and that is to change the audience's mind about a controversial issue. Being comprehensive or taking the broad view is not the objective here. If opposing viewpoints are considered it is usually to show their inadequacies and thereby strengthen the writer's own position. This is the kind that we usually think of as the traditional argument.

Action-Oriented Argument

This type of argument is highly persuasive and attempts to accomplish a specific task. This is the vote-for-me-because-I-am-the-only-candidate-who-can-lower-your-taxes type of argument. The language is emotionally charged, and buzz words designed to arouse the emotions of the audience, as well as such propaganda devices as glittering generalities (broad, sweeping statements) and bandwagonism (everyone else is voting for me, don't be left out) may even be used.

Quiet or Subtle Argument

Some arguments do not immediately appear to the audience to be arguments at all. They set out to be informative and objective, but when closely examined they reveal that the author has consciously, sometimes subconsciously, shaped and slanted the evidence in such a manner as actually to favor a particular position. Such shaping may be the result of choices in diction that bend the audience to the writer's perspective, or they may be the result of decisions not to include certain types of evidence while admitting others. Such arguments can, of course, be quite convincing as there are always those who distrust efforts to convince them in favor of making "their own" decisions on the issues.

Reconciliation Argument

Increasingly popular today is a form of argumentation in which the writer attempts to explore all facets of an issue in order to find areas of agreement or common ground. Of course, one way of viewing that common ground is to see it as itself a new argumentative thrust, a new assertion, about which there may yet be more debate. The object, nevertheless, is to lessen stridency, emotionalism, and the hardening of positions, and to mediate opposing views into a rational and, where appropriate, even practical outcome.

WHY DO WRITERS USE ARGUMENT?

True arguments are limited to assertions about which there is a legitimate and recognized difference of opinion. It is unlikely that anyone will ever need to convince a reader that falling in love is a rare and intense experience, that crime rates should be reduced, or that computers are changing the world; most everyone would agree with such assertions. But not everyone would agree that women experience love more intensely than men, that reinstating the death penalty will reduce the incidence of crime, or that computers are changing the world for the worse; these assertions are arguable and admit of differing perspectives. Similarly, a leading heart specialist might argue in a popular magazine that too many doctors are advising patients to have pacemakers implanted when they are not necessary; the editorial writer for a small-town newspaper could write urging that a local agency supplying food to poor families be given a larger percentage of the tax budget; in a lengthy and complex book, a foreign policy specialist might attempt to prove that the current administration exhibits no consistent policy in its relationship with other countries and that the Department of State is in need of overhauling. No matter what its forum or its structure, an argument has as its chief purpose the detailed setting forth of a particular point of view and the rebuttal of any opposing views.

Classical thinkers believed that there are three key components in all rhetorical situations or attempts to communicate: the *speaker* (and for us the *writer*) who comments about a *subject* to an *audience*. For purposes of discussion we can isolate each of these three entities but in actual rhetorical situations they are really inseparable, each inextricably tied to and influencing the other two. The ancients also recognized the importance of qualities attached to each of these components that are especially significant in the case of argumentation: *ethos*, which is related to the speaker; *logos*, which is related to the subject; and *pathos*, which is related to the audience. Let's look a little closer at each of these:

Ethos (Greek for "character") has to do with the authority, credibility, and to a certain extent, the morals of the speaker or writer.

Aristotle and Cicero, Greek rhetoricians, believed that it was important for the speaker to be credible and to argue for a worthwhile cause. Putting one's argumentative skills in the service of a questionable cause was simply not acceptable. But how did one establish credibility? Sometimes it was gained through achievements outside the rhetorical arena. That is, the speaker had experience with an issue, had argued the subject before, and had been judged to be sincere and honest.

In the case of your own writing, such credentials are not always possible, so you will need to be more concerned than usual with presenting your argument reasonably, sincerely, and in language untainted by excessive emotionalism. Finally, it is well worth remembering that you should at all points in your writing show respect for your audience.

Logos (Greek for "word"), related as it is to the subject, is the effective presentation of the argument itself. Is the thesis or claim a worthwhile one, is it logical, consistent, and well buttressed by supporting evidence? Is the evidence itself factual, reliable, and convincing? Finally, is the argument so thoughtfully organized and clearly presented that it impacts the audience and has the possibility of changing minds? Indeed, this aspect of argumentation is the most difficult to accomplish but is, at the same time, the most rewarding.

Pathos (Greek for "emotion") has most to do with audience. The essential question is, how does the speaker or writer present an argument or persuasion essay so as to maximize its appeal for a given audience? One answer, of course, is through the artful and strategic use of well-crafted language. Certain buzz words, slanted diction, or loaded language may become either rallying cries or causes of resentment in an argument.

It is worth remembering at this point that although one can never be certain who one's audience is, readers range along a spectrum from extremely friendly and sympathetic to extremely hostile and resistant, with a myriad of possibilities in between. The friendly audience will welcome new information and support the writer's position; the hostile audience will look for just the opposite: flaws in logic and examples of dishonest manipulation by the writer. With many arguments there is the potential for a considerable audience of interested parties who are uncommitted. If the targeted audience is judged to be friendly, then the writer need not be as concerned with *logos* and can be less cautious and more free-wheeling. If the audience is thought to be hostile, the *logos* must be the writer's immediate concern and the language should be straightforward and objective. Greatest caution, subtlety, and critical thinking must be applied to the attempt to win over an uncommitted audience.

In general, writers of argument are interested in explaining aspects of a subject as well as in advocating a particular view. Consequently, argumentation frequently utilizes the other rhetorical strategies. In your efforts to argue convincingly, you may find it necessary to define, to compare and contrast, to analyze causes and effects, to classify, to describe, to narrate. Nevertheless, it is the writer's attempt to convince, not explain, that is of primary importance in an argumentative essay. In this respect, it is helpful to keep in mind that there are two basic patterns of thinking and the presentation of our thoughts that are followed in argumentation: *induction* and *deduction*.

Inductive reasoning moves from a set of specific examples to a general statement or principle. As long as the evidence is accurate, pertinent, complete, and sufficient to represent the assertion, the conclusion of an inductive argument can be regarded as valid; if, however, you can spot inaccuracies in the evidence or point to contrary evidence, you have good reason to doubt the assertion as it stands. Inductive reasoning is the most common of argumentative structures.

Deductive reasoning, more formal and complex than inductive, moves from an overall premise, rule, or generalization to a more specific conclusion. Deductive logic follows the pattern of the syllogism, a simple three-part argument consisting of a major premise, a minor premise, and a conclusion. For example, notice how the following syllogism works:

a. All humans are mortal. *(major premise)*
b. Carolann is a human. *(minor premise)*
c. Carolann is mortal. *(conclusion)*

The conclusion here is true because both premises are true and the logic of the syllogism is valid.

Obviously, a syllogism will fail to work if either of the premises is untrue:

a. All living creatures are mammals. *(major premise)*
b. A lobster is a living creature. *(minor premise)*
c. A lobster is a mammal. *(conclusion)*

The problem is immediately apparent. The major premise is obviously false: there are many living creatures that are not mammals, and a lobster happens to be one of them. Consequently, the conclusion is invalid.

Syllogisms, however, can fail in other ways, even if both premises are objectively true. Such failures occur most often when the arguer jumps to a conclusion without taking obvious exceptions into account:

a. All college students read books. *(major premise)*
b. Kristin reads books. *(minor premise)*
c. Kristin is a college student. *(conclusion)*

Both the premises in this syllogism are true, but the syllogism is still invalid because it does not take into account that other people besides college students read books. The problem is in the way the major premise has been interpreted: if the minor premise was instead "Kristin is a college student," then the valid conclusion "Kristin reads books" would logically follow.

It is fairly easy to see the problems in a deductive argument when its premises and conclusion are rendered in the form of a syllogism. It is often more difficult to see errors in logic when the argument is presented discursively or within the context of a lengthy essay. If you can reduce the argument to its syllogistic form, however, you will have much less difficulty testing its validity. Similarly, if you can isolate and examine out of context the evidence provided to support an inductive assertion, you can more readily evaluate the written inductive argument.

Consider the following excerpt from "The Draft: Why the Country Needs It," an article by James Fallows that first appeared in the *Atlantic* magazine:

> The Vietnam draft was unfair racially, economically, educationally. By every one of those measures, the volunteer Army is less representative still. Libertarians argue that military service should be a matter of choice, but the plain fact is that service in the volunteer force is too frequently dictated by economics. Army enlisted ranks E1 through E4, the privates and corporals, the cannon fodder, the ones who will fight and die, are 36 percent black now. By the Army's own projections, they will be 42 percent black in three years. When other "minorities" are taken into account, we will have, for the first time, an army whose fighting members are mainly "non-majority," or more bluntly, a black and brown army defending a mainly white nation. The military has been an avenue of opportunity of many young blacks. They may well be firstclass fighting men. They do not represent the nation.
>
> Such a selective sharing of the burden has destructive spiritual effects in a nation based on the democratic creed. But its practical implications can be quite as grave. The effect of a fair, representative draft is to hold the public hostage to the consequences of its decisions, much as the children's presence in the public schools focuses parents' attention on the quality of the schools. If the citizens are willing to countenance a decision that means that *someone's* child may die, they may contemplate more deeply if there is the possibility that the child will be theirs. Indeed, I would like to extend this principle even fur-

ther. Young men of nineteen are rightly suspicious of the congressmen and columnists who urge them to the fore. I wish there were a practical way to resurrect provisions of the amended Selective Service Act of 1940, which raised the draft age to forty-four. Such a gesture might symbolize the desire to offset the historic injustice of the Vietnam draft, as well as suggest the possibility that, when a bellicose columnist recommends dispatching the American forces to Pakistan, he might also realize that he could end up as a gunner in a tank.

Here Fallows presents an inductive argument against the volunteer army and in favor of reinstating a draft. His argument can be summarized as follows:

ASSERTION: The volunteer army is racially and economically unfair.

EVIDENCE: The disproportionate percentage of blacks in the army, and projections which indicate that, within three years of the article's publication, more than half of the army's fighting members will be nonwhite.

CONCLUSION: "Such a selective sharing of the burden has destructive spiritual effects in a nation based on the democratic ideal." Not until there is a fair, representative draft will the powerful majority be held accountable for any decision to go to war.

Fallows's inductive scheme here is, in fact, very effective—the evidence is convincing and the conclusion strong. But his argument also depends on a more complicated deductive syllogism:

a. The democratic ideal requires equal representation in the responsibilities of citizenship. *(major premise)*
b. Military service is a responsibility of citizenship. *(minor premise)*
c. The democratic ideal requires equal representation in military service. *(conclusion)*

In order to attack Fallows's argument, it would be necessary to deny one of his premises.

Fallows also employs a number of more persuasive techniques, including an analogy: "The effect of a fair, representative draft is to hold the public hostage to the consequences of its decisions, much as children's presence in the public schools focuses parents' attention on the quality of the schools." The use of such an analogy proves nothing, but it can force readers to reconsider their viewpoint and make them more open-minded. The same is true of Fallows's almost entirely unserious suggestion about raising the draft age to forty-four. Like most writers, Fallows uses persuasive arguments to complement his more important logical ones.

LOOKING AT ARGUMENTS

Before attempting to write an argument of your own, it is helpful to analyze arguments written by others. As you have already seen, argumentative writing is a complex form, relying as it does on all the other rhetorical modes and writing strategies discussed thus far in *Subject and Strategy*. The following directions for analyzing an argumentative essay are designed to encourage close scrutiny and your critical thinking skills.

Examine the Thesis or Proposition

First, look for the thesis statement or the proposition of the argument. In other words, ask yourself, "What is the issue addressed in this argument?" Remember that the thesis of an essay is not always obvious nor placed at the beginning of argumentative essays.

You may also want, at this point, to write a short one- or two-sentence statement of your own position concerning the issue both to fix it in your mind and to make it easy to refer to as you continue your analysis. Having that statement in front of you will also make it possible to measure how much the argument has changed your thinking, if at all.

Review and Evaluate the Supporting Evidence

Next, try to come to an understanding of the way the author has supported the argument's claim or issue. It may help you to restate the claim and make a list of the reasons and evidence provided. Look for the following types of evidence: facts, statistics, reasons, examples, testimony from experts (either from interviews or from written sources), explanations, and personal anecdotes.

Assess the quality of the evidence you find. Do you have any reason to be suspicious of the validity of any portion of the evidence? What can you do to check on the validity of the evidence?

Determine the System of Argumentation That Is Used

Determine whether the argument is based on inductive or deductive reasoning or on some combination of these methods. Understanding how these systems work in your reading will better prepare you for using them in your own writing. Consider the quality of the evidence that is presented. Is that evidence factual, or are assumptions made in the evidence that you do not share?

Shared Assumptions

To the extent that there are assumptions in the argument that you agree with, you are a friendly audience. To the extent that you do not share those assumptions you will not be convinced of the validity of the argument. What assumptions are made by the writer? What assumptions do you bring as a reader? What in your background accounts for your assumptions, or prevents you from making certain ones? These are not easy questions to answer and you may have to ponder what you are reading in order to come to a useful assessment. Again, it is worthwhile to jot down notes as often as possible.

Areas of Agreement

Is there any common ground for understanding between you as a reader and the author of the argument? Of what use is the knowledge of that common ground in your assessment of the success of the argument?

Evaluation

How successful has the writer been? Are you convinced by the argument? By what portions of the argument in particular? Has your position hardened, softened, or remained the same? What have you learned about the issue by reading the argument? Is the writer informed, sincere, trustworthy, unbiased, and logical?

READING ARGUMENT IN AN ANNOTATED STUDENT ESSAY

Born in Buffalo, New York, Don Wynns now lives in Naples, Florida. Although he majored in English, Wynns took a number of electives in environmental studies. After completing his graduate studies in journalism, he hopes to combine his interests in writing and the environment by securing a position with an environmental publication. In this essay, Wynns argues that more environmental education is needed at all levels, if future generations are to solve the problems currently facing the world. To support his points, Wynns relies on information he discovered in the course of library research; he has used MLA in-text citations to document his essay whenever he quotes or paraphrases outside sources.

ENVIRONMENTAL EDUCATION:
TOWARD AN ETHIC OF STEWARDSHIP
Don Wynns

Shared assumption: we need to protect our environment.

Most Americans today seem to agree that, as a nation, we should follow an ethic of environmental stewardship. We nod our heads complacently and say, yes, we need to conserve our finite natural resources and protect our environment from becoming unfit to live in. Unfortunately, we don't live this way. 1

Claim: we don't live that way.

Grants that Americans are capable of living by environmental ethic

Reason 1: Apathy. Evidence

Perhaps the United States came closest to living by this ethic in 1973, the year of the Arab oil embargo. The resulting marathon gas lines and soaring heating bills left us no choice but to limit our ravenous consumption of oil and conserve our own natural resources. We had discovered the reality of a finite environment. Apathy, though, soon set in. A mere six years after the embargo, a Gallup poll showed that only half of Americans felt our energy situation was "fairly serious." Incredibly, 33% didn't even realize that the U.S. imports oil! (Miller 258). Today forgetfulness seems to be running rampant. The big auto makers' marketing tests show that people again want big, soft-riding gas-guzzlers, probably because of greater gas supplies and lower prices resulting from the temporary oil glut. And so Detroit, instead of producing cars that get sixty miles per gallon (this would raise a car's price about $800, but the money would be returned to the owner in only fifteen months through fuel savings [Lovins]), has reverted to the 1960 mentality of making large, lower-mileage cars and vans. 2

Evidence

Reason 2: no government leadership.

Shortsightedness is the rule of the day, and nowhere is this more evident than in Washington. Whether it be zero-budgeting a program for insulating 3

Evidence
the homes of low-income citizens, an Interior Department that all but invites coal-mining interests to strip-mine public land, or an Environmental Protection Agency which has chosen to ignore the illegal dumping of toxic wastes, our government itself has proven to be at best a weak supporter of the ethic of environmental stewardship. With such a model, no wonder the general public has not acted more responsibly.

Reassertion of claim: in spite of increased news coverage, American public remains uncommitted to idea of stewardship of the environment.
This national myopia of the 1980s has occurred   4
despite newspaper exposés and editorials, TV series and specials, environmental magazines and newsletters, and an increase in the number of basic environmental-awareness courses in our universities. Obviously, such publicity has succeeded in raising the environmental consciousness of some; but the message tends to reach a limited audience of people who either already live according to an environmental ethic or sincerely wish to do so. Most of us, however, have remained uncommitted to environmental stewardship of even the lowest order.

Reason 3: lack of environmental courses in our public schools.
Perhaps this is because the stewardship ethic is   5
not presented early enough in our schools, and because what is done is not of adequate quality. There is evidence to support such a belief. In 1974 and 1981, two concerned teachers surveyed all fifty state education agencies, forty-two of which returned both

Evidence
surveys. The responses show that on the average each agency's coordinator for environmental education spent 59% of his or her time working on other projects, such as devising new general science programs (Disinger and Bouquet 19). Between 1974 and 1981, the "decreasing priority for environmental education is lucidly demonstrated by the data evidencing decreasing percentages of staff time for its coordination in the state education agencies"; this results at least partly from the "lack of priority for environmental education within the federal establishment" combined with "state education agencies following federal funding priorities (Disinger and Bouquet 20).

Reason 4: lack of teacher training.

Moreover, the teachers of environmental studies courses in our primary and secondary schools have themselves never had to take environmental studies in college. There is no such thing as a mandatory environmental curriculum for future elementary and high school teachers. In fact, from the peak of environmental awareness on Earth Day in 1970 through late 1979, there was no increase in the number of state universities that offered certifiable majors and minors in environmental education (Trent 15). So youngsters are not receiving the quality of instruction that they should from their teachers. No matter how hard a teacher tries, if he or she is not versed in a subject the students cannot learn it well.

Evidence

6

Conclusion: without adequate education, few students will understand or live by environmental ethic, or will choose to become an environmental professional.

It seems reasonable to infer that without adequate programs in elementary and high schools, few students will understand what an environmental ethic is, much less choose to live by it; fewer still will want to become environmental or natural resources professionals. Even if a high school graduate does aspire to such a career, there is a scarcity of college and university programs offering specialization in environmental science and engineering. In a recent survey of 206 U.S. and Canadian universities, only 48% were found to have a viable curriculum in environmental studies (as opposed to a few scattered courses). And only 11% had such programs leading to a degree (Klee 34). Thus, the options for students seriously interested in scientific research or policy-making are rare indeed.

Evidence

7

Call to action: educators need to renew their commitment to education courses at all levels.

It is time to fill this void. Universities along with state and local governments must share the responsibility. By renewing their commitment to environmental courses at the introductory and advanced levels and by developing programs for future elementary and high school teachers, universities can help prepare the way. With adequate public funding at all levels, such curricula could lead to better and more numerous courses in the schools, a key to the devel-

8

opment of widespread environmental consciousness
and responsibility.

Our best hope to eliminate igno- rance and apathy is education.

As things are, it seems that only some major   9
environmental catastrophe will break through the
ignorance and apathy of most people about the environment and its problems. But surely it is better to
avert a disaster than to cause one and then learn from
it. Thanks to fifteen years of consciousness-raising
and hard experience, the foundation exists for better
understanding through better education. But we cannot afford to leave it at that. The system can work;
whether it will, however, remains to be seen.

Works Cited: al- phabetical listing of the sources Wynns uses in this essay.

Works Cited

Disinger, J., and W. Bouquet. "Environmental Education and State Education Agencies." *Journal of
   Environmental Education* (Spring 1982).

Klee, G. "The Status of Environmental Studies in U.S.
   and Canadian Geography Departments." *Journal
   of Environmental Education* (Winter 1982–83).

Lovins, Hunter. Speech. University of Vermont, 3 Apr.
   1984.

Miller, Tyler. *Living in the Environment.* Belmont, CA:
   Wadsworth, 1982.

Trent, J. "Environmental Education in Our Schools
   During the 1970's." *Journal of Environmental
   Education* (Fall 1983).

Don Wynns has always been interested in the environment. While
at the University of Vermont he took several environmental studies
courses even though he was an English major. While he was doing some
preliminary work for this argumentative essay, he found himself, as he
later related, "paging through a copy of *Environmental Management*
magazine and read an editorial by Robert DeSanto. There was a sentence that struck me: 'The concept of environmental stewardship en-
capsulates the idea that there is a need for (a) the public to better sense
our environment and its ecology, (b) the politician to better sense the
capacities and limitations of applied science, (c) the scientist to better
sense the practical need for applied ecology, and (d) the means by which
we can better communicate and instill these sensitivities.' That one

sentence got me started. In fact, I quoted it at the beginning of my first draft."

Wynns admits that he "had lots of problems" while working on this essay. "I made a lot of assertions without any supporting evidence, and I made a lot of proposals without explaining why they should be adopted. My teacher pointed out that what seemed obvious to me would be new and possibly controversial to my readers, and suggested that I share my facts and reasoning with them." And as Wynns did more research in the library, his paper changed shape. "There's almost no comparison between my first and last drafts. Along the way, I included and then dropped a history of changing American attitudes about and use of the land, and I included and dropped a detailed proposal for what the schools should teach. I also finally dropped the DeSanto quotation that began the whole thing." In the end, Wynns focused on the bad state of affairs in our public schools and educational bureaucracies and called for more environmental education at all levels.

WRITING AN ARGUMENTATIVE ESSAY

Writing an argument is a difficult assignment but one that can be very rewarding. By nature, an argument must be carefully reasoned and thoughtfully structured in order to have maximum effect. In other words, the *logos* of the argument needs to be carefully tended. Allow yourself, therefore, enough time to think about your thesis, to gather the evidence you need, and to draft, revise, edit, and proofread your essay. Fuzzy thinking, confused expression, and poor organization will be immediately evident to your reader and will diminish your chances for completing the assignment successfully. The following steps will remind you of some key features of arguments and will help you sequence your activities as you research and write.

Determine the Thesis or Proposition

Begin by determining a topic that interests you and about which there is some significant difference of opinion or about which you have a number of questions. Find out what's in the news, what people are talking about, what authors and instructors are emphasizing as important intellectual arguments. As you pursue your research, consider what assertion or assertions you can make about the topic you choose. The more specific this thesis or proposition, the more directed your research can become and the more focused your ultimate argument will be.

Don't hesitate at any point along the way to modify or even reject an initial thesis as continued research warrants.

A thesis can be placed anywhere in an argument, but it is probably best while learning to write arguments to place the statement of your controlling idea somewhere near the beginning of your composition. Explain the importance of the thesis, and make clear to your reader that you share a common concern or interest in this issue. You may wish to state your central assertion directly in your first or second paragraph, so that there is no possibility for your reader to be confused about your position. You may, as well, wish to lead off with a particularly striking piece of evidence, to capture your reader's interest.

Take Account of Your Audience

It is well worth remembering that in no other type of writing is the question of audience more important than in argumentation. Here, again, the *ethos* and *pathos* aspects of argumentation comes into play. The tone you establish, the type of diction you choose, the kinds of evidence selected to buttress your assertions, and indeed the organizational pattern you design and follow will all influence your trustworthiness and believability with your audience. If you make good judgments about the nature of your audience, respect its knowledge of the subject, and correctly envision whether it is likely to be hostile, neutral, complacent, or receptive, you will be able to tailor the various aspects of your argument appropriately.

Gather the Necessary Supporting Evidence

For each point of your argument, be sure to provide appropriate and sufficient supporting evidence: verifiable facts and statistics, illustrative examples and narratives, or quotations from authorities. Don't overwhelm your reader with evidence, but don't skimp either; it is important to demonstrate your command of the topic and control of the thesis by choosing carefully amongst all the evidence at your disposal.

Settle on an Organizational Pattern

Once you think that you have sufficient evidence to make your assertion convincing, consider how best to organize your argument. To some extent, your organization will depend on your method of reasoning: inductive, deductive, or a combination of the two. For example, is it necessary to establish a major premise before moving on to discuss a minor premise? Should most of your evidence precede your direct statement of an assertion, or follow it? Will induction work better with the particular audience you have targeted? Don Wynns, for example, in his essay "Environmental Education: Toward an Ethic of Stewardship," moves from a series of examples to the presentation of his assertion and a call to action regarding the need for environmental education. As you present your primary points, you may find it effective to move from those that are least important to those that are most important, or from those that are least familiar to those that are most familiar. A scratch outline can help; but it is often the case that a writer's most crucial revisions in an argument involve rearranging its components into a sharper, more coherent order. Very often it is difficult to tell what that order should be until the revision stage of the writing process.

Consider Refutations to Your Argument

As you proceed with your argument, you may wish to take into account well-known and significant opposing arguments. To ignore them would be to suggest to your readers any one of the following: you don't know about them, you know about them and are obviously and unfairly weighting the argument in your favor, or you know about them and have no reasonable answers to them. Grant the validity of the opposing argument or refute it but respect your reader's intelligence by addressing the problems. Your readers will in turn respect you for doing so.

Avoid Faulty Reasoning

Have someone read your argument for errors in judgment and reasoning. Sometimes others can see easily what you can't because you are so intimately tied to your assertion. Review the following list of errors in reasoning, making sure that you have not committed any of those errors in logic.

OVERSIMPLIFICATION. A foolishly simple solution to what is clearly a complex problem: *The reason we have a balance of trade deficit is that foreigners make better products than we do.*

HASTY GENERALIZATION. In inductive reasoning, a generalization that is based on too little evidence or on evidence that is not representative: *It was the best movie I saw, and so it should get an Academy Award.*

POST HOC ERGO PROPTER HOC. "After this, therefore because of this." Confusing chance or coincidence with causation. The fact that one event comes after another does not necessarily mean that the first event caused the second: *After I went to the hockey game, I caught a cold.*

BEGGING THE QUESTION. Assuming in a premise something that needs to be proven: *Parking fines work because they keep people from parking illegally.*

FALSE ANALOGY. Making a misleading analogy between logically connected ideas: *Of course he'll make a fine coach. He was an all-star basketball player.*

EITHER/OR THINKING. Seeing only two alternatives when there may in fact be other possibilities: *Either you love your job or you hate it.*

NON SEQUITUR. "It does not follow." An inference or conclusion that is not clearly related to the established premises or evidence: *She is very sincere; she must know what she is talking about.*

Conclude Forcefully

In the conclusion of your essay, be sure to restate in new language your position, at least briefly. Besides persuading your reader to accept your point of view, you may also want to encourage some specific course of action. Above all, your conclusion should not introduce new information that may surprise your reader; it should seem to follow naturally, almost seamlessly, from the series of points that have been carefully established in the body of the essay. Don't overstate your case, but at the same time don't qualify your conclusion with the use of too many words or phrases like *I think, in my opinion, maybe, sometimes,* and *probably.* Rather than rational and sensible, these words can often make you sound indecisive and fuzzy-headed.

The Declaration of Independence

THOMAS JEFFERSON

President, governor, statesman, diplomat, lawyer, architect, phi-losopher, thinker, and writer, Thomas Jefferson is one of the most important figures in United States history. He was born in Albemarle County, Virginia, in 1743 and attended the College of William and Mary. After being admitted to law practice in 1767, he began a long and illustrious career of public service to the colonies and, later, the new republic.

Jefferson drafted the Declaration of Independence in 1776. Although it was revised by Benjamin Franklin and his colleagues in the Continental Congress, in its sound logic and forceful, direct style the document retains the unmistakable qualities of Jefferson's prose.

When in the course of human events, it becomes necessary for one people to dissolve the political bands which have connected them with another, and to assume among the Powers of the earth, the separate and equal station to which the Laws of Nature and of Nature's God entitle them, a decent respect to the opinions of mankind requires that they should declare the causes which impel them to the separation.

We hold these truths to be self-evident, that all men are created equal, that they are endowed by their Creator with certain unalienable Rights, that among these are Life, Liberty and the pursuit of Happiness. That to secure these rights, Governments are instituted among Men deriving their just powers from the consent of the governed. That whenever any Form of Government becomes destructive of these ends, it is the Right of the People to alter or to abolish it, and to institute new Government, laying its foundation on such principles and organizing its powers in such form, as to them shall seem most likely to effect their Safety and Happiness. Prudence, indeed, will dictate that Governments long established should not be changed for light and transient causes; and accordingly all experience hath shown, that mankind are more disposed to suffer, while evils are sufferable, than to right themselves by abolishing the forms to which they are accustomed. But when a long train of abuses and usurpations pursuing invariably the same Object evinces a design to reduce them under absolute Despotism, it is their right, it is their duty, to throw off such government, and to provide new Guards for their future security. Such has been the patient sufferance of these Colonies; and such is now the necessity which constrains them to alter their former Systems of Government. The history of the present King of Great Britain is a history of repeated injuries and usurpations, all having in direct object the establishment of an absolute Tyranny over these States. To prove this, let Facts be submitted to a candid world.

He has refused his Assent to Laws, the most wholesome and nec- 3 essary for the public good.

He has forbidden his Governors to pass Laws of immediate and 4 pressing importance, unless suspended in their operation till his Assent should be obtained; and when so suspended, he has utterly neglected to attend to them.

He has refused to pass other Laws for the accommodation of large 5 districts of people, unless those people would relinquish the right of Representation in the Legislature, a right inestimable to them and formidable to tyrants only.

He has called together legislative bodies at places unusual, uncom- 6 fortable, and distant from the depository of their Public Records, for the sole purpose of fatiguing them into compliance with his measures.

He has dissolved Representative Houses repeatedly, for opposing 7 with manly firmness his invasions on the rights of the people.

He has refused for a long time, after such dissolutions, to cause 8 others to be elected; whereby the Legislative Powers, incapable of An- nihilation, have returned to the People at large for their exercise; the State remaining in the mean time exposed to all the dangers of invasion from without, and convulsions within.

He has endeavoured to prevent the population of these States; for 9 that purpose obstructing the Laws of Naturalization of Foreigners; re- fusing to pass others to encourage their migration hither, and raising the conditions of new Appropriations of Lands.

He has obstructed the Administration of Justice, by refusing his 10 Assent to Laws for establishing Judiciary Powers.

He has made Judges dependent on his Will alone, for the tenure of 11 their offices, and the amount and payment of their salaries.

He has erected a multitude of New Offices, and sent hither swarms 12 of Officers to harass our People, and eat out their substance.

He has kept among us, in time of peace, Standing Armies without 13 the Consent of our Legislature.

He has affected to render the Military independent of and superior 14 to the Civil Power.

He has combined with others to subject us to jurisdictions foreign 15 to our constitution, and unacknowledged by our laws; giving his Assent to their acts of pretended Legislation:

For quartering large bodies of armed troops among us: 16

For protecting them, by a mock Trial, from Punishment for any 17 Murders which they should commit on the Inhabitants of these States:

For cutting off our Trade with all parts of the world: 18

For imposing Taxes on us without our Consent: 19

For depriving us in many cases, of the benefits of Trial by Jury: 20

For transporting us beyond Seas to be tried for pretended offenses: 21

For abolishing the free System of English Laws in a Neighbouring 22 Province, establishing therein an Arbitrary government, and enlarging its boundaries so as to render it at once an example and fit instrument for introducing the same absolute rule into these Colonies:

For taking away our Charters, abolishing our most valuable Laws, 23 and altering fundamentally the Forms of our Governments:

For suspending our own Legislatures, and declaring themselves 24 invested with Power to legislate for us in all cases whatsoever.

He has abdicated Government here, by declaring us out of his 25 Protection and waging War against us.

He has plundered our seas, ravaged our Coasts, burnt our towns 26 and destroyed the Lives of our people.

He is at this time transporting large Armies of foreign Mercenaries 27 to compleat works of death, desolation and tyranny already begun with circumstances of Cruelty & perfidy scarcely paralleled in the most barbarous ages, and totally unworthy the Head of a civilized nation.

He has constrained our fellow Citizens taken Captive on the high 28 Seas to bear Arms against their Country, to become the executioners of their friends and Brethren, or to fall themselves by their Hands.

He has excited domestic insurrections amongst us, and has endeav- 29 oured to bring on the inhabitants of our frontiers, the merciless Indian Savages, whose known rule of warfare is an undistinguished destruction of all ages, sexes and conditions.

In every stage of these Oppressions We Have Petitioned for Re- 30 dress in the most humble terms: Our repeated petitions have been answered only by repeated injury. A Prince, whose character is thus marked by every act which may define a Tyrant, is unfit to be the ruler of a free People.

Not have We been wanting in attention to our British brethren. We 31 have warned them from time to time of attempts by their legislature to extend an unwarrantable jurisdiction over us. We have reminded them of the circumstances of our emigration and settlement here. We have appealed to their native justice and magnanimity and we have conjured them by the ties of our common kindred to disavow these usurpations, which would inevitably interrupt our connections and correspondence.

They too have been deaf to the voice of justice and of consanguinity. We must, therefore acquiesce in the necessity, which denounces our Separation, and hold them, as we hold the rest of mankind, Enemies in War, in Peace Friends.

We, therefore, the Representatives of the United States of America, 32 in General Congress, Assembled, appealing to the Supreme Judge of the world for the rectitude of our intentions, do, in the Name, and by Authority of the good People of these Colonies, solemnly publish and declare, That these United Colonies are, and of Right ought to be Free and Independent States; that they are Absolved from all Allegiance to the British Crown, and that all political connection between them and the State of Great Britain, is and ought to be totally dissolved; and that as Free and Independent States, they have full power to levy War, conclude Peace, contract Alliances, establish Commerce, and to do all other Acts and Things which Independent States may of right do. And for the support of this Declaration, with a firm reliance on the protection of Divine Providence, we mutually pledge to each other our lives, our Fortunes and our sacred Honor.

QUESTIONS ON SUBJECT

1. Where, according to Jefferson, do rulers get their authority? What does Jefferson believe is the purpose of government?

2. In paragraph 2, Jefferson presents certain "self-evident" truths. What are these truths, and how are they related to the intent of his argument?

3. What argument does the Declaration make for overthrowing any unacceptable government? What assumptions underlie this argument?

4. In paragraphs 3 through 29, Jefferson lists the many ways King George has wronged the colonists. Which of these "injuries and usurpations" do you feel are just cause for the colonists to declare their independence?

5. According to the Declaration, how did the colonists try to persuade the English king to rule more justly?

6. What are the specific points of Jefferson's Declaration in the final paragraph?

QUESTIONS ON STRATEGY

1. The Declaration of Independence is a deductive argument; it is, therefore, possible to present it in the form of a syllogism. What is the major premise, the minor premise, and the conclusion of Jefferson's argument? (Glossary: *Syllogism*)

2. The list of charges against the king is given as evidence in support of Jefferson's minor premise. Does he offer any evidence in support of his major premise? Why, or why not? (Glossary: *Supporting Evidence*)

3. What pattern do you see to the list of grievances in paragraphs 3 through 29? Try to group them into categories. Describe the cumulative effect of this list on you as a reader.

4. Who is Jefferson's audience and in what tone does he address this audience? Discuss why this tone is or isn't appropriate for this document? (Glossary: *Audience*)

5. Explain how Jefferson uses cause and effect thinking to justify the colonist's desire to declare their independence. (Glossary: *Cause and Effect*)

QUESTIONS ON LANGUAGE

1. Paraphrase the following excerpt and comment on Jefferson's diction and syntax: "They too have been deaf to the voice of justice and of consanguinity. We must, therefore acquiesce in the necessity, which denounces our separation, and hold them, as we hold the rest of mankind, Enemies in War, in Peace Friends." Describe the author's tone in these two sentences.

2. Is the language of the Declaration of Independence coolly reasonable or emotional, or does it change from one to the other? Give examples to support your answer.

3. Refer to your desk dictionary to determine the meanings of the following words as they are used in this selection: *effect* (paragraph 2), *prudence* (2), *transient* (2), *usurpations* (2 and 31), *evinces* (2), *despotism* (2), *candid* (2), *affected* (14), *perfidy* (27), *excited* (29), *redress* (30), *magnanimity* (31), *conjured* (31), *disavow* (31), *too* (31), *consanguinity* (31), *acquiesce* (31), *rectitude* (32), *levy* (32).

WRITING SUGGESTIONS

1. To some people the Declaration of Independence still accurately reflects America's political philosophy and way of life; to others it does not. What is your position? Discuss your analysis of the Declaration's contemporary relevance.

2. The adoption of the Declaration of Independence was, among other things, a matter of practical politics. Using library sources, research the deliberations of the Continental Congress and explain how and why the final version of the Declaration differs from Jefferson's first draft.

The Playthings of Tyrants

MARY WOLLSTONECRAFT

Mary Wollstonecraft (1759–1797) moved away from her family in 1778, at the age of nineteen. Her father had squandered much of the family's resources trying to make the social jump from trade to gentleman farmer. He became an alcoholic, and Mary often protected her family from his abuse but finally left, disgusted with the situation. Between this time and her first publication in 1787, she worked as a lady's companion, returned home to care for her mother, helped to open a school with her two sisters and close friend, Fanny Blood, traveled with Fanny to Portugal, where Fanny died in childbirth, and worked as a governess in Ireland. This diversity of experience placed her in contact with people from all social classes and levels of education and served as the foundation of her social and political writing. Wollstonecraft bore William Godwin a child on August 30, 1797, and died eleven days later. Their daughter Mary became the wife of poet Percy Bysshe Shelley and authored the novel Frankenstein.

In this selection, taken from the second chapter of her most famous work A Vindication of the Rights of Woman *(1792), Wollstonecraft begins with the premise of the equality of souls and proceeds to examine the nature of virtue and education.*

To account for, and excuse the tyranny of man, many ingenious 1 arguments have been brought forward to prove, that the two sexes, in the acquirement of virtue, ought to aim at attaining a very different character: or, to speak explicitly, women are not allowed to have sufficient strength of mind to acquire what really deserves the name of virtue. Yet it should seem, allowing them to have souls, that there is but one way appointed by Providence to lead *mankind* to either virtue or happiness.

If then women are not a swarm of ephemeron triflers, why should 2 they be kept in ignorance under the specious name of innocence? Men complain, and with reason, of the follies and caprices of our sex, when they do not keenly satirize our headstrong passions and groveling vices.—Behold, I should answer, the natural effect of ignorance! The mind will ever be unstable that has only prejudices to rest on, and the current will run with destructive fury when there are no barriers to break its force. Women are told from their infancy, and taught by the example of their mothers, that a little knowledge of human weakness, justly termed cunning, softness of temper, *outward* obedience, and a scrupulous attention to a puerile kind of propriety, will obtain for them the protection of man; and should they be beautiful, every thing else is needless, for, at least, twenty years of their lives.

Thus Milton describes our first frail mother; though when he tells 3 us that women are formed for softness and sweet attractive grace, I cannot comprehend his meaning, unless, in the true Mahometan strain, he meant to deprive us of souls, and insinuate that we were beings only designed by sweet attractive grace, and docile blind obedience, to gratify the senses of man when he can no longer soar on the wing of contemplation.

How grossly do they insult us who thus advise us only to render 4 ourselves gentle, domestic brutes! For instance, the winning softness so warmly, and frequently, recommended, that governs by obeying. What childish expressions, and how insignificant is the being—can it be an immortal one? who will condescend to govern by such sinister methods! 'Certainly,' says Lord Bacon, 'man is of kin to the beasts by his body; and if he be not of kin to God by his spirit, he is a base and ignoble creature!' Men, indeed, appear to me to act in a very unphilosophical manner when they try to secure the good conduct of women by attempting to keep them always in a state of childhood. Rousseau was more consistent when he wished to stop the progress of reason in both sexes, for if men eat of the tree of knowledge, women will come in for a taste; but, from the imperfect cultivation which their understandings now receive, they only attain a knowledge of evil.

Children, I grant, should be innocent; but when the epithet is ap- 5 plied to men, or women, it is but a civil term for weakness. For if it be allowed that women were destined by Providence to acquire human virtues, and by the exercise of their understandings, that stability of character which is the firmest ground to rest our future hopes upon, they must be permitted to turn to the fountain of light, and not forced to shape their course by the twinkling of a mere satellite. Milton, I grant, was of a very different opinion; for he only bends to the indefeasible right of beauty, though it would be difficult to render two passages which I now mean to contrast, consistent. But into similar inconsistencies are great men often led by their senses.

'To whom thus Eve with *perfect beauty* adorn'd.
'My Author and Disposer, what thou bidst

'Unargued I obey; So God ordains;
'God is *thy law; thou mine:* to know no more
'Is Woman's *happiest* knowledge and her *praise.'*

These are exactly the arguments that I have used to children; but I 6
have added, your reason is now gaining strength, and, till it arrives at
some degree of maturity, you must look up to me for advice—then you
ought to *think,* and only rely on God.

Yet in the following lines Milton seems to coincide with me; when 7
he makes Adam thus expostulate with his Maker.

'Hast thou not made me here thy substitute,
'And these inferior far beneath me set?
'Among *unequals* what society
'Can sort, what harmony or true delight?
'Which must be mutual, in proportion due
'Giv'n and receiv'd; but in *disparity*
'The one intense, the other still remiss
'Cannot well suit with either, but soon prove
'Tedious alike: of *fellowship* I speak
'Such as I seek, fit to participate
'All rational delight—'

In treating, therefore, of the manners of women, let us, disregard- 8
ing sensual arguments, trace what we should endeavour to make them
in order to cooperate, if the expression be not too bold, with the
supreme Being.

By individual education, I mean, for the sense of the word is not 9
precisely defined, such an attention to a child as will slowly sharpen the
senses, form the temper, regulate the passions as they begin to ferment,
and set the understanding to work before the body arrives at maturity;
so that the man may only have to proceed, not to begin, the important
task of learning to think and reason.

To prevent any misconstruction, I must add, that I do not believe 10
that a private education can work the wonders which some sanguine
writers have attributed to it. Men and women must be educated, in a
great degree, by the opinions and manners of the society they live in. In
every age there has been a stream of popular opinion that has carried all
before it, and given a family character, as it were, to the century. It may
then fairly be inferred, that, till society be differently constituted, much
cannot be expected from education. It is, however, sufficient for my
present purpose to assert, that, whatever effect circumstances have on
the abilities, every being may become virtuous by the exercise of its own
reason; for if but one being was created with vicious inclinations, that

WOLLSTONECRAFT: *The Playthings of Tyrants*   **395**

is positively bad, what can save us from atheism? or if we worship a God, is not that God a devil?

Consequently, the most perfect education, in my opinion, is such   11
an exercise of the understanding as is best calculated to strengthen the body and form the heart. Or, in other words, to enable the individual to attain such habits of virtue as will render it independent. In fact, it is a farce to call any being virtuous whose virtues do not result from the exercise of its own reason. This was Rousseau's opinion respecting men: I extend it to women, and confidently assert that they have been drawn out of their sphere by false refinement, and not by an endeavour to acquire masculine qualities. Still the regal homage which they receive is so intoxicating, that till the manners of the times are changed, and formed on more reasonable principles, it may be impossible to convince them that the illegitimate power, which they obtain, by degrading themselves, is a curse, and that they must return to nature and equality, if they wish to secure the placid satisfaction that unsophisticated affections impart. But for this epoch we must wait—wait, perhaps, till kings and nobles, enlightened by reason, and, preferring the real dignity of man to childish state, throw off their gaudy hereditary trappings: and if then women do not resign the arbitrary power of beauty—they will prove that they have *less* mind than man. . . .

Many are the causes that, in the present corrupt state of society,   12
contribute to enslave women by cramping their understandings and sharpening their senses. One, perhaps, that silently does more mischief than all the rest, is their disregard of order.

To do every thing in an orderly manner, is a most important pre-   13
cept, which women, who, generally speaking, receive only a disorderly kind of education, seldom attend to with that degree of exactness that men, who from their infancy are broken into method, observe. This negligent kind of guess-work, for what other epithet can be used to point out the random exertions of a sort of instinctive common sense, never brought to the test of reason? prevents their generalizing matters of fact—so they do to-day, what they did yesterday, merely because they did it yesterday.

This contempt of the understanding in early life has more baneful   14
consequences than is commonly supposed; for the little knowledge which women of strong minds attain, is, from various circumstances, of a more desultory kind than the knowledge of men, and it is acquired more by sheer observations on real life, than from comparing what has been individually observed with the results of experience generalized by speculation. Led by their dependent situation and domestic employments more into society, what they learn is rather by snatches; and as

learning is with them, in general, only a secondary thing, they do not pursue any one branch with that persevering ardour necessary to give vigour to the faculties, and clearness to the judgment. In the present state of society, a little learning is required to support the character of a gentleman; and boys are obliged to submit to a few years of discipline. But in the education of women, the cultivation of the understanding is always subordinate to the acquirement of some corporeal accomplishment; even while enervated by confinement and false notions of modesty, the body is prevented from attaining that grace and beauty which relaxed half-formed limbs never exhibit. Besides, in youth their faculties are not brought forward by emulation; and having no serious scientific study, if they have natural sagacity it is turned too soon on life and manners. They dwell on effects, and modifications, without tracing them back to causes; and complicated rules to adjust behaviour are a weak substitute for simple principles.

As a proof that education gives this appearance of weakness to 15 females, we may instance the example of military men, who are, like them, sent into the world before their minds have been stored with knowledge or fortified by principles. The consequences are similar; soldiers acquire a little superficial knowledge, snatched from the muddy current of conversation, and, from continually mixing with society, they gain, what is termed a knowledge of the world; and this acquaintance with manners and customs has frequently been confounded with a knowledge of the human heart. But can the crude fruit of casual observation, never brought to the test of judgment, formed by comparing speculation and experience, deserve such a distinction? Soldiers, as well as women, practice the minor virtues with punctilious politeness. Where is then the sexual difference, when the education has been the same? All the difference that I can discern, arises from the superior advantage of liberty, which enables the former to see more of life.

It is wandering from my present subject, perhaps, to make a politi- 16 cal remark; but, as it was produced naturally by the train of my reflections, I shall not pass it silently over.

Standing armies can never consist of resolute, robust men; they 17 may be well disciplined machines, but they will seldom contain men under the influence of strong passions, or with very vigorous faculties. And as for any depth of understanding, I will venture to affirm, that it is as rarely to be found in the army as amongst women; and the cause, I maintain, is the same. It may be further observed, that officers are also particularly attentive to their persons, fond of dancing, crowded rooms, adventures, and ridicule. Like the *fair* sex, the business of their lives is gallantry.—They were taught to please, and they only live to please. Yet they do not lose their rank in the distinction of sexes, for they are still reckoned superior to women, though in what their superiority consists, beyond what I have just mentioned, it is difficult to discover.

The great misfortune is this, that they both acquire manners before 18 morals, and a knowledge of life before they have, from reflections, any acquaintance with the grand ideal outline of human nature. The consequence is natural; satisfied with common nature, they become a prey to prejudices, and taking all their opinions on credit, they blindly submit to authority. So that, if they have any sense, it is a kind of instinctive glance, that catches proportions, and decides with respect to manners; but fails when arguments are to be pursued below the surface, or opinions analyzed.

May not the same remark be applied to women? Nay, the argument 19 may be carried still further, for they are both thrown out of a useful station by the unnatural distinctions established in civilized life. Riches and hereditary honours have made cyphers of women to give consequence to the numerical figure; and idleness has produced a mixture of gallantry and despotism into society, which leads the very men who are the slaves of their mistresses to tyrannize over their sisters, wives, and daughters. This is only keeping them in rank and file, it is true. Strengthen the female mind by enlarging it, and there will be an end to blind obedience; but, as blind obedience is ever sought for by power, tyrants and sensualists are in the right when they endeavor to keep women in the dark, because the former only want slaves, and the latter a play-thing. The sensualist, indeed, has been the most dangerous of tyrants, and women have been duped by their lovers, as princes by their ministers, whilst dreaming that they reigned over them.

QUESTIONS ON SUBJECT

1. How does Wollstonecraft see women gaining distinction in her society? Why is this distinction specious?

2. Why does the author argue that it would be inequitable to judge the virtue of women in her own time?

3. What impediment for both men and women does Wollstonecraft see vis-à-vis private education? Explain the resolution she offers.

4. According to Wollstonecraft, what role do the senses play in the education of both men and women? Do you agree with her? Why or why not?

5. The author writes that "[the education of women] is acquired more by sheer observations on real life, than from comparing what has been individually observed with the results of experience generalized by specula-

tion." What is the author saying here? Write this sentence, taken from paragraph 14, in your own words.

6. According to the author, what circumstances create the similarities between the education of women and soldiers?

QUESTIONS ON STRATEGY

1. Examine the author's major premise, the equality of souls. Does she support this premise? If so, where? If not, why do you think she chose not to? Is this premise convincing for modern readers? Explain your answer.

2. Wollstonecraft makes the concession that men have merit to their complaints about women. How does this point work into her argument? Where else do you see the author establishing a premise and then arguing her point?

3. What is the author trying to show by quoting Lord Bacon and Milton? What inconsistencies does the author find, and how do they relate to her argument?

4. In paragraph 16, Wollstonecraft writes, "It is wandering from my present subject, perhaps, to make a political remark; but, as it was produced naturally by the train of my reflections, I shall not pass it silently over." What does the following paragraph add to this essay? Does this essay read as a natural train of reflections, one point leading to the next? Explain your answer using examples from the text.

5. Where and to what advantage does the author use comparison and contrast in this essay? (Glossary: *Comparison and Contrast*)

QUESTIONS ON LANGUAGE

1. What for you is unusual about Wollstonecraft's style? What, in particular, identifies her prose as a product of the eighteenth century?

2. Refer to your desk dictionary to determine the meanings of the following words as they are used in this selection: *ephemeron* (paragraph 2), *specious* (2), *caprices* (2), *current* (2 and 15), *puerile* (2), *propriety* (2), *Mahometan* (3), *insinuate* (3), *epithet* (5 and 13), *indefeasible* (5), *expostulate* (7), *remiss* (7), *sanguine* (10), *placid* (11), *gaudy* (11), *baneful* (14), *desultory* (14), *enervated* (14), *sagacity* (14), *punctilious* (15), *cyphers* (19), *duped* (19).

WRITING SUGGESTIONS

1. Does the author's characterization of the education of women hold true today? Compare your own experiences with Wollstonecraft's observations in an essay addressing this question.

2. Wollstonecraft writes that women educated in a disorderly fashion "dwell on effects, and modifications, without tracing them back to causes." What influences do you see today that encourage this kind of behavior, both in and outside of school? Do teachers encourage students to reflect upon information? Do schools teach students how to complete their work in an orderly fashion? Write an essay in which you present your thoughts on this subject.

Where Do We Go from Here: Community or Chaos?

MARTIN LUTHER KING JR.

Martin Luther King Jr. (1929–1968), was the son of a Baptist minister. Ordained at the age of eighteen, King went on to study at Morehouse College, Crozer Theological Seminary, Boston University, and Chicago Theological Seminary. He came to prominence in 1955 in Montgomery, Alabama, when he led a successful boycott against the city's segregated bus system. The first president of the Southern Christian Leadership Conference, King became the leading spokesman for the civil rights movement during the 1950s and 1960s. He also championed women's rights and protested the Vietnam War. In 1964 he was awarded the Nobel Peace Prize for his policy of nonviolent resistance to racial injustice. King was assassinated in April 1968 after he spoke at a rally in Memphis, Tennessee.

In the following selection, taken from the book Where Do We Go from Here: Community or Chaos? *(1967), King addresses the Cold War and U.S. intervention in Vietnam. He argues that peaceful goals can only be achieved through peaceful means and exhorts his readers to study the lessons of history and reexamine their own feelings.*

A final problem that mankind must solve in order to survive in the world house that we have inherited is finding an alternative to war and human destruction. Recent events have vividly reminded us that nations are not reducing but rather increasing their arsenals of weapons of mass destruction. The best brains in the highly developed nations of the world are devoted to military technology. The proliferation of nuclear weapons has not been halted, in spite of the limited-test-ban treaty.

In this day of man's highest technical achievement, in this day of dazzling discovery, of novel opportunities, loftier dignities and fuller freedoms for all, there is no excuse for the kind of blind craving for power and resources that provoked the wars of previous generations. There is no need to fight for food and land. Science has provided us with adequate means of survival and transportation, which make it possible to enjoy the fullness of this great earth. The question now is, do we have the morality and courage required to live together as brothers and not be afraid?

One of the most persistent ambiguities we face is that everybody 3 talks about peace as a goal, but among the wielders of power peace is practically nobody's business. Many men cry "Peace! Peace!" but they refuse to do the things that make for peace.

The large power blocs talk passionately of pursuing peace while 4 expanding defense budgets that already bulge, enlarging already awesome armies and devising ever more devastating weapons. Call the roll of those who sing the glad tidings of peace and one's ears will be surprised by the responding sounds. The heads of all the nations issue clarion calls for peace, yet they come to the peace table accompanied by bands of brigands each bearing unsheathed swords.

The stages of history are replete with the chants and choruses of 5 the conquerors of old who came killing in pursuit of peace. Alexander, Genghis Khan, Julius Caesar, Charlemagne and Napoleon were akin in seeking a peaceful world order, a world fashioned after their selfish conceptions of an ideal existence. Each sought a world at peace which would personify his egotistic dreams. Even within the life span of most of us, another megalomaniac strode across the world stage. He sent his blitzkrieg-bent legions blazing across Europe, bringing havoc and holocaust in his wake. There is grave irony in the fact that Hitler could come forth, following nakedly aggressive expansionist theories, and do it all in the name of peace.

So when in this day I see the leaders of nations again talking peace 6 while preparing for war, I take fearful pause. When I see our country today intervening in what is basically a civil war, mutilating hundreds of thousands of Vietnamese children with napalm, burning villages and rice fields at random, painting the valleys of that small Asian country red with human blood, leaving broken bodies in countless ditches and sending home half-men, mutilated mentally and physically; when I see the unwillingness of our government to create the atmosphere for a negotiated settlement of this awful conflict by halting bombings in the North and agreeing unequivocally to talk with the Vietcong— and all this in the name of pursuing the goal of peace—I tremble for our world. I do so not only from dire recall of the nightmares wreaked in the wars of yesterday, but also from dreadful realization of today's possible nuclear destructiveness and tomorrow's even more calamitous prospects.

Before it is too late, we must narrow the gaping chasm between our 7 proclamations of peace and our lowly deeds which precipitate and perpetuate war. We are called upon to look up from the quagmire of military programs and defense commitments and read the warnings on history's signposts.

One day we must come to see that peace is not merely a distant 8
goal that we seek but a means by which we arrive at that goal. We must
pursue peaceful ends through peaceful means. How much longer must
we play at deadly war games before we heed the plaintive pleas of the
unnumbered dead and maimed of past wars?

President John F. Kennedy said on one occasion, "Mankind must 9
put an end to war or war will put an end to mankind." Wisdom born
of experience should tell us that war is obsolete. There may have been
a time when war served as a negative good by preventing the spread
and growth of an evil force, but the destructive power of modern weapons eliminates even the possibility that war may serve any good at all.
If we assume that life is worth living and that man has a right to survive,
then we must find an alternative to war. In a day when vehicles hurtle
through outer space and guided ballistic missiles carve highways of
death through the stratosphere, no nation can claim victory in war. A
so-called limited war will leave little more than a calamitous legacy
of human suffering, political turmoil and spiritual disillusionment. A
world war will leave only smoldering ashes as mute testimony of a human race whose folly led inexorably to ultimate death. If modern man
continues to flirt unhesitatingly with war, he will transform his earthly
habitat into an inferno such as even the mind of Dante could not
imagine.

Therefore I suggest that the philosophy and strategy of nonvio- 10
lence become immediately a subject for study and for serious experi-
mentation in every field of human conflict, by no means excluding the
relations between nations. It is, after all, nationstates which make war,
which have produced the weapons that threaten the survival of mankind and which are both genocidal and suicidal in character.

We have ancient habits to deal with, vast structures of power, in- 11
describably complicated problems to solve. But unless we abdicate our
humanity altogether and succumb to fear and impotence in the presence of the weapons we have ourselves created, it is as possible and as
urgent to put an end to war and violence between nations as it is to put
an end to poverty and racial injustice.

The United Nations is a gesture in the direction of nonviolence on 12
a world scale. There, at least, states that oppose one another have
sought to do so with words instead of with weapons. But true nonviolence is more than the absence of violence. It is the persistent and
determined application of peaceable power to offenses against the community—in this case the world community. As the United Nations
moves ahead with the giant tasks confronting it, I would hope that it
would earnestly examine the uses of nonviolent direct action.

I do not minimize the complexity of the problems that need to be 13
faced in achieving disarmament and peace. But I am convinced that we
shall not have the will, the courage and the insight to deal with such
matters unless in this field we are prepared to undergo a mental and
spiritual re-evaluation, a change of focus which will enable us to see that
the things that seem most real and powerful are indeed now unreal and
have come under sentence of death. We need to make a supreme effort
to generate the readiness, indeed the eagerness, to enter into the new
world which is now possible, "the city which hath foundation, whose
Building and Maker is God."

It is not enough to say, "We must not wage war." It is necessary to 14
love peace and sacrifice for it. We must concentrate not merely on the
eradication of war but on the affirmation of peace. A fascinating story
about Ulysses and the Sirens is preserved for us in Greek literature. The
Sirens had the ability to sing so sweetly that sailors could not resist
steering toward their island. Many ships were lured upon the rocks, and
men forgot home, duty and honor as they flung themselves into the
sea to be embraced by arms that drew them down to death. Ulysses,
determined not to succumb to the Sirens, first decided to tie himself
tightly to the mast of his boat and his crew stuffed their ears with wax.
But finally he and his crew learned a better way to save themselves:
They took on board the beautiful singer Orpheus, whose melodies were
sweeter than the music of the Sirens. When Orpheus sang, who would
bother to listen to the Sirens?

So we must see that peace represents a sweeter music, a cosmic 15
melody that is far superior to the discords of war. Somehow we must
transform the dynamics of the world power struggle from the nuclear
arms race, which no one can win, to a creative contest to harness man's
genius for the purpose of making peace and prosperity a reality for all
the nations of the world. In short, we must shift the arms race into a
"peace race." If we have the will and determination to mount such a
peace offensive, we will unlock hitherto tightly sealed doors of hope
and bring new light into the dark chambers of pessimism.

QUESTIONS ON SUBJECT

1. Why, according to the author, have we reached a point where we must
   decide between community and chaos?
2. Why was King opposed to U.S. intervention in Vietnam? What motives
   does he think drove this intervention?
3. What does the author refer to when he writes in paragraph 13, "But I am
   convinced that we shall not have the will, the courage and the insight to

deal with such matters unless in this field we are prepared to undergo a mental and spiritual re-evaluation, a change of focus which will enable us to see that *the things which seem most real and powerful are indeed now unreal and have come under sentence of death.*" Has the author prepared us for the italicized portion of this quote? Explain.

4. King writes that nationstates make war and the weapons of war. What fear in relationship to nationstates does he address?

QUESTIONS ON STRATEGY

1. King makes "I" and "we" statements throughout this essay. What advantages do you see in his use of the first person.

2. Comment on the author's use of irony in paragraph 4. Does King only implicate the leaders of nations? Explain your answer. Where does the author present a logical contrast to paragraph 4?

3. How would you describe the author's variations in tone? Is there a dominant tone to this essay? (Glossary: *Tone*)

4. How does the author's analogy of Ulysses and the Sirens provide closure for this essay? (Glossary: *Beginnings and Endings*) What does King's analogy of Ulysses and the Sirens add to this essay? (Glossary: *Analogy*) What historical insights do you see in the story of the Sirens?

5. What functions do King's many examples serve in this essay? (Glossary: *Illustration*) Which examples do you find most effective? Why?

QUESTIONS ON LANGUAGE

1. King's powerful rhetorical style shines in this piece. What do you see in the author's diction that suggests this would read well as a speech? Explain your answer using examples from the text.

2. Refer to your desk dictionary to determine the meanings of the following words as they are used in this selection: *clarion* (paragraph 4), *brigands* (4), *unsheathed* (4), *replete* (5), *akin* (5), *megalomaniac* (5), *precipitate* (7), *quagmire* (7), *inexorably* (9).

WRITING SUGGESTIONS

1. Nationstates, as King writes, make war and the weapons of war. How do you see your relationship with your own nationstate? What would you like to see changed in this relationship?

2. King begins his essay urging the historical significance of the moment. More than twenty-five years later, how pertinent do you find the issues that King raises in this essay? What has changed in this interim and what has remained the same? Write an essay in which you address these questions.

Ending the Abortion War: A Modest Proposal

FRANCES KISSLING

A social activist and pro-choice advocate, Frances Kissling was born in New York City in 1943. Kissling's interest in women's issues led her to become active in the abortion debate. In 1979 she wrote Rosie: The Investigation of a Wrongful Death *with Ellen Frankfort. A managing partner for Reproductive Health Consultants, she has written introductions to* Abortion: A Guide to Making Ethical Choices *(1983),* A New Rite: Conservative Catholic Organizations and Their Allies *(1994), and* The Catholic Health Care System and National Health Care Reform *(1994).*

The following article first appeared in The Christian Century *on February 21, 1990. While insisting on abortion rights, Frances Kissling thinks the pro-choice movement must go beyond an absolutist interpretation of those rights if it wants to forge public policy that is practical and morally sound. At the time she wrote this article, Kissling was president of Catholics for a Free Choice in Washington, D.C.*

As we enter the 1990s with modest hopes for world peace, a particularly bitter and seemingly intractable domestic war continues unabated. The U.S. Supreme Court decision in *Webster v. Reproductive Health Services* has mobilized armies of supporters and opponents of legal abortion.

Explicitly, the court let stand a provision of a Missouri law that required testing to determine fetal viability in pregnancies of 20 weeks duration and longer (it should be noted that no such tests exist). The court further curtailed poor women's ability to choose abortion by substantially expanding its prior rulings on public funding. It ruled that states are free to prohibit abortions at any health-care facility that receives any public funding. Even private doctors who perform abortions on private patients with private funds will be affected by the ruling if their admission privileges happen to be at a hospital that receives public money or has contractual arrangements with state or local governments.

In a move troubling to most religious groups, the court also let stand the preamble to the Missouri law, which declared that life begins at conception, saying that the preamble represented a permissible value judgment by the state that would have no effect on the legality of abortion.

Implicitly, the five-justice plurality opinion warned that the court 4 would no longer apply strict scrutiny to limitations on a woman's right to choose abortion. No longer would legislatures or regulatory bodies need to show a compelling state interest in order to intervene in women's decisions. The decision was interpreted by those who favor and those who oppose legal abortion as an open invitation to state legislatures to enact restrictive legislation designed to test further and possibly overturn *Roe*.

Both sides responded aggressively and passionately. Faye Wat- 5 tleton, president of the Planned Parenthood Federation of America, declared, "Make no mistake about it. This is war." Kate Michelman, director of the National Abortion Rights Action League, told elected officials, "Take our rights, lose your jobs." Randall Terry, leader of the controversial Operation Rescue, said: "We're calling on thousands of pro-life Americans to peacefully blockade these killing centers with their bodies to prevent children from dying and we will launch an equal force against state legislatures to chip away at *Roe*." (By quoting Terry alongside Wattleton and Michelman, I do not mean to imply any philosophical or strategic equivalence in their viewpoints or actions. It is simply that these were the voices most frequently heard and quoted in the last half of 1989.)

By any reasonable measure, so far, my side, the side that favors legal 6 abortion, is winning the war. On the electoral front, not only have candidates like Governor Douglas Wilder (Virginia) and Governor James Florio (New Jersey) made their pro-choice positions central to a winning strategy, but politicians considered pro-life are defecting to the pro-choice camp daily.

Perhaps more significant—and substantial—is that pro-choicers 7 have partially shifted the terms of the debate from the question of whose rights will prevail, the woman's or the fetus's, to who will decide, women or the government. This is not to say that questions of rights or of the moral value of fetal life are insignificant in evaluating the act of abortion. However, to claim that the central conflict in the debate is between women and fetuses incorrectly and unfortunately casts a woman as the adversary of the fetus and in no way acknowledges her role as moral agent. Moreover, in light of the growing attempt to subordinate individual rights to a somewhat undefined "community," even opponents of legal abortion should exercise caution in making rights arguments paramount. In framing the question "who decides?" NARAL has moved subtly from the concept of "choice," a principle that has come to be seen as related to the trivial or selfish, to the concept of "decision making," which implies greater seriousness and complexity.

Webster's threat to legal abortion has also significantly increased the 8 number of organizations, generally liberal to progressive, adding abortion to their portfolio of issues. The pro-choice coalition is bigger, stronger, more cohesive and better financed than ever before. It is convinced that given enough time and money it has the capacity to build the political machine necessary to win the war and preserve *Roe*.

Pro-life leaders, while stung by the losses of 1989, are equally com- 9 mitted to the long war and will surely win some victories in the next (or some subsequent) foray into the courts or state legislatures. The Catholic bishops have re-entered the political arena with a bang, declaring abortion—not the degradation of the planet, the economy or racism—their number one concern. Catholic legislators got a hint of the kind of political muscle the bishops are prepared to use when Bishop Leo T. Maher of San Diego announced in the midst of a special election for the California state senate that candidate Lucy Killea could no longer receive communion in the Roman Catholic church because of her pro-choice position. Catholic legislators in Montana, Rhode Island, Washington, Connecticut and Minnesota have reported that their bishops have warned them that public pro-choice positions create "problems" for the church. With 28 professional statewide lobbying offices from Hartford to Sacramento, the bishops have a political machine capable of seriously restricting *Roe* at the state level.

How all this hardball political gamesmanship and bellicosity will 10 contribute to sound, stable public policy on abortion remains to be seen. If the past 20 years are any model for the next 20, we can expect abortion to remain both an issue that is ideologically shaped and a problem that is unsolved.

One would hope, however, that this new moment in the abortion 11 debate could be seen not only as a time of crisis by those of us who are pro-choice (and I speak only to that group, having neither the right nor the interest to suggest a course of action for the opposition) but as an opportunity to examine our own beliefs in light of the signs of the times and the experience of 17 years of legal abortion. Perhaps it is time, as one good friend so aptly put it, for those of us who are pro-choice to "take the high dive"; that is, to resist the temptation to think and act in 30-second sound bites and engage instead in serious moral discourse on abortion.

Perhaps we need to listen to the wisdom of more than 50 percent 12 of our population. They hold in creative tension a basic sense of fair play in wanting women, with consultation, to make the decision about abortion or childbirth and a concern for the value of fetal life and the quality of women's decisions. Only then will we be in a position to advocate public policy that respects each individual woman and expresses our concern for human life and the community at large.

Abortion is not fundamentally a political question; it deals with 13 people's deepest, most unconscious feelings about life, the power of creation and the survival of our species. Those in the so-called "muddled middle" understand this better than those at either end of the public opinion spectrum. They understand abortion—and reproduction—as both a private and a social phenomenon. They wait for one side or the other to answer such questions as: "How will we bring new life onto this planet?" "How will we treat the rest of life?" These elements are not unconnected. Just as we challenge pro-lifers to care about more than prenatal life, so must we challenge ourselves to talk about more than the life that is here. We must also talk with reverence of the life that is to come. Most important, this conversation cannot be viewed as a threat to the rights of women, but as an enhancement of the responsible exercise of those rights. We must not let our own justifiable fear of the opposition shape the dialogue.

Concretely, we must stop criticizing moderate pro-choice voices: 14 public officials (like Governor Mario Cuomo) who speak of the "tragedy" of abortion; columnists (like Anna Quindlen of the *New York Times*) who express concerns about late-term abortions; and theologians (like Giles Milhaven of Brown University) who speak of women's sadness after abortion. All contribute a richness of spirit to the debate that needs to be encouraged not crushed.

Our own inability to acknowledge the tragedy of abortion makes us 15 suspect. Our continuous talk about *wanted* children does not inspire confidence but fear. We live in a world where our value is increasingly equated with wealth, brilliance or success. Many rightly perceive that they are powerless and unwanted. For the powerless, the fetus is a ready symbol of their own vulnerability—a symbol exploited by right-wing leaders.

Acknowledging fetal life as valuable and as an important factor in 16 decision making about abortion need not be linked to a specific religious doctrine. The Christian respect for life has never required the absolute protection of life. It does not require conferring personhood or rights on the fetus, nor does it suggest limiting the legal rights of women to decide whether to bring new life into the world or to have an abortion.

On the other hand, an enhanced sense of the value of fetal life 17 should move us beyond the status quo on abortion and beyond an absolutist interpretation of the fundamental rights articulated in *Roe v.*

Wade. On both principled and practical grounds, pro-choice advocates need to see *Roe* as a framework for good policy on abortion, not as a fortress against policy.

By no means should the pro-choice movement abandon, at this 18 time, the rights framework implicit in *Roe.* Given the unrelentingly punitive, hostile approach to women in our society, we continue to need the strongest legal protection available to enable our full and equal participation in society. This includes legal control over fertility.

An equally compelling reason for maintaining a rights framework is 19 the unprecedented assault on individual rights mounted by the Reagan administration. Individual rights for women are inseparable from individual rights for people of color. Efforts in both progressive and conservative circles (from Stanley Hauerwas to George Will) to portray individual rights as a threat to the community must be resisted. Individual rights, once they include women and people of color, are a threat not to the whole community but to the community of white men.

A theory of community that places unequal burdens on women in 20 welcoming and respecting new life is inherently unjust and doomed to fail. That injustice is obvious in our society and while lip service is paid to sharing the burden, there is little evidence that the architects of communitarian models or their admirers are moving toward a concrete embodiment of equality and responsibility.

Individual rights cannot, however, be slavishly pursued. Even the 21 most fundamental rights are regulated under the Constitution. Many of us support even more regulation for any number of rights, such as the right to bear arms. Pro-choice advocates—not just those whose goal is prohibition—need to explore regulations that will enhance women's decision making in a manner that respects fetal life without making protection of fetal life absolute. (At the same time, we must strongly reject policy measures whose only purpose is to limit or prohibit access to legal abortion.) We must see that such regulations, once enacted, are enforced scrupulously and noncoercively and that penalties for deliberately misinforming, coercing or unfairly influencing a woman's ability to make good decisions are promulgated and used.

Finally, all regulations need to be looked at individually and cumu- 22 latively to ensure that they do not prevent the poor or people of color from exercising their right to act as decision makers. Walter Dellinger, professor of law at Duke University, pointed out recently in the *University of Pennsylvania Law Review:*

> A 48-hour waiting period, for example, may not be an 'undue burden'
> for affluent professional women, and a hospitalization requirement

may only serve to make her abortion more expensive. But for an 18-year-old girl in the rural South, unmarried, pregnant, hoping to finish school and build a decent life, who has little or no access to transportation, a hospitalization requirement can mean an abortion that will cost nearly $1,000 and involve a trip of hundreds of miles; a waiting period can mean two long trips and an overnight stay in a strange and distant city. For such a woman, the burden would be absolute.

While it is premature to move from a brief exposition of some of 23 the principles needed to inform public policy initiatives on abortion to a recommendation of specific measures, the state legislative season is upon us. Many legislators and advocates will not stop to reflect before running headlong to pass new laws. And it is important, as many rush to the "middle" on abortion, that those who seek to be consensus-builders or compromisers be held to a high standard of specificity. What do we think policy on abortion should be? Are we really listening to the middle or simply attempting to co-opt it?

Here, then, are some immediate guidelines and specific elements of 24 a sound, stable public policy that can be implemented now and con-tribute to a balanced, long-term approach to the issue.

First, abortion laws need to acknowledge women's right—and 25 need—to make reproductive health decisions free from coercion, as well as both women's and society's responsibility to create conditions for women to bring life into the world.

Either in the body of the law or by reference to other existing leg- 26 islation, the community's reverence for life should be expressed in sup-port of social and economic programs for children and families. A good model for this can be found in the legislative program of the Children's Defense Fund.

The balance between women's rights and reverence for life is best 27 expressed by making resources available to assist women in good deci-sion making and in preventing pregnancy. We should advocate a series of initiatives that signal government *involvement* as opposed to *inter-vention*. Among them: funding for voluntary nondirective, comprehen-sive and confidential counseling services for women and their partners who are contemplating abortion (no funds should be made available to groups that favor one decision over the other or that preclude any legal option from the range of choices offered); funding for more mea-sures designed to prevent pregnancy, including contraceptive research and testing as well as contraceptive education and services; and equi-tably distributing funds for adoption, abortion, childbearing and child rearing.

These funding proposals represent a major shift in policy and 28 would be a significant compromise for both sides of the debate. Pro-choice advocates will need to accept greater government involvement as an expression of community consensus; in turn, the community, through the government, will need to back up its involvement with resources.

Among the particularly thorny issues confronting legislatures this 29 year are requirements for parental consent for minors' abortions, prohibitions on gender selection and postviability abortions, and so-called informed consent statutes. Critical to the pro-choice movement's ability to forge consensus on the general question of legal abortion will be its ability to respond rationally and concretely to these issues. Up to now, a fundamental rights approach and our fear of the "slippery slope" has led us to reject outright all regulation in these areas. But a blanket No is simply not a sufficient response to these complex questions.

In the case of parental consent requirements, we need to acknowl- 30 edge young women's special need for adult involvement. Indeed, we want to protect teens from either coercive abortion or coercive child-bearing. Form letters mailed to parents do not adequately or effectively discharge our obligation to these women. Neither does the absence of policy.

Provisions for nondirective, confidential counseling by health-care 31 workers, ministers and other qualified professionals would enhance decision making, and a record of such counseling could be kept as part of the medical file. Statutes similar to that passed in Maine, which demand involvement by a parent—or, when that is inappropriate, an adult family member, minister, teacher or counselor—should be applauded.

While there is no evidence that some women seek abortions solely 32 for gender selection, pro-lifers have seized on this possibility as a convenient and gruesome example of the extremes to which abortion liberty will drive us. But in fact the devaluation of women in society is the cause of gender-selection abortion. The few reports of abortion in which gender was a factor point to those communities, primarily Asian and African, where male children are still considered a necessity. Indeed, in Africa a woman is called infertile if she does not produce boys, while some Asian wives are abused and abandoned. As odious as I would find the practice of gender selection even in these hard cases, I would be loathe to take responsibility for any prohibition that could cost these women dearly.

However, the notion that women would seek abortions in the mid 33 to late second trimester because the nursery is painted blue or hubby's family has had firstborn boys for generations is ludicrous. It really deserves no response. It also deserves no defense. I would seek no laws to prevent that which does not happen, but I would not oppose such laws. This is an area for self-regulation, and one hopes that responsible providers of abortion would decline their services in such cases.

In a similar vein, I think the question of postviability abortions is 34 of little practical significance and of enormous symbolic importance. In practice, it is extremely difficult to find a physician who will perform such abortions unless there is a serious, physical, life-threatening condition for the woman or the fetus is diagnosed with profound abnormalities. There is no evidence that the right to such abortions is necessary for women's well-being or full participation in society. These facts, combined with the growing sense that fetal life deserves increasing respect as it develops should lead pro-choice advocates to accept legislation limiting postviability abortions to life-threatening or disabling cases.

Another frequently cited set of regulations on abortions are those 35 requiring "informed consent." Up to now, the court has struck down such measures. In the post-*Webster* climate they will once again be raised. Without exception, all past informed consent laws were drafted by opponents of legal abortion—not to assist in good decision making but to prevent abortion. The information mandated was often biased, inaccurate and simplistic: "life begins at conception," "the heart beats at eight weeks," "abortion is dangerous and will make you sterile." Nondirective counseling is far more appropriate and respectful of women's capacity to make good decisions than existing informed consent approaches. Moreover, I cannot stress too strongly my belief that if the government is to be involved in the process of women's decision making, those who are entrusted with helping women need to be held to the highest standard of care.

For those whose interest is in outlawing abortion, the rather mod- 36 est shift in both laws and values set forth here offers little. In the short run, these policy measures will not reduce the current number of abortions, which is troubling. It is important, however, that we not reduce abortion policy and values to a numbers game. The goal of caring people—eliminating all abortions—will require a radical transformation of society. We should focus our efforts on correcting the disease, not the symptom.

QUESTIONS ON SUBJECT

1. According to Kissling, what is the implicit significance of the *Webster* ruling?
2. What evidence does the author present to show that her side is winning politically? Do you find this evidence convincing? Explain your answer.

3. What change has Kissling's side made in their argument?

4. Kissling argues that the tactics of pro-choicers have inspired fear in the "muddled-middle." How have pro-choicers done this, and what new approach does the author put forward to change this situation?

5. Why does Kissling believe that those in favor of legal abortion must maintain a rights framework?

6. Why does the author urge her side to consider laws that regulate abortion? What criticism does she make of the opposition's approach to regulation?

QUESTIONS ON STRATEGY

1. The author presents her argument as an open letter to those in favor of legal abortion. Do you think this is the only audience her essay appeals to? Explain. (Glossary: *Audience*)

2. Among other things, Kissling outlines the political ramifications of the *Webster* ruling and argues a political course of action for those in favor of legal abortion. Would you characterize her essay as political? Do you think she is inconsistent when she writes in paragraph 13 that "abortion is not fundamentally a political question"? Explain your answer using, wherever possible, quotations from the essay.

3. The author remains critical of the opposition's tactics while suggesting that her side has let these tactics shape their own policy. How do you see Kissling go about setting a new course for those in favor of legal abortion?

4. In what ways has Kissling tried to accommodate both sides of the abortion debate? Identify specific passages in her essay in which she does this?

5. What is Kissling's tone in this essay? (Glossary: *Tone*) Do you find her tone appropriate for both her topic and her audience?

6. Kissling uses a number of specific examples and quotations in her argument. What exactly do these examples add to her argument? (Glossary: *Illustration*) Pick out several examples that work particularly well for you, and explain what you think makes them so effective.

QUESTIONS ON LANGUAGE

1. Kissling brings an awareness not only of the concerns surrounding abortion, but also the discourse in which these concerns have been and will be argued. Find examples of this latter awareness in the word choices that Kissling makes.

2. The author uses the pronoun "we" in her essay. To whom is she referring here? Is this an effective strategy? Why, or why not?

3. Refer to your desk dictionary to determine the meanings of the following words as they are used in this selection: *intractable* (paragraph 1),

unabated (1), *viability* (2), *curtailed* (2), *preamble* (3), *moreover* (7 and 35), *foray* (9), *bellicosity* (10), *discourse* (11), *punitive* (18), *slavishly* (21), *promulgated* (21), *cumulatively* (22), *exposition* (23), *loathe* (32).

WRITING SUGGESTIONS

1. In conclusion, the author writes, "The goal of caring people—eliminating all abortions—will require a radical transformation of society. We should focus our efforts on correcting the disease, not the symptom." What is the disease the author mentions, and where does she refer to it in the body of her essay? What measures has the author suggested as a means toward this goal? Do you agree with the policy she argues for? Write an essay in which you address these questions.

2. Kissling stresses the importance of making non-directional counseling available to every woman. Do some research into this type of counseling. What are the range of possibilities presented? Where is this counseling currently available and how, if at all, is it growing? Has the political session the author mentions in her essay made an impact in this field? Present your findings in an essay.

Should Drugs Be Legalized?

WILLIAM BENNETT

Current co-director of Empower America *and senior editor of* The National Review, *William Bennett was born on July 31, 1943. As an undergraduate at Williams College, Bennett played football, joined a fraternity, and played guitar in the rock band* Plato and the Guardians. *It was at Williams that he "first fell in love with the world of ideas." Bennett went on to earn his Ph.D. in philosophy at the University of Texas and his J.D. at Harvard Law School. A classroom teacher by inclination, Bennett taught philosophy at the University of Southern Mississippi, the University of Wisconsin, and Boston University and coauthored the book* Counting by Race: Equality in American Thought from the Founding Fathers to Bakke. *He served as chairperson of The National Endowment for the Humanities from 1981–1985 before becoming Secretary of Education in the Reagan administration. In 1989 he was appointed the first director of the National Drug Control Policy by President Bush. Recently he has edited* The Book of Virtues: A Treasury of Great Moral Stories (1994).*

Bennett wrote the following essay for the March 1990 issue of Reader's Digest, *while still heading the nation's war on drugs. He challenges the assumptions of legalizers and argues that the plea to legalize drugs is nothing short of an outright call to surrender.*

Since I took command of the war on drugs, I have learned from 1 former Secretary of State George Shultz that our concept of fighting drugs is "flawed." The only thing to do, he says, is to "make it possible for addicts to buy drugs at some regulated place." Conservative commentator William F. Buckley, Jr., suggests I should be "fatalistic" about the flood of cocaine from South America and simply "let it in." Syndicated columnist Mike Royko contends it would be easier to sweep junkies out of the gutters "than to fight a hopeless war" against the narcotics that send them there. Labeling our efforts "bankrupt," federal judge Robert W. Sweet opts for legalization, saying, "If our society can learn to stop using butter, it should be able to cut down on cocaine."

Flawed, fatalistic, hopeless, bankrupt! I never realized surrender 2 was so fashionable until I assumed this post.

Though most Americans are overwhelmingly determined to go toe- 3 to-toe with the foreign drug lords and neighborhood pushers, a small minority believe that enforcing drug laws imposes greater costs on society than do drugs themselves. Like addicts seeking immediate euphoria, the legalizers want peace at any price, even though it means the inevitable proliferation of a practice that degrades, impoverishes and kills.

I am acutely aware of the burdens drug enforcement places upon 4 us. It consumes economic resources we would like to use elsewhere. It is sometimes frustrating, thankless and often dangerous. But the consequences of *not* enforcing drug laws would be far more costly. Those consequences involve the intrinsically destructive nature of drugs and the toll they exact from our society in hundreds of thousands of lost and broken lives . . . human potential never realized . . . time stolen from families and jobs . . . precious spiritual and economic resources squandered.

That is precisely why virtually every civilized society has found it 5 necessary to exert some form of control over mind-altering substances and why this war is so important. Americans feel up to their hips in drugs now. They would be up to their necks under legalization.

Even limited experiments in drug legalization have shown that 6 when drugs are more widely available, addiction skyrockets. In 1975 Italy liberalized its drug law and now has one of the highest heroin-related death rates in Western Europe. In Alaska, where marijuana was decriminalized in 1975, the easy atmosphere has increased usage of the drug, particularly among children. Nor does it stop there. Some Alaskan schoolchildren now tout "coca puffs," marijuana cigarettes laced with cocaine.

Many legalizers concede that drug legalization might increase use, 7 but they shrug off the matter. "It may well be that there would be more addicts, and I would regret that result," says Nobel laureate economist Milton Friedman. The late Harvard Medical School psychiatry professor Norman Zinberg, a longtime proponent of "responsible" drug use, admitted that "use of now illicit drugs would certainly increase. Also, casualties probably would increase."

In fact, Dr. Herbert D. Kleber of Yale University, my deputy in 8 charge of demand reduction, predicts legalization might cause "a five-to-sixfold increase" in cocaine use. But legalizers regard this as a necessary price for the "benefits" of legalization. What benefits?

1. Legalization will take the profit out of drugs. The result suppos- 9
edly will be the end of criminal drug pushers and the big foreign drug
wholesalers, who will turn to other enterprises because nobody will
need to make furtive and dangerous trips to his local pusher.

But what, exactly, would the brave new world of legalized drugs 10
look like? Buckley stresses that "adults get to buy the stuff at carefully
regulated stores." (Would you want one in *your* neighborhood?) Others,
like Friedman, suggest we sell the drugs at "ordinary retail outlets."

Former City University of New York sociologist Georgette Bennett 11
assures us that "brand-name competition will be prohibited" and that
strict quality control and proper labeling will be overseen by the Food
and Drug Administration. In a touching egalitarian note, she adds that
"free drugs will be provided at government clinics" for addicts too
poor to buy them.

Almost all the legalizers point out that the price of drugs will fall, 12
even though the drugs will be heavily taxed. Buckley, for example, argues
that somehow federal drugstores will keep the price "low enough to
discourage a black market but high enough to accumulate a surplus to
be used for drug education."

Supposedly, drug sales will generate huge amounts of revenue, 13
which will then be used to tell the public not to use drugs and to treat
those who don't listen.

In reality, this tax would only allow government to *share* the drug 14
profits now garnered by criminals. Legalizers would have to tax drugs
heavily in order to pay for drug education and treatment programs.
Criminals could undercut the official price and still make huge profits.
What alternative would the government have? Cut the price until it was
within the lunch-money budget of the average sixth-grade student?

2. Legalization will eliminate the black market. Wrong. And not 15
just because the regulated prices could be undercut. Many legalizers
admit that drugs such as crack or PCP are simply too dangerous to
allow the shelter of the law. Thus criminals will provide what the government will not. "As long as drugs that people very much want remain
illegal, a black market will exist," says legalization advocate David Boaz
of the libertarian Cato Institute.

Look at crack. In powdered form, cocaine was an expensive indul- 16
gence. But street chemists found that a better and far less expensive—
and far more dangerous—high could be achieved by mixing cocaine
with baking soda and heating it. Crack was born, and "cheap" coke
invaded low-income communities with furious speed.

An ounce of powdered cocaine might sell on the street for $1200. 17
That same ounce can produce 370 vials of crack at $10 each. Ten bucks

seems like a cheap hit, but crack's intense ten- to 15-minute high is followed by an unbearable depression. The user wants more crack, thus starting a rapid and costly descent into addiction.

If government drugstores do not stock crack, addicts will find it in the clandestine market or simply bake it themselves from their legally purchased cocaine. 18

Currently crack is being laced with insecticides and animal tran- 19 quilizers to heighten its effect. Emergency rooms are now warned to expect victims of "sandwiches" and "moon rocks," life-threatening smokable mixtures of heroin and crack. Unless the government is prepared to sell these deadly variations of dangerous drugs, it will perpetuate a criminal black market by default.

And what about children and teen-agers? They would obviously be 20 barred from drug purchases, just as they are prohibited from buying beer and liquor. But pushers will continue to cater to these young customers with the old, favorite come-ons—a couple of free fixes to get them hooked. And what good will anti-drug education be when these youngsters observe their older brothers and sisters, parents and friends lighting up and shooting up with government permission?

Legalization will give us the worst of both worlds: millions of *new* 21 drug users *and* a thriving criminal black market.

3. *Legalization will dramatically reduce crime.* "It is the high price 22 of drugs that leads addicts to robbery, murder and other crimes," says Ira Glasser, executive director of the American Civil Liberties Union. A study by the Cato Institute concludes: "Most, if not all, 'drug-related murders' are the result of drug prohibition."

But researchers tell us that many drug-related felonies are commit- 23 ted by people involved in crime *before* they started taking drugs. The drugs, so routinely available in criminal circles, make the criminals more violent and unpredictable.

Certainly there are some kill-for-a-fix crimes, but does any rational 24 person believe that a cut-rate price for drugs at a government outlet will stop such psychopathic behavior? The fact is that under the influence of drugs, normal people do not act normally, and abnormal people behave in chilling and horrible ways. DEA agents told me about a teen-age addict in Manhattan who was smoking crack when he sexually abused and caused permanent internal injuries to his one-month-old daughter.

Children are among the most frequent victims of violent, drug- 25 related crimes that have nothing to do with the cost of acquiring the drugs. In Philadelphia in 1987 more than half the child-abuse fatalities involved at least one parent who was a heavy drug user. Seventy-three percent of the child-abuse deaths in New York City in 1987 involved parental drug use.

In my travels to the ramparts of the drug war, I have seen nothing 26 to support the legalizers' argument that lower drug prices would reduce crime. Virtually everywhere I have gone, police and DEA agents have told me that crime rates are highest where crack is cheapest.

4. Drug use should be legal since users only harm themselves. Those 27 who believe this should stand beside the medical examiner as he counts the 36 bullet wounds in the shattered corpse of a three-year-old who happened to get in the way of his mother's drug-crazed boyfriend. They should visit the babies abandoned by cocaine-addicted mothers— infants who already carry the ravages of addiction in their own tiny bodies. They should console the devastated relatives of the nun who worked in a homeless shelter and was stabbed to death by a crack addict enraged that she would not stake him to a fix.

Do drug addicts only harm themselves? Here is a former cocaine 28 addict describing the compulsion that quickly draws even the most "responsible" user into irresponsible behavior: "Everything is about getting high, and any means necessary to get there becomes rational. If it means stealing something from somebody close to you, lying to your family, borrowing money from people you know you can't pay back, writing checks you know you can't cover, you do all those things— things that are totally against everything you have ever believed in."

Society pays for this behavior, and not just in bigger insurance 29 premiums, losses from accidents and poor job performance. We pay in the loss of a priceless social currency as families are destroyed, trust between friends is betrayed and promising careers are never fulfilled. I cannot imagine sanctioning behavior that would increase that toll.

I find no merit in the legalizers' case. The simple fact is that drug 30 use is wrong. And the moral argument, in the end, is the most com- pelling argument. A citizen in a drug-induced haze, whether on his back-yard deck or on a mattress in a ghetto crack house, is not what the founding fathers meant by the "pursuit of happiness." Despite the legalizers' argument that drug use is a matter of "personal freedom," our nation's notion of liberty is rooted in the ideal of a self-reliant citi- zenry. Helpless wrecks in treatment centers, men chained by their noses to cocaine—these people are slaves.

Imagine if, in the darkest days of 1940, Winston Churchill had 31 rallied the West by saying, "This war looks hopeless, and besides, it will cost too much. Hitler can't be *that* bad. Let's surrender and see what happens." That is essentially what we hear from the legalizers.

This war *can* be won. I am heartened by indications that education   32
and public revulsion are having an effect on drug use. The National
Institute on Drug Abuse's latest survey of current users shows a 37-
percent *decrease* in drug consumption since 1985. Cocaine is down 50
percent; marijuana use among young people is at its lowest rate since
1972. In my travels I've been encouraged by signs that Americans are
fighting back.

I am under no illusion that such developments, however hopeful,   33
mean the war is over. We need to involve more citizens in the fight,
increase pressure on drug criminals and build on anti-drug programs
that have proved to work. This will not be easy. But the moral and social
costs of surrender are simply too great to contemplate.

QUESTIONS ON SUBJECT

1. What concessions on the part of certain legalizers does Bennett cite in his essay?

2. Why, according to Bennett, would drug legalization fail to stop the perpetuation of a black market?

3. What administrative problems does the author foresee should legalization become a reality?

4. Why does the author argue that legalization will not dramatically reduce drug-related crime?

5. What irony does Bennett find in the drug education plans proposed by legalizers?

6. What evidence does Bennett present to support his claim that we are winning the war on drugs?

QUESTIONS ON STRATEGY

1. What is Bennett's thesis, and where is it stated? (Glossary: *Thesis*)

2. How do paragraphs 1 through 4 serve as an introduction to this essay? What advantages do you see in Bennett's decision to begin his essay by quoting prominent figures in favor of legalization? (Glossary: *Beginnings and Endings*)

3. In paragraph 3, the author writes that "most Americans are overwhelmingly determined to go toe-to-toe with the foreign drug lords and neighborhood pushers," and only "a small minority" favors legalization. Do you think Bennett wrote this essay solely for the former category? (Glossary: *Audience*) Cite examples from the essay to support your answer, and explain the significance of these examples.

4. Bennett uses many powerful true stories in arguing his case. What was your reaction to these examples? (Glossary: *Examples*) To what extent do you feel the legalizers can argue with similar examples of their own?

5. What tone does the author use when writing about the proposals of legalizers? (Glossary: *Tone*) Give examples from the text.

6. How has Bennett organized his essay? Did you find it an effective plan? How else might he have presented his argument? (Glossary: *Organization*)

7. Explain why Bennett uses cause and effect analysis to discuss possible consequences or costs of not rigorously enforcing our drug laws. (Glossary: *Cause and Effect Analysis*)

QUESTIONS ON LANGUAGE

1. Bennett writes in paragraph 24, "Certainly there are some kill-for-a-fix crimes, but does any rational person believe that a cut-rate price for drugs at a government outlet will stop such psychopathic behavior?" Comment on the relationship between Bennett's diction and his tone in this quotation.

2. Bennett, as director of the National Drug Control Policy under President Bush, was committed to winning the war on drugs. Cite examples of Bennett's word choice in this essay that show he, indeed, thinks of his task in warlike terms. (Glossary: *Diction*)

3. Refer to your desk dictionary to determine the meanings of the following words as they are used in this selection: *fatalistic* (paragraphs 1 and 2), *acutely* (4), *intrinsically* (4), *exact* (4), *furtive* (9), *garnered* (14), *clandestine* (18), *perpetuate* (19), *default* (19), *cater* (20).

WRITING SUGGESTIONS

1. Bennett writes, "The simple fact is that drug use is wrong. And the moral argument, in the end, is the most compelling argument." Does the author make a convincing moral argument? Do you agree with the author that the moral argument is the most compelling? What distinction do you see between making a moral argument and moralizing? Write an essay addressing these questions.

2. What has been your experience with drug education in school? Do your own observations support Bennett's claim that education is working? What kind of drug education do you consider effective, ineffective, and why?

It Isn't Working

WILLIAM F. BUCKLEY JR.

Best known as an articulate spokesman for the political right,
William F. Buckley Jr. was born in New York City in 1925. Upon
graduating from Yale in 1950 Buckley published his first book,
God and Man at Yale: The Superstitions of Academic Freedom
(1951). Since then Buckley has been editor-in-chief of The
National Review, *the country's leading conservative publication,*
has had a syndicated newspaper column, has written several books
of nonfiction, and has been the host of the popular television
interview program "Firing Line." On the show, as with his
writings, Buckley exhibits an impressive grasp of pertinent facts
as well as an ability to separate overriding principles from topical
and practical considerations in the important political and
social issues he addresses. Recently Buckley has published A Very
Private Plot: A Blackford Oakes Novel *(1994), an adventure/*
espionage novel, and Happy Days Were Here Again: Reflections
of a Libertarian Journalist *(1993).*

In the following essay, first published in 1989 in his column
On the Right, *Buckley outlines the problems facing our war on*
drugs and argues that drug legalization will bring an end to
drug-related crime and illegal profits.

We are with reason angry at the Mexican officials who ho-hummed 1
their way through an investigation of the torture and killing of a U.S.
drug agent who did what in Mexico is intolerable, namely stand in the
way of graft. In Mexico, to do this is on the order of standing in the way
of sex. Sex will prevail, graft will prevail.

It is true that a few years ago the government of Mexico cooper- 2
ated in a program designed to spray the marijuana crop, but it proved
temporary. Somewhat like wage and price controls. If for a season the
marijuana crop from Mexico declines, then marijuana from elsewhere—
Hawaii, for instance—will increase. If there is less marijuana being
smoked today than 10 years ago, it is a reflection not of law enforcement but of creeping social perception. It has gradually transpired that
the stuff is more harmful than originally thought, and a culture that
spends billions of dollars on health foods and barbells is taking a longer,
critical look at marijuana.

We read about cocaine. In a vivid image, someone recently said that ₃ the big radars along the 2,000-mile border between Mexico and the United States begin, night after night, to track what looks like a swarm of locusts headed our way. Private planes, carrying coke to the American market.

So we bag a large number of them today, and they show up on the ₄ television news. That plane over there was carrying $10 million (or was it $100 million?) worth of coke, hurray for the Drug Enforcement Agency. But then the sober evaluation comes through. Last year—a splendid year for drug apprehension—resulted in interdicting, oh, maybe 10 percent, 20 percent of the stuff coming in.

And of course the measure of success in the drug business, like that ₅ in the business of robbing banks, is, what are your chances of getting through? Answer: terrific. The odds will always be high, when you consider that the amount of coke you can stuff into a single pocket of a man's jacket can fetch $200,000, and that the cost of the stuff where picked up can be as low as $1,000. A profit of 2,000 percent (modest in the business) is a powerful engine to attempt to try to stop in a free society. In other societies the answer is as simple as executing anybody caught smuggling or using dope, exit the dope problem.

So what are we going to do about it? My resourceful brother Wil- ₆ liam Safire has a hot bundle of ideas aimed at catching the people who launder the profits from drugs. These ideas include changing the color of our currency, so that the boys with big sacksful of green under their mattresses will be forced to bring them out, revealing their scarlet letters. Maybe we should breed 50 million drug-trained dogs to sniff at everyone getting off a boat or an airplane, what a great idea!

No, we are face to face with the rawest datum of them all, which is ₇ that the problem would not exist, except that in the United States there is a market for the stuff, and that the stuff is priced very high. If we cannot effectively prevent its insinuating its way into the country, what is it that we can prevent? The answer, of course, is its price. The one thing that could be done, overnight, is to legalize the stuff. Exit crime, and the profits from vice.

It is hardly a novel suggestion to legalize dope. Shrewd observers ₈ of the scene have recommended it for years. I am on record as having opposed it in the matter of heroin. The accumulated evidence draws me away from my own opposition, on the purely empirical grounds that what we have now is a drug problem plus a crime problem plus a problem of a huge export of capital to the dope-producing countries.

Congress should study the dramatic alternative, which is legaliza- ₉ tion followed by a dramatic educational effort in which the services of

all civic-minded, and some less than civic-minded, resources are mobilized. Television, for instance. Let the Federal Communications Commission make it a part of the overhead of a TV license to broadcast 30
minutes a week, prime time, what dope does to you.

Ours is a free society in which oodles of people kill themselves with   10
tobacco and booze. Some will do so with coke and heroin. But we
should count in the lives saved by having the deadly stuff available at the
same price as rat poison.

QUESTIONS ON SUBJECT

1. To what does Buckley attribute a decline in marijuana smoking?
2. What observation does the author make about the images of the drug war
   shown on television?
3. In Buckley's opinion, why is drug smuggling so enticing in a free society?
4. Why has the author changed his stance on the legalization of heroin?
5. What alternatives to legalization does the author mention? How does he
   treat these alternatives?

QUESTIONS ON STRATEGY

1. Buckley's tone is one of frustrated, sometimes flippant, acceptance
   throughout much of this essay. Where do you see him changing tone, and
   why do you think it is or isn't to his advantage to change from this tone?
2. Make an outline of this essay. How does the author work his way to the
   conclusion that with the legalization of drugs drug-related crime and
   profits will end? Do you think he supports this conclusion? Explain.
3. Comment on the examples the author gives in his essay. Which examples do
   you find most successful in furthering his argument? (Glossary: *Examples*)
4. Buckley suggests that "Congress should consider the dramatic alternative"
   of legalization followed by an intensive educational program. What about
   the length and structure of this essay seem tailored to encouraging further
   general and legislative discussion?
5. Buckley uses cause and effect analysis to discuss the current drug scene in
   this country. What does his proposal of legalization do to the causal chain
   he describes? (Glossary: *Cause and Effect*)

QUESTIONS ON LANGUAGE

1. Buckley's tone and syntax are both informal in this essay. Find examples of
   each and explain what is informal about them. Did you find this infor-
   mality appropriate for his subject and audience?

2. Buckley uses the pronoun "we" in his essay. How did you react to this usage? Does it help or hinder the persuasiveness of his argument? Explain.

3. Refer to your desk dictionary to determine the meanings of the following words as they are used in this selection: *graft* (paragraph 1), *transpired* (2), *interdicting* (4), *launder* (6), *insinuating* (7), *empirical* (8).

WRITING SUGGESTIONS

1. Do you agree with Buckley that the decision over legalization is primarily empirical? Are you convinced by the empirical evidence he presents? Write a reaction to this essay.

2. Consider Buckley's proposal of "legalization followed by a dramatic educational effort," possibly requiring television stations to broadcast 30 minutes, prime time, a week on the effects of drugs. How successful do you think this solution would be? What other means might be employed in an educational program? Do you think that drug use under the protection of the law would prove too strong a pressure for an educational program to counteract? Write an essay addressing these questions.

A Heretic's View on the New Bioethics

JEREMY RIFKIN

Jeremy Rifkin, social activist, editor, and author, was born on January 26, 1945, in Denver, Colorado. He received his B.A. in economics from the University of Pennsylvania and his Master's in international affairs from the Fletchner School of Law and Diplomacy. Rifkin helped to organize the first national protest against the Vietnam War in 1967. As a member of Volunteers in Service to America, Rifkin worked in New York City's Harlem ghetto. He then moved to Washington, D.C., to begin work on a project to celebrate the bicentennial. Rifkin didn't agree with the politics of this project and founded his own organization, the People's Bicentennial Commission, which called for a redistribution of wealth in America. Rifkin remains active in opposition to large corporations and genetic engineering. Recently he has published The End of Work: The Decline of the Global Labor Force and the Dawn of the Post-Market Era, *a work examining technological unemployment.*

In the following selection, taken from Rifkin's book Algeny, *he argues that a new ethics has been established that is paving the way to uncontrollable use of biotechnology.*

Darwin's world was populated by machine-like automata. Nature 1 was conceived as an aggregate of standardized, interchangeable parts assembled into various functional combinations. If one were to ascribe any overall purpose to the entire operation, it would probably be that of increased production and greater efficiency with no particular end in mind.

The new temporal theory of evolution replaces the idea of life 2 as mere machinery with the idea of life as mere information. By resolving structure into function and reducing function to information flows, the new cosmology all but eliminates any remaining sense of species identification. Living things are no longer perceived as carrots and peas, foxes and hens, but as bundles of information. All living things are drained of their aliveness and turned into abstract messages. Life becomes a code to be deciphered. There is no longer any question of sacredness or inviolability. How could there be when there are no longer any recognizable boundaries to respect? Under the new temporal theory, structure is abandoned. Nothing exists at the moment. Everything is pure activity, pure process. How can any living thing be deemed sacred when it is just a pattern of information?

By eliminating structural boundaries and reducing all living things 3 to information exchanges and flows, the new cosmology provides the proper degree of desacralization for the bioengineering of life. After all, in order to justify the engineering of living material across biological boundaries, it is first necessary to desacralize the whole idea of an organism as an identifiable, discrete structure with a permanent set of attributes. In the age of biotechnology, separate species with separate names gradually give way to systems of information that can be reprogrammed into an infinite number of biological combinations. It is much easier for the human mind to accept the idea of engineering a system of information than it is for it to accept the idea of engineering a dog. It is easier still, once one has fully internalized the notion that there is really no such thing as a dog in the traditional sense. In the coming age it will be much more accurate to describe a dog as a very specific pattern of information unfolding over a specific period of time.

Life as information flow represents the final desacralization of 4 nature. Conveniently, humanity has eliminated the idea of fixed biological borders and reduced matter to energy and energy to information in its cosmological thinking right at the very time that bioengineers are preparing to cut across species boundaries in the living world.

THE NEW ETHICS

Civilization is experiencing the euphoric first moments of the next 5 age of history. The media are already treating us to glimpses of a future where the engineering of life by design will be standard operating procedure. Even as the corporate laboratories begin to dribble out the first products of bioengineering, a subtle shift in the ethical impulse of society is becoming perceptible to the naked eye. As we begin to reprogram life, our moral code is being similarly reprogrammed to reflect this profound change in the way humanity goes about organizing the world. A new ethics is being engineered, and its operating assumptions comport nicely with the activity taking place in the biology laboratories.

Eugenics is the inseparable ethical wing of the age of biotechnol- 6 ogy. First coined by Charles Darwin's cousin Sir Francis Galton, eugenics is generally categorized in two ways, negative and positive. Negative eugenics involves the systematic elimination of so-called biologically undesirable characteristics. Positive eugenics is concerned with the use of genetic manipulation to "improve" the characteristics of an organism or species.

Eugenics is not a new phenomenon. At the turn of the century the 7 United States sported a massive eugenics movement. Politicians, celebrities, academicians, and prominent business leaders joined together in support of a eugenics program for the country. The frenzy over eugenics reached a fever pitch, with many states passing sterilization statutes and the U.S. Congress passing a new immigration law in the 1920s based on eugenics considerations. As a consequence of the new legislation, thousands of American citizens were sterilized so they could not pass on their "inferior" traits, and the federal government locked its doors to certain immigrant groups deemed biologically unfit by then-existing eugenics standards.

While the Americans flirted with eugenics for the first thirty years 8 of the twentieth century, their escapades were of minor historical account when compared with the eugenics program orchestrated by the Nazis in the 1930s and '40s. Millions of Jews and other religious and ethnic groups were gassed in the German crematoriums to advance the Third Reich's dream of eliminating all but the "Aryan" race from the globe. The Nazis also embarked on a "positive" eugenics program in which thousands of S.S. officers and German women were carefully selected for their "superior" genes and mated under the auspices of the state. Impregnated women were cared for in state facilities, and their offspring were donated to the Third Reich as the vanguard of the new super race that would rule the world for the next millennium.

Eugenics lay dormant for nearly a quarter of a century after World 9 War II. Then the spectacular breakthroughs in molecular biology in the 1960s raised the specter of a eugenics revival once again. By the mid-1970s, many scientists were beginning to worry out loud that the potential for genetic engineering might lead to a return to the kind of eugenics hysteria that had swept over America and Europe earlier in the century. Speaking at a National Academy of Science forum on recombinant DNA, Ethan Signer, a biologist at M.I.T., warned his colleagues that

> this research is going to bring us one more step closer to genetic engineering of people. That's where they figure out how to have us produce children with ideal characteristics. . . . The last time around, the ideal children had blond hair, blue eyes and Aryan genes.

The concern over a re-emergence of eugenics is well founded but 10 misplaced. While professional ethicists watch out the front door for tell-tale signs of a resurrection of the Nazi nightmare, eugenics doctrine has quietly slipped in the back door and is already stealthily at work reorganizing the ethical priorities of the human household. Virtually overnight, eugenics doctrine has gained an impressive if not an impregnable foothold in the popular culture.

Its successful implantation into the psychic life of civilization is 11 attributable to its going largely unrecognized in its new guise. The new eugenics is commercial, not social. In place of the shrill eugenic cries for racial purity, the new commercial eugenics talks in pragmatic terms of increased economic efficiency, better performance standards, and improvement in the quality of life. The old eugenics was steeped in political ideology and motivated by fear and hate. The new eugenics is grounded in economic considerations and stimulated by utilitarianism and financial gain.

Like the ethics of the Darwinian era, the new commercial eugenics 12 associates the idea of "doing good" with the idea of "increasing efficiency." The difference is that increasing efficiency in the age of biotechnology is achieved by way of engineering living organisms. Therefore, "good" is defined as the engineering of life to improve its performance. In contrast, not to improve the performance of a living organism whenever technically possible is considered tantamount to committing a sin.

For example, consider the hypothetical case of a prospective mother 13 faced with the choice of programming the genetic characteristics of her child at conception. Let's assume the mother chooses not to have the fertilized egg programmed. The fetus develops naturally, the baby is born, the child grows up, and in her early teenage years discovers that she has a rare genetic disease that will lead to a premature and painful death. The mother could have avoided the calamity by having that defective genetic trait eliminated from the fertilized egg, but she chose not to. In the age of biotechnology, her choice not to intervene might well constitute a crime for which she might be punished. At the least, her refusal to allow the fetus to be programmed would be considered a morally reprehensible and irresponsible decision unbefitting a mother, whose duty it is always to provide as best she can for her child's future well-being.

Proponents of human genetic engineering contend that it would 14 be irresponsible not to use this powerful new technology to eliminate serious "genetic disorders." The problem with this argument, says *The New York Times* in an editorial entitled "Whether to Make Perfect

Humans," is that "there is no discernible line to be drawn between making inheritable repairs of genetic defects, and improving the species." The *Times* rightly points out that once scientists are able to repair genetic defects, "it will become much harder to argue against adding genes that confer desired qualities, like better health, looks or brains."

Once we decide to begin the process of human genetic engineer- 15 ing, there is really no logical place to stop. If diabetes, sickle cell anemia, and cancer are to be cured by altering the genetic makeup of an individual, why not proceed to other "disorders": myopia, color blindness, left-handedness? Indeed, what is to preclude a society from deciding that a certain skin color is a disorder?

As knowledge about genes increases, the bioengineers will inevitably 16 gain new insights into the functioning of more complex characteristics, such as those associated with behavior and thoughts. Many scientists are already contending that schizophrenia and other "abnormal" psychological states result from genetic disorders or defects. Others now argue that "antisocial" behavior, such as criminality and social protest, are also examples of malfunctioning genetic information. One prominent neurophysiologist has gone so far as to say, "There can be no twisted thought without a twisted molecule." Many sociobiologists contend that virtually all human activity is in some way determined by our genetic makeup, and that if we wish to change this situation, we must change our genes.

Whenever we begin to discuss the idea of genetic defects, there is 17 no way to limit the discussion to one or two or even a dozen so-called disorders, because of a hidden assumption that lies behind the very notion of "defective." Ethicist Daniel Callahan penetrates to the core of the problem when he observes that "behind the human horror at genetic defectiveness lurks . . . an image of the perfect human being. The very language of 'defect,' 'abnormality,' 'disease,' and 'risk,' presupposes such an image, a kind of proto-type of perfection."

The idea of engineering the human species is very similar to the 18 idea of engineering a piece of machinery. An engineer is constantly in search of new ways to improve the performance of a machine. As soon as one set of imperfections is eliminated, the engineer immediately turns his attention to the next set of imperfections, always with the idea in mind of creating a perfect piece of machinery. Engineering is a process of continual improvement in the performance of a piece of machinery, and the idea of setting arbitrary limits to how much "improvement" is acceptable is alien to the entire engineering conception.

The question, then, is whether or not humanity should "begin" 19 the process of engineering future generations of human beings by technological design in the laboratory. What is the price we pay for embarking on a course whose final goal is the "perfection" of the human species? How important is it that we eliminate all the imperfections, all the defects? What price are we willing to pay to extend our lives, to ensure our own health, to do away with all the inconveniences, the irritations, the nuisances, the infirmities, the suffering, that are so much a part of the human experience? Are we so enamored with the idea of physical perpetuation at all costs that we are even willing to subject the human species to rigid architectural design?

With human genetic engineering, we get something and we give up 20 something. In return for securing our own physical well-being we are forced to accept the idea of reducing the human species to a technologically designed product. Genetic engineering poses the most fundamental of questions. Is guaranteeing our health worth trading away our humanity?

People are forever devising new ways of organizing the environ- 21 ment in order to secure their future. Ethics, in turn, serves to legitimize the drive for self-perpetuation. Any organizing activity that a society deems to be helpful in securing its future is automatically blessed, and any activity that undermines the mode of organization a society uses to secure its future is automatically damned. The age of bioengineering brooks no exception. In the years to come a multitude of new bioengineering products will be forthcoming. Every one of the breakthroughs in bioengineering will be of benefit to someone, under some circumstance, somewhere in society. Each will in some way appear to advance the future security of an individual, a group, or society as a whole. Eliminating a defective gene trait so that a child won't die prematurely; engineering a new cereal crop that can feed an expanding population; developing a new biological source of energy that can fill the vacuum as the oil spigot runs dry. Every one of these advances provides a modicum of security against the vagaries of the future. To forbid their development and reject their application will be considered ethically irresponsible and inexcusable.

Bioengineering is coming to us not as a threat but as a promise; not 22 as a punishment but as a gift. We have already come to the conclusion that bioengineering is a boon for humanity. The thought of engineering living organisms no longer conjures up sinister images. What we see before our eyes are not monstrosities but useful products. We no longer feel dread but only elated expectation at the great possibilities that lie in store for each of us.

How could engineering life be considered bad when it produces 23 such great benefits? Engineering living tissue is no longer a question of great ethical import. The human psyche has been won over to eugenics with little need for discussion or debate. We have already been convinced of the good that can come from engineering life by learning of the helpful products it is likely to spawn.

As in the past, humanity's incessant need to control the future in order to secure its own well-being is already dictating the ethics of the age of biotechnology. Engineering life to improve humanity's own prospects for survival will be ennobled as the highest expression of ethical behavior. Any resistance to the new technology will be castigated as inhuman, irresponsible, morally reprehensible, and criminally culpable. 24

QUESTIONS ON SUBJECT

1. According to Rifkin, how are ethics and technology changing?
2. In paragraph 5 the author writes, "a new ethics is being engineered." In Rifkin's opinion, who is doing the engineering?
3. In paragraph 11 Rifkin writes, "The new eugenics is commercial, not social." What does he mean here? How does this quote relate to information he has given up to this point?
4. What course of action does Rifkin argue for in his essay?

QUESTIONS ON STRATEGY

1. How would you describe the author's tone in this essay? (Glossary: *Tone*) Do you find this tone persuasive? Explain.
2. The reader doesn't always have an understanding of the field that an author addresses. When this is the case, contextual information becomes essential. How well does Rifkin provide context for his claims? Defend your answer with examples from the text.
3. Successful use of quotations clarify and support an author's argument, whereas a quote that appears out of context or that the author could just have easily put in his or her own words detracts from an argument. Comment on Rifkin's use of quotation in this essay.
4. A strong argumentative essay has a logical foundation without any non sequiturs. Make an outline of this essay and comment on its strength or weakness.
5. In an increasingly complicated and information glutted society, Rifkin's denunciation of a new scientific view that sees life as no more than information is guaranteed an audience. In your opinion, how broad of an audience does this essay appeal to? Explain. (Glossary: *Audience*)

6. Explain how Rifkin uses examples to argue against the new bioengineering? (Glossary: *Illustration*)

QUESTIONS ON LANGUAGE

1. What point does the author make about how a term like *defective* gets its meaning?

2. In paragraph 2 Rifkin refers to the "sacredness" and "inviolability" of life. Does Rifkin's choice of words support this view of life elsewhere in his essay? In your opinion, does such diction help or hinder his argument? Explain.

3. Refer to your desk dictionary to determine the meanings of the following words as they are used in this selection: *automata* (paragraph 1), *ascribe* (1), *temporal* (2), *cosmology* (2 and 3), *abstract* (2), *euphoric* (5), *comport* (5), *auspices* (8), *vanguard* (8), *impregnable* (10), *shrill* (11), *tantamount* (12), *confer* (14), *enamored* (19), *perpetuation* (19), *brooks* (21), *modicum* (21), *vagaries* (21), *boon* (22), *elated* (22), *spawn* (23), *ennobled* (24), *castigated* (24).

WRITING SUGGESTIONS

1. Rifkin's position as a heretic rests on his assertion that those who resist eugenics will "be castigated as inhuman, irresponsible, morally reprehensible, and criminally culpable." Write a response to this essay. Do you see the author's work as insightful, or, as Gould suggests, the result of sloppy research?

2. Do some research in your library on the eugenics movement in this country in the twentieth century, and write a paper reporting your findings.

On the Origin of Specious Critics

STEPHEN JAY GOULD

Stephen Jay Gould, a paleontologist and writer, has taught geology, biology, and the history of science at Harvard University since 1967. Born in New York City in 1941 and educated at Antioch College and Columbia University, Gould has gained a considerable reputation for his ability to explain scientific theories clearly and concisely. He writes a regular column in Natural History *magazine and has collected many of his essays in* Ever Since Darwin *(1977),* The Panda's Thumb *(1980),* The Mismeasure of Man *(1981),* Hen's Teeth and Horse's Toes *(1983),* The Flamingo's Smile *(1985),* An Urchin in the Storm *(1987),* Bully for Brontosaurus *(1991), and* Eight Little Piggies *(1993), among others.*

In the following essay, first published in the January 1985 issue of Discover, *he critically analyzes Jeremy Rifkin's* Algeny, *a book examining biotechnology. Gould shares Rifkin's concern over the use of genetic engineering, yet he believes that Rifkin uses poor scholarship and argumentation in arriving at the conclusion that science should not pursue advances in biotechnology.*

Evolution has a definite geometry well portrayed by our ancient 1 metaphor, the tree of life. Lineages split and diverge like the branches of a tree. A species, once distinct, is permanently on its own; the branches of life do not coalesce. Extinction is truly forever, persistence a personal odyssey. But art does not always imitate nature. Biotechnology, or genetic engineering, has aroused fear and opposition because it threatens to annul this fundamental property of life—to place genes of one species into the program of another, thereby combining what nature has kept separate from time immemorial. Two concerns—one immediate and practical, the other distant and deep—have motivated the opposition.

Some critics fear that certain conjunctions might have potent and 2 unanticipated effects—creating a resistant agent of disease or simply a new creature so hardy and fecund that, like Kurt Vonnegut's *ice-nine,* it spreads to engulf the earth in a geological millisecond. I am not persuaded by these excursions into science fiction, but the distant and deeper issue does merit discussion: What are the consequences, ethical, aesthetic, and practical, of altering life's fundamental geometry and permitting one species to design new creatures at will, combining bits and pieces of lineages distinct for billions of years?

Jeremy Rifkin has been the most vocal opponent of genetic engineering in recent months. He has won court cases and aroused fury in the halls of science with his testimony about immediate dangers. However, his major statement, a book titled *Algeny* (for the modern alchemy of genes), concentrates almost entirely on the deep and distant issue. His activities based on immediate fears have been widely reported and rebutted. But *Algeny*, although it was published more than a year ago, has not been adequately analyzed or dissected. Its status as prophecy or pretension, philosophy or pamphleteering, must be assessed, for *Algeny* touts itself as the manifesto of a movement to save nature and simple decency from the hands of impatient and rapacious science.

I will state my conclusion—bald and harsh—at the outset: I regard *Algeny* as a cleverly constructed tract of anti-intellectual propaganda masquerading as scholarship. Among books promoted as serious intellectual statements by important thinkers, I don't think I have ever read a shoddier work. Damned shame, too, because the deep issue is troubling and I do not disagree with Rifkin's basic plea for respecting the integrity of evolutionary lineages. But devious means compromise good ends, and we shall have to save Rifkin's humane conclusion from his own questionable tactics.

The basic argument of *Algeny* rests upon a parody of an important theme advanced by contemporary historians of science against the myth of objectivity and inexorable scientific progress: science is socially embedded; its theories are not simple deductions from observed facts of nature, but a complex mixture of social ideology (often unconsciously expressed) and empirical constraint. This theme is liberating for science; it embodies the human side of our enterprise and depicts us as passionate creatures struggling with limited tools to understand a complex reality, not as robots programmed to convert objective information into immutable truth. But in Rifkin's hands the theme becomes a caricature. Rifkin ignores the complex interplay of social bias with *facts* of nature and promotes a crude socioeconomic determinism that views our historical succession of biological worldviews—from creationism to Darwinism to the new paradigm now supposedly under construction—as so many simple reflections of social ideology.

From this socioeconomic determinism, Rifkin constructs his specific brief: Darwinian evolutionism, he asserts, was the creation of industrial capitalism, the age of pyrotechnology. Arising in this context as a simple reflection of social ideology, it never had any sound basis in reason or evidence. It is now dying because the age of pyrotechnology is yielding to an era of biotechnology—and biotech demands a new view of life. Darwinism translated the industrial machine into nature; biotech models nature as a computer and substitutes information for material parts.

Darwinism spawned (or reflected) evil in its support for exploita- 7 tion of man and nature, but at least it respected the integrity of species (while driving some to extinction) because it lacked the technology to change them by mixture and instant transmutation. But the new paradigm dissolves species into strings of information that can be reshuffled at will.

The new temporal theory of evolution replaces the idea of life as 8 mere machinery with the idea of life as mere information. All living things are drained of their aliveness and turned into abstract messages. There is no longer any question of sacredness or inviolability. How could there be when there are no longer any recognizable boundaries to respect? In the age of biotechnology, separate species with separate names gradually give way to systems of information that can be reprogrammed into an infinite number of biological combinations.

But what can we do if we wish to save nature as we know it—a 9 system divided into packages of porcupines and primroses, cabbages and kings? We can seek no help from science, Rifkin claims, for science is a monolith masquerading as objective knowledge, but really reflecting the dominant ideology of a new technological age. We can only make an ethical decision to "re-sacralize" nature by respecting the inviolability of its species. We must, for the first time in history, decide *not* to institute a possible technology, despite its immediately attractive benefits in such areas as medicine and agriculture.

I have devoted my own career to evolutionary biology, and I have 10 been among the strongest critics of strict Darwinism. Yet Rifkin's assertions bear no relationship to what I have observed and practiced for 25 years. Evolutionary theory has never been healthier or more exciting. We are experiencing a ferment of new ideas and theories, but they are revising and extending Darwin, not burying him. How can Rifkin construct a world so different from the one I inhabit and know so well? Either I am blind or he is wrong—and I think I can show, by analyzing his slipshod scholarship and basic misunderstanding of science, that his world is an invention constructed to validate his own private hopes. I shall summarize my critique in five charges:

1. Rifkin does not understand Darwinism, and his arguments refute 11 an absurd caricature, not the theory itself. He trots out all the standard

mischaracterizations, usually confined nowadays to creationist tracts. Just three examples: "According to Darwin," Rifkin writes, "everything evolved by chance." Since the complexity of cellular life cannot arise by accident, Darwinism is absurd: "According to the odds, the one-cell organism is so complex that the likelihood of its coming together by sheer accident and chance is computed to be around $1/10^{78436}$." But Darwin himself, and Darwinians ever since, always stressed, as a cardinal premise, that natural selection is not a theory of randomness. Chance may describe the origin of new variation by mutation, but natural selection, the agent of change, is a conventional deterministic process that builds adaptation by preserving favorable variants.

Rifkin then dismisses Darwinism as a tautology; fitness is defined by survival, and the catch phrase "survival of the fittest" reduces to "survival of those that survive"—and therefore has no meaning. Darwin resolved this issue, as Darwinians have ever since, by defining fitness as predictable advantage before the fact, not as recorded survival afterward (as we may predict the biomechanical improvements that might help zebras outrun or outmaneuver lions; survival then becomes a testable consequence). 12

Rifkin regards Darwinism as absurd because "natural selection makes no room for long-range considerations. Every new trait has to be immediately useful or it is discarded." How, therefore, can natural selection explain the origin of a bird's wing, since the intermediate forms cannot fly: What good is five per cent of a wing? The British biologist St. George Jackson Mivart developed this critique in 1871 as the argument about "incipient stages of useful structures." Darwin met the challenge by adding a chapter to the sixth edition of the *Origin of Species*. One need not agree with Darwin's resolution, but one does have a responsibility to acknowledge it. Darwin argued that intermediate stages performed different functions; feathers of an incipient wing may act as excellent organs of thermoregulation—a particular problem in the smallest of dinosaurs, which evolved into birds. 13

Rifkin displays equally little comprehension of basic arguments about evolutionary geometry. He thinks that *Archaeopteryx* has been refuted as an intermediate link between reptiles and birds because some true birds have been found in rocks of the same age. But evolution is a branching bush, not a ladder. Ancestors survive after descendants branch off. Dogs evolved from wolves, but wolves (though threatened) are hanging tough. And a species of *Australopithecus* lived side by side with its descendant *Homo* for more than a million years in Africa. 14

Rifkin doesn't grasp the current critiques of strict Darwinism any better. He caricatures my own theory of punctuated equilibrium [that 15 evolution moves in fits and starts rather than by slow, steady change] as a sudden response to ecological catastrophe: "The idea is that these catastrophic events spawned monstrous genetic mutations within existing species, most of which were lethal. A few of the mutations, however, managed to survive and become the precursors of a new species." But punctuated equilibrium, as Niles Eldredge and I have always emphasized, is about ordinary speciation (taking tens of thousands of years) and its abrupt appearance at low scales of geological resolution, not about ecological catastrophe and sudden genetic change.

Rifkin, it appears, understands neither the fundamentals of Darwinism, its current critiques, nor even the basic topology of the evolutionary tree.   16

2. Rifkin shows no understanding of the norms and procedures of   17
science: he displays little comprehension of what science is and how scientists work. He consistently misses the essential distinction between fact (claims about the world's empirical content) and theory (ideas that explain and interpret facts)—using arguments against one to refute the other. Against Darwinism (a theory of evolutionary mechanisms) he cites the British physiologist Gerald Kerkut's *Implications of Evolution,* a book written to refute the factual claim that all living creatures have a common ancestry, and to argue instead that life may have arisen several times from chemical precursors—an issue not addressed by Darwinism. (Creationist lawyers challenged me with the same misunderstanding during my cross-examination at the Arkansas "equal time" trial three years ago, in which the creationists unsuccessfully fought for compulsory presentation of their views in science classrooms.) Rifkin then suggests that the entire field of evolution may be a pseudo science because the great French zoologist Pierre-Paul Grassé is so critical of Darwinism (the theory of natural selection might be wrong, but Grassé has devoted his entire life to study the fact of evolution).

Science is a pluralistic enterprise, validly pursued in many modes.   18
But Rifkin ignores its richness by stating that direct manipulation by repeatable experiment is the only acceptable method for reaching a scientific conclusion. Since evolution treats historically unique events that occurred millions of years ago, it cannot be a science. Rifkin doesn't seem to realize that he is throwing out half of science—nearly all of geology and most of astronomy, for instance—with his evolutionary bath water. Historical science is a valid pursuit, but it uses methods different from the controlled experiment of Rifkin's all-encompassing caricature—search for an underlying pattern among unique events, and retrodiction (predicting the yet undiscovered results of past events), for example.

3. Rifkin does not respect the procedures of fair argument. He uses 19 every debater's trick in the book to mischaracterize and trivialize his opposition, and to place his own dubious claims in a rosy light. Just four examples:

The synecdoche (trying to dismiss a general notion by citing a single 20 poor illustration). He suggests that science knows nothing about the evolutionary tree of horses, and has sold the public a bill of goods (the great horse caper, he calls it), because one exhibit, set up at the American Museum of Natural History in 1905, arranged fossil horses in order of size, not genealogy. Right, Jeremy, that was a lousy exhibit, but you might read George Gaylord Simpson's book *Horses* to see what we do know.

The half quote (stopping in the middle so that an opponent ap- 21 pears to agree with you, or seems merely ridiculous). Rifkin quotes me on the argument about incipient stages of useful structures discussed a few paragraphs ago: "Harvard's Stephen Jay Gould posed the dilemma when he observed, 'What good is half a jaw or half a wing?' " Sure, I posed the dilemma, but then followed it with an entire essay supporting Darwin's resolution based on different function in intermediate stages. Rifkin might have mentioned it and not adduced me in his support. Rifkin then quotes a famous line from Darwin as if it represented the great man's admission of impotence: "Darwin himself couldn't believe it, even though it was his own theory that advanced the proposition. He wrote: 'To suppose that the eye, with all of its inimitable contrivances . . . could have been formed by natural selection, seems, I freely confess, absurd in the highest possible degree.' " But Rifkin might have mentioned that Darwin follows this statement with one of his most brilliant sections—a documentation of nature's graded intermediates between simple pinhole eyes and the complexity of our own, and an argument that the power of new theories resides largely in their ability to resolve previous absurdities.

Refuting what your opponents never claimed. In the 1950s, Stanley 22 Miller performed a famous experiment that synthesized amino acids from hypothetical components of the earth's original atmosphere. Rifkin describes it with glaring hype: "With great fanfare, the world was informed that scientists had finally succeeded in forming life from non-life, the dream of magicians, sorcerers, and alchemists from time immemorial." He then points out, quite correctly, that the experiment did no such thing, and that the distance from amino acid to life is immense. But Miller never claimed that he had made life. The experiment stands in all our text books as a demonstration that some simple components of living systems can be made from inorganic chemicals. I was taught this 25 years ago; I have lectured about it for 15 years. I have never in all my professional life heard a scientist say that Miller or anyone else has made life from non-life.

Refuting what your opponents refuted long ago. Rifkin devotes a 23 whole section to ridiculing evolution because its supporters once advanced the "biogenetic law" that embryos repeat the adult stages of their ancestry—now conclusively refuted. But Darwinian evolutionists did the refuting more than 50 years ago (good science is self-correcting).

4. Rifkin ignores the most elementary procedures of fair scholar- 24 ship. His book, brought forth as a major conceptual statement about the nature of science and the history of biology, displays painful ignorance of its subject. His quotations are primarily from old and discredited secondary sources (including some creationist propaganda tracts). I see no evidence that he has ever read much of Darwin in the original. He obviously knows nothing about (or chooses not to mention) all the major works of Darwinian scholarship written by modern historians. His continual barrage of misquotes and half quotes records this partial citation from excerpts in hostile secondary sources.

His prose is often purple in the worst journalistic tradition. When 25 invented claims are buttressed by such breathless description, the effect can be quite amusing. He mentions the geneticist T. H. Morgan's invocation of the tautology argument discussed previously in this essay: "Not until Morgan began to suspect that natural selection was a victim of circular reasoning did anyone in the scientific community even question what was regarded by all as a profound truth. . . . Morgan's observation shocked the scientific establishment." Now, I ask, how does he know this? He cites no evidence of any shock, even of any contemporary comment. He quotes Morgan himself only from secondary sources. In fact, everything about the statement is wrong, just plain wrong. The tautology argument dates from the 1870s. Morgan didn't invent it (and Darwin, in my opinion, ably refuted it when Morgan was a baby). Morgan, moreover, was no noble knight sallying forth against a monolithic Darwinian establishment. When he wrote his critique in the 1920s, natural selection was a distinctly unpopular theory among evolutionists (the tide didn't turn in Darwin's favor until the late 1930s). Morgan, if anything, *was* the establishment, and his critique, so far as I know, didn't shock a soul or elicit any extensive commentary.

5. *Algeny* is full of ludicrous, simple errors. I particularly enjoyed 26 Rifkin's account of Darwin in the Galapagos. After describing the "great masses" of vultures, condors, vampire bats, jaguars, and snakes that Darwin saw on these islands, Rifkin writes: "It was a savage, primeval scene, menacing in every detail. Everywhere there was bloodletting,

and the ferocious, unremittent battle for survival. The air was dank and foul, and the thick stench of volcanic ash veiled the islands with a kind of ghoulish drape." Well, I guess Rifkin has never been there; and he obviously didn't bother to read anything about these fascinating islands. Except for snakes, none of those animals live on the Galapagos. In fact, the Galapagos house no terrestrial predators at all; as a result, the animals have no fear of human beings and do not flee when approached. The Galapagos are unusual, as Darwin noted, precisely because they are not scenes of Hobbes's *bellum omnium contra omnes* (the war of all against all). And, by the way, no thick stench or ghoulish drape either; the volcanic terrains are beautiful, calm, and peaceful— not in eruption when Darwin visited, not now either.

Jeremy Rifkin, in short, has argued himself, inextricably, into a corner. He has driven off his natural allies by silly, at times dishonest, argument and nasty caricature. He has saddled his legitimate concern with an extremism that would outlaw both humane and fascinating scientific research. His legitimate brief speaks for the integrity of organisms and species. It would be a bleak world indeed that treated living things as no more than separable sequences of information, available for disarticulation and recombination in any order that pleased human whim. But I do not see why we should reject all of genetic engineering because its technology might, one day, permit such a perversion of decency in the hands of some latter-day Hitler—you may as well outlaw printing because the same machine that composes Shakespeare can also set *Mein Kampf.* The domino theory does not apply to all human achievements. If we could, by transplanting a bacterial gene, confer disease or cold resistance upon an important crop plant, should we not do so in a world where people suffer so terribly from malnutrition? Must such an event imply that, tomorrow, corn and wheat, sea horses and orchids will be thrown into a gigantic vat, torn apart into genetic units, and reassembled into rows of identical human servants? Eternal vigilance, to recombine some phrases, is the price of technological achievement.

The debate about genetic engineering has often been portrayed, falsely, as one of many battles between the political left and right— leftists in opposition, rightists plowing ahead. It is not so simple; it rarely is. Used humanely for the benefit of ordinary people, not the profits of a few entrepreneurs, this technology need not be feared by the left. I, for one, would rather campaign for proper use, not abolition. If Rifkin's argument embodies any antithesis, it is not left versus right, but romanticism, in its most dangerous anti-intellectual form, versus respect for knowledge and its humane employment. In both its content and presentation, *Algeny* belongs in the sordid company of anti-science.

Few campaigns are more dangerous than emotional calls for proscription rather than thought.

I have been so harsh because I believe that Rifkin has seriously 29 harmed a cause that is very dear to me and to nearly all my scientific colleagues. Rifkin has placed all of us beyond the pale of decency by arguing that scientific paradigms are simple expressions of socioeconomic bias, that biotech implies (and will impose) a new view of organisms as strings of separable information (not wholes of necessary integrity), and that all scientists will eventually go along with this heartless idea. Well, Mr. Rifkin, who then will be for you? Where will you find your allies in the good fight for respect of evolutionary lineages? You have rejected us, reviled us, but we are with you. We are taxonomists, ecologists, and evolutionists—most of us Darwinians. We have devoted our lives to the study of species in their natural habitats. We have struggled to understand—and we greatly admire—the remarkable construction and operation of organisms, the product of complex evolutionary histories, cascades of astounding improbability stretching back for millions of years. We know these organisms, and we love them—as they are. We would not dissolve this handiwork of four billion years to satisfy the hubris of one species. We respect the integrity of nature, Mr. Rifkin. But your arguments lack integrity. This we deplore.

QUESTIONS ON SUBJECT

1. What concern does the author feel he shares with Rifkin? What doesn't Gould find acceptable about the way Rifkin argues this concern?
2. What important point does Gould make in paragraph 5 about the paradigm Rifkin employs throughout *Algeny*?
3. According to Gould, did Darwin believe that evolution occurred by chance? Explain.
4. According to Gould, how do fact and theory differ?
5. What approach to biotechnology does Gould advocate?

QUESTIONS ON STRATEGY

1. Explain how the first ten paragraphs serve as an introduction to this essay? (Glossary: *Beginnings and Endings*)
2. What order do you see to the five charges the author makes against Rifkin? Why do you think Gould waits until paragraph eleven to begin listing these charges?

3. Gould harshly criticizes Rifkin in this essay. Would you characterize his tone as caustic, or would you choose some other adjective? Explain using examples from the text. (Glossary: *Tone*)

4. Assess the role of illustration in this argumentative essay. (Glossary: *Illustration*)

5. Comment on Gould's use of comparison and contrast to examine Rifkin's portrayal of the scientific community and Rifkin's own knowledge of his subject. (Glossary: *Comparison and Contrast*)

QUESTIONS ON LANGUAGE

1. What criticism does Gould make concerning Rifkin's prose? Compare Gould's diction in this essay with Rifkin's essay, "A Heretic's View of the New Bioethics." Do you agree or disagree with Gould? Explain.

2. Would you describe Gould's diction as that of a scientist? Why, or why not? Does his diction reveal the audience Gould intended this review essay for? Explain.

3. Refer to your desk dictionary to determine the meanings of the following words as they are used in this selection: *specious* (title), *coalesce* (paragraph 1), *odyssey* (1), *annul* (1), *practical* (1), *fecund* (2), *aesthetic* (2), *rebutted* (3), *touts* (3), *manifesto* (3), *rapacious* (3), *inexorable* (5), *empirical* (5 and 17), *immutable* (5), *paradigm* (5, 7, and 29), *determinism* (5, 6, and 11), *brief* (6 and 27), *pyrotechnology* (6), *spawned* (7 and 15), *temporal* (8), *monolith(ic)* (9 and 25), *ferment* (10), *refute* (11, 14, 17, 22, and 23), *cardinal* (11), *tautology* (12), *incipient* (13), *precursors* (15 and 17), *topology* (16), *pluralistic* (18), *adduced* (21), *inimitable* (21), *purple* (25), *sallying* (25), *saddled* (27), *legitimate* (27), *sordid* (28), *proscription* (28), *pale* (29), *reviled* (29), *hubris* (29).

WRITING SUGGESTIONS

1. Write an essay in which you explore the "common ground" that exists between Gould and Rifkin. What are their common concerns? What are their areas of major disagreement?

2. Write an argumentative essay addressing a topic of your choice. Consider Gould's well-reasoned and illustrated essay as a model. Keep in mind the following questions while working on your essay: What order do you see to the argument you wish to make? What background information will you need to give your reader? Should you give this information at the beginning of your essay or will it fall more logically within the context of a specific point that you will make in your essay?

Imagebusters

TODD GITLIN

Todd Gitlin, author, sociology professor, and director of the mass communications program at the University of California, Berkeley, was born on January 6, 1943, in New York City. He received his B.A. from Harvard University in 1963, his M.A. from the University of Michigan in 1966, and his Ph.D. from the University of California, Berkeley in 1977. He served as president of Students for a Democratic Society, wrote for the San Francisco Express Times *from 1968–1969, lectured at San Jose State College from1970–1976, and lectured at the University of California, Santa Cruz from 1974–1977 before becoming an assistant professor at the University of California, Berkeley in 1978. He has written two books and edited another examining the relationship between the mass media and society:* The Whole World Is Watching: Mass Media in the Making and Unmaking of the New Left *(1980),* Inside Prime Time *(1983), and* Watching Television *(editor, 1986). Recently he has written* The Sixties: Years of Hope, Days of Rage *(1987), a book blending research and personal experience, and a novel,* The Murder of Albert Einstein *(1992).*

In this selection, taken from the Winter 1994 issue of The American Prospect, *Gitlin contends that the liberal campaign against television violence is a cop-out, offering the appearance of action against violence, while failing to address the determining factors of violence in America.*

I have denounced movie violence for more than two decades, 1 all the way back to *The Wild Bunch* and *The Godfather.* I consider Hollywood's slashes, splatters, chain saws, and car crashes a disgrace, a degradation of culture, and a wound to the souls of producers and consumers alike.

But I also think liberals are making a serious mistake by pursu- 2 ing their vigorous campaign against violence in the media. However morally and aesthetically reprehensible today's screen violence, the crusades of Senator Paul Simon and Attorney General Janet Reno against television violence are cheap shots. There are indeed reasons to attribute violence to the media, but the links are weaker than recent headlines would have one believe. The attempt to demonize the media distracts attention from the real causes of—and the serious remedies for—the epidemic of violence.

The sheer volume of alarm can't be explained by the actual violence 3 generated by the media's awful images. Rather, Simon and Reno—not to mention Dan Quayle and the Reverend Donald Wildmon—have signed up for a traditional American pastime. The campaign against the devil's images threads through the history of middle-class reform movements. For a nation that styles itself practical, at least in technical pursuits, the United States has always been remarkably quick to become a playground of moral prohibitions and symbolic crusades.

If today's censorious forces smell smoke, it is not in the absence of 4 fire. In recent years, market forces have driven screen violence to an amazing pitch. But the question the liberal crusaders fail to address is not whether these violent screen images are wholesome but just how much real-world violence can be blamed on the media. Assume, for the sake of argument, that *every* copycat crime reported in the media can be plausibly traced to television and movies. Let us make an exceedingly high estimate that the resulting carnage results in 100 deaths per year that would not otherwise have taken place. These would amount to 0.28 percent of the total of 36,000 murders, accidents, and suicides committed by gunshot in the United States in 1992.

That media violence contributes to a climate in which violence is 5 legitimate—and there can be no doubt of this—does not make it an urgent social problem. Violence on the screens, however loathsome, does not make a significant contribution to violence on the streets. Images don't spill blood. Rage, equipped with guns, does. Desperation does. Revenge does. As liberals say, the drug trade does; poverty does; unemployment does. It seems likely that a given percent increase in decently paying jobs will save thousands of times more lives than the same percent decrease in media bang-bang.

Now, I also give conservative arguments about the sources of 6 violence their due. A culture that despises and disrespects authority is disposed to aggression, so people look to violence to resolve conflict. The absence of legitimate parental authority also feeds a culture of aggression. But aggression per se, however unpleasant, is not the decisive murderous element. A child who shoves another child after watching a fistfight on television is not committing a drive-by shooting. Violence plays on big screens around the world without generating epidemics of carnage. The necessary condition permitting a culture of aggression to flare into a culture of violence is access to lethal weapons.

It's dark out there in the world of real violence, hopelessness, 7 drugs, and guns. There is little political will for a war on poverty, guns, or family breakdown. Here, under the light, we are offered instead a crusade against media violence. This is largely a feel-good exercise, a moral panic substituting for practicality. It appeals to an American propensity that sociologist Philip Slater called the Toilet Assumption: Once the appearance of a social problem is swept out of sight, so is the problem. And the crusade costs nothing.

There is, for some liberals, an additional attraction. By campaign- 8 ing against media violence, they hope to seize "family values" from conservatives. But the mantle of anti-violence they wrap themselves in is threadbare, and they are showing off new clothes that will not stop bullets.

The symbolic crusade against media violence is a confession of 9 despair. Those who embrace it are saying, in effect, that they either do not know how, or do not dare, to do anything serious about American violence. They are tilting at images. If Janet Reno cites the American Psychological Association's recently published report, *Violence and Youth,* to indict television, she also should take note of the following statements within it: "Many social science disciplines, in addition to psychology, have firmly established that poverty and its contextual life circumstances are major determinants of violence. . . . It is very likely that socioeconomic inequality—not race—facilitates higher rates of violence among ethnic minority groups. . . . There is considerable evidence that the alarming rise in youth homicides is related to the availability of firearms." The phrase "major determinant" does not appear whenever the report turns to the subject of media violence.

The question for reformers, then, is one of proportion and focus. 10 If there were nothing else to do about deadly violence in America, then the passionate crusade against TV violence might be more justifiable, even though First Amendment absolutists would still have strong counterarguments. But the imagebusting campaign permits politicians to fulminate photogenically without having to take on the National Rifle Association or, for that matter, the drug epidemic, the crisis of the family, or the shortage of serious jobs.

So let a thousand criticisms bloom. Let reformers flood the net- 11 works and cable companies and, yes, advertisers, with protests against the gross overabundance of the stupid, the tawdry, and the ugly.

But not least, let the reformers not only turn off the set, but also 12 criticize the form of life that has led so many to turn, and keep, it on.

QUESTIONS ON SUBJECT

1. Why does the author think that "the crusades of Senator Paul Simon and Attorney General Janet Reno against television violence are cheap shots?"

2. How does the author see liberals using the issue of television violence to their advantage? What argument, according to Gitlin, have conservatives put forward?

3. What will and won't the author grant concerning the effects of television violence?

4. What is the Toilet Assumption and how does it relate to a crusade against television violence?

5. What alternative does Gitlin offer to the crusade against TV violence?

QUESTIONS ON STRATEGY

1. What is the author's thesis, and where does he state it? (Glossary: *Thesis*)

2. Sometimes agreeing with your opponents can be more damaging to their argument than disagreeing. Comment on the author's use of a "yes, but . . ." strategy in his essay? How does his opening paragraph function to set up or introduce his argument?

3. Gitlin tries to present the issue of television violence using empirical evidence. Consider the evidence he presents in paragraph 4. Is the author making a generous concession in this paragraph? What response do you think those waging the crusade against television violence would give to this? How convincing do you find the author's example? Explain your answer. (Glossary: *Illustration*)

4. In paragraph 5, what effect does Gitlin achieve with his repeated use of the verbs "does not make" and "does"? (Glossary: *Parallelism*)

5. How has Gitlin organized his argument against the liberals' "vigorous campaign against violence in the media"? (Glossary: *Organization*)

6. In this essay Gitlin not only argues that the liberals are in the wrong, but also that they have chosen their path, the crusade against violence on television, as an easy solution. Which accusation do you consider more damaging, and which do you feel the author places more emphasis on? How well does the author support the latter claim? (Glossary: *Illustration*)

QUESTIONS ON LANGUAGE

1. Gitlin stresses the importance of proportion and focus. Find examples of his diction that suggest that the liberal crusade against TV violence is out of proportion and lacks focus.

2. Would it be accurate in your opinion to describe Gitlin's tone in this essay as reasonable and logical? Point to specific language that he uses to support your answer.

3. Refer to your desk dictionary to determine the meanings of the following words as they are used in this selection: *vigorous* (paragraph 2), *aesthetically* (2), *reprehensible* (2), *propensity* (7), *tilting at* (9), *indict* (9), *absolutists* (10), *fulminate* (10), *tawdry* (11).

WRITING SUGGESTIONS

1. Gitlin writes, "Violence on the screens, however loathsome, does not make a significant contribution to violence on the streets." Do some research of your own, and write an essay either questioning or defending the author's statement.

2. As the author suggests, research is what has led so many people to turn, and keep, television on. Write an essay addressing what factors play an important role in who watches television. Feel free to include your own reasons for watching or not watching TV as well as any other observations pertinent to the subject.

The Visual Media: Mirror or Mold of American Culture?

SUMNER M. REDSTONE

Sumner M. Redstone was born in Boston on May 27, 1923. He is chairman of the board of Viacom International Inc. and its parent company Viacom Inc. Together, these companies own several cable networks, including MTV, VH-1, and Nickelodeon/ Nick at Nite. In 1944 Redstone received his B.A. and in 1947 his Bachelor of Laws from Harvard University. He has worked as a lawyer, taught law and labor management at the University of San Francisco, worked as special assistant to the attorney general, partnered in a law firm, been the CEO of National Amusements Inc. since 1967, served as founder and trustee for several charitable organizations, and taught law at the Boston University Law School. His awards include Graduate of the Year from the Boston Latin School (1989), Pioneer of the Year from the Motion Picture Pioneers (1991), and an honorary Doctor of Laws degree from Boston University (1994).

In the following selection, a shortened version of a speech he gave at Brandeis University on January 20, 1994, Redstone addresses how the visual media both mirror and mold American culture and highlight a future of exciting possibilities.

"The Visual Media: Mirror or Mold of American Culture?" is 1 about the escalating debate as to whether movies and television shape our society or simply reflect it. The question, of course, is simplistic, indeed inaccurate. It is not an either/or proposition. Both are obviously true.

And then, of course, were we to have the intellectual capacity and 2 insight needed to address the question's implications in the proper proportions, what would we do about it? Would we have a Czar of Violence? How about a Czar of Sex?

In our effort to shield, particularly the young, from violence, who 3 would decide what was good violence and bad violence? According to Senator Hollings, "violence and sex translate into profits and market share. It's the corporate bottom line." He does a disservice, I submit, to those of us in the corporate world who simply want to do the right thing and who believe in the doctrine that there is a course to human events, and that disciplined, well-motivated human beings can make a difference. But, as *The New York Times* observed recently, we cannot even agree on which violence children should not see. Should we ban the violence in *Roots;* in *Lonesome Dove;* and in *The War of the Roses?* Does it matter if the movie is *Glory* or *Gettysburg,* or if it is *Nightmare on Elm Street?* Should we ban any program or film with any violence whether it has artistic value or potential social benefit at hours when most adults are available to watch television?

Perhaps Justice Powell said it best in an opinion written 17 years 4 ago when he stated, "Speech that is neither obscene as to youths nor subject to some other legitimate prescription cannot be suppressed solely to protect the young from ideas or images that a legislative body thinks unsuitable for them." To some it may seem unfortunate, but the depiction of violence is contained in many of the great works of literature and film.

The debate as to the effect or non-effect of movies and television 5 on our society; how we deal with the subject matter and how we, society, respond to the question, is all the more profound in its implications because we are indeed, today, at the frontier of an impending revolution in telecommunications—a massive revolution, a global revolution in the dissemination of information and entertainment and visual images—a revolution that is escalating at a wild pace and has already changed and will continue to change the behavioral and social customs of the world's population. And while we cannot determine the exact course and parameters of the explosion in telecommunications, we can discern some of its direction and forecast with certainty that the world of telecommunications will be vastly different than it is today, vastly more pervasive, vastly more powerful in its capacity to affect the culture, not only of America, but of the world.

Many thoughtful people took exception to James Dean's portrayal 6 of the alienated teenager in the 1955 film *Rebel Without a Cause* for its presumed affect on American youth and the rise of juvenile delinquency. No less thoughtful people are attributing to movies and television the cause of the current explosion of violence among young people. They may have a point. There may be an effect. I wish I had the power to exclude the wrong kind of violence from the wrong people at the wrong time, but if I were that omnipotent, I think that I could more easily deal with the control of guns, the need for education, the removal of the root causes of violence in our society, and the need for parental control. I concede that this also is simplistic, but clearly more to the point.

That the power of the media is pervasive is one of the few sim- 7 plistics not subject to debate. Clearly, few would argue that movies and television are not omnipresent in our popular culture. Just look at the numbers: the average American household watches approximately 49 hours of TV weekly; the average American movie-goer attends between five and six movies per year; more than two-thirds of all TV households own VCRs and those homes rent on average between 18 and 19 videocassettes annually. And the business world, cognizant of the influence of TV on the consumer, spent about $29 billion in 1992 on television advertising—including approximately $2 billion in cable network advertising buys.

Nor is it easy to shield oneself from the influence of the visual 8 media; 98 percent of Americans own TV sets—close to two-thirds own two or more sets, and there are more than 25,000 movie theaters across the country.

The pervasive nature of movies and television is not in question. 9 What is less clear is the extent to which the visual media simply mirror our attitudes and behavior, or shape our culture.

Movie genres often seem to reflect the times in which they were 10 popular. Comedies and musicals reigned at the box office during the Great Depression. War films predominated during the 1940s; *Easy Rider, The Graduate,* and *Alice's Restaurant* typified the counterculture of the 1960s and early 1970s. And today we're witnessing an increase in family features as "baby-boomers" become parents.

Conversely, certain movies have been identified for their role in 11 starting trends and shaping cultural attitudes. Arnold Schwartzenegger's *Pumping Iron* introduced mainstream America to body-building. Film students have held up D.W. Griffith's *Birth of a Nation* as a benchmark for exploiting and expanding racism in our culture. Contemporary films, like Oliver Stone's *JFK,* have been criticized by those who fear its vivid interpretation of history will be substituted by some people for historical truth.

Television is no less immune to the debate. Self-appointed censors 12 have routinely attacked the networks for espousing the morals and philosophies of the "Hollywood" and "East Coast" elite. Those under such attack have responded that they merely reflect society—rather than create cultural values.

Of course, neither is telling the truth. Certainly not the whole truth 13 and nothing but the truth, for they have their own agendas.

The truth does lie somewhere in between. A 1991 study, *Watching* 14 *America,* by Robert and Linda Lichter and Stanley Rothman, concludes that television programs do tend to reflect the lifestyles and viewpoints in our culture—but that mirror is typically held up to the East and West Coast urban centers, where most television producers, directors, and writers live. It may not necessarily reflect the values of other parts of the country and smaller cities and rural areas.

The Lichter/Rothman study also suggests that television's eager- 15
ness to tackle controversy has made TV entertainment a more significant part of the trend-making machine. Indeed, 30 years ago, television,
in fact, avoided controversy but the result was that its content lagged
behind social trends.

One thing seems clear. The power to shape the culture becomes 16
awesome when the media can successfully create a special bond with its
audience. Because of the bond that MTV has with the young adult, it
was able by its "choose or lose" campaign to motivate hundreds and
hundreds of thousands of young adults who had given up on the political process, to register as voters and rejoin the system upon which
this country is founded, and probably affect, to some extent, the
presidential election.

Please indulge me if I often use MTV as a reference point, but I 17
understand it better than any of the other networks, as I should, and
I particularly understand it in the context of shaping rather than mir-
roring our culture and the culture of the world.

You have only to consider the impact movies and TV have had on 18
fashion to concede that the visual media is more than a mirror. What
Shirley Temple did for curls and Diane Keaton's Annie Hall character
did for ties and vests, Sean Connery's "007" did for the white dinner
jacket and Steven Segal has done for ponytails. In New Delhi today, certain tailors dress the mannequins in their store windows each afternoon
depending on the outfits worn the prior evening by MTV's veejays!

MTV represents a particularly strong case for the ability of the 19
visual media to influence our culture. From its revolutionary development 12 years ago, MTV provided a 24-hour environment for the
"new" and "experimental" in art and music. MTV did not follow the
linear television programming model. Rather than define itself in a narrative sense, MTV introduced a new form of television based on sensate
impressions.

The network's development has had a profound impact on the way 20
pop music is produced and marketed. MTV's on-air look has become a
genuine reference point for graphic artists the world over. The quick-
paced, rapid edit style of MTV's programming has become a trademark.
The language of "image/word/idea" developed at MTV has become
a language adopted by advertisers, politicians, and other media to effectively communicate with their audiences.

MTV has earned this reputation for trend-setting, in part, because 21
trends that go through our culture are most likely to originate with the

same group—young adults 18-34 years of age—which provide the core audience for MTV.

Most significantly, the special relationship which MTV has fostered 22 with its target audience has put the network in a unique position in terms of pro-social activities. Because MTV communicates with young people in their language, on their terms, and in a way that shows respect for them as individuals and for their generation as a whole, it can more easily, with more relevance, and with a greater likelihood of success, reach its viewers on important social issues. But we have also learned that the young adult population of America cannot be preached to— cannot, nor should not, be preached to.

I am a lucky guy. I run a company that, for the most part, is peopled 23 with human beings who are compassionate and decent and truly want to make a difference, people who believe, I hope not naively, that they have an opportunity to affect the course of human events for the better. The world, no doubt in exaggerated form, has credited our company with having an extraordinary reach into the minds and hearts of children and young adults. And when I witness our efforts to utilize that strength and power responsibly, to educate and inform those whom we reach for the better, it makes me proud to be a part of the company and makes me feel better about myself. This may sound maudlin, but it is true.

The visual media will continue to both reflect these new times and 24 serve as a catalyst for cultural change. Television, movies, and the multimedia promises of the future are only segments of the complex process that define our culture. And, whatever its effect on society, it is the world population's right to entertainment and information that must be vigilantly protected as the revolution in telecommunications proceeds on its global path.

QUESTIONS ON SUBJECT

1. What objection does Redstone have to censoring violence and sex on television?

2. What promise does the author see in the future of telecommunications?

3. According to the author, how has television made a positive impact on the lives of 18-34 year olds?

4. How does Redstone differentiate between "good violence" and "bad violence"? Do you believe that there is good violence? Explain.

5. What proof does Redstone present to show that the visual media both mirror and mold American culture?

QUESTIONS ON STRATEGY

1. What is Redstone's point in this essay? What is he arguing for?

2. Paragraph 2 is composed of three questions. How do these questions function in the context of Redstone's essay? What, in your opinion, is his intent in mentioning a Czar of Violence and a Czar of Sex? Explain.

3. One sign of a weak argument is the degree to which opponents are able to take issue with and raise questions about the examples an author cites. Examine this essay with an eye for playing devil's advocate. How well do the author's examples hold up to scrutiny? Do you find anything vague in the author's optimistic view of television?

4. Reread paragraph 23. What purpose does this paragraph serve within this argumentative essay? What pertinent information does the author present?

5. Redstone is quick to criticize the subjective assessments of entertainment industry critics. How objective is his own assessment of the industry and its leaders?

6. Redstone presents a question in his title. Does he answer it to your satisfaction or does he answer it in the manner you might expect an industry representative to answer it? Explain.

7. The author admits his bias toward MTV and uses several examples from MTV. How well do you think these examples speak for the whole spectrum of programs available through the visual media? (Glossary: *Illustration*)

QUESTIONS ON LANGUAGE

1. Give examples that show how the author's diction reflects the optimism he feels for the future of television and global communications.

2. Refer to your desk dictionary to determine the meanings of the following words as they are used in this selection: *dissemination* (paragraph 5), *parameters* (5), *took exception* (6), *cognizant* (7), *pervasive* (9), *espousing* (12), *linear* (19), *sensate* (19), *maudlin* (23).

WRITING SUGGESTIONS

1. One critic writes, "a generation continually entertained, exposed to decontextualized information, and firm in its belief in the right to be entertained will not have the capacity for critical analysis." Write an essay responding to this statement.

2. The 1991 television study *Watching America* concluded that "television programs do tend to reflect the lifestyles and viewpoints in our culture." How well does television reflect your lifestyle? Write an essay in which you compare your lifestyle with characters your age on television.

3. The author writes that "the young adult population of America cannot be preached to—cannot, nor should not, be preached to." Conversely, critics of MTV might argue that the very same "language of 'image/word/idea' developed at MTV" that Redstone praises, ensures that young people will not take an interest in issues unless they are presented as entertainment. Write an essay in which you address these two conflicting opinions.

Violence Is Us

ROBERT SCHEER

Robert Scheer, a contributing editor for the Los Angeles Times *and nonfiction writer, was born on April 14, 1936, in New York City. He received his B.A. from City College of New York in 1958, and did graduate work at Syracuse University and then at the University of California, Berkeley. After a four-year stint as managing editor of* Ramparts, *he became the editor-in-chief of this radical journal in 1969. His second book,* How the U.S. Got Involved in Vietnam, *was adapted for the magazine's first exposé. A Marxist, Scheer ran for Congress as an antiwar candidate in 1965 and in 1970 as a Peace and Freedom candidate for the Senate. He has authored* America After Nixon: The Age of Multinationals *(1974),* With Enough Shovels: Reagan, Bush, and Nuclear War *(1982), and* Thinking Tuna Fish, Talking Death: Essays on the Pornography of Power—*a book of essays on the Vietnam War.*

In the following selection, first published in the November 15, 1994, issue of The Nation, *Scheer hints at the complications of a legal attack on television violence. He asks his readers to consider simply eschewing violent programming and supporting good television.*

Once again Congressional committees are holding hearings on TV 1
violence, and network executives, sincere visages firmly in place, are
promising to clean up their act. Attorney General Janet Reno testified
that if they don't, "government should respond."

There is something so beside the point about this handwringing, 2
which has gone on since 1952, when the first Congressional hearing on
TV violence was held. In 1968 a national commission headed by Milton
Eisenhower warned: "We are deeply troubled by the television's constant portrayal of violence . . . in pandering to a public preoccupation
with violence that television itself has helped to generate."

Of course, violence and base stupidity on TV and in the movies is 3
excessive and getting worse. With the proliferation of cable channels,
the market has become much more competitive, and violence sells.
Hardly a night of channel-flipping goes by when my cable service

doesn't offer up several truly grotesque chainsaw massacre–type films complete with dismembered parts and spurting blood.

Then, too, there are the cleaner assassinations presented on the 4 networks both in their entertainment and local news hours. Remember the orgy of voyeurism, with three separate network movies devoted to the Amy Fisher–Joey Buttafuoco story? So-called news shows featuring real-life crime represent a major segment of entertainment scheduling. The fatal graveside shooting of a woman by her ex-spouse, captured by a television news camera, was gratuitously "teased" during the evening in many markets to get people to watch the news that night.

Nor do I deny the claims of most experts that viewing violence de- 5 sensitizes people, particularly children, to the actual effects of violence, leaving them more likely to act out in antisocial ways. As the American Psychological Association reported to Congress in 1988, "Virtually all independent scholars agree that there is evidence that television can cause aggressive behavior."

More than 200 major studies support the common-sense suspicion 6 that watching endless hours of violence is a public health menace. Those same studies demonstrate, although the pro-censorship prudes will never accept it, that the violent R-rated movies—not the sexually explicit X-rated ones—desensitize men to sexual violence. (As an example of this weirdly skewed double standard, wannabe censor Rev. Donald Wildmon took out full-page ads attacking *NYPD Blue,* not for its explicit violence—six homicides in the first episode—but rather because of a nude lovemaking scene, calling it "soft-core pornography.")

Another thing those studies show is that the poorer a family is, 7 meaning the more vulnerable and desperate, the more hours they will spend in front of the television set. Children in poverty are most often left alone with the TV as the only available babysitter.

It can hardly be a good thing that children's shows two years ago 8 reached an all-time high of thirty-two violent incidents per hour and that nine in ten children's programs involve violence. An authoritative study by George Gerbner of the University of Pennsylvania indicated that the average 16-year-old has witnessed 200,000 violent acts on TV, including 33,000 murders. Given the ease with which children can get guns in this society, there has to be some connection between the ease with which citizens are blown away by teenagers on television and in what passes for real life. And when they do it in real life they can be assured of their fifteen minutes of fame with top billing on the nightly local news.

Wayne LaPierre, vice president of the National Rifle Association, 9 had a good point when he complained recently, "It galls us that every night we get lectured by ABC, NBC and CBS News, and then they go to their entertainment programming and show all kinds of gratuitous violence." Hypocrites they are, and the voluntary labeling code that the network executives recently adopted in an effort to head off Congressional prohibitions on violent programming will change nothing. Although 72 percent of Americans polled by Times-Mirror say that we have too much violence on TV and it leads to higher crime rates, many of them must be tuning in, or the television moguls wouldn't be scheduling such fare.

Maybe it is time to face the fact that we have all this mayhem in our 10 art and our lives because we like violence. Or if we don't actually like it, we need it. Why else would we favor local news programs that stress ambulance-chasing "action news"? Whether it's local or foreign news, our attention is grabbed completely only when death and destruction are at hand. That's what the endless focus groups conducted by news organizations report. It is true, as Steven Bochco, creator of *NYPD Blue,* has stated, that the violence issue on prime time is a "bogus issue," because "there's more violence on the 5 o'clock news than anything you'll see on the networks during prime time."

Anyway, how can you control it without putting decision-making 11 into the hands of small-minded censors? What are the guidelines? Some reasonable ones, to cut the harmful effects on children, were suggested by University of Michigan psychology professor Leonard Eron, who is the dean of research in this area. "Gratuitous violence that is not necessary to the plot should be reduced or eliminated," is one that the networks say they accept. Another we can all agree on is that the "devastating effects of violence, the permanence of its consequences . . . should be made clear," meaning you hurt or die from gunshot wounds. So far so good, but what about when he tells us, "Perpetrators of violence should not be rewarded for their violent acts," and that "those who act aggressively should be punished"? Those last two, while admirable goals, would distort a reality in which many criminals do get away with their crimes. Do we want television writers to lie to us? Don't we adults need to face up to the truth that crime is out of control?

Maybe adults should watch what they want, but should children, 12 who are by definition impressionable, be exposed to a steady diet of mind-numbing violence laced with general stupidity? No, they shouldn't, but is this an issue the government or other would-be censors ought to get involved with?

The answer is, They are already involved, but despite endless guide- 13 lines for children's television, the fare is nastier than ever. The reason is that every regulation produces just that much more ingenuity on the part of the so-called creative people who make this junk. They are a crafty bunch and will always find some way of getting to the kids with the most primitive jolt.

Take the much-discussed *Beavis and Butt-Head* show, which now 14 leads the race for the lowest common denominator. When a 5-year-old in Ohio burned the family trailer to the ground, his mother blamed the show, her son's favorite, which had shown the two idiot characters setting fire to all sorts of objects. Hey, no problem, arson was taken out of the show in response to public outrage. There were the expected calls to ban *Beavis*, but no one stopped to ask the obvious question: Why had that mother let her 5-year-old watch endless hours of this repulsive show?

I asked the same question after reading a story in the *Los Angeles* 15 *Times* about firefighters having to visit the schools of Orange County, California, to warn the kids that setting fires at home is a no-no. In one class, almost all the 12-year-olds said they watched *Beavis and Butt-Head* regularly and then began chanting the call of the show's lead, "Burn, burn, burn." That was in the conservative white upper-middle-class community of Mission Viejo, one of those planned paradises. Again, why did all those parents allow their kids to watch the show? It is absurd to suggest that the government step in to censor viewing that parents have acquiesced in.

The more important question is, Why do the children of paradise 16 delight in this and other stupidities? I don't really know the full answer but it can't be, as Dan Quayle charged in the last election, that the cultural elite of Hollywood has seized their minds. Orange County voted overwhelmingly for Quayle and his running mate, the parents have thrown up the strongest defenses against Satan and his permissiveness, and church, Little League and Boy Scout attendance is very high.

One answer provided by the creators of this stuff is that it doesn't 17 mean a thing. Kids have always tuned in to cartoons and movies in which characters are splattered or blown away. They concede that things are a bit wilder now, with far more blood and gore and nastier images, but that's modern technology for you. The demand is there and the supply will follow, but no harm is done—it's just a picture.

I don't buy this argument, because the impact of television and 18 movies is too pervasive to be so easily dismissed. For many kids the electronic picture is their world, the result of an ever more technically effective medium having drowned out all other avenues of learning and stimulation.

It does desensitize and, yes, I don't think young kids should be 19 watching *Beavis and Butt-Head* scenes featuring a poke in the eye with a pencil with blood spurting out, or a dog thrown into a washing machine followed by an insane giggle of approval. I doubt very much that *Beavis* creator Mike Judge will allow his little girls to watch the show.

But "we," collectively, can't and should not do anything about it. 20 We can't because we live in a market economy in which blood lust and other primitive needs of people will be met one way or another, and trying to ban something just makes it more attractive and marketable. We shouldn't because it is the adults' right to flick on whatever they want on the increasingly responsive cable smorgasbord. And it is parents' responsibility to monitor what kids watch. The "we" as represented by the state should do nothing.

The alternative is for the public, or rather some segment of it, to 21 demand something better on at least a few of the many channels that are opening up. There are plenty of good television programs and movies that aim higher and do well at the box office. Since the market is master, people need not be passive about expressing their tastes. Where I live, for example, people have demanded successfully that the cable company carry the excellent Bravo channel, which it was threatening to drop.

"In the final analysis, it is still the law of supply and demand on all 22 this stuff," says Norman Lear, whose *All in the Family* series first upped the ante for thoughtful prime-time programming. "It goes back to the advertisers; they are the people who pay for this stuff. If they didn't want it, it wouldn't be there. They are just dealing with product. They know from experience that something hard and outrageous will sell faster than something soft.

"It's no secret that there's a lot of baseness to human nature, but 23 we don't always pander to it, and reasonable people don't wish to pander to it. But there is nothing reasonable about the bottom line and about needing to please Wall Street by the quarter—to find the instant rating successes that satisfy the bottom line.

"The network goes to someone to make a pilot, then they take it 24 to Madison Avenue, and people look at it and say, 'That's a fucking hit.' They're the first people to look at it and say, 'I want in. I will spend my millions of dollars here because I think it will rate.'"

He adds that because no single sponsor is identified with a show, as 25 was the case in the "Golden Age" of the *Philco Playhouse* and the *Alcoa Hour,* "no sponsor is seriously associated with the quality of the show."

That's what happened with *Beavis and Butt-Head*—its creator, 26 Judge, had originally prepared it as a one-time entry for a festival of "sick and twisted" cartoons. He had no intention of turning his one-liner into a series, but MTV execs saw it and ordered up thirty-five episodes, and soon it was a multinational operation with teams of animators in New York and Korea frantically turning the stuff out.

The MTV execs were right. The demand was there. It's MTV's 27 hottest show, and sixty-five more episodes are on the way for 1994 and worldwide distribution. If you don't like that because you think it represents the dumbing-down of American and world culture, then vote—by just turning the damn thing off. Don't beg Big Brother to do it for you.

QUESTIONS ON SUBJECT

1. How does Scheer observe "action news" chasing higher ratings? In Scheer's opinion, what image of reality do these programs create?
2. What is the "weirdly skewed double standard" of R and X-ratings?
3. What relationship have studies shown between poverty and television? What implications do you see in this conclusion?
4. Why does Scheer call the three major networks hypocrites?
5. Why doesn't the author think the networks' decision to impose labeling upon themselves will have an impact on TV violence?
6. Which recommendations for censoring TV violence does the author endorse? Why? Which ones does he criticize?
7. How do advertisers escape accountability for the content of programming?

QUESTIONS ON STRATEGY

1. What is the author's thesis and where does he state it? (Glossary: *Thesis*)
2. What use does the author make of the information from hundreds of studies which links television violence and real-life violence? How is this material related to his thesis? Explain.
3. Scheer encourages his reader to reevaluate his or her relationship with television. Does this essay make you think? Does it make you uncomfortable? Comment on the author's level of success in creating interest in this subject and persuading you to his point of view.
4. Reread paragraphs 22 through 24 in which the author quotes Norman Lear. Do you think that this quotation precipitates despair on this issue, or encourages a realistic course of action? Explain.
5. Scheer makes extensive use of the *Beavis and Butt-Head* example in his essay. How does this example serve to further his argument? (Glossary: *Illustration*)

QUESTIONS ON LANGUAGE

1. Scheer plays with the language of problem-solving on an issue that, as he demonstrates in a quotation from an early commission on TV violence, seems locked in its own dialectic. Using examples from the text, comment on his use of irony. (Glossary: *Irony*)

2. How would you characterize Scheer's diction in this essay—formal or informal? Did you find his diction appropriate in terms of his subject and audience? Explain.

3. Comment on Scheer's use of the pronoun "we" in paragraph 20.

4. Refer to your desk dictionary to determine the meanings of the following words as they are used in this selection: *visages* (paragraph 1), *pander* (2 and 23), *base* (3), *voyeurism* (4), *gratuitous* (4, 9, and 11), *galls* (9), *moguls* (9), *fare* (13), *acquiesced* (15).

WRITING SUGGESTIONS

1. Do you believe that the goal of providing clear, pertinent information has been sacrificed by the "action news" programs the author writes about? How do you define what news is pertinent? What would you consider an ideal news program? Write an essay in which you address these questions.

2. Scheer raises many of the same problems as Barbara Hattemer does in her essay "Cause and Violent Effect: Media and Our Youth." Both authors stress the cardinal importance of the individual adult's actions, but they disagree on censorship. Write an essay in which you compare the views of these two authors on television censorship, and offer your own view on the subject.

Cause and Violent Effect:
Media and Our Youth

BARBARA HATTEMER

Nonfiction writer and founder and president of the National Family Foundation, Barbara Hattemer studies the effects of the media on individuals and families. Her articles have appeared in Yankee Magazine, Guideposts, *and* Parents Magazine.

In the following selection, first published in the July 1994 issue of The World and I, *Hattemer drew heavily from material in her book,* Don't Touch That Dial: The Impact of the Media on Children and the Family *(1993). She points to several studies demonstrating the link between television violence and real-life violence, and argues that the vigilance of individuals will always have more effect than labeling.*

Recent headlines proclaim increasing youth violence: "Four Teen- 1 agers Charged in Murder of Tourist," "Pupils Told to Run for Their Lives—Teacher Describes Terror in Classroom," "FSU Student Murdered, Sister Raped—Eighteen-year-old Beaten to Death, Sister Tied to Tree in Ocala National Forest."

Youth crime is on everyone's mind. It is the focus of virtually every 2 political campaign of 1994. There is talk of boot camps, stricter laws, trying children as adults for committing serious crimes, larger prisons, harsher sentences, gun control, curfews. Take the kids off the streets so we can feel safe again! Keep them home! Why? So they can watch more murder and rape on television and video?

How weary we have grown of the statistics on how many murders 3 every high school graduate has seen. According to the American Psychological Association, even before leaving elementary school, the average child has seen eight thousand murders and one hundred thousand acts of violence on television.

Social science, clinical concepts, and common sense all agree that 4 what children watch affects who they become, what they believe, what they value, and how they behave.

EARLY INFLUENCE OF TV

Television's influence on our children starts earlier than most of us 5 realize. Andrew Meltzoff found that fourteen-month-old infants can watch an unfamiliar toy being dismantled and reassembled on television and repeat the actions twenty-four hours later. Even at this early age, television acts as a guide to real-life behavior. Throughout childhood, children learn by imitating what they see others doing.

Two- to six-year-old children cannot evaluate the messages they 6 receive from the media they watch. They simply accept what they see as normal behavior. Children cannot tell the difference between reality and fantasy until the fifth or sixth grade. Six- to twelve-year-olds imitate what they see and hear without fully understanding the consequences of what they are doing. Most adolescents do not have a fully developed, internal set of morals and values. They accept the conduct they see in the media as the social norm and integrate it into their own behavior patterns.

What are the predominant messages of television, movies, and other 7 media that our children are accepting and imitating? That violence is an everyday occurrence and an acceptable way of solving problems and that promiscuous sex is normal and expected of everyone, including younger and younger children. These two messages merge as the philosophy of pornography, once thought to be limited to sleazy adult bookstores and out-of-the-way art cinemas, has been mainstreamed. The rape myth—that women secretly want to be raped and that they enjoy forced sex—has so permeated our children's minds that 65 percent of boys and 47 percent of girls agreed with a survey question that "it was acceptable for a man to force sex with a woman if he had been dating her more than six months."

While television has unlimited potential for good, at the present 8 time its influence on children's lives is largely negative. Television programming, according to Dr. Paul Howard, prominent Boston psychiatrist, is so hostile and aggressive it produces tremendous anxiety in young watchers. "One weekend of children watching television," he declared, "undoes a whole week of psychotherapy for my young patients."

Television and violence have been almost synonymous since tele- 9 vision became a part of nearly every home. As far back as 1977, 9 of every 10 TV programs contained violence. Today, while there is more variety, there are more sources of violence than ever before. In addition to violent action-adventure movies and television dramas, violence pervades music videos, rap songs, documentaries, commercials, and news broadcasts. The networks provide up to 10 violent acts per hour; cable, up to 18 violent acts per hour; and children's cartoons, 32 violent acts per hour. Movies like *Teenage Mutant Ninja Turtles* raise the count to 133 violent acts per hour. The body count is rising, too: *Total Recall*, 74 dead; *Robocop 2*, 81 dead; *Rambo III*, 106 dead; and *Die Hard 2*, 264 dead.

Mass-produced, cheap industrial violence is something quite new 10
in our culture. The new heroes glamorize violence for its own sake. The
violence is the story, not an element necessary to the telling of a story.
Add to this the influence of violent video games and fantasy games that
encourage children to spend hours planning how to kill or maim more
successfully. Mix in violent comic books and serial-killer trading cards,
and you have a culture that gives its children a steady diet of violent role
models but very little old-fashioned nurture and direction from parents.

VIOLENT YOUTH

For nearly a decade, judges and police officers have been exclaim- 11
ing that they have never before seen rapists and murderers who are so
young. The news, in its promotion of the sensation, keeps the tragic
headlines ever before us. What some feared might one day happen is
indeed happening. The subculture that has long been singing about
beating up women, killing parents, and murdering for fun has surfaced.

One-half of the sex offenders in this country are now under the age 12
of eighteen! A 1988 Michigan crime report stated that 681 juveniles
who averaged fourteen years of age were convicted of sexually assaulting children who averaged seven years of age. These are not always violent or deeply troubled children; they are children who have been
exposed too early to material they cannot process without imitating.
They see it on cable in their own homes, they hear it on the telephone.
Dial-a-porn companies have admitted that 75 to 85 percent of their
customers are children. Overstimulated by what they see and hear, they
act it out on younger siblings or playmates.

Violent crime is up 560 percent since 1960 and is rising. There are 13
three million incidents of school crime every year. In 1993 alone, the
rate of violent encounters in schools rose 34 percent in the state of
Florida. Rape, assault, and murder have replaced chewing gum, talking
in class, and throwing wads of paper, the greatest school problems in
the forties. From 1987 to 1991, teenagers arrested for murder increased 85 percent. In 1990, 4,200 teenagers were killed by guns. In
New York City, one in five teenagers carries a weapon to school, and
one in twenty, a gun. On any one day, 135,000 children carry guns to
school across the nation.

It is said that we have always been a violent society, but there is a 14
new callousness among our young people. Many studies have found
that using pornography increases men's callousness toward and distrust
of women, as well as their inclination to rape. Research also has revealed

that 100 percent of our high schoolers have seen soft-core pornography, and 90 percent of high school boys and 80 percent of girls have seen hard-core pornography. The younger they are when they see it, the more likely they are to want to imitate it.

Horror movies aimed at young teens desensitize them to violence 15 and create an ever-increasing appetite for it. If the camera angle allows the child to see the action through the eyes of the madman, a subtle shift takes place. He identifies not with the passive victim but with the active perpetrator. In his imagination, it is the child himself who wields the knife, the ax, or the deadly weapon. Identifying with the aggressor, he senses the thrill of momentary power over another and learns to enjoy committing a crime.

Park Dietz declares that exposing boys to films showing women 16 being mutilated in the midst of sex scenes is the best way to raise a generation of sexual sadists. One study found that Freddy of *Nightmare on Elm Street* and Jason of *Friday the 13th* are better known to ten- to thirteen-year-olds than Abraham Lincoln and George Washington. Seven- to twelve-year-olds name horror movies as their favorites and say they like seeing people killed and enjoy watching pain and torture. Freddy is the star of not only a series of movies, but a television series, comic book, 900 number, toys, and trading cards. The mayor of Los Angeles named a holiday for him. We are teaching our children to look to mass murderers as their role models.

Film critic Roger Ebert sees a basic change taking place in society 17 regarding women in danger. The sympathy of the audience has moved from the woman to the killer. As the camera takes the killer's point of view, the lust to kill is placed, not in the character of the killer, but in the audience.

Too often, that audience is full of impressionable children. They 18 can buy a ticket to any G or PG film and often slip into R-rated films in a mall complex. (They laugh when asked if they have trouble getting to see R-rated movies, and producers boast that if they make the movies, children will find a way to see them.) At video stores and libraries, even the pretense of restricting children from R-rated movies is gone. With the notable exception of Blockbuster video stores, there is no age restriction for obtaining violent movies.

REAL-LIFE AGGRESSION

No one today doubts that our children are seeing massive amounts 19 of violence in a wide variety of media presentations. Moreover, a vast amount of scientific research proves that watching violence on the screen is causally related to real-life aggression. Since the 1968 National Commission on the Causes and Prevention of Violence, a series of government commissions and reports and a consensus of medical associations have all found a link between screen violence and violent behavior.

The television and motion picture industries have been successful 20 in casting doubt on such findings by saying that some studies show an effect and others do not, but the studies that show the fewest effects have been sponsored by the industry. We now have over three thousand studies telling us that watching violent films increases violent behavior. Research has found that preschool children who frequently watch violent cartoons behave aggressively. First-graders who watch aggressive cartoons exhibit more hostile behavior in school than first-graders who watch neutral programming or even a football game. Because the impact is greater the more realistic the violent scenes are, researchers fear the more realistic human characters in today's cartoons may have an even greater influence on children.

Leonard Eron and Rowell Huesman conducted an important 21 longitudinal study, following eight-year-olds for twenty-two years. They found that children who watched large amounts of violent television at age eight were more likely to be engaged in criminal behavior at age thirty. Not only did they commit serious crimes, they also punished their children more harshly and were much more aggressive when drinking.

Studies before and after the introduction of television in an area 22 reveal an increase in aggressive behavior after the arrival of television. Two years after television was introduced into Notel, Canada, physical aggression among children increased 160 percent.

A study by Brandon Centerwall focused on the effects of childhood 23 exposure to television violence on adult criminal behavior in larger populations, comparing the effect of television on the roughly comparable white populations of the United States, Canada, and South Africa. Fifteen years after television was introduced into the United States and Canada, white homicide deaths had risen 93 percent and 92 percent, respectively. At the same time, in South Africa, where there was no TV, the white homicide rate had dropped 7 percent. Yet, eight years after South Africa received TV, the rate had already increased 56 percent, indicating that, in fifteen years, it would be close to that of the United States and Canada. In fact, by 1987, twelve years after television had been introduced into South Africa, the white homicide rate had risen by 130 percent.

Centerwall looked for every possible alternative explanation, com-   24
pleting another eleven studies on factors such as the baby boom, urban-
ization, economic trends, alcohol consumption, capital punishment,
civil unrest, and the availability of firearms, but he could find none. He
ruled out such factors as the U.S. civil rights movement and the Vietnam War because these did not affect Canada. He concluded that exposure to violent programming on television is causally related to
roughly one-half the twenty thousand yearly homicides in the United
States and one-half the rapes and assaults as well.

His conclusions held up when he looked at populations within the   25
United States that acquired television at different times. When television appeared in the early 1950s, it was an expensive luxury. Since
blacks tended to lag behind whites by about five years in acquiring
television sets, he predicted that the white homicide rate would rise
before the black homicide rate in the United States. In fact, the white
homicide rate began to rise in 1958, while the black homicide rate
dropped consistently throughout the next four years. Similarly, those
regions of the United States like New York and New Jersey that acquired television before other sections of the country were also found
to have an earlier increase in the homicide rate.

Centerwall believes that the lag of ten to fifteen years between the   26
introduction of television and the rise in the homicide rate indicates
that the greatest effect is on children under the age of twelve. In the
past, it took these children ten to fifteen years to grow up before they
were old enough to commit homicide. Today, however, children are
not waiting to become adults to begin committing adult crimes. Youth
crime is growing at a much faster rate than adult crime. The past ten
years have seen an increase of 55 percent in the number of children arrested for murder. Centerwall explains this as the snowballing
effect. The first generation raised on television learned values from the
adults in their lives as well as from the TV set. With the increasing dominance of the media in society, the passing on of values from the older
generation has diminished, while the second and third generations
raised on TV have increasingly taken their values from the media
culture.

LETHAL VIOLENCE

The increase in the seriousness of juvenile crime may be explained   27
further by the fact that violence has become increasingly graphic and

gory. According to journalist David Barry, the juvenile delinquency portrayed in 1950s movies "consisted almost entirely of assaults with fists and weapons which left victims injured, but alive. It was nonlethal violence. The notion of American teenagers as killers was beyond the threshold of credibility."

Since then, he says, the level of criminal violence reported in 28 everyday news stories has become almost unrecognizable. He offers the following statistics as evidence of the effect of the first twenty-nine years of television on crime in the United States. In 1951, there were 6,820 murders, 16,800 rapes, and 52,090 robberies. By 1980, these had increased to 23,000 murders, 78,920 rapes, and 548,220 robberies—vastly more than the 47 percent population increase from 150 million to 220 million. The murder rate is increasing six times faster than the rate of population growth. It is now the leading cause of death for black youths and the second leading cause of death of all fifteen- to twenty-four-year-olds. Violence is the leading cause of injury to fifteen- to forty-four-year-old women. The U.S. Centers for Disease Control calls it both a leading public health issue and an epidemic.

Researchers offer numerous explanations of how and why media 29 violence translates into real-life violence. They theorize that when a child observes violence used as a means of solving conflicts, the event is recorded in his brain and stored in his memory bank. This scene can be reinforced by subsequent violent scenes, which eventually blend into a general script of how to react to conflict. The more graphic the violence, the more likely it will catch the child's attention and become part of a script stored in his memory, waiting to be retrieved when he faces a similar conflict situation in real life.

Older children are particularly responsive to violence that is realistic 30 or close to their personal experience and thus seems likely to happen in real life. Younger children are more likely to identify with and imitate violent behavior if the character is attractively portrayed. The more that children of all ages identify with a violent character, the more likely they are to be aggressive themselves.

Watching violence primes the pump and starts a network of asso- 31 ciations. As media violence is absorbed into a person's thoughts, it activates related aggressive ideas and emotions that eventually lead to aggressive behavior. What a child observes as the associative networks in his brain are developing is of paramount importance.

Violence that is rewarded or left unpunished appears to be sanc- 32 tioned in a child's mind. It is, therefore, much more likely to be imitated. Violence that appears to be justified or portrayed as necessary for a good cause is even more likely to be imitated. One reason the large amount of violence in Japanese films does not produce as much real-life violence as in the United States is the way that Japanese films portray violence, highlighting the pain, suffering, and tragic consequences that follow. They teach an altogether different lesson than America's glamorized violence.

Not everyone reacts the same way to violence. Poorly nurtured 33 children with few inner strengths and without internalized boundaries are more susceptible to its influence than well-nurtured children who have received a strong value system from their parents. Children who are undersupplied with parental love are often angry and chaotic inside. They are drawn to violent films, heavy metal music, and gangster rap because it reflects their inner turmoil. It both reinforces and offers approval for their negative attitudes. The combination of being undersupplied with parental nurture and overstimulated by violent media can be deadly.

VIOLENCE IN MUSIC

In 1989, the American Medical Association concluded that music 34 is an even greater influence on teens than television. This is because they have more exposure to heavy metal music than to either pornography or horror films. MTV has introduced a whole generation of children to songs that glorify pleasure seeking and irresponsibility. Its videos contain thirteen violent acts per hour, and four out of five of them mix violence with sex.

Rock stars are always available to young people starving for atten- 35 tion and understanding. They offer children unqualified acceptance. They appear to meet their needs and understand their chaotic emotions better than their parents. Prolonged listening to hard-rock music correlates with many negatives, from the mildly troubling to the very serious: increasing discomfort in family situations, a preference for friends over family, poor academic performance, increased chemical dependency, violence, stealing, and sexual activity. It makes disturbed adolescents feel powerful and in charge.

There is a strong relationship between antisocial or destructive 36 behavior and listening to rock music with destructive themes. The preference for heavy metal music among juvenile delinquents is almost three times as high as among the general population of high schoolers. This music is filling our children's heads with rebellion, raw sex, violence, and a hatred and abuse of women of a degree never seen before. . . .

Newsweek speaks of the ability of rap music to alienate, of its 37 imagery and lyrics as "pure confrontation." It educates our children on the crime and rage of inner-city life and fills their heads with rebellion, hate, and more raw sex. While the courts rule in favor of hateful speech, our culture struggles with how to deal with entertainment that spews hatred into children's minds.

THE FAMILY ANTIDOTE

Research has found that the best defense against the media is a 38 strong family that makes an effort to impart values and gives children clear boundaries. Youths from families with well-defined value systems use them to interpret what they observe. Teenagers from homes in which family members communicate openly and engage in an active viewing style, discussing programs with their children, are less influenced by what they see.

Violent programming has a greater impact on boys than on girls, a 39 greater impact on young men who are already callous than on those who are sensitive, and a greater impact on those from the inner city who experience violence in their daily lives. The latter, by their own admission, are more aroused by filmed violence, give it higher approval ratings, and watch more of it. With thousands of violent models stored in their memories and more aggressive associations implanted in their minds, why are we surprised when they react violently to real-life situations?

The entertainment industry could help our troubled children by 40 cutting back on the number of violent portrayals, by making them less graphic and attention-getting, and by emphasizing the sorrowful consequences of violence rather than glamorizing and making heroes of violent men.

A possible solution is granting the Federal Communications Com- 41 mission the power to include excessive violence in the broadcasting standard that limits indecency and obscenity on radio and television. Government censorship cannot raise the moral tone of the nation. A better answer is the return to standards and voluntary limits. Nothing shows so clearly how far we have fallen as a nation from the values we once agreed upon than a look at the old Motion Picture Production Code [see p. 250], in force from 1930 to 1966, which stated:

> Motion picture producers recognize the high trust and confidence which have been placed in them by the people of the world. . . . They recognize their responsibility to the public because of this trust and because entertainment and art are important influences in the life of the nation.

But a code should apply to television, cable, and satellite as well. Government hearings and citizen complaints could serve to pressure the industry to consider an updated and revised code for all its products.

For this to become a reality, citizens must demand a better balance 42 between creative freedom and social responsibility, between anything for a profit and serving the public interest. The industry must stop the "Can you top this!" mentality, which makes each sequel more graphic and gory than the one before. We must become more discriminating viewers and stop watching violent programs. We must enter into dialogue with the industry, thanking studios and networks for every good offering and supporting them at the box office and in the ratings races. We must support the sponsors of good programs and protest irresponsible companies at stockholders' meetings.

A return to standards is a better solution than labels. Parental 43 advisories give permission to label and then go ahead and produce even more violent material. We need to recapture the essence of the old motion picture code, which declared that "there is no real substitute for successful self-government in industry" and that "self-regulation is wholly consonant with freedom of expression."

QUESTIONS ON SUBJECT

1. What relationship does Hattemer delineate between television and the cognitive abilities of children?

2. According to the author, what characterizes the violence and heroes children see on television and in movies?

3. In Hattemer's opinion, how have horror movies encouraged children to identify with the aggressor?

4. Hattemer writes, "Not everyone reacts the same way to violence." What explanation does she offer for this occurrence?

5. How does the study by Brandon Centerwall account for the rise in children arrested for murder in the past ten years?

6. What action does the author advocate to combat violence in the media, and why does she find parental advisory labeling futile?

QUESTIONS ON STRATEGY

1. What is Hattemer's thesis, and where is it stated? (Glossary: *Thesis*)
2. How has Hattemer organized her essay? What function do her headings serve within this organizational pattern? (Glossary: *Organization*)
3. Consider the various ways in which Hattemer makes transitions from one paragraph to the next. (Glossary: *Transitions*) What do these transitions add to her essay?
4. Who is Hattemer addressing in this essay? (Glossary: *Audience*) Do you see the author's examples as aimed at this audience? Explain.
5. Which of the author's examples do you find most convincing in this essay? What do you think makes these examples so persuasive? (Glossary: *Illustration*)
6. Explain how the author uses cause and effect analysis to enhance her argumentative essay. (Glossary: *Cause and Effect Analysis*)

QUESTIONS ON LANGUAGE

1. What is Hattemer's attitude toward violence in the media, and how is this attitude reflected in her diction? Cite specific examples to support your answer.
2. How would you characterize Hattemer's tone in this essay? (Glossary: *Tone*)
3. Refer to your desk dictionary to determine the meanings of the following words as they are used in this selection: *permeated* (paragraph 7), *pervades* (9), *callousness* (14), *perpetrator* (15), *moreover* (19), *causally* (19 and 24), *longitudinal* (21), *paramount* (31), *sanctioned* (32), *spews* (37), *discriminating* (42), *consonant* (43).

WRITING SUGGESTIONS

1. According to Hattemer, television and popular music send the message "that violence is an everyday occurrence and an acceptable way of solving problems and that promiscuous sex is normal and expected of everyone, including younger and younger children." Write an essay in which you either support or contest Hattemer's opinion.
2. Hattemer believes that television has unlimited potential for good although nothing in her examples seems to suggest this potential. What potential do you see for television? Given that so much of the criticism of television centers around children imitating bad examples shown on TV, do you think that television can, at its best, encourage critical analysis or do

you find that it encourages passivity regardless of the programming? Write an essay addressing these questions.

3. Hattemer writes, "MTV has introduced a whole generation of children to songs that glorify pleasure seeking and irresponsibility." Write an essay comparing Hattemer's opinion with that of Sumner M. Redstone as expressed in his essay "The Visual Media: Mirror or Mold of American Culture?"

WRITING SUGGESTIONS FOR ARGUMENTATION

1. Think of a product that you like and want to use even though it has an annoying feature. Write a letter of complaint in which you attempt to persuade the manufacturer to improve the product. Your letter should include the following points:

   a. a statement concerning the nature of the problem
   b. evidence supporting or explaining your complaint
   c. suggestions for improving the product

2. Select one of the position statements that follow, and write an argumentative essay in which you defend that statement:

   a. Living in a dormitory is (*or* is not) as attractive as living off-campus.
   b. Grain sales should (*or* should not) be used as a political weapon.
   c. Student government shows (*or* does not show) that the democratic process is effective.
   d. America should (*or* should not) be a refuge for the oppressed.
   e. School spirit is (*or* is not) as important as it ever was.
   f. Interest in religion is (*or* is not) increasing in the United States.
   g. We have (*or* have not) brought air pollution under control in the United States.
   h. The need to develop alternative energy sources is (*or* is not) serious.
   i. America's great cities are (*or* are not) thriving.
   j. Fraternities and sororities do (*or* do not) build character.
   k. We have (*or* have not) found effective means to dispose of nuclear or chemical wastes.
   l. Fair play is (*or* is not) a thing of the past.
   m. Human life is (*or* is not) valued in a technological society.
   n. The consumer does (*or* does not) need to be protected.
   o. The family farm in America is (*or* is not) in danger of extinction.
   p. Grades do (*or* do not) encourage learning.
   q. America is (*or* is not) a violent society.
   r. Television is (*or* is not) a positive cultural force in America.
   s. America should (*or* should not) feel a commitment to the starving peoples of the world.
   t. The federal government should (*or* should not) regulate all utilities.
   u. Money is (*or* is not) the path to happiness.
   v. Animals do (*or* do not) have rights.
   w. Competition is (*or* is not) killing us.
   x. America is (*or* is not) becoming a society with deteriorating values.

10
COMBINING
STRATEGIES

WHAT IS COMBINING STRATEGIES?

Previous chapters in *Subject and Strategy* emphasize a specific rhetorical mode or writing strategy—narration, description, illustration, process analysis, and so forth. The essays we have selected within each of those chapters use the given mode or strategy as the dominant method of development. It is important to remember, however, that the dominant method is usually not the only one used to develop an essay. To reinforce this point, after each essay in *Subject and Strategy* we have asked specific questions about the author's use of other developmental strategies. For example, in Paul Roberts's "How to Say Nothing in 500 Words," an essay demonstrating process analysis, we ask a question about illustration: "Roberts's writing style is clearly well-suited to his student audience. How would you describe his writing style? What are some of the ways he uses humor, diction, and illustration to make the process analyses easy to follow? (Glossary: *Diction; Illustration*)" In Marie Winn's "Television and Family Life," a cause and effect essay, we ask a question about definition: "Before talking about the effects of television on family rituals, Winn offers several sociological definitions of *ritual*. Why do you suppose she thought it necessary to define the term? (Glossary: *Definition*)" Although some essays are developed through the use of a single mode, it is more the norm in good writing that writers take advantage of several of the strategies available to them, using whatever means of development will further their purpose and thesis to produce an essay that is informative, persuasive, and interesting.

READING A COMBINATION OF STRATEGIES IN AN ANNOTATED STUDENT ESSAY

In reading the work of other writers you can learn how multiple strategies can be used to your advantage in your own writing—how a paragraph of narration, a passage of description, a clarifying point of comparison and contrast, or the helpful definition of a key word or concept can vary the terrain of an essay, contribute to its interest level, and answer a reader's need to comprehend your purpose and thesis.

The first step in analyzing an essay for its use of rhetorical modes is to identify what appears to be the essay's dominant mode. Simply, what approach is most in evidence? To what has the writer devoted the most time or space? For example, is the writer clearly telling a story, describing a process, looking into the causes of a particular event or action? Next, you will want to look at what the writer does when not using the dominant strategy. If you are familiar with the various rhetorical strategies, and you should be by the time you turn to this chapter, this will be an easy and, in fact, enjoyable exercise.

The writers of the essays in this chapter each approach their subjects with a wide variety of modes: Joan Didion, while narrating the story of going home to her family, uses definition, description, and comparison and contrast to come to a better understanding of herself. Henry Louis Gates Jr. argues for a sensible approach to multiculturalism and in the process uses definition, comparison and contrast, and illustrative examples as developmental strategies. Similarly, Annie Dillard in "Living Like Weasels" narrates a story about a weasel but then goes on to use comparison and contrast, as well as description, a mode of development for which she has become widely known as a writer. Finally, in her "When Language Dies: 1993 Nobel Prize for Literature Lecture," Toni Morrison argues against any efforts, conscious or subconscious, that tend to diminish the importance of language and in favor of our recognition of the power of language to create and to enter into the mysteries of our lives. Morrison, by narrating a story and by providing various illustrations of the point the story makes uses a mixture of rhetorical modes that enhances her argument and actually puts before her readers the very power of language of which she speaks.

Just as you have found with all the essays in *Subject and Strategy*, reading and analyzing how writers work will lead you to a greater understanding of your own writing. Not only will you find that you have in the modes useful tools for development, but also the means to sharpen and make more effective the strategies that are already a natural part of your writing process.

Tara Ketch, a senior English major at the University of Vermont, took a Children's Literature course and was asked to write a term paper on some aspect of the literature she was studying. She knew that she would soon be looking for a teaching position and realized that any teaching job she accepted would bring her face-to-face with the difficult task of selecting appropriate reading materials. Ketch understood, as well, that she would have to confront criticism of her choices, so she decided to delve a little deeper into the subject of censorship, particularly as it related to children's and adolescent literature. She was interested in learning more about why people want to censor certain books and what her response to those efforts would be. In a way, she wanted to begin to develop her own teaching philosophy with respect to text selection. Her essay naturally involved several rhetorical modes working in combination: definition, cause and effect, illustration, and argumentation. As you read her essay, notice how naturally she has used these rhetorical strategies in combination to develop her ideas about censorship and teaching.

KIDS, YOU CAN'T READ THAT BOOK!
Tara E. Ketch

Definition of censorship and censors' activities

Censorship is the restriction or suppression of speech or writing that is thought to have a negative influence. In the case of children's and adolescent literature these censors are very often school officials, parents, or adults in the community who wish to monitor and influence what children are reading. For

Cause and effect: Pressure is put on school boards and questions are raised

whatever reason, they are saying, "Kids, you can't read that book; it is not fit for your eyes." To ensure that these books do not end up in the schools, pressure groups influence school boards not to purchase them, or restrict their use if they have already been

Argumentation: Who will decide how to deal with censorship issues?

purchased. Such actions present serious questions for educators. Who will decide what materials are fit for American school children? The federal government has set limits on censorship and encouraged local

1

communities to make educational decisions. In the
1968 case of <u>Epperson v. Arkansas,</u> the Supreme
Court stated, "Public education in our nation is committed to the control of state and local authorities.
Courts do not and cannot intervene in the resolution
of conflicts which arise in the daily operation of
school systems and which do not directly and sharply
implicate basic constitutional values" (Reichman 3).
In 1982, the Supreme Court ruled that, "Local school
boards may not remove books from school library
shelves simply because they dislike the ideas contained in those books and seek by their removal to
prescribe what shall be orthodox in politics, nationalism, religion, or other matters of opinion (Reichman

3). These two rulings contradict each other. The outcome is that children's books continue to be banned
in school systems for many reasons.

One important reason books are banned is family 2
values. The censor may attack a book because it goes
against his or her personal values. For example, it
may contain "offensive" language. Most problems
with books seem to come out of the author's use of

language. This is especially true of adolescent literature. In a list of the most frequently banned books in
the 1990's, J.D. Salinger's <u>Catcher in the Rye</u> took the
number three slot because of objections to its language. A parent found words such as <u>hell</u>, <u>Chrissakes</u>,
<u>bastard</u>, <u>damn</u>, and <u>crap</u> to be unacceptable (Foerstel
147). The fear was that such language was being con-
doned by the school when such a book was taught. In
a debate about Katherine Paterson's <u>Bridge to Ter-
abithia</u>, a woman protested the use of the words
<u>snotty</u> and <u>shut up</u> along with <u>Lord</u> and <u>damn</u>. She
said, "Freedom of speech was not intended to guaran-
tee schools the right to intrude on traditional family

values without warning and regardless of the availability of non-offensive alternatives" (Reichman 38).
The school board in this case decided that the book
had a value that transcended the use of the few offen-

sive words. That a book has redeeming value is the primary argument against such censorship. If we ignore all books that contain profanity, we are missing out on a lot of valuable literature.

Cause and effect: Second reason why children's and adolescent books are banned is presented

Illustration: Violence in fairy tales is presented

Other people hold dear the value that children   3 should not be exposed to anything depressing or violent. Not surprisingly, several communities have tried to get certain fairy tales banned because they are violent in nature. Jack and the Beanstalk and Little Red Riding Hood came under attack for this reason. In both cases the books were kept in the school system (Burress 283–91). The argument against their removal involved the fact that the violence was tied to fantasy. It was not in the child's everyday realm and therefore not threatening. Judy Blume's Blubber has been ques-

Illustration: Unhappy characters in literature is presented

tioned for its portrayal of unhappy child characters. Some parents refuse to recognize the fact that not all children have a happy and carefree existence. Judy Blume has her own ideas about childhood that she uses as an attack against such censorship. She argues,

Argumentation: Counter-argument by Judy Blume is presented

"Children have little control over their lives, and this causes both anger and unhappiness. Childhood can be a terrible time of life. No kid wants to stay a kid . . . the fantasy of childhood is to be an adult" (West 12).

Illustration: Death of child character is presented

Bridge to Terabithia has also been seen as a harsh portrayal of life because it deals with the death of a child. Some parents want to shelter their children from the reality of death. Others find that a book such as Bridge to Terabithia is a natural way for children to be exposed to that sensitive topic.

Cause and effect: Third reason why children's and adolescent books are banned is presented

Illustration: Sexuality topic is presented

Another family value that comes into play in cen-   4 sorship is the idea that children should be protected from sexuality. Maurice Sendak's In the Night Kitchen shows a naked little boy, and, although there is no sexual connotation, many people were incensed by the book. In New York, in 1990, parents tried to have the book removed from an elementary school. In Maine, a parent wanted the book removed because she felt it encouraged child molestation (Foerstel

201). Many of Judy Blume's books have also come under fire for their portrayal of sexual themes in adolescence. Are You There God? It's Me, Margaret has been blacklisted for its frank discussion of menstruation and adolescent development. Forever is even worse to some because it mentions intercourse and abortion.

Cause and Effect: Explanation of reasons for banning books with sexuality as topics is presented

As topics of discussion, these subjects are alien to many adults who grew up in environments where sex was not talked about; therefore, they try to perpetuate the cycle of silence by keeping these kinds of books from children. They may also worry that these books will encourage sexual activity. This fear extends to textbooks that educate children and adolescents about their bodies and sexual reproduction. Many try to ban gay and lesbian literature because they feel that homosexuality is obscene and that books about these subjects might encourage homosexual behavior and lifestyles.

Illustration: Books that discuss gay and lesbian lifestyles

All American Boys was donated to a California high school but when administrators realized that it discussed homosexuality, the book was seized and then "lost" (Reichman 43). Alyson Wonderland Publications has also published two children's books to explain the gay lifestyle to children: Michael Willhoite's Daddy's Roommate and Leslea Newman's Heather Has Two Mommies. These, not surprisingly, have met with a lot of opposition.

Cause and effect: The fourth reason why children's and adolescent books are banned is presented

Often there are religious concerns as well. Religion is in many cases the foundation for people's moral beliefs. Censorship of books because of their language, violence, and sexuality happens as much in the name of religion as family values. Religion is also used as an issue in censorship for other reasons. Some people want the Bible when used as literature

Illustration: Books that have been banned for religious reasons

banned from classrooms. Not only does teaching the Bible as literature present a problem for parents who want the Bible focused on as sacred material, but it is equally offensive to people who feel that religious documents should be kept out of the classroom (Burress 219). Sometimes religious considerations take the

5

form of censorship of books that in any way involve the occult. The picture book <u>Witches, Pumpkins, and Grinning Ghosts</u> was considered inappropriate because it "interests little minds into accepting the Devil with all his evil works" (Reichman 51). Ironically, "witches" sought the banning of <u>Hansel and Gretel</u> because it portrayed their religion in a negative light (Reichman 50). Greek and Roman mythology has also been attacked by religious groups because it discusses gods other than the Christian one. Christians also fought to ban books on evolution that called into question their religious beliefs.

Cause and effect: The fifth reason that children's and adolescent books are banned is presented

Yet another reason for the censorship of children's books is concern over racism and sexism. Minority groups have often made efforts to combat stereotypes and racial prejudices through censorship. The idea is that if children are exposed to sexism and racism in books, they will learn it. Mark Twain's <u>The Adventures of Huckleberry Finn</u> is a good example of a text that has been banned because of its racist language. The use of the term <u>nigger</u> has offended many African Americans. The problem with this criticism is that the novel was not examined for its intention, which was to question the racist attitude of the South. Twain was not a racist. Nevertheless, <u>Huckleberry Finn</u> has become one of the most frequently banned books in the United States. Women have also tried to censor nursery rhymes and children's stories that reinforce negative images of women. Some have argued in opposition that to remove all books that are sexist and racist would be to remove a piece of our history that we can learn from.

6

Illustration: Books that have been banned for racial reasons

Counter-argument is presented

Argumentation regarding gender bias

Counter-argument is presented

Central Question is raised: Should we censor children's books? Answers are given.

With this brief background and a review of some of the reasons used to ban children's books, how might the question "Should we censor children's books?" be answered? On the one hand, we should realize that there are age-appropriate themes for children. For example, elementary school children should not be exposed to the ideas of rape and abortion that

7

occur in some young adult novels. Young adults should not be exposed to extremely violent novels like Anthony Burgess's A Clockwork Orange, which they may not understand at such a young age. Does this mean these books should be removed from school libraries? Perhaps not. Libraries should be resources for children to broaden their horizons. If a child independently seeks out a controversial novel, the child should not be stopped from doing so. Exposure to a rich diversity of works is always advisable. A good way to decide if a book should be taught is if its message speaks to the children. What if this message is couched in profanity? If it is in a character representation, kids can understand the context without feeling compelled to emulate the behavior. If children are constantly exposed to books that throw reality in their faces in a violent way, then their attitudes will reflect it. So, it is the job of educators to present different types of materials to balance the children's exposure.

Argumentation: The author provides various criteria for making decisions about what is appropriate reading for children. Discussion of these criteria generally follows the author's sequencing of the discussion of the reasons why people attempt to censor children's and adolescent books.

As far as sexuality goes, it's fine for libraries to include children's books that focus on this subject if the objective is to educate or make transitions easier for the child. Religion, however, should not be focused on in the classroom because it causes too much conflict for different groups. This does not mean that religious works should be banned from school libraries. Children should have access to different religious materials to explore world religions and various belief systems. Lastly, if sexism and racism appear in books, those books should not automatically be banned. They can be useful tools for increasing understanding in our society. 8

Argumentation: Concluding statement calls for understanding and sensitivity in dealing with censorship and book selection for children and adolescents

The efforts to censor what our children are reading can turn into potentially explosive situations and cause a great deal of misunderstanding and hurt feelings within our schools and communities. If we can gain an understanding of the major reasons why people have sought to censor what our kids are reading, we will be better prepared to respond to those 9 efforts in a sensitive and reasonable manner. More importantly, we will be able to provide the best educational opportunity for our children through a sensible approach, one that neither overly restricts the range of their reading nor allows them to read any and all books no matter how inappropriate they might be for them.

Works Cited

Burress, Lee. Battle of the Books: Literary Censorship in the Public Schools, 1950–1985. New Jersey: Scarecrow, 1989.

Foerstel, Herbert. Banned in the U.S.A.: A Reference Guide to Book Censorship in Schools and Public Libraries. London: Greenwood, 1994.

Reichman, Henry. Censorship and Selection: Issues and Answers to Schools. Chicago: American Library Association, 1993.

West, Mark. Trust Your Children: Voices against Censorship in Children's Literature. London: Neal-Schuman, 1988.

WRITING AN ESSAY COMBINING STRATEGIES

Let's suppose you wanted to write an essay focusing on the college slang you have heard being used around you on campus. Depending on your purpose and your thesis, you might want to use definition to explain what slang is, illustration to give examples of it, comparison and contrast to separate slang from other types of speech, such as dialects and jargon, and perhaps division and classification to sort out the different types of slang you find or the different areas of campus life where you find slang used. Or, to give another example, let's say you wanted to write a paper on the injustice done to Japanese Americans who were sent to internment camps during World War II. You would naturally want to use illustration to recall several particular cases of families who were sent to the camps and narration if you were fortunate enough to interview some former camp inhabitants and have them recount their experiences. Your essay might also lead you into a closer examination of the reasons why all of this happened in the first place, in which case you would need to use cause and effect analysis, as well as argumentative reasoning. In short, you will need to have at your disposal the means, the strategic rhetorical devices, to accomplish whatever demands the purpose and thesis you establish for your essay make on you as a writer.

If you rely on a single mode or approach to an essay, you lose the opportunity to come at your subject from a variety of angles, any one of which might be the most insightful or engaging and, therefore, the most memorable for your reader. Perhaps no where is this more true than with essays that attempt to argue or persuade your reader. So strong is the need, and so difficult the task, of changing readers' beliefs and thoughts and of persuading readers to a particular action that you must use a combination of strategies to develop your subjects.

On Going Home

JOAN DIDION

Essayist, novelist, short story writer, and journalist, Joan Didion was born in Sacramento, California, in 1934 and educated at the University of California at Berkeley. Before moving to New York she wrote often on aspects of life in California and the West. She has written for a wide spectrum of magazines, from Mademoiselle, *to the* National Review, *and her essays have been collected in* Slouching toward Bethlehem *and* The White Album. *Her novels include* Run River, Play It As It Lays, *and* A Book of Common Prayer. *Her most recent book is a collection of essays,* After Henry.*

As you read Didion's narrative about going home at the time of her daughter's first birthday, pay particular attention to the way she uses definition, comparison and contrast, and description to better understand herself and her place within her larger family.

I am home for my daughter's first birthday. By "home" I do not 1
mean the house in Los Angeles where my husband and I and the baby live, but the place where my family is, in the Central Valley of California. It is a vital although troublesome distinction. My husband likes my family but is uneasy in their house, because once there I fall into their ways, which are difficult, oblique, deliberately inarticulate, not my husband's ways. We live in dusty houses ("D-U-S-T," he once wrote with his finger on surfaces all over the house, but no one noticed it) filled with mementos quite without value to him (what could the Canton dessert plates mean to him? how could he have known about the assay scales, why should he care if he did know?), and we appear to talk exclusively about people we know who have been committed to mental hospitals, about people we know who have been booked on drunk-driving charges, and about property, particularly about property, land, price per acre, and C-2 zoning and assessments and freeway access. My brother does not understand my husband's inability to perceive the advantage in the rather common real-estate transaction known as "sale-leaseback," and my husband in turn does not understand why so many of the people he hears about in my father's house have recently been committed to mental hospitals or booked on drunk-driving charges.

Nor does he understand that when we talk about sale-leasebacks and right-of-way condemnations we are talking in code about the things we like best, the yellow fields and the cottonwoods and the rivers rising and falling and the mountain roads closing when the heavy snow comes in. We miss each other's points, have another drink and regard the fire. My brother refers to my husband, in his presence, as "Joan's husband." Marriage is the classic betrayal.

Or perhaps it is not any more. Sometimes I think that those of us 2 who are now in our thirties were born into the last generation to carry the burden of "home," to find in family life the source of all tension and drama. I had by all objective accounts a "normal" and a "happy" family situation, and yet I was almost thirty years old before I could talk to my family on the telephone without crying after I had hung up. We did not fight. Nothing was wrong. And yet some nameless anxiety colored the emotional charges between me and the place that I came from. The question of whether or not you could go home again was a very real part of the sentimental and largely literary baggage with which we left home in the fifties; I suspect that it is irrelevant to the children born of the fragmentation after World War II. A few weeks ago in a San Francisco bar I saw a pretty young girl on crystal take off her clothes and dance for the cash prize in an "amateur-topless" contest. There was no particular sense of moment about this, none of the effect of romantic degradation, of "dark journey," for which my generation strived so assiduously. What sense could that girl possibly make of, say, *Long Day's Journey into Night?* Who is beside the point?

That I am trapped in this particular irrelevancy is never more 3 apparent to me than when I am home. Paralyzed by the neurotic lassitude engendered by meeting one's past at every turn, around every corner, inside every cupboard, I go aimlessly from room to room. I decide to meet it head-on and clean out a drawer, and I spread the contents on the bed. A bathing suit I wore the summer I was seventeen. A letter of rejection from *The Nation,* an aerial photograph of the site for a shopping center my father did not build in 1954. Three teacups hand-painted with cabbage roses and signed "E.M.," my grandmother's initials. There is no final solution for letters of rejection from *The Nation* and teacups hand-painted in 1900. Nor is there any answer to snapshots of one's grandfather as a young man on skis, surveying around Donner Pass in the year 1910. I smooth out the snapshot and look into his face, and do and do not see my own. I close the drawer, and have another cup of coffee with my mother. We get along very well, veterans of a guerrilla war we never understood.

Days pass. I see no one. I come to dread my husband's evening call, 4
not only because he is full of news of what by now seems to me our
remote life in Los Angeles, people he has seen, letters which require
attention, but because he asks me what I have been doing, suggests
uneasily that I get out, drive to San Francisco or Berkeley. Instead I
drive across the river to a family graveyard. It has been vandalized since
my last visit and the monuments are broken, overturned in the dry
grass. Because I once saw a rattlesnake in the grass I stay in the car and
listen to a country-and-Western station. Later I drive with my father to
a ranch he has in the foothills. The man who runs his cattle on it asks
us to the roundup, a week from Sunday, and although I know that I will
be in Los Angeles I say, in the oblique way my family talks, that I will
come. Once home I mention the broken monuments in the graveyard.
My mother shrugs.

I go to visit my great-aunts. A few of them think now that I am my 5
cousin, or their daughter who died young. We recall an anecdote about
a relative last seen in 1948, and they ask if I still like living in New York
City. I have lived in Los Angeles for three years, but I say that I do. The
baby is offered a horehound drop, and I am slipped a dollar bill "to buy
a treat." Questions trail off, answers are abandoned, the baby plays with
the dust motes in a shaft of afternoon sun.

It is time for the baby's birthday party: a white cake, strawberry- 6
marshmallow ice cream, a bottle of champagne saved from another
party. In the evening, after she has gone to sleep, I kneel beside the crib
and touch her face, where it is pressed against the slats, with mine. She
is an open and trusting child, unprepared for and unaccustomed to the
ambushes of family life, and perhaps it is just as well that I can offer her
little of that life. I would like to give her more. I would like to promise
her that she will grow up with a sense of her cousins and of rivers and
of her great-grandmother's teacups, would like to pledge her a picnic
on a river with fried chicken and her hair uncombed, would like to give
her *home* for her birthday, but we live differently now and I can promise
her nothing like that. I give her a xylophone and a sundress from
Madeira, and promise to tell her a funny story.

QUESTIONS ON SUBJECT

1. What does Didion mean by *home?* In what ways is her house in Los Angeles
   different from her family's place in the Central Valley of California?

2. How does Didion feel about her home, the place where she grew up? In
   what ways is she of two minds about home?

3. Didion ends paragraph 1 with the statement, "Marriage is the classic betrayal." What do you think she means?

4. Eugene O'Neill's *Long Day's Journey into Night* is an autobiographical domestic tragedy that, as Didion correctly implies, finds "in family life the source of all tension and drama." Why do you suppose Didion thinks that the pretty young girl who dances in the "amateur-topless" contest would have difficulty making any sense of O'Neill's play? Explain.

5. Didion gave her daughter a xylophone and a sundress from Madeira for her birthday. What would she have really liked to give her? Why does Didion feel that she could not make a promise "like that"?

QUESTIONS ON STRATEGY

1. Good narrative tells when an action happened, where it happened, and to whom it happened. (Glossary: *Narration*) Where does Didion give us this information?

2. Why do you suppose Didion felt compelled to define *home* early on in her essay. (Glossary: *Definition*) What would have been lost had she not done so?

3. To what end does Didion use comparison and contrast in her opening paragraph? (Glossary: *Comparison and Contrast*) Does she use this strategy elsewhere in the essay? If so, where, and to what effect?

4. In paragraph 3, Didion carefully describes the contents of a drawer in her room. Why do you suppose she has chosen the details she has? How does this paragraph of description function in the context of her narrative essay? (Glossary: *Description*) Explain.

5. What does Didion mean when she says of her relationship with her mother, "We get along very well, veterans of a guerrilla war we never understood"? What descriptive details does Didion provide to "show" us that this is what their relationship is like instead of contenting herself to "tell" us?

QUESTIONS ON LANGUAGE

1. Didion talks about the "vital although troublesome distinction" between her "house" in Los Angeles and her "home" in the Central Valley. What for you are the distinctions between these two words. What are their denotations? Connotations? (Glossary: *Connotation/Denotation*)

2. Comment on the appropriateness of each of the following substitutes for Didion's diction. Which word is better in each case, and why? (Glossary: *Diction*)
   a. *important* for *vital* (1)
   b. *bothersome* for *troublesome* (1)
   c. *dirty* for *dusty* (1)

d. *heirlooms* for *mementos* (1)
e. *weight* for *burden* (2)
f. *uncertainty* for *fragmentation* (2)
g. *immobilized* for *paralyzed* (3)
h. *obscure* for *oblique* (1, 4)
i. *outing* for *picnic* (6)

3. Refer to your desk dictionary to determine the meanings of the following words as they are used in this selection: *inarticulate* (1), *objective* (2), *sentimental* (2), *degradation* (2), *lassitude* (3), *engendered* (3).

WRITING SUGGESTIONS

1. Drawing on your own experience of home life, write a brief narrative in which you explore your feelings about "going home." Like Didion, do you carry the "burden of 'home'" with you; do you find "family life the source of all tension and drama"? Whenever possible, use description and illustration to enhance your narrative.

2. In "On Going Home" Didion willingly accepts responsibility for her own life. She honestly confronts her feelings about her parents, her husband, her brother, her child, and the passage of time. In short, she displays character and self-understanding. Write an essay in which you develop your own definition of what it means to be an adult. Be watchful for opportunities to use illustration and comparison and contrast to enhance your definition.

Living Like Weasels

ANNIE DILLARD

Annie Dillard was born in Pittsburgh and attended Hollins College. A naturalist, poet, and journalist, Dillard has written Tickets for a Prayer Wheel, Holy the Firm, Teaching a Stone to Talk: Expeditions and Encounters, An American Childhood, A Writer's Life, *and* Encounters with Chinese Writers. *In 1974 she published* Pilgrim at Tinker Creek, *a fascinating collection of natural observations for which she was awarded the Pulitzer Prize for nonfiction.*

In "Living Like Weasels" Dillard narrates the story of a chance encounter with a weasel. Notice how in developing her essay she also makes use of description and comparison and contrast to give a feel for the weasel, the place where they met, and her reactions to the meeting.

A weasel is wild. Who knows what he thinks? He sleeps in his 1 underground den, his tail draped over his nose. Sometimes he lives in his den for two days without leaving. Outside, he stalks rabbits, mice, muskrats, and birds, killing more bodies than he can eat warm, and often dragging the carcasses home. Obedient to instinct, he bites his prey at the neck, either splitting the jugular vein at the throat or crunching the brain at the base of the skull, and he does not let go. One naturalist refused to kill a weasel who was socketed into his hand deeply as a rattlesnake. The man could in no way pry the tiny weasel off, and he had to walk half a mile to water, the weasel dangling from his palm, and soak him off like a stubborn label.

And once, says Ernest Thompson Seton—once, a man shot an 2 eagle out of the sky. He examined the eagle and found the dry skull of a weasel fixed by the jaws to his throat. The supposition is that the eagle had pounced on the weasel and the weasel swiveled and bit as instinct taught him, tooth to neck, and nearly won. I would like to have seen that eagle from the air a few weeks or months before he was shot: was the whole weasel still attached to his feathered throat, a fur pendant? Or did the eagle eat what he could reach, gutting the living weasel with his talons before his breast, bending his beak, cleaning the beautiful airborne bones?

I have been reading about weasels because I saw one last week. I [3] startled a weasel who startled me, and we exchanged a long glance.

Twenty minutes from my house, through the woods by the quarry [4] and across the highway, is Hollins Pond, a remarkable piece of shallowness, where I like to go at sunset and sit on a tree trunk. Hollins Pond is also called Murray's Pond; it covers two acres of bottomland near Tinker Creek with six inches of water and six thousand lily pads. In winter, brown-and-white steers stand in the middle of it, merely dampening their hooves; from the distant shore they look like miracle itself, complete with miracle's nonchalance. Now, in summer, the steers are gone. The water lilies have blossomed and spread to a green horizontal plane that is terra firma to plodding blackbirds, and tremulous ceiling to black leeches, crayfish, and carp.

This is, mind you, suburbia. It is a five-minute walk in three [5] directions to rows of houses, though none is visible here. There's a 55 mph highway at one end of the pond, and a nesting pair of wood ducks at the other. Under every bush is a muskrat hole or a beer can. The far end is an alternating series of fields and woods, fields and woods, threaded everywhere with motorcycle tracks—in whose bare clay wild turtles lay eggs.

So. I had crossed the highway, stepped over two low barbed-wire [6] fences, and traced the motorcycle path in all gratitude through the wild rose and poison ivy of the pond's shoreline up into high grassy fields. Then I cut down through the woods to the mossy fallen tree where I sit. This tree is excellent. It makes a dry, upholstered bench at the upper, marshy end of the pond, a plush jetty raised from the thorny shore between a shallow blue body of water and a deep blue body of sky.

The sun had just set. I was relaxed on the tree trunk, ensconced in [7] the lap of lichen, watching the lily pads at my feet tremble and part dreamily over the thrusting path of a carp. A yellow bird appeared to my right and flew behind me. It caught my eye; I swiveled around—and the next instant, inexplicably, I was looking down at a weasel, who was looking up at me.

Weasel! I'd never seen one wild before. He was ten inches long, [8] thin as a curve, a muscled ribbon, brown as fruitwood, soft-furred, alert. His face was fierce, small and pointed as a lizard's; he would have made a good arrowhead. There was just a dot of chin, maybe two brown hairs' worth, and then the pure white fur began that spread down his underside. He had two black eyes I didn't see, any more than you see a window.

The weasel was stunned into stillness as he was emerging from [9] beneath an enormous shaggy wild rose bush four feet away. I was stunned into stillness twisted backward on the tree trunk. Our eyes locked, and someone threw away the key.

Our look was as if two lovers, or deadly enemies, met unexpectedly 10 on an overgrown path when each had been thinking of something else: a clearing blow to the gut. It was also a bright blow to the brain, or a sudden beating of brains, with all the charge and intimate grate of rubbed balloons. It emptied our lungs. It felled the forest, moved the fields, and drained the pond; the world dismantled and tumbled into that black hole of eyes. If you and I looked at each other that way, our skulls would split and drop to our shoulders. But we don't. We keep our skulls. So.

He disappeared. This was only last week, and already I don't re- 11 member what shattered the enchantment. I think I blinked, I think I retrieved my brain from the weasel's brain, and tried to memorize what I was seeing, and the weasel felt the yank of separation, the careening splashdown into real life and the urgent current of instinct. He vanished under the wild rose. I waited motionless, my mind suddenly full of data and my spirit with pleadings, but he didn't return.

Please do not tell me about "approach-avoidance conflicts." I tell 12 you I've been in that weasel's brain for sixty seconds, and he was in mine. Brains are private places, muttering through unique and secret tapes—but the weasel and I both plugged into another tape simulta- neously, for a sweet and shocking time. Can I help it if it was a blank?

What goes on in his brain the rest of the time? What does a weasel 13 think about? He won't say. His journal is tracks in clay, a spray of feathers, mouse blood and bone: uncollected, unconnected, loose-leaf, and blown.

I would like to learn, or remember, how to live. I come to Hollins 14 Pond not so much to learn how to live as, frankly, to forget about it. That is, I don't think I can learn from a wild animal how to live in particular—shall I suck warm blood, hold my tail high, walk with my footprints precisely over the prints of my hands?—but I might learn something of mindlessness, something of the purity without bias or motive. The weasel lives in necessity and we live in choice, hating necessity and dying at the last ignobly in its talons. I would like to live as I should, as the weasel lives as he should. And I suspect that for me the way is like the weasel's: open to time and death painlessly, noticing everything, remembering nothing, choosing the given with a fierce and pointed will.

I missed my chance. I should have gone for the throat. I should 15 have lunged for that streak of white under the weasel's chin and held on, held on through mud and into the wild rose, held on for a dearer life. We could live under the wild rose wild as weasels, mute and uncomprehending. I could very calmly go wild. I could live two days in the den, curled, leaning on mouse fur, sniffing bird bones, blinking, licking, breathing musk, my hair tangled in the roots of grasses. Down is a good place to go, where the mind is single. Down is out, out of your ever-loving mind and back to your careless senses. I remember muteness as a prolonged and giddy fast, where every moment is a feast of utterance received. Time and events are merely poured, unremarked, and ingested directly, like blood pulsed into my gut through a jugular vein. Could two live that way? Could two live under the wild rose, and explore by the pond, so that the smooth mind of each is as everywhere present to the other, and as received and as unchallenged, as falling snow?

We could, you know. We can live any way we want. People take 16 vows of poverty, chastity, and obedience—even of silence—by choice. The thing is to stalk your calling in a certain skilled and supple way, to locate the most tender and live spot and plug into that pulse. This is yielding, not fighting. A weasel doesn't "attack" anything; a weasel lives as he's meant to, yielding at every moment to the perfect freedom of single necessity.

I think it would be well, and proper, and obedient, and pure, to 17 grasp your one necessity and not let it go, to dangle from it limp wherever it takes you. Then even death, where you're going no matter how you live, cannot you part. Seize it and let it seize you up aloft even, till your eyes burn out and drop; let your musky flesh fall off in shreds, and let your very bones unhinge and scatter, loosened over fields, over fields and woods, lightly, thoughtless, from any height at all, from as high as eagles.

QUESTIONS ON SUBJECT

1. Dillard begins her essay with two paragraphs about weasels. What dominant impression of the weasel does she create in these paragraphs? (Glossary: *Dominant Impression*) Is this impression developed later on in the essay?

2. Under what circumstances did Dillard encounter the weasel? Why was this meeting important for her? What does Dillard mean when she says, "I tell you I've been in that weasel's brain for sixty seconds, and he was in mine"?

3. If not about weasels, what then is Dillard's essay about? What does Dillard mean when she says, "The weasel lives in necessity and we live in choice, hating necessity and dying at the last ignobly in its talons"?

4. What for a weasel is its "single necessity"? According to Dillard, what is it that we can learn from weasels?

QUESTIONS ON STRATEGY

1. What is Dillard's purpose in writing this essay? (Glossary: *Purpose*)

2. The dominant strategy in this essay is narration. (Glossary: *Narration*) What exactly is the story being told?

3. One of Dillard's strengths as a writer is her power of description. (Glossary: *Description*) Because of her effective use of descriptive details readers are able to "see" what Dillard herself experienced. Identify several passages of description in this essay that you found particularly powerful. What is it about each passage that makes it so effective. In what ways do these passages of description enhance Dillard narrative?

4. In paragraph 10 Dillard compares her encounter with the weasel to the sudden meeting of "two lovers" or "deadly enemies." (Glossary: *Comparison and Contrast*) In what ways does this comparison give you a better understanding of what Dillard and the weasel felt when they met by the fallen tree near the marshy end of the pond?

QUESTIONS ON LANGUAGE

1. Identify several metaphors and similes in Dillard's essay, and explain how each one works in context. (Glossary: *Figures of Speech*)

2. Dillard likes to use strong action verbs in her writing. Circle the verbs in two or three of her paragraphs. What do the verbs have in common? Collectively, what do they add to her prose? Explain.

3. Refer to your desk dictionary to determine the meanings of the following words as they are used in this selection: *swiveled* (2), *nonchalance* (4), *jetty* (6), *musk* (15), and *supple* (16).

WRITING SUGGESTIONS

1. In her final paragraph Dillard says, "I think it would be well, and proper, and obedient, and pure, to grasp your one necessity and not let it go, to dangle from it limp wherever it takes you." What does this statement mean to you? What do you think is your "one necessity"? Do you find Dillard's conclusion realistic? Why, or why not? Write a brief essay in which you explore what lessons the weasel has for you.

2. Write an essay about a chance encounter that you have had with a creature in the wild—a spider, a snake, a colony of ants, or a baby bird that had fallen from its nest, for example. Why was the meeting significant for you? Like Dillard, did you have insights into how we might all live better as a result of your encounter?

The Debate Has Been Miscast from the Start
HENRY LOUIS GATES JR.

Winner of the American Book Award for his book The Signifying
Monkey and the Language of Signify(ing): Towards a Theory
of Afro-American Literary Criticism, *Henry Louis Gates Jr. is a
pre-eminent black scholar. Born in Keyser, West Virginia, and
educated at Yale and Cambridge, Gates went on to teach at
Yale, Cornell, Duke, and is now at Harvard University where he
is W. E. B. Du Bois Professor of Humanities. In 1994 Gates
published a widely acclaimed memoir,* Colored People.

*In his essay "The Debate Has Been Miscast from the Start,"
first published in the* Boston Globe Magazine *on October 13,
1991, Henry Louis Gates Jr. argues for a balanced equilibrium
of the opposing forces in the debate over multiculturalism. In
developing his argument, Gates uses definition to establish what
he means by multiculturalism, comparison and contrast to describe the proponents and antagonists of multiculturalism, and
illustration to support or document many of his general points.*

What is multiculturalism and why are they saying such terrible 1
things about it?

We've been told that it threatens to fragment American culture 2
into a warren of ethnic enclaves, each separate and inviolate. We've
been told that it menaces the Western tradition of literature and the
arts. We've been told that it aims to politicize the school curriculum,
replacing honest historical scholarship with a "feel good" syllabus
designed solely to bolster the self-esteem of minorities. The alarm has
been sounded, and many scholars and educators—liberals as well as
conservatives—have responded to it. After all, if multiculturalism is just
a pretty name for ethnic chauvinism, who needs it?

But I don't think that's what multiculturalism is—at least, I don't 3
think that's what it ought to be. And because the debate has been
miscast from the beginning, it may be worth setting the main issues
straight.

To both proponents and antagonists, multiculturalism represents— 4
either refreshingly or frighteningly—a radical departure. Like most claims
for cultural novelty, this one is more than a little exaggerated. For the
challenges of cultural pluralism—and the varied forms of official resistance to it—go back to the very founding of our republic.

In the university today, it must be admitted, the challenge has taken 5
on a peculiar inflection. But the underlying questions are time-tested.
What does it mean to be an American? Must academic inquiry be sub-
ordinated to the requirements of national identity? Should scholarship
and education reflect our actual diversity, or should they, rather, forge
a communal identity that may not yet have been achieved?

For answers, you can, of course, turn to the latest jeremiad on the 6
subject from, say, George Will, Dinesh D'Souza, or Roger Kimball. But
in fact these questions have always occasioned lively disagreement
among American educators. In 1917, William Henry Hulme decried
"the insidious introduction into our scholarly relations of the political
propaganda of a wholly narrow, selfish, and vicious nationalism and
false patriotism." His opponents were equally emphatic in their beliefs.
"More and more clearly," Fred Lewis Pattee ventured in 1919, "is it
seen now that the American soul, the American conception of democracy, Americanism, should be made prominent in our school curricu-
lums, as a guard against the rising spirit of experimental lawlessness."
Sound familiar?

Given the political nature of the debate over education and the 7
national interest, the conservative penchant for charging the multicul-
turalists with "politics" is a little perplexing. For conservative critics, to
their credit, have never hesitated to provide a political defense of what
they consider to be the "traditional" curriculum: The future of the
republic, they argue, depends on the inculcation of proper civic virtues.
What these virtues are is a matter of vehement dispute. But to imagine
a curriculum untouched by political concerns is to imagine—as no one
does—that education can take place in a vacuum.

So where's the beef? Granted, multiculturalism is no panacea for 8
our social ills. We're worried when Johnny can't read. We're worried
when Johnny can't add. But shouldn't we be worried, too, when
Johnny tramples gravestones in a Jewish cemetery or scrawls racial
epithets on a dormitory wall? And it's because we've entrusted our
schools with the fashioning of a democratic polity that education has
never been exempt from the kind of debate that marks every other aspect of American political life.

Perhaps this isn't altogether a bad thing. As the political theorist 9
Amy Gutmann has argued: "In a democracy, political disagreement is
not something that we should generally seek to avoid. Political controversies over our educational problems are a particularly important
source of social progress because they have the potential for educating
so many citizens."

And while I'm sympathetic to what Robert Nisbet once dubbed 10
the "academic dogma"—the ideal of knowledge for its own sake—I
also believe that truly humane learning, unblinkered by the constraints
of narrow ethnocentrism, can't help but expand the limits of human
understanding and social tolerance. Those who fear that "Balkaniza-
tion" and social fragmentation lie this way have got it exactly backward.
Ours is a world that already is fissured by nationality, ethnicity, race, and
gender. And the only way to transcend those divisions—to forge, for
once, a civic culture that respects both differences and commonali-
ties—is through education that seeks to comprehend the diversity of
human culture. Beyond the hype and the high-flown rhetoric is a pretty
homely truth: There is no tolerance without respect—and no respect
without knowledge.

The historical architects of the university always understood this. 11
As Cardinal Newman wrote more than a century ago, the university
should promote "the power of viewing many things at once as one
whole, of referring them severally to their true place in the universal
system, of understanding their respective values, and determining their
mutual dependence." In just this vein, the critic Edward Said has
recently suggested that "our model for academic freedom should
therefore be the migrant or traveler: for if, in the real world outside the
academy, we must needs be ourselves and only ourselves, inside the
academy we should be able to discover and travel among other selves,
other identities, other varieties of the human adventure. But, most
essentially, in this joint discovery of self and other, it is the role of the
academy to transform what might be conflict, or context, or assertion
into reconciliation, mutuality, recognition, creative interaction."

But if multiculturalism represents the culmination of an age-old 12
ideal—the dream known in the seventeenth century, as *mathesis uni-
versalis*—why has it been the target of such ferocious attacks? On this
point, I'm often reminded of a wonderfully wicked piece of nineteenth-
century student doggerel about Benjamin Jowett, the great Victorian
classicist and master of Balliol College, Oxford:

> Here stand I, my name is Jowett,
> If there's knowledge, then I know it;
> I am the master of this college,
> What I know not, is not knowledge.

Of course, the question of how we determine what is worth 13
knowing is now being raised with uncomfortable persistence. So that in
the most spirited attacks on multiculturalism in the academy today,

there's a nostalgic whiff of the old sentiment: We are the masters of this college; what we know not is not knowledge.

I think this explains the conservative desire to cast the debate in 14 terms of the West vs. the Rest. And yet that's the very opposition that the pluralist wants to challenge. Pluralism sees cultures as porous, dynamic, and interactive, rather than the fixed property of particular ethnic groups. Thus the idea of a monolithic, homogenous "West" itself comes into question (nothing new here: Literary historians have pointed out that the very concept of "Western culture" may date back only to the eighteenth century). But rather than mourning the loss of some putative ancestral purity, we can recognize what's valuable, resilient, even cohesive, in the hybrid and variegated nature of our modernity.

Genuine multiculturalism is not, of course, everyone's cup of tea. 15 Vulgar cultural nationalists—like Allan Bloom or Leonard Jeffries—correctly identify it as the enemy. These polemicists thrive on absolute partitions: between "civilization" and "barbarism," between "black" and "white," between a thousand versions of Us and Them. But they are whistling in the wind.

For whatever the outcome of the culture wars in the academy, the 16 world we live in is multicultural already. Mixing and hybridity is the rule, not the exception. As a student of African-American culture, of course, I've come to take this kind of cultural palimpsest for granted. Duke Ellington, Miles Davis, John Coltrane have influenced popular musicians the world over. Wynton Marsalis is as comfortable with Mozart as he is with jazz; Anthony Davis writes operas in a musical idiom that combines Bartok with the blues.

In dance, Judith Jamison, Alvin Ailey, Katherine Dunham all 17 excelled at "Western" cultural forms, melding these with African-American styles to produce performances that were neither, and both. In painting, Romare Bearden and Jacob Lawrence, Martin Puryear and Augusta Savage learned to paint and sculpt by studying Western masters, yet each has pioneered the construction of a distinctly African-American visual art.

And in literature, of course, the most formally complex and com- 18 pelling black writers—such as Jean Toomer, Sterling Brown, Langston Hughes, Zora Hurston, Richard Wright, Ralph Ellison, James Baldwin, and Gwendolyn Brooks—have always blended forms of Western literature with African-American vernacular and written traditions. Then, again, even a vernacular form such as the spiritual took for its texts the King James version of the Old and New Testaments. Toni Morrison's master's thesis was on Virginia Woolf and Faulkner; Rita Dove is as comfortable with German literature as she is with the blues.

Indeed, the greatest African-American art can be thought of as an 19
exploration of that hyphenated space between the African and the
American. As James Baldwin once reflected during his long European
sojourn, "I would have to appropriate these white centuries, I would
have to make them mine. I would have to accept my special attitude, my
special place in this scheme, otherwise I would have no place in any
scheme."

"Pluralism," the American philosopher John Dewey insisted early 20
in this century, "is the greatest philosophical idea of our times." But he
recognized that it was also the greatest problem of our times: "How are
we going to make the most of the new values we set on variety, difference, and individuality—how are we going to realize their possibilities in every field, and at the same time not sacrifice that plurality to the
cooperation we need so much?" It has the feel of a scholastic conundrum: How can we negotiate between the one and the many?

Today, the mindless celebration of difference has proven as unten- 21
able as that bygone model of monochrome homogeneity. If there is an
equilibrium to be struck, there's no guarantee we will ever arrive at it.
The worst mistake we can make, however, is not to try.

QUESTIONS ON SUBJECT

1. What does Gates believe is wrong with the debate about multiculturalism?
2. According to Gates, what does *multiculturalism* mean? Did you find Gates using it interchangeably with *cultural pluralism* or does he make a distinction between the two terms?
3. What for Gates are the main issues in the debate over multiculturalism?
4. What are the "time-tested" questions that multiculturalism poses for American universities today? How does Gates answer each of these questions?
5. What do you think Gates means when he says, "the greatest African-American art can be thought of as an exploration of that hyphenated space between the African and the American"?
6. Does Gates give any hint how we might strike equilibrium between "the mindless celebration of difference" and the "bygone model of mono-chrome homogeneity"? What do you see as solutions to this stand-off?

QUESTIONS ON STRATEGY

1. Why is it necessary for Gates to provide a definition of *multiculturalism*? (Glossary: *Definition*)

2. Explain how and where Gates uses comparison and contrast to draw the lines between the proponents and antagonists of multiculturalism. (Glossary: *Comparison and Contrast*)

3. In paragraph 12 Gates quotes four lines of student doggerel about Benjamin Jowett. What point is he illustrating with this example? (Glossary: *Illustration*) How is this point related to his overall argument?

4. How does Gates support the generalization: "The world we live in is multicultural already. Mixing and hybridity is the rule, not the exception"? (Glossary: *Illustration*)

QUESTIONS ON LANGUAGE

1. What is Gates's tone in this essay? (Glossary: *Tone*) Cite examples of his diction that led you to this conclusion.

2. In paragraph 15 Gates mentions the cultural nationalists Allan Bloom and Leonard Jeffries. What is Gates's attitude toward these two men and the position they represent? What words in that paragraph led you to your conclusion?

3. Refer to your desk dictionary to determine the meanings of the following words as they are used in this selection: *inviolate* (2), *penchant* (7), *epithets* (8), *unblinkered* (10), *fissured* (10), *porous* (14), *monolithic* (14), *putative* (14), *palimpsest* (16), *vernacular* (18), and *conundrum* (20).

WRITING SUGGESTIONS

1. Using the statement "There is no tolerance without respect—and no respect without knowledge" as your thesis, write an essay in which you describe a college curriculum that "seeks to comprehend the diversity of human culture."

2. How would you answer Gates's question: "What does it mean to be an American"? And to this question you might add another: What responsibilities do you have as an American in the 1990s? Present your answers to these two questions in a well-organized essay.

When Language Dies: 1993 Nobel Prize for Literature Lecture

Toni Morrison

It came as no surprise to her critics and fans alike when, in accepting the 1993 Nobel Prize for literature, Toni Morrison turned to language as her subject. She has long been known for her curiosity about the magical properties of words and her rich use of them in her work. Morrison was born Chloe Anthony Wofford near Lake Erie in Lorain, Ohio. She published her first novel, The Bluest Eye, *in 1969; it was followed by* Sula *in 1973,* Song of Solomon *in 1977,* Tar Baby *in 1981,* Beloved *in 1987, and* Jazz *in 1992. As a novelist Morrison has risen to a pre-eminent position in American letters for her portrayals of the black experience in myth and reality.*

In "When Language Dies: 1993 Nobel Prize for Literature Lecture" Morrison speaks to us of our responsibility not to violate the power and beauty of language, but to maximize its magical and generative properties.

"Once upon a time there was an old woman. Blind but wise." Or 1 was it an old man? A guru, perhaps. Or a griot soothing restless children. I have heard this story, or one exactly like it, in the lore of several cultures.

"Once upon a time there was an old woman. Blind. Wise." 2

In the version I know the woman is the daughter of slaves, black, 3 American, and lives alone in a small house outside of town. Her reputation for wisdom is without peer and without question. Among her people she is both the law and its transgression. The honor she is paid and the awe in which she is held reach beyond her neighborhood to places far away; to the city where the intelligence of rural prophets is the source of much amusement.

One day the woman is visited by some young people who seem to 4 be bent on disproving her clairvoyance and showing her up for the fraud they believe she is. Their plan is simple: they enter her house and ask the one question the answer to which rides solely on her difference from them, a difference they regard as a profound disability: her blindness. They stand before her, and one of them says, "Old woman, I hold in my hand a bird. Tell me whether it is living or dead."

She does not answer, and the question is repeated. "Is the bird I am ₅
holding living or dead?"

Still she doesn't answer. She is blind and cannot see her visitors, let ₆
alone what is in their hands. She does not know their color, gender or
homeland. She only knows their motive.

The old woman's silence is so long, the young people have trouble ₇
holding their laughter.

Finally she speaks and her voice is soft but stern. "I don't know," ₈
she says. "I don't know whether the bird you are holding is dead or
alive, but what I do know is that it is in your hands. It is in your hands."

Her answer can be taken to mean: if it is dead, you have either ₉
found it that way or you have killed it. If it is alive, you can still kill it.
Whether it is to stay alive, it is your decision. Whatever the case, it is
your responsibility.

For parading their power and her helplessness, the young visitors ₁₀
are reprimanded, told they are responsible not only for the act of
mockery but also for the small bundle of life sacrificed to achieve its
aims. The blind woman shifts attention away from assertions of power
to the instrument through which that power is exercised.

Speculation on what (other than its own frail body) that bird-in- ₁₁
the-hand might signify has always been attractive to me, but especially
so now, thinking as I have been, about the work I do that has brought
me to this company. So I choose to read the bird as language and the
woman as a practice writer. She is worried about how the language she
dreams in, given to her at birth, is handled, put into service, even with-
held from her for certain nefarious purposes. Being a writer she thinks
of language partly as a system, partly as a living thing over which one
has control, but mostly as agency—as an act with consequences. So the
question the children put to her: "Is it living or dead?" is not unreal because she thinks of language as susceptible to death, erasure; certainly
imperiled and salvageable only by an effort of the will. She believes that
if the bird in the hands of her visitors is dead the custodians are responsible for the corpse. For her a dead language is not only one no
longer spoken or written, it is unyielding language content to admire its
own paralysis. Like statist language, censored and censoring. Ruthless
in its policing duties, it has no desire or purpose other than maintaining
the free range of its own narcotic narcissism, its own exclusivity and
dominance. However, moribund, it is not without effect for it actively
thwarts the intellect, stalls conscience, suppresses human potential. Un-
receptive to interrogation, it cannot form or tolerate new ideas, shape
other thoughts, tell another story, fill baffling silences. Official language
smitheryed to sanction ignorance and preserve privilege is a suit of

armor, polished to shocking glitter, a husk from which the knight departed long ago. Yet there it is: dumb, predatory, sentimental. Exciting reverence in schoolchildren, providing shelter for despots, summoning false memories of stability, harmony among the public.

She is convinced that when language dies, out of carelessness, disuse, and absence of esteem, indifference or killed by fiat, not only she herself, but all users and makers are accountable for its demise. In her country children have bitten their tongues off and use bullets instead to iterate the voice of speechlessness, of disabled and disabling language, of language adults have abandoned altogether as a device for grappling with meaning, providing guidance, or expressing love. But she knows tongue-suicide is not only the choice of children. It is common among the infantile heads of state and power merchants whose evacuated language leaves them with no access to what is left of their human instincts for they speak only to those who obey, or in order to force obedience. 12

The systematic looting of language can be recognized by the tendency of its users to forgo its nuanced, complex, mid-wifery properties for menace and subjugation. Oppressive language does more than represent violence; it is violence; does more than represent the limits of knowledge; it limits knowledge. Whether it is obscuring state language or the faux-language of mindless media; whether it is the proud but calcified language of the academy or the commodity driven language of science; whether it is the malign language of law-without-ethics, or language designed for the estrangement of minorities, hiding its racist plunder in its literary cheek—it must be rejected, altered and exposed. It is the language that drinks blood, laps vulnerability, tucks its fascist boots under crinolines of respectability and patriotism as it moves relentlessly toward the bottom line and the bottomed-out mind. Sexist language, racist language, theistic language—all are typical of the policing languages of mastery, and cannot, do not permit new knowledge or encourage the mutual exchange of ideas. 13

The old woman is keenly aware that no intellectual mercenary, nor insatiable dictator, no paid-for politician or demagogue; no counterfeit journalist would be persuaded by her thoughts. There is and will be rousing language to keep citizens armed and arming; slaughtered and slaughtering in the malls, courthouses, post offices, playgrounds, bedrooms and boulevards; stirring, memorializing language to mask the pity and waste of needless death. There will be more diplomatic language to countenance rape, torture, assassination. There is and will be more seductive, mutant language designed to throttle women, to pack their throats like paté-producing geese with their own unsayable, 14 transgressive words; there will be more of the language of surveillance disguised as research; of politics and history calculated to render the suffering of millions mute; language glamorized to thrill the dissatisfied and bereft into assaulting their neighbors; arrogant pseudo-empirical language crafted to lock creative people into cages of inferiority and hopelessness.

Underneath the eloquence, the glamour, the scholarly associations, 15 however, stirring or seductive, the heart of such language is languishing, or perhaps not beating at all—if the bird is already dead.

She has thought about what could have been the intellectual 16 history of any discipline if it had not insisted upon, or been forced into, the waste of time and life that rationalizations for and representations of dominance required—lethal discourses of exclusion blocking access to cognition for both the excluder and the excluded.

The conventional wisdom of the Tower of Babel story is that the 17 collapse was a misfortune. That it was the distraction, or the weight of many languages that precipitated the tower's failed architecture. That one monolithic language would have expedited the building and heaven would have been reached. Whose heaven, she wonders? And what kind? Perhaps the achievement of Paradise was premature, a little hasty if no one could take the time to understand other languages, other views, other narratives. Had they, the heaven they imagined might have been found at their feet. Complicated, demanding yes, but a view of heaven as life; not heaven as post-life.

She would not want to leave her young visitors with the impression 18 that language should be forced to stay alive merely to be. The vitality of language lies in its ability to limn the actual, imagined and possible lives of its speakers, readers, writers. Although its poise is sometimes in displacing experience it is not a substitute for it. It arcs toward the place where meaning may lie. When a President of the United States thought about the graveyard his country had become, and said "The world will little note nor long remember what we say here. But it will never forget what they did here." His simple words are exhilarating in their life-sustaining properties because they refused to encapsulate the reality of 600,000 dead men in a cataclysmic race war. Refusing to monumentalize, disdaining the "final word", the precise "summing up", acknowledging their "poor power to add or detract", his words signal deference to the uncapturability of the life it mourns. It is the deference that moves her, that recognition that language can never live up to life once and for all. Nor should it. Language can never "pin down" slavery, genocide, war. Nor should it yearn for the arrogance to be able to do so. Its force, its felicity is in its reach toward the ineffable.

Be it grand or slender, burrowing, blasting, or refusing to sanctify; 19 whether it laughs out loud or is a cry without an alphabet, the choice word, the chosen silence, unmolested language surges toward knowledge, not its destruction. But who does not know of literature banned because it is interrogative; discredited because it is critical; erased because alternate? And how many are outraged by the thought of a self-ravaged tongue?

Word-work is sublime, she thinks, because it is generative; it makes 20 meaning that secures our difference, our human difference—the way in which we are like no other life.

We die. That may be the meaning of life. But we do language. That 21 may be the measure of our lives.

"Once upon a time, . . ." visitors ask an old woman a question. 22 Who are they, these children? What did they make of that encounter? What did they hear in those final words: "The bird is in your hands"? A sentence that gestures toward possibility or one that drops a latch? Perhaps what the children heard was "It's not my problem. I am old, female, black, blind. What wisdom I have now is in knowing I can not help you. The future of language is yours."

They stand there. Suppose nothing was in their hands? Suppose the 23 visit was only a ruse, a trick to get to be spoken to, taken seriously as they have not been before? A chance to interrupt, to violate the adult world, its miasma of discourse about them, for them, but never to them? Urgent questions are at stake, including the one they have asked: "Is the bird we hold living or dead?" Perhaps the question meant: "Could someone tell us what is life? What is death?" No trick at all; no silliness. A straightforward question worthy of the attention of a wise one. An old one. And if the old and wise who have lived life and faced death cannot describe either, who can?

But she does not; she keeps her secret; her good opinion of herself; 24 her gnomic pronouncements; her art without commitment. She keeps her distance, enforces it and retreats into the singularity of isolation, in sophisticated, privileged space.

Nothing, no word follows her declarations of transfer. That silence 25 is deep, deeper than the meaning available in the words she has spoken. It shivers, this silence, and the children, annoyed, fill it with language invented on the spot.

"Is there no speech," they ask her, "no words you can give us that 26 helps us break through your dossier of failures? Through the education you have just given us that is no education at all because we are paying close attention to what you have done as well as to what you have said? To the barrier you have erected between generosity and wisdom?

"We have no bird in our hands, living or dead. We have only you 27
and our important question. Is the nothing in our hands something
you could not bear to contemplate, to even guess? Don't you remember being young when language was magic without meaning? When
what you could say, could not mean? When the invisible was what
imagination strove to see? When questions and demands for answers
burned so brightly you trembled with fury at not knowing?

"Do we have to begin consciousness with a battle heroines and 28
heroes like you have already fought and lost leaving us with nothing in
our hands except what you have imagined is there? Your answer is
artful, but its artiness embarrasses us and ought to embarrass you. Your
answer is indecent in its self-congratulation. A made-for-television
script that makes no sense if there is nothing in our hands.

"Why didn't you reach out, touch us with your soft fingers, delay 29
the sound bite, the lesson, until you knew who we were? Did you so
despise our trick, our modus operandi you could not see that we were
baffled about how to get your attention? We are young. Unripe. We
have heard all our short lives that we have to be responsible. What
could that possibly mean in the catastrophe this word has become;
where, as a poet said, "nothing needs to be exposed since it is already
barefaced." Our inheritance is an affront. You want us to have your old,
blank eyes and see only cruelty and mediocrity. Do you think we are
stupid enough to perjure ourselves again and again with the fiction of
nationhood? How dare you talk to us of duty when we stand waist deep
in the toxin of your past?

"You trivialize us and trivialize the bird that is not in our hands. Is 30
there no context for our lives? No song, no literature, no poem full of
vitamins, no history connected to experience that you can pass along to
help us start strong? You are an adult. The old one, the wise one. Stop
thinking about saving your face. Think of our lives and tell us your
particularized world. Make up a story. Narrative is radical, creating us
at the very moment it is being created. We will not blame you if your
reach exceeds your grasp; if love so ignites your words they go down in
flames and nothing is left but their scald. Or if, with the reticence of a
surgeon's hands, your words suture only the places where blood might
flow. We know you can never do it properly—once and for all. Passion
is never enough; neither is skill. But try. For our sake and yours forget
your name in the street; tell us what the world has been to you in the
dark places and in the light. Don't tell us what to believe, what to fear.
Show us belief's wide skirt and the stitch that unravels fear's caul. You,
old woman, blessed with blindness, can speak the language that tells us

what only language can: how to see without pictures. Language alone protects us from the scariness of things with no names. Language alone is meditation.

"Tell us what it is to be a woman so that we may know what it is   31
to be a man. What moves at the margin. What it is to have no home on this place. To be set adrift from the one you knew. What it is to live at the edge of towns that cannot bear your company.

"Tell us about ships turned away from shorelines at Easter, placenta   32
in a field. Tell us about a wagonload of slaves, how they sang so softly their breath was indistinguishable from the falling snow. How they knew from the hunch of the nearest shoulder that the next stop would be their last. How, with hands prayered in their sex they thought of heat, then suns. Lifting their faces, as though is was there for the taking. Turning as though there for the taking. They stop at an inn. The driver and his mate go in with the lamp leaving them humming in the dark. The horse's void steams into the snow beneath its hooves and its hiss and melt is the envy of the freezing slaves.

"The inn door opens: a girl and a boy step away from its light. They   33
climb into the wagon bed. The boy will have a gun in three years, but now he carries a lamp and a jug of warm cider. They pass it from mouth to mouth. The girl offers bread, pieces of meat and something more: a glance into the eyes of the one she serves. One helping for each man, two for each woman. And a look. They look back. The next stop will be their last. But not this one. This one is warmed."

It's quiet again when the children finish speaking, until the woman   34
breaks into the silence.

"Finally," she says, "I trust you now. I trust you with the bird that   35
is not in your hands because you have truly caught it. Look. How lovely it is, this thing we have done—together."

QUESTIONS ON SUBJECT

1. What, for Morrison, is a dead language? What does she think happens when language dies?

2. In paragraph 13, Morrison says "oppressive language does more than represent violence; it is violence." What does she mean?

3. Who is responsible for the "looting of language" to which Morrison refers in paragraph 13?

4. What is the story of the Tower of Babel? How is the story usually interpreted? What does Morrison see as an alternative interpretation? Which interpretation do you find more persuasive? Explain why?

5. At the end of the essay why does the old woman believe she can trust the young people? What have they "done—together"?

QUESTIONS ON STRATEGY

1. What is Morrison's purpose in this selection? (Glossary: *Purpose*) How do you know?

2. Morrison begins her lecture with a story about the old, blind, wise woman and her young visitors. Why does the old woman reprimand her young visitors? How does this story function both as a beginning and in the context of her argument? (Glossary: *Narration*)

3. In paragraph 22, Morrison explicitly returns to the story of the old woman and her visitors, but now posits the idea that maybe the children's hands were empty. How does this second scenario serve to further her argument about language? In what ways does this part of the story illustrate how language is meant to work, a topic Morrison discusses in the first half of her essay?

4. In paragraph 18, Morrison use the example of Lincoln's "Gettysburg Address" to illustrate a point. (Glossary: *Example*) What is that point? And how is that point related to her argument about the importance of language?

5. The questions that Morrison asks through the young people turn slowly into a narrative about slaves in a wagon. How does this story function within the context of Morrison's argument? (Glossary: *Narration*) Explain.

6. Morrison makes many claims about the power and vitality of language. She believes that "Its force, its felicity is in its reach toward the ineffable." What does she mean by this statement? Does Toni Morrison herself show in her address signs of the sensitivity to language that she argues for? Identify several examples that helped you arrive at your conclusion.

QUESTIONS ON LANGUAGE

1. On a literal level, what is the meaning of the story about the old woman? How does Morrison interpret the story figuratively? (Glossary: *Figures of Speech*) Explain.

2. At various points in her essay, Morrison personifies language. Identify several instances of her use of personification and discuss what it adds to her portrayal of language. (Glossary: *Personification*)

3. Refer to your desk dictionary to determine the meanings of the following words as they are used in this selection: *transgression* (3), *nefarious* (11), *narcissism* (11), *limn* (18), *interrogative* (19), *ruse* (23), *miasma* (23), *caul* (30), and *placenta* (32).

WRITING SUGGESTIONS

1. Perhaps one of the greatest benefits of language is the ability to imagine, to envision what might be, what could be achieved. Language gives us the power to imagine a different world. Write an essay in which you analyze this extraordinary power and discuss the special demands it places on us as humans.

2. The young people in Morrison's essay ask the old woman, "Don't you remember being young when language was magic without meaning? When what you could say, could not mean? When the invisible was what imagination strove to see? When questions and demands for answers burned so brightly you trembled with fury at not knowing?" Does that description of the sense of language for young people sound familiar to you? What was language for you as you grew older? What was lost? Gained? Write an essay describing your experiences with language as you were growing up.

WRITING SUGGESTIONS
FOR COMBINING STRATEGIES

1. Select a piece you have written for this class in which you used one primary writing strategy, and rewrite it using another. For example, choose a description you wrote in response to the exercises at the end of Chapter 2, and redraft it as a process analysis. Remember that the choice of a writing strategy influences the writer's "voice"—a descriptive piece might be very lyrical, while process analysis might be very straightforward. How does your voice change along with the strategy? Does your assumed audience change as well?

   If time allows, try this exercise with someone else in your class. Exchange a piece of writing with another student, and rewrite it using a different strategy. Discuss the choices you each made.

2. Select an essay you have written this semester, either for this class or another class. What was the primary writing strategy you used? Build upon this essay by integrating another strategy. For example, if you wrote an argument paper for a political science class, you might try using narrative to give some historical background to the paper. For a paper in the natural sciences, you could use subjective description to open the paper up to nonscientists. How does this new strategy affect the balance of your paper? Does the new strategy require you to change anything else about your paper?

3. The choice of a writing strategy reflects an author's voice—the persona he or she assumes in relation to the reader. Read back through any personal writing you've done this semester—a journal, letters to friends, e-mail. Can you identify the strategies you use outside of "formal" academic writing, as part of your natural writing voice? Write a few pages analyzing these strategies and your writing "voice," using one of the rhetorical modes studied this term. For example, you could compare and contrast your e-mail postings to your letters home. Or you could do a cause-and-effect analysis of how being at college has changed the tone or style of your journal writing.

GLOSSARY OF
RHETORICAL TERMS

Abstract   See *Concrete/Abstract.*

Allusion   An allusion is a passing reference to a familiar person, place, or thing drawn from history, the Bible, mythology, or literature. An allusion is an economical way for a writer to capture the essence of an idea, atmosphere, emotion, or historical era, as in "The scandal was his Watergate," or "He saw himself as a modern Job," or "Everyone there held those truths to be self-evident." An allusion should be familiar to the reader, for if it is not, it will add nothing to the meaning.

Analogy   Analogy is a special form of comparison in which the writer explains something unfamiliar by comparing it to something familiar: "A transmission line is simply a pipeline for electricity. In the case of a water pipeline, more water will flow through the pipe as water pressure increases. The same is true of a transmission line for electricity." See also the discussion of analogy on pages 212–213.

Analytical Reading   Reading analytically means reading actively, paying close attention to both the content and structure of the text. Analytical reading often involves answering several basic questions about the piece of writing under consideration:

1. What does the author want to say? What is his or her main point?

2. Why does the author want to say it? What is his or her purpose?

3. What strategy or strategies does the author use?

4. Why and how does the author's writing strategy suit both the subject and purpose?

5. What is special about the way the author uses the strategy?

6. How effective is the essay? Why?

For a detailed example of analytical reading, see pages 5–7 in the Introduction.

Appropriateness   See *Diction*.

Argument   Argument is one of the four basic types of prose. (Narration, description, and exposition are the other three.) To argue is to attempt to convince a reader to agree with a point of view, to make a given decision, or to pursue a particular course of action. Logical argument is based on reasonable explanations and appeals to the reader's intelligence. See Chapter 9 for further discussion of argumentation. See also *Persuasion* and *Logical Fallacies*.

Assertion   The thesis or proposition that a writer puts forward in argument.

Assumption   A belief or principle, stated or implied, that is taken for granted.

Attitude   A writer's attitude reflects his or her opinion of a subject. For example, a writer can think very positively or very negatively about a subject. In most cases, the writer's attitude falls somewhere between these two extremes. See also *Tone*.

Audience   An audience is the intended readership for a piece of writing. For example, the readers of a national weekly newsmagazine come from all walks of life and have diverse opinions, attitudes, and educational experiences. In contrast, the readership for an organic chemistry journal is made up of people whose interests and educations are quite similar. The essays in this book are intended for general readers, intelligent people who may lack specific information about the subject being discussed.

Beginnings   See *Beginnings/Endings*.

Beginnings/Endings   A *beginning* is that sentence, group of sentences, or section that introduces an essay. Good beginnings usually identify the thesis or controlling idea, attempt to interest the reader, and establish a tone. Some effective ways in which writers begin essays include (1) telling an anecdote that illustrates the thesis, (2) providing a controversial statement or opinion that engages the reader's interest, (3) presenting startling statistics or facts, (4) defining a term that is central to the discussion that follows, (5) asking thought-provoking questions, (6) providing a quotation that illustrates the thesis, (7) referring to a current event that helps to establish the thesis, or (8) showing the significance of the subject or stressing its importance to the reader.

An *ending* is the sentence or group of sentences that brings an essay to closure. Good endings are purposeful and well planned. Endings satisfy readers when they are the natural outgrowths of the essays themselves and convey a sense of finality or completion. Good essays do not simply stop; they conclude.

Cause and Effect Analysis Cause and effect analysis is one of the types of exposition. (Process analysis, definition, division and classification, and comparison and contrast are the others.) Cause and effect analysis answers the question *why?* It explains the reasons for an occurrence or the consequences of an action. See Chapter 8 for a detailed discussion of cause and effect analysis. See also *Exposition*.

Claim The thesis or proposition put forth in argument.

Classification Classification is one of the types of exposition. (Process analysis, definition, comparison and contrast, and cause and effect analysis are the others.) When classifying, the writer arranges and sorts people, places, or things into categories according to their differing characteristics, thus making them more manageable for the writer and more understandable for the reader. See Chapter 6 for a detailed discussion of classification. See also *Exposition* and *Division*.

Cliché A cliché is an expression that has become ineffective through overuse. Expressions such as *quick as a flash, dry as dust, jump for joy,* and *slow as molasses* are all clichés. Writers normally avoid such trite expressions and seek instead to express themselves in fresh and forceful language.

Coherence Coherence is a quality of good writing that results when all sentences, paragraphs, and longer divisions of an essay are naturally connected. Coherent writing is achieved through (1) a logical sequence of ideas (arranged in chronological order, spatial order, order of importance, or some other appropriate order), (2) the thoughtful repetition of key words and ideas, (3) a pace suitable for your topic and your reader, and (4) the use of transitional words and expressions. Coherence should not be confused with unity. (See *Unity*.) Also see *Transitions*.

Colloquial Expressions A colloquial expression is characteristic of or appropriate to spoken language or to writing that seeks its effect. Colloquial expressions are informal, as *chem, gym, come up with, be at loose ends, won't,* and *photo* illustrate. Thus, colloquial expressions are acceptable in formal writing only if they are used purposefully.

Comparison and Contrast   Comparison and contrast is one of the types of exposition. (Process analysis, definition, division and classification, and cause and effect analysis are the others.) In comparison and contrast, the writer points out the similarities and differences between two or more subjects in the same class or category. The function of any comparison and contrast is to clarify—to reach some conclusion about the items being compared and contrasted. See Chapter 5 for a detailed discussion of comparison and contrast. See also *Exposition.*

Conclusions   See *Beginnings/Endings.*

Concrete   See *Concrete/Abstract.*

Concrete/Abstract   A *concrete word* names a specific object, person, place, or action that can be directly perceived by the senses: *car, bread, building, book, William Jefferson Clinton, Chicago,* or *hiking.* An *abstract word,* in contrast, refers to general qualities, conditions, ideas, actions, or relationships that cannot be directly perceived by the senses: *bravery, dedication, excellence, anxiety, stress, thinking,* or *hatred.*

   Although writers must use both concrete and abstract language, good writers avoid too many abstract words. Instead, they rely on concrete words to define and illustrate abstractions. Because concrete words affect the senses, they are easily comprehended by the reader.

Connotation   See *Connotation/Denotation.*

Connotation/Denotation   Both connotation and denotation refer to the meanings of words. *Denotation* is the dictionary meaning of a word, the literal meaning. *Connotation,* on the other hand, is the implied or suggested meaning of a word. For example, the denotation of *lamb* is "a young sheep." The connotations of lamb are numerous: *gentle, docile, weak, peaceful, blessed, sacrificial, blood, spring, frisky, pure, innocent,* and so on. Good writers are sensitive to both the denotations and the connotations of words and use these meanings to advantage in their writing. See also *Slanting.*

Controlling Idea   See *Thesis.*

Deduction   Deduction is the process of reasoning from a stated premise to a conclusion that follows necessarily. This form of reasoning moves from the general to the specific. See Chapter 9 for a discussion of deductive reasoning and its relation to argumentative writing. See also *Syllogism* and *Induction.*

Definition   Definition is one of the types of exposition. (Process analysis, division and classification, comparison and contrast, and cause and effect analysis are the others.) Definition is a statement of the meaning of a word. A definition may be either brief or extended, part of an essay or an entire essay itself. See Chapter 7 for a detailed discussion of definition. See also *Exposition*.

Denotation See *Connotation/Denotation*.

Description Description is one of the four basic types of prose. (Narration, exposition, and argument are the other three.) Description tells how a person, place, or thing is perceived by the five senses. Objective description reports these sensory qualities factually, whereas subjective description gives the writer's interpretation of them. See Chapter 2 for a detailed discussion of description.

Dialogue Dialogue is the conversation that is recorded in a piece of writing. Through dialogue writers reveal important aspects of characters' personalities as well as events in the plot.

Diction Diction refers to a writer's choice and use of words. Good diction is precise and appropriate—the words mean exactly what the writer intends, and the words are well suited to the writer's subject, intended audience, and purpose in writing. The word-conscious writer knows that there are differences among *aged, old,* and *elderly; blue, navy,* and *azure;* and *disturbed, angry,* and *irritated.* Furthermore, this writer knows in which situation to use each word. See also *Connotation/Denotation*.

Division Like comparison and contrast, division and classification are separate yet closely related mental operations. Division involves breaking down a single large unit into smaller subunits or breaking down a large group of items into discrete categories. For example, the student body at your college or university can be divided into categories according to different criteria (by class, by home state or country, by sex, and so on).

Dominant Impression A dominant impression is the single mood, atmosphere, or quality a writer emphasizes in a piece of descriptive writing. The dominant impression is created through the careful selection of details and is, of course, influenced by the writer's subject, audience, and purpose. See also the discussion in Chapter 2.

Draft A draft is a version of a piece of writing at a particular stage in the writing process. The first version produced is usually called the rough draft or first draft and is a writer's beginning attempt to give overall shape to his or her ideas. Subsequent versions are called revised drafts. The copy presented for publication is the final draft.

Editing During the editing stage of the writing process, the writer makes his or her prose conform to the conventions of the language. This includes making final improvements in sentence structure and diction and proofreading for wordiness and errors in grammar, usage, spelling, and punctuation. After editing, the writer is ready to type a final copy.

Emphasis Emphasis is the placement of important ideas and words within sentences and longer units of writing so that they have the greatest impact. In general, the end has the most impact, and the beginning nearly as much; the middle has the least. See also *Organization.*

Endings See *Beginnings/Endings.*

Essay An essay is a relatively short piece of nonfiction in which the writer attempts to make one or more closely related points. A good essay is purposeful, informative, and well organized.

Ethos A type of argumentative proof having to do with the ethics of the arguer: honesty, trustworthiness, even morals.

Evaluation An evaluation of a piece of writing is an assessment of its effectiveness or merit. In evaluating a piece of writing, you should ask the following questions: What is the writer's purpose? Is it a worthwhile purpose? Does the writer achieve the purpose? Is the writer's information sufficient and accurate? What are the strengths of the essay? What are its weaknesses? Depending on the type of writing and the purpose, more specific questions can also be asked. For example, with an argument you could ask: Does the writer follow the principles of logical thinking? Is the writer's evidence convincing?

Evidence Evidence is the data on which a judgment or argument is based or by which proof or probability is established. Evidence usually takes the form of statistics, facts, names, examples or illustrations, and opinions of authorities.

Examples Examples illustrate a larger idea or represent something of which they are a part. An example is a basic means of developing or clarifying an idea. Furthermore, examples enable writers to show and not simply tell readers what they mean. The terms *example* and *illustration* are sometimes used interchangeably. See also the discussion of examples in Chapter 3.

Exposition Exposition is one of the four basic types of prose. (Narration, description, and argument are the other three.) The purpose of exposition is to clarify, explain, and inform. The methods of exposition presented in this text are process analysis, definition, division and classification, comparison and contrast, and cause and effect analysis. For a detailed discussion of each of these methods of exposition, see the appropriate section.

Fact   A piece of information presented as having a verifiable certainty or reality.

Fallacy   See *Logical Fallacies.*

Figures of Speech   Figures of speech are brief, imaginative comparisons that highlight the similarities between things that are basically dissimilar. They make writing vivid and interesting and therefore more memorable. The most common figures of speech are:

   Simile—An implicit comparison introduced by *like* or *as:* "The fighter's hands were *like* stone."

   Metaphor—An implied comparison that uses one thing as the equivalent of another: "All the world's a stage."

   Personification—A special kind of simile or metaphor in which human traits are assigned to an inanimate object: "The engine coughed and then stopped."

Focus   Focus is the limitation that a writer gives his or her subject. The writer's task is to select a manageable topic given the constraints of time, space, and purpose. For example, within the general subject of sports, a writer could focus on government support of amateur athletes or narrow the focus further to government support of Olympic athletes.

General   See *Specific/General.*

Idiom   An idiom is a word or phrase that is used habitually with a particular meaning in a language. The meaning of an idiom is not always readily apparent to non-native speakers of that language. For example, *catch cold, hold a job, make up your mind,* and *give them a hand* are all idioms in English.

Illustration   See *Examples.* Also see Chapter 3.

Induction   Induction is the process of reasoning to a conclusion about all members of a class through an examination of only a few members of the class. This form of reasoning moves from the particular to the general. See Chapter 9 for a discussion of inductive reasoning and its relation to argumentative writing. Also see *Deduction.*

Introductions   See *Beginnings/Endings.*

Irony   The use of words to suggest something different from their literal meaning. For example, when Jonathan Swift proposes in "A Modest Proposal" that Ireland's problems could be solved if the people of Ireland fattened their babies and sold them to the English landlords for food, he meant that almost any other solution would be preferable. A writer can use irony to establish a special relationship with the reader and to add an extra dimension or twist to the meaning.

Jargon   See *Technical Language.*

Logical Fallacies   A logical fallacy is an error in reasoning that renders an argument invalid. Some of the more common logical fallacies are:

> *Oversimplification*—The tendency to provide simple solutions to complex problems: "The reason we have inflation today is that OPEC has unreasonably raised the price of oil."
>
> *Non sequitur* ("It does not follow")—An inference or conclusion that does not follow from established premises or evidence: "It was the best movie I saw this year, and it should get an Academy Award."
>
> *Post hoc, ergo propter hoc* ("After this, therefore because of this")—Confusing chance or coincidence with causation. Because one event comes after another one, it does not necessarily mean that the first event caused the second: "I won't say I caught cold at the hockey game, but I certainly didn't have it before I went there."
>
> *Begging the question*—Assuming in a premise that which needs to be proven: "If American autoworkers built a better product, foreign auto sales would not be so high."
>
> *False analogy*—Making a misleading analogy between logically unconnected ideas: "He was a brilliant basketball player; therefore, there's no question in my mind that he will be a fine coach."
>
> *Either/or thinking*—The tendency to see an issue as having only two sides: "Used car salespersons are either honest or crooked."

See also Chapter 9.

Logical Reasoning   See *Deduction* and *Induction.*

Logos   A type of argumentative proof having to do with the logical qualities of an argument: data, evidence, factual information.

Metaphor   See *Figures of Speech.*

Narration   One of the four basic types of prose. (Description, exposition, and argument are the other three.) To narrate is to tell a story, to tell what happened. Although narration is most often used in fiction, it is also important in nonfiction, either by itself or in conjunction with other types of prose. See Chapter 1 for a detailed discussion of narration.

Objective/Subjective   *Objective* writing is factual and impersonal, whereas *subjective* writing, sometimes called impressionistic, relies heavily on personal interpretation. For a discussion of objective description and subjective description, see Chapter 2.

Opinion   An opinion is a belief or conclusion not substantiated by positive knowledge or proof. An opinion reveals personal feelings or attitudes or states a position. Opinion should not be confused with argument.

Organization   In writing, organization is the thoughtful arrangement and presentation of one's points or ideas. Narration is often organized chronologically. Exposition may be organized from simplest to most complex or from most familiar to least familiar. Argument may be organized from least important to most important. There is no single correct pattern of organization for a given piece of writing, but good writers are careful to discover an order of presentation suitable for their audience and their purpose.

Paradox   A paradox is a seemingly contradictory statement that may nonetheless be true. For example, *we little know what we have until we lose it* is a paradoxical statement. For a detailed discussion of paradox that includes additional examples, see Laurence Perrine's "Paradox," pages 5–6.

Paragraph   The paragraph, the single most important unit of thought in an essay, is a series of closely related sentences. These sentences adequately develop the central or controlling idea of the paragraph. This central or controlling idea, usually stated in a topic sentence, is necessarily related to the purpose of the whole composition. A well-written paragraph has several distinguishing characteristics: a clearly stated or implied topic sentence, adequate development, unity, coherence, and an appropriate organizational strategy.

Parallelism   Parallel structure is the repetition of word order or form either within a single sentence or in several sentences that develop the same central idea. As a rhetorical device, parallelism can aid coherence and add emphasis. Roosevelt's statement, "I see one third of the nation ill-housed, ill-clad, and ill-nourished," illustrates effective parallelism.

Pathos   A type of argumentative proof having to do with audience: emotional language, connotative diction, and appeals to certain values.

Personification   See *Figures of Speech*.

Persuasion   Persuasion, or persuasive argument, is an attempt to convince readers to agree with a point of view, to make a given decision, or to pursue a particular course of action. Persuasion heavily appeals to the emotions whereas logical argument does not. For the distinction between logical argument and persuasive argument, see Chapter 9.

Point of View   Point of view refers to the grammatical person of the speaker in an essay. For example, a first-person point of view uses the pronoun *I* and is commonly found in autobiography and the personal essay; a third-person point of view uses the pronouns *he, she,* or *it* and is commonly found in objective writing. See Chapter 1 for a discussion of point of view in narration.

Prewriting   Prewriting encompasses all the activities that take place before a writer actually starts a rough draft. During the prewriting stage of the writing process, the writer selects a subject area, focuses on a particular topic, collects information and makes notes, brainstorms for ideas, discovers connections between pieces of information, determines a thesis and purpose, rehearses portions of the writing in the mind and/or on paper, and makes a scratch outline. For some suggestions about prewriting, see pages 8–11 in the Introduction.

Process Analysis   Process analysis is a type of exposition. (Definition, division and classification, comparison and contrast, and cause and effect analysis are the others.) Process analysis answers the question *how?* and explains how something works or gives step-by-step directions for doing something. See Chapter 4 for a detailed discussion of process analysis. See also *Exposition.*

Publication   The publication stage of the writing process is when the writer shares his or her writing with the intended audience. Publication can take the form of a typed or an oral presentation, a dittoed or xeroxed copy, or a commercially printed rendition. What's important is that the writer's words are read in what amounts to their final form.

Purpose   Purpose is what the writer wants to accomplish in a particular piece of writing. Purposeful writing seeks to *relate* (narration), to *describe* (description), to *explain* (process analysis, definition, division and classification, comparison and contrast, and cause and effect analysis), or to *convince* (argument).

Revision   During the revision stage of the writing process, the writer determines what in the draft needs to be developed or clarified so that the essay says what the writer intends it to say. Often the writer needs to revise several times before the essay is "right." Comments from peer evaluators can be invaluable in helping writers determine what sorts of changes need to be made. Such changes can include adding material, deleting material, changing the order of presentation, and substituting new material for old.

Rhetorical Question   A rhetorical question is asked but requires no answer from the reader. "When will nuclear proliferation end?" is such a question. Writers use rhetorical questions to introduce topics they plan to discuss or to emphasize important points.

Rough Draft   See *Draft*.

Sequence   Sequence refers to the order in which a writer presents information. Writers commonly select chronological order, spatial order, order of importance, or order of complexity to arrange their points. See also *Organization*.

Simile   See *Figures of Speech*.

Slang   Slang is the unconventional, very informal language of particular subgroups in our culture. Slang, such as *zonk, split, rap, cop,* and *stoned,* is acceptable in formal writing only if it is used purposefully.

Slanting   The use of certain words or information that results in a biased viewpoint.

Specific/General   *General words* name groups or classes of objects, qualities, or actions. *Specific words,* in contrast, name individual objects, qualities, or actions within a class or group. To some extent the terms *general* and *specific* are relative. For example, *dessert* is a class of things. *Pie,* however, is more specific than *dessert* but more general than *pecan pie* or *chocolate cream pie.*

Good writing judiciously balances the general with the specific. Writing with too many general words is likely to be dull and lifeless. General words do not create vivid responses in the reader's mind as concrete specific words can. However, writing that relies exclusively on specific words may lack focus and direction, the control that more general statements provide.

Strategy   A strategy is a means by which a writer achieves his or her purpose. Strategy includes the many rhetorical decisions that the writer makes about organization, paragraph structure, syntax, and diction. In terms of the whole essay, strategy refers to the principal rhetorical mode that a writer uses. If, for example, a writer wishes to show how to make chocolate chip cookies, the most effective strategy would be process analysis. If it is the writer's purpose to show why sales of American cars have declined in recent years, the most effective strategy would be cause and effect analysis.

Style   Style is the individual manner in which a writer expresses his or her ideas. Style is created by the author's particular selection of words, construction of sentences, and arrangement of ideas.

Subject   The subject of an essay is its content, what the essay is about. Depending on the author's purpose and the constraints of space, a subject may range from one that is broadly conceived to one that is narrowly defined.

Subjective   See *Objective/Subjective*.

Supporting Evidence   See *Evidence*.

Syllogism   A syllogism is an argument that utilizes deductive reasoning and consists of a major premise, a minor premise, and a conclusion. For example:
All trees that lose leaves are deciduous. *(major premise)*
Maple trees lose their leaves. *(minor premise)*
, Therefore, maple trees are deciduous. *(conclusion)*
See also *Deduction.*

Symbol   A symbol is a person, place, or thing that represents something beyond itself. For example, the eagle is a symbol of America, and the bear, a symbol of Russia.

Syntax   Syntax refers to the way in which words are arranged to form phrases, clauses, and sentences as well as to the grammatical relationship among the words themselves.

Technical Language   Technical language, or jargon, is the special vocabulary of a trade or profession. Writers who use technical language do so with an awareness of their audience. If the audience is a group of peers, technical language may be used freely. If the audience is a more general one, technical language should be used sparingly and carefully so as not to sacrifice clarity. See also *Diction.*

Thesis   A thesis is a statement of the main idea of an essay. Also known as the controlling idea, a thesis may sometimes be implied rather than stated directly.

Title   A title is a word or phrase set off at the beginning of an essay to identify the subject, to capture the main idea of the essay, or to attract the reader's attention. A title may be explicit or suggestive. A subtitle, when used, extends or restricts the meaning of the main title.

Tone   Tone is the manner in which a writer relates to an audience, the "tone of voice" used to address readers. Tone may be described as friendly, serious, distant, angry, cheerful, bitter, cynical, enthusiastic, morbid, resentful, warm, playful, and so forth. A particular tone results from a writer's diction, sentence structure, purpose, and attitude toward the subject. See also *Attitude.*

Topic Sentence   The topic sentence states the central idea of a paragraph and thus limits and controls the subject of the paragraph. Although the topic sentence most often appears at the beginning of the paragraph, it may appear at any other point, particularly if the writer is trying to create a special effect. Also see *Paragraph.*

Transitions   Transitions are words or phrases that link sentences, paragraphs, and larger units of a composition in order to achieve coherence. These devices include parallelism, pronoun references, conjunctions, and the repetition of key ideas, as well as the many conventional transitional expressions such as *moreover, on the other hand, in addition, in contrast,* and *therefore.* Also see *Coherence.*

Unity Unity is achieved in an essay when all the words, sentences, and paragraphs contribute to its thesis. The elements of a unified essay do not distract the reader. Instead, they all harmoniously support a single idea or purpose.

Writing Process The writing process consists of five major stages: prewriting, writing drafts, revision, editing, and publication. The process is not inflexible, but there is no mistaking the fact that most writers follow some version of it most of the time. Although orderly in its basic components and sequence of activities, the writing process is nonetheless continuous, creative, and unique to each individual writer. See pages 8–35 in the Introduction. See also *Prewriting, Draft, Revision, Editing,* and *Publication.*

mission of the author and the author's agent, Molly Friedrich, The Aaron M. Priest Literary Agency, Inc., 122 East 42nd Street, Suite 3902, New York, NY 10168.

Lewis Thomas, "The Attic of the Brain," from *Late Night Thoughts on Listening to Mahler's Ninth* by Lewis Thomas. Copyright © 1980 by Lewis Thomas. Used by permission of Viking Penguin, a division of Penguin Books USA Inc.

James Thurber, "Courtship through the Ages," from *My World—and Welcome to It.* Harcourt Brace and Company, Inc. Copyright © 1942 by James Thurber. Copyright © 1970 by Helen Thurber and Rosemary A. Thurber. Reprinted by permission.

Judith Viorst, "The Truth about Lying." Originally appeared in *Redbook* magazine. Copyright © 1981 by Judith Viorst. Reprinted by permission.

Alice Walker, "My Daughter Smokes," from *Living by the Word: Selected Writings 1973–1987.* Harcourt Brace and Company, Inc. Copyright © 1987 by Alice Walker. Reprinted by permission of Harcourt Brace and Company, Inc.

Eudora Welty, "A Worn Path," from *A Curtain of Green and Other Stories* by Eudora Welty. Copyright © 1941 and renewed 1969 by Eudora Welty. Reprinted by permission of Harcourt Brace and Company, Inc.

E. B. White, "Once More to the Lake," pages 74–79 from *One Man's Meat* by E. B. White. Copyright © 1941 by E. B. White. Reprinted by permission of Harper-Collins Publishers, Inc.

Marie Winn, "Television and Family Life," pages 140–150 from *The Plugged-In Drug,* revised edition, by Marie Winn. Copyright © 1977, 1985 by Marie Winn Miller. Used by permission of Viking Penguin, a division of Penguin Books USA, Inc.

Virginia Woolf, "The Death of the Moth," from *The Death of the Moth and Other Essays* by Virginia Woolf. Harcourt Brace and Company, Inc. Copyright © 1942 by Harcourt Brace and Company, Inc. Renewed 1970 by Marjorie T. Parsons, Executrix, reprinted by permission of the publisher.

Malcolm X, "Coming to an Awareness of Language," from *The Autobiography of Malcolm X* by Malcolm X, with the assistance of Alex Haley. Copyright © 1964 by Alex Haley and Malcolm X. Copyright © 1965 by Alex Haley and Betty Shabazz. Reprinted by permission of Random House, Inc.

INDEX